VCP5-DCV

VMware® Certified Professional-Data Center Virtualization on vSphere® 5.5
Study Guide: VCP-550

D1368770

VCP5-DCV

VMware® Certified Professional-Data Center Virtualization on vSphere® 5.5
Study Guide: VCP-550

Brian Atkinson

SYBEX®
A Wiley Brand

Senior Acquisitions Editor: Jeff Kellum
Development Editor: Jim Compton
Technical Editors: André Pett and Phillip Jones
Production Editor: Eric Charbonneau
Copy Editor: Liz Welch
Editorial Manager: Pete Gaughan
Vice President and Executive Group Publisher: Richard Swadley
Associate Publisher: Chris Webb
Media Project Manager 1: Laura Moss-Hollister
Media Associate Producer: Marilyn Hummel
Media Quality Assurance: Josh Frank
Book Designers: Judy Fung and Bill Gibson
Proofreader: Josh Chase, Word One New York
Indexer: Ted Laux
Project Coordinator, Cover: Todd Klemme
Cover Designer: Wiley

Dear Reader,

Thank you for choosing *VCP5-DCV: VMware Certified Professional-Data Center Virtualization on vSphere 5.5 Study Guide: VCP-550*. This book is part of a family of premium-quality Sybex books, all of which are written by outstanding authors who combine practical experience with a gift for teaching.

Sybex was founded in 1976. More than 30 years later, we're still committed to producing consistently exceptional books. With each of our titles, we're working hard to set a new standard for the industry. From the paper we print on to the authors we work with, our goal is to bring you the best books available.

I hope you see all that reflected in these pages. I'd be very interested to hear your comments and get your feedback on how we're doing. Feel free to let me know what you think about this or any other Sybex book by sending me an email at contactus@sybex.com. If you think you've found a technical error in this book, please visit http://sybex.custhelp. com. Customer feedback is critical to our efforts at Sybex.

Best regards,

Chris Webb
Associate Publisher
Sybex, an Imprint of Wiley

Acknowledgments

Writing the update for this book has been another great learning experience for me. In many ways it was familiar for me, and in many ways it was still new. I forgot how writing still requires me to strike some sort of balance with work, family, and friends. I also learned that updating a book is not much less work than originally writing the book. Every exercise, image, case study, paragraph, sentence had to be reviewed for accuracy. As with the first edition of this book, I learned a great deal. This time my learning was about the specific changes in VMware vSphere 5.1 and 5.5, and there are a lot of them. I also was reminded how other people played a key role in helping me complete this book.

I would like to thank Jeff Kellum for his patience and willingness to listen to my ideas. This was a difficult project in many ways, and Jeff was a huge help in shaping how the book came together.

I would like to thank Jim Compton for his editing expertise. Jim offered lots of advice and allowed to me to view things through the non-techie lens in many instances.

I would like to thank my technical editor André Pett for his detailed and extremely thorough contributions to this book. André contributed so many valuable things to this book, and occasionally verified that I was not losing my mind. André's technical expertise is amazing, and I simply can't thank him enough!

I would like to thank my production editor, Eric Charbonneau, for his help with the last-minute updates—there were lots of them! I would also like to thank my copyeditor, Liz Welch, for her help in catching the mistakes that managed to slip past me and all of the other editors.

I must thank my family for their support in this project. I know it isn't easy, or always comprehensible, why I have to spend another weekend in front of a computer. I look forward to having the time to spend with them now.

About the Author

Brian Atkinson is a Senior Enterprise Engineer with over 15 years of experience in the IT field. Along the way, he has been a computer lab manager, programmer, network engineer, and systems engineer, and he has worked in education, government, healthcare, finance, and manufacturing environments. For the past seven years, he has been focused on virtualization and storage solutions.

Brian holds the VCP3, VCP4-DCV, and VCP5-DCV certifications and has been awarded the VMware vExpert designation from VMware for 2009, 2010, 2011, 2012, and 2013. He is a VMware Technology Network (VMTN) Moderator and Guru. He is also one of the VMUG leaders in Richmond, VA. He maintains his personal blog in the VMTN communities at:

http://communities.vmware.com/blogs/vmroyale

and occasionally can be found on Twitter (@vmroyale).

Contents at a Glance

Contents

Table of Exercises

Introduction

Obtaining the VCP5-DCV certification is a key step for the vSphere administrator. Having the VCP5-DCV proves that you know how to install, configure, and administer a VMware vSphere 5.5 datacenter environment. Gaining the VCP5-DCV certification is challenging and rewarding, and the process will teach you many things about vSphere that you may not have previously known.

Regardless of the experience level you bring to this book, I aim to provide you with additional experience by including multiple labs per chapter. Some of these labs may seem easy to those of you with more vSphere experience, but I believe there is no better way to learn vSphere than to actually perform the tasks these labs demonstrate. The labs line up directly with the VCP5-DCV exam objectives, and knowing how to do the steps in these labs will be very beneficial when you take the VCP5-DCV exam.

Except for Chapter 1, which previews the new vSphere 5.5 features, each chapter also includes 20 review questions. By the time you work your way through this book, you will have been presented with 200 questions. There are also an additional 150 questions included in the Sybex test engine, along with 150 flashcards. Keep in mind that these questions are not meant to provide you with real exam-type questions; rather, they are meant to test your understanding of the material presented in this book. The chapters also include case studies, warnings, tips, and notes that encompass many of the things I have seen in my experiences with vSphere.

Choosing the VCP5-DCV certification is a great decision, and with this book you are that much closer to achieving this goal. Certification is extremely valuable for a variety of professional and personal reasons, and obtaining the VCP5-DCV certification will reward you with a wealth of knowledge about vSphere 5.5. Becoming a VCP5-DCV is an exciting step in the VMware certification path, and I wish you the best of luck!

What You Need to Perform the Exercises

Access to a test lab is an essential part of using this book, but a copy of VMware Workstation 9 or later on a host system with plenty of memory can make an excellent physical lab substitute in most cases. Many of the labs in this book actually utilized VMware Workstation 9 and nested ESXi 5.5 hosts. In some ways using VMware Workstation can even teach you more about virtualization, as it forces you to think about the additional layer of abstraction in use.

What Is the VCP5-DCV Certification?

VCP5-DCV is one of the certifications offered in VMware's datacenter virtualization certification area. The VCP5-DCV will test your ability to install, configure, and administer a vSphere 5.5 environment. VMware believes VCP5-DCV candidates will have approximately 6 months of vSphere experience and a general IT experience level of 2–5 years. This general IT experience is expected because virtualization incorporates so many different aspects of IT. Experience with networking, storage, systems, security, programming, command-line interfaces, and more will all serve a vSphere administrator well.

Although having general IT experience and familiarity with vSphere 5.5 is a step in the right direction, there is also the requirement of a VMware-authorized course to obtain VCP5-DCV certification. This course requirement ensures that anyone who passes the VCP5-DCV exam have some hands-on experience with the products. The classes are comprehensive and very good at introducing students to subjects they might not otherwise have experience with. The courses are a great learning experience, but do not assume that these few days of coursework will be a suitable substitute for months or years of real-world experience. There is no substitute for actually knowing how and when to use vSphere.

The VCP5-DCV exam blueprint is the official guide to be used for the VCP5-DCV. Any objective listed in the VCP5-DCV exam blueprint is fair game for the exam, and you should expect to be tested on each objective. This book very closely follows the VCP5-DCV exam blueprint, as it was versioned at the time this book was written. Some objectives were moved to chapters where they made more contextual sense.

The VCP-DCV exam blueprint does change periodically. It has likely changed since this book was first published. Make sure you are always working off the latest copy of the VCP5-DCV exam blueprint, which is available here: http://mylearn.vmware.com/portals/certification/.

Why Become VCP5-DCV Certified?

Hopefully it's because you have a strong desire to be a VCP5-DCV! Becoming a VCP5-DCV shows that you have the skills necessary to install, configure, and administer a vSphere 5 data center environment. These skills, along with the VCP5-DCV certification, can lead to your ability to stand out among your peers, lead to career advancement opportunities, and ultimately increase your market value. Perhaps the most important reason is the simple fact that in this journey you will learn more about vSphere 5.5 than you ever thought possible.

Becoming VCP5-DCV Certified

If you are new to VMware certifications or have a VCP certification earlier than VCP4-DCV, then the following requirements exist for the VCP5-DCV certification:

- Required training course
- VCP5-DCV exam

If you have a previous VCP4-DCV certification or if you have taken an authorized VMware VCP4-DCV qualifying course, then the following requirements exist for the VCP5-DCV certification:

- VMware vSphere: What's New [V5.x]
- VCP5-DCV exam

> This information was accurate as of this writing, but it is subject to change. Always consult the VMware certification website for the latest information on the VCP5 requirements: http://mylearn.vmware.com/portals /certification/.

The VCP5-DCV exam now consists of 135 questions, and there is a time limit of 120 minutes. The exam is offered in English, but an additional 30 minutes is offered to candidates who live in a country where English is not a primary language. There is also a pre-exam survey that consists of eight questions, and you will have 15 minutes to complete these questions and the pre-exam agreements. Note that this survey has no effect on the types of questions offered in your exam. The passing score for the VCP exam is 300; a scaled scoring method is used that ranges from 100 to 500. If you need to retake the exam, you must wait seven calendar days before you are allowed to do so. Once you have passed the VCP5-DCV exam, you are not allowed to take the exam again.

> The VCP5-DCV exam is administered through Pearson VUE. For registration and more information about the exam, visit the VMware page at the Pearson VUE website: www.pearsonvue.com/vmware.

In addition to experience, coursework, and studying, another part of ensuring success on the VCP5-DCV exam is preparation for the test. Here are a few helpful hints:

- Schedule the test on a date that offers you plenty of time to prepare and when you can focus 100 percent on the exam.
- Be sure to get good consistent sleep in the days leading up to the exam.
- Eat breakfast, lunch, or a snack before going in. You want to be fresh, focused, and not distracted in any way.

- Know exactly where the testing center is and be sure to arrive there early.

- If possible, bring this book or your notes along with you to the testing center. This will allow you to review if you have time prior to the exam start.

- Relax and focus on what you know.

- Read each exam question carefully, and then read it again. Make sure you understand exactly what is being asked. I've tried to provide some misleading questions in this book to prepare you for this possibility on the VCP5-DCV exam.

- If you are unsure of a question or it is simply taking too much of your time, flag it for review and move on.

- If you don't know the answer to a question, make an educated guess. Never leave questions unanswered!

- For those difficult questions, make a mental note of them. Write them down as soon as you leave the testing center, while they are fresh in your mind. This will allow you to find the answers when you are ready.

This book aims to provide the missing pieces required to pass the VCP5-DCV exam. You bring the experience and the desire to learn, and I will cover the objectives in detail and have you ready to pass the exam! This book contains a wealth of resources, but knowing how to use them is also important. Here are my recommendations for using these resources:

1. Compare the most current VCP5-DCV exam blueprint with the exam blueprint listed in this book. Make notes of any objectives that have changed.

2. Also make notes of the objectives and rate where you think you are with each objective. Be honest in your assessment; the ultimate goal is to learn and improve.

3. Take the assessment test located at the end of this introduction. Be honest here, and when the assessment test is complete adjust your ratings from the previous step. Remember that the goal is to identify where you are strong and weak. The assessment test should help with this.

4. Take your time and read each chapter attentively. Allocate extra time to objectives you don't understand as well. Rushing through the chapters for the sake of completing them does you no favor. If there are sections that you don't understand, read them again.

5. Take time to complete the labs in each chapter. Think about how features work and how you could modify the labs for different results. Understand what each lab is trying to teach you, and do not view the labs as obstacles in the way of your completing the chapter. Be prepared to tear your lab configuration down and rebuild it several times!

6. Take your time at the end of each chapter to answer the review questions. Think of them as mini-VCP5-DCV exams. Take these tests only after reading the chapter and feeling confident that you understand the material presented in the chapter.

7. Use the flashcards included with this book. Think of them as easy questions you might receive on the exam, or facts that you may need in order to answer actual exam questions. The flashcards cover the objectives!

8. Review additional materials, specifically the tools listed in the VCP5-DCV exam blueprint. These official VMware resources contain significant detail and can provide answers to just about any question you may have.

9. Use the VMTN communities and ask questions. I have learned as much, or possibly more, from these communities than all other resources I have used. It might even be me who answers your question, as I spend a great deal of time in the VMTN communities!

10. Experiment with your lab. Break it! Never consider your lab a permanent setup. Learn how vSphere works, and understand its abilities and limitations. This is experience that will pay dividends on exam day.

Obtaining your VCP5-DCV certification will require experience, hard work, and time. There is no quick route to the VCP5-DCV, and any shortcut is simply shorting you of the benefits of this certification. Take your time and study this book. Understand the content and ask questions if you have them. It is this process of learning and experimenting that will help you become VCP5-DCV certified. Follow this advice and you will do well!

Who Should Buy This Book

Any experienced vSphere administrator who is preparing to pass the VCP5-DCV exam should read this book. This book covers each objective of the VCP5-DCV exam, as was listed in the exam blueprint at the time of publishing. Using this book as your study guide for the VCP5-DCV exam will streamline your studying process and increase your odds of passing the VCP5-DCV exam.

How This Book Is Organized

There are 11 chapters in this book, and they are as follows:

Chapter 1: What's New in vSphere 5.5   This chapter offers a quick look at what is new and what has changed in vSphere 5.5. This chapter doesn't include assessment questions or chapter review questions; it is intended to get you up to speed on what is new with vSphere 5.5.

Chapter 2: Planning, Installing, Configuring, and Upgrading vCenter Server and VMware ESXi   This chapter covers planning, installing, and configuring vCenter Server 5.5 and ESXi 5.5. Upgrading vCenter Server and ESXi are also included here.

Chapter 3: Securing vCenter Server and ESXi and Identifying vSphere Architecture and Solutions   This chapter covers securing vCenter Server and ESXi and also discusses vSphere architecture and solutions. Here you will learn more about the design of the products you installed in the previous chapter. Securing these products after installation is also covered.

Chapter 4: Planning and Configuring vSphere Networking   This chapter focuses on vSphere networking and covers vSwitches, dvSwitches, and the various aspects of configuring each.

Chapter 5: Planning and Configuring vSphere Storage   This chapter explores vSphere storage. VMFS, NFS, and the various connectivity options are discussed, along with how to use the different datastore options.

Chapter 6: Creating and Deploying Virtual Machines and vApps   This chapter covers creating and deploying virtual machines and vApps in vSphere 5.

Chapter 7: Managing and Administering Virtual Machines and vApps   This chapter covers managing and administering virtual machines and vApps. Clones, templates, and more are discussed in this chapter.

Chapter 8: Establishing Service Levels with Clusters, Fault Tolerance, and Resource Pools   This chapter covers HA, DRS, FT, vSphere Flash Read Cache, and resource pools.

Chapter 9: Maintaining Service Levels   This chapter covers migrating virtual machines, implementing backup and restores with VMware Data Protection, and patching ESXi hosts with vSphere Update Manager.

Chapter 10: Performing Basic Troubleshooting   This chapter covers troubleshooting for ESXi hosts, storage, networking, HA, DRS, vMotion, and Storage vMotion.

Chapter 11: Monitoring a vSphere Implementation and Managing vCenter Server Alarms   The final chapter in this book covers monitoring ESXi hosts and vCenter Server, in addition to using vCenter Server alarms and vCenter Operations Manager.

Each chapter also includes tips, notes, warnings, case studies, and 20 review questions. This book includes many helpful items intended to prepare you for the VCP5-DCV exam:

Assessment Test   There is a 40-question assessment test at the conclusion of the introduction that can be used to quickly evaluate where you are with vSphere 5.5. This test should be taken prior to beginning your work in this book, and will help you identify areas that you are either strong or weak in. Note that these questions are intentionally simpler than the types of questions you will see on the actual VCP5-DCV exam.

Objective Map and Opening List of Objectives   Immediately before the assessment test, you'll find a detailed exam objective map showing you where each exam objective is covered, but remember that the exam blueprint is subject to change. Each chapter, excluding Chapter 1, also includes a list of the exam objectives that are covered, along with the related VMware resources.

Exam Essentials   The end of each chapter also includes a listing of exam essentials. These are essentially repeats of the objectives, but remember that any objective on the exam blueprint could show up on the exam.

Chapter Review Questions   Chapters 2–11 include 20 review questions each. These are used to assess your understanding of the chapter and are taken directly from the chapter. These questions are based on the exam objectives, and are meant to review your understanding of the material presented in the chapter.

Bonus Contents

This book has a web page that provides several additional elements. Items available among these companion files include the following:

Sybex Test Engine   There are 150 questions included as practice exams in the Sybex test engine. These questions are taken from chapters 2–11 and cover the exam objectives. It may be helpful to wait and take these tests after you have completed the book and are feeling ready for the VCP5-DCV. If you do well on these tests, then you should also be prepared for the VCP5-DCV exam.

Electronic Flashcards   The flashcards are included for quick reference and are great tools for learning quick facts. You can even consider these as 150 additional simple exam questions, which is essentially what they are.

Glossary of Terms   A glossary is included that covers the key terms used in this book.

 You can download all these resources from www.sybex.com/go/vcp5dcvsg.

Conventions Used in This Book

This book uses certain typographic styles in order to help you quickly identify important information and to avoid confusion over the meaning of words such as on-screen prompts. In particular, look for the following styles:

- *Italicized text* indicates key terms that are described at length for the first time in a chapter. (Italics are also used for emphasis.)

- A monospaced font indicates the contents of configuration files, messages displayed at a command prompt, filenames, text-mode command names, and Internet URLs.

- **Bold monospaced text** is information that you're to type into the computer, usually at a command prompt. This text can also be italicized to indicate that you should substitute an appropriate value for your system.

In addition to these text conventions, which can apply to individual words or entire paragraphs, a few conventions highlight segments of text:

A note indicates information that's useful or interesting but that's somewhat peripheral to the main text. A note might be relevant to a small number of networks, for instance, or it may refer to an outdated feature.

A tip provides information that can save you time or frustration and that may not be entirely obvious. A tip might describe how to get around a limitation or how to use a feature to perform an unusual task.

Warnings describe potential pitfalls or dangers. If you fail to heed a warning, you may end up spending a lot of time recovering from a bug, or you may even end up restoring your entire system from scratch.

 Real World Scenario

Real World Scenario

A real world scenario is a type of sidebar that describes a task or example that's particularly grounded in the real world. This may be a situation I or somebody I know has encountered, or it may be advice on how to work around problems that are common in real, working virtual infrastructure environments.

EXERCISES

An exercise is a procedure you should try out on your own computer to help you learn about the material in the chapter. Don't limit yourself to the procedures described in the exercises, though! Try other commands and procedures to learn about vSphere.

VCP5-DCV Exam Objectives

The following list of exam objectives was taken directly from the VCP5-DCV exam blueprint version 3.1, which was the most recent version available at the time this book was published. Please note that these objectives may have changed by the time you read this.

Always ensure that you are using the latest version of the VCP5-DCV exam blueprint. The exam blueprint is available here: http://mylearn.vmware .com/portals/certification/.

Section 1: Plan, Install, Configure and Upgrade vCenter Server and VMware ESXi

Exam Objective	Chapter
1.1: Identify and Explain vSphere Architecture and Solutions	3
Identify available vSphere editions and features	3
Identify the various data center solutions that interact with vSphere (Horizon, SRM, etc.)	3
Explain ESXi and vCenter Server architectures	3
Determine appropriate vSphere edition based on customer requirements	3
1.2: Install and Configure vCenter Server	2
Identify available vCenter Server editions	2
Identify vCenter Server and vCenter Server database requirements	2
Identify Single Sign-On requirements	2
Deploy the vCenter Appliance	2
Install vCenter Server into a virtual machine	2
Size the vCenter Server database	2
Install and Configure the vSphere Client/vSphere Web Client	2
Install additional vCenter Server components	2
Install/Remove vSphere Client plug-ins	2
Enable/Disable vSphere Client plug-ins	2

(continued)

Exam Objective	Chapter
License vCenter Server	2
Create a database connection to the vCenter Server database	2
Determine availability requirements for a vCenter Server in a given vSphere implementation	2
1.3: Install and Configure VMware ESXi	**2**
Identify ESXi host requirements	2
Perform an interactive installation of ESXi using media or PXE	2
Configure NTP on an ESXi Host	2
Configure DNS and routing on an ESXi Host	2
Enable/Configure/Disable hyperthreading	2
Select a CPU power management policy	2
Enable/Size/Disable memory compression cache	2
License an ESXi host	2
1.4: Plan and Perform Upgrades of vCenter Server and VMware ESXi	**2, 4, 6, 9**
Identify upgrade requirements for ESXi hosts	2
Identify steps required to upgrade a vSphere implementation	2
Upgrade a vSphere Distributed Switch	4
Upgrade VMware Tools	6
Upgrade Virtual Machine hardware	6
Upgrade an ESXi Host using vCenter Update Manager	9

Exam Objective	Chapter
Stage multiple ESXi Host upgrades	9
Determine whether an in-place upgrade is appropriate in a given upgrade scenario	2
1.5: Secure vCenter Server and ESXi	**2, 3, 9**
Identify common vCenter Server privileges and roles	3
Describe how permissions are applied and inherited in vCenter Server	3
Describe Single Sign-On architecture	2
Configure and administer the ESXi firewall	3
Enable/Configure/Disable services in the ESXi firewall	3
Enable Lockdown Mode	3
Configure network security policies	4
View/Sort/Export user and group lists	3
Add/Modify/Remove permissions for users and groups on vCenter Server inventory objects	3
Create/Clone/Edit vCenter Server Roles	3
Add an ESXi Host to a directory service	3
Apply permissions to ESXi Hosts using Host Profiles	9
Differentiate Single-Sign-On Deployment Scenarios	2
Configure and administer Single Sign-On	2
Manage Single Sign-On users and groups	2
Determine the appropriate set of privileges for common tasks in vCenter Server	3

Section 2: Plan and Configure vSphere Networking

Exam Objective	Chapter
2.3: Configure vSS and vDS Policies	**4, 7**
Identify common vSS and vDS policies	4
Describe vDS Security Polices/Settings	4
Configure dvPort group blocking policies	4
Configure load balancing and failover policies	4
Configure VLAN/PVLAN settings	4
Configure traffic shaping policies	4
Enable TCP Segmentation Offload support for a virtual machine	7
Enable Jumbo Frames support on appropriate components	4
Determine appropriate VLAN configuration for a vSphere implementation	4

Section 3: Plan and Configure vSphere Storage

Exam Objective	Chapter
3.1: Configure Shared Storage for vSphere	**5**
Identify storage adapters and devices	5
Identify storage naming conventions	5
Identify hardware/dependent hardware/software iSCSI initiator requirements	5
Compare and contrast array thin provisioning and virtual disk thin provisioning	5
Describe zoning and LUN masking practices	5
Scan/Rescan storage	5
Configure FC/iSCSI LUNs as ESXi boot devices	5

(continued)

Exam Objective	Chapter
Create an NFS share for use with vSphere	5
Enable/Configure/Disable vCenter Server storage filters	5
Configure/Edit hardware/dependent hardware initiators	5
Enable/Disable software iSCSI initiator	5
Configure/Edit software iSCSI initiator settings	5
Configure iSCSI port binding	5
Enable/Configure/Disable iSCSI CHAP	5
Determine use case for hardware/dependent hardware/software iSCSI initiator	5
Determine use case for and configure array thin provisioning	5
3.2: Create and Configure VMFS and NFS Datastores	**5**
Identify VMFS and NFS Datastore properties	5
Identify VMFS5 capabilities	5
Create/Rename/Delete/Unmount a VMFS Datastore	5
Mount/Unmount an NFS Datastore	5
Extend/Expand VMFS Datastores	5
Upgrade from VMFS3 to VMFS5	5
Place a VMFS Datastore in Maintenance Mode	5
Select the Preferred Path for a VMFS Datastore	5
Disable a path to a VMFS Datastore	5
Determine use case for multiple VMFS/NFS Datastores	5
Determine appropriate Path Selection Policy for a given VMFS Datastore	5

Section 4: Deploy and Administer Virtual Machines and vApps

Exam Objective	Chapter
4.1: Create and Deploy Virtual Machines	6
Identify capabilities of virtual machine hardware versions	6
Identify VMware Tools device drivers	6
Identify methods to access and use a virtual machine console	6
Identify virtual machine storage resources	6
Place virtual machines in selected ESXi hosts/Clusters/Resource Pools	6
Configure and deploy a Guest OS into a new virtual machine	6
Configure/Modify disk controller for virtual disks	6
Configure appropriate virtual disk type for a virtual machine	6
Create/Convert thin/thick provisioned virtual disks	6
Configure disk shares	6
Install/Upgrade/Update VMware Tools	6
Configure virtual machine time synchronization	6
Convert a physical machine using VMware Converter	6
Import a supported virtual machine source using VMware Converter	6
Modify virtual hardware settings using VMware Converter	6
Configure/Modify virtual CPU and Memory resources according to OS and application requirements	6
Configure/Modify virtual NIC adapter and connect virtual machines to appropriate network resources	6
Determine appropriate datastore locations for virtual machines based on application workloads	6

(continued)

Section 5: Establish and Maintain Service Levels

(continued)

(continued)

Section 6: Perform Basic Troubleshooting

(continued)

Section 7: Monitor a vSphere Implementation

Exam Objective	Chapter
7.1: Monitor ESXi, vCenter Server and Virtual Machines	**11**
Describe how Tasks and Events are viewed in vCenter Server	11
Identify critical performance metrics	11
Explain common memory metrics	11
Explain common CPU metrics	11
Explain common network metrics	11
Explain common storage metrics	11
Compare and contrast Overview and Advanced Charts	11
Configure SNMP for vCenter Server	11
Configure Active Directory and SMTP settings for vCenter Server	11
Configure vCenter Server logging options	11
Create a log bundle	11
Create/Edit/Delete a Scheduled Task	11
Configure/View/Print/Export resource maps	11
Start/Stop/Verify vCenter Server service status	11
Start/Stop/Verify ESXi host agent status	11
Configure vCenter Server timeout settings	11
Monitor/Administer vCenter Server connections	11
Create an Advanced Chart	11
Determine host performance using guest Performance Monitor	11
Given performance data, identify the affected vSphere resource	11

(continued)

Exam domains and objectives are subject to change at any time without prior notice and at VMware's sole discretion. For the most current information, please visit the VMware website at http://mylearn.vmware.com /portals/certification/.

Assessment Test

1. Which of the following are supported methods for providing high availability for vCenter Server? (Choose all that apply.)

   A. vCenter in a VM protected with HA and DRS

   B. vCenter in a VM protected with HA and FT

   C. vCenter Server Heartbeat

   D. vCenter Operations Manager

2. Which of the following admission control policies in HA offers the most customization for capacity in the cluster?

   A. Define failover capacity by static number of hosts

   B. Define failover capacity by reserving a percentage of the cluster resources

   C. Use Dedicated Failover Hosts

   D. Do not reserve failover capacity

3. What is the maximum number of ports in a vSwitch?

   A. 4,084

   B. 4,088

   C. 4,095

   D. 4,096

4. What are the preferred methods for configuring and administering the ESXi firewall? (Choose two.)

   A. DCUI

   B. vSphere Web Client

   C. esxcli

   D. esxcfg-firewall

5. Storage array thin provisioning can be configured through which feature of the vSphere Web Client?

   A. VMFS datastore properties

   B. NFS datastore properties

   C. Storage adapter properties

   D. None of these

6. To install vCenter Server 5, which of the following is required?

   A. Compatible 32-bit Windows OS

   B. Compatible 32-bit Linux OS

   C. Compatible 64-bit Windows OS

   D. Compatible 64-bit Linux OS

7. Which of the following vSphere editions are available for purchase?

   A. Essentials

   B. Essentials Plus

   C. Enterprise

   D. Enterprise Plus

8. Which of the following may be used to perform operations against an ESXi host that is in lockdown mode?

   A. vSphere CLI commands

   B. vSphere Management Assistant (vMA)

   C. vSphere Client connected directly to ESXi host

   D. vSphereWeb Client connected to vCenter Server managing the ESXi host in lockdown mode

9. Which of the following are alarm-type monitors? (Choose all that apply.)

   A. Datastore cluster

   B. Datacenters

   C. Datastores

   D. Distributed port groups

10. Which of the following are port binding types used in a dvSwitch? (Choose all that apply.)

    A. Static binding

    B. Dynamic binding

    C. Persistent binding

    D. Ephemeral binding

11. What is the minimum system requirement for memory in an ESXi 5.5 host?

    A. 1GB

    B. 2GB

    C. 3GB

    D. 4GB

12. Supported storage adapters in ESXi 5.5 include which of the following?

   A. iSCSI

   B. RAID

   C. SAS

   D. All of these

13. In vSphere 5.5, what is the minimum system requirement for memory for a simple install of vCenter Server, vCenter Single Sign-On, Sphere Web Client, and the vCenter Inventory Service?

   A. 4GB

   B. 8GB

   C. 10GB

   D. 12GB

14. On an ESXi 5.5 host, what is the maximum file size allowed on a VMFS-5 datastore?

   A. 2TB

   B. 2TB minus 512 bytes

   C. 62TB

   D. 64TB

15. Which of the following terms is used to describe increasing the size of a VMDK while the virtual machine is powered on?

   A. Warm-extend

   B. Hot-extend

   C. Disk grow

   D. Disk extend

16. Disk shares can have which of the following values? (Choose all that apply.)

   A. Custom

   B. Default

   C. High

   D. Low

17. What is the virtual machine hardware version introduced in vSphere 5.5?

   A. 7

   B. 8

   C. 9

   D. 10

18. Which of the following is used to export and import virtual machines?

    A. Changed Block Tracking (CBT)

    B. vStorage APIs for Array Integration (VAAI)

    C. Raw Device Mapping (RDM)

    D. Open Virtualization Format (OVF)

19. You have a virtual machine that will be configured to use VMware FT. What is the appropriate virtual disk type to choose for this virtual machine?

    A. Flat

    B. Thick

    C. Thin

    D. None of these

20. To completely disable all time synchronization for a virtual machine, what must occur?

    A. Disable the sync device driver.

    B. Edit the VMX file.

    C. Use the vSphere Web Client to configure time properties.

    D. None of these.

21. Which of the following most accurately describes a virtual appliance?

    A. Preconfigured and ready-to-use virtual machines that include an operating system and applications

    B. Preconfigured and ready-to-use virtual machines that cannot be modified

    C. Preconfigured vApp

    D. None of these

22. Which of the following is not a valid virtual machine file?

    A. `-flat.vmdk`

    B. `-psf.vmdk`

    C. `-ctk.vmdk`

    D. `-00000#.vmdk`

23. Which vSphere component serves as an authentication broker and handles security token exchange?

    A. vCenter Server

    B. vCenter Server Single Sign-On

    C. vCenter Inventory Service

    D. vCenter Linked Mode

24. Which of the following statements is true about individual virtual machine automation levels?

    A. The automation level defined for the DRS cluster will override the individual virtual machine automation level.

    B. The automation level defined for the individual virtual machine will override the automation level defined for the DRS cluster.

    C. The automation level defined for the individual virtual machine must match that of the DRS cluster.

    D. None of these.

25. Which of the following objects can be part of the resource pool hierarchy? (Choose all that apply.)

    A. Virtual machines

    B. vApps

    C. Folders

    D. Resource pools

26. When creating VMFS datastores, what is the relationship that should be maintained between VMFS datastore and LUN?

    A. 1-1

    B. 1-2

    C. 2-1

    D. None of these

27. Which of the following can be used to increase performance on ESXi hosts?

    A. vSphere Data Protection Advanced

    B. vSphere HA

    C. vSphere Flash Read Cache

    D. vSphere App HA

28. vSphere Data Protection can back up to which of the following media types?

    A. Tape only

    B. Disk only

    C. Tape and disk

    D. Optical media

29. You add a new NIC to a vSwitch used for virtual machine network traffic. What additional actions must be taken before virtual machines will begin to use this NIC?

   A.   Refresh networking.

   B.   Reboot ESXi host.

   C.   Restart ESXi Management Network.

   D.   None of the above.

30. A virtual infrastructure administrator has been asked to restore a virtual machine to its previous configuration from a single snapshot. Which of the following actions should she take?

   A.   Delete

   B.   Delete All

   C.   Revert

   D.   Consolidate

31. Which of the following can be used to troubleshoot storage contention issues? (Choose all that apply.)

   A.   esxtop

   B.   resxtop

   C.   The vSphere Client

   D.   vCenter Operations Manager

32. VMware FT supports which of the following virtual machines? (Choose two.)

   A.   Windows Server 2008 with one vCPU

   B.   Windows Server 2008 with two vCPUs

   C.   Windows Server 2000 with one vCPU

   D.   Windows Server 2000 with two vCPUs

33. vSphere Update Manager can be used to update which of the following? (Choose all that apply.)

   A.   The VMware Tools

   B.   ESXi 4 hosts

   C.   Virtual machine hardware

   D.   ESX 3.5 hosts

34. Which of the following commands can be used to test connectivity of a vMotion interface?

   A.   ping

   B.   vmkping

   C.   esxcli network

   D.   All of these

35. Which of the following should be used for ESXi hosts that will participate in HA-enabled clusters?

A. Static IP addresses

B. DHCP-assigned IP addresses

C. IPv6

D. vMotion

36. When the vSphere Client is used and directly connected to an ESXi host, which of the following tabs is used to view tasks and events?

A. Events

B. Tasks & Events

C. Scheduled Tasks

D. None of these

37. Which of the following is used to control the vCenter Server services on the Windows host that it is installed on?

A. services.exe

B. services.msc

C. services.cpl

D. services.chm

38. Which load-balancing policy is available only in the dvSwitch?

A. Route Based On IP Hash

B. Route Based On Source MAC Hash

C. Route Based On Physical NIC Load

D. Use Explicit Failover Order

39. Where do you manage vSphere Replication from?

A. vSphere Client

B. vSphere Web Client

C. vSphere Replication Management URL

D. vSphere Data Protection Management URL

40. vCenter Operations Manager uses which of the following to provide information about objects in the virtual environment?

A. Workflows

B. Tags

C. Badges

D. Symbols

Answers to Assessment Test

1. A and C. vCenter Server is supported in a VM protected with HA and DRS. VMware vCenter Server Heartbeat is a VMware product and will be fully supported by VMware.

2. B. "Define failover capacity by reserving a percentage of the cluster resources" allows the percentage of CPU and memory resources to be reserved, making it the most customizable option available.

3. B. A vSwitch can have a maximum of 4,088 ports.

4. B and C. The vSphere Web Client and the `esxcli` command are the preferred methods for configuring the ESXi firewall.

5. D. The configuration of thin provisioning on storage devices is not supported in VMware software. You will have to use the vendor's management tools instead.

6. C. The installation of vCenter Server 5 requires a compatible 64-bit Windows OS, like Windows Server 2008 SP2 or Windows Server 2008 R2.

7. A, B, C and D. All of these editions are available.

8. D. All operations performed against an ESXi host in lockdown mode must originate from the vCenter Server that is managing the ESXi host.

9. A, B, C and D. All of these are alarm-type monitors.

10. A, B and D. Static, dynamic, and ephemeral are the three types of port binding used in a dvSwitch.

11. D. ESXi 5 hosts require a minimum of 4GB of RAM.

12. D. iSCSI, RAID, and SAS are all supported adapter classes used to provide storage connectivity in ESXi 5.5.

13. D. A simple install of vCenter Server requires 12GB of RAM.

14. C. 62TB is the maximum file size allowed on a VMFS-5 datastore with an ESXi 5.5 host.

15. B. The process of increasing the size of a VMDK while a VM is powered on is known as hot-extending.

16. A, C and D. Shares may have the values of Low, Normal, High, and Custom.

17. D. Virtual machine hardware version 10 is the latest version.

18. D. Open Virtualization Format is an open standard that can be used to import and export virtual machines.

19. B. A thick-provisioned disk, which is also known as a Thick Provision Eager Zeroed disk, is a VMDK file that is created and all of the space is provisioned and zeroed immediately. This type of disk is required for VMware FT.

20. B. To completely disable all the VMware Tools–initiated time synchronization functionality for a VM, the virtual machine's VMX file must be modified.

21. A. Virtual appliances are preconfigured and ready-to-use virtual machines that include an operating system and applications.

22. B. There is no -psf.vmdk file type.

23. B. vCenter Single Sign-On (SSO) was first introduced in vSphere 5.1 to improve authentication services in vSphere.

24. B. Individual virtual machine automation level settings override the settings defined in the DRS cluster.

25. A, B and D. Virtual machines, vApps, and other resource pools can all be members of the resource pool hierarchy.

26. A. When creating VMFS datastores, it is important to maintain a one-to-one relationship between each VMFS datastore and LUN.

27. C. The vSphere Flash Read Cache is used to provide a server-side read cache layer that increases performance.

28. B. vSphere Data Protection is a disk-based backup solution.

29. D. The addition of a vmnic to a vSwitch is a nondisruptive action, and virtual machine network traffic will begin to use this NIC immediately with no further action.

30. C. Revert will restore the virtual machine to its previous state.

31. A, B, C and D. All of these tools can be used to troubleshoot storage contention issues.

32. A and C. Windows Server 2000 and Windows Server 2008 are both supported guest operating systems for use with VMware FT, but only a single vCPU configuration is supported.

33. A, B and C. vSphere Update Manager can update virtual machine hardware, the VMware Tools, and ESX/ESXi 4.0 and newer hosts.

34. B. The vMotion interface is a VMkernel connection type, and the vmkping command can be used to test its connectivity.

35. A. It is always a good idea to use static IP addresses for any server.

36. D. When the vSphere Client is connected directly to an ESXi host, there's only an Events tab to view recent events. Tasks are only shown in the Recent Tasks pane.

37. B. The Services MMC snap-in, or `services.msc`, is used to control services in Windows.

38. C. The Route Based On Physical NIC Load policy is available only when using a dvSwitch.

39. B. vSphere Replication is managed from the vSphere Web Client.

40. C. Badges are used to provide information in vCenter Operations Manager.

Chapter 1

What's New in vSphere 5.5

✓ **vSphere ESXi Hypervisor Enhancements**

- Hot-Pluggable SSD PCI Express (PCIe) Devices
- Support for Reliable Memory Technology
- Enhancements for CPU C-States

✓ **Virtual Machine Enhancements**

- VM Compatibility with ESXi 5.5
- Expanded vGPU Support
- Graphic Acceleration for Linux Guests

✓ **vCenter Server Enhancements**

- VMware vCenter Single Sign-On
- VMware vCenter Server Appliance
- VMware vSphere Web Client
- vSphere App HA
- HA Compatibility with DRS VM-VM Affinity Rules
- vSphere Big Data Extensions

✓ **Storage Enhancements**

- Support for 62TB VMDK
- MSCS Updates
- vSphere 5.1 Feature Updates
- 16Gb E2E Support
- PDL AutoRemove
- vSphere Replication Interoperability
- vSphere Replication Multi-Point-in-Time Snapshot Retention
- VAAI UNMAP Improvements
- VMFS Heap Improvements
- vSphere Flash Read Cache

✓ **Networking Enhancements**

- Link Aggregation Control Protocol Enhancements
- Traffic Filtering
- Quality of Service Tagging
- SR-IOV Enhancements
- Enhanced Host-Level Packet Capture
- 40Gb NIC Support

✓ **VMware Data Protection Improvements**

✓ **vCenter Operations Manager**

vSphere 5.5 continues to build on the rich feature sets of both vSphere 5.0 and vSphere 5.1. There are new capabilities at all levels of the product, and the introduction of these new features will in many ways be what will differentiate the updated VCP5-DCV exam from the prior version. This chapter briefly reviews the new vSphere 5.5 features. The purpose here is simply to get everyone introduced to what is new and different in vSphere 5.5. Many of these features will be covered in greater detail in the following chapters.

vSphere ESXi Hypervisor Enhancements

vSphere 5.5 introduces several improvements to the hypervisor. These changes were introduced to provide greater performance, reliability, and efficiency.

Hot-Pluggable PCIe SSD Devices

PCIe SSDs (Peripheral Component Interconnect Express solid-state drives) can be used to provide high-performance local storage options in ESXi. Allowing administrators to hot-swap these drives should offer advantages in uptime and host resiliency. Hot-add or hot-remove of an SSD on an ESXi host is now supported, and the ESXi storage stack will detect these operations.

Support for Reliable Memory Technology

Reliable Memory Technology is a CPU hardware feature that the ESXi hypervisor can use to place the VMkernel on what is reported as more reliable memory. Because the ESXi hypervisor is loaded into memory, using Reliable Memory Technology should provide greater protection from memory errors. In addition to the VMkernel, certain processes like hostd and watchdog are also protected. Figure 1.1 shows how ESXi might use Reliable Memory Technology.

FIGURE 1.1   Reliable Memory Technology and VMkernel

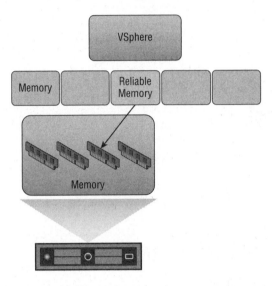

Enhancements to CPU C-States

vSphere 5.5 introduces the ability to leverage both the performance state (P-state) and the deep processor power state (C-state) in the balanced as well as the low power policy for host power management. vSphere 5.1 and prior leveraged only the performance state (P-state). These changes provide additional power savings as well as potentially enhanced CPU performance.

Virtual Machine Enhancements

Virtual machine enhancements are included in ESXi 5.5 to provide the ability to run even more Tier 1 workloads, and to provide additional abilities to VMs. Many of these enhancements are introduced to provide better end-user experiences for VM consumers, such as applications that have graphic-intensive workloads.

VM Compatibility with VMware ESXi 5.5

A new virtual machine compatibility level (or virtual machine hardware version 10) is introduced in vSphere 5.5. A new virtual-SATA Advance Host Controller Interface (AHCI) controller that supports both virtual disks and CD-ROM devices can now be used, which allows you to connect up to 30 devices per controller. With a maximum of four controllers, your VMs can now have 120 disk devices.

Expanded vGPU Support

A virtual graphics processor unit (vGPU) is a processor for rendering graphics on a VM network's host instead of an endpoint PC, with comparable performance. vGPU support in vSphere 5.5 includes GPUs based on both Intel and AMD. This support provides more flexibility for VMs or applications that have graphic-intensive workloads. vMotion of virtual machines configured with automatic rendering is possible across a mix of GPU vendors and also between ESXi hosts that use software-backed graphics rendering.

Graphic Acceleration for Linux Guests

With vSphere 5.5, VMware introduces a new guest driver that will accelerate the entire Linux graphics stack. This guest driver code is also open source, which means that any modern Linux distribution could be packaged with the guest driver. Modern distributions that are supported include Ubuntu 12.04 and later, Fedora 17 and later, and Red Hat Enterprise Linux (RHEL) 7.

vCenter Server Enhancements

vCenter Server 5.5 also has new features that improve installation ease, increase performance, improve scalability, and reduce complexity. Improvements to vCenter Single Sign-On (SSO) include a complete rewrite of the product.

vCenter Single Sign-On

vCenter Single Sign-On (SSO) was introduced in vSphere 5.1 with the intention of providing a single sign-on experience to products in the vCloud Suite. In vSphere 5.5, a single installation model is now offered and the requirement for a separate database has been eliminated. These changes, coupled with enhanced Microsoft Active Directory integration, have greatly improved SSO in this release.

vCenter Server Appliance

The vCenter Server Appliance (VCSA) included with vSphere 5.5 uses an embedded vPostgres database. This embedded database supports 100 hosts and 3000 virtual machines.

If an external Oracle database is used, those numbers increase to 1000 hosts and 10,000 virtual machines. These changes allow the standalone VCSA with the vPostgres database to be supported with very large environments.

vSphere Web Client

The vSphere Web Client is still on track to replace the traditional vSphere Client. All of the new vSphere 5.5 features can be managed only with the vSphere Web Client. Drag-and -drop, filters, and recent items are new features of the vSphere Web Client, in addition to full client support for Mac OS X. It is also important to note that in vSphere 5.5, Linux OS support has been removed. This is due to the fact that Adobe has dropped support for Flash on Linux.

vSphere App HA

vSphere 5.5 introduces vSphere App HA, which works with vSphere HA host monitoring and virtual machine monitoring to provide improved application uptime. vSphere App HA works with VMware vFabric Hyperic Server to restart an application when issues are detected. Note that App HA requires Enterprise Plus licensing.

HA Compatibility with DRS VM-VM Affinity Rules

Prior to vSphere 5.5, in the event of an ESXi host failure vSphere HA would not honor VM-VM anti-affinity rules defined in vSphere DRS when restarting virtual machines. This behavior is now more intelligent and should provide a better recovery experience following a host failure.

vSphere Big Data Extensions

Big Data Extensions (BDE) is another new feature of vSphere 5.5 that allows the deployment and management of Hadoop clusters from within the vSphere Web Client. This feature is available only with the vSphere Enterprise and Enterprise Plus editions, and it requires the vSphere Web Client.

Storage Enhancements

With the release of vSphere 5.5, VMware introduces many new features aimed at making storage more scalable, capable, resilient, and available. The first feature, which was long overdue, is the capability to create virtual machine disk (VMDK) files greater than 2TB minus 512 bytes.

Support for 62TB VMDK

In vSphere 5.1 and earlier, the maximum VMDK size was limited to 2TB minus 512 bytes. With vSphere 5.5, the new maximum size is 62TB. This means you could have a 62TB VMDK on a 64TB VMFS volume. This also includes support for virtual mode Raw Device Mappings (RDMs) as well. You may recall that support for large physical mode RDMs was first introduced in vSphere 5.0.

MSCS Updates

With vSphere 5.5, support is also expanded for Microsoft Server Cluster (MSCS). In vSphere 5.1 and earlier, only Fibre Channel was supported as the storage protocol in MSCS environments. In vSphere 5.5, both iSCSI and Fibre Channel over Ethernet (FCoE) are now supported, in addition to Fibre Channel. Microsoft Windows 2012 and the Round-Robin path policy for shared storage are both also supported in vSphere 5.5. Also, MSCS is now supported for protecting a backend Microsoft SQL vCenter Server database.

16Gb E2E Support

VMware introduces 16Gb end-to-end FC support in vSphere 5.5. This means that both the host bus adapters (HBAs) and array controllers can run at 16Gb, as long as the switch between the initiator and target also supports 16Gb.

PDL AutoRemove

PDL AutoRemove is a feature that helps prevent an all-paths-down (APD) event on an ESXi host. When a storage device is improperly removed from an ESXi host, it enters a permanent device loss (PDL) state. vSphere hosts are limited to 256 disk devices, and too many PDLs can lead to an exhaustion of device slots. This can result in an APD event, which will generally lead to an ESXi host reboot. PDL AutoRemove automatically removes a device from a host when it enters a PDL state, and thus helps prevent an APD event.

vSphere Replication Interoperability

In vSphere 5.5, vSphere Replication has been improved to allow virtual machines at the primary site to be migrated with Storage vMotion and participate in Storage DRS datastore clusters.

vSphere Replication Multi-Point-in-Time (MPIT) Snapshot Retention

In vSphere 5.5 there is a feature that enables retention of historical points in time. This is accomplished with a multi-point-in-time (MPIT) retention policy, and it allows for multiple recovery points, as illustrated in Figure 1.2.

FIGURE 1.2   vSphere Replication Recovery Settings

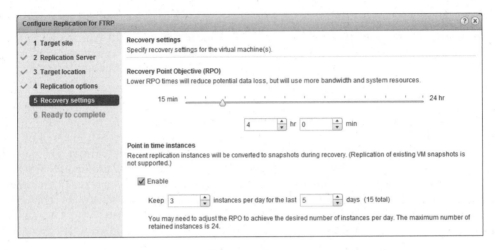

VAAI UNMAP Improvements

vStorage APIs for Array Integration (VAAI), first introduced in vSphere 4.1, is a feature that allows the hypervisor to offload certain storage functions to a supported storage array. In vSphere, one of the commands, UNMAP, has been optimized so that now the reclaim size is specified as blocks rather than a percentage value. Dead space is also now claimed in increments rather than all at once. UNMAP can also handle much larger dead space areas, now that 62TB VMDKs are possible in vSphere 5.5.

VMFS Heap Improvements

vSphere 5.5 has an improved heap eviction process, which means there is no longer a need for large heap sizes. vSphere 5.5 with 256MB of heap allows ESXi hosts to access all address space of a 64TB VMFS volume.

vSphere Flash Read Cache

The vSphere Flash Read Cache is a flash-based storage solution that pools multiple flash-based devices into a vSphere Flash Resource, as illustrated in Figure 1.3. It is used to accelerate read-intensive workloads and improve virtual machine performance. This feature is also supported with vMotion, HA, and DRS.

FIGURE 1.3   vSphere Flash Read Cache

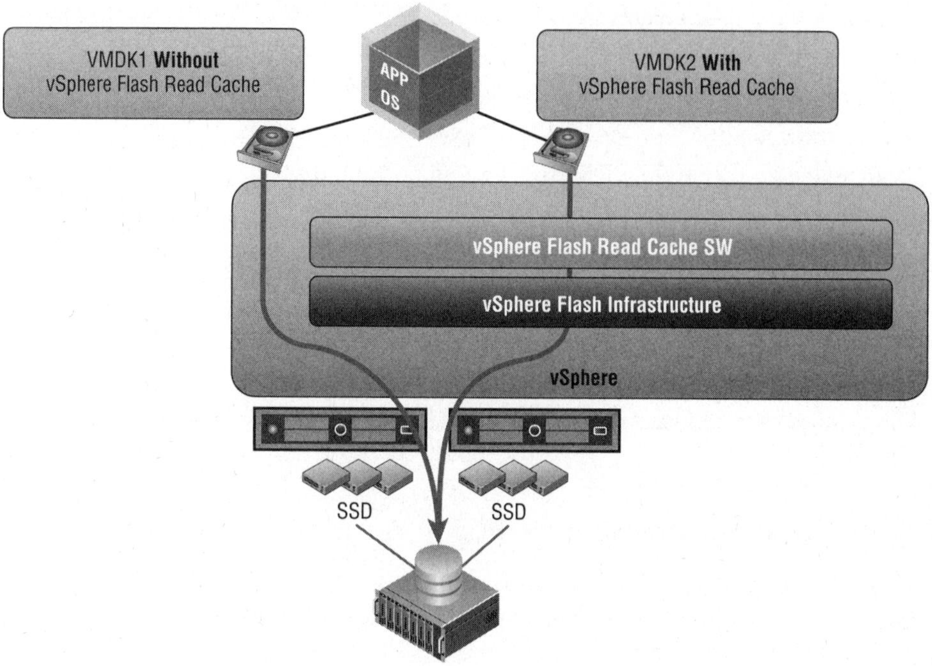

Networking Enhancements

Like many of the other improvements in vSphere 5.5, the networking of the dvSwitch has been updated to simplify operations, improve performance, and enhance security.

Link Aggregation Control Protocol (LACP) Enhancements

LACP is used to aggregate multiple network connections into a single logical connection that is used to provide increased throughput and redundancy. In vSphere 5.5, the dvSwitch now supports 22 new hashing algorithms. As many as 64 Link Aggregation Groups (LAGs) are now also supported. There are also new workflows that can be used to configure LACP across multiple ESXi hosts.

Traffic Filtering

One of the security enhancements introduced in the dvSwitch in vSphere 5.5 is the ability to support packet classification based on three different qualifiers:

- MAC Source Address and Destination Address qualifiers
- System traffic qualifiers—vMotion, FT, vSphere management
- IP qualifiers: Protocol type, IP SA, IP DA, and port number

Traffic filtering can be used to allow port-level security and provides the ability to filter ingress traffic, egress traffic, or both.

Quality of Service Tagging

Support has been added for Differentiated Service Code Point (DSCP) marking in vSphere 5.5. This enables users to insert tags in the IP header, which can be useful with certain physical routers.

SR-IOV Enhancements

In vSphere 5.5, the configuration workflow for single root I/O virtualization (SR-IOV)–enabled physical NICs has been simplified. Also introduced is the ability to propagate port group properties from the virtual switch to the virtual functions.

Enhanced Host-Level Packet Capture

A host-level CLI packet capture tool, which is the equivalent of the Linux tcpdump utility, is now available.

40Gb NIC Support

Support for Mellanox ConnextX-3 Virtual Protocol Interconnect (VPI) adapters configured in Ethernet mode is introduced in vSphere 5.5.

VMware Data Protection (VDP) Enhancements

VMware Data Protection was introduced in vSphere 5.1 and replaced VMware Data Recovery, which was introduced in vSphere 5.0. The vSphere 5.5 release of VDP has been improved to include:

- Replication of backup data to EMC Avamar
- Direct-to-host emergency restore

- Backup and restore of individual VMDKs
- Granular scheduling of backup/replication jobs
- Flexible VDP storage management

vCenter Operations Manager

While the product has been around for many years, vCenter Operations Manager Foundation was first bundled with vSphere in the 5.1 release. vCenter Operations Manager Foundation includes performance analytics and health monitoring for your virtual infrastructure. It is deployed as a vApp and includes two virtual machines, as shown in Figure 1.4. vCenter Operations Manager will be covered in great detail in Chapter 11, "Monitoring a vSphere Implementation and Managing vCenter Server Alarms."

FIGURE 1.4   vCenter Operations Manager vApp

vCenter Operations Manager vApp

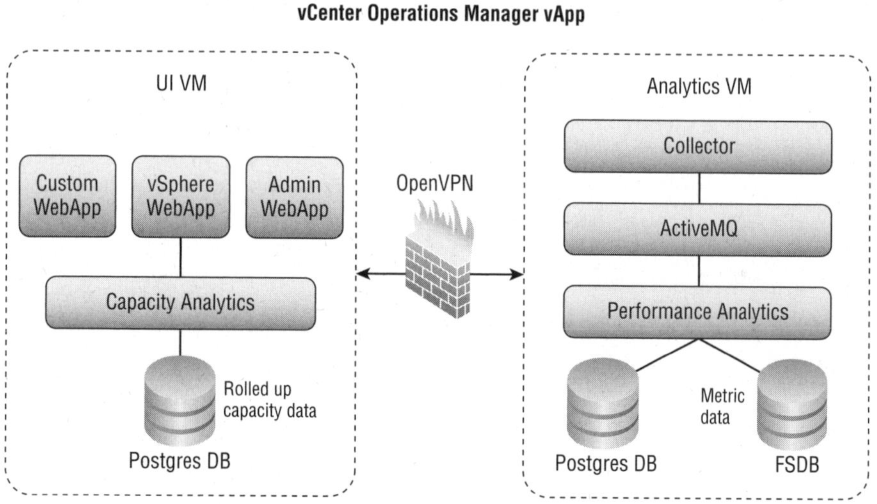

Summary

Many changes and new features were introduced in vSphere 5.5. Like previous versions of vSphere, many of the new features are targeted at being able to support larger and larger Tier 1 workloads. Some of the features are also targeted at being able to support virtual desktops or the more graphic-demanding applications running on them.

There are three significant changes in terms of what has changed for the VCP5-DCV exam and its update to be relevant to vSphere 5.5. The first of these changes is the inclusion of vCenter Single Sign-On objectives. The second change is the reintroduction of

VMware Data Protection objectives. VMware Data Recovery (released in vSphere 5.0) objectives were removed shortly after the release of vSphere 5.1 and VDP. The third change is the introduction of vCenter Operations Manager objectives. These changes represent the majority of the changes that you are likely to encounter on the new VCP5-DCV exam. Also keep in mind that other new features like vSphere Flash Read Cache and vSphere Replication, while not as extensively listed in the objectives, will also be important to learn and know for the exam.

Although there are many changes to vSphere 5.5, many of which we will explore in the coming chapters of this book, there are also features that are not covered by the VCP5-DCV exam blueprint. To think that these features omitted on the blueprint are not likely to show up on the exam could be a mistake. I encourage you to learn all of the vSphere 5.5 products and explore the feature sets as you move through this book. Learn how the products work and where they might effectively be used in your virtual infrastructure, but also be mindful of the "why" of these products and feature sets.

Chapter

2

Planning, Installing, Configuring, and Upgrading VMware ESXi and vCenter Server

VCP5.5-DCV EXAM OBJECTIVES COVERED IN THIS CHAPTER:

✓ **1.2 Install and Configure vCenter Server**

- Identify available vCenter Server editions
- Identify vCenter Server and vCenter Server database requirements
- Identify Single Sign-On requirements
- Create a database connection to the vCenter Server database
- Size the vCenter Server database
- Install vCenter Server into a virtual machine
- Deploy the vCenter Appliance
- Install and Configure the vSphere Client / vSphere Web Client
- Install additional vCenter Server components
- Install/Remove vSphere Client plug-ins
- Enable/Disable vSphere Client plug-ins
- License vCenter Server
- Determine availability requirements for a vCenter Server in a given vSphere implementation

✓ **1.3 Install and Configure VMware ESXi**

- Identify ESXi host requirements
- Perform an interactive installation of ESXi using media or PXE

- Configure NTP on an ESXi Host
- Configure DNS and Routing on an ESXi Host
- Enable/Configure/Disable hyperthreading
- Select a CPU power management policy
- Enable/Size/Disable memory compression cache
- License an ESXi host

✓ **1.4 Plan and Perform Upgrades of vCenter Server and VMware ESXi**

- Identify steps required to upgrade a vSphere implementation
- Identify upgrade requirements for ESXi hosts
- Determine whether an in-place upgrade is appropriate in a given upgrade scenario

✓ **1.5 Secure vCenter Server and ESXi**

- Describe Single Sign-On architecture
- Differentiate Single-Sign-On Deployment Scenarios
- Configure and administer Single Sign-On
- Manage Single Sign-On users and groups

TOOLS

- VMware vSphere Basics guide (Objectives 1.1, 1.2, 1.4, 1.5)
- vSphere Installation and Setup guide (Objectives 1.1, 1.2, 1.4, 1.5)
- vCenter Server and Host Management guide (Objectives 1.1, 1.2, 1.5)
- VMware Virtualization Toolkit (Objective 1.1)
- vSphere Client/vSphere Web Client (Objectives 1.1, 1.2, 1.5)
- vSphere PowerCLI (Objective 1.2)
- vSphere Upgrade guide (Objective 1.4)
- VMware vSphere Examples and Scenarios guide (Objective 1.4)

This chapter will cover installing VMware ESXi, vCenter Server, vCenter Server Single Sign-On, and many additional components. You can use this information to build your lab, and this chapter will be the starting point for all the labs in this book. We'll also cover licensing and upgrades in this chapter. When you finish reading this chapter, you will have a working vSphere lab. Let's get started!

Introducing VMware ESXi

ESXi is VMware's bare-metal hypervisor used to run virtual machines on x86 hardware. ESXi abstracts the underlying hardware on these x86 servers and allows multiple virtual machines to share these resources. ESXi is offered in two editions:

- ESXi Installable, the version that you download directly from VMware and install on your compatible x86 servers, either interactively, via script, or by using Auto Deploy

- ESXi Embedded, which is installed on USB or SD cards in servers by the server OEM

We'll begin by identifying the ESXi 5.5 host system requirements.

Identifying ESXi Host Requirements

Before you install ESXi 5.5 on a physical server or in a nested virtual machine, you must ensure that you meet the system requirements. These include the following specifications:

- A server with 64-bit x86 CPUs that is listed in the VMware Compatibility Guide (HCL)

- Two cores

- 4GB of RAM

- A supported Gigabit or 10GbE NIC

- A supported disk controller for local storage

- A boot device with a minimum size of 1GB

as well as the following requirements:

- The processor must contain only LAHF (Load AH from Flags) and SAHF (Store AH into Flags) CPU instructions.

- The NX/XD bit (a CPU feature called Never eXecute) must be enabled for the CPU in the system BIOS.

- Hardware virtualization (Intel VT-x or AMD RVI) must be enabled on x64 CPUs, if 64-bit guests are to be used.

A 5.2GB disk/LUN is required when using the local disk or booting from SAN. Now that we have covered the system requirements for ESXi 5.5, let's move on to interactively installing ESXi.

Performing an Interactive Installation of ESXi

Carrying out an interactive installation of ESXi 5 is an essential part of any virtual infrastructure administrator's duties, and it is a fairly straightforward task. In fact, if you have previously installed other ESXi versions, the procedure will be familiar. In Exercise 2.1, you will interactively install ESXi 5.5 from the installation media.

EXERCISE 2.1

Interactively Installing ESXi 5.5

1. Download or obtain a copy of the ESXi installation media. This file will have the words "VMware-VMvisor-Installer" included in the filename.

2. Connect to a console session on the server that ESXi will be installed on.

3. In the server system's BIOS, verify that the server hardware clock is set to *UTC±0*. ESXi uses UTC, which is not affected by daylight saving changes on the host but displays the time in the GUI adjusted to the client's time zone settings. Also verify that the system is configured to boot to the installation media you have available.

   If you need assistance with these steps, consult the documentation for your particular system or check the following VMware Knowledge Base (KB) articles:

   http://kb.vmware.com/kb/1003944

   http://kb.vmware.com/kb/2032756

4. Insert the optical or USB media on which the ESXi installer is located (or connect remotely if using out-of-band management), and ensure that the ESXi Embedded edition is not already installed on this server. These two editions cannot coexist.

5. Restart the system so that the ESXi installer will boot.

6. After reviewing the information on the welcome screen, press the Enter key to continue.

7. If you agree to the terms of the license agreement, press the F11 key to accept the EULA and continue.

8. On the Select A Disk To Install Or Upgrade page, select the drive that ESXi will be installed on. You can press F1 for more information about the selected disk. Be absolutely certain that the correct disk is selected here before continuing.

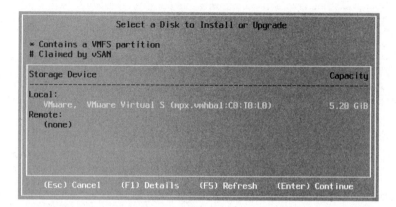

9. Once you are certain that the correct disk is selected, press Enter to continue. If the disk you selected had data from a previous installation, a Confirm Disk Selection dialog will appear. If you are sure that you want to overwrite the disk, press Enter.

10. Select a keyboard layout and press Enter. Although you can change the keyboard layout after the install from the ESXi console, keep in mind that the password you are going to enter in the next step—especially when using special characters—is based on the selected layout.

11. Enter a password for the ESXi root account, and then confirm the password. Passwords must be at least seven characters long. Once the "Passwords Match" message appears on this screen, press Enter to continue.

12. The system will be scanned for a few moments. If any errors or warnings appear on the following screen, please review and correct them if applicable. Here's an example:

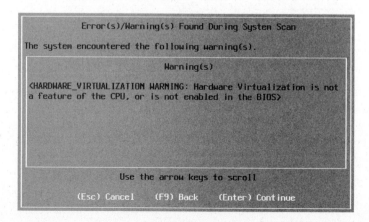

13. If warnings or errors are found on your system, press Enter to continue or Esc to cancel the install. If no errors or warnings are encountered on your system, you will see the Confirm Install screen.

14. If you are ready to begin the ESXi installation, press F11.

15. When the installation completes, read the information on the Installation Complete summary screen. After removing your installation media, press Enter to reboot the host.

> The interactive installation option is intended to be used for small deployments of fewer than five ESXi hosts. For larger installations you'll likely want to use either a scripted install or the Auto Deploy feature. We will cover Auto Deploy a bit later in this chapter.

Now that the interactive installation of ESXi is complete, you will need to wait for the system to reboot and verify that network connectivity is in place for this ESXi host. If your host is connected to a network with DHCP (Dynamic Host Configuration Protocol) running, then no further action should be required. The console of the ESXi host will display both the IPv4 and IPv6 addresses, as shown in Figure 2.1.

FIGURE 2.1 ESXi host's IP addresses

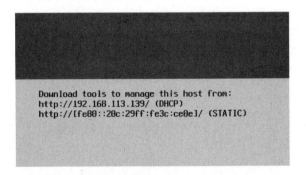

```
Download tools to manage this host from:
http://192.168.113.139/ (DHCP)
http://[fe80::20c:29ff:fe3c:ce0e]/ (STATIC)
```

If you don't have DHCP services available for your ESXi hosts or if you want to implement the VMware best practice of assigning static IP addresses to ESXi hosts, some additional configuration will be required. Exercise 2.2 covers the steps to manually configure the ESXi host management network. Although this configuration step is not a VCP5-DCV exam objective, it is very useful for the VMware administrator to know.

EXERCISE 2.2

Configuring the ESXi Host Management Network

1. Obtain local console access to the ESXi host and press F2 to log into the Direct Console User Interface (DCUI).

2. Enter the root password specified during the ESXi installation, and then press Enter to log into the DCUI.

3. Use the arrow keys on your keyboard to navigate to the Configure Management Network option on the left side of the screen. Note that the right side of the screen shows the current networking configuration. Press Enter to select this option.

4. Use the arrow keys to select the Network Adapters option on the left side of the screen and press Enter to configure the network adapters.

5. Ensure that the correct network adapter(s) selection is made on this screen. It may be necessary to connect and disconnect network cables to determine which physical network interface controller (NIC) is associated with which virtual machine NIC (VMNIC).

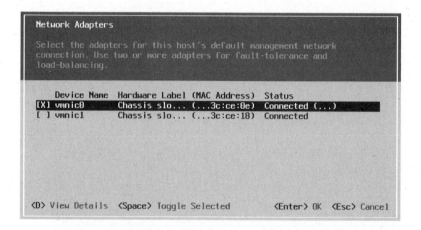

6. Use the arrow keys to select the correct network adapter(s) and the spacebar to toggle the selection(s), shown with an X in the left brackets. Once the correct network adapter is selected, press Enter to save this configuration.

7. You will return to the Configure Management Network screen. If a virtual LAN (VLAN) is required for the management network, you can use the VLAN (optional) option to set the VLAN ID.

    Most labs will probably not require this step, and there is much more additional information on VLANs in Chapter 4, "Planning and Configuring vSphere Networking."

EXERCISE 2.2 *(continued)*

8. On the Configure Management Network screen, select either IP Configuration or IPv6 Configuration and press Enter to configure the ESXi host's management network IP address. Note that if you choose to disable IPv6, a host reboot is necessary.

9. Use the arrow keys to select the DHCP or Static IP addressing option and the space-bar to toggle the selection. If a static IP address is desired, select the Static IP address option. This will activate the lower portion of the screen, where you can specify an IP address, subnet mask, and default gateway. Enter the appropriate information here and press Enter to set the configuration.

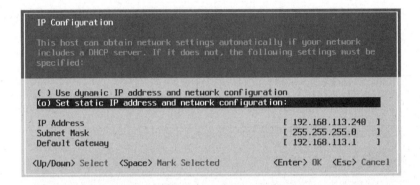

10. You will return to the Configure Management Network screen. Press Esc to return to the System Customization screen. If you made changes to your management network, you will now be prompted to confirm these changes.

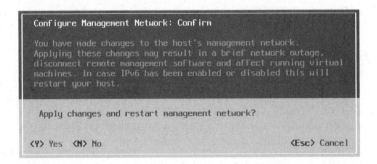

11. Press Y to save your changes and restart the management network. Exiting the Configure Management Network screen is the way to save any changes that were just made.

12. On the System Customization screen, use the arrow keys to select Test Management Network and then press Enter to continue.

13. Enter up to three IP addresses that should be reachable via ping from your ESXi host management network and press Enter to run the tests. If the tests complete successfully, press Enter to exit the tests and return to the System Customization screen.

14. If the pings failed, review your network configuration on the ESXi host and possibly upstream to your physical switches or other gear.

15. Press Esc to log out of the DCUI. Verify that the IP address shown on the landing page for the DCUI is correct.

You probably noticed that Exercise 2.2 omitted DNS configuration when you configured the management network. DNS is important, but you don't absolutely require it just yet. Don't worry, though—configuring DNS is a VCP5-DCV exam objective, and it will be covered in detail a bit later in this chapter.

As just demonstrated in Exercise 2.2, an ESXi host can be managed directly from the console via the DCUI. You could've used the ESXi Shell, but for most VMware administrators the vSphere Client is the day-to-day tool used to manage standalone ESXi hosts. It is important to know that the vSphere Client is a Windows-only application. The system requirements for the vSphere Client are as follows:

- One CPU (500MHz or faster Intel or AMD processor; 1GHz recommended)
- 500MB of RAM (1GB recommended)
- 1.5GB of free disk space for a complete installation
- No instances of Microsoft Visual J#
- GbE networking

You can download the vSphere Client from the VMware website or by accessing the local IP address of your ESXi 5.5 host over HTTPS. Now that you know your ESXi host has management network connectivity, let's take a moment to install the vSphere Client in Exercise 2.3.

EXERCISE 2.3

Installing the vSphere Client

1. Download a copy of the vSphere Client installation media from the VMware website or from https://<YOUR_ESXi_HOST_IP_ADDRESS>

2. Launch the installer on a Windows client system.

3. After the files finish extracting, select the language for the installation from the drop-down menu. Click OK to continue.

4. Review the information on the Welcome screen and click Next.

5. Review the information on the License Agreement screen, and if you agree, select the appropriate radio button. Click Next.

EXERCISE 2.3 *(continued)*

6. Select a directory for the vSphere Client to be installed in and click Next.

7. Click Install to begin the installation.

8. Click Finish on the Installation Completed screen.

> Security warnings about certificates will appear when you log into ESXi hosts and/or vCenter Server, because the vSphere Client detects certificates self-signed by an ESXi host or vCenter Server. This is the default behavior, and if you trust these certificates, you may safely ignore these warnings.

Whereas the interactive installation is a good solution for installing a few ESXi hosts, other options are better suited for mass ESXi deployments. One of these is the Auto Deploy feature.

Performing a PXE Installation of ESXi with Auto Deploy

Whereas the interactive installation we performed in this chapter is intended for smaller environments, Auto Deploy can be used to scale to large environments very quickly. Auto Deploy is used to provision ESXi hosts via *Preboot Execution Environment* (PXE) at boot. The PXE boot installation workflow is shown in Figure 2.2.

Beginning with vSphere 5.1, Auto Deploy can be configured in three different operational modes:

Stateless   Auto Deploy stores no ESXi state on the ESXi host disk(s) and allows diskless ESXi host configurations.

Stateless Caching   The ESXi image loaded into memory is also cached to a dedicated boot device (local disk, SAN, or via USB), in case the host cannot boot due to a problem with either the PXE environment or the Auto Deploy server.

Stateful Installs   Auto Deploy is used as a provisioning tool, and a onetime PXE boot occurs, but subsequent reboots will take place from a dedicated boot device.

FIGURE 2.2   PXE boot installation workflow

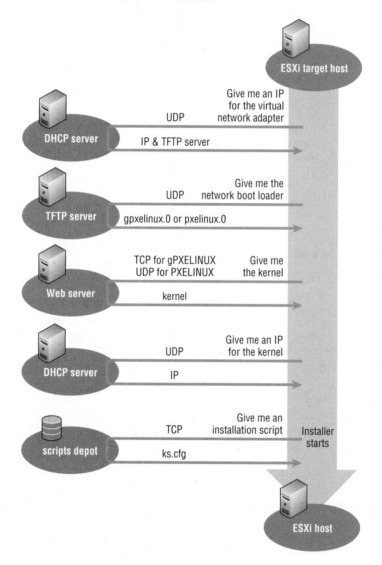

Auto Deploy can save you lots of time, but be aware that it also has a number of prerequisites. For some shops, the most time-consuming part of using Auto Deploy could be the configuration of all the components required to make it work successfully. These configuration stages, at a minimum, include the following:

1. Install vSphere Auto Deploy, using the procedure shown in Exercise 2.20 later in this chapter. Auto Deploy is a plug-in to vCenter Server, so vCenter Server is a requirement.

2. Install the VMware PowerCLI, which includes the Auto Deploy cmdlets and the Auto Deploy snap-in.

3. Install a *TFTP* (Trivial File Transfer Protocol) server on the network and make it available to both the DHCP server and the vCenter Server system.

4. Download the TFTP zip file from the Auto Deploy page in the vCenter Server and extract the file to a directory on the TFTP server.

5. Set up your DHCP scope to include option 66 and to specify the TFTP server.

6. Set up your DHCP scope to include option 67 and to specify the boot filename of `undionly.kpxe.vmw-hardwired`.

7. Set each ESXi host to be provisioned with Auto Deploy to PXE boot, following the manufacturer's instructions.

8. Use *Image Builder* to create an image profile.

9. Write rules that will assign an image profile and optional *host profile* to ESXi hosts provisioned with Auto Deploy.

Once installed and configured, Auto Deploy can be used in conjunction with host profiles to deliver fully configured ESXi hosts. Think of Auto Deploy as having the ability to add capacity on-demand for a cluster by simply powering on a server and letting it PXE boot.

Configuring Auto Deploy is outside the scope of the VCP5-DCV exam objectives and this book. Remember that for the exam, you will be expected to understand the PXE boot process and not necessarily how to configure the various aspects of Auto Deploy.

There is an excellent Auto Deploy demo featured at VMware's official You-Tube site: `www.youtube.com/watch?v=G2qZl-760yU`. The configuration of Auto Deploy is also covered in detail in *Mastering VMware vSphere 5.5*, by Scott Lowe, Nick Marshall, Forbes Guthrie, Matt Liebowitz, and Josh Atwell (Sybex, 2013).

Now that you have installed ESXi, configured the management network, and installed the vSphere Client, let's begin to configure the ESXi host. The first step we'll cover is configuring NTP on an ESXi host.

Configuring NTP on an ESXi Host

ESXi hosts use Coordinated Universal Time (UTC) for system time, and time zones are not used in ESXi. To ensure that ESXi hosts have accurate system time, you should configure ESXi hosts to use the Network Time Protocol (NTP).

In Exercise 2.4, you will configure NTP on an ESXi host using the vSphere Client.

EXERCISE 2.4

Configuring NTP on an ESXi Host

1. Open the vSphere Client and connect to the ESXi host.

2. You will likely see the VMware Evaluation Notice screen appear after logging in. This reminds you of the time left on your default 60-day evaluation license of ESXi 5. For now, click OK to continue.

3. Select the Configuration tab in the right pane of the screen, and then choose Time Configuration in the Software panel.

4. Review the current configuration. Are the date and time both correct? The NTP client should show a status of Stopped, and there should be no value shown for NTP Servers, as shown here:

5. To configure the NTP settings, click Properties.

6. Manually set the time and date in the Date And Time section of the properties.

7. You will also want to set up this ESXi host to use NTP so that it will have consistently accurate time from this point forward. Start by checking the NTP Client Enabled check box in the NTP Configuration settings. NTP is now enabled, but you will need to click the Options button to configure additional NTP settings.

8. When the NTP *Daemon* (ntpd) Options screen opens, select the NTP Settings option from the left column.

EXERCISE 2.4 *(continued)*

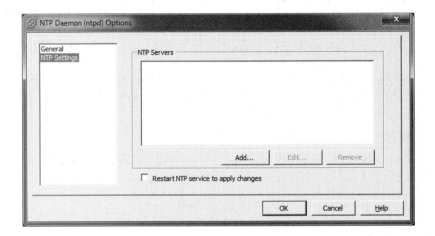

9. Click Add to add an NTP server.

    This will be the NTP server with which this ESXi host will sync its time. There may be a standard NTP server that the environment uses, and it may be located internally or externally.

10. After adding the NTP server's IP address or fully qualified domain name (FQDN), click OK.

11. In the NTP Daemon (ntpd) Options window, select Restart NTP Service To Apply Changes and then select General Settings from the left column.

12. For the General Settings of the NTP Daemon (ntpd) Options screen, select the Start Automatically If Any Ports Are Open, And Stop When All Ports Are Closed option. This is the option recommended by VMware. Click OK to continue and click OK again on the Time Configuration properties screen.

13. Review the current configuration. Is the time correct now? The NTP client should show a status of Running, and the NTP server you entered should now be listed beside the NTP servers.

NTP configuration is now complete. Repeat this process for any and all ESXi hosts running in the environment to ensure consistent and accurate timing in your virtual infrastructure. Next let's configure DNS and routing for an ESXi host.

Configuring DNS and Routing on an ESXi Host

Earlier in this chapter you used the DCUI to configure the management network for an ESXi host. You did not configure DNS at that time, but let's cover it now. DNS is very important in most environments, and without accurate name resolution, your ESXi hosts will likely run into issues in short order.

We will explore two ways to configure DNS and routing on an ESXi host—using the VSphere Client and using the ESXi DCUI. In Exercise 2.5, we will use the vSphere Client to configure DNS and routing for an ESXi host.

EXERCISE 2.5

Configuring DNS and Routing Using the vSphere Client

1. Open the vSphere Client and connect to the ESXi host by its IP address.

2. From the Inventory screen, select the ESXi host and click the Configuration tab in the right pane.

3. Choose the DNS And Routing option from the Software panel.

4. Review the current information listed for Host Identification, DNS Servers, Search Domains, and Default Gateway. Is this information currently complete and correct? To modify the DNS and Routing settings, click the Properties link in the top-right corner of the panel. A DNS And Routing Configuration window will appear.

5. The DNS Configuration tab is shown first by default. Review the information in the DNS Configuration tab.

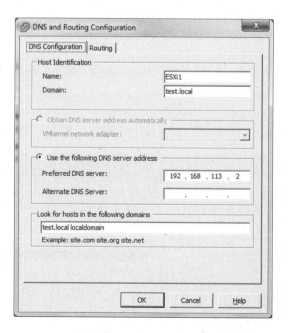

6. If changes need to be made to the Host Identification, DNS Servers, or Search Domain fields, make them on this tab. Once you've done so, click the Routing tab.

EXERCISE 2.5 (continued)

7. Verify that the default gateway listed is correct. If this information is incorrect, you can modify it here.

8. Once all changes have been made, click OK in the DNS And Routing window.

9. Depending on the changes made, an Update DNS Configuration task and/or an Update IP Route Configuration task may start. Wait for these tasks to complete and then review the DNS and routing information.

> Make sure that DNS records are created for all ESXi hosts in your environment before continuing.

In Exercise 2.5, you configured DNS and routing for an ESXi host using the vSphere Client. In Exercise 2.6, you will revisit the ESXi DCUI and configure DNS and routing from there.

EXERCISE 2.6

Configuring DNS and Routing from the ESXi DCUI

1. Obtain local console access to the ESXi host and press F2 to log into the Direct Console User Interface (DCUI).

2. You will see the System Customization menu. Scroll down to the Configure Management Network option and then press Enter to configure the management network.

3. Scroll down to the DNS Configuration option and review the DNS servers and ESXi hostname listed on the right. Press Enter to configure the DNS settings for this ESXi host. This will launch the DNS Configuration window, as shown here:

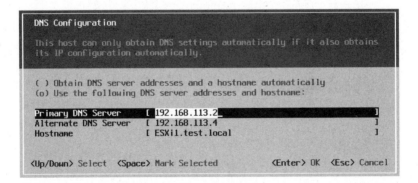

4. Use the Up and Down arrow keys to toggle between the Obtain DNS Server and Use The Following DNS Server options. To select either option, make sure the line is highlighted and press the spacebar.

5. To change the DNS servers and/or the hostname, you will have to select the Use The Following DNS Server option. Once you do, scroll down to the Primary DNS Server, Alternate DNS Server, and Hostname items and modify them as necessary. Enter the ESXi host's fully qualified name as the hostname.

6. Once you are satisfied with the changes, press Enter to save them and exit the DNS Configuration window. If you make any mistakes, simply press Esc to discard the changes.

7. You will return to the Configure Management Network menu. Scroll down to the Custom DNS Suffixes option and review the information listed on the right. Press Enter to configure the Custom DNS Suffixes for this ESXi host. This will launch the Custom DNS Suffixes window.

8. Modify the Custom DNS Suffixes as necessary. Once you are satisfied with the changes, press Enter to save the changes and exit the Custom DNS Suffixes window. If you make any mistakes, simply press Esc to discard the changes.

9. You will now return to the Configure Management Network screen. Press Esc to exit. A Configure Management Network Confirmation screen will appear. This is the same screen you saw in Step 10 of Exercise 2.2.

10. For the purpose of this exercise, press the Y key to save all changes and exit the Configure Management Network screen.

Alternatively, press the N key to discard all changes and exit the Configure Network Management screen, or press Esc if you need to return to the Configure Management Network screen.

11. You will return to the System Customization menu, where you can use the Configure Management Network option to verify any changes you made. You can also use the Test Management Network option to verify that DNS and routing are working properly.

12. After verifying that the DNS and routing changes were successfully made, press Esc to exit the DCUI. Open the vSphere Client and connect to the ESXi host where DNS and routing were just configured.

13. Verify that the DNS and routing changes that were just performed in the DCUI are also reflected properly in the vSphere Client.

WARNING Restarting the management network can result in brief network outages. This could lead to service interruptions or unplanned downtime. Always proceed with caution when using this option. Even more important to remember is that if IPv6 is enabled or disabled, the ESXi host will be restarted automatically (without prompting) by the restart management network process.

In the next section, we'll continue configuring our ESXi hosts and discuss hyperthreading.

Enabling, Configuring, and Disabling Hyperthreading

As it relates to vSphere, hyperthreading is an Intel-proprietary technology used to allow a processor/core to appear as two logical processors to the ESXi hypervisor. Before you can enable hyperthreading in ESXi, you must first enable it in the ESXi host system's BIOS. If you need assistance with enabling hyperthreading in your system's BIOS, consult the documentation for your particular system. Once the hardware is ready, you can use the vSphere Client to configure hyperthreading settings for ESXi.

In Exercise 2.7, you will configure hyperthreading for an ESXi host.

 If you have an AMD processor or you're using a VMware Workstation lab, you will not be able to perform this exercise. Fortunately, this is a simple objective and reading the steps should suffice.

EXERCISE 2.7

Enabling, Configuring, and Disabling Hyperthreading

1. Open the vSphere Client and connect to the ESXi host.

2. From the Inventory screen, select the ESXi host you want to configure hyperthreading for and then click the Configuration tab in the right pane.

3. Click the Processors link in the Hardware panel.

4. Review the current information. What is the current status of hyperthreading? To configure hyperthreading, click the blue Properties link in the top-right corner of the panel.

5. In the dialog box, you can turn hyperthreading on or off by selecting or deselecting the Enabled check box. Hyperthreading is enabled by default for host systems that fully support it, as shown here:

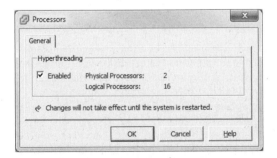

6. Once hyperthreading is enabled or disabled, click OK to save the changes. While using the vSphere Client, you can review the hyperthreading status in either the Processors section of the Hardware Configuration screen or on the Summary tab for the ESXi host server.

Hyperthreading changes will not take effect until the ESXi host is rebooted.

In addition to hyperthreading, another CPU feature that you can use in ESXi 5.5 is vSphere Host Power Management (HPM).

Selecting a CPU Power Management Policy

vSphere Host Power Management (HPM) can be implemented on ESXi 5.5 hosts to conserve power. It works by forcing certain parts of a computer system or device into reduced power states when the system or device is not fully using its capacity. Do not confuse vSphere Host Power Management with vSphere Distributed Power Management (DPM). DPM works by offloading VMs to fewer ESXi hosts and then powering off the host completely. HPM works on individual hosts and is a much more real-time energy conservation tool.

Configuring HPM is a fairly straightforward process, but it does require specific BIOS configuration on each ESXi host. Once the power management settings have been configured properly in the host's BIOS, the ESXi host can then control the power management. The power management or power profile settings in the BIOS should be configured for "OS control mode" or the equivalent. Figure 2.3 shows these settings in a Dell server's BIOS.

FIGURE 2.3   Dell server power settings in BIOS

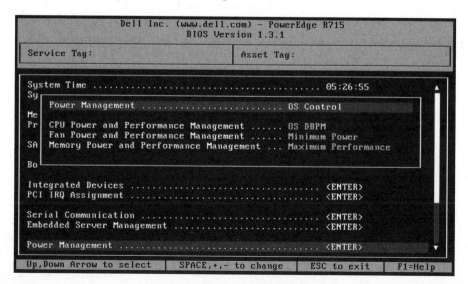

Exercise 2.8 covers the steps to modify the current HPM policy from within the vSphere Client. If your host does not support power management in its BIOS, or if it is not configured properly, you will either want to configure the BIOS first or simply follow along on this exercise.

EXERCISE 2.8

Configuring Host Power Management

1. Open the vSphere Client and connect to the ESXi host.

2. From the Inventory screen, select the ESXi host you want to configure and then click the Configuration tab in the right pane.

3. Click the Power Management link in the Hardware panel.

4. Review the current Technology and Active Policy settings.

5. Click the Properties link to the right. An Edit Power Policy Settings window will open.

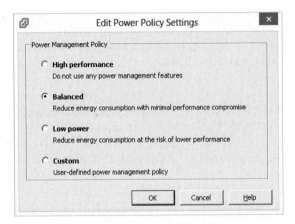

6. Change the power policy to your preferred setting and click OK.

7. A Configure Host Power Management Policy task will begin. When this task completes, verify that the Active Policy setting has been updated.

You can also define custom power policies; their use requires additional configuration under the Software panel's Advanced Settings.

Like hyperthreading and HPM, another important feature is the memory compression cache in ESXi. Let's turn our attention to this topic next.

Enabling, Sizing, and Disabling Memory Compression Cache

When memory *overcommitment* is used, virtual machine performance can be improved through the use of memory compression. Memory compression works by compressing virtual pages and storing them in memory when an ESXi host becomes overcommitted. This is significantly faster than accessing the same pages from disk, and it can improve performance in overcommitted environments during periods of memory contention.

Like many of the features in ESXi, the settings for the memory compression cache can be customized. Memory compression is enabled by default in ESXi, but it can be disabled using the vSphere Client. In Exercise 2.9, you will disable the memory compression cache and then enable it again.

EXERCISE 2.9

Enabling and Disabling the Memory Compression Cache

1. Open the vSphere Client and connect to the ESXi host.

2. From the Inventory screen, select the ESXi host for which you want to disable the memory compression cache and then click the Configuration tab in the right pane.

3. Choose the Advanced Settings link in the Software panel.

4. In the left pane of the Advanced Settings window, select Mem. Now scroll down and locate the Mem.MemZipEnable option in the right pane.

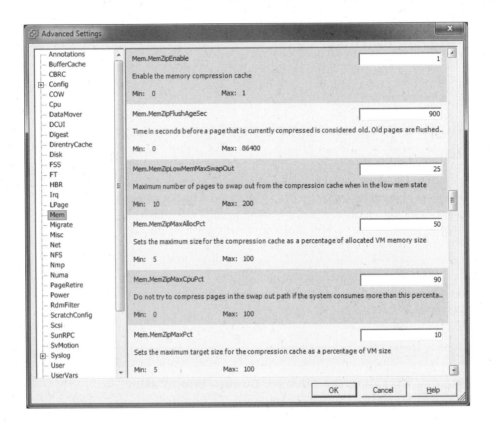

5. The Mem.MemZipEnable setting is used to enable or disable the memory compression cache. Notice the default value of 1. This means the memory compression cache is enabled. Enter **0** to disable the memory compression cache and click OK. An Update Option Values task will begin. When it completes, open the Advanced Settings window again and verify that the value of Mem.MemZipEnable has been changed to 0. The memory compression cache is now disabled.

6. Finally, change the Mem.MemZipEnable value back to a value of **1** to re-enable it. Unless you have a very robust test lab, the memory compression cache will likely be put to good use.

You've just seen how to turn the memory compression cache off and on. We will next turn our attention to sizing the compression cache. When virtual pages need to be swapped, ESXi will first try to compress those pages instead. Compressed pages of 2KB or less are then stored in the VM's compression cache. The maximum size for the compression cache can be configured, as you'll see in Exercise 2.10.

EXERCISE 2.10

Sizing the Memory Compression Cache

1. Open the vSphere Client and connect to the ESXi host.

2. From the Inventory screen, select the ESXi host for which you want to size the memory compression cache and then click the Configuration tab in the right pane.

3. Choose the Advanced Settings link in the Software panel.

4. In the left pane of the Advanced Settings window, select Mem. Now locate the Mem. MemZipMaxPct option in the right pane.

    The value entered here determines the maximum size of the compression cache used for any individual VM. This value represents a percentage of the size of the VM's memory, and the value must be between 5 and 100. For example, if you enter 25 and a VM's memory size is 1024MB, the ESXi host can use up to 256MB of host memory to store the VM's compressed pages.

5. Click OK to save the changes.

Another configuration step that is often required for ESXi hosts is to add licensing. You'll learn how to do that in the next section.

Licensing an ESXi Host

Licensing in vSphere applies to vCenter Server, ESXi hosts, and solutions. Licensing will be discussed in detail a bit later in this chapter, but for now Exercise 2.11 shows the steps required to add a license key to your standalone ESXi host.

 To allow for readers who do not have actual license keys, this exercise provides a screenshot that details the final steps of licensing. If you do not have license keys, work through the exercise as far as you can.

EXERCISE 2.11

Adding License Keys to ESXi in Evaluation Mode

1. Connect to an ESXi host with the vSphere Client.

2. Select the ESXi host, and then select the Configuration tab from the right pane.

3. Choose the Licensed Features link in the Software panel.

4. Review the information presented on the screen, and then click the Edit link in the upper-right corner. An Assign License window will open.

5. Select Assign A New License To This Host, and then click Enter to continue.

6. In the Add New License Key dialog box, enter your ESXi host license key and click OK. The Assign License dialog box appears.

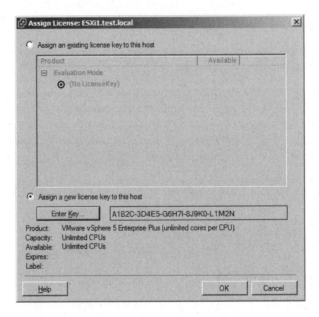

7. Click OK to assign the license.

8. Review the license information now shown in the vSphere Client to ensure that it is correct.

9. Obtain local console access to the ESXi host that was just licensed, and press the F2 key to log into the DCUI.

10. When presented with the System Customization menu, scroll down to the View Support Information option and review the license serial number information.

You've now worked through many of the stages necessary to configure an ESXi host. In the next section, we will move on to installing and configuring vCenter Server, which you can use to manage your ESXi hosts.

Introducing vCenter Server

vCenter Server is used to manage ESXi hosts and the resources they contain. vCenter Server can be installed on a supported version of Windows server, or you can use a pre-configured version known as the vCenter Server Appliance. You can use either version to manage an ESXi host's virtual machines, networks, storage systems, *resource pools*, and much more. This section will go into great detail about vCenter Server, but let's begin with discussing the available editions.

Identifying Available vCenter Server Editions

Part of planning your virtual infrastructure is being able to identify the available editions of vCenter Server in vSphere 5.5. VMware vCenter Server is available in the following editions:

- vCenter Server for Essentials
- vCenter Server Foundation
- vCenter Server Standard

Each edition of vCenter Server includes the following:

- Management service
- Database server
- Inventory service
- vSphere Web Client
- vCenter APIs and .NET Extension
- vCenter Single Sign-On
- vCenter Orchestrator
- vCenter Server Linked Mode

vCenter Server for Essentials is available only when purchased as part of one or two vSphere Essentials *Kits*: the vSphere Essentials Kit and the vSphere Essentials Plus Kit. The vSphere Essentials Kits are all-in-one solutions targeted at small-to-medium businesses (SMBs). They are, however, entirely self-contained and may not be used with other editions. These kits are limited to three hosts (two CPUs each), but otherwise include everything you need for most SMB requirements.

VMware vCenter Server Foundation is used for centralized management of up to three ESXi hosts. This version allows the purchase of the individual component of vCenter Server.

VMware vCenter Server Standard has no limits or restrictions on the number of hosts that it can be used to manage, other than those specified in the Configuration Maximums document available here:

www.vmware.com/pdf/vsphere5/r55/vsphere-55-configuration-maximums.pdf

More information on how the various editions of vCenter Server are integrated into the available vSphere editions and kits is available in Chapter 3. For the VCP5-DCV exam you should be prepared to know which edition of vCenter Server is most appropriate for the unique size of any given environment. Once you know the editions of vCenter Server, it is also important to know the vCenter Server system requirements.

Identifying vCenter Server and vCenter Server Database Requirements

The minimum system requirements for a vCenter Server Simple Install (vCenter Single Sign-On, vCenter Inventory Service, and vCenter Server all installed on a single system) are as follows:

- Intel or AMD x64 processor with two 2GHz cores
- 12GB of RAM
- 100GB of disk space, with 40GB–60GB free also required after installation
- GbE NIC

 VMware states that a Simple Install is appropriate for most deployments.

The minimum system requirements for vCenter SSO installed on a separate host are as follows:

- Intel or AMD x64 processor with two 2GHz cores
- 3GB of RAM
- 2GB of disk space
- GbE NIC
- Database connection (vSphere 5.1 only)

The minimum system requirements for the vCenter Inventory service installed on a separate host are as follows:

- Intel or AMD x64 processor with two 2GHz cores
- 3GB of RAM
- At typical activity rates, 6GB–12GB of disk space for 15,000 VMs distributed among 1,000 hosts

- GbE NIC

The minimum system requirements for vCenter Server installed on a separate host are as follows:

- Two 64-bit CPUs or a single dual-core 64-bit processor, each CPU or core rated at 2GHz or higher
- 4GB of RAM
- 4GB of free space, plus an additional 2GB if SQL Express is to be used on the same system
- GbE NIC

Keep in mind that USB and network drives are not supported for vCenter Server installation.

The minimum system requirements for the vSphere Web Client installed on a separate host are as follows:

- 2GHz 64-bit processor with four cores
- 2GB of RAM
- 2GB of free space
- GbE NIC

The minimum system requirements for the vCenter Server Appliance are as follows:

- 70GB of free space on a datastore
- GbE NIC
- 8GB of RAM if managing 10 or fewer hosts or 100 or fewer virtual machines with the embedded vPostgres database
- 16GB of RAM if managing 10–50 hosts or 100–1500 virtual machines with the embedded vPostgres database
- 24GB of RAM if managing 50–100 hosts or 1500–3000 virtual machines with the embedded vPostgres database
- 4GB of RAM if managing 10 or fewer hosts or 100 or fewer virtual machines with an external Oracle database
- 8GB of RAM if managing 10–100 hosts or 100–1000 virtual machines with an external Oracle database
- 16GB of RAM if managing 100–400 hosts or 1000–4000 virtual machines with an external Oracle database
- 32GB of RAM if managing more than 400 hosts or 4000 virtual machines with an external Oracle database

Installing vCenter Server also requires the following:

- Supported 64-bit operating system

- 64-bit system DSN
- Microsoft .NET 3.5 SP1 Framework
- Microsoft .NET Framework 3.5 Language Pack (if the server OS is not English)
- Microsoft Windows Installer version 4.5 (MSI 4.5) if the bundled SQL Express database will be used

vCenter Server Database Requirements

Both Oracle and Microsoft SQL Server are supported databases for vCenter Server and Update Manager running on Windows. Note that VMware recommends that separate databases be used for vCenter Server and Update Manager. To check for support of specific versions of these databases, see the VMware Product Interoperability Matrixes:

www.vmware.com/resources/compatibility/sim/interop_matrix.php

vCenter Server installed on a supported Windows system must have a 64-bit DSN for any supported database. For Microsoft SQL databases, create a system DSN for the SQL Native Client driver. You can also manually configure, or use the scripts included on the installation media, to create the supported databases for vCenter Server. Make sure DNS is in order, and ensure that connectivity to any external database is available.

Now that the vCenter Server requirements have been addressed, let's look a bit closer at the vCenter Single Sign-On requirements.

Identifying Single Sign-On Requirements

Generally speaking, the system requirements for vCenter Single Sign-On are the same as those of vCenter Server. One significant difference you will encounter is the database requirements between vSphere versions 5.1 and 5.5. The version of SSO shipped with vSphere 5.5 was completely rewritten and no longer requires an external database. The version of SSO shipped with vSphere 5.1 does require an external database. This can be any supported database listed on the VMware Product Interoperability Matrixes, including the bundled Microsoft SQL Express database.

There are also minimum hardware requirements for vCenter SSO, if it will be installed on a separate host:

- Intel or AMD x64 processor with two 2GHz cores
- 3GB of RAM
- 2GB of disk space
- GbE NIC

The default SSO administrator password also cannot contain non-ASCII characters, high-ASCII characters, and/or certain special characters. Check the release notes for each vCenter Server release, as the password requirements have been changing frequently. Also refer to the following VMware KB for more information.

kb.vmware.com/kb/2060746

Now that the SSO requirements have been covered, let's create an external database connection to the vCenter Server database.

Creating a Database Connection to the vCenter Server Database

Although vCenter Server can use the embedded Microsoft SQL Express database, that use is supported only for five ESXi hosts and/or 50 virtual machines. For many environments this will not be suitable and a supported external database should be used instead. Exercise 2.12 covers the steps required to connect to a vCenter Server database on an external Microsoft SQL Server 2008 R2 database. Note that this exercise assumes that an external SQL vCenter Server database has already been created, using the script DB_and_schema_creation_scripts_MSSQL.txt provided on the vCenter installation media in X:\vCenter-Server\dbschema\ and that you have a supported Windows server that meets the system requirements listed earlier. Ideally, this will be the same Windows server that you will install vCenter Server on later in this chapter.

EXERCISE 2.12

Connecting to a vCenter Database on an External Microsoft SQL 2008 R2 Database Server

1. Log on to the Windows server with a domain user account that has the required access to the vCenter Server database. This will likely be the same user specified in the database creation scripts.

2. Download the Microsoft SQL Server 2008 R2 Native Client software from Microsoft here:

   www.microsoft.com/en-us/download/confirmation.aspx?id=16978

3. Install the Microsoft SQL Server 2008 R2 Native Client software on the host that vCenter Server will be installed on.

4. Select Start ➤ Administrative Tools ➤ Data Sources (ODBC). The ODBC Data Source Administrator will open.

5. Click the System DSN tab and then click Add. A Create New Data Source window will open.

6. Select SQL Server Native Client 10.0 by clicking it and then click Finish.

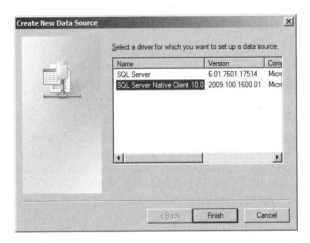

7. A Create A New Data Source To SQL Server window will open.

8. In the Name field, enter **vCenter Server 5.5 DB**.

9. Provide a description and use the drop-down menu to select the SQL Server that hosts the vCenter Server database.

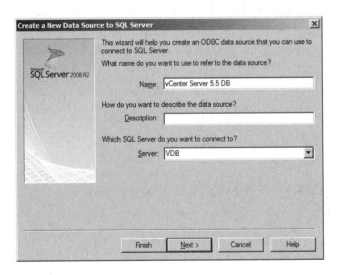

10. Click Next and choose the With Integrated Windows Authentication option. Select the Connect To SQL Server To Obtain Default Settings For The Additional Configuration Options check box and click Next.

11. Select the Change The Default Database To check box and use the drop-down menu to select the name of the vCenter Server database. Accept the defaults for all other settings.

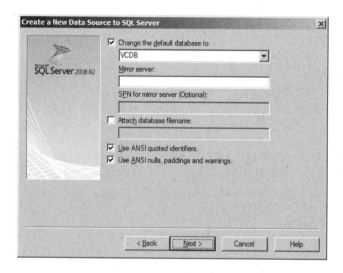

12. Click Next to continue. Accept the default settings and click Finish. An ODBC Microsoft SQL Server Setup dialog box will open.

13. Click the Test Data Source button. In the SQL Server ODBC Data Source Test window, ensure that the message TESTS COMPLETED SUCCESSFULLY! appears.

14. Click OK in this dialog box and click OK in the ODBC Microsoft SQL Server Setup dialog box.

15. Verify that the System DSN tab now shows the newly created DSN.

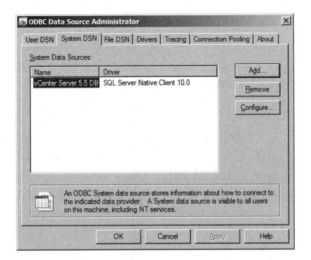

16. Click OK to close the ODBC Data Source Administrator applet.

You have now created a database connection to an external SQL Server housing the vCenter Server database. In the next section, we'll discuss sizing the vCenter Server database.

Sizing the vCenter Server Database

An important part of configuring your vCenter environment is sizing the vCenter database. Improperly sized vCenter Server databases can lead to performance issues in vCenter or even unplanned system downtime. The vCenter Server database stores many items, including host and virtual machine configurations, resources and virtual machine inventory, user permissions, roles, alarms, events, tasks, and performance statistics. This performance statistical data can account for 90 percent of the information contained in the vCenter Server database, but the amount of resources your vCenter Server database consumes will ultimately depend on the number of managed VMs and managed ESXi hosts, and the performance statistics you plan to collect.

Fortunately, vCenter Server allows you to specify the interval duration, retention, and statistics level of the statistics counters. There is even a Database Size estimator included in the vCenter Server Settings. You will need the vSphere Web Client, which we will install later in this chapter, to access this tool. From the vSphere Web Client, choose a vCenter Server's Manage tab and click Settings on the toolbar. Select General on the left and then the Edit button. In the Edit vCenter Server settings window, you will see the Database Size estimator shown at the bottom of the screen (Figure 2.4).

FIGURE 2.4   vCenter Server statistics and database size

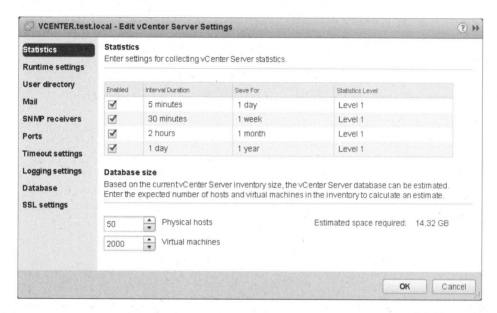

vCenter Server comes bundled with a Microsoft SQL Server 2008 R2 Express edition database. This bundled database can be used with up to five VMware ESX/ESXi hosts and 50 virtual machines in the inventory. It is important to note that the Microsoft SQL Server 2008 R2 Express database cannot be installed as part of a vCenter Server upgrade. Upgraded vCenter Server systems will require Microsoft SQL Server 2008 R2 Express to be manually installed prior to running the vCenter Server installer.

 VMware warns that exceeding the limits of the bundled database with either vCenter Server or the VCSA can cause multiple issues, including vCenter Server failure.

Keep in mind the limitations of the bundled Microsoft SQL 2008 R2 Express database when planning for your vCenter Server. If you suspect that the environment will grow beyond the limits of the included database, your design should include a supported database. You can find supported databases at the VMware Product Interoperability Matrixes website:

`http://partnerweb.vmware.com/comp_guide2/sim/interop_matrix.php`

Regardless of the database server used to house the vCenter Server database, once vCenter Server is installed and operational you should perform standard database maintenance as suggested by the database vendor. This can include actions such as monitoring the growth of the log file, compacting the database log file as needed, and scheduling regular backups of the database. See the following VMware Knowledge Base article for information on backing up the embedded vPostgres database:

http://kb.vmware.com/kb/2034505

Now that we have covered sizing and connecting to the vCenter Server database, let's install vCenter Server.

Installing vCenter Server into a Virtual Machine

vCenter Server can be installed on a physical server or a virtual machine. Both are supported configurations, and the installation process is the same once a supported 64-bit Windows Server OS is deployed. There are obvious benefits to having vCenter run in a VM, including the ability to protect it with *vSphere High Availability* (HA), *VMware Distributed Resource Scheduler* (DRS), vMotion, and the ability to *snapshot* the virtual machine. These reasons can make a strong case for running vCenter Server in a virtual machine. To install vCenter Server in a virtual machine, you have to make sure several prerequisites are met, including these:

- Installation media should be downloaded, verified, and available.

- The Microsoft .NET 3.5 SP1 Framework must be installed on the Windows server. The vCenter Server installer can install the .NET 3.5 SP1 Framework; however, the installation may require an Internet connection.

- Ensure that the vCenter Server system requirements are met, as listed earlier in this chapter.

- Verify that your Windows Server OS and remote database(s), if applicable, are both supported.

- Verify that all clocks are synchronized on any machines that will interact with this vCenter Server.

- Verify that the Windows computer name is no longer than 15 characters maximum.

- Verify that the DNS name for the Windows server matches the actual computer name. Also verify that the hostname used complies with RFC 952 guidelines. Basically you want letters, numbers, and hyphens only.

- Verify that the Windows server that will house vCenter is not a domain controller. vCenter will not install on domain controllers, because Active Directory Application Mode (ADAM) is used.

- Preferably, the vCenter Server should be installed on a Windows server that is a member of a domain.

- Ensure that the administrative account you will use to install vCenter Server is a member of the local Administrators group and that the password for this account does not contain any non-ASCII characters.

- Ensure that all required network ports are open between vCenter Server and domain controllers, SQL servers, or others as required.

- Verify that both forward and reverse DNS entries are resolving correctly for the server that vCenter server will be installed on.

- Best practice is to ensure that a static IP address is used for the Windows OS hosting the vCenter Server.

- Verify that there is no Network Address Translation between the vCenter Server system and the ESXi hosts that it will manage.

- If using an external database, have the vCenter database created.

- If using an external database, create and test a 64-bit system *data source name* (DSN) on the system where vCenter Server will be installed. If using Microsoft SQL, create the DSN using the SQL Native Client driver, as shown in Exercise 2.12.

 Verifying the checksums of your vSphere downloads can help ensure that your vSphere installs go smoothly. To verify the checksums of downloaded vSphere media, you can use free utilities like digestIT 2004 or WinMD5.

vCenter Server User Account

Once the vCenter Server prerequisites have been met, give some thought to the account that will be used to run the vCenter Server services. Either the Windows built-in SYSTEM account or a user account can be used to run vCenter Server.

Keep in mind that the Microsoft Windows built-in SYSTEM account has more permissions and rights on the server than the vCenter Server system needs, which can contribute to security problems. Also know that the SYSTEM account will not work with Windows Authentication and external databases.

The benefit of using a user account is that greater security is provided for your Windows server. User accounts can be local or be domain based. Either type of account is required to be an administrator on the Windows server that vCenter Server will be installed on. The user account must also have both the Act As Part Of The Operation System and Log On As A Service permission.

If you plan to use SQL authentication for SQL Server or if you plan to use an Oracle or DB2 database, you may want to consider setting up a local user account on the vCenter Server system. Note that security is enhanced for domain user accounts by the use of Windows Authentication for SQL Server connections.

It is also important that you log on to Windows with the correct user account when you run the vCenter Server installer. If you are going to use the bundled Microsoft SQL 2008 R2 Express database for configuration and other data, log in with any user account that has administrator privileges. If you are using either a local or external SQL database with Windows Authentication, log into Windows with the account that has access to the database to run Setup. This should be the same account you used to create the DSN for the external SQL database.

In Exercise 2.13, we will go through the process of performing a vCenter 5.5 Simple Install on a virtual machine. The Simple Install process installs vCenter Single Sign-On, vSphere Web Client, vCenter Inventory Service, and vCenter Server all on a single host. According to VMware, Simple Install is appropriate for most deployments. This exercise assumes you have a supported Windows server VM that is joined to an Active Directory domain.

EXERCISE 2.13

vCenter Server 5.5 Simple Install

1. Open a console session to a supported Windows server using the vSphere Client.

2. Ensure that the verified media for vCenter Server is attached to the VM's virtual CD-ROM drive or available locally on the virtual machine.

3. Keeping in mind the previous discussion on the user account that will run vCenter Server services, log on to the Windows server that vCenter Server will be installed on. Launch the VMware vCenter Installer application by running the autorun.exe file.

4. The VMware vCenter Installer will launch. Take note of the products listed on the vCenter Server Installer screen.

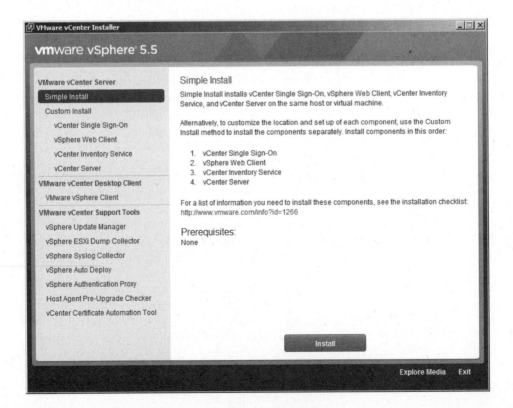

5. Select VMware vCenter Simple Install in the left pane, and then review the information in the right pane. Note the installation order.

6. Click Install to begin.

7. Review the information in the Welcome To The vCenter Server Single Sign-On Setup window and click Next.

8. Review the End-User License Agreement and accept the terms to continue.

9. Verify that the prerequisites check completes successfully, as shown in the following image:

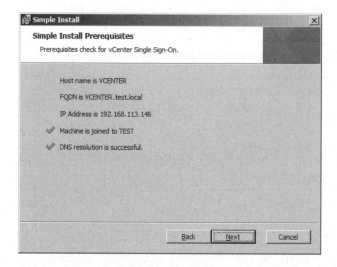

10. Enter a password for the vCenter Single Sign-On Administrator (Administrator@ vsphere.local) account and click Next to continue.

Remember the discussion earlier in this chapter about the SSO administrator password requirements.

11. Make a record of the password you just entered here. This is a very important password that you will need again.

12. Accept the default site name and click Next.

13. Accept the default HTTPS port for vCenter Single Sign-On.

14. Review and/or modify the destination directory for vCenter Single Sign-On. Note that this directory path cannot contain non-ASCII characters, commas (,), periods (.), exclamation points (!), pound signs (#), at signs (@), or percentage signs (%).

15. Review the installation options for vCenter Single Sign-On and click Install to begin the vCenter Server Single Sign-On install.

Simple Install will now install vCenter Single Sign-On, the vSphere Web Client, and the vCenter Inventory Service, in that order. No additional user interaction is required for this step.

16. When the vCenter Server installation begins, you will be prompted to enter a license key. Enter a valid key or leave this field blank to continue in evaluation mode.

17. Choose the database to be used for vCenter Server. You can use either a Microsoft SQL Server 2008 Express instance or an existing supported database. If you are using an external database, select the appropriate 64-bit DSN from the Data Source Name (DSN) drop-down menu. Click Next.

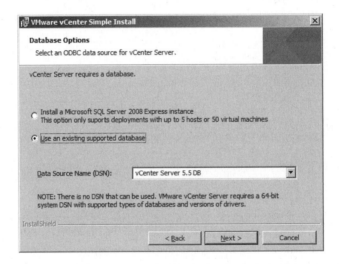

18. If you are using the bundled Microsoft SQL Server 2008 Express instance, you can select either the SYSTEM account or the currently logged-on user account for the vCenter Server service account.

If you use either a local or external SQL Server with Windows Authentication, the currently logged-on user account will be used for the vCenter Server services to run under. The option to use the SYSTEM account is not available in this case.

19. Configure the ports used for vCenter Server. These are the ports that the vCenter Server will use for various communications. Only change the default ports if you know exactly what you are doing or have a very good reason to do so. Changing ports here would typically be performed with the assistance of security and/or network personnel.

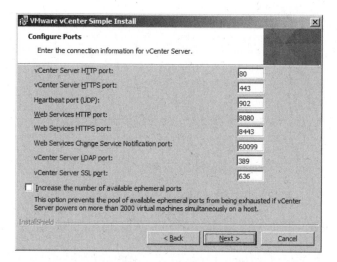

Also review the information at the bottom of this screen and decide whether to increase the ephemeral port value. Increasing the number of ephemeral ports available is important if your vCenter Server manages hosts on which there will be more than 2,000 virtual machines powered on. If this setting is appropriate for your environment, select it.

20. The vCenter Server Java Virtual Machine (JVM) memory is configured next. This setting adjusts the amount of memory allocated to the JVM. Choose the correct size for your environment, and know that this setting can be changed at any time after installation using the information you'll find here: `http://kb.vmware.com/kb/1039180`.

21. In the Ready To Install The Program window, click Install to begin the vCenter Server installation.

22. When the vCenter Server install completes, click Finish. You should now be presented with a success screen. Click OK.

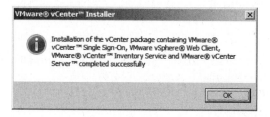

EXERCISE 2.13 *(continued)*

If you don't enter a license key during installation, vCenter Server will be in evaluation mode. Evaluation mode allows the use of the full vSphere 5.5 product feature set for 60 days. At any point within these 60 days after installation, you may enter a license key to convert vCenter Server to licensed mode.

vCenter Server 5.5 is now installed on a virtual machine and ready to use, but before we move on let's take some time to discuss the vCenter Server Appliance and how to deploy it.

Deploying the vCenter Server Appliance

The vCenter Server Appliance (VCSA) is a preconfigured Linux-based *virtual machine* (VM) that has been optimized to run only vCenter Server and its associated services. It is deployed as an *Open Virtualization Format* (OVF)–formatted VM and is supported only on ESX/ESXi 4.0/4.1 and later. An embedded vPostgres database is used in VCSA versions 5.0.1 and later, and an embedded IBM DB2 database is used in the vCenter Server Appliance 5.0. The embedded databases have the following scaling implications:

- vCenter Server Appliance 5.5 and newer: 100 hosts and 3,000 VMs
- vCenter Server Appliance 5.0 and 5.1: 5 hosts and 50 VMs

When the VCSA fails to scale to these limits, a supported external Oracle database is also supported. The VCSA supports up to 1,000 hosts and 10,000 virtual machines when used with a supported external Oracle database.

To deploy the vCenter Server Appliance, you must ensure several prerequisites are met. These include:

- The ESXi host must meet the minimum hardware requirements for the vCenter Server Appliance, which are covered earlier in this chapter.
- Either the vSphere Client or vSphere Web Client must be installed.
- The vCenter Server Appliance is supported only when installed on ESX/ESXi 4.0/4.1 and later hosts.
- All clocks used in your VMware infrastructure must be synchronized.
- There must be a minimum of 7GB of disk space and a maximum of 125GB. 70GB is a realistic expectation of the actual space used by the VCSA.
- A decision should be made on whether to use the embedded database or a supported external Oracle database.
- You must have already downloaded both the VMDK and OVF (or OVA) files for the vCenter Server Appliance from VMware's website.

NOTE DHCP should be running on the network segment where the VCSA is initially deployed, or manual network configuration of the VCSA will be required after deployment.

Once all of the prerequisites are met, you can follow the steps in Exercise 2.14 to deploy the vCenter Server Appliance.

EXERCISE 2.14

Deploying the vCenter Server Appliance

1. Decide on a hostname for the vCenter Server Appliance, and create a DNS entry for it in your environment. Verify that both forward and reverse DNS lookups resolve correctly before continuing.

2. Open the vSphere Client and connect to a supported ESXi host.

3. Choose File ➢ Deploy OVF Template to launch the Deploy OVF Template wizard.

4. Browse to the downloaded VMDK and OVF files for the vCenter Server Appliance and select the OVF file (or the single OVA file). Once you've done so, the filename will appear in the Deploy From A File Or URL field, as shown here:

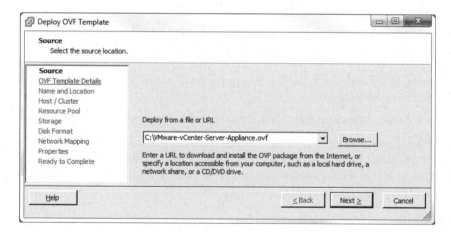

5. Click Next. Verify the OVF Template Details for accuracy and then click Next again.

6. Specify a name for the deployed template. This name will be the actual name of the deployed virtual machine. Click Next.

7. Choose a datastore and/or disk format to house the vCenter Server Appliance. Your options here depend on the type of storage your ESXi host has and/or the version of your ESXi host. Click Next.

8. For the Network Mapping setting, click on the name listed in the Destination Network column to open a drop-down menu. Select the correct network for the vCenter Server Appliance and then click Next.

9. Review the deployment settings. Select the Power On After Deployment option.

10. Click Finish to begin deploying the vCenter Server Appliance. A dialog box will appear that shows the task progress. Verify that the task completes in the vSphere Client.

    Now that the VCSA has been deployed, you have to follow some additional steps to configure it for first use. The next section of this exercise will cover changing the default root password and reviewing the VCSA network configuration.

11. In the vSphere Client, locate the vCenter Server Appliance virtual machine. Right-click the VM in the left pane and choose the Open Console option.

12. Review the information on the console.

13. Using the arrow keys on your keyboard, select the Login option and then press Enter.

14. Type the username **root** and press Enter.

15. Type the password **vmware** and press Enter.

16. At the prompt, type the command **passwd** and press Enter.

17. Enter a new password for the root account and press Enter.

18. Retype the new password to confirm and press Enter. Verify that the message Password Changed is returned.

19. Type the command **hostname** and note that the hostname for the VCSA is not set.

20. Type the command **ifconfig eth0** and note that the VCSA will have an IP address if DHCP is running on the network segment where the VCSA was deployed. If DHCP is not running on this network segment, you will need to run the following command to configure networking manually:

    /opt/vmware/share/vami/vami_config_net

21. Type the command **logout** to return to the vCenter Server Appliance landing page. Leave this console window open—you will use it again.

    You have now changed the default password for the vCenter Server Appliance and reviewed its networking setup. In the final steps of this exercise, you will complete configuration of the VCSA from its web management interface.

22. Note step 1 of the QuickStart Guide shown on the VCSA console. Open a web browser and enter the URL listed here. Make sure you use **https** and include the port number **5480**.

23. In your web browser, log into the vCenter Server Appliance using the root username and password.

24. Review the license agreement and select the Accept License Agreement check box. Click Next and wait while the EULA acceptance completes. In the VCSA console, review the activities.

25. On the Configure Options screen, click Cancel.

    Before continuing with setup of the VCSA, you need to configure a static IP address and a hostname. If you did the networking configuration from the VCSA console earlier, you can skip to step 31, where NTP will be configured for the VCSA.

26. Click the Network tab and then select Address from the toolbar. From the IP Address Type drop-down, select Static.

27. Provide the same hostname you created in step 1 of this exercise. Enter the required networking information. The final configuration should appear similar to this:

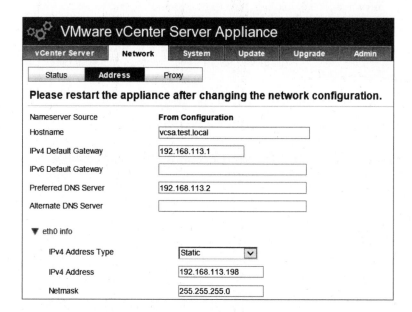

28. Click Save Settings and verify on the VCSA console that the IP address is changed under the QuickStart Guide listing.

29. Use the vSphere Client to restart the vCenter Server Appliance.

30. Connect to the vCenter Server Appliance web management interface.

31. Log in and ensure that the vCenter Server tab is selected. Select Time from the toolbar and configure either NTP or VMware Tools Synchronization. Save Settings and then select Summary on the toolbar.

32. In the Utilities panel, click the Launch button to start the Setup Wizard.

33. On the Configure Options screen, choose the Set Custom Configuration option and click Next.

34. Accept the default selection (Embedded) for Database Type and click Next. Wait for the database configuration testing to complete.

35. Accept the default selection (Embedded) for SSO (Single Sign-On) Deployment Type. Enter a password for the vCenter Single Sign On Administrator (Administrator@ vsphere.local) account.

Again, remember the discussions about non-ASCII characters, high-ASCII characters, and special characters in the default SSO administrator password.

36. Make a record of the password you just entered here. This is a very important password that you will need again. Click Next to continue.

37. Ensure that the Active Directory Enabled check box is selected, and then enter the appropriate domain name and Domain Administrator credentials. Click Next and wait for the Active Directory configuration testing to complete. If this step fails, it is likely DNS related on the VCSA.

38. Review the configuration details, and click Start to begin setup.

39. Verify the results of setup, and then click the Close button.

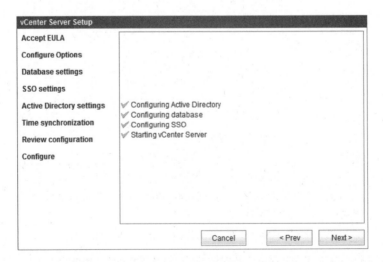

40. Select the vCenter Server tab and then click Summary on the toolbar. Review the information here.

The vCenter Server Appliance has the default username of root and the default password vmware. The password for the root account should always be changed, immediately after the VCSA is deployed.

Carefully consider the suitability of the vCenter Server Appliance for a given environment. There are certain differences that should be well understood before deployment. For example, Oracle databases are the only supported external database option, and *Linked Mode configuration* is not supported. The lack of SQL Server support alone could keep this appliance from being deployed in many Windows-based environments. For environments that want to use SQL Server and/or the Windows operating system, there is always the well-established option of installing vCenter Server on a Windows server.

Installing and Configuring the vSphere Client and vSphere Web Client

Beginning with vSphere 5.1, development of the "fat" .NET vSphere Client ceased, and its use will be phased out in future major releases of vSphere. The replacement tool for the vSphere Client is the vSphere Web Client. First introduced in vSphere 5, the vSphere Web Client is a cross-platform web application that runs in a supported web browser. Supported web browsers are listed in Table 2.1.

TABLE 2.1   vSphere Web Client–supported web browsers

Operating system	Supported web browser
Windows 32-bit and 64-bit	Internet Explorer 8, 9 (64-bit only), and 10.
	Firefox: the newest release, and the one previous release available when vSphere 5.5 was produced.
	Chrome: the latest release, and the one previous release available when vSphere 5.5 was produced.
Mac OS	Firefox: the newest release, and the one previous release available when vSphere 5.5 was produced.
	Chrome: the latest release, and the one previous release available when vSphere 5.5 was produced.

You must install Adobe Flash Player version 11.5.0 or later with the appropriate plug-in for your supported web browser.

The vSphere Web Client installer actually installs a web server. It is this web server that will host the web application known as the vSphere Web Client. So, remember that there are two distinct pieces to this feature: a web server that is installed and a client that is accessed from this web server via a supported web browser.

Note that the vSphere Web Client can connect only to vCenter Server and not to stand-alone ESXi hosts. Also note that all new features released in vSphere 5.1 and 5.5 (for example, vCenter Single Sign-On) are accessible only from the vSphere Web Client.

In Exercise 2.13, you performed a Simple Install of vCenter Server, which included the installation of the vSphere Web Client. The vSphere Web Client could have also been installed on a separate server from the vCenter Server installer. You also installed the traditional vSphere Client in Exercise 2.3 of this book and used it in subsequent exercises to configure your ESXi hosts.

For the majority of the remainder of this book, the vSphere Web Client will be used whenever possible for exercises. Before you begin to use the vSphere Web Client, you must install the Client Integration Plug-in for the vSphere Web Client. Exercise 2.15 covers the steps required to do so.

EXERCISE 2.15

Installing the vSphere Web Client Integration Plug-in

1. Log on to the Windows server where you installed the vSphere Web Client. Select Start ➢ Programs ➢ VMware ➢ VMware vSphere Web Client ➢ vSphere Web Client.

    Take a moment to note that the Use Windows Session Authentication option is currently grayed out. Installing the Client Integration Plug-in will correct this.

    If you are using Microsoft Internet Explorer, you will have to perform one additional step at this point. This is because Internet Explorer identifies the Client Integration Plug-in as located in the Internet zone instead of the local intranet zone.

2. Select Tools ➢ Internet Options in Internet Explorer and click the Security tab. Deselect Enable Protected Mode for both the Internet and local intranet zones. Click OK.

3. Click the Download Client Integration Plug-in link.

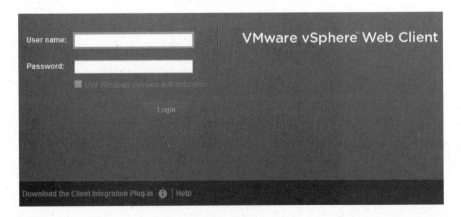

4.   Use the procedure appropriate for your web browser and OS to launch the VMware Client Integration Plug-in application. You may be prompted to close your open web browser(s).

5.   When the VMware Client Integration Plug-in application launches, click the Next button on the Welcome screen to begin.

6.   Agree to the terms of the end user license agreement, and click Next to continue.

7.   Choose a destination directory for the VMware Client Integration Plug-in, and click Next to continue.

8.   Click the Install button to install the VMware Client Integration Plug-in.

9.   Click the Finish button on the Summary screen to complete the installation.

10. Repeat this installation for any other systems where you would like to use the VMware Client Integration Plug-In by opening a supported web browser and going to `https://<vCenter Server FQDN>:9443/vsphere-client`

The VMware Client Integration Plug-in allows you to access a virtual machine console from within the vSphere Web Client. It also allows you to deploy OVF or OVA templates and transfer files to and from datastores.

You now have vCenter Server installed, but before you can configure it any further we must first discuss and configure vCenter Server Single Sign-On. This is an absolute necessity, as you simply cannot log into vCenter Server until you have configured Single Sign-On. In the next section we will discuss the Single Sign-On architecture.

Describing Single Sign-On Architecture

vCenter Single Sign-On (SSO) was first introduced in vSphere 5.1 as an authentication broker that provides single sign-on capabilities for vCenter Server and other technologies that have been registered with vCenter Single Sign-On. This can include products like vCenter Server, vCenter Orchestrator, vSphere Data Protection, or vCloud Director. It is important to remember that SSO handles authentication only, and not permissions. Each solution or component will be responsible for its own roles and permissions.

SSO is very important, because it is a required component with vSphere 5.1 and newer. It significantly changes the way vCenter Server authenticates users. Previously with vCenter Server installed on Windows servers, vCenter Server users would be granted access from membership in the local Administrators group on that server. With SSO, users must first be authenticated against an identity source configured in SSO. For this reason, SSO must be configured prior to logging into vCenter Server for the first time. In addition, SSO can be configured only from the vSphere Web Client. This makes the vSphere Web Client an essential part of vCenter Server installations in vSphere versions 5.1 and newer.

The workflow of the vCenter SSO authentication process goes like this. A user logs on to the vSphere Web Client and these credentials are sent as an authentication request to SSO. SSO verifies these credentials against a configured identity source, like Active Directory, and then exchanges the authenticated credentials for a security token. If the user is in the identity source, vCenter Single Sign-On returns this token, which represents the user to the vSphere Web Client. It is this token that is presented to the vSphere solutions and components that have been registered with vCenter Single Sign-On. The token is then verified with SSO by the solution or component to be valid and not expired. This workflow is shown in Figure 2.5.

FIGURE 2.5   vCenter Single Sign-On workflow

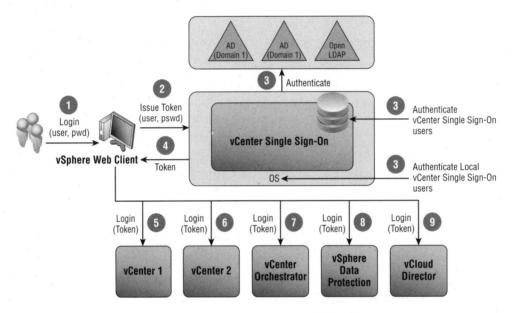

vCenter Single Sign-On consists of a set of components that are installed as part of SSO's installation:

Administration Server   Used to allow SSO administrators access to configure SSO from the vSphere Web Client

Security Token Service (STS)   Used to manage the SSO Security Assertion Markup Language (SAML) tokens

vCenter Lookup Service   Contains vSphere environmental topology information; is used to enable secure vSphere component connections

VMware Directory Service (vmdir)   The directory service for the vsphere.local domain in vSphere 5.5

When SSO is first deployed in vSphere 5.1, the only user with administrative privileges in SSO is admin@System-Domain. When SSO is first deployed in vSphere 5.5, the only user with administrative privileges in SSO is administrator@vsphere.local. The password for these accounts is created during installation of vCenter Server Single Sign-On.

Now that we have covered the architecture of vCenter SSO, let's move on to discussing the deployment types that can be used when installing it.

Differentiating Single-Sign-On Deployment Scenarios

In vSphere 5.1 when you are installing SSO, you have three different deployment types to choose from:

Standalone   Used to create a single node in a basic vCenter SSO install or the first node in a high availability or multisite installation

HA   Used to create an additional node for an existing high availability vCenter SSO installation

Multi-Site   Used to create an additional node for an existing multisite vCenter SSO installation

In vSphere 5.5 when you are installing SSO, there is a single deployment type, which is based on a multimaster model. You have three choices during the installation of SSO, as shown in Figure 2.6:

FIGURE 2.6   SSO deployment in vSphere 5.5

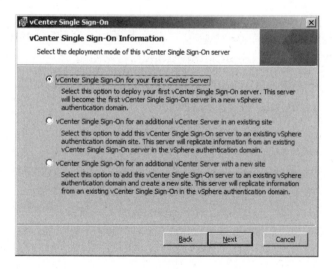

vCenter Single Sign-On For Your First vCenter Server   Used to create the first vCenter Single Sign-On site in a new vSphere authentication domain. This is what the vCenter Simple Install process will use.

vCenter Single Sign-On For An Additional vCenter Server In An Existing Site   Used to add an additional vCenter Single Sign-On server to an existing vSphere authentication domain site. This SSO server will replicate information from an existing SSO server in the vSphere authentication domain.

vCenter Single Sign-On For An Additional vCenter Server With A New Site Used to add an additional vCenter Single Sign-On server to an existing vSphere authentication domain and create a new site. This SSO server will replicate information from an existing SSO server in the vSphere authentication domain.

For a datacenter with one to five vCenter Servers, VMware recommends that vCenter Server, Inventory Service, Web Client, and the SSO Server all be installed on a single host. This is what the Simple Install option that you performed in Exercise 2.13 did. Simple Install allows each of these components to communicate locally (think fast), and will support up to 1,000 vSphere hosts and 10,000 virtual machines. We have covered the architecture and deployment scenarios for SSO, and in the next section we will discuss configuring it.

Configuring and Administering Single Sign-On

Right now, the Single Sign-On administrator is the only user who has any access to our vCenter Server environment. You will need to use this user account to first check, and possibly correct, your identity sources before continuing. Exercise 2.16 will cover the steps to confirm identity sources for AD domains. This exercise will use a vCenter Server 5.5 installed from a Simple Install on a Windows server.

EXERCISE 2.16

Confirming AD Domains for vCenter Administrators

1. Open your web browser and enter the following URL:

   `https://[WEB_CLIENT_FQDN_OR_IP]:9443/vsphere-client`

2. Enter the vCenter Single Sign On administrator (**administrator@vsphere.local**) username and provide the appropriate password. Click the blue Login button.

3. On the vSphere Web Client Home page, click the Administration option on the left side of the screen.

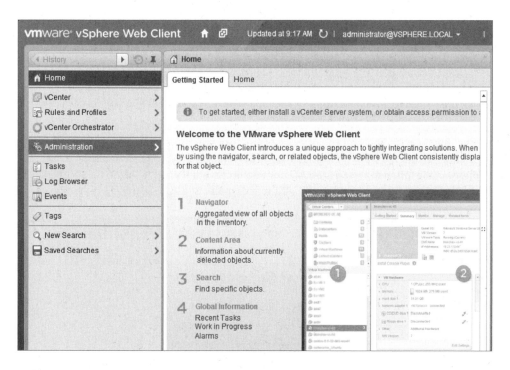

4. A new set of menus will appear; click Users And Groups and then click the Users tab in the middle pane. Using the Domain pull-down menu, verify that your AD domain is listed here. My test lab domain `test.local` is shown in the following image:

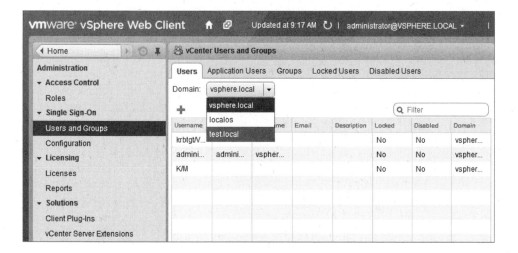

EXERCISE 2.16 *(continued)*

5. If your domain is not listed, you will need to add an identity source.

6. Click the Identity Sources tab and review the sources listed at the top of this pane. Click the plus sign to add an identity source. An Add Identity Source window will open.

7. Select the Identity Source Type of Active Directory (Integrated Windows Authentication) and ensure the Domain Name listed is correct. Select the Use Machine Account option. In the following image, an AD domain is shown. If you performed a Simple Install of vCenter Server that was joined to a domain, this is all you need to configure.

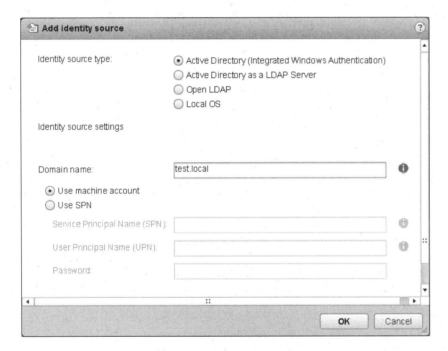

8. Click OK to add the identity source. An Add Identity Source task will begin. When it completes, verify that the domain is now listed as an identity source.

9. In the Single Sign-On menu, click Configuration.

10. Select the Policies tab and click Password Policies on the toolbar.

11. Note the current password policy, and pay particular attention to the Maximum Life-
time value.

By default, the SSO administrator password will expire in 90 days. Be sure you understand the implications of this.

 The topic of configuring Identity sources could easily fill an entire chapter
and is beyond the scope of this book. If you need assistance configuring
identity sources other than Microsoft AD, please consult the documentation specific to the directory service as well as VMware's knowledge base.

You have verified and/or added identity sources in vCenter Single Sign-On. One final
step remains before you can use the vSphere Web Client: ensuring that your vCenter Server
is accessible.

Managing Single Sign-On Users and Groups

During the Simple Install process, local administrators who are Active Directory users
should be migrated to Single Sign-On. However, there are cases where this may not happen,
so you will need to check and possibly correct this issue before continuing.

Exercise 2.17 covers the steps to verify and/or add administrative user access to vCenter.
This exercise will also assume that a Simple Install of vCenter Server 5.5 was done on a
Windows server joined to an Active Directory domain.

EXERCISE 2.17

Adding AD Domain Users as SSO Administrators

1. Open your web browser and enter the following URL:

   https://[WEB_CLIENT_FQDN_OR_IP]:9443/vsphere-client

2. Enter the vCenter Single Sign-On administrator username (**administrator@vsphere.
local**) and provide the appropriate password. Click the Login button.

3. On the vSphere Web Client Home page, click Administration on the left. Select Users
And Groups and then click the Groups tab in the middle pane.

4. Select the Administrators item in the list by clicking it. This is the Single Sign-On
administrators group.

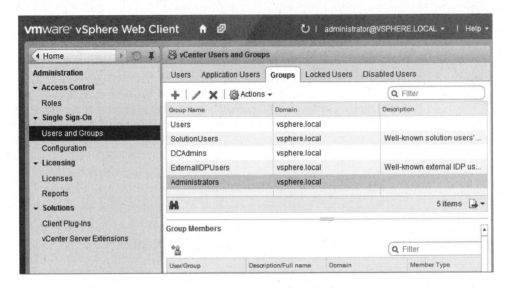

5. Note that there is a listing of Group Members for the SSO administrators group. Do you see group members listed?

6. Click the Add Member icon directory below Group Members. An Add Principals window will open.

7. In the Add Principals window, choose the correct domain and then use the Users And Groups drop-down menu to sort the users and groups.

8. Select a user or group by clicking it, and then click Add to confirm your selection.

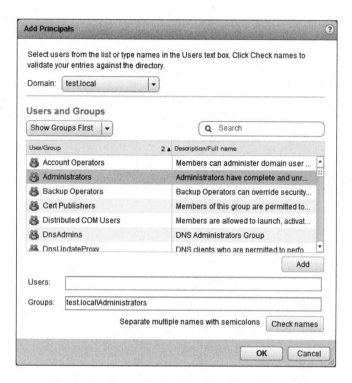

9. When all users and/or groups have been selected, click Check Names to verify. A Correct Usernames dialog box will appear. Click OK to continue.

10. Click OK in the Add Principals window to add the selected user(s) and/or group(s) to the SSO administrators group.

11. Verify that the selections you just made are now listed in the Group Members field at the bottom of the screen.

12. Use the menu at the top of the screen to log the SSO administrator out of the vSphere Web Client.

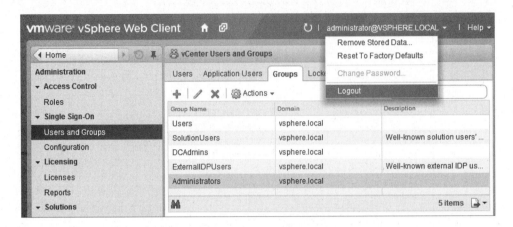

13. At the vSphere Web Client login, enter the credentials for one of the domain users who is a member of the group you just added to the SSO administrators group. Click Login.

14. Select vCenter in the left pane. Note in the Inventory list on the left that vCenter Servers is listed with a value of 0.

This is the expected behavior. SSO administrators have full administrative rights over SSO but no rights to vCenter Server. The SSO administrator account (Administrator@vsphere.local) needs to assign permissions to vCenter Server. This is the final step in allowing your domain users to log into vCenter Server via the vSphere Web Client.

15. Log out of the vSphere Web Client and log back in as Administrator@vsphere.local.

16. Select vCenter in the left pane. In the Inventory list on the left, note that vCenter Servers is listed with a value of 1.

17. Select vCenter Servers in the Inventory list on the left, and then select the vCenter Server listed below it. It should appear with its FQDN.

18. On the Manage tab, select Permissions from the toolbar.

19. Click the Add icon. An Add Permission window will open.

20. Click Add. A Select Users/Groups window will open.

21. In the Select Users/Groups window, select the correct domain from the Domain drop-down menu. Use the Users And Groups drop-down menu to sort the users and groups as desired.

22. Select a user or group by clicking it, and then click Add to confirm your selection.

23. When all users and/or groups have been selected, click Check Names to verify. A Correct Usernames dialog box will appear. Click OK to continue.

24. Click OK in the Select Users/Groups window to add the selected user(s) and/or group(s) to the Add Permission window.

25. Verify that the selections you just made are now listed in the Users And Groups field on the left.

26. Use the Assigned Role drop-down menu to select Administrator. Ensure the Propagate To Children check box is selected at the bottom of the window. The final configuration should look similar to this:

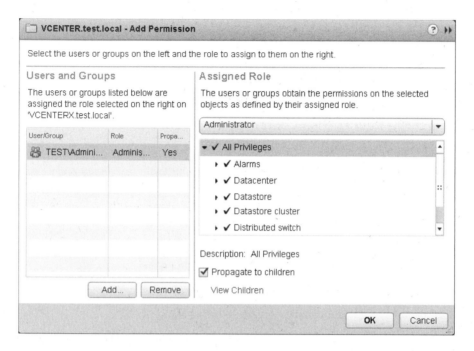

27. Click OK to add this permission to the vCenter Server root inventory object.

28. Verify that the user and/or group is now listed and that Role is set to Administrator.

29. Log out of the vSphere Web Client and log back in as a user who is a member of the group you just added the vCenter Server permission for.

30. Select vCenter in the left pane. Note in the Inventory list on the left that vCenter Servers is listed with a value of 1.

31. Take a few moments and navigate around vCenter Server.

DNS and how it is configured in your test lab can make significant differences in the success of using the passthrough authentication option in the vSphere Web Client. If you have trouble with this option, try logging in with either the *DOMAIN\USERNAME* or *USERNAME@DOMAIN*.DOM format.

Now that SSO is configured and you have access to vCenter Server, let's take a moment to add at least one ESXi host to the vCenter Server you installed in this chapter. This will help the exercises in this book flow more smoothly—and besides, vCenter without ESXi hosts to manage just isn't very exciting. Exercise 2.18 covers the steps to add an ESXi host to the vCenter Server inventory.

EXERCISE 2.18

Adding an ESXi Host to the vCenter Server Inventory

1. Connect to a vCenter Server with the vSphere Web Client.

2. Click the Go Home icon (the white house) at the top of the window. In the middle of the screen, click to select the Home tab and select Hosts And Clusters.

3. Read the information on the Getting Started tab for Step 1, and then click the Create Datacenter link at the bottom of the tab.

4. A New Datacenter window will open. Enter a unique name for your datacenter object. Note that you can rename this object without disruption later.

5. Click OK to create the datacenter object in the vCenter Server inventory.

6. Select the newly created datacenter object in the left pane.

7. The Getting Started tab will have Step 2 available. Read the information shown here, and then click the Add A Host link at the bottom of the tab.

8. The Add Host wizard will open. Enter the hostname or IP address of the ESXi host you want to add to the datacenter object created in Step 5.

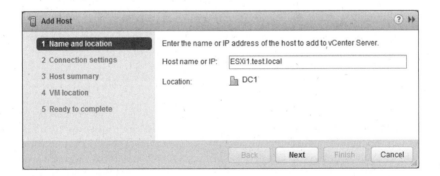

9. Click Next to continue.

10. Enter the root username and password for the ESXi host, and then click Next.

11. You will see a Security Alert popup window. Click Yes if you trust this ESXi host's default self-signed security certificates.

12. Review the information presented in the Host Summary screen, and click Next.

13. Review the license information and press Next to leave this ESXi host in evaluation mode.

14. Do not choose to enable Lockdown Mode, and click Next.

15. Accept the default object given for the VM Location and click Next.

16. Review the information on the Ready To Complete screen and click Finish to add the ESXi host to the vCenter Server's inventory.

17. Monitor this task in the top-right Recent Tasks pane.

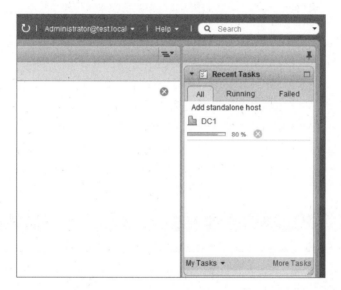

18. When the host has been successfully added, the Getting Started tab will refresh and Step 3 will now be selected.

19. For now, you may optionally proceed with Steps 3 and 4 in the Getting Started tab. However, we will cover these steps in great detail in Chapter 6, "Creating and Deploying Virtual Machines and vApps."

Now that you have access to vCenter Server, let's continue with the installation of additional vSphere components. In the next section, you will install vSphere Syslog Collector and vSphere Auto Deploy.

Installing Additional vCenter Server Components

Several additional vCenter Server components are available on the vCenter Server installer screen, and the VCP5-DCV exam objectives do not explicitly state which ones you should know. Therefore, I will cover several in this book. The first additional component that you will install is the VMware Syslog Collector.

The VMware Syslog Collector is essentially a syslog server for Windows. The idea is that ESXi system logs can be directed to a *syslog server*, rather than to a local disk on the ESXi host. As we will explore later, a local disk may not be required for an ESXi 5 host. The possibility of a diskless ESXi host makes it essential to have the ability to collect logs. The VMware Syslog Collector provides this capability.

The VMware Syslog Collector can be installed either on the same machine as the associated vCenter Server or on a different one. If it's installed on a different machine, that machine must meet the system requirements and have a network connection to the vCenter Server. There are several prerequisites for installing the VMware Syslog Collector:

- Verify membership in the Administrators group on the system.

- Verify that the system requirements are met.

- Verify that the host machine has Windows Installer 3.0 or later.

- Verify that the host machine has a valid IPv4 address.

- Determine if the Syslog Collector will be standalone or integrated with a vCenter Server 5 or later.

Once these prerequisites have been met, installation of the Syslog Collector can begin. The installation steps are covered in Exercise 2.19.

EXERCISE 2.19

Installing the VMware Syslog Collector on the vCenter Server

1. Connect to a console session on the Windows server that houses the vCenter Server. Be sure to log on with an administrator account.

2. Launch the VMware vCenter Installer and select vSphere Syslog Collector from the list of VMware vCenter Support Tools. Click the Install button to begin.

3. When the installation wizard starts, select the language.

4. On the Welcome screen, click Next to begin.

5. Agree to the terms of the end user license agreement, and click Next.

6. Choose a destination directory for the Syslog Collector. You will also need to choose a directory for the syslog repository and configure the repository settings.

   Depending on the number of hosts, and a variety of other factors, the log file size and rotation settings may need to be tweaked over time. It is also important to keep in mind that the location for the repository could potentially require significant space. For this reason, a drive other than the system drive of the server should be used.

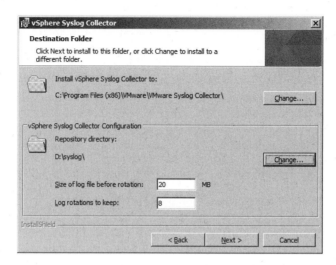

7. For this exercise, choose the VMware vCenter Server Installation setup type and click Next.

8. Enter the FQDN or IP address of the vCenter Server, along with the appropriate vCenter administrator credentials. Accept port 80 unless you have made customizations to the vCenter ports. Click Next.

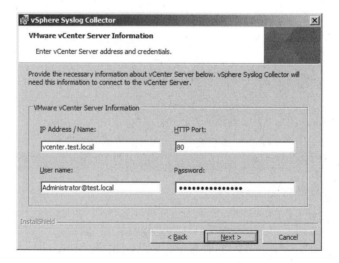

9. If you see an SSL Certificate warning, click Yes to continue.

10. Review the Syslog Collector port settings. The UDP and TCP protocols on port 514 are the defaults shown here. Once the port settings are configured, click Next.

EXERCISE 2.19 *(continued)*

11. Use the pull-down menu to specify how the Syslog Collector should be identified (which IP address or hostname) on the network, and click Next.

12. Click Install to begin the installation of the vSphere Syslog Collector, and then click Finish when the install is complete.

> We will verify the installation of the Syslog Collector after installing VMware Auto Deploy. We will do that because, although both tasks are parts of the exam objective, the steps required to configure the Syslog Collector and Auto Deploy are the same.

Earlier in the chapter, you saw that the Auto Deploy server is a component that simplifies the deployment of VMware ESXi hosts. It can be used to provision multiple physical hosts with VMware ESXi software, while specifying the exact image to deploy and the host to provision with the image.

> The Auto Deploy feature must be installed separately for each instance of vCenter Server that Auto Deploy will be used with.

There are several prerequisites for installing Auto Deploy:

- Verify membership in the Administrators group on the system.
- Verify that the system requirements are met.
- Verify that the host machine has Windows Installer 3.0 or later.

Once these prerequisites have been met for Auto Deploy, installation can begin. The steps for installing Auto Deploy are shown in Exercise 2.20.

EXERCISE 2.20

Installing VMware Auto Deploy

1. Connect to a console session on the Windows server that houses the vCenter Server. Be sure to log on with an administrator account.

2. Launch the VMware vCenter Installer and select vSphere Auto Deploy from the list of VMware vCenter Support Tools. Click Install to begin.

3. When the installation wizard starts, select the language.

4. On the Welcome screen, click Next to begin.

5. Agree to the terms of the end user license agreement, and click Next.

6. Choose a destination directory for Auto Deploy. You will also need to choose a directory for the Auto Deploy repository and configure the maximum size of the

repository. It is important to keep in mind that the location for the repository could eventually grow quite large, and so the volume selected should have plenty of free space. The default value of 2GB is designed to hold four image profiles. Click Next.

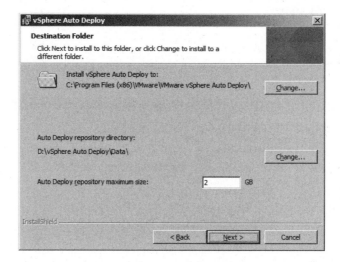

7. Enter the FQDN or IP address of the vCenter Server, along with the appropriate vCenter administrator credentials. Accept port 80 unless you have made customizations to the vCenter ports. Click Next.

8. If you see an SSL Certificate warning, click Yes to continue.

9. Review the Auto Deploy port settings, and click Next.

10. Specify how vSphere Auto Deploy should be identified on the network (which IP address or hostname), and click Next.

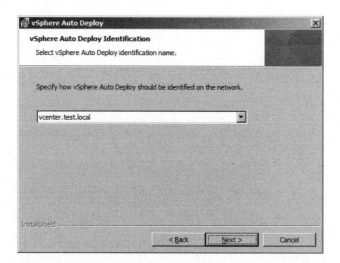

11. Click Install to begin the installation of the vSphere Auto Deploy, and then click Finish when the install is complete.

You have now installed the vSphere Syslog Collector and the vSphere Auto Deploy support tools. In the next section, we will discuss vSphere Client Plug-Ins.

Installing and Removing vSphere Client Plug-Ins

Plug-ins are applications that provide additional features and/or functionality to vCenter Server. A plug-in normally consists of a server component and a client component. The plug-in server components are installed and registered with a vCenter Server, and the plug-in client component is available to the vSphere Client and/or the vSphere Web Client.

Installing plug-ins may modify the vCenter Server management interfaces by adding further views, tabs, toolbar buttons, and menu options. These additions typically serve to add functionality, and they can be managed using the vSphere Client's *Plug-In Manager.*

Some vCenter Server features that are implemented as plug-ins include these:

- vCenter Storage Monitoring Service
- vCenter Service Status
- vCenter Hardware Status

Two additional components that make use of the vSphere Client plug-ins are the VMware Syslog Collector and VMware Auto Deploy, both of which you installed in the previous section.

Sometimes there may also be a need to remove a vSphere Client plug-in. Because vSphere Client plug-ins are essentially nothing more than Windows applications, they are quite easily uninstalled by using the native application uninstall functions in the Windows OS.

In the next section, you will configure (that is, enable and disable) both the VMware vSphere Syslog Collector and the VMware vSphere Auto Deploy client plug-ins.

Enabling and Disabling vSphere Client Plug-Ins

To verify that the Syslog Collector and Auto Deploy plug-ins are enabled, access the Plug-ins menu in the vSphere Client and choose the Manage Plug-ins option to open the Plug-in Manager shown in Figure 2.7.

FIGURE 2.7   vCenter Plug-In Manager

Plug-in Name	Vendor	Version	Status	Description
Installed Plug-ins				
VMware vCenter Storage Monitoring Service	VMware Inc.	5.5	Enabled	Storage Monitoring and Reporting
VMware vSphere Update Manager Extension	VMware, Inc.	5.5.0.17854	Enabled	VMware vSphere Update Manager extension
VMware Syslog Collector Configuration	VMware, Inc.	5.5.0	Enabled	Describes the configuration of the remote syslog collector service
vCenter Hardware Status	VMware, Inc.	5.5	Enabled	Displays the hardware status of hosts (CIM monitoring)
vCenter Service Status	VMware, Inc.	5.5	Enabled	Displays the health status of vCenter services
Auto Deploy	VMware, Inc.	5.5.0.7710	Enabled	Supports network-based deployment of ESX servers.
Available Plug-ins				

If the either the Syslog Collector or Auto Deploy plug-in is installed but shown as disabled, you will need to first enable the plug-in. To enable a plug-in, highlight it in the list of Installed Plug-ins, right-click it, and choose Enable. This same procedure also works if you need to disable an enabled plug-in.

Once you have verified that all of the listed installed plug-ins are enabled, close the Plug-In Manager and browse to the Administration section of vCenter Server Home (see Figure 2.8). You will see that icons have been added for both Network Syslog Collector and Auto Deploy. If the icons don't show up right away, you may need to log out and log in again.

FIGURE 2.8   Syslog and Auto Deploy icons

At this point in the chapter, you have installed the following items:

- ESXi
- vSphere Client

- vCenter Single Sign-On
- vCenter Server Web Client
- vCenter Server Inventory Service
- vCenter Server
- vCenter Server Appliance
- Syslog Collector support tool
- Auto Deploy support tool

In the next section, we will explore licensing vCenter Server.

Licensing vCenter Server

Licensing in vSphere applies to vCenter Server, ESXi hosts, and solutions. Solutions are applications that extend the functionality or capabilities of vCenter Server. Examples include *VMware vCenter Operations* and *VMware vCenter Site Recovery Manager*. Each vCenter Server, ESXi host, and solution will require a license after its evaluation period expires.

Every license provides a given amount of capacity. License key capacity can vary based on the number of processors in a host, the number of asset instances, and the number of virtual machines. Two types of license limits are used to enforce licensing: strong and soft. Licenses with a strong limit prevent operations that would result in exceeding the license capacity. Licenses with a soft limit allow operations that would result in exceeding the license capacity but would trigger an alarm in vCenter Server.

Major upgrades of vCenter and ESXi, such as upgrading from vSphere 4 to vSphere 5, will require obtaining new license keys. The same is true for edition upgrades, such as from Enterprise to Enterprise Plus.

You can obtain a license key from the VMware license portal at `http://my.vmware.com`. The license portal may be used to upgrade or downgrade license keys, combine or divide the capacity of keys, view the change history of license keys, and even to find license keys. License keys consist of an alphanumeric sequence of 25 characters grouped in fives with dashes between each group—for example, A1B2C-3D4E5-G6H7I-8J9K0-L1M2N. License keys contain information about the licensed product, expiration dates, license capacity, and more.

vSphere license management is centralized, and the vSphere Web Client can be used to manage all licenses available in the license inventory of a vCenter Server or Linked Mode group. To view license information for a vCenter Server, follow these steps:

1. Log in to the vCenter Server using the vSphere Web Client and click the Go home icon. Select the Home tab.

2. Select Licensing in the Administration options.

3. Click the License Keys tab to manage license keys.

The Licenses pane offers the License Keys, Products, and Solutions tabs, among others. Clicking any tab allows you to add, assign, and remove license keys. Some products and solutions may need to be installed before you can add the license key.

In Exercise 2.21, you will add a license key to vCenter Server using the vSphere Web Client.

To allow for the fact that not everyone may have a valid license key, we'll provide a screenshot in this exercise that details the final steps of licensing. If you do not have a valid license key, work through the exercise as far as you can.

EXERCISE 2.21

Adding vCenter License Keys Using the vSphere Web Client

1. Open the vSphere Web Client and log in as a user with administrative rights to the vCenter Server.

2. Read the announcement across the top of the screen about the evaluation licenses, shown here:

There are vCenter Server systems with expiring license keys in your inventory.   Details…

vmware‾ vSphere Web Client

3. Click the Details link. A License Keys Expiring window will open with the details of the license expiration. Close the License Keys Expiring window.

4. Use the left menu and choose Administration ➤ Licensing ➤ Licenses to access the current license information.

5. The licensing features will load in the middle pane. Make sure that the correct vCenter Server is listed in the vCenter Server pull-down menu at the top of this pane. Click the plus icon to add a new license.

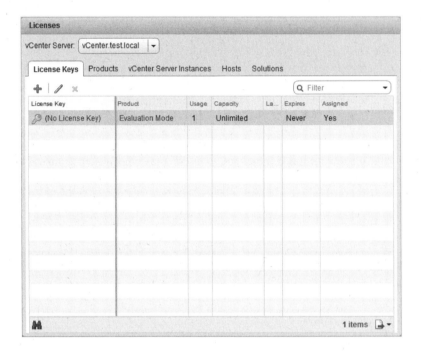

6. In the Add License Keys window, enter a valid license key for vCenter Server. Enter an optional label, and then click Next to continue. In environments with many keys, these labels can be quite useful.

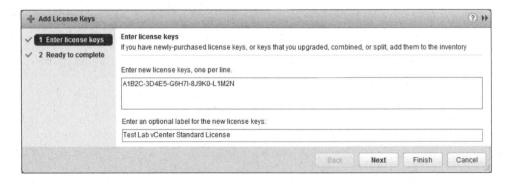

7. The license will be validated and then you will be presented with a review screen that shows the License Key, Product Name, Capacity, Label, and Expiration values. Click Finish to add this license, or click Back if you need to make changes.

8. Verify that the new license key is now listed in the Licenses pane in the middle of the vSphere Web Client.

9. Once the license has been added, it needs to be assigned to a vCenter Server instance. Select the vCenter Server Instances tab in the middle pane.

10. Select a vCenter Server instance, and then click Assign License Key. An assign License Key window will open.

11. In the Assign License Key window, select an available license from the list of license keys and click OK. An Assign License Key task will begin. When this task completes, verify the vCenter Server instance is now listed with the appropriate license.

Now that you have seen how to license a vCenter Server, let's move on to determining vCenter Server availability requirements.

Determining Availability Requirements for a vCenter Server in a Given vSphere Implementation

Depending on the vSphere implementation you are working with, it may be necessary to provide additional availability options for vCenter Server. If vCenter Server is installed in a virtual machine, you are already on your way to providing higher availability.

Installing vCenter Server in a virtual machine allows the entire virtual machine to be backed up as an image. This backup image can be restored far more quickly than a rebuild of a physical server. With the exception of vSphere Essentials, all editions of vSphere can leverage vSphere High Availability (HA) and vMotion to protect the vCenter Server virtual machine. The Enterprise and Enterprise Plus editions of vSphere can also leverage the VMware Distributed Resource Scheduler (DRS) to protect the vCenter Server virtual machine.

Although *VMware Fault Tolerance* (FT) might at first appear to be an attractive option for protecting vCenter Server, vCenter Server requires a minimum of two vCPUs or one dual-core vCPU. Running vCenter Server on a VM with a single vCPU would be an unsupported configuration.

Clustering vCenter Server using Microsoft Cluster Services (MSCS) or Veritas Cluster Services (VCS) is another option that can be used to provide high availability to a vCenter Server. The ability to cluster two physical servers, two virtual servers, or a combination of one physical server and one virtual server is also an attractive option in some environments.

VMware does not certify third-party clustering solutions. VMware will offer support for vCenter Server installed on these solutions, but if the issue is determined to be related to the third-party software, you will likely be required to open a support request with the third-party vendor's support organization.

vSphere 5.5 introduces support for MSCS to back the vCenter Server database instance, and this is an improvement over prior releases. Note that protecting the vCenter Server database with MSCS alone does not fully protect vCenter Server.

In the past, many virtual infrastructure administrators kept a cold standby vCenter Server. This involved creating an image, typically a physical-to-virtual (P2V) conversion, and having it ready to deploy in the event of an emergency. This strategy has risks associated with it; the consistency of the Active Directory Application Mode (ADAM) database cannot be guaranteed. vCenter Server uses ADAM primarily for Linked Mode, but other information is stored there as well. Making a clone or P2V of the vCenter Server may not properly copy the ADAM database. If you decide to use this strategy, thoroughly test it first. These risks may also hold true for certain image-based backups of the vCenter Server.

The most attractive option, besides using HA, vMotion, and/or DRS, might be the VMware vCenter Server Heartbeat application. VMware vCenter Server Heartbeat is a Windows-based application that delivers high availability for VMware vCenter Server, protecting it from application, configuration, operating system, network, and hardware-related problems. VMware vCenter Server Heartbeat is used to protect the vCenter Server and its database with failover and failback capabilities on both physical and virtual platforms. Most importantly, VMware vCenter Server Heartbeat is a VMware product and will be fully supported by VMware.

The best availability solution will be the one that fits the needs of the environment. Regardless of the approach taken, always be sure to have good consistent backups of the vCenter Server database.

Now that you have performed clean installs and configured both ESXi and vCenter Server, let's turn our attention to planning and performing upgrades for existing installs of ESXi and vCenter Server.

Planning and Performing Upgrades of vCenter Server and VMware ESXi

Upgrading existing ESXi and vCenter Server systems is an important task for the virtual infrastructure administrator. vSphere has been popular for quite some time, and it's quite possible you will need to perform upgrades of existing vSphere environments. We will start off with identifying the steps to upgrade a vSphere implementation.

Identifying Steps Required to Upgrade a vSphere Implementation

There are many steps required in upgrading a vSphere implementation, primarily because of the number of components involved. The first step is always to read the VMware vSphere release notes for known issues. The release notes contain valuable information that can prevent you from wasting time with known issues. The vSphere 5.5 release notes are available here:

www.vmware.com/support/vsphere5/doc/vsphere-esx-vcenter-server-55-release-notes.html

Once you have reviewed the release notes, take note of the ESXi hosts that will be upgraded. You'll need to do the following:

- Ensure that systems, and the components contained within, are all on the VMware *Hardware Compatibility List* (HCL). Just because a server is on the HCL does not guarantee that all of its cards are going to be there as well. Always verify inclusion of all components in the VMware HCL.

- Ensure that server hardware for ESXi hosts is 64 bit.

- Ensure that the current ESX and/or ESXi versions are supported for upgrade to the latest ESXi release.

- Ensure that any plug-ins, agents, VIBs, or scripts currently in use are compatible or available for the latest ESXi release.

- Run the Host Agent Pre-Upgrade Checker (Figure 2.9), available on the VMware vCenter Installer media, to check for issues with existing agents on ESXi hosts.

FIGURE 2.9:   vCenter Host Agent Pre-Upgrade Checker

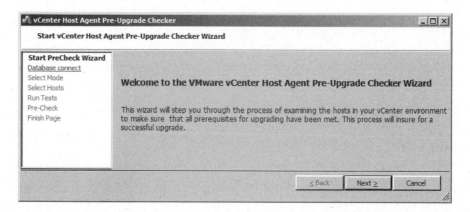

For vCenter, you must take a similar set of steps to ensure a successful upgrade. You must ensure that:

- 10GB of free space is available on the disk that vCenter Server is currently installed on.

- System requirements are met for all systems. This includes things like having two processors in your vCenter Server.

- The operating system used for vCenter Server is a supported version and that it is at the required patch level.

- The database used for vCenter Server is a supported version and that it is at the required patch level.

- A consistent full backup of the current vCenter Server database is available, prior to the vCenter upgrade.

- The database permissions are set properly on the vCenter Server database.

- The ODBC System DSN on the vCenter Server is using the proper driver and it is a 64-bit DSN.

You must be aware of a few things with vCenter upgrades in relation to the 64-bit OS requirements. These include:

- You can upgrade vCenter Server 4.x to vCenter Server 5 on the same machine if the vCenter Server 4.x instance is running on a supported 64-bit operating system.

- You cannot upgrade vCenter Server 4.x if it is running on Windows XP Professional x64, because vCenter Server 5 does not support Windows XP Professional x64.

- You can use the *data migration tool* to upgrade to vCenter Server 5.5 if vCenter Server 4.x is installed on a 32-bit system.

- You can use the data migration tool to upgrade to vCenter Server 5.5 if vCenter Server 2.5 U6 is installed on a 32-bit system.

- You can use the data migration tool to migrate an existing SQL Server Express database from a previous vCenter Server 4.x install.

- You can use the native tools provided by the database manufacturer to move a locally installed database on a 32-bit vCenter Server 4.x instance to the 64-bit OS that will house the vCenter Server 5.5 instance.

Once you've sorted out all the compatibility issues, the general sequence of events for upgrading a vSphere implementation is as follows:

1. Upgrade vCenter Single Sign-On (if applicable).

2. Upgrade vSphere Web Client (if applicable).

3. Upgrade vCenter Inventory Service (if applicable).

4. Upgrade vCenter Server.

5. Upgrade Update Manager (if applicable).

6. Upgrade ESX/ESXi hosts.

7. Upgrade vSphere Client.

8. Upgrade VMware Tools in virtual machines.

9. Upgrade virtual hardware in virtual machines.

Again, this is the general sequence of events in a vSphere upgrade, and certain environments will likely have additional steps. An example of an additional step could be "install new SAN multipathing agents" on the ESXi host. For any vSphere upgrade, a key component to success is the proper planning up front.

Now that you have learned the sequence of events in a vSphere upgrade, we will discuss the specific upgrade requirements for ESXi hosts.

Identifying Upgrade Requirements for ESXi Hosts

The first step in upgrading ESXi hosts is to identify the upgrade requirements. It is important to be able to identify which hosts can be upgraded, and to know which hosts will not be able to be upgraded. Knowing the requirements for the ESXi release is also crucial in the upgrade process. The upgrade requirements include the following:

- A supported server platform that is listed in the VMware HCL at www.vmware.com/go/hcl.

- 64-bit x86 CPUs (also called "x64 CPUs") with LAHF (Load AH from Flags) and SAHF (Store AH into Flags) CPU instructions.

- The NX/XD bit must be enabled for the CPU in the BIOS.

- Hardware virtualization (Intel VT-x or AMD RVI) must be enabled on x64 CPUs.

- You require a minimum of 4GB of RAM for ESXi 5.5.

- You require one or more Gigabit or 10Gb Ethernet controllers that are listed in the VMware HCL.

- You require a supported disk controller that is listed in the VMware HCL.

You can use the free VMware CPU Identification Utility to verify 64-bit capability with VMware. You'll find the VMware CPU Identification Utility here: www.vmware.com/download/shared_utilities.html

It is also important to note that the following storage systems are supported for ESXi 5.5 installation and boot:

- SATA disk drives on supported SAS controllers

- SATA disk drives on supported on-board SATA controllers

- SAS disk drives

- Dedicated storage LUN on SAN (Fibre Channel, FCoE or iSCSI)

- USB devices (1GB minimum size required)

ESXi supports booting from the Unified Extensible Firmware Interface (UEFI) and can boot from disks larger than 2TB, provided that the system and controller card both support it.

In addition to the hardware requirements, it is also important to note the upgrade paths for existing vSphere 5.x implementations. Table 2.2 shows the upgrade paths to upgrade from ESXi 4.x to ESXi 5.

TABLE 2.2   ESXi 5 upgrade paths

Upgrade method	Upgrade from ESXi 4.x to ESXi 5
vSphere Update Manager	Yes
Interactive upgrade from media	Yes
Scripted upgrade	Yes
vSphere Auto Deploy	No
esxcli	No

ESX/ESXi 3.x hosts are not supported for direct upgrade to ESXi 5. If you must upgrade ESX/ESXi 3.x hosts, they must first be upgraded to ESX/ESXi 4.x. It will typically be faster and easier to perform a fresh install of ESXi 5 on these systems.

Now that we have covered the requirements and paths for upgrading existing ESXi hosts, we will focus on determining whether an in-place upgrade is appropriate.

Determining Whether an In-Place Upgrade Is Appropriate in a Given Upgrade Scenario

An in-place upgrade for ESXi is an upgrade performed on the same ESX/ESXi host on which a version of ESX/ESXi is already running. Sometimes an in-place upgrade may not be appropriate for a given vSphere environment. One scenario where this would be true is for ESX/ESXi 3.x hosts. These hosts are not supported for direct upgrade to ESXi 5 and instead require a prerequisite upgrade to ESX/ESXi 4.x. In this scenario, it will likely be easier and faster to just perform a fresh install of ESXi 5.5. It is also possible that the hardware these ESX/ESXi 3.x systems are installed on may no longer be on the VMware HCL or meet the system requirements for ESXi 5.5.

Another scenario that may not be appropriate is an ESX 4.x host that was upgraded from ESX 3.x with a partition layout that is incompatible with ESXi 5.5. In many cases, especially when changing from ESX to ESXi implementations, it will be easier and less complicated to perform a fresh install of the latest ESXi release.

 Real World Scenario

Upgrading from vSphere 5

A virtual infrastructure administrator is currently administering a cluster of ESXi 5 hosts. These ESXi hosts are managed by a vCenter Server 5 instance. The virtual infrastructure administrator would like to upgrade his environment to vSphere 5.5. He consulted the VMware HCL and discovered that the hardware his ESXi hosts are running on is supported in ESXi 5.1 but not in ESXi 5.5.

He considered upgrading his vCenter Server environment to vSphere 5.1, but being a Mac OS user, he really wanted the VM console access offered by the vSphere Web Client in vCenter Server 5.5. He initially decided that this upgrade to vSphere 5.1 was not appropriate for his environment.

Later on, while discussing this issue with some people at his local VMUG, he was told about the VMware Product Interoperability Matrixes website. Upon return to the office, he consulted the website and discovered that he could upgrade his vCenter Server to 5.5 and his ESXi hosts to 5.1 and be fully supported. He ultimately decided to perform the upgrade this way, which allowed him to get the features he wanted and still remain in a supported configuration.

Another consideration is to ensure compatibility of any VMware solutions or plug-ins before upgrading the vSphere environment. This is also true for items like backup software being used in the environment. Leveraging the new features of the latest vSphere release at the cost of losing supported backup capability for VMs would likely not be an acceptable solution. Every upgrade scenario will have its own unique set of requirements, and knowing when to upgrade or start new is an important part of the virtual administrator's responsibilities.

Summary

This chapter covered the exam objectives related to installing and configuring VMware ESXi and vCenter Server. This chapter also covered installing ESXi both interactively and with Auto Deploy. You configured various settings on the ESXi hosts using the vSphere Client and the DCUI. Always be thinking about whether there are multiple ways to accomplish the same task in vSphere, and be sure you know those different ways.

We looked at the available vCenter Server editions, along with licensing, database sizing, and availability requirements for vCenter Servers. These topics are important in knowing how to plan and implement any vSphere environment.

You also installed many VMware products in this chapter. This chapter was intentionally heavy on exercises, because candidates are expected to have actual experience installing and using these VMware products. Knowing what these products do and using the products is key to doing well on the VCP5-DCV exam.

Finally, this chapter covered upgrading vCenter Server and ESX/ESXi hosts. Identifying upgrade requirements for ESX/ESXi hosts and vCenter Servers is another key part of designing and building a virtual infrastructure. We also looked at the sequence of events for upgrading a vSphere environment. This is important, as some components are dependent on other components. This chapter concluded by showing how to determine whether an in-place upgrade is appropriate.

Exam Essentials

Know how to install and configure VMware ESXi.   Understand how to perform an interactive installation of ESXi. Know how ESXi hosts can be deployed with VMware Auto Deploy. Know how to configure NTP, DNS and routing, hyperthreading, host power management, and the memory compression cache on an ESXi Host. Know how to license an ESXi host.

Know how to install vCenter Server Single Sign-On, vCenter Server, vCenter Server Appliance, vSphere Client, vSphere Web Client, and various vCenter Support Tools.   Understand the process of installing each of these products. Know the available vCenter Server editions and their differences. Know how to size the vCenter Server database. Know how to install/remove and enable/disable vSphere Client plug-ins. Know how to license vCenter Server. Know how to determine availability requirements for a vCenter Server in a given vSphere implementation. Know how SSO works, how to configure it, and how to install it.

Know how to plan and perform upgrades of vCenter Server and VMware ESXi.   Know how to identify the steps required to upgrade a vSphere implementation. Understand how to identify upgrade requirements for ESX/ESXi hosts. Know how to determine whether an in-place upgrade is appropriate in a given upgrade scenario.

Review Questions

1. The vCenter Server Appliance shipped with vSphere 5.5 contains an embedded database that supports how many VMs?

    A. 1,000

    B. 2,000

    C. 3,000

    D. 4,000

2. vCenter Server comes bundled with a Microsoft SQL Server 2008 R2 Express edition database. This bundled database is supported for up to how many hosts?

    A. 5

    B. 10

    C. 20

    D. Unlimited

3. When installing ESXi 5.5 interactively, you need to use a root password consisting of how many characters?

    A. 6

    B. 7

    C. 8

    D. 0

4. When SSO is first deployed in vSphere 5.1, what is the name of the user account that has administrative privileges in SSO?

    A. Admin@System-Domain

    B. Administrator@System-Domain

    C. Admin@vsphere.local

    D. Administrator@vsphere.local

5. You plan to install vCenter Server 5.5 in a virtual machine. The vCenter Server will use a remote SQL database and will support 2 hosts and 15 virtual machines. How many vCPUs should you start with when building this VM? (Choose two.)

    A. 1 vCPU with 2 cores

    B. 2 vCPUs with 1 core

    C. 3 vCPUs with 2 cores

    D. 4 vCPUs with 1 core

6. Which of the following is not a component of vCenter Single Sign-On?

    A. Administration Server

    B. Security Token Service

    C. vCenter Inventory Service

    D. VMware Directory Service

7. Which of the following is used to ensure accurate time on ESXi hosts?

    A. vCenter Operations Manager

    B. PXE

    C. vSphere Syslog Collector

    D. NTP

8. What is the first item to be updated in the sequence of events in a vSphere 5.1 to vSphere 5.5 upgrade?

    A. vCenter Single Sign-On

    B. ESXi hosts

    C. vCenter Server

    D. vSphere Client

9. What are two technologies that Auto Deploy relies on?

    A. RDP

    B. PXE

    C. DHCP

    D. SSL

10. ESXi 5 has a system requirement of a minimum of how many processor cores?

    A. 1

    B. 2

    C. 4

    D. 8

11. You plan to install vCenter Server on a Windows server and use an external SQL Server. Which of the following is required? (Choose two.)

    A. 32-bit DSN

    B. 64-bit DSN

    C. SQL Native Client

    D. vSphere Client

12. Which advanced setting is used to enable/disable the memory compression cache?

    A. Mem.BalancePeriod

    B. Mem.MemZipEnable

    C. Mem.ShareVmkEnable

    D. Mem.MemZipMaxPct

13. Which of the following can be used to configure DNS and routing settings for an ESXi host? (Choose all that apply.)

A. vSphere Client

B. vSphere Web Client

C. Service Console

D. DCUI

14. You have a virtual machine administrator who has Mac OS on her laptop. She needs to perform day-to-day operations of a Windows VM that she is responsible for. Which client application should she use?

A. vSphere Client

B. vCenter Client

C. vSphere Web Client

D. vCenter Remote Client

15. Which of the following vCenter Server Support Tools are available for install from the VMware vCenter installer? (Choose all that apply.)

A. VMware ESXi Dump Collector

B. VMware Syslog Collector

C. VMware Auto Deploy

D. VMware vSphere Authentication Proxy

16. VMware vCenter Server Standard is used in which of the following vSphere 5 Kits? (Choose all that apply.)

A. Essentials Plus

B. Standard

C. Advanced

D. Enterprise Plus

17. What is the minimum GB of disk space required for the vCenter Server Appliance?

A. 7

B. 25

C. 50

D. 80

18. Which of the following statements is true of vSphere Host Power Management? (Choose all that apply.)

A. It requires specific BIOS settings on each ESXi host.

B. It requires vSphere Distributed Power Management.

C. ESXi hosts can control power management.

D. It requires Intel processors.

19. When SSO is first deployed in vSphere 5.5, what is the user account that has administrative privileges in SSO?

   A. Admin@System-Domain

   B. Administrator@System-Domain

   C. Admin@vsphere.local

   D. Administrator@vsphere.local

20. Which of the following utilities are supported for ESXi 5 upgrades from ESX/ESXi 4.x versions?

   A. esxcli

   B. esxupdate

   C. vihostupdate

   D. None of the above

Chapter

3

Securing vCenter Server and ESXi and Identifying vSphere Architecture and Solutions

---

VCP5-DCV EXAM OBJECTIVES COVERED IN THIS CHAPTER:

✓ **1.1 Identify vSphere Architecture and Solutions**

- Explain ESXi and vCenter Server architectures

- Identify available vSphere editions and features

- Determine appropriate vSphere edition based on customer requirements

- Identify the various data center solutions that interact with vSphere (Horizon, SRM, etc.)

✓ **1.5 Secure vCenter Server and ESXi**

- Configure and administer the ESXi firewall

- Enable/Configure/Disable services in the ESXi firewall

- Enable Lockdown Mode

- Add an ESXi Host to a directory service

- View/Sort/Export user and group lists

- Identify common vCenter Server privileges and roles

- Describe how permissions are applied and inherited in vCenter Server

- Add/Modify/Remove permissions for users and groups on vCenter Server inventory objects

- Create/Clone/Edit vCenter Server Roles
- Determine the appropriate set of privileges for common tasks in vCenter Server

TOOLS

- vSphere Installation and Setup guide (Objective 1.5)
- vCenter Server and Host Management guide (Objective 1.5)
- VMware vSphere Examples and Scenarios guide (Objective 1.5)
- vSphere Security guide (Objective 1.5)
- VMware vCenter Single Sign-On Server (Objective 1.5)
- Replacing Default vCenter 5.1 and ESXi Certificates (Objective 1.5)
- vSphere Client / vSphere Web Client (Objective 1.5)
- Direct Console User Interface (DCUI) (Objective 1.5)
- VMware vSphere Basics guide (Objective 1.1)
- What's New in vSphere 5.5 Platform (Objective 1.1)
- Introduction to VMware vSphere 5 (Objective 1.1)
- VMware Virtualization Toolkit (Objective 1.1)
- vSphere 5.x Licensing, Pricing and Packaging Whitepaper (Objective 1.1)

Whereas Chapter 2 focused on planning, installing, configuring, and upgrading VMware ESXi and vCenter Server, this chapter will focus on securing those products. In other words, ESXi and vCenter Server are installed and running, and now you need to perform additional security configuration. A discussion of vSphere 5.5 architecture and VMware solutions will round out this chapter.

Securing vCenter Server and ESXi

Knowing how to secure ESXi hosts and vCenter Server is an essential part of any virtual infrastructure administrator's responsibilities. VMware includes many features to protect ESXi and vCenter Server and all its inventory objects, including the ability to set granular permissions, a firewall, virtual switch layer 2 security, directory authentication mechanisms, and more. Knowing the capabilities of these features and how to use them is crucial for both the planning and ongoing maintenance of vSphere 5.5 environments. This chapter begins by adding security configuration to the ESXi host you installed in Chapter 2.

Configuring and Administering the ESXi Firewall

ESXi 5 hosts include a firewall that sits between the ESXi host's management interface and the network. The access control is provided through a VMkernel network adapter (*vmknic*)–level firewall module that inspects packets against firewall rules. The firewall is enabled by default and blocks all traffic by default, except for traffic for the management services listed in Table 3.1.

TABLE 3.1   TCP and UDP port access in vSphere 5.5

Port	Purpose	Traffic type
53	DNS client	UDP in and out
68	DHCP client	UDP in and out
80	HTTP access	TCP in and out
	vSphere Fault Tolerance (FT)	UDP out

TABLE 3.1   TCP and UDP port access in vSphere 5.5 *(continued)*

Port	Purpose	Traffic type
111	RPC service used by VCSA	TCP in and out
135	Used to join VCSA to AD domain	TCP in and out
161	SNMP Server	UDP in
427	CIM client	UDP in and out
443	HTTPS access	TCP in
513	VCSA logging activity	UDP in
902	Authentication, provisioning, VM migration, VM consoles, heartbeat	TCP in and out UDP out
1234	vSphere Replication	TCP out
1235	vSphere Replication	TCP out
5988	CIM transactions over HTTP	TCP in
5989	CIM XML transactions over HTTPS	TCP in and out
8000	Requests from vMotion	TCP in and out
8100	vSphere Fault Tolerance (FT)	TCP and UDP in and out
8200	vSphere Fault Tolerance (FT)	TCP and UDP in and out

The ESXi firewall also allows Internet Control Message Protocol (ICMP) traffic.

The vSphere Web Client's GUI will be the preferred way to manage the ESXi firewall for most administrators, but you should also know that the esxcli command can be used to administer the ESXi firewall. In Exercise 3.1, you will use the vSphere Web Client to configure the ESXi firewall and disable the NTP Client. This exercise assumes that you have previously enabled NTP, as covered in Exercise 2.4.

EXERCISE 3.1

Disabling the NTP Client in the ESXi Firewall

1. Connect to a vCenter Server with the vSphere Web Client.

2. In the left menu, move your mouse cursor over the vCenter menu item. When it becomes highlighted in blue, click it.

3. Select the Hosts And Clusters option and click it.

4. In the left menu, expand Inventory Objects and then choose an ESXi host by clicking it.

5. In the middle pane, click the Manage tab and then select Settings from the toolbar. Select Security Profile from the System menu.

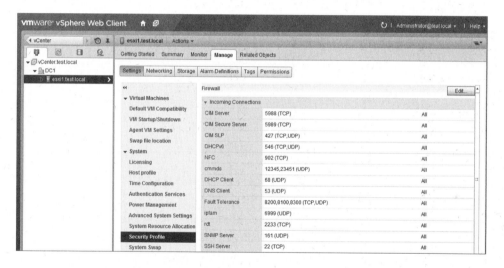

6. In the listing of the ESXi firewall's incoming and outgoing connections, locate the NTP Client entry under Outgoing Connections and click the Edit button located on the upper right. An Edit Security Profile window will open.

7. Review the firewall properties.

   A check appears in the check box next to services that are enabled. You can also review the incoming and outgoing ports used by the service, the protocol used by the service, and the status of the associated daemon (if applicable). In addition, you can sort the services (ascending and descending) by clicking any column header.

EXERCISE 3.1 *(continued)*

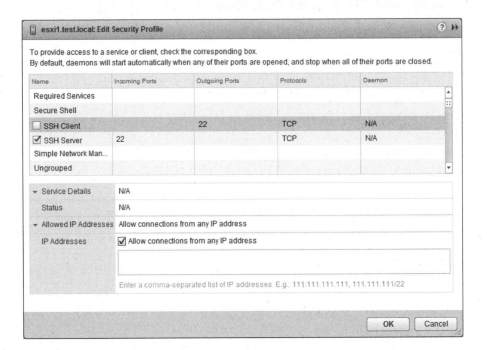

8. For the purposes of this exercise, you are going to disable the NTP Client. Scroll down and select the NTP Client entry in the Name column.

   Notice that the Service Details load at the bottom of the window. Review this information and note that the status value shows Running.

9. Deselect the NTP Client check box, and click OK to continue.

10. Monitor the Firewall Ports tasks that begin. When these tasks complete, review the list of Outgoing Connections in the middle pane, and verify that NTP Client is no longer listed there.

11. Click the Edit button again to review the NTP Client status. Scroll down and select the NTP Client entry in the Name column. Review the information in the Edit Security Profile window. Verify that the NTP Client check box is not selected and that the status shows Stopped.

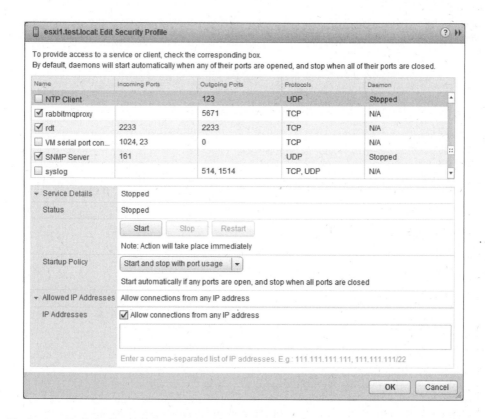

12. Leave the Edit Security Profile window open.

    At this point, you have seen the steps for disabling the NTP Client in the ESXi firewall. The same process can be used for other services in the ESXi firewall as well. In the remainder of this exercise, we will configure an advanced option in the ESXi firewall: allowing connections only from within the vCenter Server's management network. We will also enable the NTP Client again.

13. In the Edit Security Profile window, click the check box beside NTP Client.

14. In the Service Details listed at the bottom of this window, locate the Allowed IP Addresses section. Note that by default, Allow Connections From Any IP Address is selected.

15. Deselect the Allow Connections From Any IP Address check box and enter the information for the network that the vCenter Server management interface is configured for. For example, if vCenter Server has an IP address of 192.168.113.129 and a subnet mask of 255.255.255.0, enter **192.168.113.0/24**. You can list multiple networks here, using commas as separators.

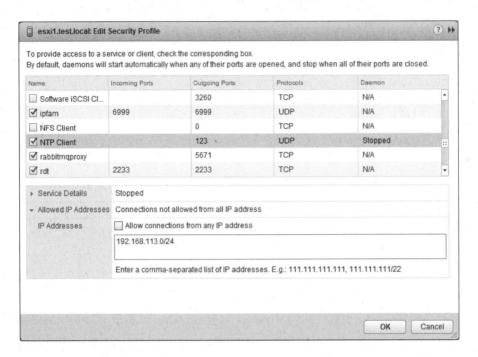

16. Click OK in the Edit Security Profile window. Wait for any tasks to complete; then review the list of Outgoing Connections in the middle pane again and verify that NTP Client is listed with the allowed network(s) shown beside it.

The NFS Client rule set has a different behavior than other ESXi firewall rule sets. NFS Client settings are automatically configured by ESXi when NFS datastores are mounted or unmounted. This means any manual changes made to the NFS Client rule set will be overridden by ESXi whenever these NFS operations occur.

Now that you have configured the ESXi firewall, we will look a little further into configuring service status and startup policies in the ESXi firewall.

Enabling, Configuring, and Disabling Services in the ESXi Firewall

In addition to the firewall settings, the ESXi security profile contains a list of services running on the ESXi host. These services can be configured to start based on the status of the firewall ports. It can be useful to control the behavior of certain services. Three startup policies are available for services:

Start And Stop With Port Usage   A service will attempt to start if any port is open and will continue to attempt to start until it successfully completes. The service will then be stopped when all ports are closed. Note that this policy is listed as Start Automatically If Any Ports Are Open, And Stop When All Ports Are Closed in the traditional vSphere Client. Regardless of the name, the functionality is the same and this is the setting VMware recommends.

Start And Stop With Host   A service will start shortly after the host starts and close shortly after the host shuts down.

Start And Stop Manually   This setting is used to manually control the service state and does not take port availability into consideration. The service status will be preserved across ESXi host reboots.

These three startup policies for services can be changed using the vSphere Web Client. Exercise 3.2 covers the procedure for changing the NTP Daemon service startup policy.

EXERCISE 3.2

Configuring Startup Policies for ESXi Services

1.   Connect to a vCenter Server with the vSphere Web Client.

2.   On the Home page, click vCenter ➢ Hosts And Clusters and select an ESXi host from the inventory.

3.   In the middle pane, click the Manage tab.

4.   At the top of the Manage tab, click Settings, and then choose Security Profile.

5.   Click the Incoming Connections header to collapse the contents, and then click the Outgoing Connections header to collapse the contents. The services are listed directly below the Firewall section.

EXERCISE 3.2 *(continued)*

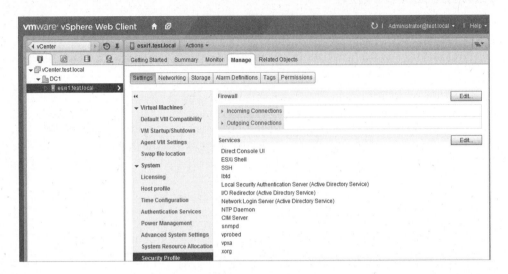

6. Click the Edit button for Services. Make sure you click the Edit button for Services here and not for the Firewall section.

7. Review the information in the Edit Security Profile window. You can sort this information by clicking either column header.

8. Select NTP Daemon from the list and review its Service Details.

9. Notice that the default startup policy for the NTP Daemon service is set to Start And Stop With Port Usage and that the service status is Running.

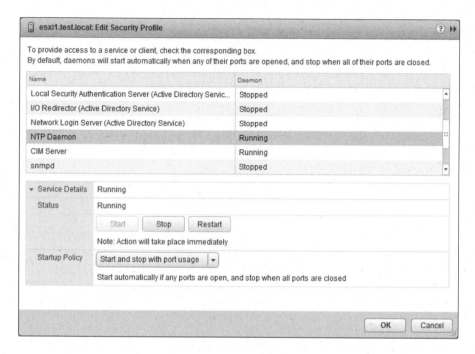

10. In the Startup Policy section, select Start And Stop Manually from the pull-down menu and click OK. An Update Service Activation Policy task will begin. When this task completes, click the Edit button for Services.

11. Verify that the Start And Stop Manually startup policy is selected, and then use the Stop button to stop the NTP Daemon service.

12. A Stop Service task will run and complete. Verify that NTP Daemon is listed as Stopped in the Edit Security Profile window and then click OK.

13. Right-click on the ESXi host that you've just edited. If there are no VMs running on this host, choose Reboot from the context menu.

14. When the ESXi host is again available in the vSphere Web Client, return to the Edit Security Profile window and verify that the NTP Daemon service is now listed as Stopped.

15. Start the NTP Daemon service and reboot the ESXi host once again.

16. When the ESXi host is again available in the vSphere Web Client, return to the Edit Security Profile window and verify that the NTP Daemon service is now listed as Running.

17. Finally, change the default startup policy for the NTP Daemon service back to Start And Stop With Port Usage.

This exercise showed how to set the startup policies for ESXi services. By setting the NTP Daemon service to the startup policy of Start And Stop Manually, you can control how the service behaves. A reboot of the ESXi host preserves these settings. This approach can be used to effectively disable a service. You also returned the NTP Daemon service to its default, and VMware-recommended, setting of Start And Stop With Port Usage. This ensures that your ESXi host has the ability to communicate with NTP servers and thus will have accurate time moving forward.

Now that you've seen how to configure ESXi services, we will discuss another security feature of ESXi. *Lockdown mode* is used to increase the security of ESXi hosts by limiting the access allowed to the host.

Enabling Lockdown Mode

All operations performed against an ESXi host in lockdown mode must originate from the vCenter Server that is managing the ESXi host. *vSphere CLI* commands, *vSphere Management Assistant* (vMA), and the vSphere Client can no longer connect to an ESXi host once it is placed in lockdown mode. This makes vCenter Server an absolute requirement to use lockdown mode. The idea behind lockdown mode is to leverage the centralized roles and privileges and event auditing present in vCenter Server to increase security, provide greater availability, and simplify operations.

Lockdown mode does not affect the availability of the ESXi Shell, SSH, or the Direct Console User Interface (DCUI) if these services are enabled. For example, the root user can still log in to the DCUI when lockdown mode is enabled. Lockdown mode can be enabled when initially adding ESXi hosts to vCenter Server, as shown in Figure 3.1.

FIGURE 3.1   The Enable Lockdown Mode option

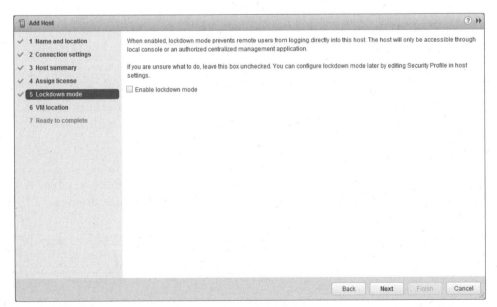

Lockdown mode can also be enabled with the DCUI, as shown in Figure 3.2.

FIGURE 3.2   Enabling lockdown mode with the DCUI

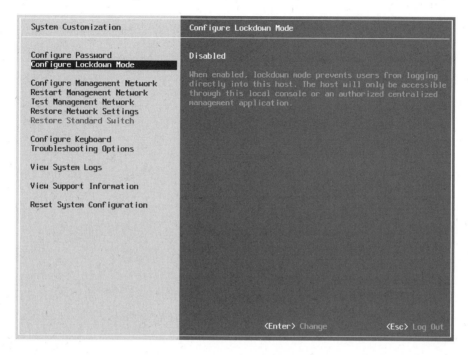

Finally, lockdown mode can be configured with the vSphere Web Client. This approach will typically be the most common way that virtual infrastructure administrators enable or disable lockdown mode. Exercise 3.3 covers the steps for enabling and disabling lockdown mode using the vSphere Web Client.

EXERCISE 3.3

Enabling Lockdown Mode Using the vSphere Web Client

1. Connect to a vCenter Server with the vSphere Web Client.

2. On the Home page, click vCenter ➢ Hosts And Clusters and select an ESXi host from the inventory.

3. In the middle pane, click the Manage tab. Choose Settings ➢ Security Profile.

4. Collapse the Incoming Connections and then the Outgoing Connections contents. Lockdown Mode is listed directly below the Services section.

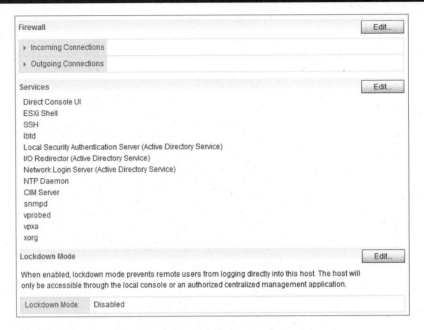

5. Review the information presented here, and then click the Edit button for Lockdown Mode. A Lockdown Mode message window will open.

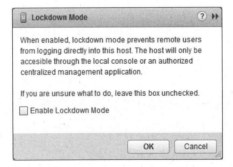

6. Place a check in the checkbox beside Enable Lockdown Mode and click OK.

7. An Enable Lockdown Mode task will start. When this task completes, the ESXi host will be in lockdown mode.

8. Verify that the ESXi host is reporting that lockdown mode is enabled in the vSphere Web Client.

9. Log in to this ESXi host's DCUI and verify that lockdown mode is also enabled there.

To disable lockdown mode, simply repeat these steps and deselect the Enable Lockdown Mode check box.

WARNING
Enabling or disabling lockdown mode from the DCUI discards permissions for any local users and/or groups defined on the ESXi host. Using the vSphere Web Client or the vSphere Client connected to vCenter Server to set lockdown mode on an ESXi host will preserve these permissions.

Another security feature that can be used to protect your ESXi hosts is adding them to a directory service.

Adding an ESXi Host to a Directory Service

ESXi can be configured to use a directory service, like Microsoft's Active Directory (AD), to manage user and group permissions. This is useful when users must have access to the ESXi host but maintaining a separate set of user accounts on the ESXi is undesirable. A directory service like AD can leverage existing directory user accounts and prevent all virtual infrastructure administrators from having to share the ESXi root credentials. This helps simplify the administration and security of the ESXi hosts. To add an ESXi host to a Microsoft Active Directory service, make sure the following prerequisites have been met:

- The Active Directory domain controllers and domain name must be resolvable in the ESXi host DNS server entries.
- Verify that the ESXi hostname is fully qualified with the domain name of the Active Directory forest, for example, esxi1.test.local.
- The time between the ESXi host and the directory service should be synchronized. This is most easily accomplished in ESXi by using NTP.

There are two methods that can be used to join an ESXi host to an Active Directory domain:

vSphere Authentication Proxy   The domain name of the Active Directory server and the IP address of the authentication proxy server are entered when joining an ESXi host to a domain. Using the vSphere Authentication Proxy allows you to avoid storing Active Directory credentials on the ESXi host.

Active Directory Credentials   The Active Directory credentials and the domain name of the Active Directory server are entered when the ESXi host is joined to the domain.

In Exercise 3.4 you will add an ESXi host to an Active Directory domain using the Active Directory credentials method. Note that this exercise requires a working Active Directory domain.

EXERCISE 3.4

Adding an ESXi Host to Active Directory

1. Connect to a vCenter Server with the vSphere Web Client.

2. On the Home page, click vCenter ➤ Hosts And Clusters and select an ESXi host from the inventory.

3. In the middle pane, click the Manage tab.

4. On the Manage tab, click Settings, and choose System ➤ Authentication Services.

5. Click the Join Domain button. A Join Domain window will open.

6. In the Domain Settings section, enter the domain name. The domain name can be entered in either of two ways:

    NAME.DOMAIN   For example, **test.local**. The computer account will be created under the default container in Active Directory.

    NAME.DOMAIN/CONTAINER/PATH   For example, **test.local/NorthAmerica /Richmond**. The account is created under the Richmond organizational unit (OU) in Active Directory.

7. Click OK to continue. A Join Windows Domain task will start. When this task completes, verify that Directory Services Type is listed as Active Directory. Also verify in Domain Settings that the domain is listed properly.

    At this point in the exercise, the ESXi host has been joined to the Active Directory domain. You can verify this by locating the ESXi computer account, using the native tools for managing the domain. In the remainder of this exercise, we will switch to the traditional vSphere Client. This is a necessary step in order to add the Active

Directory domain user and group permissions to the ESXi host. Remember that ESXi-specific permissions can be managed only with the vSphere Client connected directly to the ESXi host.

8. Open the vSphere Client and connect to the ESXi host you just configured to use Active Directory. Enter the credentials for the root user.

9. Select the ESXi host in the left pane, and then click the Configuration tab. Select the Authentication Services link in the Software panel. Verify that Directory Services Type is listed as Active Directory. Also verify in Domain Settings that the domain is listed properly.

10. Now click the Permissions tab. Right-click in the white space and choose Add Permission from the context menu. An Assign Permissions window will open.

11. Click the Add button on this screen. This will open a Select Users And Groups window. Use the pull-down menu to select the domain. Use the pull-down menu under Users And Groups to select the Show Groups First option. Select an administrative group and click Add. This will add the group to the groups listed at the bottom of this window.

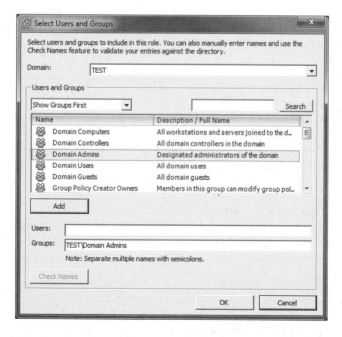

12. Once your domain administrative group has been added, the OK button will become enabled in the Select Users And Groups window. Click OK here; you will be returned to the Assign Permissions window.

13. Use the pull-down menu under Assigned Role to choose the Administrator role for your domain admin group. The final configuration should look similar to this:

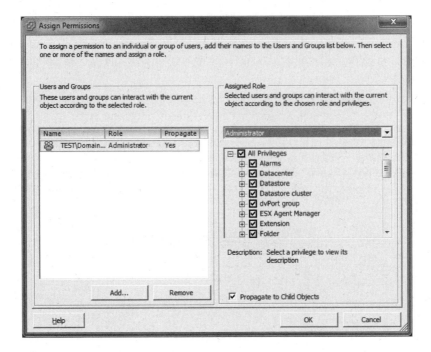

14. Click OK to add the permission. Verify in the Permissions tab that the group just added is now listed.

15. Close the vSphere Client.

16. To verify the new permission works as expected, open the vSphere Client and log in to the ESXi host with a domain account that is a member of the group you added in the previous steps.

Adding your ESXi hosts to Active Directory is a powerful security feature that allows you to leverage the capabilities of the directory service for authentication to your ESXi hosts. This capability can save you both time and effort, because you don't have to create and maintain multiple local ESXi user accounts.

As mentioned previously in the exercise, direct-access ESXi users and groups must be managed from the traditional vSphere Client connected directly to a unique ESXi host. Let's take a moment now to discuss ESXi users, and how to manage them, in more detail.

Viewing, Sorting, and Exporting User and Group Lists

There are two types of users in a vSphere environment: direct-access users and vCenter Server users. Direct-access (local) users are those who have accounts directly on an ESXi host. vCenter Server users have accounts that are authenticated by SSO and then used to access the vCenter Server. Each user type is entirely independent of the other. For example, a direct-access user on an ESXi host could have no access to the vCenter Server used to manage the same ESXi host.

ESXi direct-access users are created on each ESXi host on a per-host basis. vCenter Server cannot be used to manage direct-access users on an ESXi host. It is also important to know that individual ESXi hosts are not integrated with SSO, and neither is the traditional vSphere Client.

In environments where direct-access users have been created, it will sometimes be necessary for a virtual infrastructure administrator to view the local users and groups on an ESXi host, possibly for auditing purposes. These user and group lists may also be sorted and exported to HTML, XML, XLS, and CSV. Exercise 3.5 shows the procedure to view, sort, and export users and groups.

EXERCISE 3.5

Viewing, Sorting, and Exporting User and Group Lists from an ESXi Host

1. Connect to an ESXi host with the traditional vSphere Client.

2. Select the ESXi host in the left pane, and then click the Local Users & Groups tab. You can now use the Users and Groups buttons at the top of the panel to toggle between views, as shown here:

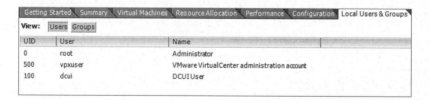

You can also sort the Users view by UID, user, or name by simply clicking the column heading. The Groups view can be sorted by UID or group, using the same procedure of clicking the column heading.

3. With the Users view selected, click the User column heading. The view is now sorted alphabetically by ESXi login.

4. To show or hide columns, right-click any of the column headings and use the check boxes to select or deselect the name of the column.

5. To export the user list, right-click anywhere in the Users view and choose the Export List option from the context menu.

6. When the Save As dialog opens, enter a filename for the exported list and choose the desired file format using the Save As Type drop-down menu.

7. Open the exported file and verify its contents.

This exercise demonstrated the steps for viewing, sorting, and exporting user lists from an ESXi host. Unlike ESXi, vCenter Server does not provide a user list for you to review. There is also no equivalent functionality in vCenter Server to create, remove, or otherwise change the vCenter Server users manually. Instead, the tools used to manage the Windows domain users or local user accounts database are used to manage vCenter Server users. vCenter Server does provide the ability to assign permissions for users and groups to inventory objects, and this will be the next topic discussed.

Identifying Common vCenter Server Privileges and Roles

When vCenter Server is installed, there will be a common set of *privileges* and *roles* available by default. It is important to know that privileges define individual user rights and that roles are a collection of privileges. By default, there are three system roles and six sample roles included in vCenter Server, as shown in Figure 3.3.

FIGURE 3.3 System and sample roles

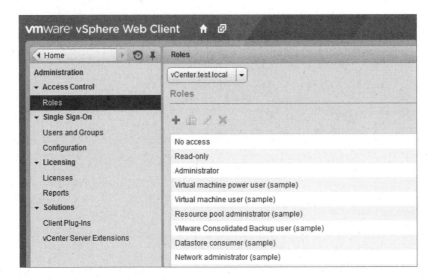

The three default system roles are as follows:

- No Access
- Read-Only
- Administrator

The three system roles are permanent, meaning they cannot be modified in any way. These three default system roles will likely be used in many environments. For example, No Access and Read-Only are very useful for quickly and effectively restricting user access.

The six default sample roles are as follows:

- Virtual Machine Power User
- Virtual Machine User
- Resource Pool Administrator
- VMware Consolidated Backup User
- Datastore Consumer
- Network Administrator

The default sample roles can be used as is or as guidelines for creating custom roles. Although it is possible to use the default sample roles, it is considered best practice not to modify them. If a sample role needs to be modified, consider cloning it instead. You can then modify the cloned sample role accordingly. The benefit of using this approach is that it allows the original sample role to be retained for future reference. We will discuss how to clone roles a bit later in this chapter.

 You can also create roles directly on ESXi hosts. However, these roles will not be accessible from within vCenter Server.

Now that I've explained the common roles, we will cover the privileges that each role can contain. Privileges define individual user rights. Figure 3.4 shows some of the available privileges that can be assigned to a role.

FIGURE 3.4 Privileges assignable to roles

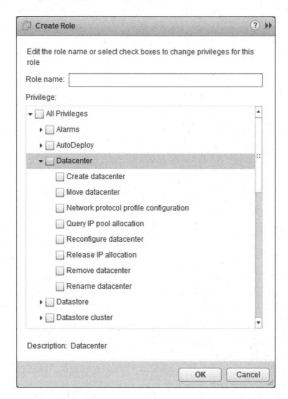

The number of privileges is quite large, and this can lead to some interesting capabilities for users. I strongly recommend that you take some time to review the available privileges that can be assigned to the sample or custom roles.

It is important to remember that privileges define individual user rights and that roles are collections of privileges. A *permission* is created by pairing a role with a user or group and associating it with an object in the vCenter Server inventory. In the next section, we will focus on how these permissions are applied and inherited in vCenter Server.

Describing How Permissions Are Applied and Inherited in vCenter Server

Now that you know how privileges and roles work in vCenter Server, you must understand how permissions work in vCenter. If you happened to skip to this section without reading the preceding discussion of roles and privileges, it might be worthwhile to review the information there. If you have a good understanding of vCenter Server roles and privileges, then read on.

Permissions are applied in vCenter Server by pairing a user or group with a role. This pair is then associated with an object in the vCenter Server inventory to create the permission. A user with Administrator privileges must assign permissions to other nonadministrative users, because these users will by default have no permissions on any of the vCenter Server inventory objects. In vSphere 5.5, the initial vCenter Server root inventory object administrative access is assigned by the SSO administrator, as you saw in Exercise 2.17.

Two forms of permissions apply to vCenter Server inventory objects: managed entities and global entities. Managed entities, which include clusters, datacenters, folders, and hosts, may have permissions assigned to them. Global entities, which include things such as licenses, roles, sessions, and custom fields, cannot have permissions assigned to them and instead will derive their permissions from the root vCenter level.

When assigning permissions to inventory objects, you must also consider permission inheritance or propagation. Permission propagation is one of the configurable settings when permissions are assigned to vCenter Server inventory objects. In the Assign Permissions window, you can select the Propagate To Child Objects check box, as shown in Figure 3.5, to enable the propagation of permissions down the inventory hierarchy.

FIGURE 3.5   Enabling the Propagate To Child Objects option

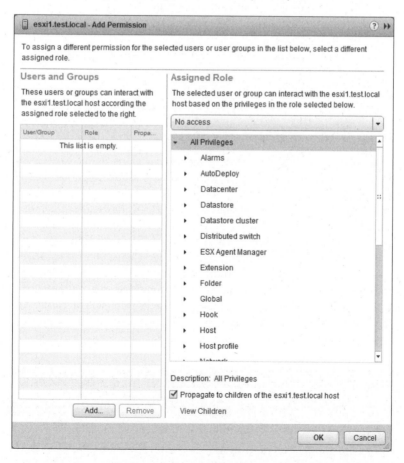

Each permission assigned will have the option available to enable propagation, but it is important to remember that propagation is not universally applied. Any permission defined directly on a child object will override permissions propagated from parent objects.

Inventory objects can inherit permissions from multiple parent objects in the hierarchy, but objects can have only one permission for each user or group. For example, assume there is a user who is a member of two groups in Active Directory. Each of these Active Directory groups is given different permissions on a single virtual machine. This user will have the union of the permissions. This is because an inventory object—the virtual machine in this case—will inherit multiple permissions.

This same example would have seen a different outcome, if there had been a permission defined on the virtual machine for this user. Remember, user permissions take precedence over any group permissions.

WARNING   Before assigning a permission with a restrictive role to a group, verify that the group does not contain the Administrator account or any other accounts with administrative privileges.

Now that you have seen how permissions are applied and inherited in vCenter Server, let's focus on the assigning permissions to vCenter Server inventory objects.

Adding, Modifying, and Removing Permissions for Users and Groups on vCenter Server Inventory Objects

In vSphere, a permission consists of a role plus the user or group name assigned to an inventory object. A permission grants the user or group the rights to perform the actions specified in the role for the inventory object to which the role is assigned. Inventory objects include vCenter Server itself, datacenters, clusters, ESX/ESXi hosts, resource pools, *vApps*, virtual machines, datastore clusters, datastores, virtual switches, and folders. The procedure to add individual user or group permissions is nearly identical, and the steps for adding permissions for a user will be covered in Exercise 3.6. The next three exercises will be built around a series of events involving a domain user named Marshall, who is assigned to a new project involving an ESXi host managed by vCenter Server. Note that this exercise requires a working Active Directory domain. The steps reference an Active Directory domain named TEST (test.local) and a domain user named Marshall; make substitutions as required for your environment.

EXERCISE 3.6

Adding Permissions for Users on vCenter Server Inventory Objects

1. Connect to a vCenter Server with the vSphere Web Client.

2. Select an ESXi host from your inventory.

3. In the middle pane, click the Manage tab and choose Permissions to review the current permissions for the ESXi host.

4. To add a new permission, click the plus sign above the User/Group column header.

5. An Add Permission window will open. In the left pane, you can add a user or group permission by clicking Add.

6. Clicking Add will open a Select Users And Groups window. You can choose the domain and sort order for users and groups, and there is even a search function. Once the desired username is found, select it and click Add. Doing so will place the name in the Users field at the bottom of the screen.

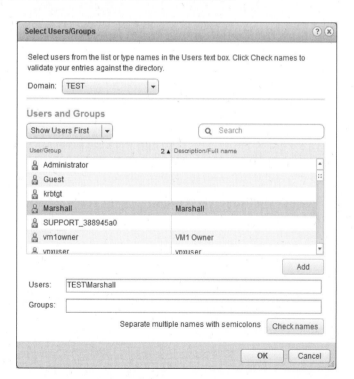

You could also skip directly to the Users field at the bottom of the screen and type in the username, in this case, **TEST\Marshall**. Use the Check Names button to verify the account. Once the desired username has been added to the Users field, click OK to continue.

7. You will return to the Add Permission window. Now that the domain user has been added, choose the Assigned Role drop-down menu and select Read-Only.

8. Accept the default value for the Propagate To Child Objects option, and click OK to add the permission to the ESXi host. Verify that the selected user is now listed on the Permissions tab with the Read-Only role.

The domain user Marshall now has the Read-Only permission to the ESXi host, and the work request is closed. A couple of months pass by, and you receive another work request to make Marshall an administrator of the ESXi host. Exercise 3.7 will modify the permissions for this ESXi host to change the user's role from Read-Only to Administrator.

EXERCISE 3.7

Modifying Permissions for Users on vCenter Server Inventory Objects

1. Connect to a vCenter Server with the vSphere Web Client.

2. Select the same ESXi host used in the previous exercise from the inventory.

3. Verify the current permissions for the ESXi host and that Marshall has the Read-Only role.

4. To modify the permission for the domain user, right-click the permission and choose Change Role from the context menu. You can also select the permission, and then use the Pencil icon above the User/Group column header.

5. A Change Role On Permissions window will open.

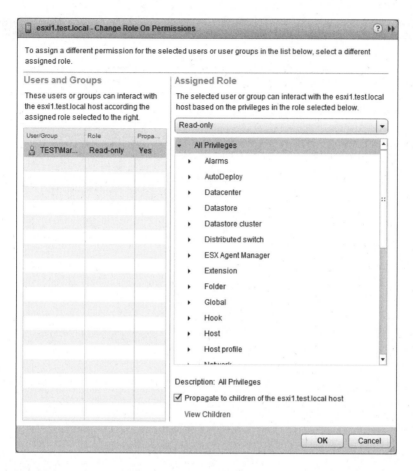

6. Use the pull-down menu under the Assigned Role to change the selection to Administrator. Notice that a series of check marks now appears beside the privileges, indicating the new access.

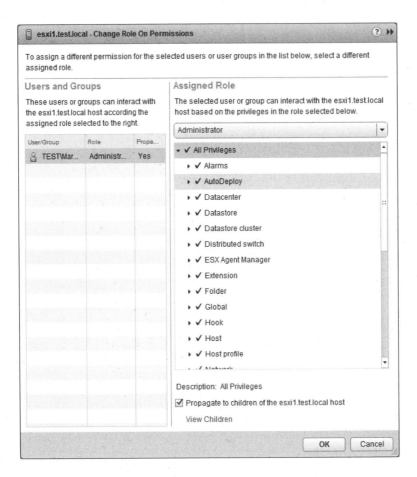

7. Click OK to modify the permission. Verify that the permission has been changed and reflects the new role of Administrator.

The domain user Marshall now has the Administrator role for the ESXi host, and the work request is closed. The next day you receive a work request to remove all access to this ESXi host from Marshall. In Exercise 3.8, you will completely remove his permissions for the ESXi host.

EXERCISE 3.8

Removing Permissions for Users on vCenter Server Inventory Objects

1. Connect to a vCenter Server with the vSphere Web Client.

2. Select the same ESXi host used in the previous exercise from the inventory.

3. Verify the current permissions for the ESXi host. Right-click the permission for Marshall, and choose the Remove option from the context menu. Note that there is no confirmation prompt on this action.

4. Verify that the domain user Marshall is no longer listed on the Permissions tab for this ESXi host.

The preceding series of exercises focused on user permissions to an ESXi host managed by vCenter Server. You saw that group permissions are configured in the same basic manner and are nearly identical to set up. Generally speaking, it is considered a better practice to use custom-defined Active Directory groups for permissions rather than user accounts.

When working with Active Directory groups in vCenter Server and/or vCenter Single Sign-On, always be sure to use security groups and not distribution groups.

Now that we have covered establishing permissions for vCenter Server inventory objects, you will learn about working with the roles that are used to define permissions in vCenter Server.

Creating, Cloning, and Editing vCenter Server Roles

Earlier in this chapter we discussed the three system roles and the six sample roles included in vCenter Server. Although these default roles may be used, VMware recommends that you create unique roles to suit the specific access control needs of your environment. In Exercise 3.9, we will follow this recommendation and create a new role.

EXERCISE 3.9

Creating a New Role in vCenter Server

1. Connect to a vCenter Server with the vSphere Web Client.

2. On the Home page, click the Administration ➢ Roles option. Note that you can use the house icon at the top left of the screen to return home at any time.

3. The current roles are listed in the middle pane. Click the plus icon above the list of roles to add a new role.

4. A Create Role window will open.

5. Give the new role the name **Snapshot Taker**. Expand the list of privileges for Datastore and select the Allocate Space privilege's check box. Now scroll down to the Virtual Machine privileges and expand the list. Expand the Snapshot Management privileges and check the Create Snapshot privilege's box. The Create Role window with the virtual machine privileges is shown here. Click OK to continue.

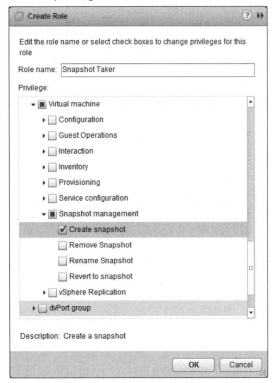

6. Click OK to create the role. Verify that the new role is now listed in the roles.

This newly created role can be used to allow a user or group to have the ability to snapshot a virtual machine. Creating new roles is a fairly straightforward process, but understanding the required privileges can often be more difficult. The vSphere Security Guide and vSphere Virtual Machine Administration Guide both contain additional information about the required privileges for common tasks. This information can be quite valuable when you are creating your own custom roles.

It is sometimes easier to use one of the provided sample roles as a starting point for creating your own custom role. VMware recommends that the default sample roles not be modified; the solution is to instead clone the default sample role. Cloning will make an exact copy of the sample role that can then be modified for your own use. Exercise 3.10 will cover both cloning and editing a sample role.

Cloning and Editing a Sample Role in vCenter Server

1. Connect to a vCenter Server with the vSphere Web Client.

2. Navigate to the vCenter Server roles.

3. Click the Virtual Machine Power User (Sample) role, and then right-click the role and choose Clone.

4. A window titled Clone Role Virtual Machine Power User (Sample) will open with the cloned role name and privileges.

5. Change Role Name to **Virtual Machine Super Power User**. Click the top-level Virtual Machine privilege and verify that the privilege now contains a check mark. The configuration should look similar to that shown here:

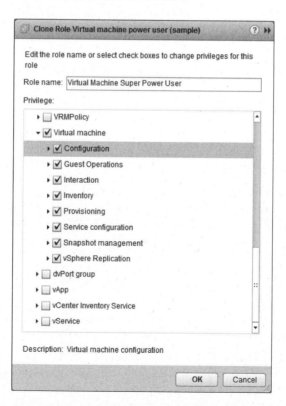

6. Click OK to save the changes made to the role, and then verify that the new role is now listed in the roles.

Now that we have covered how to create, clone, and edit roles in vCenter Server, we will discuss determining the appropriate set of privileges for common tasks in vCenter Server.

Determining the Appropriate Set of Privileges for Common Tasks in vCenter Server

Part of the virtual infrastructure administrator's responsibility is determining the appropriate set of privileges required by the various consumers of that infrastructure. These will be the users who need to create and deploy virtual machines, use virtual machine consoles, or do any other number of administrative or operational tasks. With the number of privileges available in vCenter Server, the options for users are almost endless. This section will cover the appropriate set of privileges for two different scenarios. The first will be the privileges required for creating a new virtual machine, and the second will be for a virtual machine user who needs console access.

The minimum privileges required to create a new virtual machine are as follows:

- Virtual Machine.Inventory.Create New
- Virtual Machine.Configuration.Add New Disk (if new virtual disk(s) will be created)
- Virtual Machine.Configuration.Add Existing Disk (if an existing virtual disk will be used)
- Virtual Machine.Configuration.Raw Device (if an RDM or SCSI pass-through device is used)
- Resource.Assign Virtual Machine to Resource Pool (on destination cluster, resource pool, or host)
- Datastore.Allocate Space (on destination datastore)
- Network.Assign Network

To assign this set of privileges, you would use the roles feature in vCenter Server to create a new role. From its interface, you can add any number of additional privileges to expand the capabilities of the role. Another role that often is needed in the virtual infrastructure is for virtual machine users who need access to a local console of the virtual machine.

For example, say there is a virtual machine user who must have access to the virtual machine's console to monitor an application. This user could easily be granted the Administrator role, but that would give the user too much access to the virtual machine. Instead, a new role can be created to grant only console access to this user. The following is the minimum privilege required to give a user access to a virtual machine console:

Virtual Machine.Interaction.Console Interaction

As you can see, roles can contain a single privilege or multiple privileges. Understanding the required privileges can be difficult, and a good deal of experimentation (preferably in a lab environment) with the privileges is the best way to learn them. As mentioned earlier in this chapter, both the vSphere Security Guide and the vSphere Virtual Machine

Administration Guide contain additional information about required privileges for many common tasks. When these resources can't provide the solution, it becomes helpful to understand the privileges and how they work. Doing so will allow you to create your own roles that provide only the required access.

We have now completed our coverage of securing vCenter Server and ESXi, and in the final section of this chapter we will discuss the vSphere architecture and VMware solutions.

Identifying vSphere Architecture and Solutions

As a VMware Certified Professional, you will be expected to know the architecture of VMware products and how they work. You will also be expected to identify the appropriate solution for your business and customers. In this section you will explore the architecture of vSphere and its various editions and feature sets. I will also cover data center solutions that VMware offers.

Explaining ESXi and vCenter Server Architectures

vSphere architecture is composed of three distinct layers:

Virtualization   x86 servers with ESXi hypervisor

Management   vCenter Server and associated services

Interface   Solutions that provide additional functionality such as the vSphere Client or the vSphere CLI

The Virtualization Layer

The virtualization layer consists of ESXi hosts, which abstract processor, memory, video, storage, and resources into virtual machines. ESXi hosts represent the aggregate resources of their underlying physical x86 hardware. For example, if a host has four quad-core 3GHz CPUs and 128GB of RAM, then that host has 48GHz of processing resources and 128GB of RAM resources available.

ESXi hosts can also be placed into clusters, which aggregate the resources of all hosts in the cluster. Clusters typically have access to the same networks and storage resources and can be managed as a single entity. For example, if a cluster contains two ESXi hosts each with four quad-core 3GHz CPUs and 128GB of RAM, then the cluster has 96GHz of processing resources and 256GB of RAM resources available.

ESXi hosts or clusters can also use resource pools. Resource pools are created to partition resources of ESXi hosts or clusters containing multiple ESXi hosts. This can be useful when a certain group of virtual machines needs guaranteed resources. Resource pools can be dynamically changed, and their resources can also be shared when not in use.

Real World Scenario

Using Resource Pools

A customer is currently using a single ESXi host to run four virtual machines. Two of these virtual machines are used by R&D, and the other two virtual machines are used by HR staff. The R&D virtual machines have higher resource requirements than the HR virtual machines. The virtual infrastructure administrator needs to be able to ensure that the R&D virtual machines get the resources they require.

The virtual infrastructure administrator creates two resource pools on the ESXi host and sets CPU Shares to High for the R&D resource pool and to Normal for the HR resource pool, as shown here:

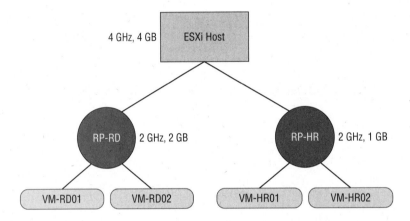

With this resource pool set up, the R&D group gets the resources required to run their workloads, whereas the HR resource pool also provides sufficient resources to these VMs to run their workloads.

The Management Layer

vCenter Server is a centralized management application used to manage ESXi hosts, but this statement does not accurately capture the extent of vCenter Server's capabilities. vCenter Server offers a single pane of glass interface that provides the following core services:

- Virtual machine provisioning
- Host and VM configuration
- Resources and virtual machine inventory management

- Statistics and logging
- Alarms and event management
- A task scheduler
- vApps

The capabilities of vCenter Server may be further extended with vCenter Server plug-ins. Certain plug-ins are included along with the base vCenter Server product, including these:

- vCenter Storage Monitoring
- vCenter Hardware Status
- vCenter Service Status

There are also other vCenter Server plug-ins that can be installed separately, including the following:

- vSphere Update Manager (VUM)
- vCenter Orchestrator
- VMware Data Protection

vCenter Server also contains interfaces that integrate it with third-party products and applications, including these:

- ESXi server management
- VMware vSphere API
- Active Directory interface
- Database interface

The Interface Layer

The management and virtualization layers can both be accessed through various interfaces. These interfaces include the following:

- vSphere Client
- vSphere Web Client
- vSphere PowerCLI
- vSphere SDK for Perl
- vSphere CLI (vCLI)
- vSphere SDK for .NET
- vSphere Web Services SDK

Understanding the architecture of ESXi and vCenter Server will be important for the VCP5-DCV exam, and it is important to know how these three layers interoperate with each other. Now that you have seen the ESXi and vCenter Server architectures, let's move our discussion to identifying the available vSphere editions and features.

Identifying Available vSphere Editions and Features

Many editions of vSphere are available, and for the exam it is important to know the differences between these editions. Figure 3.6 lists the vSphere editions and their associated features.

Three editions of vSphere are bundled with vCenter Server Operations Manager. Known as vSphere with Operations Management, these bundled editions are available with vCenter Standard, Enterprise, or Enterprise Plus. These editions offer an easier and possibly more cost-effective way to purchase and manage your vCenter Operations Manager licenses. vCenter Operations Manager will be covered in detail in Chapter 11, "Monitoring a vSphere Implementation and Managing vCenter Server Alarms."

Although knowing the editions and features listed in Figure 3.6 is helpful for the exam, it is equally important to understand what the features are and how they are actually used. You are much more likely to see an implementation question on the VCP5-DCV exam than a simple "What is the difference between these two editions?" question.

In addition to becoming familiar with the various vSphere editions and feature sets, you should understand which edition of vSphere to use. We will cover this topic in the next section.

Determining Appropriate vSphere Edition Based on Customer Requirements

Part of successfully designing any virtual infrastructure is determining which edition of vSphere will fit the specific requirements. Smaller businesses will often have an entirely different set of business requirements and budgets for their infrastructure than a large enterprise. Knowing how to leverage the correct edition of vSphere based on these requirements is important. Various factors can come into play here, such as virtual machine availability, advanced storage functionality, backup strategy, and even the number of virtual machines that will be powered on.

FIGURE 3.6 vSphere 5.5 editions and features

	Essentials Kit	Essentials Plus Kit	Standard	Enterprise	Enterprise Plus
Centralized Management	vCenter for Essentials	vCenter for Essentials	vCenter Foundation or Standard (Sold Separately)	vCenter Foundation or Standard (Sold Separately)	vCenter Foundation or Standard (Sold Separately)
Included Entitlement	3 servers with up to 2 processors each	3 servers with up to 2 processors each			
SUSE Linux Enterprise Server for VMware			YES	YES	YES
Product Features					
Thin Provisioning	YES	YES	YES	YES	YES
Update Manager	YES	YES	YES	YES	YES
vStorage APIs for Data Protection	YES	YES	YES	YES	YES
Data Protection		YES	YES	YES	YES
High Availability		YES	YES	YES	YES
vMotion		YES	YES	YES	YES
vSphere Replication		YES	YES	YES	YES
Storage vMotion		YES	YES	YES	YES
Hot Add			YES	YES	YES
vShield Endpoint			YES	YES	YES
Fault Tolerance			YES	YES	YES
Storage APIs for Array Integration				YES	YES
Storage APIs for Multipathing				YES	YES
Distributed Resources Scheduler (DRS)				YES	YES
Distributed Power Management (DPM)				YES	YES
Reliable Memory				YES	YES
Big Data Extensions					YES
Storage I/O Control					YES
Network I/O Control					YES
Distributed Switch					YES
Host Profiles					YES
Auto Deploy					YES
Storage DRS					YES
App HA					YES
Profile-Driven Storage					YES
Flash Read Cache					YES

Real World Scenario

Choosing the Appropriate vSphere Edition for Customer Needs

A customer is currently using the free VMware vSphere Hypervisor on two x86 hosts to house five virtual machines. The customer has been using this setup for some time but has decided on virtualization as the infrastructure of choice for the future. So the customer plans to eliminate its remaining non-ESXi physical servers in the next year and expects to double the virtual infrastructure as a result. Virtual machine backups have been a pain point for this customer. The customer has an existing SAN and wants to leverage a centralized management solution for these ESXi hosts and to provide high uptime for the virtual machines in this environment.

Two editions of vSphere were immediately considered. The Essentials edition would allow the customer to meet the centralized management requirement with vCenter Server, but this edition would not adequately address the high availability requirements. The Essentials Plus edition would meet the centralized management requirement and could leverage the customer's SAN to provide HA and vMotion. Another value of the Essentials Plus edition is the inclusion of VMware Data Protection, which would allow the customer to obtain image-level virtual machine backups.

The three other available editions of vSphere would have also worked for this customer, but the Essentials Plus edition currently best meets this customer's requirements. This solution also gives the customer room to grow and should serve them quite well in the future.

We have now covered how to determine the appropriate vSphere edition based on specific customer requirements. It is important to know the feature sets of each vSphere edition to ensure that you always choose the appropriate edition. Another important aspect of meeting customer requirements is understanding the many additional VMware solutions that are available.

Identifying the Various Datacenter Solutions That Interact with vSphere (Horizon, SRM, Etc.)

In the licensing section of Chapter 2, you saw that solutions are applications that extend the functionality or capabilities of vCenter Server. These solutions include VMware vCenter Operations and VMware vCenter Site Recovery Manager. The following is an overview of some of the VMware solutions currently available:

Horizon View   A virtual desktop infrastructure (VDI) solution

Horizon Workspace   A workspace portal solution

Horizon Mirage   A layered OS image management solution

Site Recovery Manager   A disaster recovery solution

vCenter Operations Management Suite   A performance, capacity, and health monitoring solution

vCloud Director   A software-defined data center provisioning solution

VMware offers many solutions, as do third-party vendors. Becoming familiar with all of these solutions would be an enormous task, and you will not likely need such knowledge for the VCP5-DCV exam. It is beneficial to know what some widely used VMware solutions are, though, and to at least understand what they are used for.

Summary

This chapter covered the topics of securing vCenter Server and ESXi and identifying the vSphere architectures and solutions. Knowing how to secure the virtual infrastructure is an extremely important skillset for the virtual infrastructure administrator. To address this, we covered vCenter Server privileges, roles, and permissions. We discussed securing ESXi with its built-in firewall, services, lockdown mode capability, and directory services integration.

Knowing the architecture of vSphere and other VMware solutions is helpful in designing your virtual infrastructure. Equally important is knowing the available vSphere editions, features, and VMware solutions. For the VCP5-DCV exam, you will be expected to know what vSphere editions and features are available, when to use these features and editions, and how to integrate solutions to meet additional requirements.

Exam Essentials

Know how to secure ESXi 5.5 and vCenter Server 5.5.   Understand the difference between a permission, a privilege, and a role. Be able to identify the common vCenter Server privileges and roles and know how to create, clone, and edit roles. Understand how permissions are applied and inherited in vCenter Server and know what permissions override others. Know how to configure and administer the ESXi firewall and ESXi services in the ESXi firewall. Understand what lockdown mode is used for and how to implement it. Know how to view, sort, and export user and group lists in vCenter Server, as well as how to add, modify, and remove permissions for users and groups on vCenter Server inventory objects. Know how to add an ESXi host to a directory service and why you would do so. Be able to determine the appropriate set of privileges for common tasks in vCenter Server.

Know how to identify vSphere architecture and solutions.   Know both the ESXi and vCenter Server architectures. Understand the available vSphere editions and features, and be able to determine the appropriate vSphere edition based on specific customer requirements. Know how to use different VMware solutions to meet additional customer virtual infrastructure requirements.

Review Questions

1. How many default system roles are available in vCenter?

   A. 2

   B. 3

   C. 4

   D. 5

2. In vCenter Server, which of the following items defines individual user rights?

   A. Role

   B. Permission

   C. Privilege

   D. None of these

3. In vCenter Server, a role is a collection of _____.

   A. Roles

   B. Permissions

   C. Privileges

   D. User rights

4. What is created by pairing a vCenter Server role with a user or group and then associating it with an object in the vCenter Server inventory?

   A. Role

   B. Permission

   C. Privilege

   D. User right

5. In vCenter Server, which of the following statements are true about permission inheritance? (Choose two.)

   A. Any permission defined directly on a child object will override permissions propagated from parent objects.

   B. Any permission defined directly on a parent object will override permissions propagated from child objects.

   C. Virtual machines do not inherit multiple permissions.

   D. Virtual machines inherit multiple permissions.

6. Which of the following statements about the ESXi firewall is true?

   A. The firewall is disabled by default and must be enabled using the vSphere Web Client.

   B. The firewall is enabled by default and blocks all traffic by default, except for traffic for the default management services.

    C. The firewall is enabled by default, allows all outbound traffic, and blocks all inbound traffic.

    D. The firewall is disabled by default and must be enabled using the `esxcli` command.

7. Which of the following is the VMware-recommended startup policy for ESXi services?

    A. Start And Stop With Port Usage

    B. Start And Stop With Host

    C. Start And Stop Manually

    D. VMware does not specifically recommend any single startup policy.

8. Operations performed against an ESXi host in lockdown mode can originate from which of the following?

    A. vMA

    B. vSphere Client connected directly to ESXi host

    C. vCenter Server

    D. vSphere CLI commands

9. Which of the following are valid reasons to join ESXi hosts to a directory service? (Choose all that apply.)

    A. Allows vSphere Web Client access directly to ESXi host

    B. Simplifies user management

    C. Improved security for root account

    D. Enables vCenter lockdown mode

10. To export the list of local ESXi users to an HTML file, which of the following approaches could be used?

    A. vSphere Client connected to a vCenter Server

    B. vSphere Client connected to ESXi host

    C. vSphere Web Client connected to a vCenter Server

    D. vSphere Web Client connected to ESXi host

11. Which of the following is the preferred method to manage user permissions in vCenter Server?

    A. Using Local Windows groups

    B. Using Active Directory distribution groups

    C. Using Active Directory security groups

    D. Using Active Directory users

12. When working with the vSphere Web Client, which of the following is true of the vCenter Server default system roles?

    A. They can be cloned.

    B. They can be edited.

    C. They can be removed.

    D. None of these.

13. Which of the following groups must be created in Active Directory before an ESXi can successfully use Active Directory for authentication?

    A. ESXi Admin

    B. ESXi Admins

    C. ESX Admin

    D. ESX Admins

14. Which of the following is VMware's virtual desktop infrastructure solution?

    A. Horizon View

    B. Site Recovery Manager

    C. vCenter Operations Management Suite

    D. vCloud Director

15. Which of the following privileges are required for taking a virtual machine snapshot? (Choose all that apply.)

    A. Virtual Machine.Snapshot Management.Create Snapshot

    B. Virtual Machine.Provisioning.Allow Disk Access

    C. Datastore.Allocate Space

    D. Datastore.Update Virtual Machine Files

16. Which features of the Enterprise Plus Edition of vSphere are not included with the Enterprise Edition of vSphere? (Choose all that apply.)

    A. Storage APIs for Multipathing

    B. Storage I/O Control

    C. Storage vMotion

    D. Storage DRS

17. Which features of the Enterprise Edition of vSphere are not included with the Standard Edition of vSphere? (Choose all that apply.)

    A. Storage APIs for Array Integration

    B. Storage APIs for Multipathing

    C. Distributed Resources Scheduler (DRS)

    D. Distributed Power Management (DPM)

18. The vSphere architecture is composed of which layers? (Choose all that apply.)

    A. Virtualization

    B. Client access

    C. Management

    D. Interface

19. Which features of the Essentials Plus Edition of vSphere are not included with the Essentials Edition of vSphere? (Choose all that apply.)

A. Data Protection

B. High Availability

C. vMotion

D. vSphere Replication

20. A customer needs to implement a virtual infrastructure that meets the following requirement: the customer wants to have both diskless and stateless ESXi hosts implemented. Which vSphere edition is required?

A. Enterprise Plus

B. Enterprise

C. Standard

D. None of the above

Chapter

4

Planning and Configuring vSphere Networking

VCP5-DCV EXAM OBJECTIVES COVERED IN THIS CHAPTER:

✓ **1.4: Plan and Perform Upgrades of vCenter Server and VMware ESXi**

  ▪ Upgrade a vNetwork Distributed Switch

✓ **1.5: Secure vCenter Server and ESXi**

  ▪ Configure network security policies

✓ **2.1: Configure vNetwork Standard Switches**

  ▪ Identify vNetwork Standard Switch (vSS) capabilities

  ▪ Create/Delete a vNetwork Standard Switch

  ▪ Add/Configure/Remove vmnics on a vNetwork Standard Switch

  ▪ Configure vmkernel ports for network services

  ▪ Add/Edit/Remove port groups on a vNetwork Standard Switch

  ▪ Determine use case for a vNetwork Standard Switch

✓ **2.2: Configure vNetwork Distributed Switches**

  ▪ Identify vNetwork Distributed Switch (vDS) capabilities

  ▪ Create/Delete a vNetwork Distributed Switch

  ▪ Add/Remove ESXi hosts from a vNetwork Distributed Switch

  ▪ Add/Remove uplink adapters to dvUplink Groups

  ▪ Add/Configure/Remove dvPort groups

  ▪ Create/Configure/Remove virtual adapters

- Migrate virtual adapters to/from a vNetwork Standard Switch
- Migrate virtual machines to/from a vNetwork Distributed Switch
- Determine Use Case for a vNetwork Distributed Switch

✓ **2.3: Configure vSS and vDS Policies**

- Identify common vSS and vDS policies
- Configure load balancing and failover policies
- Configure traffic shaping policies
- Configure VLAN settings
- Determine appropriate VLAN configuration for a vSphere implementation
- Configure dvPort group blocking policies
- Enable Jumbo Frames support on appropriate components

TOOLS

- vSphere Installation and Setup guide (Objectives 2.1, 2.2, 2.3)
- vSphere Networking guide (Objectives 2.1, 2.2, 2.3)
- vSphere Client

In this chapter, we will configure vSphere networking. So far, we have built and configured ESXi hosts and vCenter Server, but now we will cover how to connect these ESXi hosts to various networks in your environment.

Configuring vNetwork Standard Switches

Networking in vSphere is a key concept to understand for the VCP5-DCV exam. Knowing how to configure networking allows you to use advanced features like vMotion, Fault Tolerance (FT), and more. The networking configuration is also used to provide load-balanced and highly available virtual machine network traffic. Securing network storage communications, management interfaces, and virtual machines is another important aspect of networking. When ESXi is installed, a virtual switch is created by default. This is a standard vSwitch, and the first topic we will cover in this chapter.

Identifying vNetwork Standard Switch Capabilities

vNetwork standard switches, or vSwitches, are software constructs of the local ESXi host that process layer 2 Ethernet headers. Figure 4.1 shows the architecture of a vSwitch. It is important to note that each ESXi host has its own set of vSwitches and maintains a separate configuration for each vSwitch located on the host.

> You will see the terms *vNetwork standard switch*, *vSS*, and *vSwitch* throughout this chapter. It is important to remember that these terms are all referring to the same thing. For the sake of consistency, the term *vSwitch* will be used most often.

vSwitches are used in ESXi to provide two types of networking:

Virtual Machine   This connection type is used to allow virtual machines to communicate and applies exclusively to virtual machines.

VMkernel   This connection type is used for host-based connections such as ESXi management traffic, vMotion, FT, iSCSI, and NFS.

These two *connection types* are provided by *port groups* in the vSwitch. The default port groups created during ESXi installation are shown in Figure 4.2.

FIGURE 4.1   vSwitch architecture

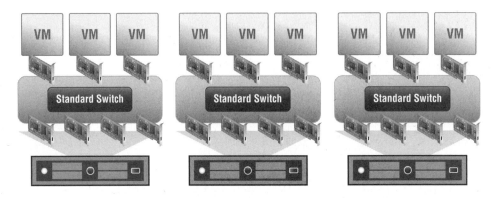

FIGURE 4.2   Default vSwitch port groups

In the vSphere Web Client, you can obtain the properties for a vSwitch by selecting it in the Virtual Switches list (by default there is only one switch initially) and then clicking the yellow pencil (Edit Settings) icon. To obtain the properties for a port group, hover the mouse over the port group name in the vSwitch diagram. The text descriptor of the port group will turn to a blue link. Click this link, and then click the yellow pencil icon that appears above the vSwitch to view the selected port group properties. When working with vSwitches, it is important to remember that properties defined on a port group will override properties defined on the vSwitch containing the port group.

A vSwitch has a maximum of 4,088 ports.

One capability of a vSwitch is the ability to move layer 2 virtual machine traffic internally. This means that two VMs on the same subnet and also residing on the same ESXi host can communicate directly; their traffic does not need to leave the ESXi host. An additional capability of a vSwitch is that VMs can communicate with other external networks. vSwitches are also capable of supporting virtual local area networks (VLANs) and 802.1Q VLAN encapsulation.

vSwitches can also be used to provide security via security policies. Three security policies are available:

- Promiscuous Mode

- MAC Address Changes

- Forged Transmits

The final section of this chapter discusses these security policies in detail.

Outbound traffic shaping is another capability of a vSwitch. ESXi can use traffic shaping policies to restrict network bandwidth available and allow bursts of traffic. These traffic shaping policies are applied to each VM network adapter connected to the standard switch. It is important to remember that ESXi can shape only outbound network traffic on vSwitches and that traffic shaping is disabled by default. Figure 4.3 shows the configurable options for traffic shaping.

FIGURE 4.3   Options for traffic shaping

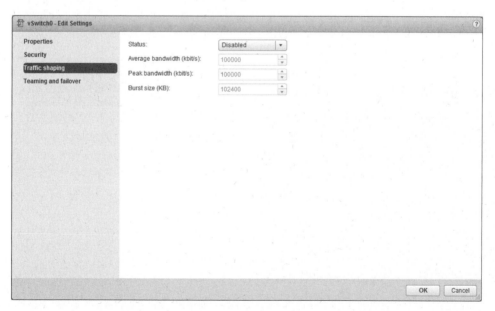

NIC teaming is another capability of a vSwitch. In ESXi, virtual machine network redundancy is provided by the vSwitch. Instead of the virtual machine having multiple network adapters set up in a teamed configuration, a vSwitch can instead be set up on the ESXi host to provide this fault tolerance. The options to configure this redundancy are found in the Teaming And Failover vSwitch settings, as shown in (Figure 4.4).

FIGURE 4.4   Options for NIC teaming

vSwitches also have the ability to use Cisco Discovery Protocol (CDP), which is Cisco's proprietary discovery protocol. To obtain CDP information for peer devices connected to the physical network adapters on vNetwork standard switches, click the information icon beside the physical adapter(s) assigned to the vSwitch, as shown in Figure 4.5.

FIGURE 4.5   CDP information

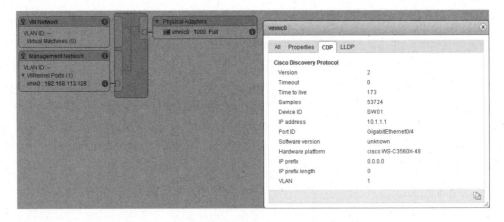

Note that if your upstream network devices do not support CDP, there will be no CDP information available to review. vSwitches have many powerful capabilities, and many of the capabilities just covered will be discussed in much greater detail later in this chapter. Before exploring those details, let's create a vSwitch.

Creating and Deleting a vNetwork Standard Switch

When ESXi is installed interactively, a single vSwitch named vSwitch0 is created by default. This vSwitch contains two port groups: one for virtual machines and one for management. This default vSwitch will get you started, but at some point you will likely need to add additional networks. Exercise 4.1 shows how to create a new vSwitch that will be dedicated for virtual machine network traffic.

EXERCISE 4.1

Creating a vSwitch

1. Connect to a vCenter Server with the vSphere Web Client.

2. On the Home page, click the vCenter ➤ Hosts And Clusters option and select an ESXi host from the inventory.

3. Click the Manage tab and then select the Networking option from the tab's toolbar.

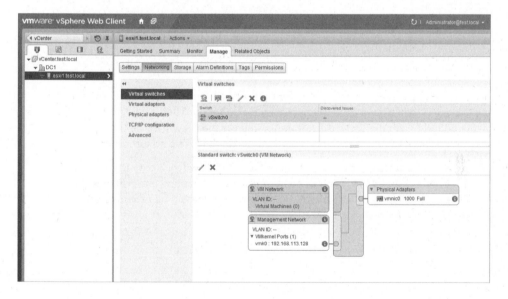

4. Click the Add Host Networking icon, which is the blue and green globe icon with the plus sign on it, to add host networking. The Add Networking wizard will begin.

5. Select the Virtual Machine Port Group For A Standard Switch connection type and click the Next button to continue.

6. Choose the New Standard Switch option and click Next to continue.

7. On the Create A Standard Switch screen, click the plus icon to assign a physical network adapter. An Add Physical Adapters To The Switch window will open.

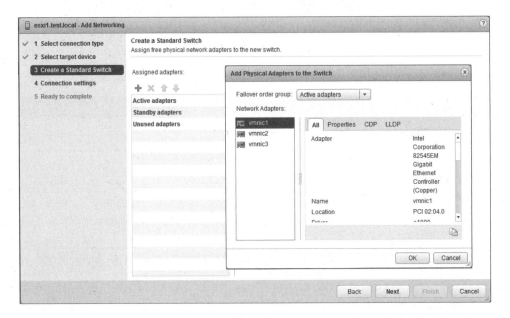

8. In the Add Physical Adapters To The Switch window, select the Unused Adapters option from the Failover Order Group drop-down menu. Then select an unused network adapter from the list in the left pane. Review the network adapter information, properties, and CDP/LLDP information (if applicable) for this adapter.

9. Click OK to add the physical network adapter to the vSwitch. Verify that a (New) vmnicX entry is listed in the left pane in the Unused Adapters list. Select this entry and then use the blue up arrow to move the entry to the Active Adapters section, as shown in the following image:

EXERCISE 4.1 *(continued)*

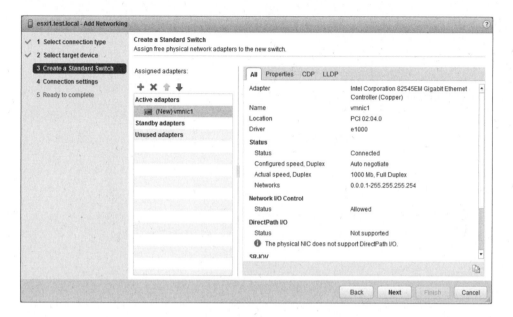

10. Click the Next button to continue.

11. Provide a network label for the default port group that will be added to this vSwitch. If using multiple ESXi hosts with vCenter and vMotion, make sure this network label is consistent across all of your ESXi hosts to ensure vMotion works properly. Choose a VLAN ID for this network if applicable and click Next to continue.

12. Review the information on the Ready To Complete screen and click the Finish button to add the vNetwork standard switch to the ESXi host.

13. An Add Virtual Machine Port Group To vSwitch1 task will begin. When this task completes, select the vSwitch and review the information shown for accuracy.

EXERCISE 4.1 *(continued)*

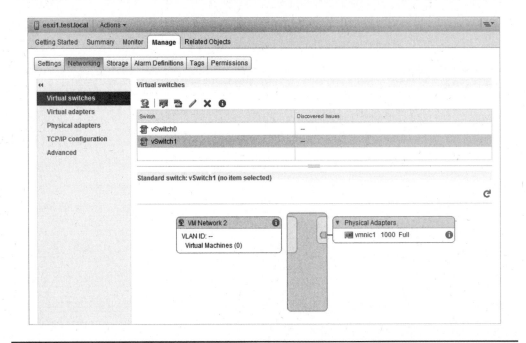

One part of this exercise that can be somewhat confusing is the use of the terms *connection type* and *port group*. In step 5 of this exercise, you were asked to choose a connection type. In step 11, you were asked to provide a label for the port group. The connection type you choose will determine the type of port group (Virtual Machine or VMkernel) that is created.

When you add a new vSwitch, a port group will be created by default. This is because a vSwitch without port groups would be like a physical switch without any ports.

It is always best to select at least two NICs for a vSwitch used for virtual machine network traffic in order to provide both redundancy and load distribution.

Now that you have created a new vSwitch, it's also important to know how to remove a vSwitch. (Since future exercises in this chapter will build on the vSwitch you just created, I will describe the steps but not demonstrate them.)

To remove a vSwitch, locate it on the Manage tab and click to select it. Then click the red X icon located directly above. You will be prompted to confirm the removal of the vSwitch (Figure 4.6). Click the Yes button to continue.

FIGURE 4.6   Removing a vSwitch

 Attempting to delete a vSwitch will fail if virtual machines are actively using the vSwitch.

Now that we have created a vSwitch, I will cover adding, configuring, and removing *vmnics* on a vSwitch.

Adding, Configuring, and Removing vmnics on a vNetwork Standard Switch

As your virtual environment grows, you will want to ensure that it can scale to meet the virtual machine's networking demands. In the event that virtual machine networking traffic were to approach capacity, it is possible to add additional physical adapters to a vSwitch. Physical network adapters are also referred to as vmnics. Exercise 4.2 covers how to add an additional vmnic to an existing vSwitch and configure it.

EXERCISE 4.2

Adding a vmnic to a vSwitch and Configuring It

1. Connect to a vCenter Server with the vSphere Web Client.

2. On the Home page, click the vCenter ➤ Hosts And Clusters option and select an ESXi host from the inventory.

3. Click the Manage tab and then select the Networking option from the tab's toolbar.

4. Select the vSwitch created in Exercise 4.1 and then click the Manage The Physical Network Adapters Connected To The Selected Switch icon, which is the green network adapter icon with the wrench on it.

5. The Manage Physical Network Adapters For vSwitch1 window opens.

6. Click the plus icon to add additional network adapters to the vSwitch. The Add Physical Adapters To The vSwitch window launches. This is the same process we used in the previous exercise to add the initial network adapter to the vSwitch.

7. Use the Failover Order Group drop-down menu to select the Unused Adapters option. Then select an unused network adapter from the list in the left pane. You can select multiple adapters by clicking while holding the Ctrl key.

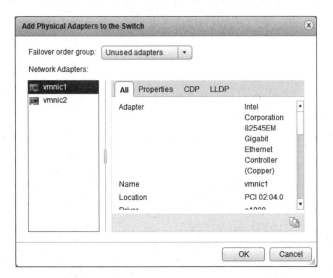

8. Click OK to add the physical network adapter to the vSwitch. Since the usual purpose of creating new vmnics is to add network capacity for virtual machines, ensure that a (New) vmnicX entry is listed in the left pane under Active Adapters and that there are at least two adapters listed here.

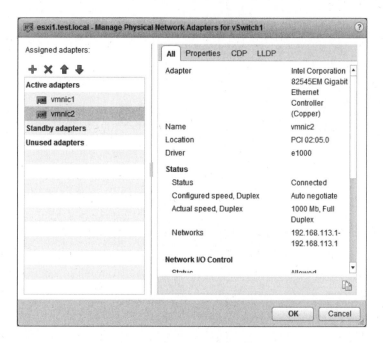

Standby adapters could also be used, but they would become active only if an active adapter failed. If you wanted to make one or more adapters active and one or more standby, you could do so by selecting the physical adapter and then using the blue up and down arrow icons.

9. Click OK to add the network adapter to the vSwitch.

10. Wait for the screen to refresh or use the blue refresh arrow icon to manually refresh the screen. Verify that the newly added physical network adapter is now listed in the vSwitch Physical Adapters field.

EXERCISE 4.2 *(continued)*

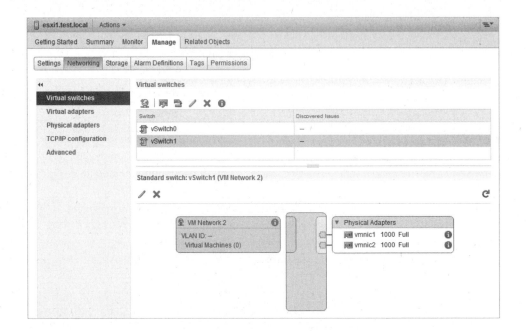

At this point, the new NIC has been added to the vSwitch, and virtual machine network traffic will begin to use it but also know that existing VMs will not be automatically rebalanced across or moved to this new NIC. The addition of a vmnic is a nondisruptive action for virtual machines.

Another situation that you may encounter is the need to remove a vmnic from a vSwitch. This could happen when a vSwitch was built with too many NICs or is experiencing low utilization with the number of NICs currently available, and this capacity could now be better utilized on another vSwitch. Exercise 4.3 shows how to remove a physical adapter from an existing vSwitch.

EXERCISE 4.3

Removing a vmnic from a vSwitch

1. Connect to a vCenter Server with the vSphere Web Client.

2. On the Home page, click the vCenter ➤ Hosts And Clusters option and select an ESXi host from the inventory.

3. Click the Manage tab and then select the Networking option from the tab's toolbar.

4. Select the vSwitch created in Exercise 4.1 and then click the Manage The Physical Network Adapters Connected To The Selected Switch icon.

5. The Manage Physical Network Adapters For vSwitch1 window will open.

6. Select the physical adapter you want to remove and then click the red X icon. The physical adapter will be removed from the list of assigned adapters. You will not be prompted to confirm this action, but you can click the Cancel button if you make a mistake here.

7. Click OK to confirm the removal of the physical adapter.

8. Wait for the screen to refresh or use the blue refresh arrow to manually refresh the screen. Verify that the selected physical network adapter is no longer listed in the vSwitch Physical Adapters field.

At this point, the NIC has been removed from the vSwitch, and any virtual machine network traffic that was using this vmnic will be moved to an active vmnic in the vSwitch. The removal of a vmnic is a nondisruptive action for virtual machines.

Now that you have created, configured, and removed a physical adapter from a vSwitch, it should be easier to see how vSwitches have the ability to scale with your environment. You can now turn your attention to configuring VMkernel ports for network services.

Configuring VMkernel Ports for Network Services

As mentioned at the beginning of this chapter, the VMkernel (vmknic) is used for host-based connections such as ESXi management traffic, vMotion, FT, iSCSI, and NFS. The process for configuring VMkernel ports differs from configuring virtual machine connection types in that an IP address is assigned to the VMkernel as part of the configuration. In Exercise 4.4, you will create a new vSwitch and configure a VMkernel port for vMotion use.

EXERCISE 4.4

Configuring a vSwitch with a VMkernel Port Group for vMotion

1. Connect to a vCenter Server with the vSphere Web Client.

2. On the Home page, click the vCenter ➤ Hosts And Clusters option and select an ESXi host from the inventory.

3. Click the Manage tab and then select the Networking option from the toolbar located on the Manage tab.

EXERCISE 4.4 *(continued)*

4. Click the Add Host Networking icon to add host networking. The Add Networking wizard will begin.

5. Select the VMkernel Network Adapter connection type and click Next to continue.

6. Choose the New Standard Switch option and click Next to continue.

7. On the next screen, click the green plus icon to add a physical network adapter. An Add Physical Adapters To The Switch window will open.

8. In the Add Physical Adapters To The Switch window, select the Unused Adapters option from the Failover Order Group drop-down menu. Then select an unused network adapter from the list in the left pane.

9. Click OK to add the physical network adapter to the vSwitch. Verify that a (New) vmnicX entry is listed in the left pane in the Active Adapters section.

10. Click Next to continue.

11. Provide a network label of vMotion. It is important to remember that this network label must be consistent across all ESX/ESXi hosts that vMotion will be used with. Choose a VLAN ID for this network if applicable. Choose the appropriate IP Settings and TCP/IP Stack for your network, and select the vMotion Traffic check box.

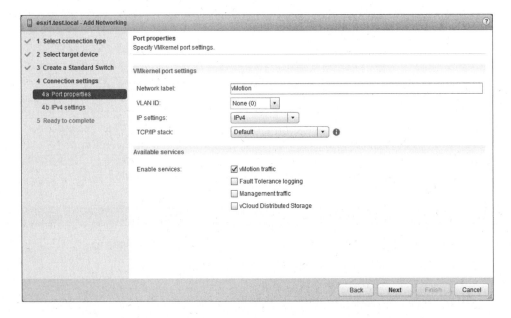

12. Click Next to continue. Provide an appropriate static IP address and subnet mask; then click Next to continue. In the following example, an isolated network is used for the vMotion traffic.

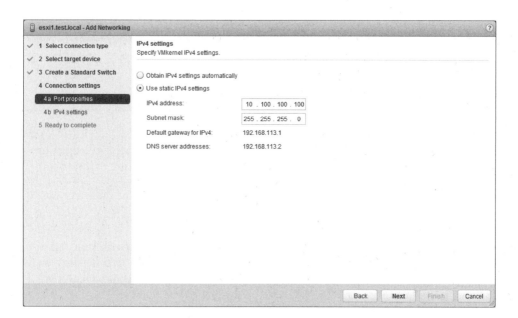

13. Review the information on the Ready To Complete screen and click Finish to add the new vSwitch to the ESXi host.

14. Select the vSwitch and review the information shown for accuracy.

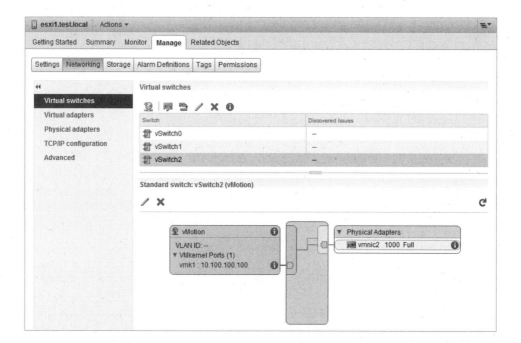

EXERCISE 4.4 *(continued)*

When an isolated layer 2 network is used for vMotion or other VMkernel connections, a default gateway is not required.

VMware best practices recommend that vMotion traffic be isolated on a dedicated separate network. This is because the contents of the guest operating system's memory are transmitted unencrypted over the network during a vMotion. Not isolating vMotion traffic could have serious security implications and should always be considered in network designs.

The same best practices of isolation generally apply for any VMkernel connection type. vMotion, storage, and FT traffic are all best configured in isolation. The previous exercise covered how to add a new vSwitch with a VMkernel port group used for vMotion, but a vMotion port group could have easily been configured on any existing vSwitch. The configuration for any VMkernel connection type, such as FT, iSCSI, NFS, and management traffic, is very similar; I will now discuss the setup for each VMkernel type.

In step 11 of Exercise 4.4, we enabled the service for vMotion Traffic. Figure 4.7 shows the available services.

FIGURE 4.7   VMkernel available services

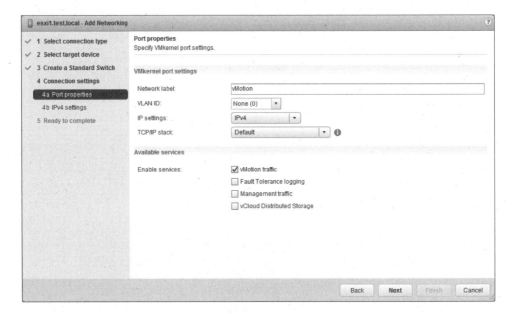

These four options are as follows:

vMotion Traffic   To enable vMotion traffic to be used with the port group

Fault Tolerance Logging   To enable FT traffic to be used with the port group

Management Traffic   To enable HA heartbeat traffic to be used with the port group

vCloud Distributed Storage   To enable vCloud Distributed Storage traffic to be used with the port group

 To use the VMkernel for network storage (iSCSI or NFS), you would simply omit any of the services listed previously when configuring the VMkernel.

Now that you have seen how to configure VMkernel port groups and some of the best practices, we will move on to adding, editing, and removing port groups on a vSwitch.

Adding, Editing, and Removing Port Groups on a vNetwork Standard Switch

In Exercise 4.4 you created a vSwitch and a VMkernel port group to be used for vMotion. For Exercise 4.5, let's assume that you added this vMotion port group too soon in your setup; it turns out that you need to add NFS storage to this ESXi host immediately. In Exercise 4.5, you will edit the vMotion port group to allow it to be used for accessing NFS storage instead of vMotion.

EXERCISE 4.5

Editing a Port Group in a vSwitch

1. Connect to a vCenter Server with the vSphere Web Client.

2. On the Home page, click the vCenter ➤ Hosts And Clusters option and select an ESXi host from the inventory.

3. Click the Manage tab and then select the Networking option from the toolbar.

4. Locate the vSwitch created in Exercise 4.4 and select it by clicking it.

5. In the vSwitch diagram at the bottom of the tab, hover the mouse over the VMkernel port on the left in the vMotion box. This will be listed with a vmkX descriptor and an IP address. The text will turn blue and become a link. Click this link. Note that two icons will appear above the vSwitch now. Click the yellow pencil icon to edit the port group properties.

EXERCISE 4.5 *(continued)*

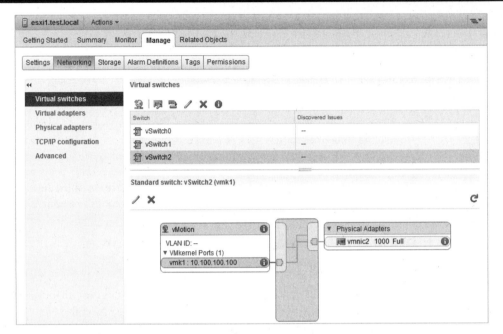

6. An Edit Settings window will appear. The port properties are shown by default. Clear the vMotion Traffic check box. In the left pane, click Validate Changes. Ensure that Overall Validation Status shows a value of Passed. Click OK to save the changes to the virtual NIC.

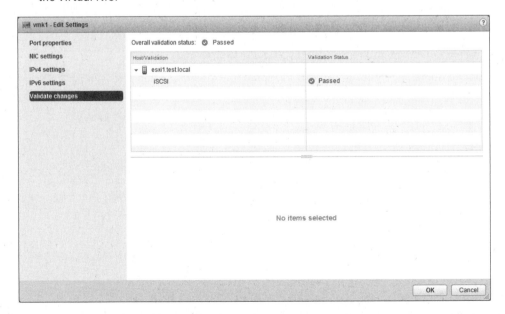

7. Wait for the Update Virtual NIC task to complete. In the vSwitch diagram at the bottom of the tab, hover the mouse over the vMotion label on this port group. The text will turn blue and become a link. Click this link, and then click the yellow pencil icon to edit the port group properties.

8. An Edit Settings window will appear. The properties are shown by default. Change the Network Label entry from vMotion to NFS, and then click OK to save this change.

9. Wait for the Update Port Group task to complete and then verify the changes made to this vSwitch.

You have now edited what was a VMkernel port group configured for vMotion to become a VMkernel port group configured for NFS storage access instead. This is a simple task that consists of only changing the port group label and the VMkernel enabled service.

For the purposes of the next exercise, assume that you also need to configure your NFS appliance via its web management interface. The problem is that this management interface is sitting on the same network on which you just set up a VMkernel connection type to access the NFS volumes, but you can't use the VMkernel connection type for virtual machine networking. To get around this, you will temporarily create a virtual machine port group on this network. This will allow you to access the NFS server's web management interface from a virtual machine. Exercise 4.6 shows the steps to add a virtual machine network port group to a vSwitch. This exercise will be very similar to Exercise 4.1, except that instead of creating a new vSwitch we will add the port group to an existing vSwitch.

EXERCISE 4.6

Adding a Port Group in a vSwitch

1. Connect to a vCenter Server with the vSphere Web Client.

2. On the Home page, click the vCenter ➤ Hosts And Clusters option and select an ESXi host from the inventory.

3. Click the Manage tab and then select the Networking option from the tab's toolbar.

4. Locate the vSwitch that you modified in Exercise 4.5 and select it by clicking it.

5. Click the Add Host Networking icon to add host networking. The Add Networking wizard will begin.

6. Select the Virtual Machine Port Group For A Standard Switch connection type and click Next to continue.

7. Choose the Select An Existing Standard Switch option and click Next to continue. Note that you can use the Browse button to choose a different vSwitch here if the correct vSwitch was not already selected. Click Next to continue.

EXERCISE 4.6 *(continued)*

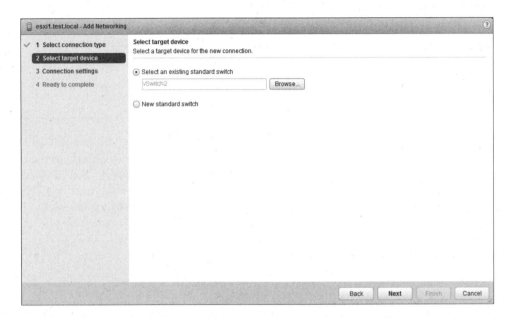

8. Provide a network label for the port group that will be added to the vSwitch. Choose a VLAN ID for this network if applicable and click Next to continue.

9. Review the information on the Ready To Complete screen and click Finish to add the port group to the vSwitch.

10. An Add Virtual Machine Port Group To vSwitch task will begin. When this task completes, select the vSwitch and review the information shown for accuracy. It should have one VMkernel port group for NFS traffic and one virtual machine port group for virtual machine networking traffic.

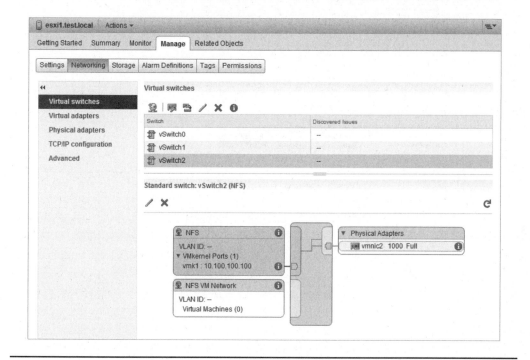

Now you have a virtual machine port group on the vSwitch used for the NFS storage network, and this virtual machine port group may be presented to any virtual machine on your ESXi host(s). This is accomplished through the virtual machine settings, as shown in Figure 4.8.

For the purposes of Exercise 4.7, assume that you are done using the virtual machine to configure the NFS server. Now for security purposes, you want to power off the virtual machine and remove this virtual machine network from the vSwitch. Exercise 4.7 shows the procedure to remove this virtual machine port group from the vSwitch.

FIGURE 4.8 VM network labels

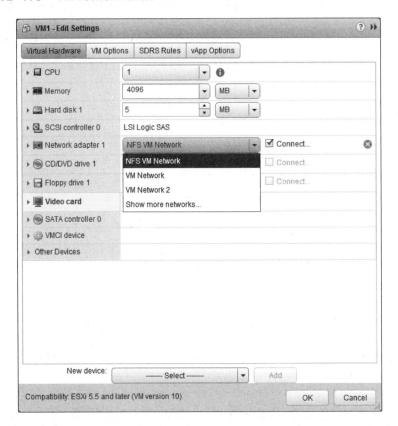

Removing a Port Group from a vSwitch

1. Connect to a vCenter Server with the vSphere Web Client.

2. On the Home page, click the vCenter ➢ Hosts And Clusters option and select an ESXi host from the inventory.

3. Click the Manage tab and then select the Networking option from the tab's toolbar.

4. Locate the vSwitch that we modified in Exercise 4.5 and select it.

5. In the vSwitch diagram at the bottom of the tab, hover the mouse over the virtual machine networking port group label. The text will turn blue and become a link. Click this link, and then click the X icon that appears directly above the vSwitch.

6. You will be prompted to confirm removal of the port group. Click Yes to proceed.

7. A Remove Port Group On vSwitch task will start. When this task completes, verify that the port group is no longer listed in the vSwitch properties.

 vSwitches can also still be configured via the traditional vSphere Client connected directly to an ESXi host.

We have covered creating vSwitches, and adding, removing, and editing port groups on vNetwork standard switches. Now let's take a moment to discuss determining the use case for a vSwitch.

Determining the Use Case for a vNetwork Standard Switch

You know that vSwitches are software constructs of the local ESXi host that process layer 2 Ethernet headers. Since the vSwitch is a software construct of ESXi, a vCenter Server is never required to use a vSwitch. vSwitches are used to provide network services to the ESXi host and virtual machines. The two types of network services are virtual machine and VMkernel, which are also known as connection types and port groups.

The virtual machine connection type is used to provide connections for virtual machines. This can be VM-to-VM traffic on the same ESXi host or VM to other external network traffic. Virtual machine connection types are the simpler type; the VLAN ID is the only unique configurable option.

VMkernel connection types are used to provide management network access, vMotion, FT, iSCSI, and NFS connections for ESXi hosts. These connection types have an IP address, whereas virtual machine connection types do not.

In summary, any virtual environment that needs networking capability could be a use case for a vSwitch. One exception to keep in mind is regarding *converged adapters* and 10 Gigabit Ethernet (GbE) adapters. If the ESXi host has a limited number of adapters, you may run into certain limitations when using vSwitches to manage multiple networks on fewer adapters. The next section of this chapter will move away from the vSwitch and focus on the vNetwork Distributed Switch (vDS), or dvSwitch.

Configuring vNetwork Distributed Switches

Understanding how to use and configure the vNetwork Distributed Switch (also known as dvSwitch or vDS) is another key requirement for the VCP5-DCV exam. It will also be important to know the distinguishing capabilities of the dvSwitch. While many of the concepts are the same between vSwitch and dvSwitch, the dvSwitch adds many new features and functionalities that simply are not available with the vSwitch. The first topic I will cover in this section is identifying the capabilities of the vNetwork Distributed Switch.

Identifying vNetwork Distributed Switch Capabilities

A dvSwitch differs from a vSwitch in that it allows a single virtual switch representation to span multiple ESXi hosts. This is a significant difference from the vSwitch, which relies on each ESXi host to have specific networking configured. Figure 4.9 shows the architecture of the dvSwitch. It is important to remember that in order to use a dvSwitch, you are required to have both vCenter Server and the Enterprise Plus edition of vSphere.

You will see the terms *vNetwork Distributed Switch*, *vDS*, and *dvSwitch* throughout this chapter. It is important to remember that these terms are all referring to the same thing. For the sake of consistency, the term *dvSwitch* will be used most often.

FIGURE 4.9   dvSwitch architecture

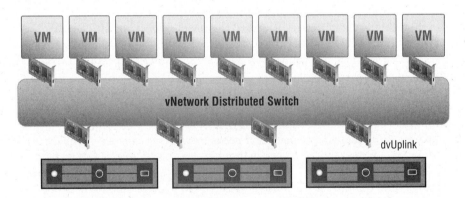

The dvSwitch includes all of the capabilities of the vSwitch, discussed earlier in this chapter, plus the following additional capabilities:

Bidirectional Virtual Machine Rate Limiting (Traffic Shaping)　Where the vSwitch can shape only outbound (also known as *egress* or *TX*) traffic, the dvSwitch can also shape inbound (also known as *ingress* or *RX*) traffic. Traffic shaping is used when bandwidth limits need to be imposed on virtual machines.

Centralized vCenter Administration and Provisioning　dvSwitches are administered and provisioned from within vCenter, meaning that there is a single configuration to manage. This approach offers advantages over maintaining multiple vSwitch configurations on multiple ESXi hosts, especially in large environments.

Cisco Nexus 1000V Virtual Switch　In addition to the features of the dvSwitch, there is the possibility of using third-party dvSwitches. For example, the Cisco Nexus 1000V can be implemented inside your virtual infrastructure. The Cisco Nexus 1000V brings many enhancements, such as the use of ACLs, port security, and more. But possibly the biggest change this technology brings is in the management of the virtual networks. With the Cisco Nexus 1000V, the network staff can manage a Cisco network device and realize the benefits of using a platform that they already understand how to use.

Dynamic Adjustment for Load-Based NIC Teaming　Load-based NIC teaming uses a load-balancing algorithm to regularly check the load on teamed NICs. If one NIC is overloaded, a port-NIC mapping reassignment will occur to attempt to balance the load. This process can keep the load on teamed NICs balanced and is a significant improvement over how teaming is performed on the standard vSwitch.

Enhanced Security and Monitoring for vMotion Traffic　Virtual machine networking state, including counters and port statistics, is tracked as virtual machines are migrated with vMotion from host to host in a dvSwitch. This provides a more consistent view of the virtual machine's network interfaces, regardless of the VM's location or migration history, and simplifies the troubleshooting and network monitoring for virtual machines.

IEEE 802.1p Tagging　IEEE 802.1p tagging is a standard used to provide quality of service (QoS) at the media access control (MAC) level. This capability can be used to guarantee I/O resources and is applied to outbound network traffic.

LLDP　dvSwitches include support for Link Layer Discovery Protocol (LLDP), which is a standard-based (IEEE 802.1AB) and vendor-neutral discovery protocol. Much like Cisco's proprietary discovery protocol CDP, LLDP is used to discover information about network devices.

NetFlow　NetFlow is another new feature of the dvSwitch version available in vSphere 5. It allows the monitoring of application flows (or IP traffic). This NetFlow data helps in capacity planning and in ensuring that I/O resources are properly used in the virtual infrastructure.

Network I/O Control　Network I/O Control allows the creation of resource pools containing network bandwidth. Administrators can create new resource pools to associate with port groups and specify 802.1p tags, allowing different virtual machines to be in different resource pools. This allows a subset of virtual machines to be given a higher or lower share of bandwidth than the others.

Port Mirror Port mirroring is when a network switch sends a copy of network packets seen on switch ports, or an entire VLAN, to a network monitoring device connected to another switch port. This is also known as Switched Port Analyzer (SPAN) on Cisco switches. Port mirroring is used for monitoring or troubleshooting.

Private VLAN Support   dvSwitches include support for *Private VLAN (PVLAN)*, which is used to provide isolation between computers on the same IP subnet. A PVLAN can be described as a nested VLAN, or a VLAN located within a VLAN. The first VLAN is known as the primary, whereas the nested VLANs are known as secondary. There are three types of PVLAN ports:

> **Promiscuous**   Can communicate with all ports, including the isolated and community ports
>
> **Isolated**   Can communicate with only promiscuous ports
>
> **Community**   Can communicate with all ports in the same secondary PVLAN and the promiscuous PVLAN

> Many of the features of the Enterprise Plus edition of vSphere are geared toward large environments. If you have never worked in a large environment, some of these features may not seem applicable to your situation. For the exam, it will be still be necessary to understand these features and their uses. You may have to think outside of your comfort zone to understand how powerful some of these features could be to an environment with hundreds of ESXi hosts and thousands of virtual machines.

Management Network Rollback and Recovery   This feature is used to ease management network use in the dvSwitch. It works by detecting configuration changes to the management network. If the ESXi host cannot communicate with its associated vCenter Server, the network will automatically revert to its previous working configuration.

Network Health Check   This feature is used to help vSphere administrators quickly identify configuration errors in the network. It monitors VLAN, MTU, and network adapter teaming at regular intervals. If these checks fail, a warning will be displayed in the vSphere Web Client.

Link Aggregation Control Protocol (LACP)   LACP is a standards-based link aggregation protocol used to group physical network adapters into a single logical link. The dynamic implementation included in the dvSwitch allows verification of correct setup and features automatic configuration, negotiation, and reconfiguration of detected link failures.

Traffic Filtering and Marking   This feature is used for filtering and priority tagging for network traffic to virtual machines, VMkernel adapters, or physical adapters. It can be used to protect these connections from security attacks, to filter out unwanted traffic, or to establish QoS.

As you can see, the dvSwitch offers many advanced capabilities that the vSwitch does not. Although the dvSwitch may not be suitable for every environment, it is still important to know its capabilities for the exam. It is also important to know that not all of these dvSwitch features are available with every dvSwitch version. We'll discuss the dvSwitch versions and the features they include further in the next section, where you will also see how to create a dvSwitch.

Creating and Deleting a vNetwork Distributed Switch

dvSwitches can be created at the vCenter Server datacenter level. In vCenter Server 5.5, you can create five versions of the dvSwitch:

Distributed Switch 5.5.0   This version is compatible with vSphere 5.5 and newer, and it introduces Traffic Filtering and Marking, as well as enhanced LACP support.

Distributed Switch 5.1.0   This version is compatible with vSphere 5.1 and newer, and it introduces Management Network Rollback and Recovery, Health Check, Enhanced Port Mirroring, and LACP.

Distributed Switch 5.0.0   This version is compatible with vSphere 5.0 and newer, and it introduces user-defined network resource pools in Network I/O Control, NetFlow, and Port Mirroring.

Distributed Switch 4.1.0   This version is compatible with vSphere 4.1 and newer, and it introduces load-based teaming and Network I/O Control.

Distributed Switch 4.0   This version is compatible with vSphere 4.0 and newer, but features supported by later versions of the dvSwitch will not be available.

You may have noticed that the distributed switch versions follow the same versioning as vSphere. It is important to remember that features supported by later versions of the dvSwitch are not available in prior versions. For example, NetFlow was introduced in dvSwitch 5.0.0 and would only work with dvSwitch versions 5.0.0, 5.1.0, and 5.5.0.

Exercise 4.8 shows how to create a version 5.5.0 dvSwitch. The requirements for the exercises in the remainder of this chapter are vCenter Server 5.5 either with Enterprise Plus licensing or running in *Evaluation Mode*. A minimum of two ESXi 5.5 hosts with two available/unassigned physical NICs is also required. Also note that the exercises in the remainder of this chapter will build on each other sequentially, beginning with Exercise 4.8.

EXERCISE 4.8

Creating a dvSwitch

1. Connect to a vCenter Server with the vSphere Web Client.

2. On the Home page, click vCenter ➤ Distributed Switches in the left pane.

3. On the Objects tab, click the Create A New Distributed Switch icon, which is the switch icon with the green plus icon on it. The New Distributed Switch wizard will launch.

4. Provide a name for the dvSwitch and select a datacenter to place the dvSwitch in.

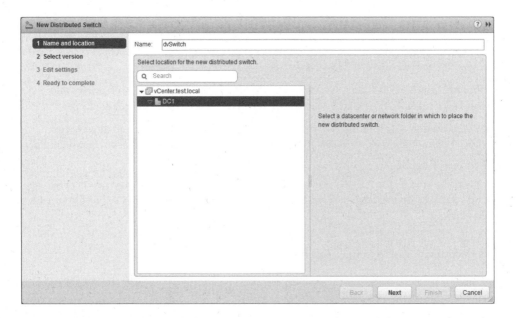

5. Click the Next button to continue.

6. Accept the default selection of Distributed Switch 5.5.0 and click Next to continue.

7. Accept the default values for the dvSwitch settings and click Next to continue.

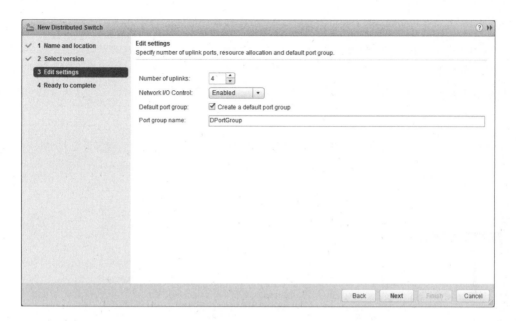

Uplink ports are used to connect the dvSwitch to physical NICs on ESXi hosts and represent the maximum number of per-host physical NICs that may be connected the dvSwitch.

8. Review the information on the Ready To Complete screen and click Finish to add the dvSwitch to the datacenter.

9. A Create vSphere Distributed Switch task, an Add Distributed Port Groups task, and an Update Network I/O Control task will each begin. When these tasks have completed, verify that the dvSwitch is listed on the Objects tab.

10. Select the dvSwitch you just created, and right-click on it. Choose Edit Settings from the context menu.

11. Review the General settings, and then click Advanced in the left pane. Review the Advanced settings.

12. Click Cancel to close the dvSwitch - Edit Settings window.

At this point, the dvSwitch is created, but additional configuration is still needed before we can use it. Before we get to these steps, let's take a moment to discuss deleting or removing a dvSwitch. To delete a dvSwitch, you select it on the Object tab, right-click, and choose All vCenter Actions ➤ Remove From Inventory, as shown in Figure 4.10.

FIGURE 4.10   Deleting a dvSwitch

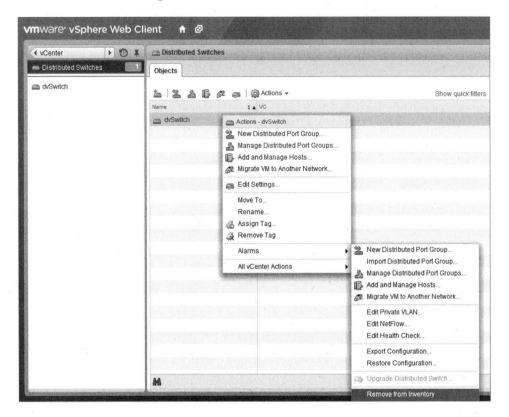

You will be prompted before the dvSwitch is deleted. Note that deleting a dvSwitch also removes its port groups, alarms, and tasks. If you actually delete your dvSwitch, be sure to re-create it before continuing to the next section.

Now that we have discussed how to create and delete a dvSwitch, we will move on to configuring the dvSwitch for use. The first step will be to cover how to add to and remove ESXi hosts from the dvSwitch.

Adding and Removing ESXi Hosts to/from a vNetwork Distributed Switch

In Exercise 4.8, we created a dvSwitch. Before we can start to use this dvSwitch, we need to first add ESXi hosts to its configuration. Exercise 4.9 shows how to add ESXi hosts to the dvSwitch created in Exercise 4.8.

EXERCISE 4.9

Adding an ESXi Host to a dvSwitch

1. Connect to a vCenter Server with the vSphere Web Client.

2. On the Home page, click vCenter ➤ Distributed Switches in the left pane.

3. On the Objects tab, right-click the dvSwitch that we created in the previous exercise. Choose Add And Manage Hosts from the context menu.

4. The Add And Manage Hosts wizard will appear.

5. Choose the Add Hosts option and click the Next button to continue.

6. On the Select Hosts screen, click the green plus icon to select an ESXi host. A Select New Hosts window will appear.

7. Select two ESXi 5.5 hosts by placing checks in the check boxes to the left of each server name. You can also use the gray Incompatible Hosts link at the top left of this screen to verify whether the hosts you plan to use are compatible with the version of the dvSwitch selected.

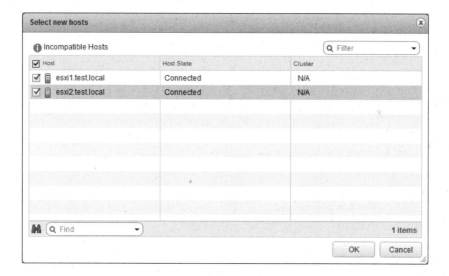

8. Once the two hosts have been selected, click OK to continue.

9. Verify that the selected ESXi hosts are now listed on the Select Hosts screen and show a Host Status value of Connected. Click the Next button to continue.

10. Review the information on the Select Network Adapter Tasks screen, and then click Next to continue.

EXERCISE 4.9 *(continued)*

11. Review the information on the Manage Physical Network Adapters screen, as shown here:

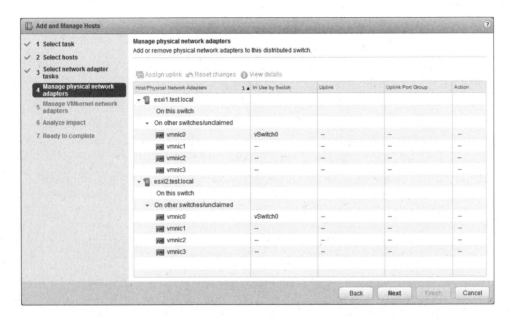

In the example, there are two ESXi hosts, each with four physical network adapters (vmnic0, vmnic1, vmnic2, vmnic3). vmnic0 is assigned to the default vSwitch0, which is the standard vSwitch created during ESXi installation. The remaining three physical network adapters can be assigned to our dvSwitch.

12. Select one additional physical network adapter under the first ESXi host by clicking it. Now click the icon for Assign Uplink listed above the column headers here. A Select An Uplink For vmnicX window will open. Click Uplink1 to select it and then click OK.

13. Repeat step 12 for the second ESXi host.

14. You should now have a configuration similar to the following:

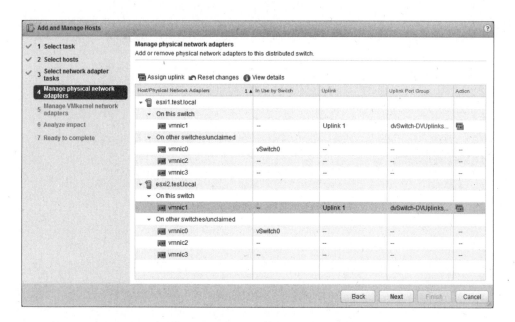

15. Click the Next button to continue. On the Manage VMkernel Network Adapters screen, review the information and then click Next.

16. Review the information on the Analyze Impact screen and ensure that the Overall Impact Status values show No Impact. Click Next to continue.

17. Review the information on the Ready To Complete screen and click Finish to add the ESXi hosts to the dvSwitch.

18. A Manage Host Networking On Distributed Switch task will begin. When this task completes, return to the left pane and choose vCenter ➤ Hosts And Clusters. Select one of the hosts that were added to the dvSwitch and then select the Manage tab. Click the Networking option on the toolbar, and then select the Virtual Switches option in the left pane.

19. Select the dvSwitch just created and then review the dvSwitch diagram displayed at the bottom of the screen.

EXERCISE 4.9 *(continued)*

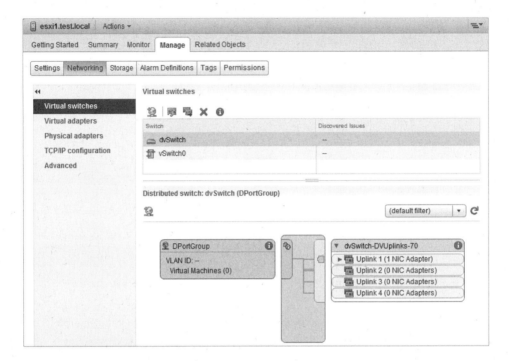

20. Also verify the dvSwitch settings on the second ESXi host before continuing.

We have now added two ESXi hosts and one physical network adapter to our dvSwitch. We still need to add additional network adapters to complete the dvSwitch configuration. Before we get to these steps, let's take a moment to discuss removing an ESXi host from a dvSwitch. You may recall from earlier in this chapter that a vSwitch cannot be removed if virtual machines are connected to it. This is also true when removing an ESXi host from a dvSwitch. Ensure that no virtual machines—running on the host you are going to remove—are connected to the dvSwitch before removing it or you will receive an error. Exercise 4.10 demonstrates removing an ESXi host from the dvSwitch.

EXERCISE 4.10

Removing an ESXi Host from a dvSwitch

1. Connect to a vCenter Server with the vSphere Web Client.

2. On the Home page, click vCenter ➢ Distributed Switches in the left pane.

3. On the Objects tab, right-click the dvSwitch that we created in the previous exercise. Choose Add And Manage Hosts from the context menu.

4. The Add And Manage Hosts wizard will start.

5. Choose the Remove Hosts option and click Next to continue.

6. On the Select Hosts screen, click the green plus icon to select an ESXi host. A Select New Hosts window will appear.

7. Select a single ESXi 5.5 host by checking the box to the left of the ESXi server name and click OK to continue.

8. Verify that the selected ESXi host is now listed on the Select Hosts screen and shows a Host Status value of Connected.

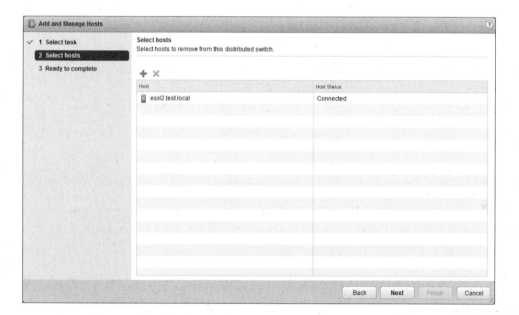

9. Click Next to continue.

10. Review the information on the Ready To Complete screen and then click the Cancel button. Optionally, you can click the Finish button and then repeat Exercise 4.9 to add the ESXi host back to the dvSwitch.

Another option for removing a single ESXi host from a dvSwitch is to navigate to vCenter ➢ Hosts And Clusters and then select the desired ESXi host. Click the Manage tab and the Networking option on the toolbar at the top of the screen. Select Virtual Switches from the left pane, and then select the dvSwitch. There is a red icon located above the column headers that can be used to remove the ESXi host from the dvSwitch (Figure 4.11).

FIGURE 4.11   Removing an ESXi host from a dvSwitch

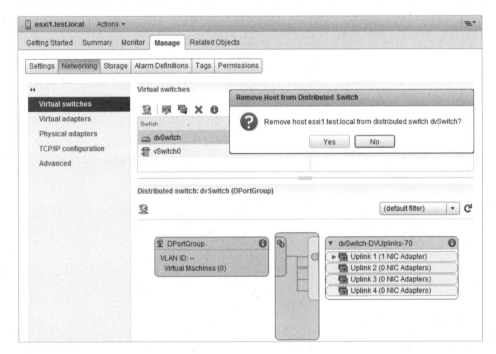

We have now covered adding ESXi hosts to a dvSwitch and removing them. We have also added one uplink adapter from each ESXi host to our dvSwitch. To follow best practices and provide a fault-tolerant design for our dvSwitch, we will add a second physical network adapter to the dvSwitch. In the next section you will learn how to add uplink adapters to and remove them from our dvSwitch.

Adding and Removing Uplink Adapters to/from dvUplink Groups

A Distributed Virtual Uplink (*dvUplink*) is used to provide a level of abstraction between the physical network adapters (vmnics) on the ESXi host and dvSwitches. This allows ESXi hosts using the same dvSwitch to have differing vmnic configurations and still use the same teaming, load balancing, and failover policies.

An uplink adapter is a physical network adapter used to provide external network connectivity to a dvSwitch. One uplink adapter on each ESXi host may be assigned to each uplink port on a dvSwitch. In Exercise 4.9, you added a single uplink adapter to your dvSwitch. In Exercise 4.11, we will cover adding an additional uplink adapter to a dvUplink group.

EXERCISE 4.11

Adding an Uplink Adapter to a dvUplink Group

1. Connect to a vCenter Server with the vSphere Web Client.

2. On the Home page, click vCenter ➤ Hosts And Clusters. Select one of the ESXi hosts that we added to the dvSwitch and then select the Manage tab. Click the Networking option on the toolbar, and then select the Virtual Switches option in the left pane.

3. Select the dvSwitch and then click the green network adapter icon with the wrench on it.

4. The [Host] - Manage Physical Network Adapters For dvSwitch window will open.

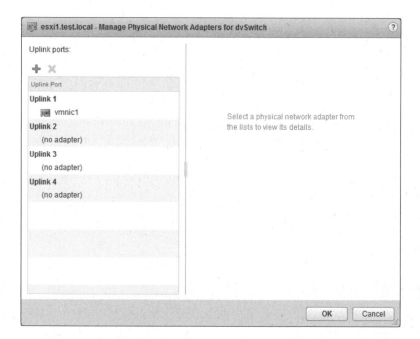

5. Click the green plus icon to add additional network adapters to the dvSwitch. The Assign Physical Adapters To The Switch window will launch.

6. Use the Uplink drop-down menu to select a single available uplink, and then select the physical network adapter from the list of network adapters in the left pane. Uplink 2 and vmnic2 are selected in the following image:

EXERCISE 4.11 *(continued)*

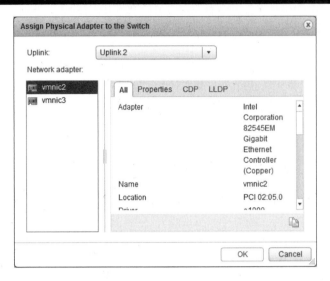

7. Click OK to add the physical network adapter to uplink on the dvSwitch. Ensure that the selections you just made are shown in the left pane under Uplink Ports and click OK to continue.

8. Verify that the uplink and vnmic are shown in the dvSwitch diagram at the bottom of the Manage tab.

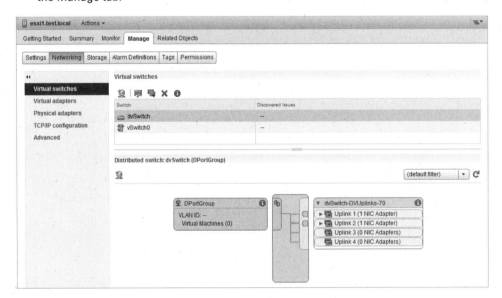

9. Repeat steps 2–8 for each ESXi host that will use this dvSwitch.

As a virtual infrastructure administrator, you could also find yourself in a situation where too many uplinks were provided to a dvSwitch and you need to remove an uplink adapter from a dvSwitch for use elsewhere. The steps to perform this operation are shown in Exercise 4.12.

EXERCISE 4.12

Removing an Uplink Adapter from a dvUplink Group

1. Connect to a vCenter Server with the vSphere Web Client.

2. On the Home page, click vCenter ➤ Hosts And Clusters. Select one of the ESXi hosts that we added to the dvSwitch and then select the Manage tab. Click the Networking option on the toolbar, and then select the Virtual Switches option in the left pane.

3. Select the dvSwitch and then click the Manage The Physical Network Adapters Connected To The Selected Switch icon.

4. The [Host] - Manage Physical Network Adapters For dvSwitch window will appear.

5. Click the vmnic you want to remove to select it. Then click the red X icon to remove the physical adapter. You will not be prompted to confirm the removal.

6. Click the Cancel button, unless you really want to remove the uplink adapter.

After this exercise is completed, review the dvSwitch settings on the Manage tab and ensure that your dvSwitch is configured with at least two uplink adapters. If you didn't click the Cancel button in step 6 of the previous exercise, you will want to add the uplink adapter back to the dvSwitch before continuing.

We now have a usable dvSwitch with a default dvPort group, two ESXi hosts, and two uplink adapters configured for it. Next we will discuss adding, configuring, and removing a dvPort group to be used for virtual machine network traffic.

Adding, Configuring, and Removing dvPort Groups

Distributed port groups (*dvPort groups*) are similar to port groups in the vSwitch. They are used to provide networking for virtual machines and to the VMkernel in dvSwitches. However, the way in which dvPort groups are configured in the dvSwitch is different from the way in which port groups are configured in the vSwitch. To demonstrate these differences, Exercise 4.13 will add a dvPort group used for virtual machine traffic to a dvSwitch.

EXERCISE 4.13

Adding a dvPort Group to a dvSwitch

1. Connect to a vCenter Server with the vSphere Web Client.

2. On the Home tab, click Networking. Select the dvSwitch that we have been work-ing with in the left pane. Right-click the dvSwitch and choose New Distributed Port Group. The New Distributed Port Group window will appear.

3. Give the distributed port group a descriptive name and verify that Location is set to the dvSwitch to which you will add the distributed port group. Click Next to continue.

4. Review the properties of the new distributed port group. Accept all default values and click Next.

5. Review the information on the Ready To Complete Screen. It should appear similar to the following image:

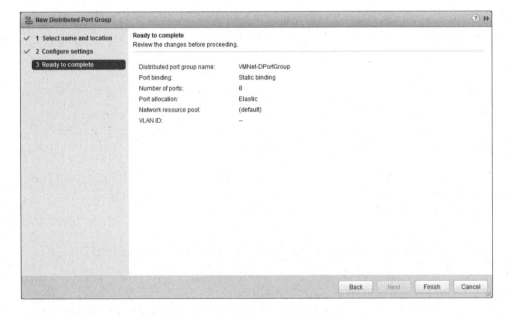

6. Click Finish to add the distributed port group to the dvSwitch.

7. An Add Distributed Port Groups task will begin. When this task completes, click the name of your dvSwitch shown on the Objects tab.

8. On the Manage tab, click Settings on the toolbar and then verify that the new dis-tributed port group is now listed in the dvSwitch. It should appear similar to the following image, where the newly created distributed port group is named VMNet-DPortGroup:

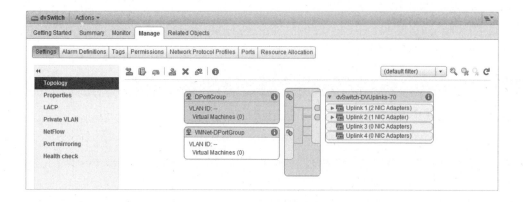

In step 4 of Exercise 4.13, we accepted the defaults. Two of these settings were the port binding and VLAN type. We will discuss port binding settings in the next section, but now let's take a moment to cover the four VLAN type options that were available on this screen:

None   No VLAN will be used. This is the equivalent of leaving the optional VLAN ID field blank when creating a port group in a vSwitch.

VLAN   This option is used to enter a VLAN ID with a value between 1 and 4094. This is the equivalent of setting a value for the optional VLAN ID when creating a port group in a vSwitch.

VLAN Trunking   This option is used to enter a VLAN trunk range. This is different from a vSwitch in that a single dvPort group may be used to handle all of the trunked VLANs. A vSwitch would require a port group per VLAN to achieve the same result.

Private VLAN   This option is used to select a private VLAN. If private VLANs have not been established, this option cannot be used. There is no equivalent functionality in the vSwitch.

 Real World Scenario

Simplifying VLAN Trunking with dvSwitches

A customer has 250 VLANs that are being trunked to a vSwitch with 250 port groups. The customer is expecting to grow in the next 6 months and will need to add 50 VLANs to this trunk. In vSphere 5, the maximum number of port groups per standard vSwitch is 256.

You meet with this customer to discuss how to plan for this change. You discover that the customer has Enterprise Plus licensing, and you discuss how moving from a vSwitch to a dvSwitch could solve this problem. A dvPort group can use a VLAN trunk range, which would allow the 256 limit present in the vSwitch to be exceeded. This would also simplify switch configuration and allow the customer to scale out for quite some time.

Once a dvPort group has been added to the dvSwitch, you also have the ability to configure additional options. In Exercise 4.14 you will configure additional options for the dvPort group added in Exercise 4.13.

EXERCISE 4.14

Configuring a dvPort Group

1. Connect to a vCenter Server with the vSphere Web Client.

2. On the Home tab, click Networking. Click the dvSwitch that we have been working with on the Objects tab.

3. On the Manage tab, click Settings on the toolbar. Click the name of the newly added dvPort group we added in Exercise 4.13.

4. Click the Edit Distributed Port Group Settings icon. The Edit Settings window will appear.

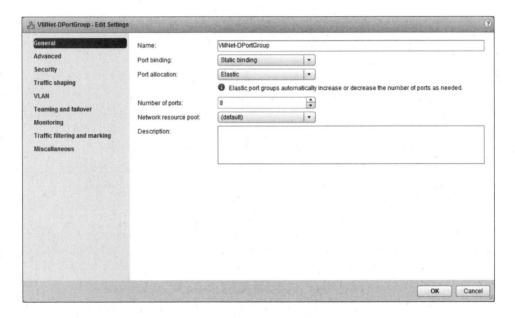

5. Review the information in the General section. Note the Port Binding drop-down menu and the default setting of Static Binding. Port binding will be discussed in detail at the conclusion of this exercise. Provide a description for this distributed port group in the Description field.

6. Review each of the remaining items in the left pane of the Edit Settings window.

7. Click OK to save the distributed port group description settings. A Reconfigure Distributed Port Group task will begin.

You have now reviewed the configuration of a dvPort group and provided a description for it. Many of the settings here will be covered later in this chapter, but right now let's take a moment to discuss port binding. *Port binding* determines when dvPorts in a dvPort group are assigned and unassigned to a virtual machine. There are three types of port binding:

- Static binding
- Dynamic binding
- Ephemeral binding

Static binding is the default port binding and is recommended by VMware for general use. With static binding, a dvPort is immediately assigned and reserved when the virtual machine is connected to the dvPort. This guarantees connectivity for the VM, and the dvPort is freed only when the virtual machine is removed from the dvPort group. With static binding, network statistics are kept when using vMotion or power cycling the virtual machine.

Dynamic binding was deprecated in vSphere 5 and was primarily used in situations where there were more virtual machines than available dvPorts but the number of available ports was not ultimately expected to be exceeded. An example of this would be an environment with 150 virtual machines connected to a dvPort group with 128 ports but where only 75 of these virtual machines would ever be powered on simultaneously. With dynamic binding, a dvPort is assigned only when a virtual machine is both powered on and has its NIC connected. The dvPort is freed when the virtual machine is powered off or its NIC is disconnected. With dynamic binding, network statistics are kept when using vMotion but lost if the virtual machine is powered off.

Ephemeral binding is more similar to the behavior of a vSwitch and can be managed either from vCenter Server or directly from the ESXi host. VMware recommends that ephemeral binding be used only for recovery purposes or in situations where vCenter Server is unavailable. With ephemeral binding, a dvPort is created and assigned when a virtual machine is both powered on and has its NIC connected. The dvPort is deleted when the virtual machine is powered off or its NIC is disconnected. With ephemeral binding, network statistics are lost when using vMotion or power cycling the virtual machine.

Now that we have covered configuring a dvPort group and discussed port binding in detail, we will move to the next topic, removing a dvPort group. In step 6 of Exercise 4.8, when we first created a dvSwitch, we accepted the default port group creation. Now that we have created a dvPort group specifically for virtual machine traffic, we will remove this default distributed port group. Exercise 4.15 shows how to do this.

EXERCISE 4.15

Removing a dvPort Group

1. Connect to a vCenter Server with the vSphere Web Client.

2. On the Home tab, click Networking. Click the dvSwitch that we have been working with on the Objects tab.

3. On the Manage tab, click Settings on the toolbar. Click the name of the default dvPort group. The box that shows the dvPort group will turn blue.

4. Click the red X icon to remove this distributed port group. Click Yes to confirm the removal.

5. A Delete Distributed Port Group task will begin. When this task completes, use the blue refresh arrow at the upper right to refresh the screen. The dvSwitch should look similar to the following image, with only the virtual machine networking dvPort group remaining:

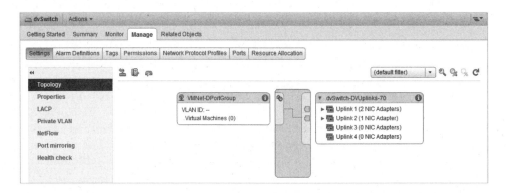

We have now covered adding, configuring, and removing dvPort groups in dvSwitches. I also covered VLAN options and discussed how port binding works in the dvSwitch. At this point in the chapter, you should have a dvSwitch that can provide networking for your VMs. If you recall from earlier in this chapter, there are two types of networking connection types (virtual machine and VMkernel). In the next section, I will cover how to add a VMkernel connection type to this dvSwitch.

Creating, Configuring, and Removing Virtual Adapters

In a dvSwitch, *virtual adapters* are used to provide VMkernel connections such as ESXi management traffic, vMotion, FT, iSCSI, and NFS. In Exercise 4.16, you will create a virtual adapter that will be used for vMotion traffic. In the first part of this exercise we will create a dvPort group, which we covered in Exercise 4.13.

EXERCISE 4.16

Adding a Virtual Adapter to a dvSwitch

1. Connect to a vCenter Server with the vSphere Web Client.

2. On the Home tab, click Networking. Navigate to the dvSwitch that we have been working with in the left pane. Right-click on the dvSwitch in the left pane and choose New Distributed Port Group from the context menu. The New Distributed Port Group window will open.

3. Give the distributed port group a descriptive name and verify that Location is set to the dvSwitch that we have been working with in this chapter. Click Next to continue.

4. Review the properties of the new distributed port group. Accept all default values and click Next to continue.

5. Review the information on the Ready To Complete Screen, and click Finish to add the distributed port group to the dvSwitch.

6. An Add Distributed Port Groups task will begin. When this task completes, navigate to the Manage tab for the dvSwitch.

7. On the Manage tab, click Settings on the toolbar and then verify that the new distributed port group is now listed in the dvSwitch. It should appear similar to the following image, where the newly created distributed port group is named vmk-DPortGroup:

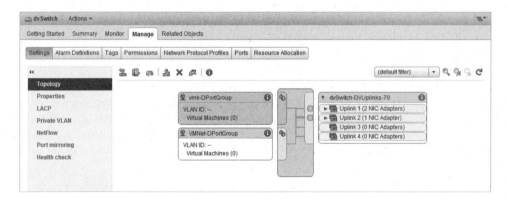

8. Click the Related Objects tab, and then select Hosts from the toolbar. Click an ESXi host to select it. You will be taken to the host's Manage tab.

9. Select Networking from the toolbar, and then select VMkernel Adapters in the left menu on the Manage tab. Click the Add Host Networking icon to add a virtual adapter. The Add Networking wizard will begin.

Note that in this step the VMkernel adapter and the virtual adapter are the same thing.

10. Choose the VMkernel Network Adapter option for the connection type and click Next.

11. Accept the default option of Select An Existing Distributed Port Group and click the Browse button to select the distributed port group we created in the first part of this exercise. Click Next once the group has been selected.

12. Check the box for vMotion traffic in the Enable Services section and click Next.

13. Provide a static IP address and subnet mask for the VMkernel.

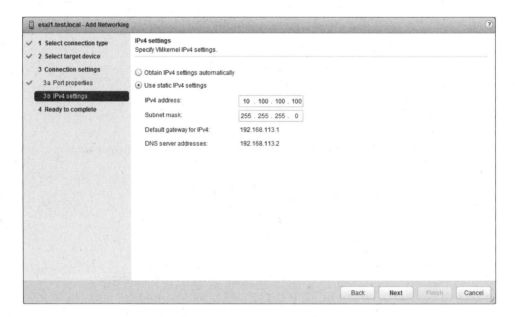

14. Click Next to continue, and then review the information on the Ready To Complete Screen.

15. Click the Finish button to add the virtual adapter to the dvSwitch.

16. An Add Virtual NIC task will begin. When this task completes, verify that the newly created virtual adapter is now listed on the Manage tab.

17. Repeat steps 8–16 for all remaining ESXi hosts that will use this dvSwitch.

18. In the left pane, click the name of your dvSwitch and then review the dvSwitch topology. Note the value of the VMkernel ports in the VMkernel distributed port group we just created.

TIP Multi-NIC vMotion is a valuable feature of vSphere 5 that can be used to increase the performance of vMotion. See the following VMware KB for more information on how to configure it:

`http://kb.vmware.com/kb/2007467`

You have now added a virtual network adapter (VMkernel adapter) to your dvSwitch. Exercise 4.17 shows the steps to configure this virtual adapter.

EXERCISE 4.17

Configuring a Virtual Adapter

1. Connect to a vCenter Server with the vSphere Web Client.

2. On the Home tab, click Networking. Click the dvSwitch that we have been working with in the left pane.

3. On the Related Objects tab, choose Hosts from the toolbar and then select one of your ESXi hosts by clicking it.

4. On the Manage tab, ensure that Networking is selected on the toolbar and that VMkernel Adapters is selected in the left pane.

5. Click to select the virtual adapter created in the previous exercise.

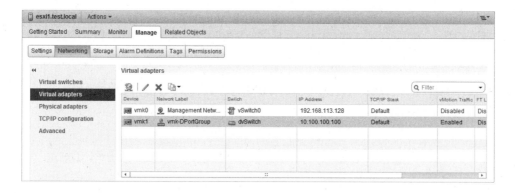

6. Click the pencil icon to edit the settings for the virtual adapter. The Edit Settings window will appear.

7. Review the information in Port Properties and NIC settings. Select the IPv4 Settings option.

8. Change the IP address of this virtual adapter and then click OK to continue.

9. An Update Virtual NIC task will begin. When this task completes, verify that the IP address was changed in the IP Address column of the VMkernel Adapters list.

You may also need to remove a virtual adapter; this can be done from the same VMkernel Adapters view where we just edited the virtual adapter. To remove a virtual adapter here, make sure it is highlighted and then click the red X icon above the column headers. You will be prompted to confirm removal, as shown in Figure 4.12.

FIGURE 4.12   The Remove VMkernel Network Adapter confirmation prompt

The Analyze Impact button can be used to ensure that the removal will not disrupt other operations. Clicking OK will remove the virtual adapter.

Unlike distributed port groups in a dvSwitch, virtual adapters are removed or configured at the ESXi host level, so multiple host operations may sometimes be required when working with virtual adapters.

We now have a dvSwitch with virtual machine networking and a VMkernel adapter for vMotion traffic. In Exercise 4.16, we added a new dvPort group and virtual adapter by using the Add Networking wizard. It is also possible to migrate an existing virtual adapter to a dvSwitch or vSwitch on a per-host basis. The virtual adapter migration process will be covered in the next section of this chapter.

Migrating Virtual Adapters to and from a vNetwork Standard Switch

Sometimes it may be necessary to migrate networking to and from a virtual switch. Exercise 4.18 shows the steps involved in migrating a virtual adapter used for vMotion from a dvSwitch to an existing vSwitch.

EXERCISE 4.18

Migrating a Virtual Adapter to a vSwitch

1.   Connect to a vCenter Server with the vSphere Web Client.

2.   On the Home page, click the vCenter ➤ Hosts And Clusters option and select an ESXi host from the inventory.

3. Click the Manage tab and then select the Networking option from the tab's toolbar.

4. Ensure that Virtual Switches is selected in the left pane, and then click the desired target vSwitch to select it.

5. Review the vSwitch topology for the selected vSwitch. It should appear similar to what is shown in the following image:

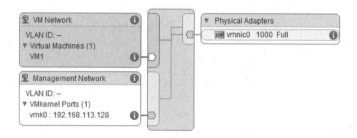

6. Click the Migrate A VMkernel Network Adapter To The Selected Switch icon to migrate a VMkernel network adapter to the selected switch. A Migrate VMkernel Network Adapter To vSwitchX wizard will begin.

7. Click to select the virtual network adapter that we added to the dvSwitch in Exercise 4.16.

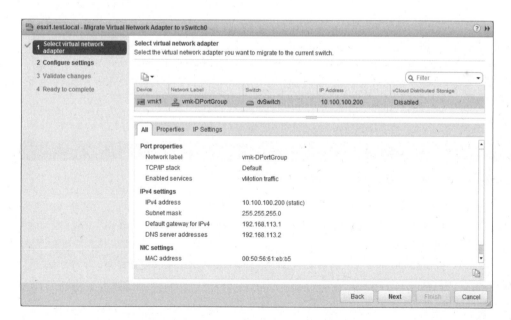

8. Review the information in the lower portion of the screen and then click the Next button to continue.

EXERCISE 4.18 *(continued)*

9. Provide a unique network label, like **vMotion**, and then click Next to continue.

10. Review the information in the Analyze Impact section and click Next to continue.

11. Review the information on the Ready to Complete section and then click the Finish button to migrate the virtual adapter from the dvSwitch to the vSwitch.

12. Review the vSwitch topology again. It should now appear similar to the following image:

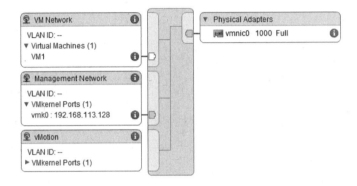

We have now moved a VMkernel connection from our dvSwitch to a standard vSwitch. This can be a useful practice when an existing virtual switch is already assigned a virtual adapter, because it streamlines the process of removing and adding the virtual adapter into one wizard. Now, let's reverse the operation and return this virtual adapter back to the dvSwitch in Exercise 4.19.

EXERCISE 4.19

Migrating a Virtual Adapter to a dvSwitch

1. Connect to a vCenter Server with the vSphere Web Client.

2. On the Home tab, click Networking, and then select the dvSwitch that we have been working with in the left pane.

3. On the Related Objects tab, select the same ESXi host used in the previous exercise.

4. On the Manage tab, ensure that Networking is selected on the toolbar and that Virtual Switches is selected in the left pane.

5. Click the dvSwitch that we have been working with in this chapter to select it.

6. Review the dvSwitch topology. It should appear similar to the following image.

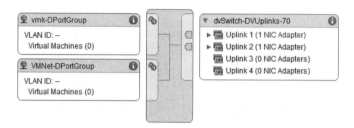

7. Click the Migrate Physical Or Virtual Network Adapters To This Distributed Switch icon to migrate the virtual adapter to this distributed switch. The Migrate Networking wizard will launch.

8. Accept the defaults in the Select Network Adapter Tasks screen and click Next.

9. Review the information on the Manage Physical Network Adapters screen and click Next to continue.

10. On the Manage Virtual Network Adapters screen, click to select the virtual adapter from the list, and then click the Assign Port Group link located above the column headers.

11. The Assign Destination Port Group window will open. Select the VMkernel distributed port group.

12. Click OK to continue. Review the changes now listed on the Manage Virtual Network Adapters screen and then click Next.

13. Make sure the Analyze Impact screen shows a Validation Status of No Impact, and then click Next.

14. Review the information on the Ready To Complete screen and then click the Finish button to migrate the virtual adapter from the vSwitch to the dvSwitch.

15. Review the dvSwitch topology again. It should now appear similar to the following image:

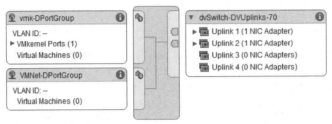

 NOTE   Just like moving and configuring virtual adapters, migrating them also occurs at the ESXi host level.

We have now successfully migrated a virtual adapter between virtual switches. Remember that virtual adapters are only used for VMkernel connections. We still need to cover the steps to migrate virtual machines to and from a dvSwitch.

Migrating Virtual Machines to and from a vNetwork Distributed Switch

Sometimes it may also be necessary to migrate virtual machine networking to and from a vSwitch. In the following case study, you will examine a scenario where this capability would be useful.

 Real World Scenario

Migrating Virtual Machine Networking to a dvSwitch

In an earlier case study in this chapter, you looked at a company that had outgrown an existing vSwitch implementation. The company had decided to use dvSwitches for their virtual machine networks and has now performed the prerequisite work required for the move. It is time to make the transition.

Migrating virtual machine networking will seamlessly allow this company to move all of their virtual machines on the current vSwitch to the new dvSwitch in a few simple steps. The migration is entirely automated, and there is no resulting virtual machine downtime as a result of this move.

Exercise 4.20 covers the steps involved in migrating virtual machine networking from a vSwitch to a dvSwitch. This exercise assumes that you have at least one virtual machine connected to the default vSwitch VM network created during ESXi installation. If you do not have any VMs, you will need to create one that uses this networking setup. You can expedite this process by simply creating a VM and not installing a guest OS. You could use the vCenter Server or vCenter Server Appliance VMs, but in this case be very careful to ensure that your networking is correct in the dvSwitch or you could lose access to the vSphere Web Client.

EXERCISE 4.20

Migrating Virtual Machines to a dvSwitch

1. Connect to a vCenter Server with the vSphere Web Client.

2. On the Home page, click the vCenter ➢ Hosts And Clusters option and right-click on a datacenter name in the left pane.

3. Choose the Migrate VM To Another Network option from the context menu. The Migrate Virtual Machine Networking wizard will launch.

4. For the Source Network, browse to select the default VM network that was created during ESXi installation. Click OK to confirm this selection.

5. For Destination Network, browse to select the virtual machine networking distributed port group that we created in Exercise 4.13. Click OK to confirm this selection.

6. Ensure that the final configuration on the Select Source And Destination Networks screen resembles the following image:

EXERCISE 4.20 *(continued)*

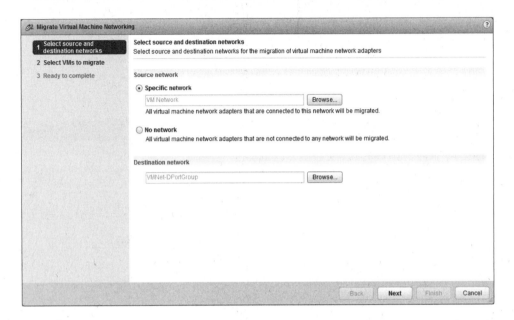

7. Click the Next button to continue. Select a virtual machine by expanding the list of VMs and checking its box. You can also expand the VM to view its NICs and view details about them.

8. Click the Next button to continue, and then review the information on the Ready To Complete screen.

9. Click the Finish button to begin the VM network migration. A Migrate Virtual Machine Networking task will begin. When this task completes, verify in the VM's properties that it is now using the dvSwitch network.

The same procedure detailed in Exercise 4.20 can also be used to migrate virtual machine networking from a dvSwitch to a vSwitch. The Source and Destination Networks fields in the Migrate Virtual Machine Networking wizard would simply be reversed, as shown in Figure 4.13.

FIGURE 4.13   Migrating VM networking from a dvSwitch

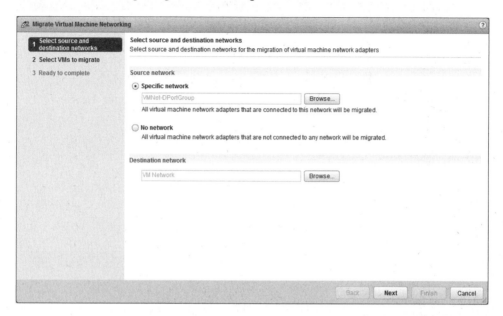

We have now covered migrating virtual machine networking to and from both a vSwitch and a dvSwitch. In this chapter, we have been working with the latest version of the dvSwitch, but in some cases you may have older dvSwitches that are in need of upgrade. In the next section, we will explain how to upgrade an older version of the dvSwitch.

Upgrading a vNetwork Distributed Switch

A version 4.0.0, 4.1.0, 5.0.0 or 5.1.0 vSphere *distributed switch* (dvSwitch) may be upgraded to the 5.5.0 version, after the vCenter 5.5 and ESXi 5.5 upgrades are both complete. This is because the version 5.5.0 dvSwitch is only compatible with ESXi 5.5 and later and will be available only after vCenter Server is running at version 5.5.

The dvSwitch upgrade will allow the distributed switch to take advantage of the latest set of features available in the vSphere 5.5 release, and dvSwitch upgrades are nondisruptive. This means that virtual machines and ESXi hosts attached to the dvSwitch being upgraded experience no downtime during the upgrade. Exercise 4.21 details the procedure of upgrading an existing version 5.0.0 dvSwitch to the 5.5.0 version. Don't worry if you don't already have an older dvSwitch, as we will create one first in the exercise.

EXERCISE 4.21

Upgrading a vNetwork Distributed Switch

1. Connect to a vCenter Server with the vSphere Web Client.

2. On the Home page, click vCenter ➤ Distributed Switches in the left pane.

3. On the Objects tab, click the switch icon with a green plus sign to begin. The New Distributed Switch wizard will launch.

4. Provide a name for the dvSwitch and select a datacenter to place the dvSwitch in. Click the Next button to continue.

5. Specify Distributed Switch Version 5.0.0 and click Next to continue.

6. Accept the default values for the dvSwitch settings and click Next.

7. Review the information on the Ready To Complete screen.

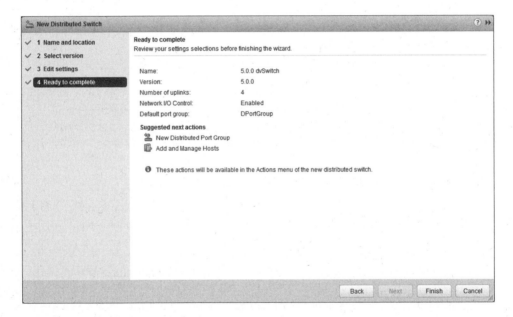

8. Click the Finish button to add the dvSwitch to the datacenter. A series of tasks will begin. Wait for these tasks to complete and the new dvSwitch to appear.

9. On the Objects tab, select the version 5.0.0 dvSwitch you just created. Right-click it and choose Upgrade Distributed Switch from the context menu. The Upgrade Distributed Switch wizard will begin.

10. Select Version 5.5.0 for the upgrade version and click the Next button to continue.

11. Since no ESXi hosts were actually added to this dvSwitch, there will be no compatibility issues. In live environments, ensure that all compatibility checks pass on this step. Click the Next button to continue.

12. Review the information on the Ready To Complete screen and click the Finish button to begin the dvSwitch upgrade.

13. Click the name of the dvSwitch that was just upgraded. Now click the Summary tab and verify the dvSwitch version listed.

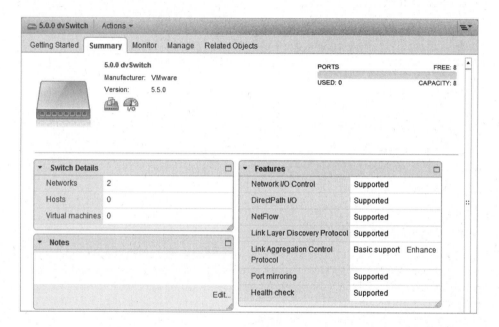

 vNetwork distributed switches cannot be downgraded to previous vSphere dvSwitch versions, and older incompatible ESXi hosts cannot be used with the latest dvSwitch version.

We have covered a great deal about distributed virtual switches in this chapter. Before we move on to the next section of this chapter, let's take a moment to discuss the use cases for a dvSwitch.

Determining the Use Case for a vNetwork Distributed Switch

The use case for dvSwitches could ultimately come down to the size of the environment. Larger environments will be more likely to benefit from many of the advanced features available only in the dvSwitch. To review from earlier, these features include the following:

- Bidirectional virtual machine rate limiting (traffic shaping)
- Centralized vCenter administration and provisioning
- Cisco Nexus 1000V virtual switch
- Dynamic adjustment for load-based NIC teaming
- Enhanced security and monitoring for vMotion traffic
- IEEE 802.1p tagging
- LLDP support
- LACP support
- NetFlow
- Network I/O Control
- Port Mirror
- Private VLAN support
- Health Check
- Traffic Filtering and Marking

Another use case for the dvSwitch is with converged adapters and 10GbE adapters where there simply may not be enough physical NICs to use the vSwitch effectively and maintain proper network isolation. How the network is managed can be another determining factor for dvSwitch use. If the network team is going to manage the network, they may want to use the dvSwitch for its advanced capabilities.

In summary, any virtual environment with Enterprise Plus licensing and vCenter Server that needs networking capability could be a use case for the dvSwitch. It is also important to remember that hybrid configurations are entirely possible, and sometimes this mixture of dvSwitches and vSwitches can be the best solution. The next section of this chapter will cover configuring vSwitch and dvSwitch policies.

Configuring vSS and vDS Policies

Policies may be set at the port group level on either a vSwitch or a dvSwitch. These policies apply to all of the port groups on a vSwitch or to ports in the dvPort group, but they may also be overridden. In the final section of this chapter, I will cover some of these policies, how they are used, and when to use them. The first topic in this section is identifying common vSwitch and dvSwitch policies.

Identifying Common vSwitch and dvSwitch Policies

The vSwitch and dvSwitch have four policies in common:

Failover And Load Balancing Policy   Used to determine how outbound network traffic will be distributed across network adapters and how to handle failed network adapters.

Security Policy   Used to establish layer 2 frame filtering policies.

Traffic Shaping Policy   Used to control the amount of bandwidth allowed. Remember that vSwitches offer this capability only on outbound traffic.

VLAN Policy   Used to establish VLAN ID for a network connection, but remember that private VLANs are not possible with vSwitches.

 While outbound traffic can be controlled with the vSwitch load balancing policy, keep in mind that inbound traffic is controlled by the physical switch configuration.

It is important to remember that although these four policies are common across vSwitches and dvSwitches, there are still differences in their implementation. These differences will be important to understand for the exam. Now that I have outlined the common policies between the vSwitch and the dvSwitch, we will delve a little deeper into each one. Let's start with configuring load balancing and failover policies in virtual switches.

Configuring Load Balancing and Failover Policies

Load balancing and failover policies are used to determine how network traffic will be distributed across network adapters and how to handle failed network adapters. The following options are configurable:

- Load Balancing
- Network Failover Detection
- Notify Switches
- Failback
- Failover Order

To view or configure these options for a vSwitch, use the vSwitch - Edit Settings option. Figure 4.14 shows the vSwitch Teaming and Failover settings.

FIGURE 4.14 vSwitch Teaming and Failover settings

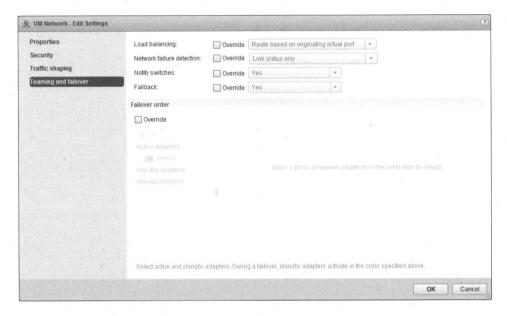

Exercise 4.22 covers the steps to view or configure the load balancing and failover policies for a dvSwitch.

EXERCISE 4.22

Viewing dvSwitch Teaming and Failover Policies

1. Connect to a vCenter Server with the vSphere Web Client.

2. On the Home page, click the vCenter ➤ Distributed Switches option in the left pane.

3. On the Objects tab, right-click the dvSwitch and choose Manage Distributed Port Groups. The Manage Distributed Port Groups window will open.

4. Select the Teaming And Failover check box, and click Next to continue.

5. Click the desired port group to select it, and then click Next.

6. The Teaming And Failover screen will list the policies, as shown here:

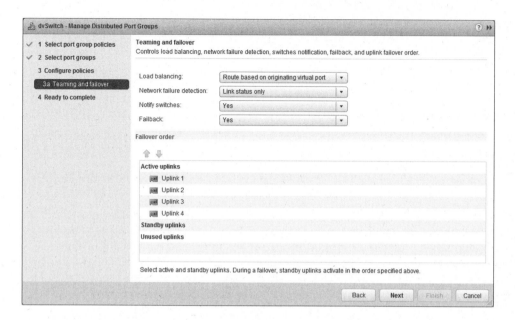

7. Review the available options and then click Cancel to close the window.

Now that you have seen how to find the load balancing and failover policies, let's examine how each of these policies can be used.

Load Balancing

The load-balancing policy is used to determine how ESXi hosts will use their uplink adapters. There are five configurable options in this policy:

Route Based On Originating Virtual Port   The wording differs slightly between the vSwitch and the dvSwitch, but the meaning is the same. An uplink will be selected based on the virtual port where the traffic entered the switch. This is the default setting.

Route Based On IP Hash   An adapter or uplink will be selected based on a hash of the source and destination IP addresses of each packet.

Route Based On Source MAC Hash   An adapter or uplink will be selected based on a hash of the source Ethernet.

Route Based On Physical NIC Load   An uplink will be selected based on the current load of the physical NICs. Note that this option is available only when using a dvSwitch.

Use Explicit Failover Order   An adapter or uplink that is listed highest in the order of active adapters and passes failover detection criteria will be used.

Route Based On IP Hash requires that EtherChannel be configured on the physical switch, and EtherChannel should be used only with the Route Based On IP Hash option.

Network Failover Detection

Network Failover Detection is a mechanism used to detect uplink failures. There are two configurable options in this policy:

Link Status Only   As the name implies, it relies only on the link status provided by the network adapter. This option can detect switch failure and cable pulls but cannot detect configuration errors or cable pulls on the other side of a physical switch.

Beacon Probing   Beacon probes are sent out and listened for on all NICs in the team. This information is used to determine link status and more, and it is capable of detecting configuration errors and cable pulls on the other side of a physical switch. Beacon probing should not be used in conjunction with the Route Based On IP Hash load-balancing policy; it is most useful when three or more adapters are used in the teaming.

Unless you have a specific reason to use beacon probing, use the default option for network failover detection of link status only.

Notify Switches

The Notify Switches option is used to notify switches in case of a failed uplink adapter on the ESXi host. There are two configurable options in this policy:

Yes   When this option is used, the physical switch is notified when a virtual NIC's location changes. This behavior is desirable most of the time, since it provides the lowest latencies.

No   This option would typically be used only when connected virtual machines are using Microsoft Network Load Balancing (NLB) in unicast mode.

Failback

Failback is used to determine what an uplink adapter does after recovering from a failure. There are two configurable options in this policy:

Yes   The adapter is put back in service immediately after recovery, and the standby adapter returns to being a standby adapter. Yes is the default setting.

No   The adapter is left out of service after recovery, until it is again needed.

Failover Order

The final configurable option is for the uplink adapter failover order. Note that the naming differs between the vSwitch, which uses the term *adapters*, and the dvSwitch, which uses the term *uplinks*. Aside from the naming differences, the three options in this policy perform the same way. The options are as follows:

Active Adapters/Uplinks   These adapters will be used as long as network connectivity is available.

Standby Adapters/Uplinks   These adapters will be used if one of the active adapters loses connectivity.

Unused Adapters/Uplinks   These adapters will never be used.

The active, standby, and unused adapters/uplinks can be organized in the virtual switch properties and overridden in the port group properties.

 Do not configure standby adapters/uplinks when using the Route Based On IP Hash load-balancing policy.

Load balancing and failover are used to provide redundant, highly available, and right-sized networking to our virtual switches. Next, let's discuss the security policies that can be used to protect virtual switches.

Configuring Network Security Policies

Virtual switches are capable of enforcing security policies to protect virtual machines connected to them from impersonation and interception attacks. These policies can be configured at the vSwitch level or at the individual port group level in the vSwitch. Figure 4.15 shows a vSwitch with the three different security policies and their default settings of Accept or Reject.

FIGURE 4.15   vSwitch security policies

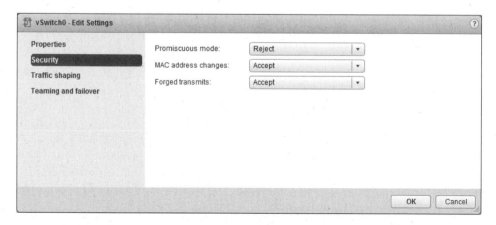

Promiscuous Mode policies allow a guest operating system with a NIC placed into promiscuous mode to observe all traffic on the same vSwitch or port group. Typically, this policy would be used only if you were running a packet sniffer or intrusion detection system on the guest operating system. When Promiscuous Mode is set to Accept, any guest operating system with a NIC placed into promiscuous mode can view traffic destined for other guests or hosts on the same network segment. Because this is a nonsecure mode of operation, the default setting for this policy is Reject.

So you can better understand how the MAC Address Changes and Forged Transmits policies function, I will first review some basic networking information. Each virtual network adapter in a virtual machine has its own unique MAC address. The MAC address is typically assigned when the adapter is created, but it can be changed or even hard-coded in a VM's network adapter settings.

The MAC address specified in the virtual machine's settings is known as the *initial MAC address*, and it cannot be changed by the guest operating system. Each virtual network adapter also has what is known as an *effective MAC address*. The guest operating system is responsible for setting the value of the effective MAC address, and it will typically match the initial MAC address. However, the initial and effective MAC addresses may be different. This is useful for virtual machines that were converted from physical hardware, where they may have been licensed to a specific MAC address. The downside to allowing the initial and effective MAC addresses to differ is that it introduces the opportunity for MAC address impersonation or spoofing. MAC address spoofing can allow network device impersonation or circumvention of access control lists. The MAC Address Changes and Forged Transmits policies work similarly, but there are a few subtle differences.

MAC Address Changes policies affect traffic that is received by a virtual machine. The MAC Address Changes policy is used to control how differentiation between the initial MAC address and the effective MAC address is handled by the vSwitch or port group. When the MAC Address Changes policy is set to Accept, the initial and effective MAC addresses can differ. In other words, the vSwitch will honor the MAC Address Change request. When the MAC Address Changes policy is set to Reject, the initial and effective MAC addresses must match or the vSwitch will disable the port the virtual machine's NIC is connected to. This virtual machine will no longer receive any traffic—until its initial MAC address and effective MAC address again match.

 WARNING If you are using the ESXi Software iSCSI initiator, be sure to set the MAC Address Changes option to Accept.

Forged Transmits policies affect traffic that is transmitted from a virtual machine. The Forged Transmits policy is used to control how differentiation between the initial MAC address and the effective MAC address is handled by the vSwitch or port group. When the Forged Transmits policy is set to Accept, the initial and effective MAC addresses can differ. In other words, the vSwitch will honor forged transmits since it won't even compare the MAC addresses. When the Forged Transmits policy is set to Reject, the initial and effective MAC addresses must match or the vSwitch will simply drop any packets received from the virtual machine.

 If Microsoft's Network Load Balancing is being used in unicast mode, set both the MAC Address Changes policy and the Forged Transmits policy to Accept.

Before we leave network security policies behind, keep in mind that the MAC Address Changes policy will affect traffic that is received by a virtual machine and that the Forged Transmits policy will affect traffic that is transmitted from a virtual machine. I find it helpful to use the completely unrelated acronym of TFTP to help keep these two straight:

Transmitted = Forged Transmits Policy

Now that we have covered the policies available for securing virtual switches, let's move on to configuring virtual switch traffic shaping policies.

Configuring Traffic Shaping Policies

Traffic shaping policies are used to control network bandwidth and can be configured in both vSwitches and dvSwitches. It is important to remember that only outbound traffic will be controlled on a vSwitch and that both inbound and outbound traffic will be controlled on a dvSwitch. A traffic shaping policy consists of the following:

Average Bandwidth   The bits per second allowed across a port. This number is measured over a period of time and represents the allowed average load.

Peak Bandwidth   The maximum bits per second allowed across a port. This number is used to limit the bandwidth during a burst and cannot be smaller than the average bandwidth number.

Burst Size   The maximum kilobytes (KB) allowed in a burst. This option can allow a port that needs more bandwidth than is specified in the average bandwidth value to gain a burst of higher-speed traffic if bandwidth is available.

Exercise 4.23 covers the steps for configuring traffic shaping on a vSwitch.

EXERCISE 4.23

Configuring Traffic Shaping Policies on a vSwitch

1.   Connect to a vCenter Server with the vSphere Web Client.

2.   On the Home page, click vCenter ➢ Hosts And Clusters and then select an ESXi host from the inventory.

3. Click the Manage tab and then the Networking option. Ensure that the Virtual Switches option is selected in the left pane on this tab, and then click to select a vSwitch.

4. Click the Edit Settings icon (the yellow pencil icon located just above the column headers) to edit the vSwitch settings. The Edit Settings window will open.

5. Click the Traffic Shaping menu option on the left. Note that Status is set to Disabled by default. Change the value to Enabled, using the drop-down menu.

6. Set the Average Bandwidth value to a value smaller than the Peak Bandwidth value. The final configuration should appear similar to the following image:

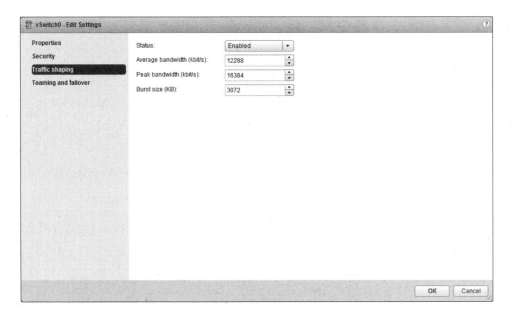

7. Click OK to save these changes. An Update Virtual Switch task will begin. When it completes, use the blue information icon to verify the traffic shaping values you just entered.

8. Using the topology map at the bottom of the Manage tab, select a port group by clicking its name. Click the Edit Settings icon located directly above the topology map to edit the port group settings.

9. In the Edit Settings window, select the Traffic Shaping tab.

10. Note that Status is set to Enabled and that the values for Average Bandwidth, Peak Bandwidth, and Burst Size are inherited from the vSwitch setting.

11. To disable traffic shaping policies for this port group, select the Override check box in the Status field, and then use the drop-down menu to change the status to Disabled.

12. The traffic shaping policy has now been overridden for this port group, and the values for Bandwidth and Burst Size are grayed out.

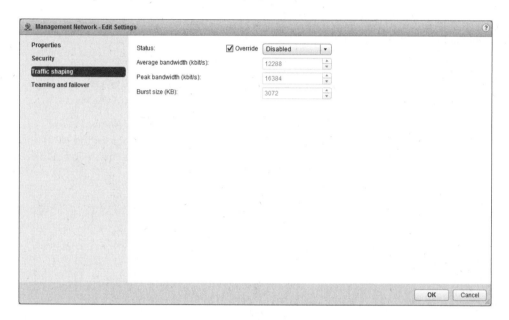

13. Click OK to save these changes. An Update Port Group task will begin. When it completes, use the information icon to verify that traffic shaping values do not exist for the port group.

The ability to override particular traffic shaping policies on the port group level provides additional granularity to the vSwitch configuration. This can be particularly useful if limits are needed on certain networks and other networks need to run as fast as possible.

 When a traffic shaping policy is applied, it will be applied to each vmnic attached to the port group and not to the vSwitch as a whole. Also remember that vSwitch changes are per-ESXi host.

Besides configuring traffic shaping policies in the vSwitch, you also need to know how to configure traffic shaping policies in the dvSwitch. This is covered in Exercise 4.24.

EXERCISE 4.24

Configuring Traffic Shaping Policies on a dvSwitch

1. Connect to a vCenter Server with the vSphere Web Client.

2. On the Home page, click vCenter ➢ Distributed Switches in the left pane.

3. On the Objects tab, right-click the dvSwitch and choose Manage Distributed Port Groups. The Manage Distributed Port Groups window will open.

4. Choose the Traffic Shaping option and click Next to continue.

5. Click the desired port group to select it, and then click Next to continue.

6. The Traffic Shaping screen will list both the ingress (network into VM) traffic shaping settings and the egress (VM out to network) traffic shaping settings.

7. Use the drop-down menu to change the Status field for both Ingress (network into VM) and Egress (VM out to network) to Enabled. Enter the same values for the Average Bandwidth, Peak Bandwidth, and Burst Size that you used in Exercise 4.23 when configuring traffic shaping on the vSwitch.

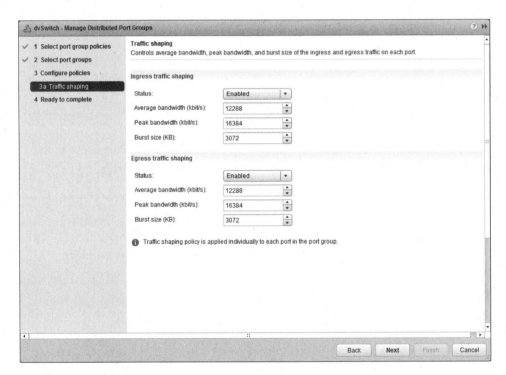

Note that Ingress and Egress do not have to be enabled as a pair. You can pick either one individually or both together.

8. Click the Next button to continue. Review the information on the Ready To Complete screen and click the Finish button to save these changes.

9. A Reconfigure Distributed Port Group task will begin. When this task completes, expand the dvSwitch in the left pane. Click Distributed Port Groups and select the appropriate port group. Verify the settings.

We have now covered load balancing and failover policies, network security policies, and traffic shaping policies. The fourth and final virtual switch policy that both switches share is the VLAN policy.

Configuring VLAN Settings

Both vSwitches and dvSwitches can be configured to use VLANs. Many of the vSwitch exercises earlier in this chapter included steps where the VLAN could have been provided. The VLAN settings for a port group in a vSwitch can be configured by obtaining the properties for the port group. This is shown in Figure 4.16, where Management Network has been assigned to VLAN 46.

FIGURE 4.16   VM port group VLAN settings

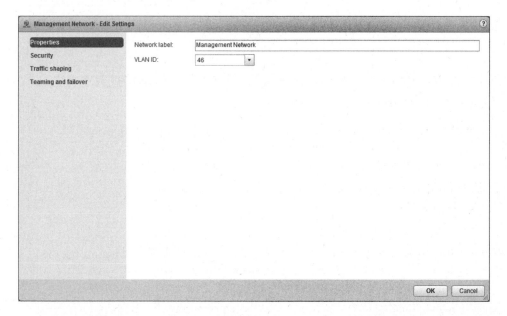

Similarly, the VLAN settings for a dvSwitch can be configured by obtaining the properties for the dvPort group. This is shown in Figure 4.17, where the dvPort group has been assigned to VLAN 46.

FIGURE 4.17   dvPort group VLAN settings

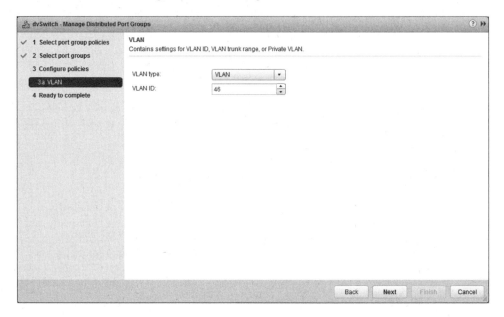

Before we leave our coverage of VLANs behind, let's take a moment to discuss determining the appropriate VLAN configuration for a vSphere implementation.

Determining Appropriate VLAN Configuration for a vSphere Implementation

A VLAN is used to segment a single physical network into multiple logical networks. VLANs are used in vSphere implementations for the following reasons:

- To simplify ESXi host integration
- To improve network security
- To reduce network congestion
- To isolate network traffic

To support VLANs in vSphere, either the physical or the virtual switch must tag the Ethernet frames with an 802.1Q tag. This tag is also known as the VLAN ID. Three configuration modes can be used to tag and untag the packets for virtual machine frames:

External Switch Tagging (EST)   The physical switch performs all VLAN tagging. ESXi host network adapters are connected to access/untagged ports on the physical switch.

Virtual Switch Tagging (VST)   The vSwitch (or dvSwitch) performs all VLAN tagging. ESXi host network adapters must be connected to trunk/tagged ports on the physical switch. This is the most common implementation.

Virtual Guest Tagging (VGT)   An 802.1Q VLAN trunking driver installed in the virtual machine performs all VLAN tagging. ESXi host network adapters must be connected to trunk/tagged ports on the physical switch. In order for the tagged traffic to be passed through to the virtual guest, either VLAN 4095 for a vSwitch port group or VLAN trunking for a dvPort group has to be configured.

Determining the appropriate VLAN configuration for a vSphere implementation will often come down to understanding both the requirements and the available infrastructure. VLAN configuration is part of the vSphere design, and there will likely always be some sort of retrofit involved to integrate vSphere into existing environments.

Keep in mind that VST is the most commonly used VLAN implementation. This is because VST can use trunked VLANs, and nothing has to be configured in the guest OS. Using trunked VLANs cuts down on the number of physical NICs required in the ESXi hosts, and not having to configure each guest OS lowers administrative effort and cuts down on complexity.

Configuring dvPort Group Blocking Policies

Port blocking policies are used to block all ports on a port group from sending and receiving data and are available only in dvSwitches. In Exercise 4.25, you will configure dvPort group blocking policies. The upgraded dvSwitch we worked with in Exercise 4.21 would be a great candidate for this lab, since it is unlikely to be in use.

EXERCISE 4.25

Configuring dvPort Group Blocking Policies

1. Connect to a vCenter Server with the vSphere Web Client.

2. On the Home page, click vCenter ➤ Distributed Switches in the left pane.

3. On the Objects tab, right-click the dvSwitch and choose Manage Distributed Port Groups. The Manage Distributed Port Groups window will open.

4. Select the Miscellaneous check box, and click Next to continue.

5. Click the desired port group to select it, and then click Next to continue.

6. The Miscellaneous option controls the port blocking configuration via a drop-down menu. Change the Block All Ports option to Yes, and click Next to continue.

EXERCISE 4.25 *(continued)*

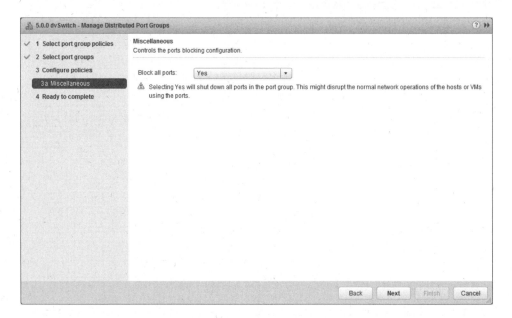

7. Review the information on the Ready To Complete screen, and then click the Finish button to apply the port blocking policy to the distributed port group. A Reconfigure dvPort Group task will begin. When this task completes, the dvPort group configuration is complete.

At this point, all connections using this dvPort group are blocked. If this is your only dvPort group or if you need these connections to work, go back through the previous exercise and undo the changes just made. There is one final topic we need to cover in this chapter: enabling jumbo frames.

Enabling Jumbo Frames Support on Appropriate Components

A *jumbo frame* is an Ethernet frame with a payload size greater than 1,500 bytes and less than or equal to 9,000 bytes. This size is also known as the *maximum transmission unit* (MTU). Jumbo frames can be enabled to improve network I/O performance and use fewer CPU resources. Jumbo frames must be supported on the network end to end, meaning that the ESXi host, the destination, and any and all physical switches between the two must support jumbo frames.

The use of jumbo frames does not automatically guarantee a performance increase. When using jumbo frames, it is always best to test performance with and without them to see if there is a benefit to using them.

In Exercise 4.26, you will create a new dvSwitch that has jumbo frames enabled. You will first configure the dvSwitch to use jumbo frames, and then you will create a new VMkernel connection type that could be used for iSCSI or NFS traffic.

EXERCISE 4.26

Enabling Jumbo Frames for a dvSwitch

1. Connect to a vCenter Server with the vSphere Web Client.

2. On the Home page, click vCenter ➤ Distributed Switches in the left pane.

3. On the Objects tab, right-click the appropriate dvSwitch and choose the Edit Settings option from the context menu. The Edit Settings window will open.

4. Choose the Advanced option in the left pane. Change the value of MTU (Bytes) to **9000** and click OK to save the changes.

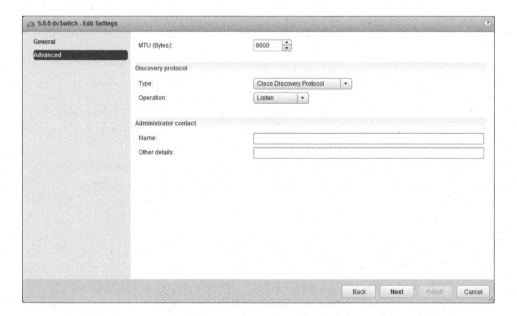

5. An Update Properties task will begin, followed by a Reconfigure vSphere dvSwitch task. Wait for these tasks to complete, and use the Edit Settings option to verify that the change was successfully made.

   You have now configured the dvSwitch to use jumbo frames; however, you still need to create a distributed port group with the same MTU size. In the following steps, you will create a distributed port group MTU size to match that of the dvSwitch.

6. Right-click the same dvSwitch and choose New Distributed Port Group. The New Distributed Port Group window will appear.

7. Give the distributed port group a descriptive name and verify that Location is set to the dvSwitch that we have been working with in this exercise. Click Next to continue.

8. Review the settings of the new distributed port group. Accept all default values and click Next to continue.

9. Review the information on the Ready To Complete Screen, and click Finish to add the distributed port group to the dvSwitch.

10. An Add Distributed Port Groups task will begin. When this task completes, click the name of the dvSwitch shown on the Objects tab.

11. In the Manage tab, click Settings on the toolbar and then select Properties in the left menu.

12. Verify that the MTU value is 9000 Bytes.

13. On the Home page, click vCenter ➢ Distributed Switches. In the left pane, select the dvSwitch that we have been working with. Right-click the dvSwitch in the left pane and choose New Distributed Port Group from the context menu. The New Distributed Port Group window will appear.

14. Give the distributed port group a descriptive name and verify that Location is set to the dvSwitch we have been working with in this chapter. Click Next to continue.

15. Review the properties of the new distributed port group. Accept all default values and click Next.

16. Review the information on the Ready To Complete Screen, and click the Finish button to add the distributed port group to the dvSwitch.

17. An Add Distributed Port Groups task will begin. When this task completes, click the name of your dvSwitch shown on the Objects tab.

18. On the Manage tab, click Settings on the toolbar and then verify that the new distributed port group is now listed in the dvSwitch. It should appear similar to the following image, where the newly created distributed port group is named vmk-DPortGroup:

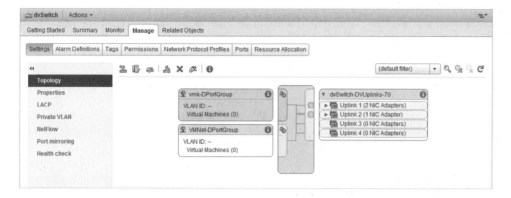

19. In the left pane, click dvSwitch ➢ Hosts and then select an ESXi host.

20. Click the Virtual Adapters option in the Networking section of the Manage tab. Click the Add Host Networking icon to add a virtual adapter. The Add Networking wizard will begin.

21. Choose the VMkernel Network Adapter option for the connection type and click Next.

22. Accept the default option of Select An Existing Distributed Port Group and click the Browse button to select the distributed port group we created in the first part of this exercise. Click Next once the group has been selected.

23. Check the box for vMotion traffic in the Enable Services section and click Next.

24. Provide a static IP address and subnet mask for the VMkernel.

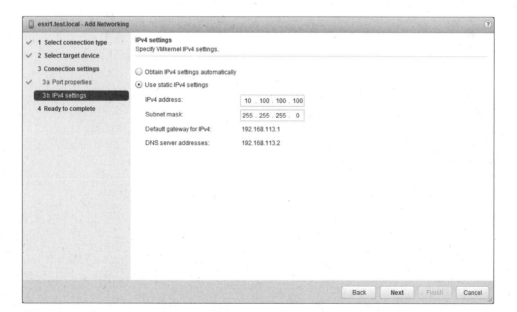

25. Click the Next button to continue, and then review the information on the Ready To Complete Screen.

26. Click the Finish button to add the virtual adapter to the dvSwitch.

27. An Add Virtual NIC task will begin. When this task completes, verify that the newly created virtual adapter is now listed on the Manage tab.

28. Repeat steps 9–16 for all remaining ESXi hosts that will use this dvSwitch.

29. In the left pane, click the name of your dvSwitch and then review the dvSwitch topology. Note the value of the VMkernel ports in the VMkernel distributed port group we just created.

The dvSwitch, dvPort group and VMkernel have now been configured to use jumbo frames. However, jumbo frames must still be enabled for all devices connected to this vSwitch—the physical switch, the NAS device, and any other physical or virtual machines that will be connected to this network.

We discussed a use case in Exercise 4.6, where a virtual machine might be used to connect to an isolated storage network running an NFS server. In the case of a jumbo frame–configured network, like the one you just built in Exercise 4.26, you would also need to make changes to the virtual machine to allow it to use jumbo frames on this network.

The process to enable a virtual machine for jumbo frames involves adding a VMXNET 2 or VMXNET 3 network adapter to the virtual machine. In addition to using a VMXNET 2 or VMXNET 3 network adapter, the following items are required to use jumbo frames in a virtual machine:

- The VMXNET 2 or VMXNET 3 network adapter must be connected to a virtual machine port group on a virtual switch with jumbo frames enabled.

- All physical switches and other devices connected to the virtual machine must support jumbo frames. Remember that jumbo frames must be supported end to end.

- The guest OS must also be configured to support jumbo frames. In Windows guests, this is accomplished by changing the MTU setting in the network adapter properties, as shown in Figure 4.18.

We have now covered enabling jumbo frames on a dvSwitch, dvPort group, and virtual machine, and with that this chapter on vSphere networking comes to an end.

FIGURE 4.18   Jumbo frames in Windows

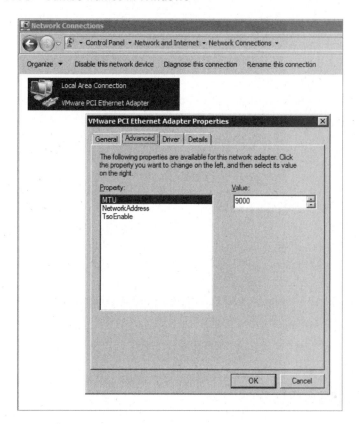

Summary

This chapter covered networking in vSphere 5.5. Knowing how to network with vSwitches and dvSwitches and when to use each is extremely important for the exam. You learned first about vSwitches and their capabilities, as well as the following tasks:

- Creating and deleting vSwitches
- Adding, configuring, and removing vmnics on vSwitches
- Configuring VMkernel ports on vSwitches for network services

- Adding, editing, and removing port groups in the vSwitch
- Determining the use case for a vSwitch

We also covered dvSwitches and identifying their capabilities. You learned the following skills:

- Creating and deleting dvSwitches
- Adding and removing ESXi hosts to/from dvSwitches
- Adding, configuring, and removing dvPort groups
- Adding and removing uplink adapters to dvUplink groups
- Creating, configuring, and removing virtual adapters
- Migrating virtual adapters and virtual machines to and from a dvSwitch
- Determining the use case for a dvSwitch

The final part of this chapter focused on configuring vSwitch and dvSwitch policies. I identified the common policies they share and covered these skills:

- Configuring load-balancing polices, security policies, traffic shaping policies and VLAN settings
- Determining the appropriate VLAN configuration for a vSphere implementation
- dvPort group blocking policies
- Enabling jumbo frames on a dvSwitch, dvPort group and virtual machine

Exam Essentials

Know how to configure vSwitches.   Be able to identify the capabilities of a vSwitch. Understand how to create and delete vSwitches. Know how to add, configure, and remove vmnics on a vSwitch. Understand how to configure VMkernel ports for different network services. Be able to add, edit, and remove port groups on a vSwitch. Be able to determine the use case for a vSwitch.

Know how to configure dvSwitches.   Be able to identify the capabilities of a dvSwitch. Understand how to create and delete dvSwitches. Know how (and when) to add and remove ESXi hosts from a dvSwitch. Know how to add, configure, and remove dvPort groups in a dvSwitch. Understand how uplink adapters work and how to add and remove them to dvUplink port groups. Be able to create, configure, and remove virtual adapters. Know how to migrate virtual adapters to/from a dvSwitch. Also know how to migrate virtual machine networking to/from a dvSwitch. Know how to upgrade a dvSwitch. Be able to determine the use case for a dvSwitch.

Know how to configure vSwitch and dvSwitch policies.   Be able to identify common policies that are shared between the vSwitch and the dvSwitch. Understand how to configure load-balancing and failover policies, security policies, and traffic shaping policies. Know how to configure VLAN settings and understand when to use VLANs. Be able to configure dvPort group blocking policies and know how to enable jumbo frames.

Review Questions

1. In a vSwitch, which of the following can be used to obtain information for peer network devices?

    A. Beacon probing

    B. LLDP

    C. CDP

    D. PVLANs

2. What are the two connection types available when creating a new vSwitch?

    A. Virtual machine

    B. Management

    C. LAN

    D. VMkernel

3. Which of the following policies are common across vSwitches and dvSwitches? (Choose all that apply.)

    A. Failover and Load Balancing policy

    B. VLAN policy

    C. Security policy

    D. Traffic Shaping policy

4. Which of the following VLAN tagging configurations require trunk/tagged ports to be configured on a physical switch? (Choose two.)

    A. EST

    B. VST

    C. VGT

    D. EXT

5. Which of the following is a use case for a vSwitch? (Choose all that apply.)

    A. Environment with ESXi hosts and no vCenter Server

    B. Environment with ESXi hosts and vCenter Server with Standard Licensing

    C. Environment with ESXi hosts and vCenter server with Enterprise Licensing

    D. Environment with ESXi hosts and vCenter Server with Enterprise Plus Licensing

6. Which load-balancing policy is available only with the dvSwitch?

    A. Route Based On IP Hash

    B. Route Based On Physical NIC Load

    C. Route Based On MAC Hash

    D. Use Explicit Failover Order

7. You need to remove one of the two physical adapters from a vSwitch that has a virtual machine port group with 25 connected virtual machines. What sequence of events should you use to accomplish this task?

   A. Leave all VMs on the ESXi host. Remove the vmnic from the vSwitch.

   B. Leave all VMs on the ESXi host. Remove the vSwitch.

   C. Migrate all VMs to another ESXi host using vMotion. Remove the vmnic from the vSwitch. Move the VMs back to this ESXi host.

   D. Migrate all VMs to another ESXi host using vMotion. Remove the vSwitch. Move the VMs back to this ESXi host.

8. You have a customer that requires Network I/O Control and NetFlow. Which version of the dvSwitch must be used?

   A. 4.0.0

   B. 4.1.0

   C. 4.1.1

   D. 5.0.0

9. When creating a dvSwitch, what are the options for adding ESXi hosts? (Choose all that apply.)

   A. Add Now

   B. Add One

   C. Add Later

   D. Add All

10. When adding a dvPort group to a dvSwitch, you use the VLAN Trunking option. How many dvPort groups will be required to support three trunked VLANS?

   A. 0

   B. 1

   C. 2

   D. 3

11. A customer has an NFS server implemented on a dedicated and isolated network. The ESXi hosts connect to this NFS server through a vSwitch configured with a VMkernel port group. You need to connect a virtual machine to the management interface on the NFS server. What are the steps you need to take?

   A. Create a virtual machine port group on the vSwitch. Connect a virtual machine to this port group. Give the VM an IP address on the storage network. Connect to and use the management interface on the NFS server. Disconnect the VM from this port group and remove the virtual machine port group.

   B. Create a virtual machine port group on a new vSwitch. Connect a virtual machine to this port group. Give the VM an IP address on the new network. Connect to and use the management interface on the NFS server.

    C. Connect the virtual machine to the VMkernel port group. Give the VM an IP address on the storage network. Connect to and use the management interface on the NFS server. Disconnect the VM from the VMkernel port group and remove the VMkernel port group.

    D. Create a virtual machine port group on the vSwitch. Connect a virtual machine to this port group. Give the VM an IP address on the storage network. Connect to and use the management interface on the NFS server. Disconnect the VM from this port group.

12. Which of the following statements is true about Etherchannel and load-balancing policies? (Choose two.)

    A. Route Based On IP Hash requires EtherChannel.

    B. Route Based On MAC Hash requires EtherChannel.

    C. Do not configure standby adapters/uplinks when using the Route Based On MAC Hash load-balancing policy.

    D. Do not configure standby adapters/uplinks when using the Route Based On IP Hash load-balancing policy.

13. Which of the following network adapters are required for virtual machines to utilize TSO? (Choose all that apply.)

    A. e1000

    B. vlance

    C. VMXNET 2 (Enhanced)

    D. VMXNET 3

14. What types of traffic can a vmknic be used for? (Choose all that apply.)

    A. vMotion

    B. Virtual Machine

    C. iSCSI

    D. Management

15. Which of the following is a use case for the dvSwitch? (Choose all that apply.)

    A. An environment with ESXi hosts and no vCenter Server

    B. An environment with ESXi hosts and vCenter Server with Standard licensing

    C. An environment with ESXi hosts and vCenter server with Enterprise licensing

    D. An environment with ESXi hosts and vCenter Server with Enterprise Plus licensing

16. What is used to allow ESXi hosts using the same dvSwitch to have differing vmnic configurations and still use the same teaming, load-balancing, and failover policies?

    A. dvPort group

    B. dvUplink

    C. Uplink adapters

    D. dvPort

17. You have a customer that requires the use of virtual machine traffic shaping on both inbound and outbound connections. Which of the following solutions provide this capability?

   A. dvSwitch

   B. vSwitch

   C. Both of these

   D. None of these

18. Which of the following are required to use jumbo frames in a virtual machine? (Choose all that apply.)

   A. VMXNET 2

   B. Guest OS configuration changes

   C. Ensuring that all devices on the network segment support jumbo frames

   D. VMware Tools

19. Which statement best describes static port binding?

   A. A dvPort is created and assigned when a virtual machine is created.

   B. A dvPort is created and assigned when a virtual machine is both powered on and has its NIC connected.

   C. A dvPort is immediately assigned and reserved when the virtual machine is connected to the dvPort.

   D. A dvPort is immediately assigned and reserved when the dvSwitch is created.

20. Which of the following describes the use for virtual adapters in the dvSwitch? (Choose all that apply.)

   A. Used to provide virtual machine connections

   B. Used to provide vMotion traffic

   C. Used to provide FT traffic

   D. Used to provide NFS traffic

Chapter 5

Planning and Configuring vSphere Storage

VCP5-DCV EXAM OBJECTIVES COVERED IN THIS CHAPTER:

✓ **3.1: Configure Shared Storage for VSphere**

- Identify storage adapters and devices
- Identify storage naming conventions
- Scan/Rescan storage
- Enable/Configure/Disable vCenter server storage filters
- Describe zoning and lun masking practices
- Identify hardware/dependent hardware/software iSCSI initiator requirements
- Determine use case for hardware/dependent hardware/software iSCSI initiator
- Configure/Edit hardware/dependent hardware initiators
- Enable/Disable software iSCSI initiator
- Configure/Edit software iSCSI initiator settings
- Configure iSCSI port binding
- Enable/Configure/Disable iSCSI CHAP
- Configure FC/ISCSI LUNs as ESXi boot devices
- Compare and contrast array thin provisioning and virtual disk thin provisioning
- Create an NFS share for use with vSphere
- Determine use case for and configure array thin provisioning

✓ **3.2: Create and Configure VMFS and NFS Datastores**

- Identify VMFS-5 capabilities
- Create/Rename/ Delete/Unmount a VMFS datastore

- Identify VMFS and NFS Datastore properties

- Extend/Expand VMFS Datastores

- Upgrade from VMFS3 to VMFS5

- Place a VMFS Datastore in Maintenance Mode

- Determine appropriate Path Selection Policy for a given VMFS Datastore

- Select the Preferred Path for a VMFS Datastore

- Disable a path to a VMFS Datastore

- Mount/Unmount an NFS Datastore

- Determine use case for multiple VMFS/NFS Datastores

TOOLS

- vSphere Installation and Setup guide (Objectives 3.1, 3.2)

- vSphere Storage guide (Objectives 3.1, 3.2)

- VMware vSphere Examples and Scenarios guide (Objective 3.1)

- vSphere Client / vSphere Web Client (Objectives 3.1, 3.2)

This chapter will cover the objectives of section 3 of the VCP5-DCV exam blueprint. It will focus completely on configuring storage in vSphere 5.5.

Configuring Shared Storage for vSphere

Knowing how to configure shared storage for a vSphere environment is an essential part of the virtual infrastructure administrator's duties. Many of the advanced features of vSphere—including HA, DRS, Storage vMotion, and FT—rely on shared storage. This shared storage can be in the form of Virtual Machine File System (VMFS) datastores on a storage area network (*SAN*), raw device mappings on a SAN, or Network File System (*NFS*) volumes on networked-attached storage (*NAS*) devices. The first topic in this chapter is identifying storage adapters and devices in ESXi.

Identifying Storage Adapters and Devices

ESXi abstracts physical storage from virtual machines and uses storage adapters to provide connectivity between ESXi hosts and storage. The connected storage is also known as a target. SCSI, SAS, iSCSI, RAID, Fibre Channel, Ethernet, and Fibre Channel over Ethernet (FCoE) are all supported adapter classes used to provide storage connectivity in ESXi. The storage adapters are accessed by ESXi through device drivers in the VMkernel. In ESXi, a device is simply storage space on a target. A device may often be referred to as a logical unit number (*LUN*).

 Not all storage adapters are supported by ESXi. Always check the hardware compatibility list (HCL) for device compatibility, and never assume that a device will work.

Exercise 5.1 demonstrates how to use the vSphere Web Client to identify storage adapters and how to obtain information about the devices connected through these storage adapters.

EXERCISE 5.1

Identifying Storage Adapters and Devices in ESXi

1. Connect to a vCenter Server with the vSphere Web Client.

2. On the Home page, click the vCenter ➤ Hosts And Clusters option and select an ESXi host from the inventory.

EXERCISE 5.1 *(continued)*

3. Click the Manage tab and then select the Storage option from the toolbar.

4. Make sure that Storage Adapters is selected, and review the list of storage adapters. As with other listings in vSphere, you can customize the columns by right-clicking any column header. Click each entry in the list and then review the details listed below it. Here, the local disks in the ESXi server are listed for adapter vmhba1:

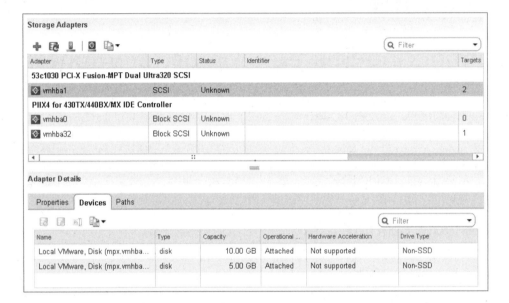

Any storage adapters that are present in the system, such as HBA cards, DVD-ROM drives, and RAID adapters, will be listed under the Storage Adapters section. Also remember that certain adapters, such as software iSCSI and FCoE, must first be enabled before they will be visible in the Storage Adapters list.

5. Select the Storage Devices option. Review the Name, Type, Capacity, and Operational State settings and more here.

6. In the lower portion of the screen, click the Paths tab to view the path information for a chosen storage device. Review the information presented for details about the paths to the devices.

In the last step of Exercise 5.1, you looked at viewing the path information for a device. In the next section, I will discuss the storage device naming conventions used in this tab.

Identifying Storage Naming Conventions

In ESXi, each device is identified by a device identifier. The device identifiers are as follows:

- SCSI INQUIRY
- Path-based

- Legacy
- Runtime Name

Let's take a closer look at each of these device identifiers. With SCSI INQUIRY, the storage system generates an identifier for the device that is both persistent and unique. The prefixes `eui`, `naa`, and `t10` are used with this identifier. Table 5.1 shows the naming convention and examples for the SCSI INQUIRY device identifiers.

TABLE 5.1   SCSI INQUIRY identifier naming conventions and examples

Naming convention	Example
`eui.<EUI>:<Partition>`	`eui.5577bd49251ddb52`
`naa.<NAA>:<Partition>`	`naa.6006016094602800e07ff528b73ae011:2`

In Table 5.1, the `eui` example is using the entire device, so the unique part of this identifier is `5577bd49251ddb52`. The `naa` example is also shown with its own unique part of the identifier, but it is using a specific partition (partition 2) on the device.

With the Path-based identifier, the ESXi host generates an identifier for devices that do not provide `eui`, `naa`, or `t10` data. This identifier is not unique or persistent. The prefix `mpx` is used with this identifier. Table 5.2 shows the naming convention and an example for the Path-based device identifier.

TABLE 5.2   Path-based identifier naming convention and example

Naming convention	Example
`mpx.vmhba<Adapter>:C<Channel>:T<Target>:L<LUN>` : `<Partition>`	`mpx.vmhba2:C0:T0:L0`

In Table 5.2, the example is using storage adapter 2, storage channel number 0, target number 0, and LUN 0, and no partition is specified.

With the Legacy identifier, the ESXi host issues an identifier that includes a series of unique digits. The prefix `vml` is used with this identifier. Table 5.3 shows the naming convention and an example for the Legacy device identifier.

TABLE 5.3   Legacy identifier naming convention and example

Naming convention	Example
`vml.<VML>:<Partition>`	`vml.02000600006006016094602800364ce22e38 25e011524149442030:1`

In Table 5.3, the example is shown with its own unique part of the identifier, but it is also using a specific partition (partition 1) on the device.

Runtime Name is an identifier used exclusively to identify the name of the first path to a device. It is not reliable or persistent. Table 5.4 shows the naming convention and an example for the Runtime Name path identifier.

TABLE 5.4   Runtime Name identifier naming convention and example

Naming convention	Example
vmhba<*Adapter*>:C<*Channel*>:T<*Target*>:L<*LUN*>	vmhba1:C0:T1:L0

In Table 5.4, the example is using storage adapter 1, storage channel number 0, target number 1, and LUN 0.

To help you better understand these naming conventions, some important terms are defined here:

vmhba<*Adapter*>   The name of the storage adapter used by the ESXi host.

C<*Channel*>   The number of the storage channel.

T<*Target*>   The target number, as determined by the ESXi host.

L<*LUN*>   The number that shows the position of the LUN within the target. Note that if a target has only a single LUN, the LUN number will always be 0.

Now that the naming conventions used in ESXi have been covered, let's turn our attention to scanning and rescanning for storage devices.

Scanning and Rescanning Storage

Adding and modifying storage are common events in any virtual environment. While certain operations on VMFS datastores and raw device mapping (RDM) devices are discovered by automatic rescans, sometimes a manual rescan is required. For example, manual rescans are required for any of the following changes:

- A new disk array is zoned on a SAN.
- A new device (LUN) is created on a SAN.
- The path masking on a host is changed.
- A cable is reconnected.
- CHAP settings in iSCSI environments are modified.
- Static or dynamic addresses in iSCSI environments are modified.

The rescan options are used any time these types of changes are made. The rescan operation allows ESXi hosts to have up-to-date and accurate information about storage devices. Exercise 5.2 shows how to use the rescan functions.

EXERCISE 5.2

Rescanning Storage in ESXi

1. Connect to a vCenter Server with the vSphere Web Client.

2. In the left pane, select an ESXi host from the inventory.

3. Click the Manage tab and then select the Storage option from the toolbar.

4. Make sure that Storage Adapters is selected, and then click the Rescan All Storage Adapters On The Host To Discover Newly Added Storage Devices And/Or VMFS Volumes button, which is a server icon with a green gradient line beneath it.

5. A Rescan Storage window will appear, as shown here:

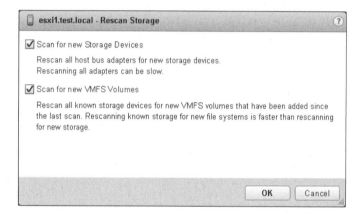

6. By default, both the Scan For New Storage Devices and Scan For New VMFS Volumes options are selected. Accept these defaults; then click OK to begin the rescan operations.

7. A Rescan Storage task will begin, and it will be immediately followed by a Rescan All HBAs task and a Rescan VMFS task.

    In steps 5–6, the Scan For New Storage Devices option rescanned all storage adapters in the host for new storage devices. When this task completed, the Scan For New VMFS Volumes task began to scan all known storage devices for new VMFS volumes. There may be times when you simply need to scan a single storage adapter for new devices, without scanning every storage adapter in the system.

8. Select a single storage adapter on the Storage Adapters screen, and then click the Rescans The Host's Storage Adapter To Discover Newly Added Storage Devices button, which is a gray square icon with a green gradient line beneath it.

9. A Rescan HBA task will begin.

    You also may need to simultaneously scan many ESXi hosts for new devices and VMFS volumes.

EXERCISE 5.2 *(continued)*

10. Return to the Hosts And Clusters view in the vSphere Web Client. In the left pane, right-click a datacenter, cluster, or folder that contains ESXi hosts and select the All vCenter Actions ➤ Rescan Storage option from the context menu.

11. A Rescan For Datastores Warning window will appear, as shown here:

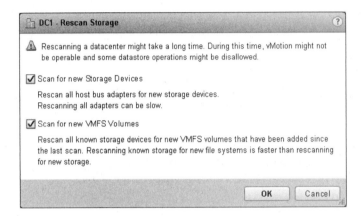

Review the warning information to understand the implications of this operation. Note that by default, both the Scan For New Storage Devices and Scan For New VMFS Volumes options are selected. Accept these defaults; then click OK to begin the rescan operations.

12. For each host contained in the datacenter, cluster, or folder you chose, a Rescan All HBAs task will begin. This task will be immediately followed by a Rescan VMFS task for each host. When these tasks complete, review each ESXi host for any changes.

 VMFS datastores are also referred to as VMFS volumes. In this book, the term VMFS *datastores* will be used most often, following the naming convention used in the VCP5-DCV exam blueprint.

Exercise 5.2 covered three distinct rescan operations performed with the vSphere Web Client. First it covered scanning all storage adapters in a single ESXi host for new storage devices and VMFS volumes. It next covered how to rescan a single storage adapter, and the exercise concluded with how to rescan all storage adapters in multiple ESXi hosts. Now that you understand scanning for devices and VMFS volumes, let's look at enabling, configuring, and disabling vCenter Server storage filters.

Enabling, Configuring, and Disabling vCenter Server Storage Filters

Storage filters are used in vCenter Server to help prevent storage corruption and performance issues caused by the unsupported use of storage devices. In essence, the storage filters will allow only particular types of devices to be listed for particular operations. Table 5.5 lists the four storage filters and their associated keys.

TABLE 5.5   vCenter Server storage filters and keys

Filter name	Key
VMFS filter	`config.vpxd.filter.vmfsFilter`
RDM filter	`config.vpxd.filter.rdmFilter`
Same Host and Transports filter	`config.vpxd.filter.SameHostAndTransportsFilter`
Host Rescan filter	`config.vpxd.filter.hostRescanFilter`

The VMFS filter is used to filter out devices that are already in use as VMFS datastores on any host managed by vCenter Server. These devices cannot be reused as new VMFS volumes or RDMs. In other words, when a scan for new devices operation is performed, existing VMFS volumes will not be listed. This prevents the accidental reuse of VMFS volumes.

The RDM filter is used to filter out devices that are already in use as RDM devices on any host managed by vCenter Server. These devices cannot be reused as new VMFS volumes or different RDMs. In other words, when a scan for new devices operation is performed, existing RDMs will not be listed.

The Same Host and Transports filter is used to filter out devices that have some type of incompatibility. For example, adding an extent when the device is not exposed to all hosts or adding a Fibre Channel extent to a VMFS datastore on local storage would be prevented and thus filtered.

The Host Rescan filter is used to automatically rescan for VMFS datastores after datastore management operations are performed.

 You should consult with the VMware support team before making any changes to the storage filters. Exercise 5.3 should definitely not be performed in any production environment.

The vCenter Server storage filters have specific use cases and will most likely be used in conjunction with VMware support. With that being said, the Host Rescan filter is the least likely of the four filters to cause problems. In Exercise 5.3, you will disable, configure, and then enable the Host Rescan filter.

Disabling, Configuring, and Enabling vCenter Server Storage Filters

1. Connect to a vCenter Server with the vSphere Web Client.

2. Select a vCenter Server from the left pane, and then select the Settings option from the toolbar located on the Manage tab. Select Advanced Settings, and then type the following in the Filter box:

   `config.vpxd.filter`

3. When the filtered results display, notice that only a single result is returned.

4. If additional results are returned, look through the list of keys and verify whether any of the vCenter Server storage filter keys in Table 5.5 are listed. By default, none of the four filters will be listed.

5. Click the Edit button. An Edit Advanced vCenter Server Settings window will open.

6. At the bottom of this window, enter the text **config.vpxd.filter .hostRescanFilter** in the Key field. Enter the text **false** in the Value field. The final configuration is shown here:

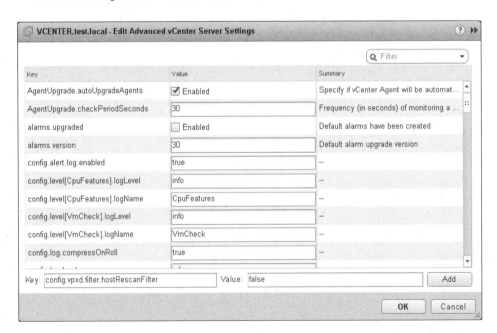

7. Click the Add button to add this key and disable the Host Rescan Filter storage filter. Verify that the new key has been added in the list of keys on the screen.

8. Click OK to close the Edit Advanced vCenter Server Settings window.

The Host Rescan Filter is now disabled, and datastore management operations will no longer result in automatic VMFS rescans. Because having the Host Rescan Filter disabled is not a recommended practice, you will now change this setting back.

9. Type the following in the Filter box:

`config.vpxd.filter`

10. When the filtered results display, verify that `config.vpxd.filter` `.hostRescanFilter` is listed and the value is `false`.

11. Click the Edit button again, and when the Edit Advanced vCenter Server Settings window opens, filter the results again or scroll through the list of keys and locate this key:

`config.vpxd.filter.hostRescanFilter`

12. Highlight the `config.vpxd.filter.hostRescanFilter` key and then click the Value field. Change the text to the value **true** and then click OK in the Edit vCenter Server Settings window. The Host Rescan filter is now enabled again.

Note that it is not possible to remove keys once they have been added to the Advanced Settings section of the vCenter Server Settings window. If the keys have been added, then their behavior must be controlled with the `true` and `false` values. Remember, the value `false` will turn off the filter, and the value `true` will turn on the filter.

 Regardless of the value specified in the `config.vpxd.filter` `.hostRescanFilter` key, an ESXi host will automatically rescan when a new device is presented to it.

Now that I have covered vCenter Server storage filters, I will describe zoning and LUN masking practices.

Describing Zoning and LUN Masking Practices

Zoning and LUN masking are used to secure devices located on Fibre Channel (FC) SANs. Zoning is a process used at the switch level in FC SANs to define which HBAs can connect to which controllers on the SAN. Another way to think of zoning is as an access control for device communications. In a typical vSphere environment, single-initiator zoning or single-initiator-single-target zoning would be used. In either of these cases, the initiator could be represented by a Fibre Channel storage adapter port in an ESXi host and the target could be represented by a port on the storage processor. The terms initiator and target are also used in iSCSI.

LUN masking is a process performed at the SAN storage processors or ESXi host level that makes LUNs hidden from certain hosts. LUN masking can also be used to reduce the number of devices presented to an ESXi host, which would make rescan operations faster.

Now that I have covered zoning and LUN masking, we will identify the hardware-dependent and software iSCSI initiator requirements.

Identifying Hardware/Dependent Hardware/Software iSCSI Initiator Requirements

An iSCSI initiator encapsulates SCSI commands into Ethernet packets. This allows ESXi hosts to communicate with an iSCSI-capable SAN over standard Ethernet cabling. In ESXi 5, there are two types of iSCSI initiators. These are known as the software iSCSI adapter and the hardware iSCSI adapter.

With the software iSCSI adapter, the initiator code is included as part of the VMkernel. This allows any standard network adapter to be used, and the processing involved in the iSCSI encapsulation is performed by the ESXi host. The result can be more resource-intensive for the ESXi host, but it does not require the purchase of a hardware iSCSI adapter to obtain iSCSI connectivity.

With the hardware iSCSI adapter, an actual piece of hardware is used to perform both networking and iSCSI offloading (or in some adapters just the iSCSI offloading). Offloading means removing the CPU load required to process iSCSI off your ESXi host. With the hardware adapter, the iSCSI processing will be performed on the adapter. These adapters will almost always require additional up-front costs. The hardware iSCSI adapters are further grouped into two additional categories:

Dependent Hardware iSCSI Adapter   This is an adapter that performs the iSCSI processing but relies on the VMkernel for networking access. Again, as the name suggests, the dependent hardware iSCSI adapter depends on VMware software interfaces for networking, configuration, and management operations. An example of this type of adapter is the Broadcom 5709 NIC.

Independent Hardware iSCSI Adapter   This is an adapter that performs both the iSCSI processing and networking. This adapter is also known as an iSCSI HBA. This adapter implements its own interfaces for networking, configuration, and management and does not depend on VMware software to provide them. An example of this type of adapter is the QLogic QLA4052 adapter.

Dependent-hardware iSCSI adapters may sometimes be included in servers, but these adapters often require separate licensing. Always check with your server vendor to determine whether there are additional costs associated with the provided dependent hardware iSCSI adapters.

Now that we have covered the three types of iSCSI adapters, let's determine the use cases for them.

Determining Use Case for Hardware/Dependent Hardware/Software iSCSI Initiator

Part of designing an iSCSI environment for the virtual infrastructure involves knowing when to use which type of initiator. Determining the use case for the different iSCSI initiators is often about finding the right balance between performance and cost.

The software iSCSI adapter typically requires the least initial investment, because any standard NIC can be used. This is useful in situations where the environment is smaller, cost matters significantly, or the ESXi hosts have sufficient processing to spare.

The dependent hardware iSCSI adapter will typically require a larger initial investment than a standard NIC, because these adapters have the ability to offload the iSCSI processing from the ESXi host. This type of adapter is useful in situations where there may not be processing to spare on the ESXi hosts. These adapters are also useful in that they can be used as standard NICs as well, so they provide flexibility. Note that because the iSCSI traffic bypasses the regular network stack, performance reporting may be inaccurate for the NIC.

The independent hardware iSCSI adapter will typically require the largest initial investment, because the adapters have the ability to both offload the iSCSI processing from the ESXi host and provide networking. This type of adapter is useful in situations where the host cannot be expected to provide processing for iSCSI traffic. This adapter is the most efficient in terms of the resource consumption on the ESXi host.

Now that you have seen the use cases for the iSCSI initiators, I will cover configuring the dependent hardware iSCSI adapter.

Configuring and Editing Hardware/Dependent-Hardware Initiators

The dependent hardware iSCSI adapter relies on VMware software to provide both networking and iSCSI configuration and management interfaces. Although the iSCSI engine of the dependent hardware iSCSI adapter will appear on the list of storage adapters as a vmhba, additional configuration must be performed before it can be used. Exercise 5.4 covers the steps required to configure and edit a dependent hardware iSCSI adapter. This exercise requires your lab to include the following:

- An independent hardware adapter, like a Broadcom BCM5709, that is listed on the VMware HCL and that meets the required firmware and driver versions specified there

- An iSCSI target to connect to

If your lab lacks either of these requirements, you may want to simply follow along on this exercise.

EXERCISE 5.4

Configuring and Editing a Dependent Hardware iSCSI Adapter

1. Connect to a vCenter Server with the vSphere Web Client.

2. Select an ESXi host and then click the Manage tab. Select Storage on the toolbar and then select Storage Adapters in the left menu.

    If a dependent hardware iSCSI adapter is installed, it will appear in the list of Storage Adapters.

3. Select the vmhba<*Number*> adapter that is listed under the <*Vendor Name*> iSCSI Adapter. Review the information in the Properties tab at the bottom of the screen. Remember which storage adapter (vmhba<*Number*>) you select.

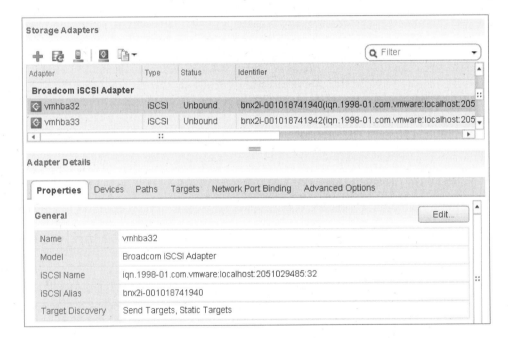

As you'll recall, to use the dependent hardware iSCSI adapter you must first configure networking for it. In the following section, you will identify the selected storage adapter's associated network component. You will then use this information to create a new VMkernel connection for iSCSI traffic.

4. Select the Network Port Binding tab at the bottom of the screen.

5. Click the Add icon (the green plus sign). A Bind vmhba<*number*> With VMkernel Adapter window will open.

6. Select the vmnic listed here and be sure to remember which vmnic number you selected. Review the information on the Status tab at the bottom of the screen.

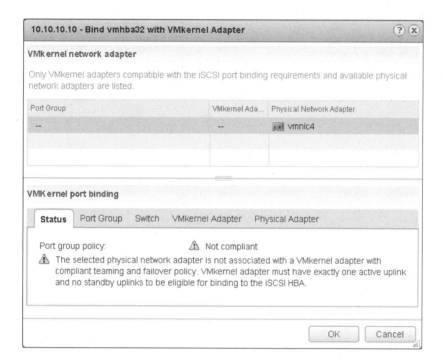

7. Click Cancel.

You have now identified which vmnic is associated with the dependent hardware iSCSI adapter. As shown in the Status tab in step 7, you will need to use this information to create a VMkernel connection that uses the appropriate vmnic for connectivity. Make sure you provide the VMkernel with an IP address on the same subnet as your iSCSI storage system. The steps to create a VMkernel connection with a vSwitch were covered in Exercise 4.4 in Chapter 4, if you need a reference.

8. Return to the same dependent hardware iSCSI storage adapter you chose in step 3 of this exercise and select it.

9. Select the Network Port Binding tab at the bottom of the screen.

10. Click the Add icon. A Bind vmhba<*number*> With VMkernel Adapter window will open.

11. Select the vmnic listed here and review the information on the Status tab at the bottom of the screen. The port group policy should now be listed as compliant, as shown here:

EXERCISE 5.4 *(continued)*

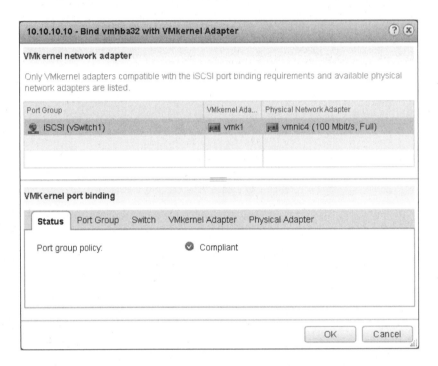

12. Click OK to bind the selected VMkernel adapter to the iSCSI adapter. An Add Virtual NIC To iSCSI Adapter task will begin.

13. Note that there is now a message indicating a storage rescan is recommended. Close this message to clear the warning, since there are no devices that a rescan operation will detect at this point.

14. Review the information on the Network Port Binding tab. It should be similar to that shown here:

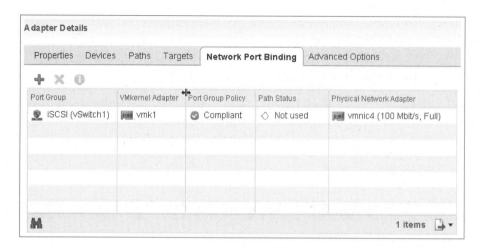

15. Repeat steps 1–14 of this exercise for each ESXi host that will have access to shared iSCSI storage.

   At this point, the dependent hardware iSCSI adapter is essentially configured. The only remaining step is to add and configure an iSCSI target. For this exercise, you will configure Dynamic Discovery with no authentication, since CHAP configuration will be covered in Exercise 5.9.

16. Navigate to the same dependent hardware iSCSI storage adapter(s) that you have been working with in this exercise.

17. Select the storage adapter and then click the Targets tab in the bottom window. Select Dynamic Discovery from the toolbar, and then click Add. An <vmhba#> - Add Send Target Server window will open.

18. Enter the IP address and port number for the iSCSI target, and click OK to add the iSCSI target. An Add Internet SCSI Send Targets task will begin.

19. There should be a message indicating that a storage rescan is recommended. Close this message and then click the Rescan The Host's Storage Adapter To Discover Newly Added Storage Devices icon. A Rescan HBA task will begin. When it completes, check for new storage devices (if applicable).

20. Repeat steps 16–19 of this exercise for each ESXi host that will have access to shared iSCSI storage.

You now know how to configure and edit a dependent hardware iSCSI adapter. In the next section, you will see how to enable and disable the software iSCSI initiator.

Enabling and Disabling a Software iSCSI Initiator

In the previous exercise, you learned how to configure and edit a dependent hardware iSCSI adapter. Some environments may not have dependent hardware iSCSI adapters or independent hardware iSCSI adapters and will instead leverage a standard NIC for iSCSI access. The software iSCSI initiator is used in this case. Exercise 5.5 will cover how to enable the software iSCSI initiator on an ESXi host.

EXERCISE 5.5

Enabling the Software iSCSI Initiator

1. Connect to a vCenter Server with the vSphere Web Client.

2. Select an ESXi host and then click the Manage tab. Select Storage on the toolbar and then select Storage Adapters in the left menu.

3. Review the current storage adapters and verify that the iSCSI Software Adapter is not listed.

   If the iSCSI Software Adapter is already listed here and you are comfortable with this process, skip to step 6. It is important to note that only a single software iSCSI adapter can be added to each ESXi host.

4. Click the Add New Storage Adapter icon, which is a green plus sign. Select Software iSCSI Adapter from the context menu.

   An Add Software iSCSI Adapter window will open, as shown here:

5. Click OK. A Change Software Internet SCSI Status task will begin.

6. When this task completes, select the vmhba<Number> adapter that is listed under iSCSI Software Adapter. Locate the Adapter Details section at the bottom of the screen.

7. In the Properties tab, ensure that the Adapter Status reports a value of Enabled, as shown here:

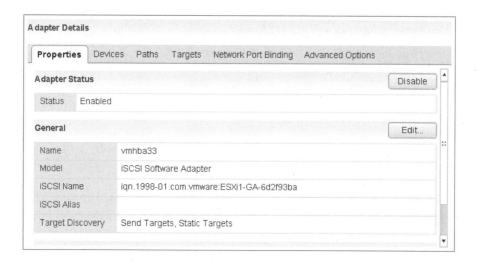

Take note of the other tabs in the iSCSI Initiator (vmhba<*Number*>) Properties window. You will be using each of these tabs later in this chapter, as you continue to configure iSCSI. At this point, the software iSCSI initiator is enabled and ready to be configured for use. The software iSCSI initiator can also be disabled and removed, if at some point in the future it is no longer required.

Exercise 5.6 covers how to disable and remove the software iSCSI initiator. It is important to note that disabling and removing the software iSCSI adapter will require an ESXi host reboot. If you do not want to reboot your host, you may simply want to read through this exercise.

EXERCISE 5.6

Disabling the Software iSCSI Initiator

1. Connect to a vCenter Server with the vSphere Web Client.

2. Select an ESXi host and then click the Manage tab. Select Storage on the toolbar and then select Storage Adapters in the left menu.

3. Select the vmhba<*Number*> adapter that is listed under the iSCSI Software Adapter. Review the information in the Properties tab at the bottom of the screen.

4. In the Properties tab, ensure that the Adapter Status reports a value of Enabled.

5. Click the Disable button located to the right of Adapter Status. A Disable iSCSI Adapter window will open, as shown here:

EXERCISE 5.6 *(continued)*

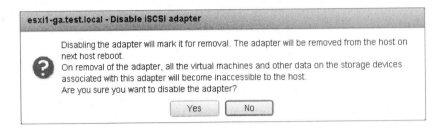

6. Click OK. A Reboot Required note will be added beside this ESXi host in the left pane of the vSphere Web Client. A warning icon will also be placed beside the iSCSI Software Adapter and a message will appear below the Storage Adapters section of the screen.

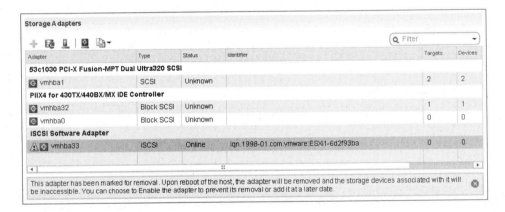

7. Place the ESXi host in maintenance mode and reboot it.

8. When the host is available again, verify that the Software iSCSI initiator is no longer listed in the Storage Adapters list. The absence of the iSCSI Software Adapter in the Storage Adapters list confirms that the software iSCSI initiator is disabled and removed.

I have now detailed how to enable and disable the software iSCSI software adapter. If you chose to disable the iSCSI software adapter in the previous exercise, you will need to enable it again before continuing. In the next section, get ready to turn your attention to configuring and editing additional software iSCSI initiator settings.

Configuring and Editing Software iSCSI Initiator Settings

Once the iSCSI software adapter has been enabled, the next step is to configure it. In Exercise 5.7, you will configure and edit additional iSCSI software adapter settings.

EXERCISE 5.7

Configuring and Editing the Software iSCSI Initiator Settings

1. Connect to a vCenter Server with the vSphere Web Client.

2. Select an ESXi host and then click the Manage tab. Select Storage on the toolbar and then select Storage Adapters in the left menu.

3. Select the vmhba<*Number*> adapter that is listed under the iSCSI Software Adapter. Review the information in the Properties tab at the bottom of the screen.

4. Note the two additional iSCSI properties, iSCSI Name and iSCSI Alias. The descriptor entered for the iSCSI Alias is simply a friendly name that can be safely modified. Click the Edit button for the General section. An Edit General window will open.

5. Enter a friendly name for the iSCSI Alias and click OK to save the changes. An Update Internet SCSI Alias task will begin. When this task completes, verify that the alias is listed in the General section of the Properties tab.

6. Click the Advanced Options tab and review the advanced options listed there. These options are not normally used and would be more likely used in conjunction with VMware support.

7. Click the Properties tab and scroll down to the bottom to view the Authentication settings. Click the Edit button to view the default CHAP settings. We will configure these settings in Exercise 5.9.

You have now configured and reviewed iSCSI software adapter settings. In the next section, we will continue to configure the iSCSI software adapter by configuring iSCSI port binding.

Configuring iSCSI Port Binding

iSCSI port binding is the process of associating an iSCSI software adapter with a VMkernel adapter used for networking. The software iSCSI adapter and the dependent hardware iSCSI adapter both require a VMkernel connection type to be established, before configuring iSCSI port binding. You performed port binding for the dependent hardware iSCSI adapter in Exercise 5.4 and will now perform port binding for the software iSCSI adapter in Exercise 5.8. Note that this exercise requires a pre-existing VMkernel that is on the same network segment as your iSCSI storage. Exercise 4.4 in Chapter 4 covers the steps required to configure VMkernel networking.

EXERCISE 5.8

Configuring iSCSI Port Binding on the Software iSCSI Initiator

1. Connect to a vCenter Server with the vSphere Web Client.

2. Select an ESXi host and then click the Manage tab. Select Storage on the toolbar and then select Storage Adapters in the left menu.

3. Select the iSCSI Software Adapter, and then select the Network Port Binding tab at the bottom of the screen.

4. Click the Add icon, which is the green plus sign. A Bind vmhba<*number*> With VMkernel Adapter window will open.

5. Select the virtual switch created prior to the start of this exercise by clicking or selecting it.

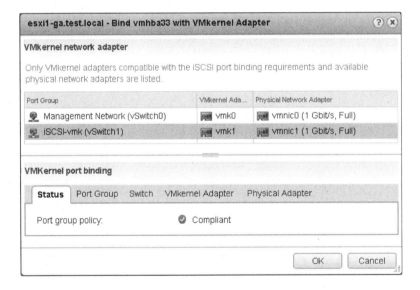

6. Click OK to bind the selected VMkernel adapter with the iSCSI adapter. An Add Virtual NIC To iSCSI Adapter task will begin.

7. Note that there is now a message indicating a storage rescan is recommended. Close this message to clear the warning, since there are no devices that a rescan operation will detect at this point.

8. Review the information in the Network Port Binding tab. It should appear similar to the following:

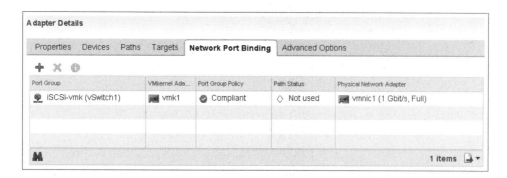

9. Complete this exercise for each ESXi host that will have access to shared iSCSI storage.

> The NIC that is used in port binding must be on the same subnet as the iSCSI target, or the ESXi host will not be able to establish sessions to it.

I have now covered nearly all of the configuration steps for the different iSCSI adapters, but there is still one final configuration item remaining. In the following section, you'll see how to enable, configure, and disable iSCSI CHAP options for iSCSI traffic.

Enabling, Configuring, and Disabling iSCSI CHAP

Challenge Handshake Authentication Protocol (CHAP) is used to provide security in iSCSI environments. CHAP uses a three-way handshake algorithm that is based on a CHAP secret that both the initiator and the target are aware of. Instead of sending the secret over the wire, this protocol uses a hash of the secret. CHAP is supported at the adapter level in ESXi. For greater security, per-target CHAP authentication is also supported for the dependent hardware iSCSI adapter and the software iSCSI adapter.

The two CHAP authentication methods supported in ESXi 5.5 are described here:

Unidirectional CHAP The target (storage system) authenticates the iSCSI adapter (initiator); however the initiator does not authenticate the target.

Bidirectional CHAP The target (storage system) authenticates the iSCSI adapter (initiator), and the initiator also authenticates the target. Mutual CHAP is supported for dependent hardware iSCSI adapters and software iSCSI adapters only.

A security level is specified for CHAP during iSCSI configuration. Table 5.6 shows the CHAP security levels used in vSphere 5.5.

TABLE 5.6   CHAP security levels

CHAP security level	Description	Supported Adapters
None	The host does not use CHAP authentication. Select this option to disable authentication if it is currently enabled.	Software Dependent hardware Independent hardware
Use unidirectional CHAP if required by target	The host prefers a non-CHAP connection but can use a CHAP connection if required by the target.	Software Dependent hardware
Use unidirectional CHAP unless prohibited by target	The host prefers CHAP but can use non-CHAP connections if the target does not support CHAP.	Software Dependent hardware Independent hardware
Use unidirectional CHAP	The host requires successful CHAP authentication. The connection fails if CHAP negotiation fails.	Software Dependent hardware Independent hardware
Use bidirectional CHAP	The host and the target support bidirectional CHAP.	Software Dependent hardware

 Each storage array's implementation of CHAP will be specific. Always consult the array documentation for the supported CHAP configurations before you specify the CHAP security level in ESXi.

Exercise 5.9 covers how to enable, configure, and disable iSCSI CHAP. In the interest of using an adapter that you most likely have access to, this exercise will focus on configuring CHAP for the iSCSI software adapter.

EXERCISE 5.9

Enabling, Configuring, and Disabling iSCSI CHAP on the Software iSCSI Adapter

1. Connect to a vCenter Server with the vSphere Web Client.

2. Select an ESXi host and then click the Manage tab. Select Storage on the toolbar and then select Storage Adapters in the left menu.

3. Select the vmhba<*Number*> adapter that is listed under the iSCSI Software Adapter. Click the Properties tab at the bottom of the screen. Scroll down to the Authentication section and click the Edit button.

4. An Edit Authentication window will open.

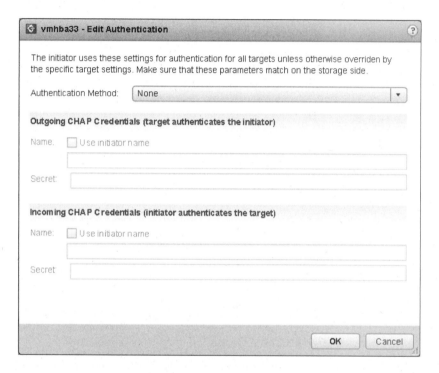

Notice that the default Authentication Method is None. As shown in Table 5.6, this setting means that CHAP is currently disabled. In the following steps, you will configure the iSCSI software adapter to use unidirectional CHAP.

5. In the Edit Authentication window, use the Authentication Method drop-down menu to select the Use Unidirectional CHAP option. Notice how the Outgoing CHAP Credentials fields become active.

6. Enter a username in the Name field. Enter a secret in the Secret field. The final configuration should look similar to this:

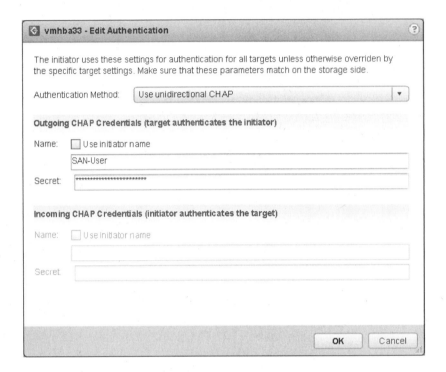

7. Click OK. An Update Internet SCSI Authentication Properties task will start.

8. When this task completes, you will be prompted to rescan the host bus adapter. Close this warning message.

   At this point, CHAP has been enabled and the iSCSI software adapter has been configured to use unidirectional CHAP. The remaining steps of the exercise will focus on returning CHAP to its default state of None, or disabled. If you have iSCSI storage and want to connect to it, you can skip to step 13 of this exercise to do so. Also note that Exercise 5.10 will require a storage device to be available to an ESXi host.

9. On the iSCSI software adapter's Properties tab, scroll down to the Authentication section and click the Edit button.

10. When the Edit Authentication window opens, use the Authentication Method drop-down menu to select the None option. Notice how the Outgoing CHAP Credentials fields now become inactive.

11. Click OK in the Edit Authentication window. An Update Internet SCSI Authentication Properties task will start.

12. When this task completes, you will be prompted to rescan the storage adapter. Close this warning message.

13. On the iSCSI software adapter's Targets tab, click Dynamic Discovery on the toolbar.

14. Click the Add button. An Add Send Target Server window will open.

15. Enter the FQDN or IP address of the iSCSI server. Modify the port value only if it has been changed from the default of 3260.

16. Under the Authentication Settings section, ensure that the Inherit Settings From Parent check box is selected. This will allow the connection to use the CHAP credentials previously configured on the adapter level. The final configuration should look like this:

17. Click OK. An Add Internet SCSI Send Targets task will begin. An Update Internet SCSI Authentication Properties task will begin. When these tasks complete, you will be prompted to rescan the storage adapter. Close this warning message.

18. Ensure that the iSCSI software adapter is selected on the Storage Adapters panel, and then click the Rescan The Host's Storage Adapter To Discover Newly Added Storage Devices icon. A Rescan HBA task will begin. When this task completes, verify that the newly added target is listed as an iSCSI Server on the Targets tab for the iSCSI software adapter.

19. Click the Paths tab. Review the information about the iSCSI server.

20. Click the Devices tab. Review the information about the storage devices available on the iSCSI server.

21. Repeat steps 13–20 on each additional ESXi host that requires access to this same shared storage.

Although this exercise focused on the software iSCSI adapter, the process for configuring CHAP is the same for all of the iSCSI adapters.

You have now seen how to configure CHAP for your iSCSI connections. In the following section, we will discuss connecting to an array with iSCSI to install and boot ESXi.

Configuring FC/iSCSI LUNs as ESXi Boot Devices

The Boot From SAN option allows your ESXi host to boot from a LUN located on your SAN storage, as opposed to local disk in the server. This is useful in certain hardware configurations, like when using blades. Diskless server configurations are often desired because they consume less power, have fewer moving parts, are more portable, and offer more flexibility than local disk can typically provide. ESXi supports booting from an iSCSI SAN LUN with either an iSCSI HBA or a NIC with specialized firmware, and booting from an FC SAN with a supported FC HBA.

 ESXi 5.1 and newer can also be configured to boot from software FCoE. In order for this to work, the adapter needs to support partial FCoE offload (software FCoE), and has to contain either an FCoE Boot Firmware Table (FBFT) or an FCoE Boot Parameter Table (FBPT).

The first step in configuring Boot From SAN is to ensure that the HBA or network adapter you intend to use is listed on the VMware HCL. It is important to know that when picking a network card for use with iSCSI boot that the card must support iBFT (*iSCSI Boot Firmware Table*). iBFT is used to communicate information about the iSCSI boot device to an OS. iBFT support in the HCL is typically listed as a footnote in the Network settings listed for the card. If in doubt, it may also be a good idea to consult with your adapter vendor.

Once a supported adapter is available, the next step is to configure the storage system. This includes the following tasks:

- Obtain and implement specific boot from SAN vendor best practices for your storage system.
- For iSCSI, use static IP addresses and avoid routing the storage traffic if possible. Verify network connectivity.
- For FC, ensure that zoning and masking are completed.
- Ensure that a unique LUN is presented to each host as a boot LUN. This boot LUN should not be accessible to any other system on the SAN fabric or IP storage network, and this LUN should not be used as a VMFS partition.
- Configure security as appropriate on the storage system.

- Configure a diagnostic partition for the ESXI host, if using either an iSCSI or FC HBA. iBFT cannot use a diagnostic partition, so if you are using the dependent hardware adapter or the iSCSI software adapter you will not be able to complete this step.

- Ensure that the first path to the storage is available. Multipathing at first boot is not supported.

If you are using a dependent hardware adapter or the iSCSI software adapter, the next step is to configure the NIC in the system BIOS to boot from SAN. Figure 5.1 shows the BIOS setup for the integrated NICs in a Dell rackmount server.

FIGURE 5.1   iSCSI boot configuration in BIOS

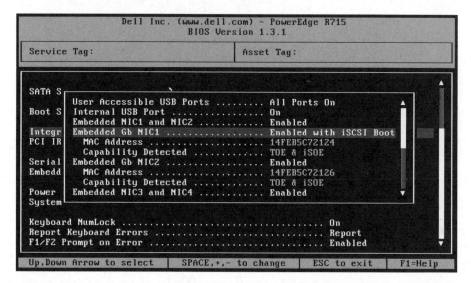

While in the server's BIOS settings, also ensure that the NIC with iSCSI Boot enabled is located before the optical media drive in the system boot order. You want the connection to the storage to be established prior to running setup from optical media, assuming that you are doing that. Once these BIOS changes have been implemented, the next step is to configure the network card itself from its configuration or setup utility. Figure 5.2 shows the configuration menu for a Broadcom NIC.

If you are using either the iSCSI or FC HBA to boot from SAN, specific configuration of these devices will also be required. Consult your system or vendor documentation, as the configuration will vary.

FIGURE 5.2 NIC configuration menu

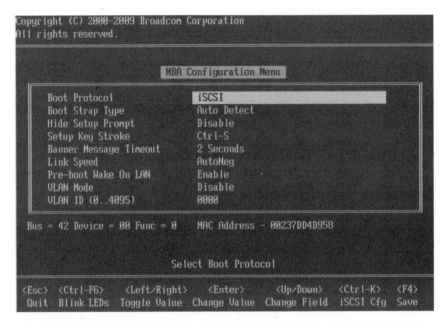

Once the storage system and server have both been configured, the final step is to install ESXi on the boot LUN. This install would be performed in much the same way as an install to local disk, but the SAN disk would be selected for the installation disk.

Now that we have covered storage systems and connectivity, let's conclude the first section of this chapter with a discussion of thin provisioning.

Comparing and Contrasting Array Thin Provisioning and Virtual Disk Thin Provisioning

Thin provisioning is the process of provisioning storage but not actually using all of the provisioned space. This can take place on SAN and NAS devices at the storage level or at the virtual disk level. Both of these approaches offer similar benefits, and both will require additional monitoring to be used with success.

With virtual disk thin provisioning in ESXi, a virtual disk is provisioned upon creation. The size is chosen as one of the options, and then the VMDK is created with this provisioned size. With this approach, the VMDK starts small and grows as necessary. For example, a virtual machine is created with a single 50GB thin-provisioned hard disk. An operating system and several applications are then installed on this VM. The provisioned storage value will report 50GB, and the Used Storage value might report 20GB. At this point, thin provisioning is saving 30GB of space on the storage system.

Thin-provisioned virtual disks are not supported with VMware FT. When turning on FT for a VM with thin-provisioned disks, the disks will be converted to the eager-zeroed virtual disk format.

With array thin provisioning, the concept is basically the same. Space allocated as devices (volumes or LUNs) is created on the storage device, but the consumption of this space is only as required. Storage array thin provisioning requires ESXi 5 and a storage device with a firmware version that supports T10-based Storage APIs: Array Integration (Thin Provisioning).

Both of these approaches allow for the overprovisioning of storage resources. This can be a powerful feature and can provide cost savings, but it must be used with caution. If a thin-provisioned storage device runs out of space, the results are never good. Because of this, monitoring is essential with both forms of thin provisioning.

Determining Use Case for and Configuring Array Thin Provisioning

Thin provisioning allows for the overprovisioning of storage and allows for greater flexibility in predicting growth. The type of disks used in your virtual machines can often help determine the use case for array thin provisioning. There are three disk types for the virtual machines:

Thin Provisioned   These disks grow as required.

Thick Provision Lazy Zeroed   These disks have all space allocated when created, but the space on the disk is not zeroed.

Thick Provision Eager Zeroed   These disks have all space allocated when created, and the space is also zeroed out upon creation.

I will discuss these disk types in more detail in Chapter 6, "Creating and Deploying Virtual Machines and vApps," but it is also useful to know some of this information now as it pertains to array thin provisioning.

If your virtual machines use mostly thin-provisioned and flat-disk formats, then array thin provisioning can save consumed space on the SAN. If you use thick-provisioned disks, thin provisioning on the SAN will be limited. Keep in mind that VMware FT and certain clustering solutions will also require thick-provisioned disks, so array thin provisioning is often not a good fit with these solutions.

Raw device mappings are often a great use case for array thin provisioning, because the file systems on these volumes will have room for growth factored into their size upon creation and will also require free space for the file system.

Many NAS servers typically use a default allocation policy of thin, and if you are using one of these units, then thin provisioning is a guaranteed use case. Another interesting new feature introduced in vSphere 5 is NFS reserve space, which allows thick disks on the NAS server. Check with your NAS vendor to see whether your storage array supports thick disks or whether thin provisioning is the only option.

The process for configuring array thin provisioning will differ from vendor to vendor and system to system, so always consult the documentation provided by your storage device vendor for the configuration and best practices.

 The configuration of thin provisioning on storage devices is not supported in ESXi. You will have to use the vendor's management tools for this.

Now let's examine creating and configuring VMFS and NFS datastores.

Creating and Configuring VMFS and NFS Datastores

As a VMware Certified Professional, you will be expected to know how to add and use VMFS and NFS datastores. In this section, I will cover how to create and configure them. You will also explore many of the operational tasks involved with both VMFS and NFS datastores.

Identifying VMFS-5 Capabilities

Virtual Machine File System (VMFS) was created by VMware as a purpose-built and optimized clustered file system that provides storage virtualization. VMFS provides many capabilities, each of which is described here:

Clustered File System   VMFS is a clustered file system that allows concurrent access from multiple hosts.

Encapsulation   Virtual machines that are housed on VMFS datastores have all of their files encapsulated in directories on VMFS.

Simplified Administration   Typically, large VMFS datastores are created on storage devices in ESXi. This simplifies interactions between virtualization administrators and storage administrators, because the virtual administrator has a pool of storage that can be used for virtual machines.

Dynamic Growth   VMFS can be expanded or extended, allowing flexibility and scalability. This process can happen while VMs are running on the datastore. VMDK files can also be expanded on VMFS volumes while the virtual machines they are assigned to are running.

Advanced Feature Enablement When combined with shared storage from a SAN, VMFS also allows advanced vSphere features such as vMotion, DRS, HA, and FT to be used.

Thin Provisioning VMFS supports thin-provisioned VMDK files, allowing for overallocated VMFS datastores.

Backup and Recoverability VMFS allows proxied backups of virtual machines while the VM is in use.

RDMs VMFS volumes provide support for RDM devices.

VMFS-5 is the version of VMFS included with vSphere 5. This version includes the following enhancements:

Unified 1MB File Block Size For newly created VMFS-5 volumes, the previous 1MB, 2MB, 4MB, or 8MB file block sizes have been replaced with a single block size of 1MB. Using this 1MB block size, VMFS-5 can support VMDK files of 2TB minus 512 bytes in vSphere 5.0 and 5.1. In vSphere 5.5, VMFS-5 can support VMDK files of 62TB. Note that the version of VMFS-5 in use does not determine these limits but rather the version of the ESXi host.

Large Single Extent Volumes Storage devices greater than 2TB are now supported for use as VMFS datastores. The new limit in VMFS-5 is 64TB.

Large Physical RDMs RDMs in physical compatibility mode now have a maximum size of 64TB in all versions of vSphere 5. RDMs in virtual compatibility mode have a maximum size of 2TB minus 512 bytes in ESXi 5.0 and 5.1. For ESXi 5.5 hosts, the maximum size for a RDM in virtual compatibility mode is 62TB.

Online In-Place Upgrades VMFS-3 datastores can be upgraded to VMFS-5 without service interruption to hosts or virtual machines.

Smaller Sub-blocks These blocks are sized at 8KB, as compared to 64KB in previous versions. This means files sized between 1KB and 8KB will consume only 8KB, rather than 64KB.

Small File Support Used for files less than or equal to 1KB. With these small files, the file descriptor location will be stored in the VMFS metadata rather than file blocks. If these files ever grow beyond 1KB, then the files will start using 8KB blocks. The idea with both smaller sub-blocks and small file support is to reduce the amount of disk space consumed in the VMFS datastore by small files.

Large File Numbers VMFS-5 introduces support for more than 100,000 files on the VMFS datastore.

ATS Enhancement Hardware assisted locking, also known as atomic test & set (ATS), is now used for file locking on storage devices that support hardware acceleration.

Although VMFS-5 supports 64TB volumes, always consult your storage vendor to ensure that sizes this large are supported on the storage device.

Now that I have covered the capabilities of VMFS and the specifics of VMFS-5, I will cover creating and performing operations on a VMFS datastore.

Creating, Renaming, Unmounting, and Deleting a VMFS Datastore

If you installed ESXi on disk, a default VMFS volume was likely created as part of the install. The local VMFS volume is also probably small and is not shared storage. One of the capabilities of VMFS is to be used with shared storage to provide the framework for the advanced features of vSphere. Exercise 5.10 details creating and renaming a VMFS datastore. While this exercise can be performed with any available storage device, the examples used will show an iSCSI disk. To complete this exercise, you should have an available LUN presented to your ESXi host.

EXERCISE 5.10

Creating and Renaming a VMFS Datastore

1. Connect to a vCenter Server with the vSphere Web Client.

2. Select an ESXi host in the left pane and right-click it. Choose the New Datastore option from the context menu. The New Datastore wizard will open.

3. Click Next on the Location screen to begin.

4. Select VMFS for the datastore type and click Next.

5. Provide a descriptive name for the datastore name, and select the appropriate device from the list by highlighting it, as shown here:

Note the Filter function available on this screen, and remember that columns can be sorted and customized here.

6. Once the appropriate device has been selected, click Next.

7. Choose the VMFS version to be used. If this is a standalone host or an all–ESXi 5 host environment, choose the VMFS-5 option. If you have legacy (pre–ESXi 5) hosts, then choose the VMFS-3 option. Once the selection has been made, click Next.

8. Review the current partition layout. It is generally a good idea to verify that the Capacity and Free Space values are equal in size. In the Datastore Details section, accept the defaults. This will create a single partition of the maximum size. Click Next.

9. Review the information on the Ready To Complete screen and click Finish to create the VMFS datastore.

10. A Create VMFS Datastore task will begin. A Rescan VMFS task will also run on any other ESXi hosts that are in the same cluster. When these tasks complete, click the Related Objects tab for the ESXi host. Select Datastores from the toolbar, and then verify that the new datastore appears in the list of datastores shown here.

You have now created a VMFS datastore, and it is ready to be used by all ESXi hosts in the cluster. In the next part of this exercise, you will rename the VMFS datastore. Renaming a datastore is nondisruptive and can be completed while VMs that are located on the datastore are powered on.

11. Select the datastore just created by clicking it. Right-click on the datastore and select Rename from the context menu.

12. A Datastore - Rename window will open. Enter the new name for the datastore and click OK. A Rename Datastore task will begin.

13. When this task completes, verify that the new datastore name is reflected in the Related Objects tab.

You have now created and renamed a VMFS datastore. If this VMFS datastore was accessible to multiple ESXi hosts being managed by vCenter, the new name would be reflected on each of these hosts.

 When creating VMFS datastores, it is important to maintain a one-to-one relationship between each VMFS datastore and LUN.

Additional operations that can be performed on VMFS datastores include unmounting and deleting them. Unmounting a datastore will not destroy the datastore but simply make it inaccessible to the ESXi host(s). If other ESXi hosts have this datastore mounted, they may continue to access the datastore as usual. The unmount operation has several prerequisites:

- Virtual machines and templates may not reside on the datastore.

- *ISOs* located on the datastore must be removed from virtual machines.

- Mapping files for RDMs on the datastore must be removed.

- The datastore cannot be part of a *datastore cluster.*

- The datastore must not be managed by Storage DRS.

- Storage I/O Control must be disabled for the datastore.

- The datastore must not be used for vSphere HA heartbeat.

- No operations, including those from scripts or third-party utilities, that would result in I/O to the datastore can be used while the unmount operation is in progress.

 Snapshots can cause issues when unmounting datastores. If you have covered all of the prerequisites previously listed and cannot unmount the datastore, check to see if a snapshot exists on any virtual machine that may have been residing on the affected datastore. Datastores used as ISO repositories are more likely to encounter this problem.

VMFS datastores can be unmounted one at a time, or you can choose the hosts that the VMFS datastore should be unmounted from. Exercise 5.11 will detail the steps for both of these approaches.

EXERCISE 5.11

Unmounting a VMFS Datastore

1. Connect to a vCenter Server with the vSphere Web Client.

2. Select an ESXi host and then click the Related Objects tab. Select Datastores from the toolbar.

3. Select the VMFS datastore created in Exercise 5.10 by clicking it.

4. Click the Actions menu and choose the All vCenter Actions ➢ Unmount Datastore option from the context menu.

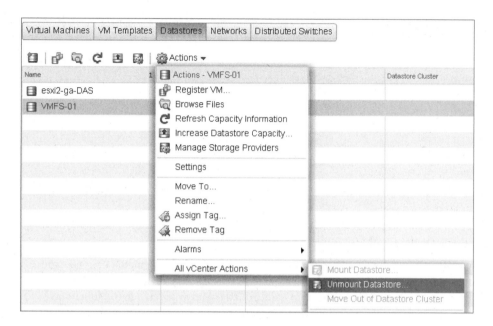

5. An Unmount Datastore window will open. Select the hosts that you want to unmount this datastore from by selecting the check box next to the server name.

6. Click OK. An Unmount VMFS task will begin. When the task completes, verify that the datastore is now listed as both Unmounted and Inaccessible.

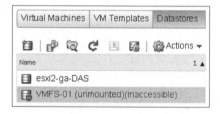

If this VMFS datastore was being shared by other ESXi hosts that you didn't select in step 5, check the status of the VMFS datastore that was just unmounted on one of these other hosts now. You will find that the VMFS datastore is still mounted and accessible. It is also worth noting that this VMFS datastore can easily be mounted again simply by right-clicking the datastore and choosing Mount.

7. If the VMFS datastore is to be permanently removed, the storage device must also be detached. Select the unmounted datastore and make a note of the SCSI INQUIRY identifier listed in the Device column.

EXERCISE 5.11 *(continued)*

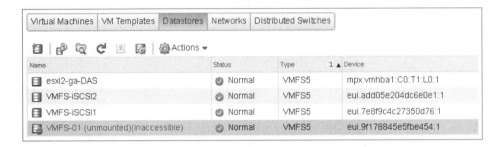

8. Click the Manage tab for the ESXi host. Select Storage on the toolbar, and then select Storage Devices in the left menu.

9. In the Name column, locate the SCSI INQUIRY identifier that matches the one used for the datastore in the previous steps. Select this storage device. Click the Detaches The Selected Device From The Host icon, which is shown circled in the following graphic, along with the SCSI INQUIRY identifier:

10. A Detach Device window will open. Review this information and then click Yes. A Detach SCSI LUN task will begin. When this task completes, verify that the Operational State column for this storage device reports a value of Detached.

   Once the storage device is reporting Detached on all ESXi hosts that had access, the LUN can be unpresented on the storage system. Even after unmounting the datastore, detaching the storage device, and unpresenting the LUN, it may still be necessary to manually remove SCSI INQUIRY identifiers from each ESXi host's configuration.

11. To obtain the list of SCSI INQUIRY identifiers for permanently detached devices, obtain access to the ESXi Shell and run the following command:

```
esxcli storage core device detached list
```

The output should appear similar to what is shown here:

```
~ # esxcli storage core device detached list
Device UID           State
--------------------  -----
eui.9f178845e5fbe454  off
~ #
```

12. To remove the permanently detached device, run the following command:

    `esxcli storage core device detached remove -d` *NAA_ID*

    where *NAA_ID* is the actual SCSI INQUIRY identifier.

13. Enter the following command to verify that the detached device has been removed:

    `esxcli storage core device detached list`

    No output means the device has been removed.

14. As a final step, a rescan of the storage adapter should be performed on all ESXi hosts that had visibility to the LUN. The storage device will then be automatically removed from the Storage Adapters list.

You have now seen how to create, rename, unmount, and detach VMFS datastores. The remaining operation that needs to be covered is how to delete VMFS datastores. This is a useful operation when the storage device needs to be reused and not completely removed from the system. For example, a VMFS-3 volume with an 8MB block size could be deleted and then added again as a VMFS-5 volume.

 WARNING Deleting a VMFS datastore will destroy the datastore and its contents, and the VMFS datastore will be removed from any host that has access to it.

To delete a VMFS datastore, all virtual machines should first be removed, and other ESXi hosts should no longer be accessing the VMFS datastore. Exercise 5.12 will cover the steps to delete a VMFS datastore. Proceed with caution, and if a test VMFS datastore isn't available, it may be best to just read through this exercise.

EXERCISE 5.12

Deleting a VMFS Datastore

1. Connect to a vCenter Server with the vSphere Web Client.

2. Select an ESXi host and then click the Related Objects tab. Select Datastores from the toolbar.

EXERCISE 5.12 *(continued)*

3. Select the VMFS datastore to be deleted, and right-click on it. Choose All vCenter Actions ➢ Delete Datastore from the context menu.

A Confirm Device Removal prompt will appear, as shown here.

Confirm Delete Datastore

Delete the selected datastore(s)?
This operation will permanently delete all the files associated with the virtual machines on the datastore.

Yes   No

4. Review this information and click Yes to continue.

5. A Remove Datastore Task will start, and it will be immediately followed by a Rescan VMFS task. When these tasks complete, verify that the VMFS datastore is no longer listed on the Related Objects tab.

I have now covered the VMFS datastore operations of create, rename, unmount, detach, and delete. Next, I will cover how to identify VMFS datastore properties.

Identifying VMFS Datastore Properties

There are several places where VMFS datastore properties can be obtained in the vSphere Web Client. On the Related Objects tab, after you choose Datastores from the toolbar the Datastores view contains several VMFS properties. Like many of the views in vCenter Server, the visible columns can be customized. Figure 5.3 shows the VMFS datastore properties available in the Datastores view.

FIGURE 5.3 VMFS datastore properties in the Datastores view

| Getting Started | Summary | Monitor | Manage | **Related Objects** |

| Virtual Machines | VM Templates | Datastores | Networks | Distributed Switches |

Name	1 ▲	Status	Type	Device	Drive Type	Capacity	Free
esxi2-ga-DAS		✓ Normal	VMFS5	mpx.vmhba1:C0:T1:L0:1	Non SSD	9.75 GB	8.75 GB
VMFS-iSCSI1		✓ Normal	VMFS5	eui.7e8f9c4c27350d76:1	Non SSD	49.75 GB	41.01 GB
VMFS-iSCSI2		✓ Normal	VMFS5	eui.add05e204dc6e0e1:1	Non SSD	49.75 GB	47 GB

By double-clicking a VMFS datastore in Datastores view, you can switch to the datastore. Select the Manage tab, and then select Settings from the toolbar. Some of the additional information available in the General menu item includes free space on the VMFS datastore, the VMFS version, and the block size used. Figure 5.4 shows all of the information available when the General menu item is selected.

FIGURE 5.4   VMFS datastore properties

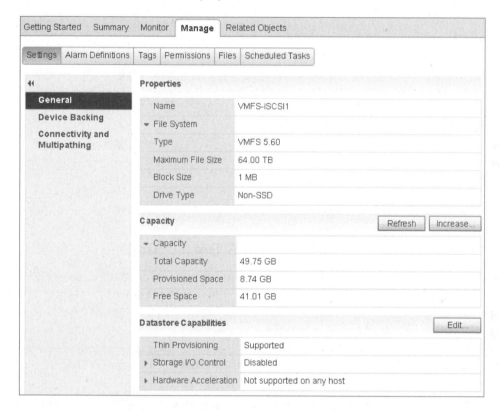

The Summary tab can also be used to obtain information about the datastore. This includes VMFS version information, the number of ESXi hosts connected, capacity information, and more. Figure 5.5 shows the Summary tab for a VMFS datastore.

 Various VMFS datastore properties are obtained in different locations, so make sure you know your way around the vSphere Web Client.

One of the options in the VMFS datastore properties shown in Figure 5.4 was the ability to increase the VMFS datastore size. In the next section, I will discuss this topic.

FIGURE 5.5 VMFS datastore Summary tab

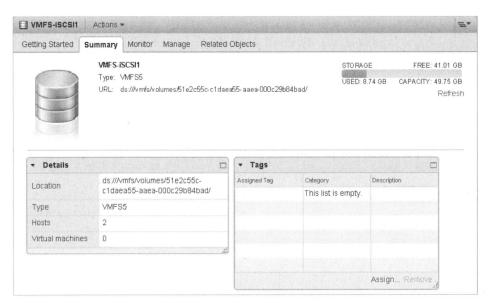

Extending and Expanding VMFS Datastores

Expanding VMFS datastores is sometimes necessary. For example, a VMFS datastore may not be sized adequately or a VM may have experienced unexpected growth. To handle these situations, VMFS datastores can be increased dynamically. There are two methods used to increase the size of VMFS datastores:

Add Extent   Also known as *extending* the VMFS datastore, this is where another storage device is coupled with the original storage device to extend a VMFS datastore that spans the devices.

Grow Extent   Also known as *expanding* the VMFS datastore, this is where the storage device backing the VMFS datastore is increased in size, and the VMFS datastore is then expanded to fill this space. This method is very similar to the functionality often used in VMware and Windows environments to increase a VMDK and then expand the NTFS volume to use this new space.

Exercise 5.13 shows how to grow an extent in a VMFS datastore. A prerequisite for this exercise is that the device backing the VMFS datastore must have already been expanded. This expansion operation will need to be performed on your storage system through its appropriate management function, and the ESXi hosts will need to have their appropriate storage adapter(s) rescanned to pick up this change.

EXERCISE 5.13

Growing an Extent in a VMFS Datastore

1. Connect to a vCenter Server with the vSphere Web Client.

2. Select a VMFS datastore and then click the Manage tab. Click Settings on the toolbar, and then select General.

3. Click the Increase button located to the right of Capacity. An Increase Datastore Capacity window will open.

4. Select the datastore that will be expanded. This datastore should be easily identifiable, as the Expandable column should report a value of Yes. This is shown in the following graphic, where a 500GB LUN has been increased to 550GB:

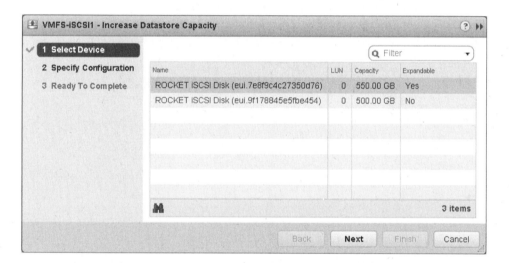

5. Click Next to continue. Review the partition layout and then use the Partition Configuration drop-down menu to change the value to 'Use Free Space 50.00 GB' To Expand The Datastore, replacing the value of 50.00GB as appropriate. Click Next to continue.

6. Review the information on the Ready To Complete screen and click the Finish button to grow the VMFS datastore.

7. A Compute Disk Partition Information For Resize task will begin, and it will be immediately followed by an Expand VMFS Datastore task and a Rescan VMFS task.

   When these tasks complete, verify on the Manage tab that the Total Capacity value is updated and correct.

Now that I have covered growing or expanding a VMFS datastore, Exercise 5.14 will cover adding a new extent to, or extending, a VMFS datastore. A prerequisite for this exercise will be an additional device that can be used as an extent. This will require additional configuration on your storage system and ESXi host storage adapter rescans.

EXERCISE 5.14

Adding an Extent in a VMFS Datastore

1. Connect to a vCenter Server with the vSphere Web Client.

2. Select a VMFS datastore and then click the Manage tab. Click Settings on the toolbar, and then select General.

3. Click the Increase button located to the right of Capacity. An Increase Datastore Capacity window will open.

4. Select the datastore that will be expanded. Since this datastore is going to have an extent added, the extent should be easily identifiable by its size. This is shown in the following graphic, where a 50GB LUN has been created to use as an extent:

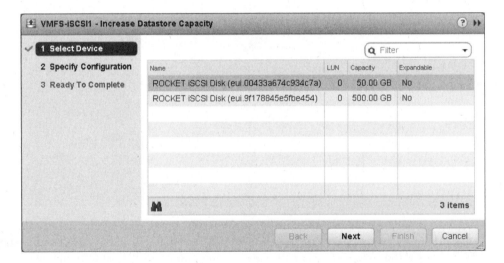

5. Click Next to continue. Review the Partition Layout and then use the Partition Configuration drop-down menu to change the value to Use All Available Partitions. Click Next to continue.

6. Review the information presented on the Ready To Complete screen and click the Finish button to add the extent to the VMFS datastore.

7. An Extend Datastore task will begin. When it completes, a Rescan VMFS task will begin for any ESXi hosts in the same cluster.

   When these tasks complete, verify on the Manage tab that the Total Capacity value is updated and correct.

I have now covered how to expand and extend VMFS datastores. In the next section, I will cover how to upgrade a VMFS-3 datastore to VMFS-5.

Upgrading a VMFS-3 Datastore to VMFS-5

To leverage the new features of VMFS-5, existing VMFS-3 datastores can be upgraded to VMFS-5. Upgraded VMFS-3 datastores will retain their given block sizes, and these datastores can be upgraded while VMs are running on them. In the VMFS-3 to VMFS-5 upgrade process, the ESXi file-locking mechanism will ensure that no processes are accessing the VMFS datastore. The ESXi 5 host will preserve all files on the VMFS datastore during the upgrade. Here are a few other points to remember:

- It is recommended that backups of all virtual machines on the VMFS datastore be taken prior to the upgrade.

- It is also important to know that the VMFS-3 to VMFS-5 upgrade is a one-way process. There is no rollback option.

- All hosts accessing the VMFS-3 datastore being upgraded must be ESXi 5 or newer. Any host connected to this VMFS-3 datastore that doesn't support VMFS-5 will lose connectivity to the datastore after the upgrade to VMFS-5 completes.

- All virtual machine snapshots on the VMFS-3 datastore should be committed or discarded prior to the VMFS-5 upgrade.

- Remove any partitions that ESXi does not recognize from the storage device, or the upgrade will fail.

Once you have ensured that the VMFS-3 datastore is ready to be upgraded to VMFS-5, you can proceed with the upgrade. Exercise 5.15 will cover upgrading a VMFS-3 datastore to the VMFS-5 format. In this exercise, you will first create a VMFS-3 datastore and then upgrade it to VMFS-5.

EXERCISE 5.15

Upgrading a VMFS-3 Datastore to VMFS-5

1. Connect to a vCenter Server with the vSphere Web Client.

2. Select a VMFS-3 datastore and then click the Manage tab. Click Settings on the toolbar, and then select General.

3. Click the Upgrade To VMFS-5 button located to the right of Properties. An Upgrade To VMFS-5 window will open.

4. Select the VMFS-3 check box.

EXERCISE 5.15 *(continued)*

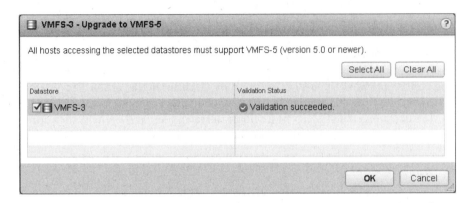

5. Click OK. An Upgrade VMFS task will begin. A Rescan VMFS task will also be started for any other ESXi hosts in the same cluster. When these tasks complete, verify that the datastore is now using VMFS-5 in the File System section of the Properties field.

 ESXi 5 offers complete read-write support for both VMFS-3 and VMFS-5 datastores, but VMFS-2 is not supported in ESXi 5. VMFS-2 datastores must first be upgraded to VMFS-3 in order to upgrade them to VMFS-5.

Now that I have covered how to upgrade a VMFS-3 datastore to VMFS-5, there are a few things worth mentioning for these datastores:

- Upgraded VMFS-5 datastores continue to use the previous block size of the VMFS-3 datastore.

- Upgraded VMFS-5 datastores can use the 1KB small-files feature.

- Upgraded VMFS-5 datastores can be grown to 64TB, exactly like newly created VMFS-5 datastores.

- Upgraded VMFS-5 datastores have all of the *VAAI* ATS improvements, exactly like newly created VMFS-5 datastores.

- Upgraded VMFS-5 datastores will continue to use 64KB sub-blocks and not the new 8K sub-blocks.

- Upgraded VMFS-5 datastores will continue to have a file limit of 30,720 files. Newly created VMFS-5 datastores can contain more than 100,000 files.

- Upgraded VMFS-5 datastores will continue to use the master boot record (MBR) type of partition. When the upgraded VMFS-5 datastore grows beyond 2TB, it will automatically switch from MBR to GUID Partition Table (GPT) with no impact to your running VMs.

- Upgraded VMFS-5 datastores continue to have their partition starting at sector 128. Newly created VMFS-5 datastores have their partition starting at sector 2048.

Now that I have shown you how to upgrade a VMFS-3 datastore to VMFS-5 and discussed the implications of doing so, you can turn your attention to placing a VMFS datastore in maintenance mode.

Placing a VMFS Datastore in Maintenance Mode

Similar to the way ESXi hosts can be placed in a cluster with DRS enabled, shared VMFS datastores can be placed in a datastore cluster with Storage DRS enabled. Storage DRS is one of the exciting new features of vSphere 5, and it is covered in detail in Chapter 8, "Establishing Service Levels with Clusters, Fault Tolerance, and Resource Pools," which also covers the exam objective of placing a VMFS datastore in maintenance mode. In the next section, I will cover how to select the preferred path for a VMFS datastore.

Determining the Appropriate Path Selection Policy for a Given VMFS Datastore

Multipathing, as its name implies, is a technique used to provide multiple paths from an ESXi host to storage devices. This is done both to increase performance and to provide fault tolerance. Multipathing is managed in ESXi through a collection of VMkernel APIs known as Pluggable Storage Architecture (PSA). Figure 5.6 provides an overview of the PSA.

FIGURE 5.6   Pluggable Storage Architecture

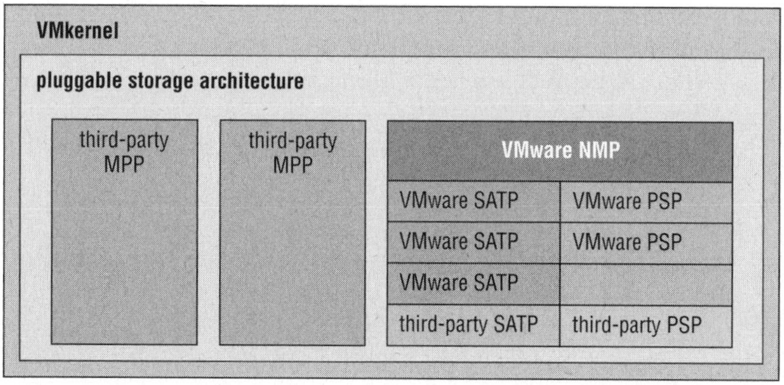

When ESXi starts up or an adapter is rescanned, the PSA uses *claim rules* to determine which multipathing plug-in (MPP) to use. The MPP will be responsible for both claiming and managing the multipathing for the device. MPPs are extensible and can be provided by third parties. ESXi also includes a Native Multipathing plug-in (NMP) by default that typically supports storage systems listed on the VMware HCL. If third-party MPPs are used, they replace the functionality included with the NMP. The NMP manages two additional types of plug-ins:

Storage Array Type Plug-in (SATP)   The SATP is responsible for performing array-specific functions in a failover situation, monitoring the health, and reporting changes of each physical path.

Path Selection Plug-in (PSP)   The PSP deals with path selection for a given device.

A PSP is assigned for each logical device by the VMware NMP. This PSP is based on information obtained by the SATP. By default, there are three PSPs:

VMW_PSP_FIXED   The ESXi host will use the first working path discovered, or it may use a designated preferred path if manually configured this way. This is used by most active-active storage devices and is displayed as Fixed (VMware) for the path selection policy in the vSphere Web Client.

VMW_PSP_MRU   The ESXi host will use the most recently used path. If this path becomes unavailable, an alternate path will be used. With MRU, there is no preferred path. This is used by most active-passive storage devices and is displayed as Most Recently Used (VMware) for the path selection policy in the vSphere Web Client.

VMW_PSP_RR   The ESXi host will use rotating paths. For active-active storage devices, this rotation will occur through all available paths. For active-passive storage devices, this rotation will occur through all active paths. This is used with both active-active and active-passive storage devices and is displayed as Round Robin (VMware) for the path selection policy in the vSphere Web Client.

As mentioned earlier, ESXi hosts will automatically select the path selection policy based on the information contained in the claim rules when ESXi starts up or an adapter is rescanned. Typically, the path selection policy will not need to be modified. If in doubt, check with your storage vendor to determine whether the appropriate path selection policy is being used by your VMFS datastores.

Now that I have covered the PSA and how multipathing works in ESXi, I will cover how to select the preferred path for a VMFS datastore.

Selecting the Preferred Path for a VMFS Datastore

The vSphere Web Client can be used to view the path information for a VMFS datastore and to modify the path(s) used by the VMFS datastore. Exercise 5.16 will cover the steps required to select the preferred path for a VMFS datastore. I recommend that you use either an empty VMFS datastore or a VMFS datastore with no running VMs on it for this exercise.

EXERCISE 5.16

Selecting the Preferred Path for a VMFS Datastore

1. Connect to a vCenter Server with the vSphere Web Client.

2. Select a VMFS datastore and then click the Manage tab. Click Settings on the toolbar, and then select the Connectivity And Multipathing option.

3. Select an ESXi host by clicking it. Review the ESXi host's Multipathing Details listed at the bottom of the screen. Note that there may be multiple entries listed here, as shown here:

4. Click the Edit Multipathing button to the right of one of the Multipathing Policies—preferably for a storage device that is not in use. An Edit Multipathing Policies window will open.

5. If your path is currently set to Fixed, as is shown in the previous graphic, you will notice that the Preferred column will have an asterisk in it.

EXERCISE 5.16 *(continued)*

6. Use the Path Selection Policy drop-down menu to change the path selection policy for this VMFS datastore.

    Any third-party PSP that is installed on the ESXi host you are working on will also appear in the drop-down menu for the path selection policy, so there could be more choices here than the default three provided.

7. Once all path selection policy changes have been made, click OK.

8. A Set Logical Unit Policy task will begin. When this task completes, verify that the new path selection policy is now listed.

WARNING

Remember that the path information typically will not need to be changed. Consult with your storage provider or VMware before making these types of changes, especially in production environments.

I have now detailed how to change the path selection policy for a VMFS datastore. Next I will cover how to disable a path to a VMFS datastore.

Disabling a Path to a VMFS Datastore

Certain maintenance operations might require the disabling of a path to a VMFS datastore. Exercise 5.17 will cover the steps required to disable a path to a VMFS datastore. As with the previous exercise, you are encouraged to use either an empty VMFS datastore or a VMFS datastore with no running VMs on it for this exercise.

EXERCISE 5.17

Disabling a Path to a VMFS Datastore

1. Connect to a vCenter Server with the vSphere Web Client.

2. Select a VMFS datastore and then click the Manage tab. Click Settings on the toolbar, and then select the Connectivity And Multipathing menu item.

3. Select an ESXi host by clicking it. Carefully review and then select your storage devices. After you are sure that you have the correct one, expand the Paths Field.

4. Select a path and then click the Disable button.

5. A Disable Multiple Path task will begin. When it completes, verify that the path has been disabled.

I have now covered how to disable a path for a VMFS datastore. The same warnings and caveats that applied to changing the path selection policy apply here. Proceed with caution when disabling paths to VMFS datastores. I will next move away from VMFS and cover the configuration of NAS and NFS for ESXi.

Creating an NFS Share for Use with vSphere

The Network File System (NFS) can be used by ESXi hosts to create datastores or to create ISO and template repositories. ESXi includes a built-in NFS client for this purpose. Creating an NFS share for use with ESXi has several caveats:

- The network-attached storage device should be listed on the VMware HCL.

- NFS version 3 over TCP must be used.

- A file system must be created on the NAS device and exported. Ensure that all VMkernel interfaces are listed in this export list.

- ESXi hosts must be able to access the NFS server in read-write mode.

- Read-write access must be allowed for the root system account.

- The NFS export must use the no_root_squash option.

- VMkernel networking over a standard physical NIC is required. Multiple NICs can be used, as long as the vSwitches/dvSwitches and physical switches are configured accordingly.

The specifics of configuring an NFS share will vary from vendor to vendor. Always consult with your vendor for their instructions on configuring an NFS share for use with vSphere. These documents will often include additional best practices, and their use is always highly recommended.

Network-attached storage is a storage device that can use different protocols to make files available. One of these protocols is NFS v3, which ESXi can use as a datastore. In Exercise 5.18, you will connect to a NAS device and mount an NFS volume. This exercise will require a properly configured NAS device to complete, and you should also ensure that a VMkernel connection has already been created on the same subnet that the NAS server is located on. If your test environment is lacking a NAS device, you may want to just read through this exercise.

EXERCISE 5.18

Connecting to a NAS Device

1. Connect to a vCenter Server with the vSphere Web Client.

2. Select an ESXi host in the left pane and then right-click on it. Choose the All vCenter Actions ➢ New Datastore option from the context menu. The New Datastore wizard will open.

3. Click Next on the Location screen to begin.

4. Select NFS for the datastore type and click Next.

5. On the Name And Configuration screen, provide this NFS datastore with a descriptive name. In the NFS Share Details section, enter the NFS server's DNS name, IP address, or NFS UUID and provide the mount point folder name in the Folder field. The final setup should look similar to this:

Datastore name: `NFS-01`

NFS Share Details

Server: `10.10.10.100`

E.g: nas, nas.it.com, 192.168.0.1 or FE80:0:0:0:2AA:FF:FE9A:4CA2

Folder: `/vols/nfs-01`

E.g: /vols/vol0/datastore-001

⚠ If a datastore already exists in the datacenter for this NFS share and you intend to configure the same datastore on new hosts, make sure that you enter the same input data (Server and Folder) that you used for the original datastore. Different input data would mean different datastores even if the underlying NFS storage is the same.

Access Mode

☐ Mount NFS as read-only

The Mount NFS As Read-Only option is often useful for ISO repositories but not for datastores. This exercise pertains to datastores, so make sure you leave this option unchecked.

6. Review the information on the Ready To Complete screen and click Finish to add the NFS share to the ESXi host.

7. A Create NAS Datastore task will begin. When this task completes, verify that the NFS datastore has been added.

Unlike VMFS datastores, NFS datastores must be manually added to each ESXi host that will connect to them. It is also crucial that the server and folder names entered in the Add Storage Wizard are identical across all ESXi hosts. If the server and folder names don't match, ESXi hosts will see these NFS mounts as different datastores.

I have now covered the steps required to connect to a NAS device and mount an NFS volume. The actual operation of connecting to an NFS share is typically quite simple, in comparison to the setup required on the NAS device. In the next section, we will cover identifying NFS datastore properties.

Identifying NFS Datastore Properties

Once an NFS datastore is mounted, the properties for the datastore can be viewed on the Manage tab by clicking Settings on the toolbar. The General menu item will show the properties for the NFS datastore. Figure 5.7 shows the NFS datastore properties.

I have now covered obtaining the properties for NFS datastores. In the next section, I will cover unmounting and mounting the NFS datastore you mounted in Exercise 5.18.

Mounting and Unmounting an NFS Datastore

Once an NFS datastore is mounted, it can also be unmounted. Unmounting a datastore will not destroy the datastore but will simply make the datastore inaccessible to the ESXi host(s). If other ESXi hosts have this datastore mounted, they can continue to access the datastore as usual.

The operation to unmount an NFS datastore is quite simple. Figure 5.8 shows the context menus used to unmount an NFS datastore.

FIGURE 5.7 NFS datastore properties

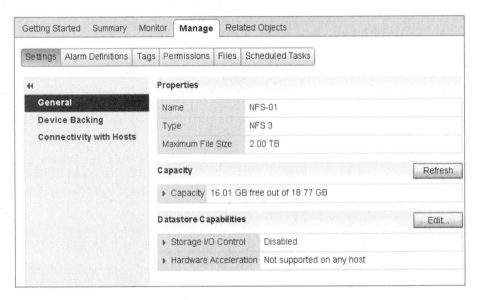

FIGURE 5.8 Unmount NFS datastore

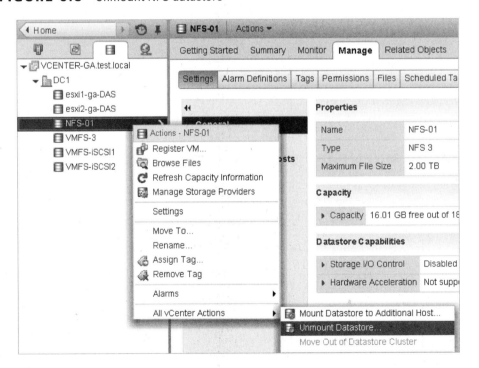

If there are running VMs located on an NFS datastore, you cannot unmount it.

Unlike a VMFS datastore, which will stay listed in the Datastore view as Inactive, when an NFS datastore is unmounted it is removed from the Datastore view. To mount an unmounted NFS datastore again, you will need to repeat the NFS mount that was covered in Exercise 5.18.

I have now covered mounting NFS datastores, obtaining NFS datastore properties, and unmounting NFS datastores. In the next section, I will cover determining the use case for multiple VMFS and NFS datastores.

Determining the Use Case for Multiple VMFS/NFS Datastores

Multiple datastores in ESXi can serve many purposes, some of which include the following:

Load Distribution   Multiple datastores can be backed by various physical disk configurations. This allows tiering of VMFS datastores and could also be leveraged by Storage DRS.

Departmental or Political   The HR or finance department may have purchased a NAS or SAN and want this storage to be dedicated to their virtual machines.

Higher Availability   Mixing SANs or NAS devices can lead to higher availability, specifically around planned maintenance. If the capacity is available, VMs could be consolidated onto one storage system for the maintenance period.

NAS and SAN Additions   Adding and retiring new storage systems could require new datastores to be added.

Differing Workloads   Desktops can have a much different set of requirements and capabilities than servers, and things such as deduplication may want to be leveraged on certain backend storage systems.

ISO or Template Repositories   Certain ISOs and templates will likely be available in the virtual environment.

Dynamic Disk Mirroring   Windows can use dynamic disks to span a boot volume across two datastores. This could make a VM more resilient to the loss of a single datastore.

Storage vMotion   Storage vMotion will require a minimum of a source and destination datastore.

VMFS-5   Certain environments may want to add new datastores for VMFS-5 volumes, as opposed to upgrading them in place.

Replication   Certain datastores can be used with VMware SRM or other replication solutions. Having multiple datastores allows the placement of only replicated VMs on a VMFS datastore that will be replicated.

We have covered multiple use cases for multiple VMFS and NFS datastores. Storage is abstracted from VMs through the use of datastores, and there is a lot of flexibility because of this. There are likely many more use cases available. See whether you can identify at least one before you move on.

Summary

This chapter covered planning and configuring vSphere storage. Knowing how to use the different storage options is an important part of any virtual infrastructure administrator's duties. We covered the following:

- Identifying storage adapters and devices

- Using storage naming conventions

- Scanning and rescanning for storage devices

- Understanding vCenter Server storage filters and zoning and LUN masking practices

- Identifying the different iSCSI adapters and their requirements, along with determining the use case for each

- Enabling, disabling, and configuring the software iSCSI initiator

- Using port binding for dependent hardware iSCSI adapters and software iSCSI adapters

- Configuring CHAP

- Determining use cases for thin provisioning

Next we focused on VMFS and NFS datastores. Specifically, you learned:

- The capabilities of VMFS-5

- How to create, rename, unmount, and delete a VMFS datastore

- How to identify VMFS datastore properties

- The options for increasing the size of VMFS datastores

- How to upgrade a VMFS-3 datastore to VMFS-5 and the caveats for the upgraded datastores

- Path selection policies, preferred paths, and disabling paths

- How to create NFS shares for use with ESXi

- How to connect to NAS devices

- How to mount and unmount NFS datastores

- How to identify NFS datastore properties

- Use cases for multiple VMFS/NFS datastores

Exam Essentials

Know how to configure shared storage for vSphere 5.   Be able to identify storage adapters and devices. Know the storage naming conventions and their formats. Be able to scan and rescan for storage devices. Know the vCenter Server storage filters and how to enable, configure, and disable them. Know what zoning and LUN masking are and what they are used for. Know the three types of iSCSI adapters, their requirements, and when to use each of them. Be able to configure and edit the three types of iSCSI adapters. Understand how to use port binding in the vSphere Client. Understand what CHAP is, why it is used, and how to use it. Understand the differences between array thin provisioning and virtual disk thin provisioning. Be able to determine the use case for array thin provisioning and know that vSphere cannot manage storage array thin provisioning.

Know how to create and configure VMFS and NFS datastores.   Be able to identify the capabilities of VMFS-5. Know how to create, rename, unmount, and delete VMFS datastores. Know the various locations that VMFS properties can be obtained. Understand the two ways that VMFS datastores may be increased in size and the differences in these two approaches. Be able to upgrade VMFS-3 volumes to VMFS-5 and know the caveats associated with upgrading them. Know how to place a VMFS datastore in maintenance mode. Be able to determine the appropriate path selection policy for a VMFS datastore, and know how to select the preferred path for a VMFS datastore. Also know how to disable a path to a VMFS datastore. Know the requirements for NFS shares created on NAS devices, and know how to connect to the NAS device and mount an NFS datastore. Also know how to unmount an NFS datastore and understand the operation for mounting it again. Be able to identify NFS datastore properties. Understand the use cases for multiple VMFS/NFS datastores.

Review Questions

1. You select the Manage tab for an ESXi host and select Storage from the toolbar. You then choose the Storage Adapters menu item, but the iSCSI Software Adapter is not listed. What could be the problem?

    A. The software iSCSI adapter must be installed as a separate VIB.

    B. The software iSCSI adapter is not enabled.

    C. The software iSCSI adapter can be viewed only from the DCUI.

    D. The software iSCSI adapter must have VMkernel networking set up before it is visible in the Storage Adapters list.

2. Which of the following is an example of a SCSI INQUIRY device identifier?

    A. eui.5577bd49251ddb52

    B. mpx.vmhba2:C0:T0:L0

    C vml.02000600006006016094602800364ce22e3

    D. vmhba1:C0:T1:L0

3. ESXi 5.5 supports booting from an iSCSI SAN LUN with which of the following adapters? (Choose all that apply).

    A. Independent iSCSI HBA

    B. Dependent iSCSI hardware adapter

    C. Software iSCSI Adapter

    D. Fibre Channel HBA

4. You create a new VMFS-5 datastore for one of your ESXi hosts. What is the largest VMDK file that can be created on this datastore?

    A. 2TB minus 512 bytes

    B. 62TB

    C. 64TB

    D. None of these

5. Which of the following are default path selection policies in ESXi? (Choose all that apply.)

    A. Fixed (VMware)

    B. Dynamic (VMware)

    C. Most Recently Used (VMware)

    D. Round Robin (VMware)

6. You have a customer that requires that the target (storage system) authenticates the iSCSI adapter (initiator) and that the iSCSI adapter also authenticates the target. Which CHAP authentication method should be used?

   A. One-way CHAP

   B. Mutual CHAP

   C. Three-way CHAP

   D. None of these

7. You have a customer that is deploying ESXi and will be using iSCSI storage. The customer wants the iSCSI implementation to use the least amount of the ESXi host resources as possible. Which of the following storage adapters would be the best choice for this set of requirements?

   A. Software iSCSI adapter

   B. Dependent hardware iSCSI adapter

   C. Independent hardware iSCSI adapter

   D. FCoE adapter

8. Your team has decided on a new naming strategy for all VMFS datastores. Currently, the names used do not adhere to this standard. How can you most easily fix this problem?

   A. Unmount the VMFS datastore and then rename it using the vSphere Web Client

   B. Rename each VMFS datastore in the vSphere Web Client

   C. Enable SSH and configure the firewall for the ESXi host using the vSphere Web Client, connect to it and then rename the VMFS datastore from the command line.

   D. Storage vMotion a virtual machine and use the advanced options available there.

9. Which of the following is a process performed at the SAN storage processors or ESXi host level that makes LUNs hidden from certain hosts?

   A. Provisioning

   B. Zoning

   C. LUN masking

   D. Multipathing

10. What are two ways that VMFS datastores can be enlarged after their initial creation? (Choose two.)

    A. Inflate

    B. Extend

    C. Expand

    D. Zeroed

11. Which of the following are vCenter Server storage filters? (Choose all that apply.)

    A. VMFS filter

    B. RDM filter

C. Same Host and Transports filter

D. Host Rescan filter

12. You upgraded a VMFS-3 volume with a block size of 8MB to VMFS-5. What is the block size of the VMFS-5 volume?

A. 8MB

B. 4MB

C. 2MB

D. 1MB

13. You need to unmount a VMFS datastore from a cluster of ESXi hosts for maintenance. Which of the following are prerequisites for performing this action? (Choose all that apply.)

A. Virtual machines and templates may not reside on the datastore.

B. Mapping files for RDMs on the datastore must be removed.

C. ISOs located on the datastore must be removed from virtual machines.

D. The datastore must not be used for vSphere HA heartbeat.

14. Which of the following information is required when adding an NFS share to be used as a datastore? (Choose all that apply.)

A. NFS server name, IP address, or NFS UUID

B. Path to the NFS share

C. NFS server credentials

D. NFS datastore name

15. You have a two node cluster of ESXi 5.5 hosts managed by vCenter 5.5. Your shared storage is a supported Fibre Channel SAN, and you have a virtual machine that requires multiple 4TB volumes for file storage. Which of the following can be used to provide the space for this file storage? (Choose all that apply.)

A. NFS

B. iSCSI

C. VMFS

D. RDM

16. As part of routine maintenance, you unmounted an NFS datastore from an ESXi host. What do you need to do to mount this NFS datastore again, when the maintenance window is complete?

A. Reboot the ESXi host.

B. Right-click the inactive datastore and choose the Mount option from the context menu that appears.

C. Use the Add Storage Wizard to mount it.

D. Rescan the ESXi host's HBAs.

17. Which of the following storage adapters performs both the iSCSI processing and the networking for iSCSI traffic?

   A. Software iSCSI adapter

   B. Dependent hardware iSCSI adapter

   C. Independent hardware iSCSI adapter

   D. FCoE adapter

18. You create a VM with a single 50GB thin-provisioned virtual disk, and your storage array also uses thin provisioning. You later decide to protect this VM with VMware FT. How much space does this VM's single virtual disk consume on the storage array?

   A. Greater than 50GB.

   B. 50GB.

   C. Less than 50GB.

   D. It depends on the amount of data in the VMDK.

19. Which of the following is used to communicate information about iSCSI boot devices to an ESXi host.

   A. iBHA

   B. iBRP

   C. iBDC

   D. iBFT

20. You have a 10-node ESXi cluster, and you just presented new devices to all 10 ESXi hosts. You need to quickly scan the adapters on all 10 hosts to find the new device. What option is the fastest?

   A. In the vSphere Web Client, rescan each individual storage adapter for each ESXi host.

   B. Write a script to perform this operation.

   C. In the vSphere Web Client, use the Rescan Storage option from the context menu that appears when you right-click on the vCenter Server root object.

   D. In the vSphere Client, use the Rescan Storage option from the context menu that appears when your right-click on the cluster object.

Chapter 6

Creating and Deploying Virtual Machines and vApps

VCP5-DCV EXAM OBJECTIVES COVERED IN THIS CHAPTER

✓ **1.4: Plan and Perform Upgrades of vCenter Server and VMware ESXi**

- Upgrade VMware Tools

- Upgrade Virtual Machine hardware

✓ **4.1: Create and Deploy Virtual Machines**

- Identify capabilities of virtual machine hardware versions

- Configure and deploy a guest os into a new virtual machine

- Place virtual machines in selected ESXi hosts/Clusters/ Resource Pools

- Identify methods to access and use a virtual machine console

- Install/Upgrade/Update VMware Tools

- Identify VMware Tools device drivers

- Configure virtual machine time synchronization

- Identify virtual machine storage resources

- Configure/Modify disk controller for virtual disks

- Configure appropriate virtual disk type for a virtual machine

- Create/Convert thin/thick provisioned virtual disks

- Configure disk shares

- Determine appropriate datastore locations for virtual machines based on application workloads

- Configure/Modify virtual CPU and memory resources according to OS and application requirements

- Configure/Modify virtual NIC adapter and connect virtual machines to appropriate network resources

- Convert a physical machine using VMware Converter

- Import a supported virtual machine source using VMware Converter

- Modify virtual hardware settings using VMware Converter

✓ 4.2: Create and Deploy vApps

- Determine when a tiered application should be deployed as a vApp

- Create/Clone/Export a vApp

- Add objects to an existing vApp

- Identify vApp settings

- Edit vApp settings

- Configure IP pools

- Suspend/Resume a vApp

TOOLS

- VMware vSphere Basics guide (Objective 1.4)

- vSphere Installation and Setup guide (Objective 1.4)

- vSphere Upgrade guide (Objective 1.4)

- VMware vSphere Examples and Scenarios guide (Objective 1.4)

- Installing and Administering VMware vSphere Update Manager (Objective 1.4)

- vSphere Client / vSphere Web Client (Objective 1.4)

- vSphere Virtual Machine Administration guide (Objectives 4.1, 4.2)

- Installing and Configuring VMware Tools Guide (Objective 4.1)

- vSphere Client / vSphere Web Client (Objectives 4.1, 4.2)

In this chapter, we will focus on creating and deploying virtual machines and vApps.

We will cover understanding virtual machine hardware versions, creating VMs, working with VMware Tools, editing VMs, and determining their resources. You'll also learn how to perform physical-to-virtual (P2V) conversions using VMware Converter, import supported sources, and modify existing virtual machine hardware settings.

The final section of this chapter will cover vApps. You will learn exactly what vApps are, when to use them, and how to create, network, clone, and export them.

Creating and Deploying Virtual Machines

Everything covered so far in this book has been about getting to this point. For the most part, the virtual infrastructure exists in its entirety to run virtual machines. Knowing how to create and deploy VMs is an essential task for any virtual infrastructure administrator. The first topic covered is identifying the capabilities of virtual machine hardware versions. Knowing the features of the various versions is often important in determining whether a specific workload can be supported.

Identifying Capabilities of Virtual Machine Hardware Versions

A virtual machine hardware version is used to designate the features of the virtual hardware. This version indicates the hardware features available in the virtual machine and can include things such as the BIOS or EFI, number of CPUs, maximum memory configuration, and more. When creating a virtual machine using the vSphere Web Client, you can use the Custom option to choose the version of the virtual machine hardware. By default, new virtual machines will be created with the latest version of the virtual hardware available on the host where the VM is being created. In vSphere 5.5, this will be virtual machine hardware version 10.

Virtual machine hardware version 10 includes the following capabilities:

64 vCPU Support   This is unchanged from virtual machine hardware version 9.

1TB Memory Support   This is unchanged from virtual machine hardware version 9.

SATA Controllers   Now a VM with a supported guest OS can have 4 SATA controllers, with 30 devices each for a total of 120 devices.

Improved vGPU Support for VMs   The virtual graphics processor will now work with both AMD-based and Intel-based graphics cards.

62TB VMDKs   This is a great change that will allow larger file and/or database servers to use virtual machine disks (VMDKs).

The capabilities of virtual machine hardware version 10 are an improvement over the capabilities of both virtual machine hardware versions 8 and 9, which were introduced in vSphere 5 and 5.1. With each vSphere release, VMware continues to push the capabilities of the virtual machine hardware to new levels. It is important to know that virtual machines using virtual machine hardware versions prior to version 10 can still be created and run on ESXi 5.5 hosts, but they will not have all of the features and capabilities of virtual machine hardware version 10. For example, a virtual machine hardware version 7 VM can be created in vSphere 5.5, but it can have a maximum of only 8 vCPUs.

Starting in vSphere 5.1, VMware tried to change the way we think about virtual machine hardware version numbers. The idea was to move to a less version-specific approach and instead use virtual machine compatibility levels. Figure 6.1 shows the virtual machine compatibility level, as seen in the Summary tab for a virtual machine.

FIGURE 6.1   VM compatibility level

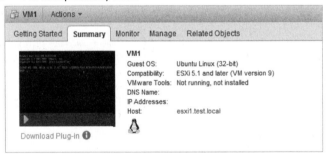

The idea behind compatibility levels is that virtual machine hardware features are married to a specific vSphere release, as opposed to just a standalone version number. This approach should simplify upgrades for the vSphere administrator, as many workloads will not benefit from the capabilities of newer virtual hardware. Those workloads that are compatible can remain at their current virtual machine hardware level and not be considered out of date; an upgrade would be unnecessary. Table 6.1 shows the extended virtual machine hardware version support matrix.

TABLE 6.1   ESXi host and virtual machine hardware compatibility

vSphere release	Supported virtual machine hardware version(s)
vSphere 4.0	4, 7
vSphere 4.1	4, 7

vSphere release	Supported virtual machine hardware version(s)
vSphere 5.0	4, 7, 8
vSphere 5.1	4, 7, 8, 9
vSphere 5.5	7, 8, 9, 10

If you want to use the latest features included in virtual machine hardware version 10, you must use ESXi 5.5 and create the VM in the vSphere Web Client. The vSphere Client cannot be used to create or edit version 10 VMs.

Now that you have seen the capabilities and compatibilities of virtual machine hardware versions, let's create a virtual machine.

Configuring and Deploying a Guest OS into a New Virtual Machine

In Exercise 6.1, we will create a new virtual machine using the vSphere Web Client. This virtual machine will be used for many of the exercises in this chapter and the remainder of the book. Keep in mind that a virtual machine is simply virtual hardware, and it does not include an operating system, or guest OS.

EXERCISE 6.1

Configuring and Deploying a New VM

1. Log in to the vSphere Web Client.

2. On the Home tab, click VMs And Templates.

3. Right-click on the Datacenter object in the left pane and choose New Virtual Machine from the context menu. The New Virtual Machine wizard will launch.

4. Select the Create A New Virtual Machine option and click Next to continue.

5. Give the virtual machine a unique name of up to 80 characters and specify an inventory location. Click Next to continue.

6. Select an ESXi host where the VM will be located. You can also search for the folder or datacenter using the provided search function. Click Next to continue.

You'll learn more about initial virtual machine placement in the next section of this chapter.

7. Select a datastore that suits the workload requirements of the VM and that is large enough to hold the entire contents of the VM. Ensure that the compatibility check icon (green circle with an arrow) appears at the bottom of the screen before continuing.

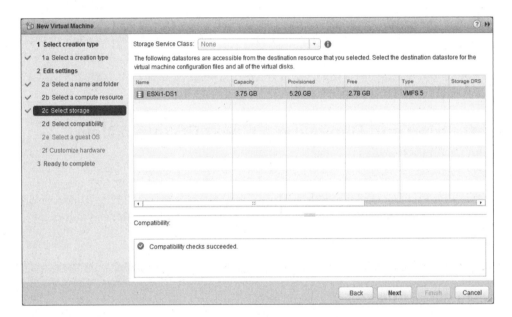

8. Click the Next button to continue.

9. Using the drop-down menu, select the compatibility level of ESXi 5.1 And Later, and then click Next.

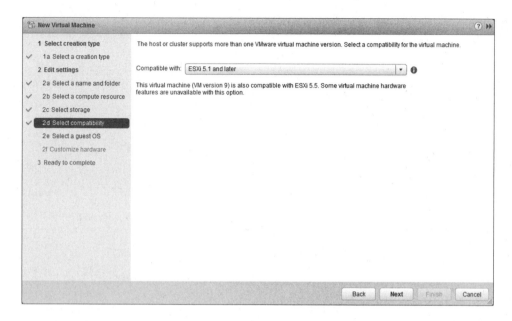

Choosing the compatibility level of ESXi 5.1 And Later will create a virtual machine hardware version 9 VM. We will upgrade this to virtual machine hardware version 10 in a later exercise in this chapter.

10. Choose Guest OS Family Of Windows and Guest OS Version Of Microsoft Windows Server 2008 R2 (64-bit), and click Next to continue.

11. On the Customize Hardware screen, review the settings for this new virtual machine.

12. Click the arrow for the New Hard Disk option to expand the new hard disk options. Locate the Disk Provisioning field in the left pane and then select the Thin Provision check box. Later in this chapter we'll examine the Provisioning options in more detail.

EXERCISE 6.1 *(continued)*

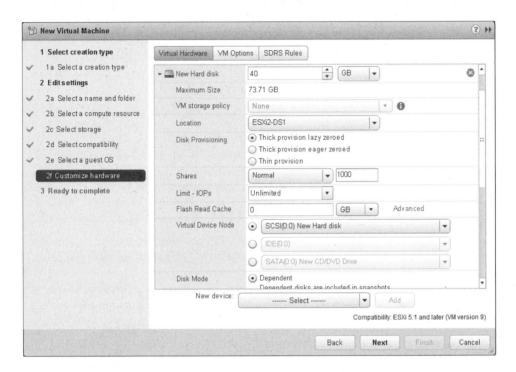

After the thin provisioning has been selected, take a few moments to explore the rest of the disk options. Also, take some time to explore the remaining screens and view the available options in the vSphere Web Client. Note that a Virtual Hardware view and a VM Options view are available, and these views can be toggled using the buttons at the top of the screen.

13. After reviewing the options in the Customize Hardware portion of the wizard, click Next to continue.

14. Review the information on the Ready To Complete screen and click Finish to deploy the new VM.

15. A Create Virtual Machine task will begin. When this task completes, the newly created VM will be listed in the left pane.

16. Click this VM to select it, and then review the virtual machine settings in the vSphere Web Client for accuracy.

 Deploying a VM will not install an operating system on the VM. Use the same procedures for installing an OS that you would use for physical hardware.

Note that future exercises in this chapter will require a virtual machine with an installed guest OS. The exercises in this chapter will use Windows 2008 R2, but any supported guest OS will work. If you don't have a VM with a guest OS installed, now might be a good time to let Setup start running!

We have now covered configuring and deploying a new virtual machine in the vSphere Web Client. In the next section, I will provide more detail about the initial placement options for virtual machines.

Placing Virtual Machines in Selected ESXi Hosts/Clusters/Resource Pools

When we created the virtual machine in Exercise 6.1, part of the process was to identify the inventory location or compute resource. Figure 6.2 shows this step when using the vSphere Web Client.

FIGURE 6.2   VM placement options

A cluster, ESXi host, vApp, or resource pool can be selected for initial placement of the virtual machine when it is created. The available options will depend on how the virtual infrastructure is designed. For example, a cluster without DRS enabled will not have the resource pools as an option. The decision you make for the initial placement is in no way permanent, and virtual machines can move about the virtual infrastructure either through manual processes such as vMotion or through automated migrations from DRS.

Now that I have shown you how to build virtual machines and discussed the options for their initial placement, I will cover identifying the methods used to access a virtual machine console.

Identifying Methods to Access and Use a Virtual Machine Console

Unlike physical machines, virtual machines don't have a keyboard, monitor, and mouse that an individual can physically sit down in front of and use to manage the VM. However, the virtual machine console can still be accessed. Several methods can be used to access virtual machine consoles. Applications such as Remote Desktop Protocol (RDP) and VNC can be used to access consoles, and vSphere also includes two built-in options. The vSphere Client and the vSphere Web Client both include the ability to access a virtual machine console.

To access the virtual machine console from the vSphere Client, simply right-click any virtual machine in the inventory and choose Open Console from the context menu, as shown in Figure 6.3.

FIGURE 6.3   Accessing the VM console with the vSphere Client

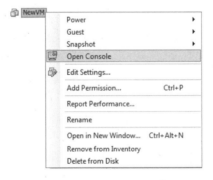

To use the vSphere Web Client to access a virtual machine console, you must first download and install the client integration plug-in. Exercise 6.2 will cover this process.

EXERCISE 6.2

Accessing a Virtual Machine Console

1. Log out of the vSphere Web Client or connect to the vSphere Web Client but do not log in.

2. Click the Download The Client Integration Plug-in link on the vSphere Web Client login page.

3. Use the procedure appropriate for your web browser to launch the VMware Remote Console Plug-in application.

4. When the VMware Remote Console Application launches, click Next to begin. If you have supported web browsers opened, you will first be prompted to close them.

5. Click Next on the Welcome screen to begin.

6. Accept the terms of the license agreement and then select a local directory where the VMware Client Integration Plug-in will be installed.

7. Click Install, and then click Finish when the installer completes.

8. Open a web browser and log in to the vSphere Web Client. Locate a powered-on VM from the inventory and select it.

9. On the VM's Summary tab, click the blue Launch Console link located directly below the thumbnail view of the console.

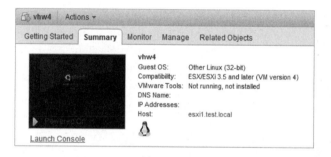

10. The Console will open in a new tab in the browser window.

If after installing the Client Integration Plug-in you still see a blue Download Plug-in link on the VM's Summary tab, ensure that your web browser is supported.

For working in the console window using the vSphere Web Client, here are some helpful commands:

- Pressing Ctrl+Alt will release the cursor from the console window.
- Pressing Ctrl+Alt+Enter will exit full-screen mode.

Now that you have seen how to access virtual machine consoles, let's turn our attention to installing the VMware Tools in a guest OS.

Installing, Upgrading, and Updating VMware Tools

Although never required for guest OS functionality, VMware Tools enhance the performance of a VM's guest operating system and provide additional management functionalities for the VM. VMware Tools can be installed manually using the vSphere Web Client, and Exercise 6.3 covers the procedure for a Windows 2008 R2 guest operating system.

EXERCISE 6.3

Installing VMware Tools in a Guest OS

1. Log in to the vSphere Web Client.

2. On the Home tab, click VMs And Templates.

3. In the left pane, click a powered-on virtual machine with a supported guest OS installed to select it.

4. On the Summary tab for the VM, note the status of VMware Tools is currently reported as Not Running, Not Installed. Also notice under the blue Launch Console link a yellow alert banner that shows the VMware Tools status.

5. Click the Install VMware Tools on this banner. Note that if this banner is missing you can also use the Actions ➤ All vCenter Actions ➤ Guest OS ➤ Install VMware Tools option available directly above the Summary tab.

6. An Install VMware Tools window will open. Review this information and then click Mount to continue.

7. Open a console session to this virtual machine and log in to the guest OS with an Administrator account.

8. The VMware Tools CD-ROM image will be mounted, and if enabled, `autorun.exe` will launch the VMware Tools Setup. If `autorun.exe` does not begin installation, browse

the contents of the mounted CD-ROM and start the installation manually with either `setup.exe` or `setup64.exe`.

9. Click Next on the VMware Tools Setup Welcome screen.

10. Choose the Custom option and click Next to continue.

11. In the left pane, expand the VMware Device Drivers and review the list of device drivers that will be installed. The complete list of device drivers is shown in the following image:

12. Note that the default installation directory can be changed for the VMware Device Drivers by selecting a component and then using the Browse button. Click Next to continue.

13. Click Install to install the VMware Tools.

14. When the installation is complete, click Finish. You will then be prompted to reboot the guest OS. Click the Yes button to reboot.

15. When the virtual machine has rebooted, view the information at the top of the Summary tab for the VM and verify that the VMware Tools status reports Running and that a version number is listed.

Now that you know how to install VMware Tools in a virtual machine, I will cover upgrading and updating the VMware Tools. These two tasks are likely also familiar to most virtual infrastructure administrators, because it is a VMware-recommended best practice to keep the VMware Tools at the latest release available.

VMware Tools can be upgraded manually, or virtual machines can be configured to check and upgrade automatically during power cycling of the VM. Update Manager is another option for upgrading the VMware Tools. Exercise 6.4 covers the steps for upgrading an existing VMware Tools installation on Windows Server 2008 R2 to the latest version. Note that unless you have an older version of VMware Tools available, you may not be able to complete this exercise.

EXERCISE 6.4

Upgrading VMware Tools to the Latest Version

1. Select a VM from the inventory.

2. On the Summary tab for the VM, note the status of VMware Tools is currently reported as Upgrade Available. Also notice under the Launch Console link an alert banner that shows the VMware Tools status as Out Of Date.

3. On the Summary tab, select Actions ➤ All vCenter Actions ➤ Guest OS ➤ Upgrade VMware Tools.

4. An Upgrade VMware Tools window will open. Review the information in this window, and then select the Interactive Upgrade option. Click Upgrade to continue.

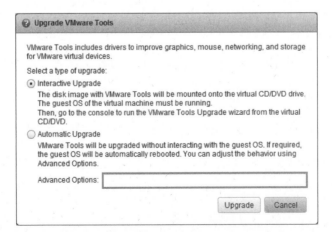

5.   Open a console session to this virtual machine and log in to the guest OS with an Administrator account.

6.   The CD-ROM image will be mounted, and if enabled, `autorun.exe` will launch the VMware Tools Setup. If `autorun.exe` does not begin installation, browse the contents of the mounted CD-ROM and start the installation manually with either `setup.exe` or `setup64.exe`.

7.   Click Next on the VMware Tools Setup Welcome screen.

8.   Choose the Typical option and click Next to continue.

9.   Click Install to install the VMware Tools.

10.   When the installation is complete, click Finish. You may then be prompted to reboot the guest OS. Click the Yes button to reboot.

11.   When the virtual machine has rebooted, view the information at the top of the Summary tab for the VM and verify that the VMware Tools status reports Running and that a version number is listed.

In the previous exercise, we chose the interactive VMware Tools upgrade instead of the automatic upgrade. The automatic option differs in two ways. First, it will not give you the opportunity to perform a custom installation, and second, if a reboot is required, it will reboot the guest OS without prompting at the conclusion of the VMware Tools install. Be sure to remember this when choosing the option you will use to upgrade the VMware Tools on production virtual machines.

One other option that is occasionally required is to update or modify the VMware Tools. This can be useful in situations where a particular device driver needs to be added or removed from the installation. Exercise 6.5 covers the steps required to update VMware Tools by removing the Audio driver. This exercise will also use the same VM running Windows Server 2008 R2 as a guest OS.

EXERCISE 6.5

Updating VMware Tools

1.   Select a VM from the inventory.

2.   Open a console session to this virtual machine and log in to the guest OS with an Administrator account.

3.   Use the native Windows Programs And Features option in Control Panel. Select VMware Tools and then click Change.

4.   Click Next on the VMware Tools Setup Welcome screen.

5.   Choose the Modify option and click the Next button to continue.

6.   Click the drop-down menu for Audio, and then select the Entire Feature Will Be Unavailable option.

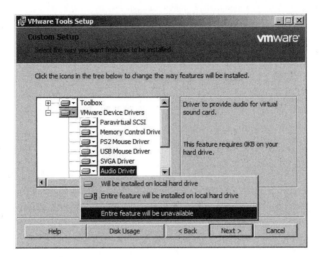

7. Note how the status changes on the Audio option. Click Next to continue.

8. On the Ready To Change VMware Tools screen, click Change to update VMware Tools.

9. When the installation is complete, click Finish. You may then be prompted to reboot the guest OS.

 On Linux guests, to install the VMware Tools you will first extract the contents of the `tar.gz` file from the mounted optical media and then run the `./vmware-install.pl` command to begin setup.

We have now covered installing, upgrading, and updating the VMware Tools. In the next section, we'll discuss the VMware Tools device drivers and the roles they play in enhancing virtual machine performance.

Identifying VMware Tools Device Drivers

The VMware Tools provide device drivers for the mouse, sound, graphics, networking, and more, but the device drivers that are installed in a typical VMware Tools installation will depend on the guest operating system. Performing a custom installation of VMware

Tools, or modifying an existing installation, will allow you to choose which device drivers are installed in the guest OS. Table 6.2 lists the VMware Tools device drivers that may be included in a VMware Tools installation and a brief description of each.

TABLE 6.2   VMware Tools device drivers

Device driver	Description
Paravirtual SCSI	Used to provide increased performance for *paravirtualized* SCSI devices.
Virtual Printing	Used to allow guests to access the host's printers.
Memory Control	Used to provide enhanced memory management functionality.
Mouse	Used to smooth mouse movement in the guest OS.
SVGA	Used to enable 32-bit displays, greater display resolutions, and improved graphics performance.
Audio	Used to provide audio for virtual sound cards.
VMXNet NIC	Used to provide increased performance for network devices.
VMXNet3 NIC	Used to provide increased performance for paravirtualized network devices.
Volume Shadow Copy Service Support	Used to enable VSS support for Windows Vista or Windows Server 2003 or newer. Older versions of Windows will use the FileSystem Sync driver instead.
VMCI	Used to enable VM-to-VM or VM-to-host communications using datagrams and shared memory.
vShield Drivers	Used to enable the vShield Endpoint thin agent for VMs to be protected by vShield Endpoint.
Shared Folders	Used to enable shared folders — disabled by default and generally not recommended for use.

Windows Vista and newer guest operating systems will use the VMware SVGA 3D (Microsoft – WDDM) driver instead of the SVGA driver. This driver adds support for Windows Aero.

Now that we have covered the VMware Tools device drivers, I will detail how to upgrade the virtual machine hardware. The virtual machine hardware upgrade should always be performed after the update to the latest VMware Tools release. This is because the newer virtual hardware may have driver requirements that would be satisfied by the latest VMware Tools release.

Upgrading Virtual Machine Hardware

Virtual machines have hardware versions associated with them. This version indicates the hardware features available in the virtual machine and can include things like the BIOS or EFI, number of CPUs, maximum memory configuration, and more. When a virtual machine is created using the vSphere Web Client, one of the options in the wizard is to choose a compatibility level. The compatibility level determines the version of the virtual machine hardware. Compatibility levels can be set at the datacenter, cluster, host or virtual machine object level. Table 6.3 shows the compatibility levels and associated virtual machine hardware versions.

TABLE 6.3 Compatibility level and virtual machine hardware versions

Compatibility level	Virtual machine hardware version
ESX/ESXi 3.5 and later	4
ESX/ESXi 4.0 and later	7
ESXi 5.0 and later	8
ESXi 5.1 and later	9
ESXi 5.5 and later	10

A normal part of any ESXi host upgrade is to upgrade virtual machines to the new virtual hardware version. The process, much like the VMware Tools upgrade, is quite familiar to experienced virtual infrastructure administrators. The virtual hardware may be upgraded as a manual process, and Update Manager may also be used to perform orchestrated VMware Tools and virtual hardware upgrades.

Recall that in Exercise 6.1 we created a virtual machine with a compatibility level of ESXi 5.1 And Later. In Exercise 6.6, we will upgrade the compatibility level for this VM to

ESXi 5.5 And Later. This will update the virtual machine hardware from version 9 to version 10.

EXERCISE 6.6

Updating the Virtual Machine Hardware Version

1. Select the VM used in Exercise 6.1 from the inventory in the vSphere Web Client.

2. In the VM Hardware panel, verify that the compatibility for this VM is reported as ESXi 5.1 And Later (VM Version 9).

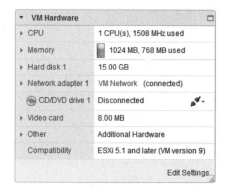

3. In the VM Hardware panel, click Edit Settings.

4. Click the arrow to expand the Upgrade menu.

5. Check the Schedule VM Compatibility Upgrade option.

6. Ensure that the Compatibility With drop-down menu contains the ESXi 5.5 And Later selection.

7. Select the Only Upgrade After Normal Guest OS Shutdown check box. This option is used to prevent the virtual machine hardware upgrade from occurring if the guest OS crashes or if the VM encounters other problems like an HA event. The final configuration should look like this:

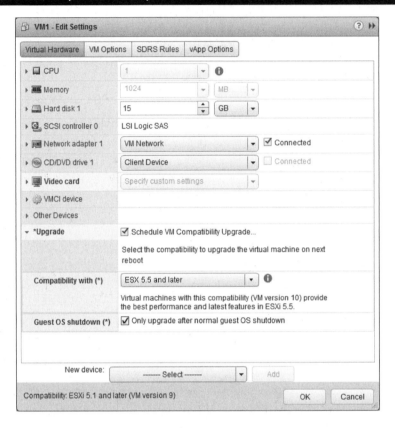

8. Click OK to confirm the VM Compatibility Upgrade. A Reconfigure Virtual Machine task will begin. When this task completes, shut down the guest OS.

9. In the VM Hardware panel, verify that the compatibility for this VM is reported as ESXi 5.5 And Later (VM Version 10).

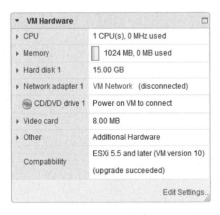

10. Power the guest OS back on and log in. Verify that all is well, and note that you may be prompted for a reboot.

 The virtual hardware upgrade is an irreversible operation that can make the VM incompatible with previous versions of vSphere. VMware Converter is a useful tool for changing virtual hardware versions. Creating a new VM with the desired virtual machine hardware version and adding the disk(s) from an existing VM is another approach that can be used.

Now that we have covered creating virtual machines, using VMware Tools and virtual machine hardware versions, we will move on to configuring our virtual machines. Let's start with time synchronization.

Configuring Virtual Machine Time Synchronization

The VMware Tools have the ability to synchronize the time of the guest OS with the time of the ESXi host that the guest is running on. This feature is known as *periodic time synchronization*. When this feature is enabled, VMware Tools will check once a minute to determine whether the clocks are synchronized. If the clocks are not in sync, the time will be adjusted in the guest OS accordingly. The VMware Tools will move the time ahead for guests that have fallen behind and will slow down the clock on guests that have moved ahead of the current host time.

In most cases, the native functions (Win32Time, NTP) used in operating systems will be more accurate than periodic time synchronization and should be used instead to guarantee accurate time in the guest OS. Regardless of the approach taken, only a single method of time synchronization should ever be used.

Exercise 6.7 will cover the steps used to determine whether VMware Tools periodic time synchronization is in use. You will also learn how to enable and disable periodic time synchronization. This exercise will use a virtual machine running a Windows Server 2008 R2 guest OS and will use the command-line tools. As a reminder, in the next major vSphere release the VMware Tools GUI will be deprecated.

EXERCISE 6.7

Configuring Periodic Time Synchronization in a Virtual Machine

1. Obtain a console session to a virtual machine with a Windows 2008 R2 guest OS and log in.

2. Open a command prompt and type the following command:

```
cd "C:\Program Files\VMware\VMware Tools"
```

EXERCISE 6.7 *(continued)*

Note that on different Windows operating systems, this path may vary. On Linux and Solaris the path will be usr/sbin, and it will vary on other operating systems as well.

3. At the command prompt, type the following command:

    VmwareToolboxCmd.exe timesync status

    Note that on Linux, Solaris, and FreeBSD the command is as follows:

    vmware-toolbox-cmd

4. The results of this command are shown here:

5. In this example, time synchronization is disabled. To enable time synchronization, enter this command:

    VmwareToolboxCmd.exe timesync enable

6. If time synchronization is enabled, enter this command to disable it:

    VmwareToolboxCmd.exe timesync disable

At this point, periodic time synchronization has been disabled. Certain operations will trigger the VMware Tools to synchronize time in the virtual machine:

- Starting VMware Tools service/daemon (reboot or power on)
- Resuming a VM from a suspend operation
- Reverting to snapshot
- Shrinking a disk

 To completely disable all VMware Tools–initiated time synchronization functionality for a VM, the virtual machine's VMX file must be modified (see http://kb.vmware.com/kb/1189).

Now that I have covered time synchronization, we will begin to explore various aspects of virtual disks and how they relate to the virtual machine. Let's start with identifying virtual machine storage resources.

Identifying Virtual Machine Storage Resources

In Exercise 6.1 you configured and deployed a virtual machine. Part of the configuration was the creation of a virtual disk for this virtual machine. Now that the VM has been deployed, let's look closer at its storage resources. Figure 6.4 shows the storage resources used by a virtual machine.

FIGURE 6.4   Virtual machine storage resources

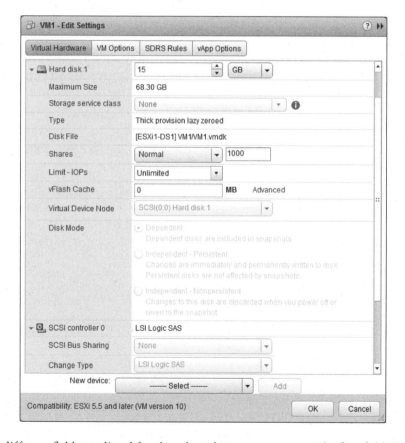

Ten different fields are listed for the selected storage resource. The first field shows the virtual disk size. The menu can be used to change the virtual disk size to a greater value here. The second field listed is the maximum size the virtual disk can be on the datastore where it is currently located. The third field has a drop-down menu that can be used to view or modify the storage service class for this virtual machine. The fourth field is the disk provisioning type. The fifth field is the Disk File, and it shows the path information of the virtual disk. The Disk File field includes the datastore, the VM directory name, and the virtual disk name.

The sixth field features a drop-down menu that shows the disk shares value and a text field that can be used to assign a numeric value. The seventh field also features a drop-down menu that shows the configured IOPS limit for the virtual disk. The disk shares and limits settings will both be covered in detail in Chapter 7. The eighth field shows the information for the configured vFlash settings, and the ninth field features another drop-down menu that can be used to view or modify the virtual device node. This represents the SCSI controller and the drive number for the selected virtual disk. In Figure 6.4, SCSI 0:0 is used, meaning SCSI controller 0 and SCSI ID 0. Note that this value is grayed out for powered-on virtual machines.

The final field is the disk mode. This is where independent disks can be configured. Like the virtual device node, the disk mode field is also grayed out for powered-on virtual machines. Independent disks are excluded from snapshot operations. Two modes can be used with independent disks:

Independent Persistent   This disk behaves just like a normal disk, and all writes are committed to disk.

Independent Nonpersistent   All changes to this type of independent disk are lost at VM power-off or reset.

Other locations are available to obtain additional information about virtual machine storage resources. In the Virtual Machines panel on the Resources tab for a selected datacenter or host you'll find two additional fields, as shown in Figure 6.5.

FIGURE 6.5   Virtual machine storage resources

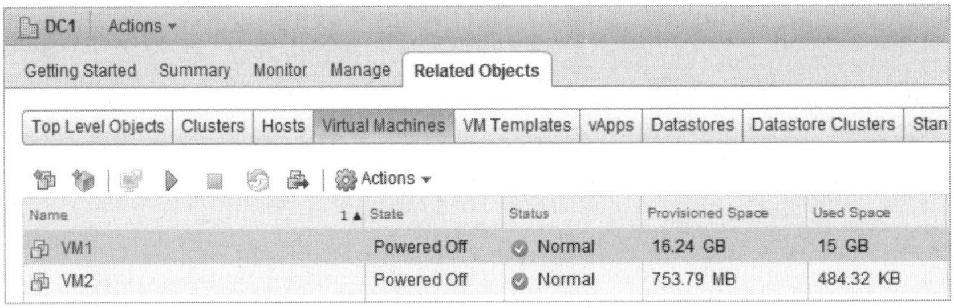

The storage resource information here consists of the following:

Provisioned Space   This value represents the provisioned size of all virtual disks in the virtual machine plus the size of the virtual machine's swap file.

Used Space   This is the amount of space consumed by all of the files that make up the virtual machine, including swap files, config files, and snapshots. For thin-provisioned disks, this value will typically report a value less than the value reported for the Provisioned Storage field.

> You can also right-click any column header in the view shown in Figure 6.5 and choose the Show/Hide Columns option to select additional fields including shares and IOPS limits.

You might have noticed in Figure 6.4 that the information for the virtual machine's SCSI controller was also visible below the virtual disk information. Let's discuss configuring and modifying the disk controllers for virtual disks in the next section.

Configuring and Modifying the Disk Controller for Virtual Disks

Virtual disk controllers are used by virtual machines to access their virtual disks. When you create a virtual machine, the default controller for the guest operating system you selected will be provided. This controller type will seldom need to be changed. The virtual disk controller types are described here:

IDE   This type is used by legacy operating systems for disk and CD/DVD ROM drives.

SATA   This type is new with hardware version 10 and is typically used for Mac OS X guests and CD/DVD ROM drives.

BusLogic Parallel   This is an emulated version of a hardware storage adapter from BusLogic. This adapter is typically used with older operating systems that include the BusLogic driver by default.

LSI Logic Parallel   This is an emulated version of a hardware storage adapter from LSI. This adapter is typically used with newer operating systems that include the LSI driver by default.

LSI Logic SAS   This controller was first introduced with vSphere 4 and is intended to provide increased performance over the BusLogic and LSI Logic Parallel controllers. It is available only for VMs that are using virtual machine hardware version 7 or newer. As some vendors phase out support for parallel SCSI, the LSI Logic SAS adapter could also be a wise choice to ensure future compatibility. Check with your OS vendor for more information.

VMware Paravirtual   This storage controller was also first introduced with vSphere 4 and is intended to provide high performance with lower CPU utilization. It is intended for use with high I/O and high-performance storage and is not supported by all operating systems.

Check the following VMware KB article to ensure operating system compatibility with the VMware Paravirtual SCSI (PVSCSI) adapter:

http://kb.vmware.com/kb/1010398

 Application-consistent quiescing (via VMware Tool snapshots) is not supported for virtual machines with IDE or SATA disks.

In addition to specifying the disk controller type, you can configure the SCSI bus sharing type to be used with the controller. SCSI bus sharing allows different virtual machines to access the same virtual disk(s) simultaneously and is useful in clustering solutions. The three types of SCSI bus sharing are as follows:

None   This is the default setting and does not allow the virtual disks to be shared.

Virtual   This setting allows virtual disks to be shared by virtual machines located on the same ESXi host.

Physical   This setting allows virtual disks to be shared by virtual machines located on any ESXi host.

The available operations for SCSI controllers are adding, removing, and changing the type, as well as setting the bus sharing options. In Exercise 6.8 you will add an additional disk controller to a virtual machine and configure the SCSI bus sharing options for it. The exercise will begin with a Windows 2008 R2 guest OS on a virtual machine with a single LSI Logic SAS controller and virtual disk.

EXERCISE 6.8

Configuring and Modifying a Disk Controller

1.   Connect to a vCenter Server with the vSphere Web Client.

2.   Right-click a powered-off virtual machine from the inventory. Choose the Edit Settings option from the context menu.

3.   The Edit Settings window will open, as shown here.

The first step is to add an additional controller to the virtual machine.

4. Click the New Device drop-down menu located at the bottom of the Edit Settings window to make the menu appear. Select SCSI Controller from the list of devices and then click Add to continue. A New SCSI Controller item will now be listed at the bottom of the list in the virtual machine properties.

5. Use the arrow to the left to expand the New SCSI Controller options. Review the options, as shown here:

6. Use the drop-down menu to change the SCSI Bus Sharing option to Virtual, and change the SCSI Controller Type option to VMware Paravirtual.

7. Click OK to add this new SCSI controller to the VM.

8. A Reconfigure Virtual Machine task will start. When this task completes, verify that the new SCSI controller is listed in the virtual machine properties, as shown in the following image:

9. In the Edit Settings window for the VM, add a new hard disk.

10. Expand the New Hard Disk to modify it. Configure the size and disk provisioning type for the virtual disk. Change the Virtual Device Node value to SCSI(1:0), and click OK to save these changes.

EXERCISE 6.8 *(continued)*

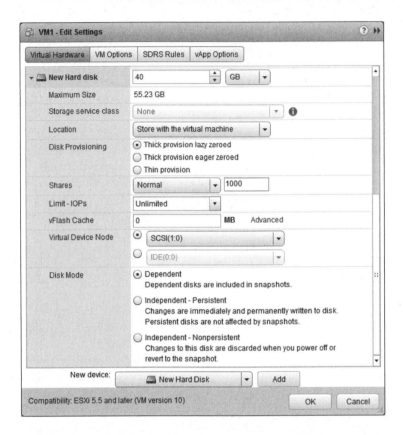

11. Verify that the new disk added is listed under the new SCSI controller.

We have covered how to add and configure virtual disks and controllers, and now we will discuss the virtual disk types in more detail.

Configuring the Appropriate Virtual Disk Type for a Virtual Machine

As you saw in Exercise 6.8, when virtual disks are created, certain properties can be specified. These properties include the size of the disk, the type of provisioning to use, the location to store the disk, the virtual device node, and the disk mode. This section discusses the different virtual disk types.

Virtual disk types, disk provisioning, and *format* are all used to refer to the type of virtual disk used in a virtual machine. The three types of virtual disks—that is, the three options for Disk Provisioning in the New Hard Disk settings—are Thick Provision Lazy Zeroed, Thick Provision Eager Zeroed, and Thin Provision.

A Thick Provision Lazy Zeroed disk is a VMDK file that is created and all of its space is provisioned immediately. Although the space is provisioned immediately, the space is actually zeroed on command. A virtual disk that is created as 20GB will consume 20GB of space on the datastore, regardless of the actual disk usage in the guest OS. This virtual disk type was known as a *flat disk* in previous vSphere versions.

Zeroing is the process in which disk blocks are overwritten with zeroes. This process is performed to ensure that no prior data is still on the volume that might cause problems with the VMDK, or introduce data security issues.

A Thick Provision Eager Zeroed disk is a VMDK file that when created has all of its space provisioned immediately. With this type of VMDK, the space is also zeroed at the time of creation. This type of disk takes the longest to create and is required for certain features like VMware FT. A virtual disk that is created as 20GB will consume 20GB of space on the datastore, regardless of the actual disk usage in the guest OS. There is a slight performance increase with this format, since the zeroing does not have to happen at runtime as it does with the other two formats.

A Thin Provision disk is a VMDK file that is created with a zero size, and it will grow on demand as required. A virtual disk that is 20GB will consume approximately the actual space used by the guest operating system. Keep in mind that although the size will increase as required, it will not shrink if files within the guest operating systems are deleted.

In addition to virtual disks, raw device mappings can be used in virtual machines. Raw device mapping (RDM) can be used to store virtual machine data directly on the storage area network (SAN), as opposed to storing it in a VMDK file on a VMFS datastore. This can be useful if SAN snapshots are required, if applications that are SAN-aware are used, or if Microsoft Cluster Service (MSCS) is used.

Adding an RDM to a virtual machine will create an RDM file that points to the raw device. This RDM file will have a ·vmdk extension and will even report the size of the raw device in the Datastore Browser, but this file contains only the mapping information. Two compatibility modes can be used with RDMs:

Physical   In this compatibility mode, the VMkernel passes through all SCSI commands with the exception of the REPORT LUNs command. This allows the VMkernel to isolate the LUN to the virtual machine that owns it. Physical Compatibility mode is used for SAN-aware applications running in a virtual machine. VMware snapshots are not possible with this compatibility mode.

Virtual This compatibility mode allows the guest OS to treat the RDM more like a virtual disk and can be used with snapshots.

Exercise 6.9 shows the steps to add an RDM to a virtual machine using the vSphere Web Client. Note that for this exercise you will need to have a storage LUN (Logical Unit Number) presented to the ESXi host, one that is not already used as a VMFS datastore. In case this LUN needs to be accessible by multiple hosts, make sure it's presented to each host with the same LUN ID.

EXERCISE 6.9

Adding an RDM Disk to a Virtual Machine

1. Connect to a vCenter Server with the vSphere Web Client.

2. Right-click a virtual machine from the inventory. Choose the Edit Settings option from the context menu.

3. The Edit Settings window will open. Click the New Device drop-down menu in the Edit Settings window to make the menu appear.

4. Select RDM Disk from the list of devices and then click Add to continue.

5. A Select Target LUN window will open. Select an available storage LUN from this list by clicking it.

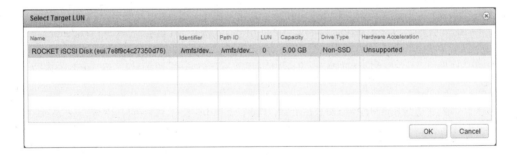

6. Click OK in the Select Target LUN window to continue.

7. Locate the New Hard Disk entry in the virtual machine properties and expand the options for it. Note that the size field is grayed out, since RDM disks must be expanded using the storage vendor's management tools.

8. Using the drop-down menu, change Compatibility Mode to Virtual, and then review the Virtual Device Node for the RDM disk.

9. Click OK to add the new RDM disk to the VM.

10. A Reconfigure Virtual Machine task will start. When this task completes, the RDM has been added to the VM.

11. To configure the RDM, use disk management tools in the guest OS to scan for new devices and to format the disk appropriately.

When configuring an RDM disk with disk management tools in the guest OS, make sure that the partition is aligned properly.

Configuring the appropriate virtual disk type for a virtual machine will depend on a variety of factors in your environment. Some of these factors could include the following:

Storage Consumption   If space or the ability to overallocate storage is a primary concern in an environment, then thin-provisioned disks would be appropriate.

Fault Tolerance (FT)   If VMware FT is required, then thick-provisioned eager zeroed disks would be appropriate.

Performance   If absolute performance is a concern, then thick-provisioned eager zeroed disks would also be appropriate.

Storage Support   If your storage is NFS and doesn't support the *VAAI* NAS extensions, then thin provisioning would be the only option.

Clustering   Clustering solutions will often require thick-provisioned eager zeroed disks and/or RDMs.

Disk Operations   While all VMs are encapsulated and generally very portable, RDMs can be easily moved or attached to other virtual or physical servers in the same SAN fabric.

Now that I have covered configuring appropriate virtual disk types for virtual machines, we will go into more detail on creating and converting virtual disks.

Creating and Converting Thin/Thick Provisioned Virtual Disks

As you have seen in previous exercises, the virtual disk formats are typically chosen upon virtual machine creation. The format chosen here is in no way permanent, and the conversion of any disk format to another disk format is easily accomplished. Exercise 6.10 shows the steps to convert a thin disk, in a powered-off virtual machine, to a thick disk.

EXERCISE 6.10

Converting a Thin Disk to a Thick Disk

1.   Connect to a vCenter Server with the vSphere Web Client.

2.   Select a powered-off virtual machine with a thin-provisioned disk from the inventory.

3.   Right-click the virtual machine and choose Edit Settings.

4.   When the Edit Settings window opens, select a thin-provisioned hard disk from the list of devices and expand it to view its properties.

5.   Verify that the Type value is reported as Thin Provision.

6. Also note the Disk File information for the virtual disk.

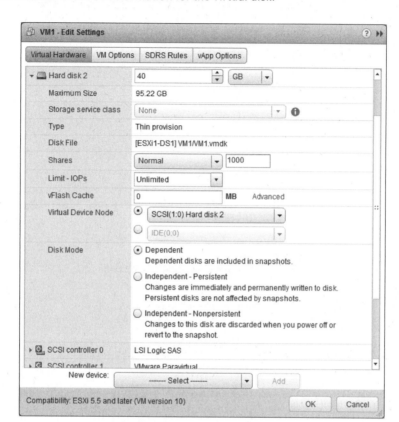

7. Click the Cancel button to exit the Edit Settings window.

8. On the virtual machine's Manage tab, click Settings and then select VM Hardware from the left pane.

9. Use the gray arrow to expand the information for the thin-provisioned hard disk, and then review the location listed for this virtual disk. This should match the Disk File information you obtained in step 6 of this exercise.

10. Click the blue datastore name. On the datastore's Manage tab, click the Files option and then click the appropriate directory for the disk file that you will be expanding.

11. The right pane will refresh with the contents of the directory you selected.

12. Locate the virtual disk file using the path information obtained in step 6, and right-click it. Choose the Inflate option from the context menu, as shown here:

EXERCISE 6.10 *(continued)*

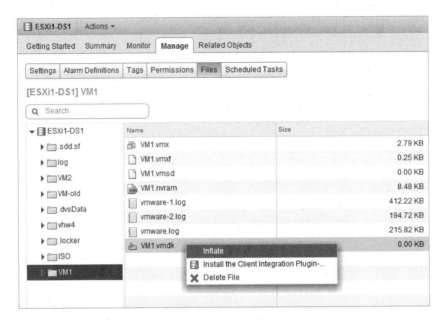

13. An Inflate Virtual Disk task will begin. Note that this task can take some time to complete for larger VMDK files.

14. When the Inflate Virtual Disk task completes, verify the value reported for the virtual disk in the Size column now reflects the full size for the virtual disk.

15. Open the virtual machine properties and expand the inflated hard disk. Verify that the Type value is now reported as Thick Provision.

As shown in Exercise 6.10, the inflate operation will convert a thin-provisioned disk to a thick-provisioned disk. The vmkfstools command, Storage vMotion, and VMware Converter could also each be used to accomplish this same task or to convert a thick disk to thin.

Now that we have covered some of the virtual disk operations, let's turn our attention to some of the performance options for virtual disks. We will begin with configuring disk shares for a virtual machine.

Configuring Disk Shares

In vSphere, shares are used to specify the relative importance of a virtual machine as it pertains to a specific resource. Shares can be configured for CPU, memory, or disk. Disk shares are used to prioritize disk access for virtual machines that access the same datastores.

It is important to note that disk shares are applicable only on a per-host basis and cannot be pooled across a cluster. Shares may have the values of Low, Normal, High, and Custom. Each of these values will be compared to the sum of all shares for all VMs on the host. Virtual machines with the highest share values will have higher throughput and lower latency than those with lower share values.

An input/output operations per second (IOPS) limit can also be set for a virtual machine. This will limit the number of disk I/O operations per second for the virtual machine.

Exercise 6.11 covers the steps required to configure disk shares for a virtual machine. In this exercise you will set the shares value to High and the IOPS limit to Unlimited, which would give this VM a very high relative priority.

EXERCISE 6.11

Configuring Disk Shares for a Virtual Machine

1. Connect to a vCenter Server with the vSphere Web Client.

2. Right-click a virtual machine and choose Edit Settings from the context menu.

3. When the Edit Settings window opens, select a virtual disk from the list of devices and expand it to view its properties.

4. Locate the Shares field and take note of the current default values.

5. Using the drop-down menu to the right of the Shares field, change the value to High. Take note of the value to the right of the drop-down menu.

EXERCISE 6.11 *(continued)*

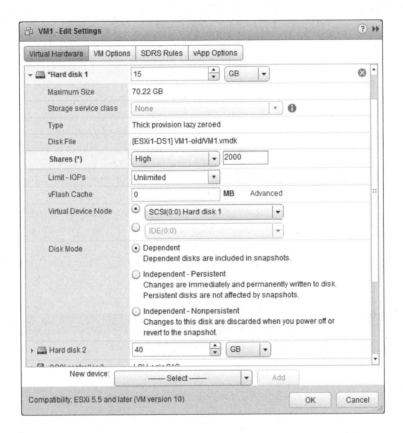

6. Click OK to save the changes. A Reconfigure Virtual Machine task will begin.

Configuring disk shares is a great way to give priority to certain virtual disks. Another great way to give performance to certain virtual disks is to place them on appropriately backed datastores.

Determining Appropriate Datastore Locations for Virtual Machines Based on Application Workloads

When adding virtual disks to virtual machines, two options are available for choosing the location used to store the virtual disk files:

Store With The Virtual Machine This option will store the virtual disk file in the virtual machine directory, along with the virtual machine's configuration and log files. This approach is generally easy to manage, since all of the virtual machine's files are in a single location.

Browse   This option will allow the virtual machine disk file to be stored on a separate datastore or datastore cluster. This approach is often useful but does add complexity to the management of the VM.

Having multiple datastores and the ability to distribute virtual disks across multiple datastores can offer many advantages. Determining the appropriate datastore location will often come down to looking at the physical storage that is backing the datastore. Certain workloads will require specific disk configurations, and knowing the capabilities of the disks behind the datastore will be beneficial in determining which datastore to use.

Microsoft SQL Server is commonly configured to use both RAID5 and RAID1+0 disk configurations. With multiple datastores on differing RAID sets, this capability can easily be provided for SQL Server or other servers that have similar requirements.

If replication is being used at the storage level, any virtual machine could have its page file placed on a different virtual disk in a different datastore. This could allow very fast page file access, in addition to excluding this constantly changing disk from replication.

Applications that are read-intensive will likely perform extremely well on a datastore backed by storage that is utilizing *SSD* disks.

Virtual desktops can be placed on datastores backed by storage that supports *deduplication.*

The key thing to remember when determining the appropriate datastore location is that you will need to understand both the application's requirements and the capability of the storage system backing the datastore. In addition to configuring your storage resources appropriately, the vCPU and memory resources for the VM should be configured appropriately for the specific applications that they run.

Configuring and Modifying Virtual CPU and Memory Resources According to OS and Application Requirements

Different virtual machines will require different resources for both CPU and memory, just as physical servers have different configurations. Although it may initially seem like a good idea to give your VMs maximum memory and maximum CPU resources, it is actually a best practice to start small and grow as required. This approach both conserves resources and creates a more scalable environment.

The first step in building out a virtual machine is to look at the system requirements for the guest OS. Windows Server 2008 R2 has the following recommended system requirements:

- Processor: Single 2GHz or faster
- Memory: 2GB

At this point, you know the virtual machine needs a single vCPU and 2GB of RAM. As the second step in sizing your virtual machine, let's look at the system requirements for the application. For this example, let's look at the minimum-sized vCenter Server installation, which has the following system requirements:

- Processor: Two 64-bit CPUs or one 64-bit dual-core processor

- Memory: 12GB

At this point, you know the virtual machine needs two vCPUs or a single dual-core vCPU and 12GB of RAM. As the final step in sizing the virtual machine, you would include any additional system requirements for things such as antivirus or other standard applications that will be installed on the server. Once the final number is totaled, the virtual machine may be sized accordingly by editing its settings.

Virtual machines have the ability to grow, and even shrink if required, in a dynamic fashion. Of course, reboots are often required, but if additional applications need to be added to a server, the system requirements can be calculated and adjusted. There is no need to oversize virtual machines when the environment is this flexible. The final step in sizing is the ongoing performance monitoring of the virtual machine. As problems are found or as the system grows beyond its original capacity, administrators can upgrade the virtual machine to continue to evolve with the actual demands of the workload.

We have covered disk, processor, and memory configuration for our VMs, so now let's focus on configuring and modifying network connections for virtual machines.

Configuring and Modifying Virtual NIC Adapters and Connecting Virtual Machines to Appropriate Network Resources

Configuring and modifying virtual NIC adapters is an important part of maintaining the virtual infrastructure. In many environments, there are multiple networks, and some environments will even have DMZ or external-facing networks connected to their ESXi hosts. Because of this, it is very important to understand the networking setup in a given vSphere environment. Configuring networking for a virtual machine involves selecting a network adapter type, a network connection, and the connection options. Before you configure a virtual NIC, take a look at some of the different NIC types:

E1000 This is an emulated version of the Intel 82545EM Gigabit Ethernet NIC. Drivers are available in most Linux versions 2.4.19 and newer, Windows XP Professional (64-bit) and newer, and Windows Server 2003 (32-bit) and newer.

E1000E This emulates a newer model of Intel Gigabit NIC (number 82574) in virtual machine hardware version 8 and later. It is known as the "e1000e" vNIC, and it is the default vNIC for Windows 8 and newer (Windows) guest operating systems.

SR-IOV Passthrough   With this NIC, the VM and an ESXi host's physical network adapter communicate directly without the use of the VMkernel. Drivers are available in Red Hat Enterprise Linux 6.x and Windows Server 2008 R2 SP2.

Vlance   This is an emulated version of the AMD 79C970 PCnet32 LANCE NIC. Drivers are available in most 32-bit guests but not for Windows Vista and newer.

Flexible   This adapter identifies itself as a Vlance adapter at boot but can function as a VMXNET adapter if the VMware Tools are installed.

VMXNET   This adapter is built for virtual machines and requires the VMware Tools to provide a driver.

VMXNET 2 (Enhanced)   This adapter is based on the VMXNET adapter but offers jumbo frames and hardware offload support. This adapter is available for limited guest operating systems running on ESX/ESXi 3.5 and newer and requires the VMware Tools to provide a driver.

VMXNET 3   This adapter is a paravirtualized NIC designed for performance. VMXNET 3 offers jumbo frames, hardware offloads, support for multiqueue, IPv6 offloads, and MSI/MSI-X interrupt delivery. It is important to note that VMXNET 3 is a completely different adapter than either VMXNET or VMXNET 2, and it requires the VMware Tools to provide a driver.

Now that we have covered virtual NIC adapters, Exercise 6.12 shows the steps required to add and configure a virtual NIC to a virtual machine and connect the virtual machine to a network. Note that this exercise will remove the currently configured NIC for the virtual machine and replace it. Before starting this exercise, ensure that this VM has the latest version of the VMware Tools installed.

EXERCISE 6.12

Adding, Configuring, and Connecting a Virtual NIC Adapter

1. Connect to a vCenter Server with the vSphere Web Client.

2. Right-click a virtual machine in the left pane. Choose Edit Settings from the context menu.

3. Click Network Adapter 1 to select it. The device properties will then appear below the device.

4. Take note of the Network Label shown for this network adapter in the drop-down menu and also note the values listed in both the Status and Adapter Type fields.

5. Hover the mouse over Network Adapter 1 and note the Remove icon that appears beside the device.

EXERCISE 6.12 *(continued)*

6. Click the Remove icon to mark the network adapter for removal. Note how the device field turns pink and the text Device Will Be Removed now appears beside it.

7. Click the New Device drop-down menu in the Edit Settings window. Select Network from the list of devices and then click Add to continue. A New Network item will now appear at the bottom of the list in the virtual machine properties.

8. Use the arrow to the left of the New Network item to expand it.

9. Using the drop-down menu, change the network label to the value noted in step 4 of this exercise. Using the drop-down menu, change Adapter Type to VMXNET 3. Select the Connect At Power On option. The final configuration should look like this:

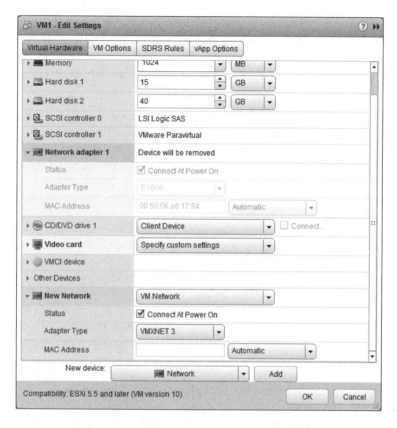

10. Click OK to save these changes. A Reconfigure Virtual Machine task will begin. When this task completes, the configuration is complete.

11. Because the NIC was replaced with a new one, the network configuration in the guest OS will need to be reconfigured before the VM can be used on the network again. Follow the procedures specific to your guest OS for this step.

> In the virtual machine settings, a field is provided that lets you specify the MAC address for a virtual NIC. Refer to the vSphere Networking Guide to view the rules for using this feature and the allowable MAC addresses that may be specified.

We have now covered creating virtual machines and configuring them. In the next section you will see how to convert existing physical servers using VMware Converter.

Converting a Physical Machine Using VMware Converter

VMware Converter is a free application provided by VMware that can be used to convert physical servers to virtual machines (P2V), convert virtual machines to virtual machines (V2V), reconfigure virtual machines, and import various image formats and convert them to virtual machines. A number of operating systems from Microsoft, Red Hat, SUSE, and Ubuntu are supported for conversion, but it is always a good idea to check the supported operating systems listed in the VMware Converter Standalone documentation.

Since vSphere 5, VMware Converter has been released as a standalone application, and these versions do not support cold cloning. Cold cloning is the process of booting a physical or virtual machine to VMware Converter media and running the conversion from it. This approach allows for consistent images, because the applications would be stopped and the operating system would be powered off. In VMware Converter Standalone 5.1, hot cloning is used. Hot cloning converts the physical server or virtual machine while it is running the guest OS and applications. To ensure consistency with hot clones, VMware recommends that you stop all services and applications while the conversion is in process. This will guarantee that the applications and data are consistent when the conversion is complete.

The cloning process will copy data over the network. Two primary modes are used for the cloning process:

Volume Based   This mode will be used if volumes are resized to a smaller (or larger) size, and it will simply copy each file on the source over the network to the destination.

Disk Based   This mode will be used if volumes remain the same size or are increased in size, and it will copy the disk blocks. This mode is much faster than the volume-based mode.

It is also important to note that Ethernet controllers will change as part of the conversion process. After a P2V operation, networks will have to be reconfigured on the guest OS. The conversion and the change of the underlying hardware can also have implications for software that is licensed on MAC addresses or some other aspect of physical hardware.

VMware Converter Standalone 5.5 can be installed on a physical server or virtual machine either as a local installation or as a client-server installation. Exercise 6.13 covers the steps required to install VMware Converter Standalone 5.5 on a Windows 2008 R2 virtual machine as a local install. If you already have VMware Converter Standalone 5.5 installed, you can skip this exercise.

EXERCISE 6.13

Installing VMware Converter Standalone

1. Open a web browser and go to www.vmware.com/go/getconverter.

2. Log in or create an account and then download the VMware vCenter Converter Standalone 5.5 binary.

3. Verify the checksum for the downloaded file and then launch the executable to begin Setup.

4. Click Next on both the Welcome screen and the End-User Patent Agreement screen. Agree to the terms in the license agreement, and click Next.

5. Select the desired installation directory and click Next.

6. Choose Local Installation for Setup Type and click Next.

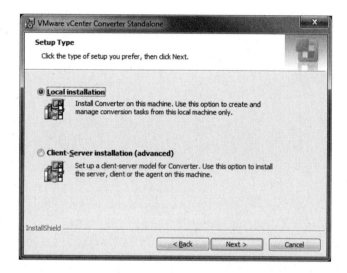

7. Click Install. When the installation completes, make sure the Run Converter Standalone Client Now option is checked and click the Finish button.

Now that VMware Converter Standalone 5.5 is installed, Exercise 6.14 will cover the steps for using it to perform a P2V conversion for a physical server. You will need a physical server with a supported operating system for this exercise. If you don't have a physical server, a VM can make a suitable substitute.

EXERCISE 6.14

Performing a P2V Conversion with VMware Converter Standalone 5.5

1. Open the VMware vCenter Converter Standalone application and click Convert Machine. The File ➢ New ➢ Convert Machine option can also be used here.

2. A Conversion Wizard will launch. Choose Powered-on Machine from the Select Source Type drop-down menu.

3. Specify a remote powered-on machine in the lower portion of the screen and enter the IP address or FQDN of the physical server to be converted. Also, enter a user-name/password that has Administrative access to the physical server. Choose the appropriate OS Family, using the drop-down menu. The final configuration should look similar to the image shown here:

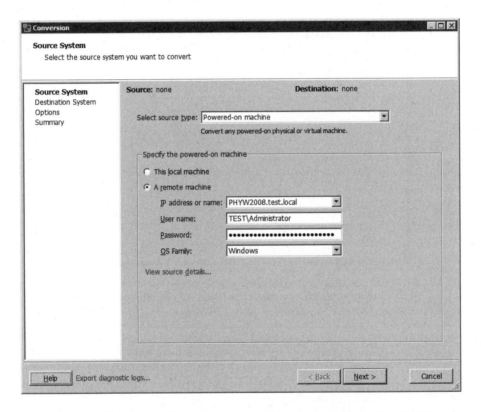

4. Click the blue View Source Details link. You will be prompted to install the VMware vCenter Converter Standalone Agent on the source machine. Choose the Automatically Uninstall The Files When Import Succeeds option and click Yes to continue.

5. The status of the agent deployment will be shown on the same window, and when complete, a Machine Details window will appear. Review the details here and click the Close button.

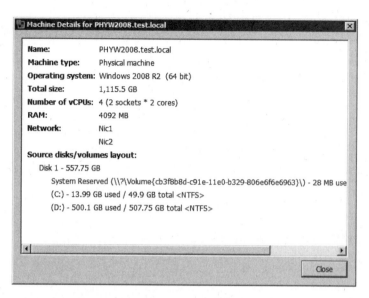

6. On the Destination System screen, select the default Destination Type of VMware Infrastructure Virtual Machine. Enter the FQDN for the vCenter Server that this virtual machine will be managed by, and enter the appropriate credentials for the vCenter Server.

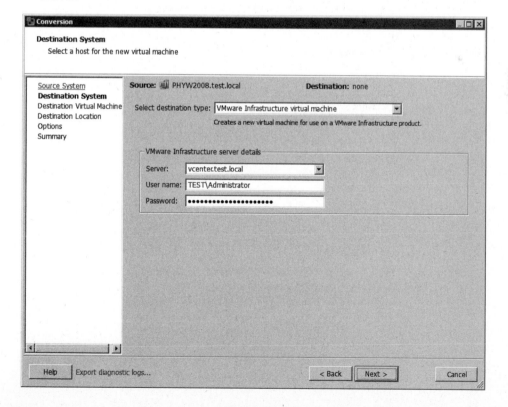

7. Click the Next button to continue. At the top of the Destination Virtual Machine screen, give the new virtual machine a unique name. Choose an inventory location for the new virtual machine and click Next.

8. Select the cluster or host that the virtual machine will be hosted on from the Inventory option in the middle of the screen. Use the drop-down menu to select a datastore and virtual machine hardware version. Click Next to continue.

9. On the Options screen, make any changes necessary. This can include reducing the number of vCPUs, changing which disks are copied, resizing the disks that are copied, connecting and disconnecting networks, and more.

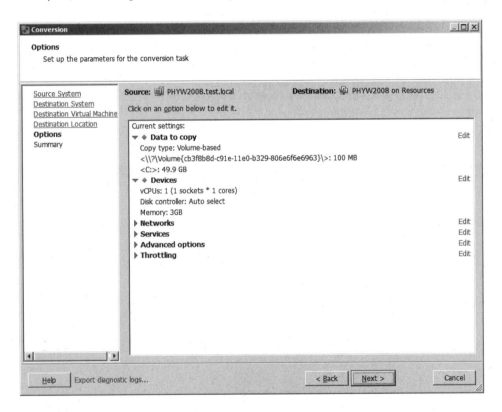

Note that any settings that are modified will have a blue diamond in front of them. When all of the changes have been made, click Next.

10. Review the information on the Summary screen and click the Finish button. A task will be listed in the VMware Converter Standalone window that shows the source, destination, progress, and more.

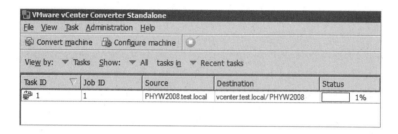

11. Selecting the task will populate the Summary and Task Progress tabs at the bottom of the screen. These tabs provide more detail on the progress.

12. When the conversion task completes, open the vSphere Web Client and locate the converted server in the inventory. Power it on and watch it boot from a console session.

> Converting a physical machine to a virtual machine involves much more than just running the VMware Converter. Any hardware agents, hardware management applications, and vendor-specific device drivers will need to be removed. Networking will need to be reconfigured, and some time will likely need to be spent with the system logs to ensure that everything is working properly. Only after this cleanup is complete should the applications on the converted virtual machine be started.

Now that you have learned how to convert a physical machine to a virtual machine using VMware vCenter Converter Standalone 5.5, I will cover another of this product's capabilities. In addition to physical servers, various supported VM source types can be imported into the vSphere environment by using VMware Converter Standalone 5.5.

Importing a Supported Virtual Machine Source Using VMware Converter

VMware Converter can convert a variety of other sources into vSphere environments. Some of these sources are as follows:

- Acronis True Image Echo 9.1 and 9.5
- Acronis True Image Home 10 and 11

- Symantec Backup Exec System Recovery 6.5, 7, 8, and 8.5
- Symantec LiveState Recovery 3 and 6 (.sv2i only)
- Norton Ghost 10, 12, and 14 (.sv2i only)
- Parallels Desktop 2.5, 3, and 4 (.pvs and .hdd)
- Parallels Workstation 2 (.pvs)
- StorageCraft ShadowProtect Desktop 2, 2.5, 3, 3.1, and 3.2 (.spf)
- StorageCraft ShadowProtect Server 2, 2.5, 3, 3.1, and 3.2 (.spf)
- StorageCraft ShadowProtect SBS 2, 2.5, 3, 3.1, and 3.2 (.spf)
- StorageCraft ShadowProtect IT 2, 2.5, 3, 3.1, and 3.2 (.spf)
- VMware Workstation 7, 8, 9 and 10
- VMware Fusion 3, 4, 5 and 6
- VMware Player 3, 4, 5 and 6
- vCenter Server 4, 4.1, 5, 5.1 and 5.5
- ESX 4 and 4.1
- ESXi 4, 4.1, 5, 5.1 and 5.5
- Hyper-V Server 2008 R2 (supported powered-off guests)
- Microsoft Virtual PC 2004, 2007 VHD (.vmc)
- Microsoft Virtual Server 2005, 2005 R2 VHD (.vmc)

Exercise 6.15 covers the steps to import a powered-off VM that is hosted by VMware Workstation into a vSphere environment by using VMware Converter. Not all test environments have a VMware Workstation VM. If you have any of the other supported sources, you can substitute that as necessary in this exercise, or you can just read along.

EXERCISE 6.15

Importing a VMware Workstation VM Using VMware Converter

1. Open the VMware vCenter Converter Standalone application.

2. Click the Convert Machine button, or choose File ➤ New ➤ Convert Machine.

3. A Conversion Wizard will launch. From the Source Type drop-down menu, choose VMware Workstation Or Other VMware Virtual Machine.

4. Browse to the VMX file for the powered-off VMware Workstation VM.

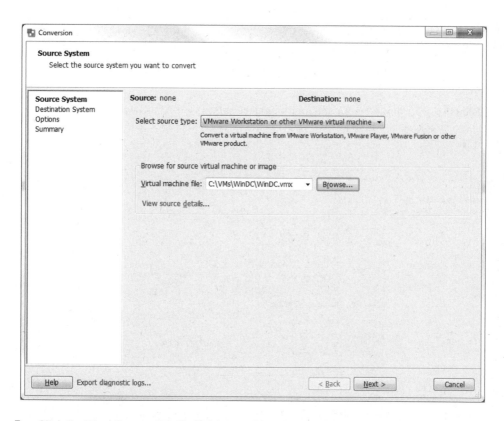

5. Click the View Source Details link located just below the field where the VMX path information is entered. A Machine Details window will open. Review the information and then click the Close button.

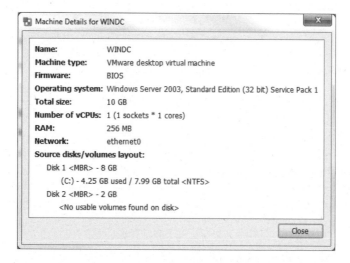

6. Click Next on the Source System screen, and then review the Destination System screen options.

7. Using the drop-down menu, ensure that a destination type of VMware Infrastructure Virtual Machine is selected and enter the FQDN and credentials for the vCenter Server.

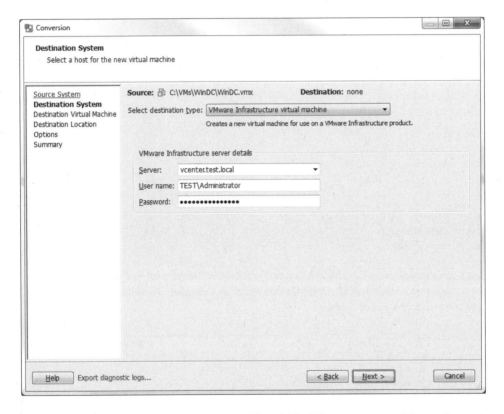

8. Click Next. At the top of the Destination Virtual Machine screen, provide a unique name for the virtual machine. Choose an inventory location for this virtual machine and click Next.

9. Select the cluster or host that the virtual machine will be hosted on from the Inventory option in the middle of the screen. Use the drop-down menus on the right to select a datastore and virtual machine hardware version. Click the Next button.

10. On the Options screen, make any changes necessary. This can include reducing the number of vCPUs, changing which disks are copied over, resizing the disks that are copied over, connecting and disconnecting networks, and more.

11. Click Next and review the information presented on the Summary screen. Click Finish to begin importing the VMware Workstation VM source.

12. A task will be listed in the VMware Converter Standalone window that shows the source, destination, progress, and more. Selecting the task will populate the Summary and Task Progress tabs at the bottom of the screen. These tabs provide more detail on the progress.

13. When this task completes, open the vSphere Web Client and locate the converted server in the inventory. Power it on and watch it boot from a console session.

Now that I have covered performing P2V conversions and importing a virtual machine from VMware Workstation into a vSphere environment, I will discuss how to use VMware Converter to modify the virtual hardware settings of a virtual machine.

Modifying Virtual Hardware Settings Using VMware Converter

So far, I have covered two ways to use VMware Converter. I showed you how to perform a P2V and import a VMware Workstation VM source. Another useful function that can be performed by VMware Converter is a virtual-to-virtual (V2V) conversion within the vSphere environment. Using VMware Converter for a V2V operation is useful in the following situations:

- Shrinking disks
- Downgrading the virtual machine hardware version
- Making clones of VMs with snapshots
- Changing hypervisors

Although virtual disks can be easily expanded, shrinking them is not as easily accomplished. Likewise, there is no mechanism in place to easily downgrade the virtual machine hardware version. A V2V operation with VMware Converter can solve both of these problems.

⊕ **Real World Scenario**

Using VMware Converter for V2V Conversions

A virtual infrastructure administrator has recently upgraded the virtual machine hardware version on a virtual machine in the production environment. Several days later an incident is reported by the owner of the application running on this virtual machine. The application owner reports that problems began immediately following the virtual machine hardware version upgrade.

The virtual infrastructure administrator decides to use VMware Converter to perform a V2V of the virtual machine. The V2V conversion will allow the virtual machine hardware version to be changed back to the prior version. The converted version of the application can then be loaded offline or on a test network to verify whether it functions correctly with the previous version of the virtual machine virtual hardware.

In Exercise 6.16, we will use VMware Converter to perform a V2V conversion on an existing powered-off virtual machine with virtual machine hardware version 10. You will convert this virtual machine to virtual machine hardware version 9, and you will also shrink the OS volume on this virtual machine in the process of the conversion. You will need a virtual machine with a supported Windows guest OS for this exercise.

EXERCISE 6.16

Performing a V2V Conversion to Modify Virtual Hardware Settings Using VMware Converter

1.   Open the VMware vCenter Converter Standalone application.

2.   Launch the Convert Machine wizard.

3. On the Source System screen, select VMware Infrastructure Virtual Machine for Source Type.

4. Enter the FQDN of the vCenter Server where the virtual machine that will be converted is located. Provide appropriate credentials for the vCenter Server and click Next.

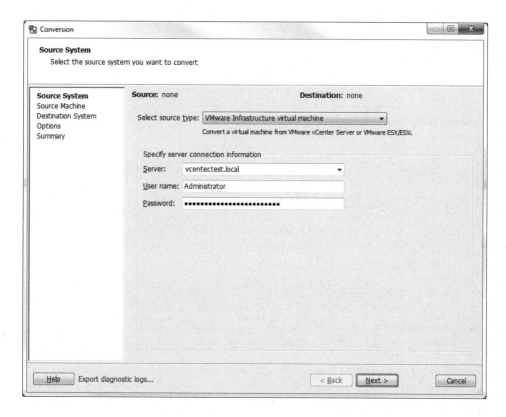

5. On the Source Machine screen, select the inventory location for the VM that will be converted. Once the VM is located in the right pane, select it and click Next.

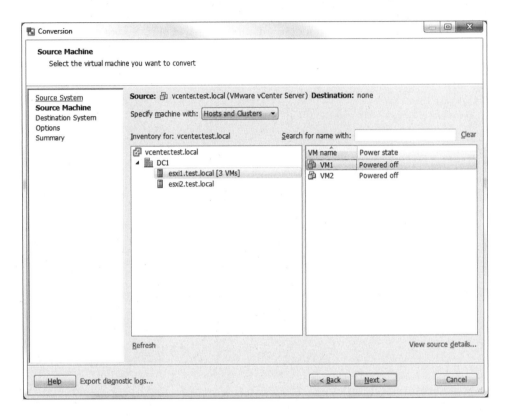

6. On the Destination System screen, select VMware Infrastructure Virtual Machine for Destination Type. Enter the FQDN for the vCenter Server that this converted virtual machine will be managed by, and enter the appropriate credentials for the vCenter Server.

   The vCenter Server you select in this step can be the same one that you specified in step 4, but it could also be a different vCenter Server. The remainder of this exercise assumes that you chose the same vCenter Server.

7. Click Next, and then at the top of the Destination Virtual Machine screen, provide a unique name for the new virtual machine. Choose an inventory location and click Next.

   The V2V operation will create a copy of the source, so either the destination VM will need to have a different name or it will have to be located in another folder if the same vCenter Server is being used.

8. Select the cluster or host that the virtual machine will be hosted on from the Inventory option in the middle of the screen, and use the drop-down menu on the right to select an appropriate datastore.

9. Change the virtual machine hardware version to Version 9 using the drop-down menu. The final configuration should look like the following:

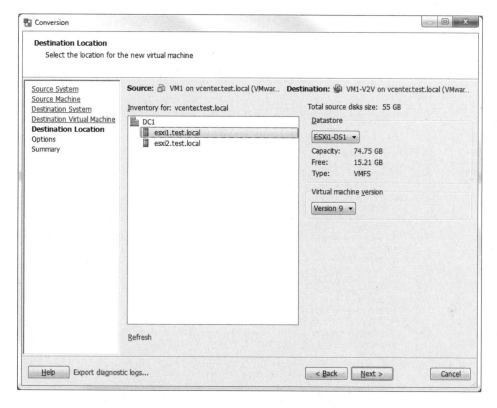

Choosing virtual machine hardware version 9 in the previous step was one objective of this exercise. In the remaining steps, you will resize the C: source volume to achieve the other objective: shrinking a virtual disk.

10. Click the Next button on the Destination Location screen.

11. On the Options screen, click the Edit link to the right of the Data To Copy item. Using the Data Copy Type drop-down menu, change the value to Select Volumes To Copy. The screen will refresh to show a new set of options.

12. In the row where the C: source volume is listed, locate the Destination Size column. Using the drop-down menu, review the current size and the minimum size values.

EXERCISE 6.16 *(continued)*

13. Decide on a new smaller size for the C: source volume and then select the <Type Size In GB> option from the drop-down menu. The drop-down menu will now allow you to enter this value. Enter the number only and then press Enter. The drop-down menu will now update to reflect the value you just entered. The final configuration will look like this:

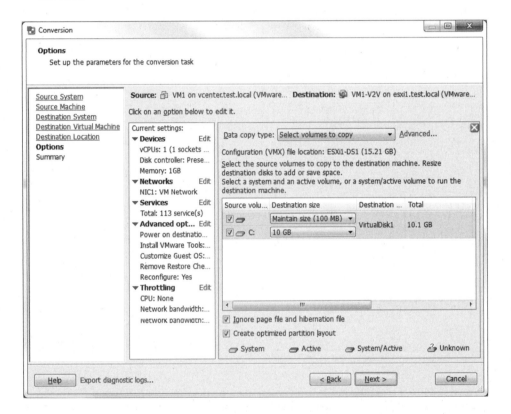

14. Review the information on the Summary screen and click the Finish button to begin the V2V conversion.

15. A task will be listed in the VMware Converter Standalone window that shows the source, destination, progress, and more. Selecting the task will populate the Sum-

mary and Task Progress tabs at the bottom of the screen. These tabs provide more detail on the progress.

16. When this task completes, open the vSphere Web Client and locate the converted virtual machine in the inventory. Right-click it and choose Edit Settings from the context menu.

17. Verify that the virtual machine hardware version has been downgraded and that the virtual disk has been resized.

You have now seen three ways to use VMware Converter in your vSphere environment. In the final section of this chapter, we will create and deploy vApps.

Creating and Deploying vApps

In addition to virtual machines, vSphere can be used as a platform for running applications. This is accomplished with a *vApp*, which is a container that consists of one or more virtual machines. These virtual machines are treated as a group in the vApp, and properties such as start order and shutdown order can be configured for the group. In this section, you will learn how to create and use vApps.

Determining When a Tiered Application Should Be Deployed as a vApp

By design, a tiered application is logically separated across multiple servers. An example of a three-tier application in vSphere might consist of a web front-end running on a virtual machine, a middleware application running on another virtual machine, and a database running in yet another virtual machine. The tiered architecture has certain dependencies, and this is true in both physical and virtual environments. For example, the web server must be able to communicate with the middleware application, which must be able to communicate with the database server. These dependencies are typically covered with application documentation and operational procedures.

The *vApp* approach can be used to simplify the dependencies of tiered applications, particularly when all tiers of the application are virtual machines. vApps may have specified start orders for the virtual machines they contain. This allows a tiered application to be encapsulated and treated as a unit rather than its parts. For example, a vApp can be powered up as a unit.

Real World Scenario

Using vApps

A new project has been requested from the R&D department of a client's business. They want to create an external web-based customer portal and have requested a set of virtual machines for this project. The list of servers includes a domain controller, a database server, an application server, and a web server. They want this environment to be self-contained and have no connectivity to any of the other networks in the company.

It is decided that a vApp will be used for this project. The virtual machines will be added to the vApp, and it will function as a unit. Start order will be used to ensure that the environment is both powered up and shut down in the proper sequence. Using a vApp will simplify both administrative and operational overheads by treating the entire set of virtual machines as an application.

Now that you have seen what a vApp is, let's create one.

Creating a vApp

A vApp must be created, and vCenter Server is a requirement to create them. A vApp can be created in the vCenter Server datacenter object from a DRS-enabled cluster with at least one host. This is shown in Figure 6.6 with vApp1. vApps can also be created on a standalone ESX 3.0 or newer host that is managed by vCenter Server. This is shown in Figure 6.6 with vApp2.

FIGURE 6.6 vApp location options

 If you plan to deploy a vApp on a DRS-enabled cluster, remember that DRS requires either the Enterprise or Enterprise Plus edition of vSphere.

Exercise 6.17 will cover the steps required to create a vApp. You will need a DRS-enabled cluster with at least one ESXi host to complete this lab.

EXERCISE 6.17

Creating a vApp

1. Connect to a vCenter Server with the vSphere Web Client.

2. Navigate to a DRS-enabled cluster in the left pane, and then right-click it. Choose New vApp from the context menu.

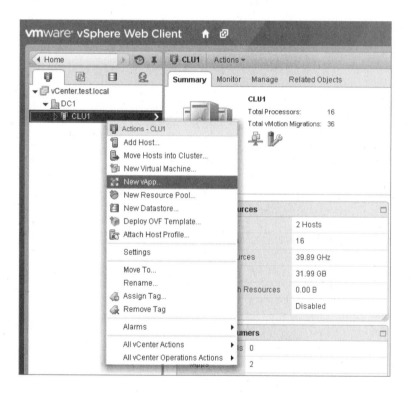

3. A New vApp Wizard will launch. On the Select A Creation Type screen, choose the Create A New vApp option and click Next.

4. Provide a unique name for the vApp and select a datacenter. Click Next to continue.

5. Configure the CPU and Memory Resources settings as necessary for your environment, or simply click Next to accept the default values.

EXERCISE 6.17 *(continued)*

6. Review the information on the Ready To Complete screen and click Finish. A Create vApp task will begin.

7. When the Create vApp task completes, verify that the vApp is listed in the left pane under the ESXi host.

 vApps can also be created with the vSphere Client.

We have now created a vApp, but it isn't really of any use just yet. Let's begin to add objects (like tiered applications) to it next.

Adding Objects to an Existing vApp

Objects that can be added to a vApp include virtual machines, resource pools, and other vApps. There are two options that you can use to add objects. To add new objects, in the vSphere Web Client right-click the vApp and select All vCenter Actions ➢ New options from the context menu. These options are shown in Figure 6.7.

The other option is to add existing objects to the vApp. This is easily accomplished in the vSphere Web Client, by dragging the objects into the vApp. For example, dragging an existing virtual machine into a vApp will happen without any prompting as long as the move is allowed. Figure 6.8 shows a virtual machine named Web-Server being dragged into a vApp named vApp2.

FIGURE 6.7   Adding a new object to a vApp

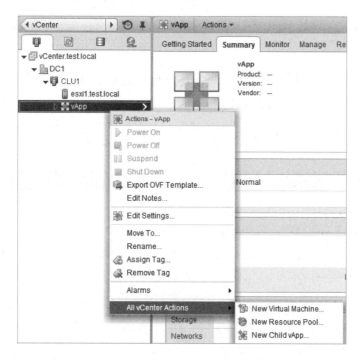

FIGURE 6.8   Dragging an object to a vApp

   Objects can also be easily removed from a vApp by dragging them to a new supported location.

Using the vSphere Web Client, take some time now and create at least one new virtual machine or add an existing virtual machine to the vApp you created in Exercise 6.17. Once the vApp has been populated with objects, you will be able to start identifying settings for the vApp.

Identifying and Editing vApp Settings

Now that you have created a vApp and added objects to it, you can identify and edit the vApp settings. Exercise 6.18 covers identifying the various vApp settings and editing the start order options.

EXERCISE 6.18

Identifying vApp Settings

1. Connect to a vCenter Server with the vSphere Web Client.

2. Right-click a vApp in the left pane. Choose Edit Settings from the context menu.

3. An Edit vApp window will open. In the Deployment section, expand the CPU Resources to view the settings.

4. Expand the Memory Resources item to view its settings.

The CPU Resources and Memory Resources settings are used to specify CPU and memory resources for the vApp. Configuring these options is similar to configuring the options for a resource pool, which will be covered in detail in Chapter 8, "Establishing Service Levels with Clusters, Fault Tolerance, and Resource Pools."

5. While still in the Deployment section, expand the IP Allocation item to view its settings. This will display the IP allocation policy that the vApp uses. This option will be discussed later in this chapter.

The Deployment settings have been covered, and the remainder of the exercise will look at the Authoring settings for the vApp. Note that you will work your way up through these settings.

6. Expand the IP Allocation item to view its settings. This will display the IP allocation scheme and IP protocol supported by this vApp. Review these settings.

7. Expand the Properties item and then expand the Product Item. Both of these items are used to provide additional details about the vApp.

8. Expand the Start Order item. This will display the order in which the virtual machines in this vApp will be both started and shut down.

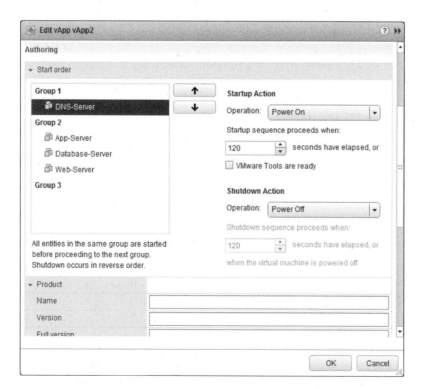

EXERCISE 6.18 *(continued)*

Notice that in this image there are two groups. The first group, Group 1, contains a DNS server. No virtual machines in Group 2 will be powered on until the DNS server is first powered up. Then in Group 2, the database server will first be powered up. It will be followed by the application server and finally the web server.

9. Select a virtual machine in the left pane. In the Startup Action section on the right, select the VMware Tools Are Ready check box.

   This option will allow the subsequent virtual machines to start up sooner than the 120-second delay if the VMware Tools start sooner. The VMware Tools starting is generally a good sign that the VM is up and running.

10. In the Shutdown Action section, use the drop-down menu to change the default operation to Guest Shutdown. When this change has been made, the Shutdown Sequence timer becomes enabled.

    These changes can be made or customized for each virtual machine in the list. This gives you finer control over how the vApp starts up.

11. Click OK in the Edit vApp window to save the changes made to the start order. When the Update vApp Configuration tasks complete, the settings have been saved.

I have now covered identifying the various vApp settings and editing the Start Order Startup and Shutdown actions. In the next section, we will discuss how IP pools are used with a vApp.

Configuring IP Pools

An IP pool is a network configuration stored in vCenter. The IP pool is associated with one or more virtual machine port groups and can be used to provide IP addresses to virtual machines in a vApp.

 An IP pool does not provide the same functionality as a DHCP server. Leveraging IP pools for addressing requires some type of support inside the guest OS of the VMs that make up the vApp.

Exercise 6.19 will cover the steps required to configure an IP pool and set up a vApp to use it.

EXERCISE 6.19

Configuring an IP Pool and vApp

1. Connect to a vCenter Server with the vSphere Web Client.

2. Navigate to and select a datacenter object in the inventory. Select the Manage tab for the datacenter and then select Network Protocol Profiles from the toolbar.

3. Click the Add icon. An Add Network Protocol Profile window will open.

4. Provide a descriptive name for the network protocol profile. Place a check in one of the checkboxes that is for a virtual machine connection type. You want to associate this network protocol profile with a virtual switch port group that virtual machines communicate on.

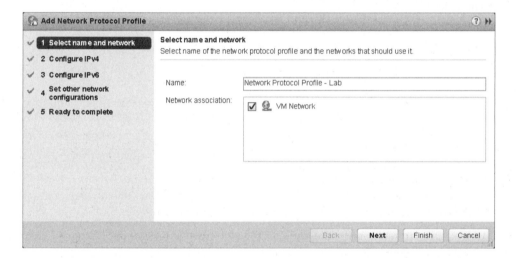

5. Click Next and configure IPv4. Provide a subnet and gateway for this network and add DNS Server Addresses.

6. Place a check in the Enable IP Pool option. Notice how the IP Pool Range field becomes active. Enter an IP Pool Range.

   Note that the range is a starting IP address, a number sign (#), and a number that represents the value of the range. In the following image, the range starts at 172.16.1.5 and includes the next 250 addresses. The gateway and broadcast address are always excluded from the range. You can also click the View Range link to view the addresses that will be available.

Configure IP v4
Supply the relevant IPv4 configuration

Subnet:	172 . 16 . 1 . 0 / 24
Subnet mask:	255.255.255.0
Address range:	172.16.1.1 to 172.16.1.254
Gateway:	172 . 16 . 1 . 1
DHCP present:	☐ Choose this option if a DHCP server is available on this network
DNS server addresses:	172.16.1.2,172.16.1.3

DNS server addresses are specified as a list of IP addresses separated by comma, semicolon, or space.

Enable IP pool:	☑ Choose this to enable the IP pool
IP pool range:	172.16.1.5#250 Hide range

Enter the address ranges as an ordered, comma separated list such as: 1.2.3.4#70, 1.2.3.80#16.

```
172.16.1.5
172.16.1.6
172.16.1.7
```

7. Click Next and then click Next again to skip IPv6 configuration. On the Set Other Network Configurations screen, enter a DNS Domain, Host Prefix, DNS Search Path and HTTP Proxy as required for your environment. Click Next to continue.

8. Review the information on the Ready To Complete screen and click Finish to create the network protocol profile.

9. The network protocol profile will now be listed on the Manage tab. Select the network protocol profile you just created and review its settings in the lower pane.

   At this point the IP pool has been created as part of the network protocol profile and is ready to be used. The remainder of this exercise will show how to associate a vApp with this network protocol profile.

10. Navigate to a vApp in the left pane and expand its contents. Verify that each VM in the vApp is connected to the same virtual machine port group that you associated with the IP pool in step 4 of this exercise.

11. Edit the settings of each VM in the vApp. Select the vApp Options toolbar item and place a check in the Enable vApp Options checkbox.

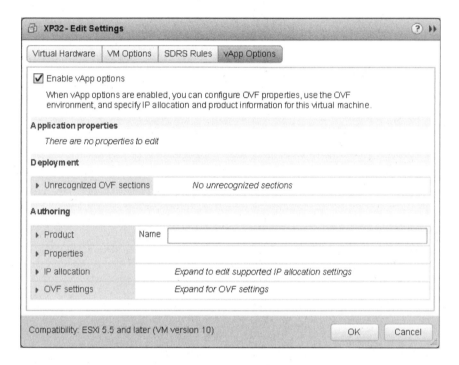

12. Click OK to save these changes. A Reconfigure Virtual Machine task will start. When this task completes, select the vApp and right-click it. Choose Edit Settings from the context menu. An Edit vApp window will open.

13. Expand the IP Allocation item under the Authoring section. Place a check in the OVF Environment option. Ensure that IPv4 is selected in the IP Protocol drop-down menu.

    In the IP Allocation Scheme settings, the DHCP option could have also been selected. Selecting this option would allow the vApp to use a DHCP Server. This DHCP server would have been entered on the same screen where the IP Pool was created back in step 6 of this exercise. Since this exercise covers IP pools, we will use only the OVF Environment option.

14. While still in the Edit vApp window, expand the IP Allocation item under the Deployment section. Verify the IP Protocol is IPv4 and then ensure that Static - Manual is selected for the IP Allocation. Click the information icon to the right of the IP Allocation drop-down menu to review the IP Allocation Policy.

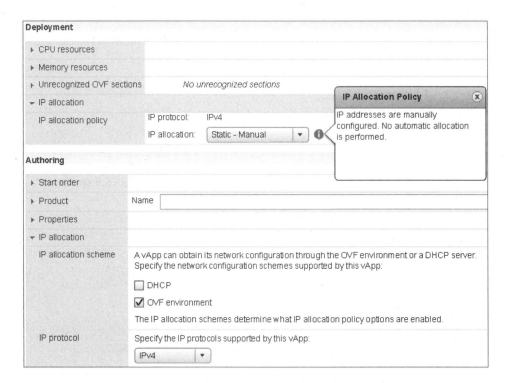

15. Click OK to save the changes. An Update vApp Resource Configuration task will begin, and it will be followed by an Update vApp Configuration task. When these tasks complete, configuration of the IP pool and the vApp is complete.

Before we leave IP pools behind, let's review the IP allocation policies for a vApp. The four available policies are as follows:

DHCP   This policy is used when the virtual machines in the vApp are configured to use an existing DHCP server to acquire IP addresses.

Static - Manual   This policy is used when the virtual machines in the vApp are configured manually with static IP addresses.

Static - IP Pool   This policy is used when the virtual machines in the vApp are configured to use IP pools. Addresses are automatically allocated at VM power on and remain allocated at VM power off.

Transient - IP Pool   This policy is used when the virtual machines in the vApp are configured to use IP pools. Addresses are automatically allocated at VM power on but are released at VM power off.

You have now created a network protocol profile and an IP Pool. Understand that certain vApps, like vCenter Operations Manager, may not deploy properly without the presence of a network protocol profile. We will cover this in more detail in Chapter 11, "Monitoring a vSphere Implementation and Managing vCenter Server Alarms." Let's now turn our attention to suspending and resuming a vApp.

Suspending and Resuming a vApp

Like virtual machines, vApps can also be suspended and resumed. To suspend a vApp, in the vSphere Web Client right-click the vApp and choose the Suspend option from the context menu. You will then be prompted to confirm suspension of the vApp. Virtual machines are suspended based on the reverse start order, and this order can be confirmed by viewing the tasks listed in the Recent Tasks pane in the vSphere Web Client. Figure 6.9 shows the Suspend option in the vSphere Web Client.

FIGURE 6.9   Suspending a vApp

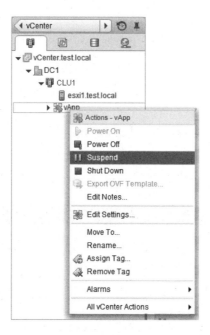

To resume a vApp, in the vSphere Web Client right-click the vApp and choose the Power On option from the context menu. Virtual machines will be resumed as specified in the start order, and this order can be confirmed by viewing the tasks listed in the Recent Tasks pane in the vSphere Web Client. Figure 6.10 shows the Power On option in the vSphere Web Client.

FIGURE 6.10   Resuming a vApp

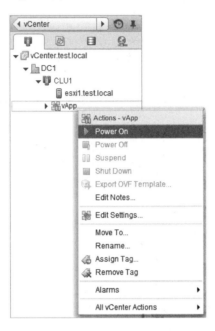

There is one final vApp topic remaining in this chapter: cloning and exporting vApps.

Cloning and Exporting a vApp

vApps can be cloned and exported, just like virtual machines can. Exercise 6.20 covers the steps required to clone a vApp using the vSphere Web Client.

EXERCISE 6.20

Cloning a vApp

1.   Connect to a vCenter Server with the vSphere Web Client.

2.   Right-click the vApp in the left pane. Choose the All vCenter Actions ➢ Clone option from the context menu.

3.   A New vApp Wizard will open. On the Select A Creation Type screen, verify that the Clone An Existing vApp option is selected and click the Next button.

4.   Select a destination ESXi host and click Next.

5.   Provide a unique name for the vApp and select a datacenter. Click Next to continue.

6. From the Select Virtual Disk Format drop-down menu, select a storage format. Also select a datastore by clicking it.

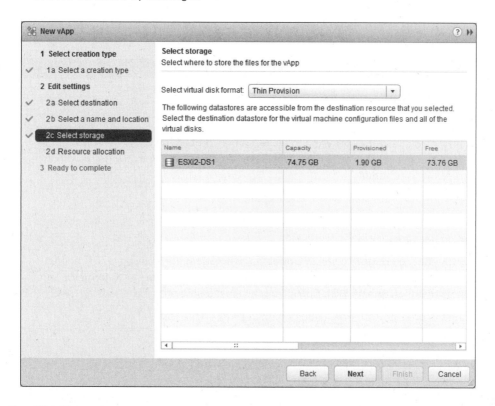

7. Click Next to continue.

8. Configure the CPU and Memory Resources settings as necessary for your environment, or simply click Next to accept the default values.

9. Review the information on the Ready To Complete screen and click the Finish button. A Clone vApp task will begin. When this task completes, verify that the vApp is listed in the inventory.

While vApps can be cloned into other vApps, a vApp cannot be cloned into itself.

Cloning vApps is useful in instances where a copy of a vApp is needed, perhaps for a new test or development environment. Exporting a vApp is often useful in the same instances that cloning a vApp is useful, but exported vApps can also be imported on different systems in different locations. It is important to note that vApps can be cloned regardless of the virtual machine power states, where exporting requires all VMs contained in the vApp to be powered off. Exercise 6.21 will cover the steps required to export a vApp.

EXERCISE 6.21

Exporting a vApp

1. Connect to a vCenter Server with the vSphere Web Client.

2. Right-click the powered-off vApp in the left pane. Choose the Export OVF Template option from the context menu. A Client Integration Access Control window will open. Click Allow to continue.

3. The Export OVF Template window will open.

4. Provide a descriptive name for the OVF template. This will be the name of the file, used in the directory in the next field.

5. Click the Choose button to select a directory with adequate free space to hold the OVF template. This directory is where the OVF template will be saved to on the same system that the vSphere Web Client from which it's being run.

6. Using the drop-down menu, choose the Single File (OVA) format option.

    Two options are available here:

    Folder Of Files (OVF)   This option is used to package the OVF template as a set of files (.ovf, .vmdk, and .mf).

    Single File (OVA)   This option is used to package the OVF template into a single OVA file.

7. Provide a detailed annotation for the OVF template.

8. If any virtual machines in the vApp are connected to an ISO file or floppy image, there will be an option allowing you to include these image files as part of the OVF template. If applicable for your vApp, choose whether to include image files.

9. Select the Enable Advanced Options check box and review these options. The final configuration should look similar to the image shown here:

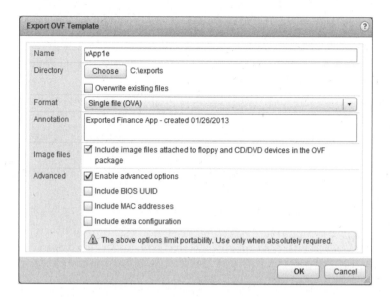

10. Click OK. An Initialize OVF Export task and an Export OVF Template task will each begin.

11. When these tasks complete, verify that the vApp was exported to the location you selected on the local filesystem.

Summary

This chapter covered creating and deploying virtual machines and vApps. Knowing how to create and deploy virtual machines is absolutely essential for any virtual infrastructure administrator, and the exam objectives include numerous specific skills:

- Identify the capabilities of the different virtual machine hardware versions
- Configure and deploy a virtual machine
- Place VMs in selected ESXi hosts, resource pools, and clusters
- Access and use a virtual machine console

- Install, upgrade, and update the VMware Tools and the VMware Tools device drivers
- Update virtual machine hardware
- Configure virtual machine time synchronization and identify virtual machine storage resources
- Configure disk controllers for virtual disks, appropriate virtual disk types, and disk shares and create and convert thin- and thick-provisioned virtual disks
- Determine appropriate datastore locations for virtual machines based on application workloads
- Configure and modify vCPU and memory resources according to OS and application requirements
- Configure and modify virtual NIC adapters and connect VMs to appropriate network resources
- Use VMware Converter to perform a P2V conversion, import a VMware Workstation virtual machine, and perform a V2V to modify virtual hardware settings

This chapter also focused on creating and deploying vApps:

- Determine when a tiered application should be deployed as a vApp
- Create a vApp and add objects to an existing vApp
- Identify and edit the settings of a vApp
- Suspend and resume a vApp
- Clone and export a vApp

In the next chapter, we will continue to work with virtual machines; you'll learn various management and administrative tasks.

Exam Essentials

Know how to create and deploy virtual machines. Be able to identify the capabilities of virtual machine hardware versions. Know how to configure and deploy a guest OS into a new virtual machine and how to place the VM in ESXi hosts, clusters, and resource pools. Be able to identify the methods used to access virtual machine consoles. Know how to install, upgrade, and update the VMware Tools and be able to identify the different VMware Tools device drivers. Know how to upgrade virtual machine hardware. Be able to configure virtual machine time synchronization and identify virtual machine storage resources. Know how to configure and modify disk controllers, virtual disk types, and disk shares. Understand how to create and convert thin-provisioned virtual disks. Be able to determine appropriate datastore locations for virtual machines based on application workloads. Know how to configure and modify vCPU and memory resources according to OS and application requirements. Understand how to configure and modify virtual NIC adapters and connect virtual machines to the appropriate network resources. Understand the P2V process using VMware Converter. Know how to import a supported VM source using VMware Converter, and know how to perform a V2V with VMware Converter to modify virtual hardware settings.

Know how to create and deploy vApps. Be able to determine when a tiered application should be deployed as a vApp. Know how to create a vApp and add objects to it. Be able to identify and edit vApp settings. Understand how to configure IP pools. Know how to suspend and resume a vApp, in addition to how to clone and export a vApp.

Review Questions

1. You updated the virtual machine hardware version for a virtual machine from version 9 to version 10. Several days later an application on this virtual machine is being reported as no longer working. You need to return the virtual machine back to the previous virtual hardware version. How do you do this?

    A. Use the vSphere Client to change the version.

    B. Use the vSphere Web Client to change the version.

    C. Use VMware Converter to change the version.

    D. None of these is correct.

2. Which of the following methods can be used to configure and deploy a new virtual machine? (Choose all that apply.)

    A. vMA

    B. vSphere Client

    C. vSphere Web Client

    D. vApp

3. You have a virtual machine with a single 20GB thin disk with 40 percent free space. The virtual machine needs to have a SAN-aware application installed that will consume 100MB of additional disk space. What type of disk should you add to this virtual machine?

    A. Physical Compatibility Mode RDM.

    B. Virtual Compatibility Mode RDM.

    C. No disk needs to be added.

    D. None of these is correct.

4. Which of the following are VMware device drivers loaded by the VMware Tools? (Choose all that apply.)

    A. Mouse

    B. VMCI

    C. VMXNet

    D. Memory Control

5. Which editions of vSphere include the VMware Converter? (Choose all that apply.)

    A. Essentials

    B. Enterprise

    C. Enterprise Plus

    D. None of these

6. Which of the following can be used to clone a vApp?

A. VMware Converter

B. vSphere Client

C. vSphere Web Client

D. vMA

7. Which type of SCSI bus sharing allows virtual disks to be shared by virtual machines located on the same ESXi host?

A. None

B. Local

C. Physical

D. Virtual

8. Which inventory objects are IP pools associated with?

A. vCenter root object

B. Datacenter

C. Cluster

D. Host

9. Which of the following NICs will always require the VMware Tools to provide drivers for them? (Choose all that apply.)

A. E1000e

B. VMXNET

C. VMXNET 2

D. VMXNET 3

10. Which of the following objects may be added to an existing vApp? (Choose all that apply.)

A. Virtual machines

B. Resource pools

C. vApps

D. Folders

11. Which of the following statements are correct about the VMware Tools? (Choose two.)

A. The VMware Tools are required for virtual machines.

B. The VMware Tools are required only for advanced functionality in virtual machines.

C. An automatic VMware Tools upgrade can reboot the guest OS without prompting.

D. An interactive VMware Tools upgrade can reboot the guest OS without prompting.

12. Which of the following statements are true about the start order for the virtual machines in a vApp? (Choose two.)

    A. Each group is started at the same time, and virtual machines in the groups are started in the order listed.

    B. Each virtual machine in the same group is started in the order listed, before the next group begins.

    C. Shutdown is performed in reverse order of the start order.

    D. Shutdown is performed as a simultaneous operation against all virtual machines in the vApp.

13. Which disk mode results in a disk that loses all changes at virtual machine power off or reset?

    A. Independent Persistent

    B. Dependent Persistent

    C. Independent Nonpersistent

    D. Dependent Nonpersistent

14. You want to use VMware Converter to import a Windows 2008 R2 Hyper-V hosted virtual machine into your vSphere 5.5 environment. Which of the following are acceptable ways to perform this operation? Choose two.

    A. Run VMware Converter with the Hyper-V virtual machine running, and treat it like you would any other physical machine.

    B. Power off the Hyper-V virtual machine and then run VMware Converter.

    C. Power off the Hyper-V virtual machine and copy its files to the system where VMware Converter is installed. Then import the Hyper-V VM locally.

    D. Use the vSphere Client with the VMware vCenter Converter plug-in to import the Hyper-V virtual machine.

15. You plan to deploy a vApp on a DRS-enabled cluster. Which editions of vSphere will you be able to accomplish this with? (Choose all that apply.)

    A. Essentials Plus

    B. Standard

    C. Enterprise

    D. Enterprise Plus

16. Which of the following are capabilities of virtual machine hardware version 10? (Choose two.)

    A. 32 vCPU

    B. 64 vCPU

    C. 512GB RAM

    D. 1TB RAM

17. What are the three options available for choosing the location used to store the virtual disk files? (Choose three.)

   A. With the virtual machine

   B. In a datastore different from the virtual machine

   C. In a datastore cluster

   D. In a resource pool

18. Which of the following methods can be used to convert a thin disk to a thick disk? (Choose all that apply.)

   A. The Datastore Browser Inflate option

   B. Storage vMotion

   C. VMware Converter

   D. vmkfstools

19. Which of the following options can be used to disable periodic time synchronization? (Choose two.)

   A. VmwareToolboxCmd.exe

   B. vmware-toolbox-cmd

   C. vSphere Client

   D. vSphere Web Client

20. Which of the following methods can be used to obtain virtual machine console access? (Choose all that apply.)

   A. vSphere Client

   B. vSphere Web Client

   C. ESXi Shell

   D. VMware Converter

Chapter

7

Managing and Administering Virtual Machines and vApps

VCP5 EXAM OBJECTIVES COVERED IN THIS CHAPTER:

✓ **2.3: Configure vSS and vDS Policies**

- Enable TCP Segmentation Offload Support for a Virtual Machine

✓ **4.3: Manage Virtual Machine Clones and Templates**

- Identify Cloning and Template Options

- Clone an existing virtual machine

- Create a template from an existing virtual machine

- Deploy a virtual machine from a template

- Update existing virtual machine templates

- Deploy virtual appliances and/or vApps from an OVF template

- Import and/or Export an OVF Template

- Determine the appropriate deployment methodology for a given virtual machine application

- Identify content types

- Create a Local/Remote Content Library with/without external storage (VMs, ISOs, Scripts, vApps)

- Publish/Subscribe/Share a Content Library

✓ **4.4: Administer Virtual Machines and vApps**

- Identify files used by virtual machines

- Identify locations for virtual machine configuration files and virtual disks

- Configure virtual machine options
- Configure virtual machine power settings
- Configure virtual machine boot options
- Configure virtual machine troubleshooting options
- Identify common practices for securing virtual machines
- Determine when an advanced virtual machine parameter is required
- Hot Extend a virtual disk
- Adjust virtual machine resources (shares, limits and reservations) based on virtual machine workloads
- Configure USB passthrough from an ESXi Host
- Configure Serial port redirection

TOOLS

- vSphere Virtual Machine Administration guide (Objectives 4.3, 4.4)
- VMware vSphere Examples and Scenarios guide (Objective 4.3)
- VMware Open Virtualization Format Tool (Objective 4.3)
- OVF Tool User Guide (Objective 4.3)
- vSphere Client / vSphere Web Client (Objectives 4.3, 4.4)
- vSphere Networking guide (Objective 2.3)

This chapter will cover the objectives of sections 4.3 and 4.4 of the VCP5-DCV exam blueprint. It will focus on managing and administering virtual machines and vApps.

We will first explore topics such as cloning, templates, and deploying OVFs. vCloud Connector, virtual machine file composition, securing VMs, and much more will also be covered.

Managing Virtual Machine Clones and Templates

Virtual infrastructure administrators can use clones and templates to both save time and ensure consistency of deployed virtual machines. Knowing how to manage virtual machine clones and templates is an essential task for any virtual infrastructure administrator. The first topic I will cover in this chapter is identifying cloning and template options.

Identifying Cloning and Template Options

Cloning in vCenter Server is the process of creating an exact copy of a virtual machine, including the virtual hardware and the guest OS. A clone can be made from a powered-on or powered-off virtual machine. Clones are often useful for testing purposes. For example, a production server could be cloned while online, and then the clone could be used in a test environment. The cloned virtual machine is its own virtual machine and in no way depends on the original. It will get a new, unique UUID and MAC address.

A virtual machine can also be converted to a template in vCenter Server, and once converted, templates cannot be powered on or have their configurations modified. Templates can be used in vCenter Server to provide simplified provisioning of virtual machines. A typical use for templates is to set up a master image of a frequently deployed server operating system, for example Windows Server 2012. This virtual machine can be modified to form a standard build for your environment, and then all future Windows Server 2012 servers can be deployed from this virtual machine template. An additional feature of deployment from a template is the ability to customize the guest operating system. Using templates both simplifies builds and nearly eliminates mistakes in the process.

Many different options can be specified while either creating a clone or deploying from a template:

- You can select a datacenter.
- You can select a cluster or an ESXi host.
- You can select a resource pool.
- You can select a virtual disk format.
- You can select a datastore.
- You can select a storage profile.
- You can select whether to disable Storage DRS.
- You can select whether to customize the guest OS.
- You can select whether to power on the VM after creation.

 vCenter Server is a requirement to use cloning and templates.

Next let's discuss how to clone an existing virtual machine.

Cloning an Existing Virtual Machine

In Exercise 7.1, you will use the vSphere Web Client to clone an existing Windows Server 2008 R2 virtual machine to a template. For the purpose of the exercise, I will assume that this Windows Server 2008 R2 virtual machine is your master image that is used for deploying new virtual machines.

EXERCISE 7.1

Cloning an Existing Virtual Machine

1. Connect to a vCenter Server with the vSphere Web Client.

2. Locate the virtual machine and right-click it. Select the Clone To Virtual Machine option from the context menu. The Clone Existing Virtual Machine Wizard will launch.

3. Provide the new virtual machine with a unique name and choose an inventory location. Click Next.

4. Choose the host or cluster that will be used to run the virtual machine. Review any issues reported in the Compatibility window before proceeding. Click Next.

5. Using the drop-down menu, select a virtual disk format for the cloned virtual machine. By default, the selection is Same Format As Source. Choose a datastore to store the virtual machine on. Review any issues reported in the Compatibility window before proceeding. Click Next.

6. On the Select Clone Options screen, select the Customize The Operating System check box. Leave both the Customize This Virtual Machine's Hardware (Experimental) and Power On Virtual Machine After Creation check boxes empty.

Not selecting Customize The Operating System would clone the virtual machine, creating an exact replica of it. This option will allow you to both customize this virtual machine and create a customization specification that can be used again. For example, you will use the customization specification you create in this exercise later in this chapter.

7. Click the Next button. The Clone Existing Virtual Machine Wizard will minimize to the right into the Work In Progress panel, and the New VM Guest Customization Spec window will open.

8. Enter a Customization Spec Name and Description, and click Next.

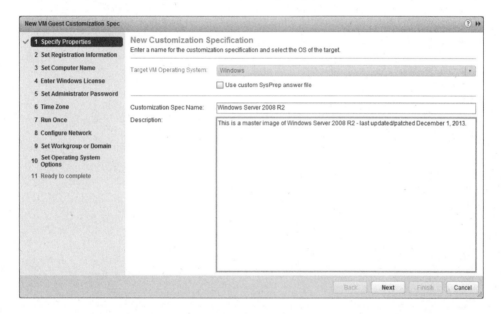

9. Complete the Name and Organization fields on the Set Registration Information screen and click Next.

10. Select the Use The Virtual Machine Name option, and click Next to continue. You can also manually provide a computer name in the Enter A Name field.

11. Enter the Windows Product Key and choose the appropriate options for the Server License Mode. Click Next.

12. Provide the password for the local Windows Administrator account and confirm. Click Next.

13. Select the appropriate time zone and click Next.

14. Click Next on the Run Once screen.

15. Choose the Use Standard Network Settings option for networking and click Next to continue.

EXERCISE 7.1 *(continued)*

16. Fill in the Windows Server Domain or Workgroup fields appropriate for your environment. If you choose to add the guest OS on this virtual machine to the domain, you will need to provide a username and password of a user with authority to join machines to the domain. Click Next.

17. Unless you have a specific reason not to, leave the Generate New Security ID (SID) option checked and click Next.

18. Review the information on the Ready To Complete screen for accuracy. The final configuration should look similar to this:

19. Click Finish to save the customization specification information.

20. The Clone Existing Virtual Machine Wizard will be restored from the Work In Progress panel, and the guest customization you just created will be displayed in the middle of the screen.

21. Click the name of the guest customization to select it and then click Next.

22. Review the information on the Ready To Complete screen for accuracy, and then click Finish to begin the clone process.

23. A Clone Virtual Machine task will begin. When this task completes, locate the new virtual machine in the inventory. Right-click it and choose Edit Settings from the context menu. Verify the settings and power it on, if you want.

24. Return to the home screen in the vSphere Web Client. Under the Monitoring section in the center of the screen, click the Customization Specification Manager icon.

25. Click the customization specification you created in this exercise to select it.

26. Right-click the customization specification and choose Edit from the context menu to launch the customization specification editor.

27. Optionally, make changes to the customization specification or click Cancel to close the editor.

The Customize This Virtual Machine's Hardware (Experimental) option in Exercise 7.1 is not recommended for use in production systems, because experimental options offer no guaranteed support from VMware.

You've now seen how to clone a virtual machine and how to use the customization specifications included in vCenter Server. In the following section, you will learn how to create a template from an existing virtual machine.

Creating a Template from an Existing Virtual Machine

In the previous exercise, you cloned a master virtual machine in order to deploy a new virtual machine from it. This process works and is acceptable, but what if another administrator were to power on the master image and make changes to it? One solution to the problem of keeping master images from being modified is to convert these virtual machines to templates.

Once a virtual machine is converted to a template, it cannot be powered on in vCenter Server. When a virtual machine is converted to a template, the ·vmx file extension changes to ·vmtx. The ·vmtx file extension designates a template VM. This is shown in Figure 7.1.

FIGURE 7.1 A template VM as seen in the File Browser

ESXi1-DS1 Actions ▾			

Getting Started | Summary | Monitor | **Manage** | Related Objects

Settings | Alarm Definitions | Tags | Permissions | **Files** | Scheduled Tasks

[ESXi1-DS1] VM1

🔍 Search

▼ ESXi1-DS1	Name	Size	Modified	Type
▶ .sdd.sf	📄 VM1.vmtx	2.52 KB	7/11/2013 11:34 AM	Template VM
▶ log	📄 VM1.vmxf	0.25 KB	6/20/2013 10:48 AM	File
▷ VM1	📄 VM1.vmsd	0.00 KB	6/20/2013 10:48 AM	File
	📄 VM1.nvram	8.48 KB	6/23/2013 3:16 PM	Non-volatile Memory File
	📄 VM1.vmdk	41,943,040.00 KB	6/24/2013 12:51 PM	Virtual Disk

Templates are also not visible in the Hosts And Clusters view in the vSphere Client. Converting a virtual machine to a template is a simple process in vCenter Server. In Exercise 7.2, you will create a template from an existing virtual machine. For the purpose of the exercise, I assume that you are using as your master image the same Windows Server 2008 R2 virtual machine used in Exercise 7.1.

EXERCISE 7.2

Creating a Template from an Existing VM

1. Connect to a vCenter Server with the vSphere Web Client.

2. Select Hosts And Clusters in the left pane, and then locate the powered-off virtual machine in the left pane. Take note of which ESXi host it is located on.

3. Right-click the virtual machine and select All vCenter Actions ➢ Convert To Template.

4. A Mark Virtual Machine As Template task will begin. When this task completes, the virtual machine will disappear from the Hosts And Clusters view.

5. In the left pane, navigate to the ESXi host that the virtual machine was located on. Click VM Templates on the Related Objects tab. Locate the template in the list, and notice how the icon for a template is different.

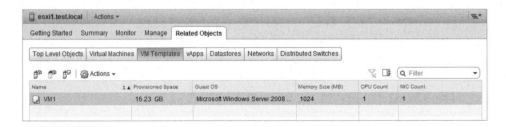

6. Return to the home screen in the vSphere Web Client. Under the Inventories section in the center of the screen, click the VMs And Templates icon.

7. Locate the template and review its properties.

Now that we have created a template, in the next section you will learn how to deploy a virtual machine from it.

Deploying a Virtual Machine from a Template

The process of deploying a virtual machine from a template is similar to the process of cloning a virtual machine. In Exercise 7.3, you will deploy a virtual machine from the template created in Exercise 7.2.

EXERCISE 7.3

Deploying a VM from a Template

1. Connect to a vCenter Server with the vSphere Web Client.

2. In the left pane, locate the template created in Exercise 7.2.

3. Right-click the template and review the options that appear in the context menu.

Note that the available operations for templates include cloning, adding permissions, renaming, removing from the inventory, and deleting.

EXERCISE 7.3 *(continued)*

4. Choose the All vCenter Actions ➢ Deploy VM From This Template option. The Deploy From Template Wizard will launch.

5. Provide the new virtual machine with a unique name and choose an inventory location. Click Next to continue.

6. Choose the host or cluster that will be used to host the virtual machine. Review any issues reported in the Compatibility window before proceeding. Click Next.

7. Using the drop-down menu, select a virtual disk format for the new virtual machine. By default, the selection is Same Format As Source. Choose a datastore to store the virtual machine on. Review any issues reported in the Compatibility window before proceeding. Click Next.

8. On the Select Clone Options screen, select the Customize The Operating System check box. Leave both the Customize This Virtual Machine's Hardware (Experimental) and Power On Virtual Machine After Creation check boxes empty. Click Next.

9. Click to select the customization specification created in Exercise 7.2, and then click Next to continue.

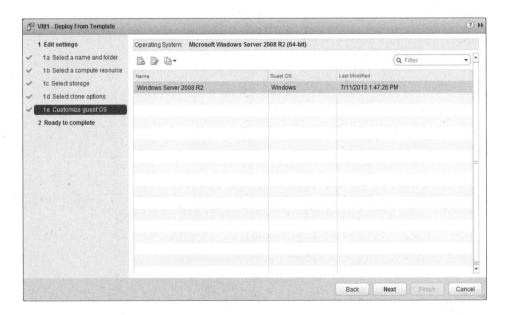

10. Review the information on the Ready To Complete screen and click Finish.

11. A Clone Virtual Machine task will begin. When it completes, locate the new virtual machine in the inventory.

Now that you know how to create templates and deploy virtual machines from them, let's discuss updating your templates.

Updating Existing Virtual Machine Templates

After a virtual machine is converted to a template, it cannot be powered on. Although this provides a degree of protection for the master virtual machine image, over time this template will certainly become stale. Build guides may change, vendor-supplied updates will likely need to be applied, and any number of changes will need to happen to get the master virtual machine image compliant with the current standards.

To address these issues, you can simply convert a template back to a virtual machine. Once converted, it can then be powered on and updated as necessary using the procedures specific to the guest OS. Exercise 7.4 shows the steps required to convert a template to a virtual machine so that it can be updated.

EXERCISE 7.4

Updating Virtual Machine Templates

1. Connect to a vCenter Server with the vSphere Web Client.

2. In the left pane, locate the template created in Exercise 7.2.

3. Right-click the template and choose Convert To Virtual Machine from the context menu.

4. The Convert Template To Virtual Machine Wizard will launch.

5. Choose the host or cluster that will be used to host the virtual machine. Review any issues reported in the Compatibility window before proceeding. Click Next to continue.

6. Review the information on the Ready To Complete screen and click Finish to convert the template to a virtual machine.

7. A Mark As Virtual Machine task will begin. When this task completes, locate the virtual machine in the inventory.

At this point, the template is no more. Browsing the datastore would reveal that the VMTX file has been replaced with a VMX file. The virtual machine is now visible again in the Hosts And Clusters view. Because you are now working with a virtual machine, its configuration can be edited. The virtual machine can also be powered on, and updates can be applied to the guest OS. When all of these changes have been made, the virtual machine can be powered off and again converted to a template.

There is still one other type of template that we need to cover: the OVF template. In the next section, we will explore deploying virtual appliances and vApps from an OVF template.

Deploying Virtual Appliances and vApps from an OVF Template

Virtual appliances are preconfigured and ready-to-use virtual machines that include an operating system and/or applications. VMware provides a virtual appliance marketplace at www·vmware·com/appliances. Virtual appliances offer convenience and portability and are often optimized for virtual infrastructures.

 Real World Scenario

Virtual Appliances

A virtual infrastructure administrator has learned that his company has just acquired another company. As part of this acquisition, his company will become responsible for more than 100 virtual machines, including 10 virtual machines with the Ubuntu desktop running as the guest OS. The administrator is somewhat apprehensive about this, because he has no experience with Linux. He decides to get an early jump on learning how Ubuntu works and plans to build a virtual machine that will run the Ubuntu guest operating system.

The administrator downloads the Ubuntu installation media, and when it completes, he creates a new virtual machine. He boots the virtual machine to the installation media and gets through the basic installation. Next he spends several hours configuring the operating system and getting VMware Tools installed. At the end of the day, he tells a co-worker about his Ubuntu experience and how long it took to get everything working. The co-worker asks him why he didn't just use a virtual appliance instead.

The virtual infrastructure administrator had never heard of virtual appliances and was surprised to hear that he could have downloaded a prebuilt virtual machine with the Ubuntu guest OS and VMware Tools already installed. Using a virtual appliance would have allowed the entire project to be completed in a fraction of the time.

Virtual appliances may sound similar to an exported vApp, which we covered in Exercise 6.21, and that is because they are. vApps are built on an industry-standard format, the Open Virtualization Format (OVF). This is the same format used for the vast majority of the virtual appliances in the VMware virtual appliance marketplace.

Deploying a virtual appliance is a simple task. If you think back to one of the first exercises in this book, you may recall that you have already deployed a virtual appliance. In Exercise 2.14, you deployed the vCenter Server Appliance. The vCenter Server Appliance was packaged in the "folder of files" format, where the OVF template consisted of a set of files.

If you don't recall Exercise 2.14, don't go back there just yet. In the next section, I will cover importing OVF templates, and the procedure is exactly the same as deploying a virtual appliance.

Importing and Exporting an OVF Template

In Exercise 6.21 from Chapter 6, you exported an OVF template for a vApp. There is no import function in the vSphere Web Client, and an exported OVF template is simply imported using the Deploy OVF Template function instead. An important thing to remember is that OVA files are nothing more than packaged versions of OVF files and folders.

 There is no difference in the operation of deploying a virtual appliance and importing an exported vApp. Both are OVF templates, and both are imported into the vSphere environment by using the Deploy OVF Template function in the vSphere Web Client.

In Exercise 7.5, you will import the OVF template you created in Exercise 6.21.

EXERCISE 7.5

Importing an OVF Template

1. Connect to a vCenter Server with the vSphere Web Client.

2. Locate the root vCenter object in the left pane and right-click it. Choose Deploy OVF Template from the context menu that appears.

3. A Client Integration Access Control pop-up may appear. If so, click the Allow button to continue.

4. The Deploy OVF Template Wizard will launch. Browse to the local file location of the exported vApp from Exercise 6.21 and choose the OVA file. Once the OVA file has been selected, it will appear in the Deploy From A File Or URL field. Click Next to continue.

5. Verify the OVF template details for accuracy and click Next.

6. Specify a name and location for the deployed template. This name will be the name of the deployed VM. Click Next.

7.   Select a host (or cluster) to run the virtual machine. Click Next.

8.   Using the drop-down menu, select a virtual disk format for the new virtual machine. Choose a datastore and click Next.

9.   Review the information on the Ready To Complete screen and ensure that the Power On After Deployment check box is empty.

10.   Click Finish to begin deploying the vApp.

11.   An Initialize OVF Deployment and a Deploy OVF Template task will each begin, and a progress window will appear. Verify that these tasks complete and then locate the vApp in the inventory.

Now that you have seen how to use the Deploy OVF Template Wizard to import a vApp, as well as other deployment options, I will summarize how to determine the appropriate deployment methodology for a given VM application.

Determining the Appropriate Deployment Methodology for a Given Virtual Machine Application

Determining the appropriate deployment methodology for the virtual machines in your environment will depend on a variety of factors. Another phrase that can be used to describe the deployment methodology is *virtual machine provisioning*. Table 7.1 covers the provisioning methods and use cases.

TABLE 7.1   Deployment methodologies for VMs

Provisioning	Use cases
On-demand	One-off deployments Small environments with few VMs Specific configurations used for testing Initially creating a VM to be used as a template
Clones	Making copies for testing Avoiding repetition of tasks
Templates	Deploying multiple consistent images from a protected virtual machine
OVF/virtual appliances	Using preconfigured virtual machines or vApps Creating portable/packaged applications

Now that you have seen how to determine the appropriate deployment methodology for a given virtual machine application, I will move on to a brief discussion of VMware's vCloud Connector product.

Identifying Content Types

VMware's vCloud Connector is a product that provides one interface to connect and oversee multiple public and private clouds and for transferring cloud content between them. These clouds could be vSphere clouds, private vCloud Director clouds, or even public vClouds. As of version 2.6 of vCloud Connector, there is a single edition that is full-featured and free. In previous versions, there were two editions and some of the features required additional licensing.

vCloud Connector consists of three components:

- vCloud Connector UI - this is a plug-in used in the vSphere Client to access the vCloud Connector user interface.

- vCloud Connector server — a single virtual appliance that is deployed and registered to a vCenter Server.

- vCloud Connector nodes — a virtual appliance that is deployed to each cloud to manage data transfer.

The vCloud Connector architecture is shown in Figure 7.2.

FIGURE 7.2 vCloud Connector architecture

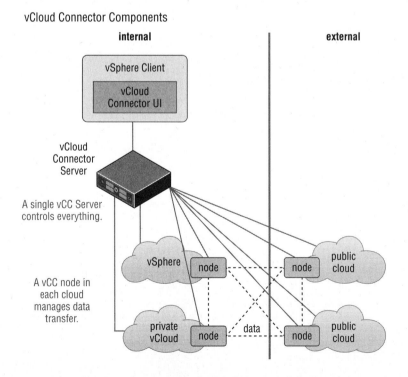

Another VMware product, vCloud Director, can also come into play, but for the sake of keeping this content concise we will focus on vCloud Connector. For the VCP5-DCV exam, remember that the role of vCloud connector is to serve as a broker between VMware private and public cloud environments. Copies of templates, vApps and VMs are also possible between these cloud environments, when using vCloud Connector. The three content types in vCloud Connector are:

- Templates
- vApps
- Virtual machines

vCloud Director offers additional content types of ISOs and scripts.

Now that I have provided an overview of vCloud Connector and its content types, let's move on to creating a content library.

Creating a Local/Remote Content Library with/without external storage (VMs, ISOs, Scripts, vApps)

A content library is used in vCloud Connector to distribute and synchronize templates across the cloud environments. One way to set this up is to use folders in vCenter Server to organize your templates. Figure 7.3 shows the vCloud Connector interface in the vSphere Client.

FIGURE 7.3   vCloud Connector folder view

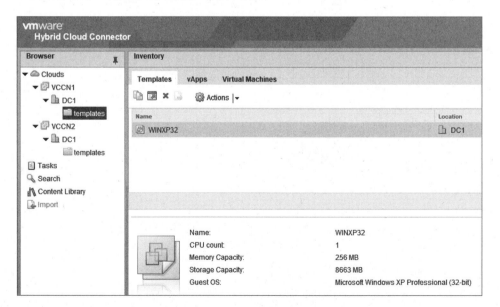

Notice how Cloud VCCN1, which is the local cloud, has a data center inventory object and a single folder named templates. This folder contains one template, which is named WINXP32. To create a content library, right-click the templates folder and choose the Publish To Content Library.

FIGURE 7.4 Creating a content library

Once the content library is created, the templates folder will appear under the Content Library. Also note how the templates folder icon in the left pane now has an up arrow icon on it.

FIGURE 7.5 Content Library contents

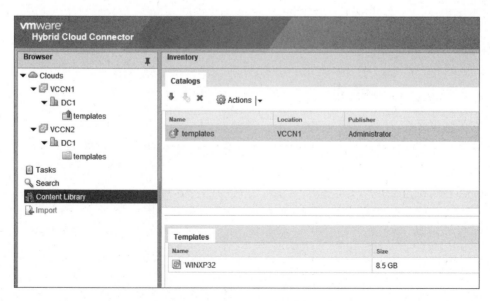

Once the content library is published, other clouds can be subscribed to it. It is this subscription that will start the synchronization of the templates.

Publishing/Subscribing/Sharing a Content Library

The final step involved in synchronizing a content library is to subscribe another cloud to it. To do this, select the item in the content library and use the Actions -> Subscribe menu option.

FIGURE 7.6 Subscribe cloud to content library

This will open a Subscribe Wizard window, where the target cloud can be selected from a drop-down menu. A folder must also be selected on the target cloud.

FIGURE 7.7 Subscribe wizard

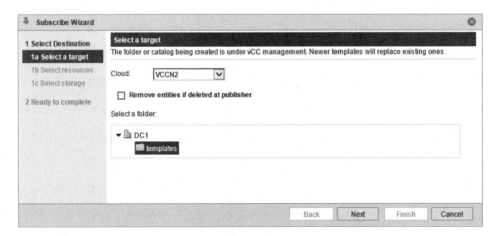

Once the target cloud is selected, the data center object and storage resources must also be selected for use on the target side. A summary screen shows all of the options selected.

FIGURE 7.8 Subscribe wizard summary

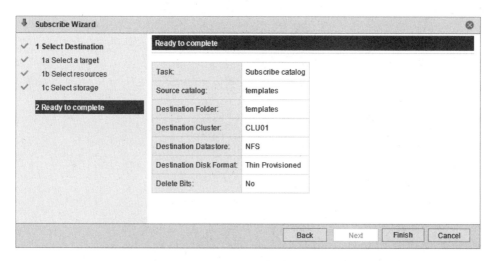

Once the subscribe Wizard is completed, an Export OVF Template task will begin in the vSphere Client. Once this task completes, the templates folder on the target cloud can be reloaded to verify the template synchronization. Also note how the templates folder icon in the left pane now has a down arrow icon on it.

FIGURE 7.9 Subscribe verification

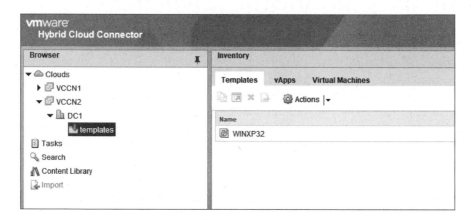

Clouds can also be unsubscribed and unpublished from content libraries by using the Actions menu.

FIGURE 7.10   Unsubscribe or unpublish a content library

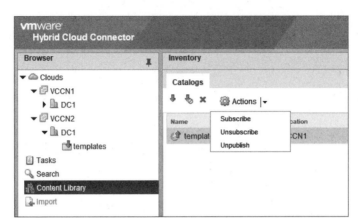

The vCloud Connector content presented in this chapter is not intended to be comprehensive. An entire chapter could have been written on how to install, configure and use this product. For the VCP5-DCV exam, remember that you are only expected to understand the content types and how content libraries are used in vCloud Connector. In the next section, we will cover administering virtual machines and vApps.

Administering Virtual Machines and vApps

Daily operations with virtual machines and vApps are among the more common tasks that most virtual infrastructure administrators perform on the job. Knowing how to administer virtual machines and vApps is an important set of skills to have for any virtual infrastructure administrator and is equally important for the VCP5-DCV exam. We will begin with identifying the virtual machine file types and locations, and then move on to configuration, security, and more.

Identifying Files Used by Virtual Machines

A virtual machine consists of a set of files stored on a storage device. The minimum files required for a virtual machine are a configuration file (VMX), a virtual disk file (VMDK), and an NVRAM file (BIOS or EFI). While these three files alone can constitute a virtual machine, there are many more file types that may be visible in a virtual machine's directory on a datastore. The most important of these additional files are described in Table 7.2.

TABLE 7.2   Virtual machine files

File extension	Description
`.vmx`	Virtual machine configuration file. This file contains every aspect of the virtual machine, including the virtual hardware assigned to it.
`.vmx~`	VMX edit file. All changes for a powered-on virtual machine are applied to this file. Once the changes are complete the file is swapped with the in-use VMX file.
`.vmxf`	Virtual machine supplemental configuration file.
`.vmdk`	Virtual disk characteristics. This is a small text file that contains descriptive data about the `-flat.vmdk` file.
`-flat.vmdk`	Virtual disk contents. This is the actual contents of the virtual hard disk and will be significantly larger than the VMDK file.
`-00000#.vmdk`	Virtual disk characteristics. This is a small text file that contains descriptive data about the `-delta.vmdk` or `-sesparse.vmdk` file.
`-delta.vmdk`	Snapshot delta files for virtual disks <2TB. These files can also be referred to as *delta links*, *redo logs*, and *child disks*.
`-sesparse.vmdk`	Snapshot delta files for virtual disks >=2TB. These files can also be referred to as *delta links*, *redo logs*, and *child disks*.
`.nvram`	Virtual machine BIOS or EFI configuration file.
`.vmsd`	A database that stores information and metadata about snapshots for a virtual machine.
`.vmsn`	Stores the memory state at the time of the snapshot.
`.vswp`	The virtual machine's swap file.
`vmx-...vswp`	VMX swap file. This file allows the VMkernel to swap virtual machine overhead memory.
`.vmss`	Virtual machine suspend file.
`.log`	The current virtual machine log file.
`-#.log`	Archived (rotated) virtual machine log files.
`-ctk.vmdk`	Holds change block tracking (CBT) information for a corresponding VMDK file.
`-aux.xml`	Snapshot manifest metadata file. In vSphere 5 and newer, this file is no longer required but is still created. The VMSD file is now used instead.
`.vmtx`	Virtual machine template configuration file.
`.hlog`	vCenter marker file for a vMotion operation.
`.psf`	Persistent state file, used with vSphere Replication feature of SRM 5 to keep pointers for changed blocks.

It is also important to note that when viewing the files in the File Browser, the virtual disk file information is abstracted. Figure 7.11 shows a listing of the files for VM1, as viewed in the File Browser.

FIGURE 7.11   VM files viewed in the File Browser

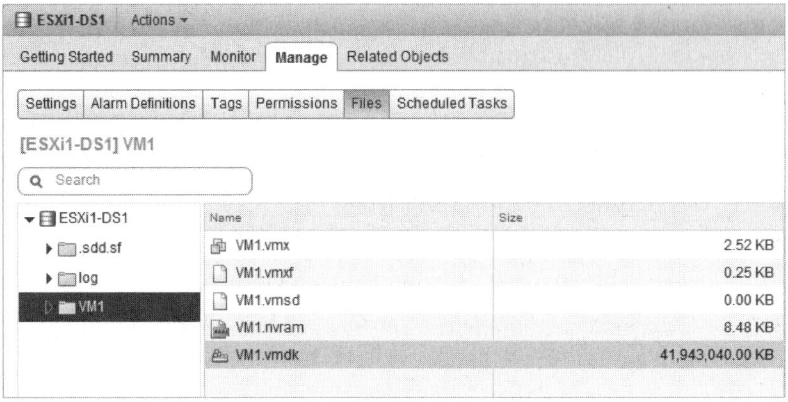

Notice that there is a single VMDK file listed that represents both the ·vmdk (its name) and -flat·vmdk file (its size). To view both of these actual files and their attributes, you can use the ESXi Shell. Figure 7.12 shows the listing of VMDK files for the virtual machine VM1.

FIGURE 7.12   Virtual disks viewed in the ESXi Shell

Note that in this listing the .vmdk and -flat·vmdk files are both visible. Always be aware of the level of abstraction present in the File Browser when working with virtual machine files.

Next we will cover identifying locations for virtual machine configuration files and virtual disks.

Identifying Locations for Virtual Machine Configuration Files and Virtual Disks

When a virtual machine is created, using any of the available methods, one of the options is to select destination storage for the virtual machine files. This location will be a VMFS or NFS datastore in your vSphere environment. The files used by the virtual machine will be stored on this datastore in a directory specified during the creation and will typically have the same name as the virtual machine. However, it is possible to store the virtual machine swap file and virtual disks in different directories.

The virtual machine swap (VSWP) file is created when a virtual machine is powered on. This file is used only if the ESXi host runs out of physical memory and is used to allow overcommitment of virtual memory for virtual machines running on the ESXi host. Initially, the size of the VSWP file will be equal to the amount of virtual machine–assigned memory minus the memory reservation set for the VM. These files can be large, and in some cases, like when troubleshooting or using replication, it is better to have them on their own storage locations and not in the same *working location* as the virtual machine. (The working location is the directory where the virtual machine's configuration files are stored.) Figure 7.13 shows the VM Working Location field.

FIGURE 7.13   VM Working Location field

Virtual machine swap files can be placed in the following locations:

Default   Selecting this option will store the virtual machine swap file at the default location, as defined in the host or cluster where the VM currently resides.

Always Store With The Virtual Machine   Selecting this option will store the virtual machine swap file in the working location. This is the same location where the VM's configuration file is stored.

Store In The Host's Swapfile Datastore   Selecting this option will store the virtual machine swap file in the swap file datastore as defined on the host or cluster where the VM currently resides. Otherwise, the virtual swap file will be stored in the virtual machine's working location.

Configuring virtual machine swap file locations will be covered in detail in Chapter 9, "Maintaining Service Levels."

In addition to the virtual machine swap file, the virtual disks for a virtual machine can be stored in different datastores. When a new virtual disk is added to a virtual machine, the virtual disk location can be specified as part of the process. It is also possible to add existing virtual disks to a virtual machine. Cold-migrating and Storage vMotion are two supported ways that a virtual disk could be moved to different datastores.

Now that the locations for virtual machine configuration files and virtual disks have been identified, I will cover configuring virtual machine options.

Configuring Virtual Machine Options

Virtual machine options are used to configure a variety of additional virtual machine properties. These options are accessed using the VM Options tab of the Virtual Machine Properties editor. You might recall that the VM Options tab was shown in Figure 7.4, where the virtual machine working location was identified. The properties that can be configured on the VM Options tab include the following:

- Virtual machine name
- Guest operating system
- Remote Console options
- VMware Tools
- Power management
- Boot options
- Logging, debugging, and statistics
- Configuration parameters
- Latency sensitivity
- Fibre Channel NPIV
- BIOS and/or EFI
- Swap file location

In Exercise 7.6, you will modify a virtual machine's configuration file (VMX) by using the Configuration Parameters functionality in the VM Options tab. In this exercise, you will add two configuration parameters intended to limit the number and size of the virtual machine log files.

EXERCISE 7.6

Configuring Virtual Machine Options

1. Connect to a vCenter Server with the vSphere Web Client.

2. Select a powered-off virtual machine from the inventory and right-click it. Choose Edit Settings from the context menu.

3. The Virtual Machine Edit Settings window will open. Click the VM Options tab.

4. Expand the Advanced section and locate the Configuration Parameters section.

5. Click the Edit Configuration button to the right of the Configuration Parameters section. The Configuration Parameters window will appear, as shown here:

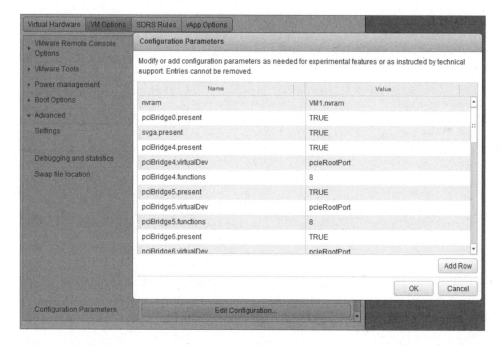

6. Click the Add Row button at the bottom of the window. A new row will be created in the list of configuration parameters. In the Name column, enter the following value: **log.rotateSize**.

EXERCISE 7.6 *(continued)*

7. Press the Tab key and enter the following value in the Value column in the same row: **1000**.

   This configuration parameter ensures that a new log file will be created when the current log file reaches the size of 1000KB. This limit is deliberately kept small for this exercise and would normally be much larger. In the next steps, you will configure log rotation settings.

8. Click the Add Row button again. Another new row will be created in the list of configuration parameters. In the Name column, enter the following value: **log.keepOld**.

9. Press the Tab key on the keyboard and enter the following value in the Value column in the same row: **10**.

   This configuration parameter ensures that no more than 10 log files will be maintained. Older log files will be deleted as necessary.

10. The configuration parameters just entered should look like this:

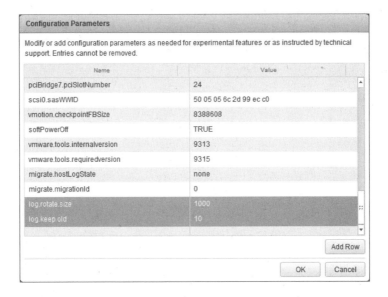

11. Click OK in the Configuration Parameters window and then click OK in the Virtual Machine Edit Settings window to save these changes.

12. A Reconfigure Virtual Machine task will start. When this task completes, browse to the working location of this virtual machine using the File Browser.

13. Expand the directory for the virtual machine and locate the virtual machine's configuration file. This is the file that ends with the .vmx extension.

14. Right-click the VMX file and choose the Download From Datastore option from the context menu. Save the file to a convenient location.

15. Open the file with WordPad or your favorite text editor. (Do not use Notepad, because it will not format the file properly.)

16. Locate the following lines in the VMX file:

```
log.keepOld = "10"
log.rotateSize = "1000"
```

These two lines are the formatted result of the two rows you added in steps 6 to 10.

17. Power on this virtual machine.

18. Return to the File Browser and refresh the contents of the working location of this VM by clicking the blue Refresh button in the upper-right toolbar.

19. Note that the directory contents now include 10 log files. Note the names of the log files. Shut down the virtual machine and refresh the datastore contents again. Take note of the names of the log files now, because they should have been rotated and include new names.

In the previous exercise, the log files were created purposely small to demonstrate the log rotation. In a real environment, you would want to size your log files much larger. Now that we have covered adding an advanced option by using the configuration parameters function, I will show you how to configure additional advanced options for the virtual machine. Let's start with power settings.

Configuring Virtual Machine Power Settings

A virtual machine has power options that are used to determine whether the VM is suspended or left powered on when the guest OS is placed in standby mode. It is important to note that these options are not applicable to all guest operating systems and that Wake On LAN is supported only for Windows guest operating systems. Figure 7.14 shows the guest power management settings for a virtual machine running a 64-bit CentOS 5 guest operating system.

In addition to supporting only Windows guests, Wake On LAN also has the following NIC requirements:

- Flexible (VMware Tools required)
- vmxnet
- Enhanced vmxnet
- vmxnet 3

FIGURE 7.14 The Wake On LAN power option is absent for CentOS VM.

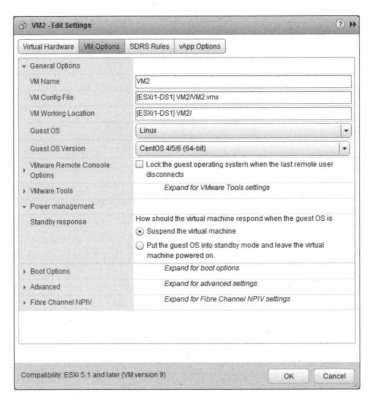

Wake On LAN can resume only those VMs that are in an S1 sleep state. S1 means the processor caches have been flushed and the CPUs have ceased all execution of instructions, but power to the CPUs and RAM is maintained. Therefore, suspended, hibernated, or powered-off VMs cannot be resumed via Wake On LAN.

In Exercise 7.7, you will configure the power settings for a powered-off virtual machine. Powering a VM off is a prerequisite to changing its power settings.

EXERCISE 7.7

Configuring VM Power Management Settings

1. Connect to a vCenter Server with the vSphere Web Client.

2. Select a powered-off virtual machine from the inventory and right-click it. Choose the Edit Settings option from the context menu.

3. The Virtual Machine Edit Settings window will open. Click the VM Options tab.

4. Expand the Power Management section and locate the Standby Response section.

5. Choose the Put The Guest OS Into Standby Mode option and select the appropriate network adapter. The final configuration should look like this:

6. Click OK to save these changes.

7. A Reconfigure Virtual Machine task will begin. When this task completes, the power settings have been modified successfully.

> Unsupported virtual network adapters might appear in the list of Wake On LAN options but will not work. Always verify that the virtual adapters listed on the Hardware tab of the virtual machine properties are supported for Wake On LAN before configuring Wake On LAN support.

Now that I have covered configuring the power settings for a virtual machine, let's move on to configuring virtual machine boot options.

Configuring Virtual Machine Boot Options

You can use the virtual machine boot options to control how a virtual machine starts. These options can be useful for obtaining access to a virtual machine's BIOS or EFI settings or for providing additional time to press the Esc key in order to obtain a boot menu. In Exercise 7.8, you will configure the boot options for a powered-off virtual machine using the vSphere Web Client.

EXERCISE 7.8

Configuring VM Boot Options

1. Connect to a vCenter Server with the vSphere Web Client.

2. Select a powered-off virtual machine from the inventory and right-click it. Choose Edit Settings from the context menu.

3. The Virtual Machine Edit Settings window will open. Click the VM Options tab.

4. Expand the Boot Options section and take a moment to review the options available here.

5. Select the Force BIOS Setup check box.

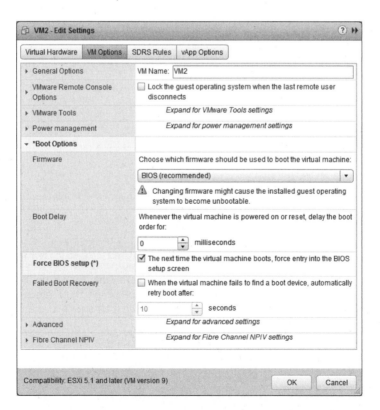

6. Click OK to save this change.

7. A Reconfigure Virtual Machine task will begin.

8. When this task completes, power on the VM and open the console (with the Web Client, the console can be opened only for a powered-on VM). Verify that the virtual machine successfully enters BIOS setup.

Next we will cover how to configure troubleshooting options for virtual machines.

Configuring Virtual Machine Troubleshooting Options

As reliable as virtual machines are, occasionally it is necessary to troubleshoot them. Fortunately, several options are available for configuring virtual machine troubleshooting. One of these options was covered in Exercise 7.6, where you ensured that virtual machine logging was enabled. Just as the virtual machine logging options were configured in the virtual machine properties' Options tab, the other available troubleshooting options are also located here. Figure 7.15 shows these options, as they appear in the vSphere Web Client.

FIGURE 7.15   Virtual machine troubleshooting options

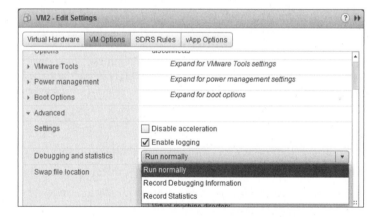

In addition to logging, the other item in the Settings field is the Disable Acceleration option. You can use this option to slow down a virtual machine if there is a problem running or installing software in it. If the problem with the software is then resolved, you can turn off the Disable Acceleration option.

In the Debugging And Statistics section, you can configure virtual machines to obtain additional debugging or statistical information. These options are typically used when working with VMware support.

We will now move away from configuring virtual machine options and identify some common practices for securing our virtual machines.

Identifying Common Practices for Securing Virtual Machines

Because the virtual infrastructure can encompass so much of the physical infrastructure, securing virtual machines can seem like a daunting task. Consider that securing a virtual machine can involve all of the following items:

- Guest operating system
- Virtual machine
- ESXi hosts
- Storage units connected to ESXi hosts
- Networks connected to ESXi hosts
- vCenter Server or other management applications
- Backup servers or applications

Securing virtual machines is in many ways no different from securing physical machines. Operations such as hardening the guest operating systems, installing periodic guest operating system updates, and updating antivirus and other applications are all good examples of this. Beyond the practices used to protect the guest OS, there are some specific protections that must be provided to the virtual machines themselves.

Virtual machines can be hardened in many additional ways. Earlier in this chapter, in Exercise 7.6, you added log rotation to a virtual machine. This is an example of one of the many hardening practices that can be applied to virtual machines. These options can be found in the most current version of the vSphere Security Hardening Guide. The following are some of the virtual machine–specific hardening options that can be added to the virtual machine configuration file:

- Preventing virtual disk shrinking
- Preventing other users from spying on administrator remote consoles
- Ensuring that unauthorized devices are not connected (unless needed/required)
- Preventing unauthorized removal, connection, and modification of devices
- Disabling VM-to-VM communication through VMCI
- Limiting VM log file size and number
- Limiting informational messages from the VM to the VMX file
- Disabling certain unexposed features
- Disabling remote operations within the guest
- Not sending host performance information to guests
- Controlling access to VMs through VM-safe APIs

The ESXi hosts also need to be protected in order to protect the virtual machines. ESXi hosts should be patched and hardened using the information contained in the vSphere Security Hardening Guide. ESXi hosts also include a firewall, which should be configured properly. ESXi hosts should use a syslog server and persistent logging, and they should also be configured for NTP to ensure accurate time. Management consoles should be on isolated networks dedicated to server management. The security of the virtual machines on the ESXi host is only as good as the security on the ESXi hosts used to run them. Much as with physical servers, if someone obtains local access to the ESXi host, then the security battle is already lost.

 To find the most current vSphere Security Hardening Guide, check VMware's Security Advisories, Certifications & Guides website:

`http://vmware.com/go/securityguides`

In addition to the ESXi hosts, the storage and networks attached to them need to be secured to protect virtual machines. vMotion traffic is sent unencrypted over the network, so to protect virtual machines, this traffic needs to be isolated. Hosts may have access to multiple networks, and understanding these networks is important in ensuring that virtual machines are not misconfigured. Virtual switch security should also be configured appropriately to minimize risks. Ethernet-based storage networks should use authentication mechanisms and be isolated. Fibre Channel SAN environments should make use of zoning and LUN masking practices to ensure that only authorized hosts have access to the storage devices. Storage system management interfaces should also be located on isolated networks dedicated to management.

Management applications, like vCenter Server, will also need to be secured to protect the virtual machines. For example, giving the local Windows Administrators group the Administrator permission in vCenter Server can provide far more access to your VMs than you would want. VM sprawl can be another problem for virtual machine security. As virtual machines are deployed and then not tracked or not placed in life-cycle management systems, there could be VMs that are forgotten. Giving virtual infrastructure operations personnel the least amount of privileges can also be helpful in securing virtual machines. This can prevent operators from performing actions such as connecting VMs to the wrong networks, attaching disks, or worse.

One final consideration for securing virtual machines is to look at the backup applications or scripts that are used to back up complete virtual machine images. A backup of a complete system is a truly portable copy of a complete working system. Encryption or other methods of protecting the backups can be useful in protecting systems with sensitive data. For systems that use a Windows proxy server, it is also critical that the proper precautions are taken to ensure that Windows does not write signatures to your VMFS volumes. In addition, backup operators and other administrators who use this machine need to understand these implications.

In the next section, we will look at determining when an advanced virtual machine parameter is required.

Determining When an Advanced Virtual Machine Parameter Is Required

In this chapter we have covered some of the virtual machine configuration file security hardening options. To apply any of the virtual machine hardening best practices listed in the vSphere Security Hardening Guide to a virtual machine, you can add advanced configuration parameters to the virtual machine. In Exercise 7.6, you added two of these advanced configuration parameters to control virtual machine logging behavior.

Another time when advanced configuration parameters might be added to a virtual machine is when working with VMware support. Advanced parameters can also be used to gain access to experimentally supported features and to create unsupported configurations. Anyone who has built a vSphere environment in a VMware Workstation lab has likely used some of these unsupported options to test advanced vSphere features.

 Real World Scenario

Virtual Machine Templates and Configuration Parameters

A virtual infrastructure administrator has decided that she wants to harden her virtual machines with certain configuration parameters contained in the vSphere Security Hardening Guide. Her vSphere environment is relatively new and contains only five virtual machines. She has manually updated these virtual machines but is looking for a solution to include these configuration parameters on all virtual machines she deploys in the future.

The administrator has two templates that she has used to deploy her five virtual machines. She decides that she will add the advanced configuration parameters to the templates so that all newly deployed virtual machines will include these settings by default. She converts her templates to virtual machines, adds the configuration parameters, and then converts the virtual machines back to templates. Now any new virtual machines deployed from these templates will automatically include the security-hardening parameters.

Next we will cover one of the powerful features that make virtual machines so flexible: hot-extending virtual disks.

Hot-Extending a Virtual Disk

Hot-extending a disk means increasing its capacity while the guest OS is running. Hot-extending a virtual disk is a task that every virtual infrastructure administrator has probably already performed. This process is simple, and end users appreciate this capability as much as the virtual infrastructure administrator does. Exercise 7.9 shows the steps to hot-extend a virtual disk. This exercise uses a Windows Server 2008 R2 virtual machine.

EXERCISE 7.9

Hot-Extending a Virtual Disk

1. Connect to a vCenter Server with the vSphere Web Client.

2. Select a powered-on virtual machine from the inventory and right-click it. Choose Edit Settings from the context menu.

3. The Virtual Machine Edit Settings window will open.

4. In the Virtual Hardware tab, locate the hard disk that will be extended.

5. Note the currently listed size shown to the right of the selected hard disk. Enter the new larger value for the hard disk, and then click OK in the Virtual Machine Edit Settings window.

6. A Reconfigure Virtual Machine task will begin. When the task completes, the disk has been extended.

   At this point, the virtual disk has tecŠically been hot-extended. But until the guest OS has been reconfigured to use this new space, there is no real benefit to simply hot-extending the disk. The remainder of this exercise will show how to make use of the extended disk (actually a partition/volume) in Windows Server 2008 R2.

7. Open a console to the Windows Server 2008 R2 VM and log in.

8. Typically when logging in to Windows Server 2008 R2, Server Manager will start automatically. If Server Manager does not automatically start, locate it in the Start menu under Administrative Tools.

9. Expand the Storage item in the left pane. Select the Disk Manager.

10. In the right pane, review the information for the extended disk. The space that was added to the virtual disk should be visible and reported as Unallocated to the right of the current volume.

   If the extended space is not visible, right-click the Disk Management icon in the left pane and choose Rescan Disks from the context menu.

11. Right-click the volume to be extended and choose Extend Volume from the context menu.

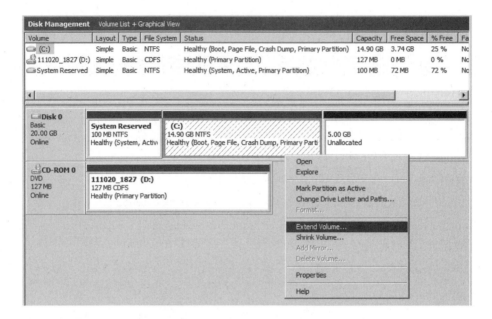

12. The Extend Volume Wizard will launch. Click Next to begin.

13. Review the information on the Select Disks screen and click Next to continue. By default, the extend operation will use all of the available space.

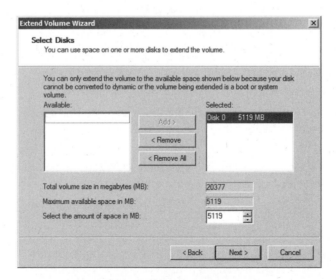

14. Click Finish to extend the volume in Windows.

15. On the Disk Management screen, verify that the volume was extended and is reporting the new size.

 Different operating systems have different support for hot-extending disks. Check with your OS vendor to see whether hot-extend is supported. If it is, the vendor should have specific instructions available.

It is also important to remember that virtual disks may not be hot-extended if the virtual machine has an active snapshot, or if the virtual machine uses an IDE disk controller. If either of these conditions is present, the disk options will be grayed out in the Virtual Machine Edit Settings window.

In the next section, we will discuss how to enable TCP segmentation offload for a VM.

Enabling TCP Segmentation Offload Support for a Virtual Machine

TCP segmentation offload (TSO) reduces the CPU overhead required by TCP/IP communications and improves network I/O performance. By default, TSO is enabled on VMkernel interfaces, but it must be enabled on virtual machines by using the *VMXNET 2* or *VMXNET 3* network adapter types. The virtual machine must also use a supported guest operating system. For a complete updated list of the supported operating systems that can be used with the VMXNET 2 and VMXNET 3 network adapters, visit http://kb·vmware ·com/kb/1001805·

Exercise 7.10 covers the steps to enable TSO for a Windows Server 2008 R2 virtual machine. It is important that the VMware Tools be installed in this VM, as we will be installing either the VMXNET2 or VMXNET3 adapter. Both of these high-performance network adapters require drivers from VMware Tools.

EXERCISE 7.10

Enabling TSO for a Virtual Machine

1. Connect to a vCenter Server with the vSphere Web Client.

2. Locate and right-click a powered-off virtual machine. Choose Edit Settings from the context menu. The Virtual Machine Edit Settings window will appear.

3. Expand the properties for a network adapter. Review the Adapter Type information, and verify that it is not listed as VMXNET 2 (Enhanced) or VMXNET 3. If either of these adapters is in use, then no further action is required to enable TSO for this virtual machine and you can skip to step 13.

4. If the network adapter is not VMXNET 2 or VMXNET 3, take note of the current network label. In the next step you will remove this adapter, and you may need this information again.

5. Hover the mouse over Network Adapter 1 and note the Remove icon that appears beside the device.

6. Click the Remove icon to mark the network adapter for removal. Note how the device field turns pink and the text Device Will Be Removed now appears beside it.

7. Click the New Device drop-down menu located at the bottom of the Edit Settings window to make the menu appear. Select Network from the list of devices and then click the Add button to continue. A New Network item will now be listed at the bottom of the list in the virtual machine properties.

8. Use the arrow to the left of the New Network item to expand it.

9. Using the drop-down menu, change the network label to the value noted in step 5 of this exercise. Using the drop-down menu, change Adapter Type to VMXNET 3. Select the Connect At Power On check box. The final configuration should appear similar to the following:

10. Click OK to save these changes. A Reconfigure Virtual Machine task will begin. When this task completes, the configuration is complete.

11. Because the network adapter was replaced with a new one, the network configuration in the guest OS will need to be reconfigured before the VM can be used on the network again. Power on the virtual machine and follow the procedures specific to your guest OS for this step.

12. In the Windows guests, you can verify TSO support by typing the following command at a command prompt:

```
netsh int ip show offload
```

The next topic we will cover is adjusting a virtual machine's resources based on workload.

Adjusting Virtual Machine Resources (Shares, Limits, and Reservations) Based on Virtual Machine Workloads

Sometimes a virtual machine needs additional resources; for example, at month-end, the finance application may require significantly more CPU and memory resources. Fortunately, there are ways to adjust the virtual machine resources for these types of situations.

You might recall the section on configuring disk shares in Chapter 6. Shares are used to specify the relative importance of a virtual machine as it pertains to a specific resource. In addition to the disk, the other two resources that may be configured for the virtual machine are CPU and memory. Just like disk shares, both CPU and memory resources can be adjusted on the Virtual Hardware tab of the Virtual Machine Edit Settings window. This tab is shown in Figure 7.16.

FIGURE 7.16   The Virtual Hardware tab of the Virtual Machine Edit Settings window

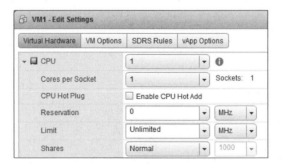

I will briefly describe each of these resource types here, but Chapter 8 covers them in much more detail. As discussed in the previous chapter, shares are used to specify relative importance of specific resources. Shares can have the values of Low, Normal, High, and Custom. Each of these values will be compared to the sum of all shares for all VMs on the host. Virtual machines with the highest share values will be able to consume more resources in periods of resource contention on the ESXi host.

In addition to shares, reservations can be used to guarantee a minimum allocation of CPU and memory for a virtual machine. This setting is used to claim a specific amount of the resource for the virtual machine so that these resources will always be available. Memory reservations can also be used to avoid overcommitment of physical memory resources. Memory reservations are required for virtual machines running in a vSphere Storage Appliance cluster, for example.

Limits are used to set an upper bound for resources. This prevents a virtual machine from using more resources than specified. This setting is by default set to Unlimited for both CPU and memory. Using this setting will ensure that the virtual machine uses close to the vCPU and memory allocations it has been granted.

Exercise 7.11 will cover the steps required to adjust virtual machine resources. For the purpose of this exercise, assume that the workload requires memory reservations to be set.

EXERCISE 7.11

Adjusting Virtual Machine Resources

1. Connect to a vCenter Server with the vSphere Web Client.

2. Locate a powered-off virtual machine in the inventory and select it. Right-click the virtual machine and choose Edit Settings from the context menu.

3. The Virtual Machine Edit Settings window will open. On the Virtual Hardware tab, expand the Memory item. Note that values can be specified for Shares, Reservation, and Limit.

4. Select the Reserve All Guest Memory (All Locked) box. The available options will all be grayed out after you make this selection.

5. Click OK to save these changes. A Reconfigure Virtual Machine task will begin. When this task completes, power on the virtual machine, and it will have a memory reservation.

 Configuring shares, reservations, and limits on individual virtual machines adds operational complexity to your environment. Resource pools are generally the preferred way of guaranteeing resources to your virtual machines. I will discuss resource pools in the next chapter.

In addition to performance options, another useful feature for virtual machines is USB passthrough.

Configuring USB passthrough from an ESXi Host

USB passthrough is used to add ESXi-host connected USB devices, such as security dongles and storage devices to VMs residing on the ESXi host. These host-connected USB devices can be presented to one VM at a time, and must be disconnected from the VM before they can be re-assigned. The USB passthrough feature consists of three components:

- USB Arbitrator — This component is installed and enabled on ESXi hosts by default. It manages connection requests, routes USB device traffic, scans the host for USB devices, and controls VM connections to USB devices. A maximum of 15 USB controllers can be monitored by the USB arbitrator.

- USB Controller — This component is a physical USB controller. ESXi hosts are required to have USB controller hardware that supports both USB 2.0 and 1.1 devices. There is also a virtual USB controller, which is a software virtualization function of the physical USB host provided to the VM. Two virtual USB controllers can be assigned to each VM, and must be added to the virtual machine before USB devices can be passed through from the ESXi host. The xHCI controller, available for Linux, Windows 8, and Windows 2012, supports USB 3.0 superspeed, 2.0, and 1.1 devices. The EHCI+UHCI controller supports USB 2.0 and 1.1 devices.

- USB Devices — This is the actual USB device that is connected to the ESXi host. A maximum of 20 USB devices can be connected to an ESXi host in a supported configuration. The same maximum of 20 also applies to the number of USB devices that can be simultaneously connected to a virtual machine.

Not all USB devices are supported for use in VMs. For a list of USB device models supported for passthrough from an ESXi host, refer to VMware KB:

http://kb.vmware.com/kb/1021345

You might think that using USB passthrough with a virtual machine would anchor it to an ESXi host, but VMs with USB passthrough devices are supported for use with vMotion and DRS. These VMs can maintain the USB passthrough connections to USB devices on the original ESXi host, under the following conditions:

- All connected USB passthrough devices must be configured for vMotion.

- If migrated VMs with USB passthrough devices are suspended or powered off, then these devices will not be reconnected when the VM is resumed or powered on again.

- Resuming Linux guests with USB passthrough devices may result in different mount points for the USB device.

- If DPM turns off a host with USB devices presented to VMs, these connections are lost.

- Migrated VMs with USB passthrough devices are possible via communication over the ESXi hosts' management networks. This is not possible if one host uses IPv4 and the other host uses IPv6, since the same IP version must be used.

Hot adding memory, CPU or PCI devices to virtual machines will disconnect USB devices.

Exercise 7.12 will cover the steps required to add a USB passthrough device to a virtual machine. This exercise requires a physical ESXi host, with a supported USB device attached to it. You will also need a virtual machine with a USB controller. If your lab doesn't meet these requirements, you may want to just read along.

EXERCISE 7.12

Adding a USB Device to a Virtual Machine

1. Connect to a vCenter Server with the vSphere Web Client.

2. Right-click a virtual machine in the inventory and select Edit Settings.

3. On the Virtual Hardware tab, select Host USB Device from the New device drop-down menu, and then click Add.

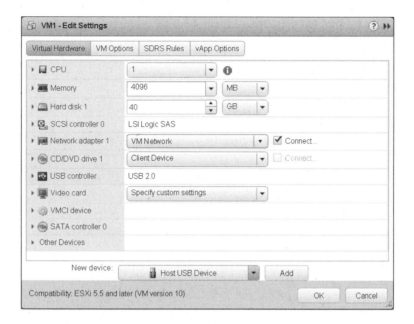

4. The new USB device appears at the bottom of the Virtual Hardware device list.

5. Expand New USB Device, and select the device to add.

6. If you do not plan to migrate a virtual machine with USB devices attached, deselect the Support vMotion option. This action reduces complexity, and results in better performance and stability for USB devices.

7. Click OK to save the changes to the VM.

8. Open the virtual machine and verify that the guest OS sees the USB device.

In addition to USB passthrough, serial port redirection can also be configured for virtual machines.

Configuring Serial port redirection

Serial ports can be used to connect additional peripherals to virtual machines. Up to four virtual serial ports can be used by a virtual machine. Virtual serial ports can be used in a variety of ways, and the chosen connection type will ultimately depend on what you are trying to accomplish. The available connection types are as follows:

- Physical serial port on the host — Allows the VM to use a physical serial port on the ESXi host. This connection type could be used for an external modem.

- Output to file — Allows output from the virtual serial port to be sent to a file on the ESXi host. This connection type could be used to capture data sent to a virtual serial port from a program running in a VM.

- Connect to a named pipe — Allows a direct connection between two VMs, a connection between a VM, and an application running on an ESXi host. This connection type mimics two devices being connected over a serial cable, and could be used for remote debugging on a virtual machine.

- Connect over the network — Allows a serial connection to and from a VM's serial port over the network. The Virtual Serial Port Concentrator (vSPC), which mimics physical serial port concentrators, can also be used here and is supported with vMotion.

ESXi firewall settings can prevent network traffic, if you add or configure a serial port that is backed by a remote network connection.

Exercise 7.13 will cover the steps required to add a serial port to a virtual machine. You will configure the connection type as Use Network and then connect to the serial port remotely with Telnet to verify its availability. This exercise requires a powered-off VM, preferably one with a modern Windows guest OS.

EXERCISE 7.13

Adding a Serial Port to a Virtual Machine

1. Connect to a vCenter Server with the vSphere Web Client.

2. Right-click a virtual machine in the inventory and select Edit Settings.

3. On the Virtual Hardware tab, click the New Device drop-down menu and select Serial Port. Click Add to add the serial port to the virtual machine.

4. Ensure that the serial port is expanded to show its configuration. Select the Use Network option from the New Serial Port drop-down menu.

5. Place a check in the Connect At Power On option.

6. Choose Server from the Connection Direction drop-down menu.

7. For the Connection Port URI, enter: **telnet://:12345**

8. Accept the defaults for all other settings; the final configuration should appear similar to this:

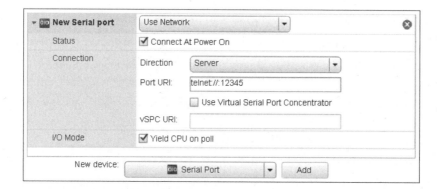

9. Click OK to add the configured serial port. A Reconfigure Virtual Machine task will start. When this task completes power on the VM.

10. When the virtual machine is powered on, telnet to port 12345 on the ESXi host where the VM is located with the following command:

```
telnet [ESXi Host} 12345
```

The previous lab demonstrates the network connection type of serial port redirection. Take some time to experiment beyond this lab with the other connection types and see what communications you can establish with serial ports.

Summary

This chapter covered managing and administering virtual machines. Knowing how to manage and administer virtual machines is essential for any virtual infrastructure administrator. Tasks covered included the following:

- Identifying the different cloning and template options.

- Cloning an existing virtual machine

- Creating a template from a virtual machine

- Deploying a virtual machine from a template

- Updating an existing virtual machine template

- Deploying virtual appliances and vApps from an OVF template

- Importing and exporting OVF templates

- Determining the appropriate deployment methodology for a given virtual machine application.

- Identifying vCloud Connector content types

- Creating, publishing, and subscribing content libraries in vCloud Connector

We also focused on administering virtual machines and vApps, including these topics:

- The files that make up virtual machines, along with the locations where these files can be stored

- Configuring different virtual machine options, including power settings, boot options, and troubleshooting options

- Common practices for securing virtual machines

- Determining when advanced configuration parameters are required

- Hot-extending a virtual disk

- Adjusting a virtual machine's resources

- Configuring USB passthrough from an ESXi host

- Configuring serial port redirection

Exam Essentials

Know how to manage virtual machine clones and templates.   Be able to identify the different cloning and template options. Know how to clone a virtual machine and create a template from a virtual machine. Understand how to deploy a new VM from a template and how to update existing templates. Be able to deploy virtual appliances and vApps from an OVF template. Know how to import and export an OVF template. Be able to determine the appropriate deployment method for a given virtual machine. Know the vCloud Connector content types, and how to create and manage a content library.

Know how to administer virtual machines and vApps.   Be able to identify the files used by a virtual machine and know the locations where the various files can be stored. Be able to configure virtual machine options, power settings, boot options, and troubleshooting options. Understand common practices for securing virtual machines and when advanced configuration parameters are required. Be able to hot-extend a disk. Know how to adjust virtual machine resources on a per-VM basis. Know how to configure USB passthrough and serial port redirection.

Review Questions

1. Which of the following items are listed as options on the context menus when right-clicking a template in the vSphere Web Client? (Choose all that apply.)

   A. Clone to Template

   B. Add Permission

   C. Rename

   D. Convert to Virtual Machine

2. Which of the following are not valid content types in vCloud Connector? (Choose two.)

   A. Virtual machine

   B. vApp

   C. Cluster

   D. Resource pool

3. You work in a 100 percent Windows virtual machine environment. You need to deploy four Linux VMs for a project. Which deployment methodology would be the least amount of work?

   A. Create four virtual machines one at a time.

   B. Create one virtual machine and clone it three times.

   C. Create one virtual machine and then convert it to a template. Deploy the remaining VMs from this template.

   D. Create a vApp.

4. You want to add several items listed in the vSphere Security Hardening Guide to a virtual machine configuration file. How will you most easily accomplish this task?

   A. Power off the virtual machine and add the options to the VM using the Configuration Parameters ➤ Edit Configuration button in the virtual machine settings.

   B. Add the options to the VM using the Security Parameters button in the virtual machine settings.

   C. Power off the virtual machine and clone it. Specify these options as part of the cloning process.

   D. Clone the virtual machine and specify these options as part of the cloning process.

5. A particular application is having a problem with installation. Which of the following options can be used to slow down a virtual machine in hopes of allowing the install to complete?

   A. Disable Acceleration

   B. Limit

   C. Shares

   D. Reservation

6. Which of the following vSphere features are available with USB passthrough? (Choose all that apply.)

   A. Distributed Power Management (DPM)

   B. Distribute Resource Scheduler (DRS)

   C. Fault Tolerance (FT)

   D. vMotion

7. vApps are built on which industry-standard format?

   A. OVA

   B. OVF

   C. OVT

   D. OVX

8. Which of the following options can be modified in the virtual machine settings while the virtual machine is powered on?

   A. Guest Operating System

   B. Force BIOS Setup

   C. CPUID Mask

   D. Power Management

9. Which of the following is the correct sequence for updating existing virtual machine templates?

   A. Using the Web Client, convert the template to a virtual machine, power on the virtual machine, make changes to the virtual machine as required, power off the virtual machine, and convert the virtual machine to a template.

   B. Using the Web Client, power on the virtual machine template, make changes to the virtual machine as required, and power off the virtual machine template.

   C. Using the Web Client, rename the virtual machine template using the File Browser, power on the virtual machine, make changes to the virtual machine as required, power off the virtual machine template, and rename the virtual machine using the File Browser.

   D. Using the Web Client, convert the template to a virtual machine using VMware Converter, power on the virtual machine, make changes to the virtual machine as required, power off the virtual machine, and convert the virtual machine to a template.

10. Which of the following are valid configuration options for a new serial port added to a virtual machine? (Choose all that apply.)

   A. Use output file

   B. Use physical serial port

   C. Use named pipe

   D. Use network

11. Which of the following items need to be secured in order to properly secure virtual machines? (Choose all that apply.)

   A. Virtual machine configuration files

   B. vMotion network(s)

   C. vCenter Server permissions

   D. ESXi hosts

12. Which of the following resources can be adjusted in the Edit Resource Settings window for a virtual machine? (Choose all that apply.)

   A. Shares

   B. Limits

   C. Reservations

   D. Allocations

13. What is the file extension for a virtual machine configuration file when the virtual machine has been converted to a template?

   A. .vmx

   B. .vmxf

   C. .vmtx

   D. .vmsd

14. A virtual machine owner is reporting that she is out of disk space on a virtual machine with a single disk running Windows Server 2008 R2. The guest OS has one volume only. What steps do you take to most quickly solve this problem?

   A. Add another virtual disk to the virtual machine and instruct the virtual machine owner to move some of her data to it.

   B. Hot-extend the virtual disk in the Web Client and then extend the volume in Windows using the Disk Manager.

   C. Instruct the user to schedule downtime and power down the virtual machine's guest OS. Hot-extend the disk.

   D. Clone the virtual machine and resize the disk.

15. You are trying to use the setup option for the BIOS of a virtual machine; however, the virtual machine starts up too fast for you to access the setup option. In the vSphere Web client, which virtual machine boot options can be used to solve this problem? (Choose all that apply.)

   A. Specify a different boot firmware.

   B. Specify a Boot Delay value.

   C. Select the Force BIOS Setup option.

   D. Set a Failed Boot Recovery value.

16. Which of the following file types can be moved outside the working location of a virtual machine? (Choose two.)

   A. VSWP

   B. LOG

   C. VMX

   D. VMDK

17. Which of the following files is a database that stores information and metadata about snapshots for a virtual machine?

   A. VMSS

   B. VMSN

   C. VSWP

   D. VMSD

18. Which of the following are required to create clones and templates? (Choose all that apply.)

   A. vCenter Server

   B. vSphere Client

   C. vSphere Web Client

   D. VMware Converter

19. Which of the following combinations are supported for Wake On LAN functionality? (Choose two.)

   A. Windows guest OS and VMXNET

   B. Linux guest OS and VMXNET 2

   C. Windows guest OS and VMXNET 3

   D. Linux guest OS and VMXNET 3

20. Which of the following can be deployed in the Web Client by using the Deploy OVF Template option? (Choose all that apply.)

   A. Virtual appliances

   B. Virtual disks

   C. vTeam

   D. vApps

Chapter 8

Establishing Service Levels with Clusters, Fault Tolerance, and Resource Pools

VCP5-DCV EXAM OBJECTIVES COVERED IN THIS CHAPTER:

✓ **5.1: Create and Configure VMware Clusters**

- Determine appropriate failover methodology and required resources for an HA implementation

- Describe DRS virtual machine entitlement

- Create/Delete a DRS/HA Cluster

- Add/Remove ESXi Hosts from a DRS/HA Cluster

- Add/Remove virtual machines from a DRS/HA Cluster

- Enable/Disable Host Monitoring

- Configure admission control for HA and virtual machines

- Enable/Configure/Disable virtual machine and application monitoring

- Configure automation levels for DRS and virtual machines

- Configure migration thresholds for DRS and virtual machines

- Create VM-Host and VM-VM affinity rules

- Configure Enhanced vMotion Compatibility

- Monitor a DRS/HA Cluster

- Configure Storage DRS

- Enable BIOS P/C states

- Enable/Configure/Disable Host Power Management /Distributed Power Management
- Determine appropriate power threshold for a given implementation

✓ **5.2: Plan and Implement VMware Fault Tolerance**

- Determine use case for enabling VMware Fault Tolerance on a virtual machine
- Identify VMware Fault Tolerance requirements
- Configure VMware Fault Tolerance networking
- Enable/Disable VMware Fault Tolerance on a virtual machine
- Test an FT configuration

✓ **5.3: Create and Administer Resource Pools**

- Describe the Resource Pool hierarchy
- Define the Expandable Reservation parameter
- Create/Remove a Resource Pool
- Configure Resource Pool attributes
- Add/Remove virtual machines from a Resource Pool
- Determine Resource Pool requirements for a given vSphere implementation
- Evaluate appropriate shares, reservations and limits for a Resource Pool based on virtual machine workloads
- Describe vFlash architecture
- Create/Delete vFlash Resource Pool
- Assign vFlash resources to VMDKs

TOOLS

- vCenter Server and Host Management guide (Objective 5.1)
- vSphere Availability guide (Objectives 5.1, 5.2)
- vSphere Resource Management guide (Objectives 5.1, 5.3)
- vSphere Virtual Machine Administration guide (Objective 5.3)
- vSphere Client/vSphere Web Client

This chapter covers the objectives of sections 5.1, 5.2, and 5.3 of the VCP5-DCV exam blueprint. It focuses on clusters, VMware Fault Tolerance (FT), and resource pools.

We will first discuss high-availability (HA) implementation resources and failover methodologies. You will learn about virtual machine entitlement, along with some basic information about Distributed Resource Scheduler (DRS) and HA. I will cover the steps required to create and delete a DRS/HA cluster, as well as how to add and remove ESXi hosts from a DRS/HA cluster and the steps to monitor a DRS/HA cluster. I will show you how to enable and disable host monitoring in a cluster and how to configure admission control for HA and VMs. You will learn about virtual machine and application monitoring, along with automation levels for DRS and virtual machines, and you'll see how to configure the migration thresholds for DRS and virtual machines. I will describe how to create VM-Host and VM-VM affinity rules. EVC compatibility, monitoring clusters, and Storage DRS will also be covered. This section will conclude with configuring Distributed Power Management for a vSphere environment.

We will then explore the VMware Fault Tolerance feature. You will learn how to determine the use cases for VMware FT and identify the requirements to implement FT in a vSphere environment. I will also cover how to create networking for the Fault Tolerance logging traffic, as well as the steps to enable and disable FT and to test it.

The final section of this chapter will focus on resource pools. I will explore the resource pool hierarchy and discuss the Expandable Reservation parameter. I will show you how to create and remove resource pools, configure their attributes, and add and remove virtual machines to and from a resource pool. I will also explain how to determine the resource pool requirements for a given vSphere implementation. You will learn how to evaluate appropriate shares, reservations, and limits for a resource pool, based on VM workloads. This chapter will conclude with a discussion of vSphere Flash Read Cache implementation.

Creating and Configuring VMware Clusters

In vSphere, a cluster is a collection of ESXi hosts and the virtual machines associated with them that have shared resources and are managed by vCenter Server. Clusters are used to enable some of the more powerful features in vSphere, such as Distributed Resource Scheduler (DRS), High Availability (HA), Fault Tolerance (FT), and vMotion. The first topic we will explore in this chapter is determining the appropriate failover methodology and required resources for an HA implementation.

Determining the Appropriate Failover Methodology and Required Resources for an HA Implementation

As you will see later in this chapter, creating clusters and configuring them in vCenter Server are both relatively simple tasks. Like many aspects of vSphere, creating a cluster involves proper up-front planning. Part of this planning is determining how you want the cluster to function. Will the cluster have both DRS and HA enabled, or perhaps just one and not the other? The answers to these questions will impact the way the cluster is designed. Remember that DRS provides load balancing and HA provides high availability. Although these two features complement each other well, they serve different functions and don't always have to be used in unison.

For clusters that will use HA, the resources that will be required are in part determined by how failures in the cluster will be handled. For example, are all virtual machines required to have a certain amount of uptime? If you have a two-node cluster, with each ESXi host running at 80 percent capacity of memory and processing, then a single host failure will not likely allow you to achieve the virtual machine availability requirements. The failover behavior is handled by admission control policies in the HA cluster and will be discussed later in this chapter.

Knowing your environment's specific availability requirements will help determine the appropriate failover methodology and the resources required for an HA implementation. In the next section, I will describe DRS virtual machine entitlement.

DRS Virtual Machine Entitlement

While each ESXi host has its own local scheduler, enabling DRS on a cluster will create a second layer of scheduling architecture. Figure 8.1 shows this architecture.

FIGURE 8.1   Global and local schedulers

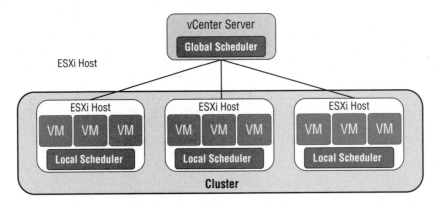

Both of these schedulers compute resource entitlement for virtual machines. This resource entitlement is based on both a static and a dynamic entitlement. The static entitlement consists of a virtual machine's shares, reservations, and limits. The dynamic entitlement for the virtual machine includes metrics such as estimated active memory and CPU demand.

If the DRS cluster is not overcommitted, the virtual machine's entitlement will be the same as its resource allocation. In periods of contention, DRS will use the virtual machine entitlement to determine how to best distribute resources.

Now that you understand failover methodologies and virtual machine entitlement, let's create a cluster.

Creating and Deleting a DRS/HA Cluster

Once the prerequisite planning and design work is complete, creating a cluster is simple. Exercise 8.1 covers the steps to create a new cluster with both HA and DRS enabled.

EXERCISE 8.1

Creating a New Cluster with HA and DRS Enabled

1. Connect to a vCenter Server with the vSphere Web Client.

2. Switch to the Hosts And Clusters view. Right-click a datacenter object and choose the New Cluster option from the context menu. The New Cluster Wizard will launch.

3. Provide the cluster with a descriptive and unique name.

4. Select the Turn ON check box for DRS. The DRS options will expand.

5. From the Set Automation Level drop-down menu, select Manual. Note the default setting of the Migration Threshold slider. The final DRS configuration should look like this:

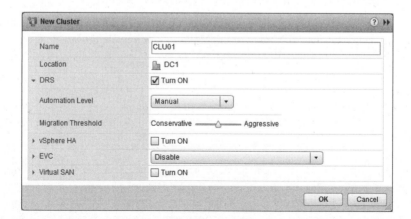

6. Select the Turn ON check box for vSphere HA. Expand the vSphere HA options.

EXERCISE 8.1 *(continued)*

7. Deselect the Enable Host Monitoring option. Ensure that the Admission Control options are expanded. Deselect the Enable Admission Control check box.

8. Review and accept the default settings for the VM Monitoring. The final vSphere HA configuration should look like this:

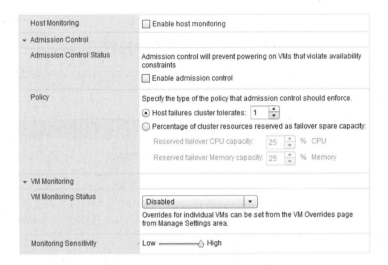

9. Accept the default settings for the EVC and Virtual SAN options and click OK to create the cluster.

10. A Create Cluster task will begin. When this task completes, verify that the new cluster has been created in the left pane of the Hosts And Clusters view.

11. Right-click the cluster in the left pane and choose Settings from the context menu. The cluster properties will be shown in the Manage tab. Review the settings and verify that vSphere HA and DRS are both turned on.

This exercise has focused on creating a cluster. Many of the cluster settings can be configured only after the initial cluster has been created.

Note that clusters can exist without shared storage, but nearly all of the functionality they provide will require shared storage. Before proceeding, please ensure that shared storage exists for any ESXi hosts that will be added to the cluster you just created. If you need assistance, Chapter 5, "Planning and Configuring vSphere Storage," showed how to configure shared storage. The remainder of the exercises in this chapter will assume that the same shared storage is available for each ESXi host in the cluster created in Exercise 8.1.

Another configuration that should exist in each ESXi host in the cluster is VMkernel networking for vMotion traffic. Having vMotion configured enables DRS to migrate virtual machines to different hosts. Exercises 4.4 and 4.5 in Chapter 4 covered configuring vMotion networking. The remainder of the exercises in this chapter will also assume that vMotion has been configured for each ESXi host in the cluster created in Exercise 8.1.

Occasionally, you might need to delete a cluster. The steps to delete a cluster are simple and consist of right-clicking the cluster in the left pane of the vSphere Web Client and choosing All vCenter Actions ➤ Remove From Inventory from the context menu. A Remove Cluster confirmation dialog will appear, and clicking the Yes button will delete the cluster.

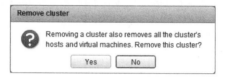

The steps to create and delete a DRS- and HA-enabled cluster have been covered. However, a cluster with no ESXi hosts is not very functional, so the next section shows you how to add ESXi hosts to this cluster.

Adding and Removing ESXi Hosts to/from a DRS/HA Cluster

Like vCenter Server, a cluster isn't nearly as interesting until ESXi hosts have been added to it. In the previous exercise, you created a new cluster with DRS and vSphere HA enabled. In Exercise 8.2, two ESXi hosts will be added to this cluster. This exercise will assume that there is one host already present in the same datacenter as the cluster and that the second host will be added to the cluster as a new host.

EXERCISE 8.2

Adding and Removing ESXi Hosts to and from a Cluster

1. Connect to a vCenter Server with the vSphere Web Client.

2. Select Hosts And Clusters in the left pane.

3. Locate an ESXi host that will be added to the cluster. Click this host and drag it into the cluster. The Move Host Into This Cluster window will open. In this example, esxi1.test.local is used.

EXERCISE 8.2 *(continued)*

4. Accept the default option for the virtual machine resources.

   Choosing the default option will put all of the ESXi host's virtual machines in the cluster's root resource pool and will delete any resource pools currently defined on the ESXi host.

5. Click OK to add this ESXi host to the cluster.

6. A Move Host Into Cluster task will begin, as will a Configuring vSphere HA task. When these tasks complete, verify that the ESXi host is now a member of the cluster by expanding the cluster in the left pane.

   You have now added an existing ESXi host from your datacenter into a new cluster. The following steps show how to add a host that was not already being managed by a vCenter Server.

7. Right-click the cluster and choose the Add Host option from the context menu. The Add Host wizard will launch.

8. Enter the FQDN of the ESXi host and verify that the Location field contains the name of your cluster. Click Next to continue.

9. Provide administrative credentials to log in to this ESXi host and click Next. A Security Alert window will appear. Click Yes if you trust the ESXi host in your lab environment.

10. Review the information on the Host Summary screen and click Next.

11. If you have licenses and want to use them, assign them on the Assign License screen. Otherwise, select the Evaluation Mode option. Click Next.

12. Leave the Enable Lockdown Mode option unchecked and click Next.

13. Choose the Root Resource Pool option, as you did in the previous exercise. Click Next.

14. Review the information on the Ready To Complete screen and click Finish to add this ESXi host to the cluster.

15. An Add Host task will begin, as will a Configuring vSphere HA task. When these tasks complete, verify that the ESXi host is now a member of the cluster by expanding the cluster in the left pane.

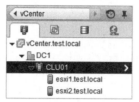

Two ESXi hosts have now been added to the cluster. The remainder of this exercise will cover the steps to delete an ESXi host from the cluster. Just as you added the first ESXi host by dragging it into the cluster, an ESXi host can be removed from a cluster by dragging it into a new supported location.

16. Select one of the two ESXi hosts that were just added to the cluster and right-click it. Choose the Enter Maintenance Mode option from the context menu.

17. A Confirm Maintenance Mode window will appear. Review this information and click OK to proceed.

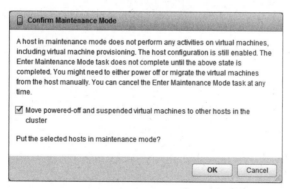

18. An Enter Maintenance Mode task will begin. When this task completes, the icon for the ESXi host will change to indicate that it is in maintenance mode.

19. Click this ESXi host and drag it into the datacenter object.

20. A Move Entities task will begin. When this task completes, verify that the ESXi host is now listed in the datacenter.

21. Select this same ESXi host and right-click it. Choose the Exit Maintenance Mode option from the context menu.

22. An Exit Maintenance Mode task will begin. When this task completes, the icon for the ESXi host will change to indicate that it is no longer in maintenance mode.

You have now added ESXi hosts to your cluster in two different ways. Any virtual machines that were already present on ESXi hosts are automatically part of the cluster. In the next section, you'll see how to add new virtual machines to the cluster and remove them.

Adding and Removing Virtual Machines to/from a DRS/HA Cluster

The process of adding a virtual machine to a cluster is similar to that of adding a virtual machine to a host or vApp. Chapters 6 and 7 covered adding virtual machines to ESXi hosts and vApps, deploying OVF templates, and moving machines with VMware Converter. Each of these deployment options allows you to choose a cluster, so adding a virtual machine to a cluster should be familiar ground by now.

To create a new VM that will be a member of a cluster, simply right-click the cluster and choose the New Virtual Machine option from the context menu. The New Virtual Machine wizard is shown in Figure 8.2 at the Select a Compute Resource screen.

FIGURE 8.2   Adding a new VM to a cluster

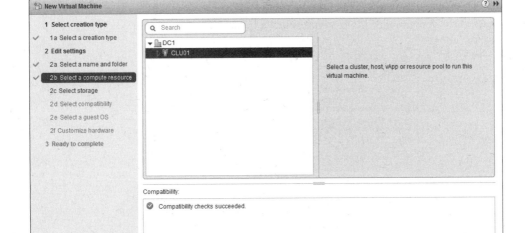

Virtual machines running on ESXi hosts in the same datacenter but not in the cluster can also be added to the cluster. This approach could be used for a VM that was in a testing or pilot program but is now ready to be moved into production and benefit from DRS and HA. Exercise 8.3 shows the steps to move a powered-on VM from another host to a cluster. This exercise requires an additional ESXi host that is not part of the cluster and, as mentioned earlier in this chapter, assumes that a vMotion network and shared storage exist for all of the ESXi hosts.

EXERCISE 8.3

Adding a VM from an Existing ESXi Host to a Cluster

1. Connect to a vCenter Server with the vSphere Web Client.

2. Locate a powered-on virtual machine. Right-click it and choose the Migrate option from the context menu.

3. The VM - Migrate wizard will open. Choose the Change Host option and click Next.

4. On the Select Destination Resource screen, select the cluster object and then select the Allow Host Selection Within This Cluster check box.

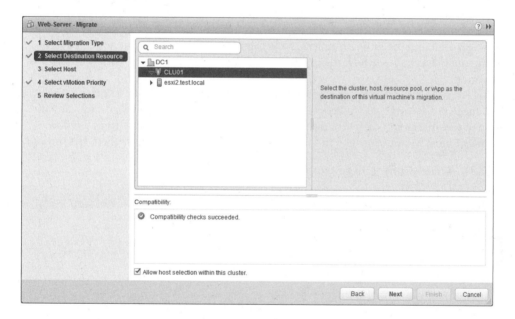

5. Click the Next button and select the desired ESXi host in the next screen. Click Next.

6. Choose the Reserve CPU For Optimal vMotion Performance (Recommended) option and click Next.

7. Review the information on the Review screen and click Finish to move the VM to the cluster.

8. A Relocate Virtual Machine task will begin. When this task completes, verify that the virtual machine is now a member of the cluster.

If a vMotion network were not available between the two ESXi hosts used in Exercise 8.3, the powered-off virtual machine could still be cold-migrated to the cluster.

Removing a virtual machine is accomplished in much the same way that a virtual machine is added to a cluster. vMotion can be used to migrate a powered-on VM from a cluster to another host that has access to both the vMotion network and the same shared storage. If the vMotion network and shared storage requirements are not met, the VM can be *cold-migrated* from the cluster to an ESXi host.

You have now created a cluster, added ESXi host(s) to it, and added virtual machines to it. Next we will explore some of the options available in the cluster settings.

Enabling and Disabling Host Monitoring

In Exercise 8.1, you created a DRS/HA cluster, and there were two HA settings that were modified from the default settings. These changes were to disable host monitoring and to disable admission control. Changing these settings initially allowed the cluster to be more flexible for a lab or similar environment. Now that the cluster is built and hosts and VMs are running in it, you'll see how to configure the HA settings, beginning with enabling host monitoring.

To start, right-click the cluster object and choose Settings from the context menu. On the Manage tab, ensure that vSphere HA is selected in the left pane, and then click the Edit button in the upper-right corner of the middle pane. In the Edit Cluster Settings window, expand the Host Monitoring item in the left pane. Figure 8.3 shows the vSphere HA settings.

FIGURE 8.3   vSphere HA settings

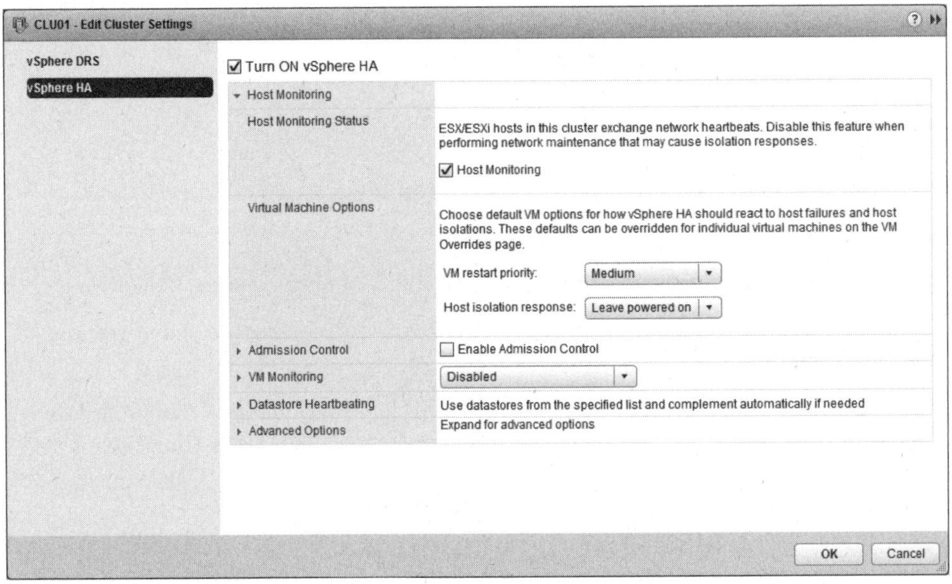

The first field is used to enable and disable host monitoring. Enable host monitoring here by selecting the Host Monitoring option. Click OK to save the changes.

Enabling host monitoring will allow ESXi hosts in the cluster to exchange network heartbeats via the HA agents over their management networks. vSphere HA uses a master-slave host design. In this design, a single member of the cluster is the master, whereas all other hosts are slaves. For network heartbeating, the master sends heartbeats to the slaves and each slave sends heartbeats to the master. In addition to the network heartbeating, HA uses *datastore heartbeating*. By default, HA selects two shared datastores (heartbeat datastores) on which each host in the HA cluster maintains an open file specifically created for this reason. Figure 8.4 shows the datastore heartbeating options.

FIGURE 8.4   vSphere HA Datastore Heartbeating settings

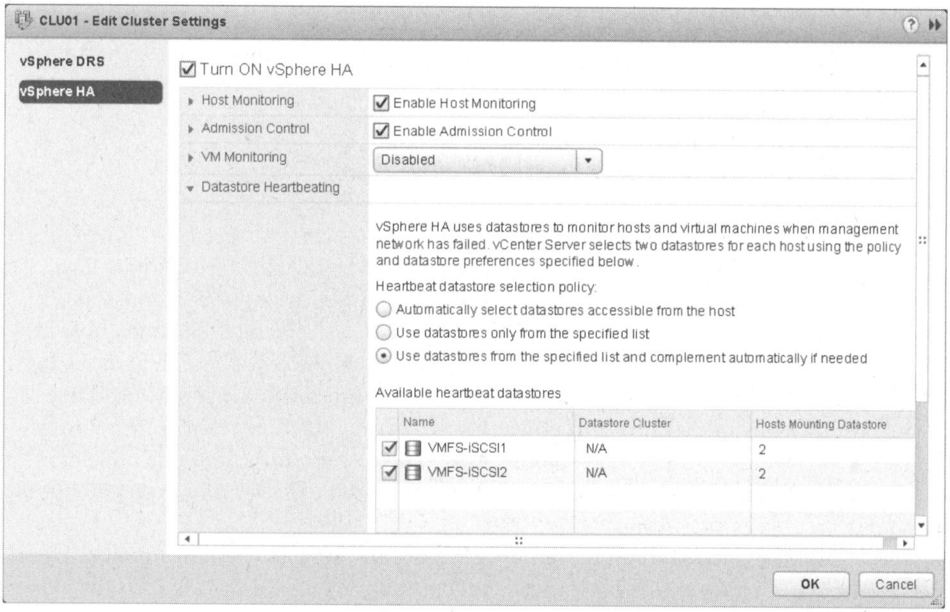

If the master stops receiving network heartbeats from a slave, it must determine whether the host has failed or is isolated. To do so, the master queries the heartbeat regions on the two datastores to find out whether the slave still has access to the heartbeat files. If the master no longer receives network heartbeats from the slave, the slave is not responding to pings, and the slave is not generating datastore heartbeats, then the slave is considered failed. HA will then try to restart the virtual machines that were running on the slave on other hosts in the cluster.

If a slave is still running and doesn't receive either the network heartbeats from the master nor election traffic from other hosts, the slave will attempt to ping the cluster isolation address. If this ping operation fails, the slave considers itself isolated and triggers an isolation response. The master host will also utilize the host isolation response settings to determine what action to take with the virtual machines.

If a slave host is no longer receiving network heartbeats from the master but receives election traffic from other slaves, then the slave is considered partitioned. An election process will take place among the slaves in the partition to determine a new master host. This is considered a degraded protection state but will allow the hosts in the cluster to again detect failed hosts or isolated hosts so that the correct HA action can be taken.

The function of vSphere HA is to restart VMs, and it does not provide stateful application-level fault tolerance.

Host monitoring can be disabled for network or ESXi host maintenance in lab settings or other configurations where you would not want HA to function as normal, such as when first building out the cluster. Now that I have covered host monitoring, let's turn our attention to admission control policy.

Configuring Admission Control for HA and Virtual Machines

Admission control is used to guarantee that capacity exists in the cluster to handle host failure situations. The current available resources of the cluster are used by admission control to calculate the required capacity, so this value will be dynamic. Placing a host in maintenance mode or experiencing a host failure will change the capacity calculations for the cluster. Admission control attempts to ensure that resources will always be available on the remaining hosts in the cluster to power on the virtual machines that were running on a failed or unavailable host. The recommended configuration for admission control is to enable it. This will allow the cluster to reserve the required capacity and keep you out of host resource saturation situations.

Admission control is further configured by selecting the admission control policy. These policies are used to further define how admission control will ensure capacity for the cluster. The four policies are as follows:

- Define Failover Capacity By Static Number Of Hosts
- Define Failover Capacity By Reserving A Percentage Of The Cluster Resources
- Use Dedicated Failover Hosts
- Do Not Reserve Failover Capacity

We'll take a closer look at each of these four policies, but also keep in mind that vSphere HA is a complex subject and that multiple chapters could easily be devoted to it.

Define Failover Capacity By Static Number Of Hosts   With this policy, a user-specified number of hosts may fail, and vSphere HA will reserve resources to fail over the virtual machines running from this number of failed hosts. The calculation used for this is based on a slot size, which is the amount of memory and CPU assigned to powered-on virtual machines. The slot size is compared to the capacity of the hosts in the cluster to determine how many total slots are available. vSphere HA will then attempt to reserve enough resources to be able to satisfy the number of needed slots.

Define Failover Capacity By Reserving A Percentage Of The Cluster Resources With this policy, a user-specified percentage of the cluster's aggregate CPU and memory resources are reserved for recovery from ESXi host failures. CPU and memory percentages can be configured separately, and the CPU and memory reservation values of the virtual machine are used in the calculation by vSphere HA.

Use Dedicated Failover Hosts With this policy, a user-specified number of hosts are reserved strictly for failover. The failover host(s) cannot have powered-on virtual machines, because the failover host(s) will be used only for an HA event. In an HA event, vSphere HA will attempt to start the virtual machines on the failover host. If the specified failover host is not available or is at capacity, then vSphere HA will attempt to use other hosts in the cluster to start virtual machines.

Do Not Reserve Failover Capacity With this policy, virtual machines will be allowed to power on that would otherwise violate availability constraints. In other words, this policy means do not use Admission Control.

Now that I have briefly discussed admission control and the admission control policies, Exercise 8.4 will show how to configure them. Note that this exercise will require a minimum of two ESXi hosts that already belong to a cluster. One of the ESXi hosts should have no running VMs on it.

EXERCISE 8.4

Configuring Admission Control and Admission Control Policies

1. Connect to a vCenter Server with the vSphere Web Client.

2. Locate a cluster in the inventory. Right-click it and choose Settings from the context menu.

3. On the Manage tab, ensure that vSphere HA is selected in the left pane, and then click the Edit button in the upper-right corner of the middle pane. In the Edit Cluster Settings window, expand the Admission Control item in the left pane.

4. Select the admission control policy Define Failover Capacity By Reserving A Percentage Of The Cluster Resources.

5. Change the values to 35% for both CPU and Memory.

6. Now select the admission control policy of Use Dedicated Failover Hosts. Notice how the previous values remain in the Define Failover Capacity By Reserving A Percentage Of The Cluster Resources policy but are now grayed out.

7. Click the green plus sign located beneath the Use Dedicated Failover Hosts policy item. An Add Failover Host window will appear.

EXERCISE 8.4 *(continued)*

8. Select the checkbox beside your ESXi host with no running VMs and click OK. The final configuration should look like this:

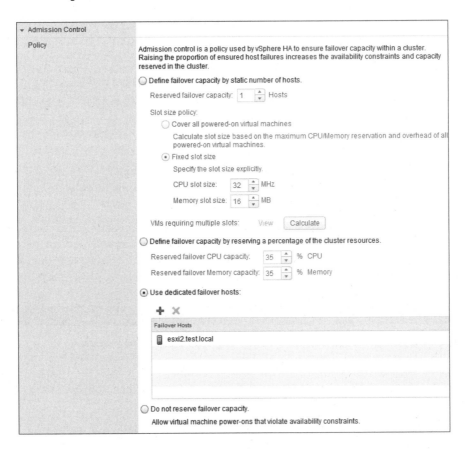

9. Click OK to save the admission control policy changes. A Reconfigure Cluster task will begin.

10. When this task completes, on the Manage tab in the Settings window, ensure that the vSphere HA is selected in the left pane. Expand the Admission Control item and verify that a value of 1 Host is listed for Number Of Failover Hosts.

11. Power on a virtual machine in the cluster. Attempt to migrate it with vMotion to the failover ESXi host. You will receive an error message stating that the operation cannot be performed.

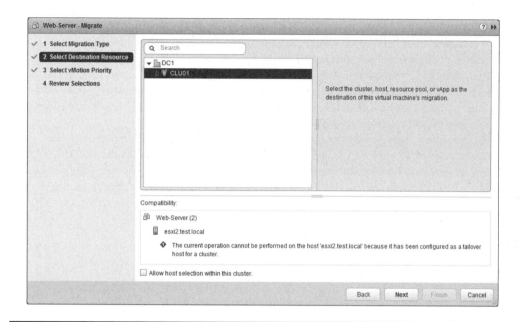

One other topic that needs to be addressed is the virtual machine options for vSphere HA. These options are also listed in the Edit Cluster Settings window and are contained in the Host Monitoring section. Figure 8.5 shows the Virtual Machine Options screen.

FIGURE 8.5   Virtual Machine Options screen for HA

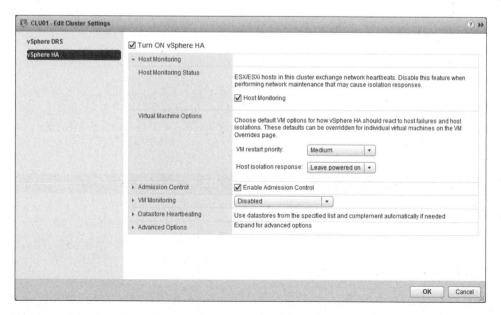

The Virtual Machine Options section of the cluster settings is used to specify the restart priority and host isolation response for both the cluster and the individual virtual machines. The virtual machine restart priority is used to specify the start order for virtual machines, if an HA event occurs. VMs with the highest restart priority are restarted first. This setting can be used to ensure that important virtual machines get powered on first. It is also useful in cases where cluster resources become exhausted in an HA event to ensure that the more important VMs are powered on.

If you recall the vApp start order options from Chapter 6, VM restart priority can be used in a somewhat similar way. In an application with a three-tiered architecture, the database server could have a High restart priority, the application server could have a Medium priority, and the web server frontend could have a Low priority. Although there will be no guarantees, as with a vApp, it is still a sound approach. The four settings for virtual machine priority are as follows:

- Disabled
- Low
- Medium
- High

The Disabled option can be used to disable HA for virtual machines. This can be useful for clusters that include nonessential virtual machines.

Host isolation response is used to configure the behavior of the ESXi host when it has lost its management network connection but has not failed. When a host is no longer able to communicate with the HA agents running on other ESXi hosts in the cluster and is also unable to ping its isolation address, it is considered isolated. Once isolated, the host will execute the isolation response. The isolation responses are as follows:

- Leave Powered On
- Power Off, Then Failover
- Shut Down, Then Failover

These options are self-explanatory, but keep in mind that the shutdown isolation response requires that the guest operating systems have the VMware Tools installed. Now that you have seen the vSphere HA options for virtual machines, Exercise 8.5 shows how to configure them.

EXERCISE 8.5

Configuring VM Options for vSphere HA

1. Connect to a vCenter Server with the vSphere Web Client.

2. Locate a cluster in the inventory. Right-click it and choose Settings from the context menu.

3. On the Manage tab, ensure that vSphere HA is selected in the left pane, and then click the Edit button in the middle pane. In the Edit Cluster Settings window, expand the Host Monitoring item in the left pane.

4. From the VM Restart Priority drop-down menu, choose Low.

5. From the Host Isolation Response drop-down menu, choose Shut Down, Then Failover.

These two options have now changed the default behavior for the cluster as a whole. In the remainder of the exercise, you will see how to modify individual virtual machine settings. This procedure also assumes the three-tiered application I discussed earlier. If you don't have a three-tiered application, complete the exercise with existing virtual machines instead.

6. On the Manage tab, ensure that Settings is selected. Select the VM Overrides option in the left pane, and then click Add to open the Cluster - Add VM Overrides window.

EXERCISE 8.5 *(continued)*

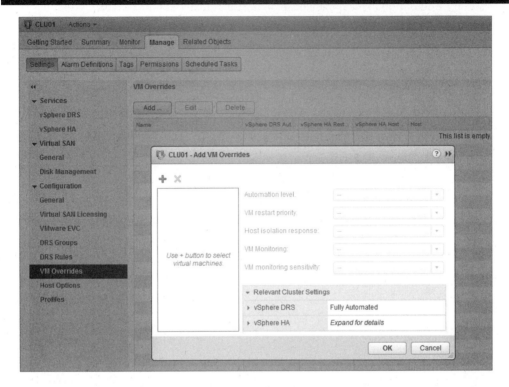

7. Click the plus icon to select the virtual machine that houses the database. Click OK to add the VM and return to the Cluster - Add VM Overrides window.

8. From the VM Restart Priority drop-down menu, choose High. Ensure that Host Isolation Response is set to Use Cluster Setting.

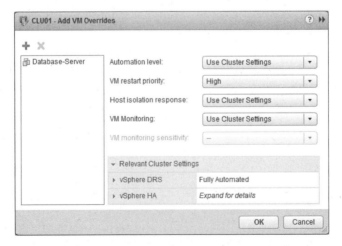

These options will configure HA to shut down the database cleanly and then restart this virtual machine with a high priority. Note that individual virtual machine priority settings will override those of the cluster.

9. Click OK to save the VM Override for the VM that has the database. A Reconfigure Cluster task will begin. Wait for this task to complete before continuing.

10. Click the Add button to open the Cluster - Add VM Overrides window again.

11. Click the plus icon to select the virtual machines that house both the middleware application and the web server. Click OK to add these two VMs and return to the Cluster - Add VM Overrides window.

12. From the VM Restart Priority drop-down menu, choose Medium. Ensure that Host Isolation Response is set to Use Cluster Setting.

    These options will configure HA to shut down both the middleware and web server virtual machines and then restart them with a medium priority. Note again that individual virtual machine priority settings will override those of the cluster.

13. Review the settings of the VM Overrides. Notice that the web server was added with a restart priority of Medium. This mistake was intentional so that we could review the edit function for VM Overrides.

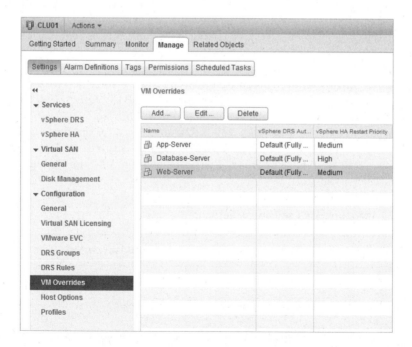

14. Select the virtual machine that houses the web server, and click the Edit button to open the Cluster - Edit VM Overrides window.

EXERCISE 8.5 *(continued)*

15. From the VM Restart Priority drop-down menu, choose Low. Ensure that Host Isolation Response is set to Use Cluster Setting.

These options will configure HA to shut down the web server frontend for the application and then restart it with a low priority.

16. Click OK to save these changes to the web server VM. A Reconfigure Cluster task will begin. When this task completes, review the VM Overrides to ensure that the three-tiered application is configured properly.

Now that we have covered VM overrides, let's turn our attention to enabling, configuring, and disabling virtual machine and application monitoring.

Enabling, Configuring, and Disabling Virtual Machine and Application Monitoring

VM monitoring is used to provide high availability for individual virtual machines. Whereas vSphere HA can restart virtual machines when a host fails or becomes isolated, VM monitoring can restart individual virtual machines when they have failed or become unresponsive. Application monitoring works in much the same way, except that a specific application is monitored rather than the virtual machine.

VM monitoring works by monitoring VMware Tools heartbeats and I/O activity from the VMware Tools process running in the guest OS. If VMware Tools heartbeats stop for the duration of the failure interval, the last 120 seconds of disk I/O activity will be checked. If there is no disk I/O in this period, the virtual machine will be reset.

Virtual machine monitoring sensitivity can also be configured for the cluster and for individual VMs. This allows you to fine-tune the monitoring sensitivity both to obtain rapid resolution and to avoid false positives. Table 8.1 shows the VM monitoring sensitivity values for the cluster setting.

TABLE 8.1 VM monitoring sensitivity settings

Setting	Failure interval	Reset period
High	30 seconds	1 hour
Medium	60 seconds	24 hours
Low	120 seconds	7 days

You can also use the Custom option for VM Monitoring Sensitivity if the defaults do not provide the functionality required for your environment.

Virtual machines can be configured individually so that an individual VM can have settings that override those of the cluster. These options are configured in the VM Monitoring section of the cluster settings and will be discussed in more detail in Exercise 8.6.

Application monitoring performs similarly to VM monitoring. It differs in that it uses heartbeats from a specific application and thus requires the application to be customized to use VMware application monitoring.

Exercise 8.6 shows how to enable and configure VM and application monitoring.

EXERCISE 8.6

Enabling and Configuring VM Monitoring and Application Monitoring

1. Connect to a vCenter Server with the vSphere Web Client.

2. Locate a cluster in the inventory. Right-click it and choose Settings from the context menu.

3. On the Manage tab, ensure that vSphere HA is selected in the left pane, and then click the Edit button in the upper-right corner of the middle pane. In the Edit Cluster Settings window, expand the VM Monitoring item in the left pane.

4. From the VM Monitoring drop-down menu, choose VM And Application Monitoring.

    Note that by default VM Monitoring is set to Disabled. To disable the VM Monitoring option at the end of this exercise, you will simply change the value here.

5. In the Monitoring Sensitivity section, select the Preset option and use the slider to adjust the setting to the center value. The presets in the Custom field below the slider will adjust to reflect the values of its current position.

    The center setting of the slider will enable the VM to be restarted if no heartbeat or I/O is detected within a 60-second interval. The virtual machine can be restarted up to three times within the reset period of 24 hours. If the VM fails a fourth time within the reset period, vSphere HA will take no further action.

EXERCISE 8.6 *(continued)*

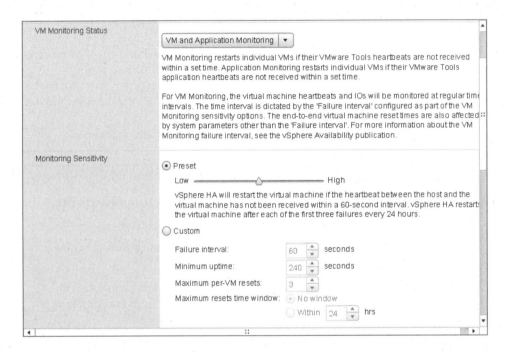

6. Click OK to save these VM Monitoring settings. A Reconfigure Cluster task will begin.

7. On the Manage tab, ensure that Settings is selected. Select the VM Overrides option in the left pane, and then select the database server listed in the VM Overrides list in the middle pane.

8. Click the Edit button to open the Cluster - Edit VM Overrides window.

9. Change the VM Monitoring value for the database server to Disabled.

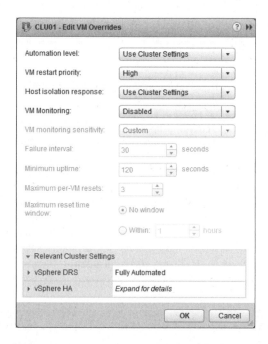

The database server has now been excluded from VM and application monitoring.

10. Click OK to save these changes. A Reconfigure Cluster task will begin. When this task completes, the virtual machine and application monitoring options for HA will be set.

In the next section we will move away from vSphere HA and turn our attention to DRS.

Configuring Automation Levels for DRS and Virtual Machines

Since DRS is responsible for both the initial placement of virtual machines and migrations using vMotion, automation levels can be configured to help control how involved the Distributed Resource Scheduler will actually be. Table 8.2 shows the available automation levels and a description of each.

TABLE 8.2   DRS Automation levels

Automation level	Description
Manual	No action will be taken, and vCenter Server will indicate suggested virtual machine migrations.
Partially auto-mated	vCenter Server will indicate suggested virtual machine migrations and place the virtual machines on ESXi hosts at VM startup.
Fully automated	vCenter Server will use vMotion to optimize resource usage in the cluster and place the virtual machines on ESXi hosts at VM startup.

The automation level can be set for the entire DRS cluster, but virtual machines may have their individual automation levels set to override the cluster settings. In Exercise 8.7, we will set the automation level for a cluster and set a virtual machine's individual automation level to differ from the cluster settings.

EXERCISE 8.7

Configuring the Automation Level for a Cluster and a VM

1. Connect to a vCenter Server with the vSphere Web Client.

2. Locate a cluster in the inventory. Right-click it and choose Settings from the context menu.

3. On the Manage tab, ensure that vSphere DRS is selected in the left pane, and then click the Edit button in the upper-right corner of the middle pane.

4. In the Edit Cluster Settings window, expand the DRS Automation item in the left pane.

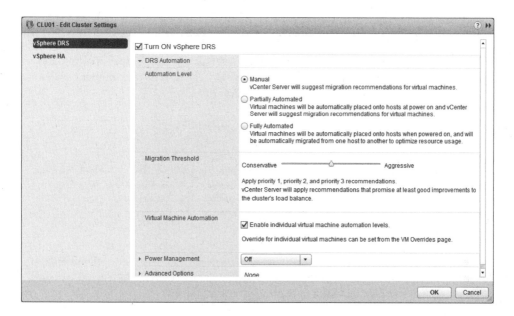

In Exercise 8.1 when you created a cluster, the automation level was set to Manual. In the following steps, you will change the automation level to Fully Automated.

5. Select the Fully Automated option and accept the default migration threshold option.

   The migration threshold settings will be covered in detail in the next section of this chapter.

6. Ensure that in the Virtual Machine Automation section, Enable Individual Virtual Machine Automation Levels is selected.

7. Click OK to save these changes.

8. A Reconfigure Cluster task will begin. Wait for this task to complete.

   Changing the automation level for the cluster and enabling virtual machine automation were the first part of this exercise. The remainder of the exercise will focus on changing the automation level for an individual virtual machine in the cluster.

9. On the Manage tab, ensure that Settings is selected. Select the VM Overrides option in the left pane, and then select one of the VMs that were added in the previous exercises.

10. Click the Edit button to open the Cluster - Edit VM Overrides window.

11. Change the Automation Level value for the VM to Disabled.

    Disabling the automation level will prevent vCenter from generating or performing migration recommendations for it. Disabling the automation level is also known as *pinning* a virtual machine to a host.

EXERCISE 8.7 (continued)

12. Click OK to save the changes to the automation level for this VM. A Reconfigure Cluster task will begin. The final configuration in the VM Overrides pane should look like this, where in my lab I changed the Database-Server VM.

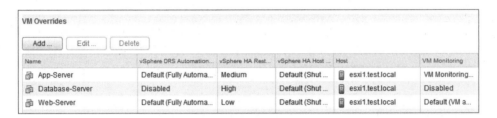

 Individual automation levels of virtual machines in a DRS cluster can be overridden by features such as vApps and/or FT.

Next we will cover how to configure migration thresholds for DRS and virtual machines.

Configuring Migration Thresholds for DRS and Virtual Machines

In the previous exercise, where we configured the cluster automation level, we accepted the default migration threshold. The migration threshold is used to specify which recommendations are applied, depending on the selected cluster automation level. For example, the manual and partially automated automation levels will result only in vMotion recommendations being generated. The migration threshold can be adjusted using the slider provided in the DRS automation-level settings.

Moving the migration threshold slider to the left will make DRS more conservative—that is, it will minimize the number of operations performed by DRS. Moving the slider to the right will make DRS more aggressive and result in more operations in the cluster. As it is with many options in vSphere, the key is to find the migration threshold setting that works best in your particular environment. Exercise 8.8 shows the steps for configuring the migration threshold for DRS.

EXERCISE 8.8

Configuring the Migration Threshold for DRS

1. Connect to a vCenter Server with the vSphere Web Client.

2. Locate a cluster in the inventory. Right-click it and choose Settings from the context menu.

3. On the Manage tab, ensure that vSphere DRS is selected in the left pane, and then click the Edit button in the upper-right corner of the middle pane.

4. In the Edit Cluster Settings window, expand the DRS Automation option in the left pane. Locate the Migration Threshold settings.

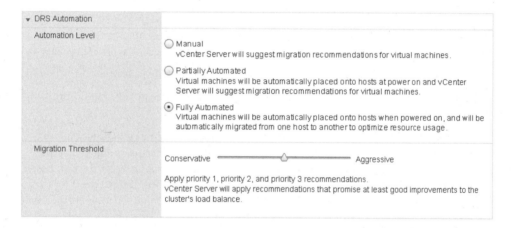

In Exercise 8.7, the automation level was set to Fully Automated and the default setting was accepted for the migration threshold.

5. Slide the Migration Threshold slider to the far left. Review the information displayed below the slider. This information will change each time the slider is moved to explain the effect of the current position.

6. Move the slider one position to the right and review the information displayed below it. Repeat these steps until the slider has reached the far-right side.

7. Click the Cancel button.

The migration threshold is applied to the cluster as a whole, and there is no option to change the migration threshold for an individual virtual machine. The closest setting that can be used to exclude virtual machines from the migration threshold setting is the individual virtual machine automation level, as shown in the previous exercise.

> Disabling the individual automation level of a virtual machine that vCenter Server is running on is often used to ensure that vCenter Server is always located, or "pinned," on a single ESXi host.

Next, let's discuss how to create VM-Host and VM-VM affinity rules.

Creating VM-Host and VM-VM Affinity Rules

Affinity rules are used in clusters to control the placement of virtual machines. Two types of relationships can be established with affinity rules:

Affinity   Used to keep VMs together and/or place VMs on predefined hosts

Anti-affinity   Used to keep VMs separated and/or prevent VMs from running on predefined hosts

For example, an affinity rule can be used to ensure that two virtual machines run on the same ESXi host. This is often used for performance reasons, because all of the traffic between virtual machines will be localized. An anti-affinity rule might be used when there are redundant virtual machines established as part of a fault-tolerant design. Keeping these VMs separated could provide protection from unplanned application downtime in the event of an ESXi host failure.

In addition to the two types of relationships established with affinity rules, there are two different types of affinity rules:

VM-Host   Used with a group of VMs and a group of hosts

VM-VM   Used between individual virtual machines

The key thing to remember with the two types of affinity rules is that the VM-Host rules apply to groups and will use DRS Groups. VM-VM rules apply to individual virtual machines and will use DRS Rules.

> Affinity rules in DRS are not the same thing as the CPU scheduling affinity that can be specified for a VM in the Virtual Machine Properties editor.

Now that you have seen what affinity rules are and the relationships that can be established with them, Exercise 8.9 will cover the steps required to create a VM-Host affinity rule for a group of VMs that we want to keep running on a single host. As mentioned previously, VM-Host affinity rules are used to group virtual machines and ESXi hosts.

Both the VM DRS Group (containing only VMs) and the Host DRS Group (containing only ESXi hosts) must be created before any rules can be created that link them, so our first steps will be to create those groups.

EXERCISE 8.9

Creating a VM-Host Affinity Rule

1. Connect to a vCenter Server with the vSphere Web Client.

2. Locate a cluster in the inventory. Right-click it and choose Settings from the context menu.

3. On the Manage tab, ensure that DRS Groups is selected in the left pane, and then click the Add button under DRS Groups.

4. A Create DRS Group window will open.

5. Give the VM DRS group a descriptive name in the Name field. Ensure that VM DRS Group is selected in the Type drop-down menu.

6. Click the Add button to select one or more virtual machines to add to the DRS Group. Click OK to return to the Create DRS Group window.

7. Once all of the applicable virtual machines have been added, the result should look similar to this:

8. Click OK and verify that the virtual machine DRS group is listed, once the Reconfigure Cluster task completes.

9. Click the Add button under DRS Groups again. A Create DRS Group window will open.

10. Give the Host DRS group a descriptive name in the Name field. Ensure that Host DRS Group is selected in the Type drop-down menu.

11. Click the Add button to select a single ESXi host to add to the Host DRS Group. Click OK to return to the Create DRS Group window.

12. Once a single ESXi host has been added, the result should look similar to this:

13. Click OK to save the Host DRS Group. A Reconfigure Cluster task will begin. When this task completes, verify that both a Virtual Machine DRS Group and a Host DRS Group are listed under DRS Groups in the middle pane.

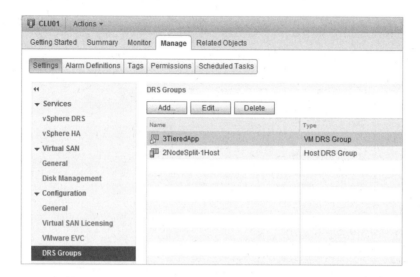

At this point, the DRS groups required to create a VM-Host affinity rule have been created. The remainder of the exercise will cover creating the affinity rule itself.

14. On the Manage tab, ensure that Settings is selected and that DRS Rules is selected in the left pane.

15. Click the Add button in the middle pane to create a new rule. A Create DRS Rule window will appear.

16. Provide the rule with a descriptive name, and ensure that the Enable Rule check box is selected.

17. Using the drop-down menu under the Type field, choose the Virtual Machines To Hosts option.

Note the three options available here, and these three components are what make up an affinity rule.

18. Using the drop-down menu located under VM Group, verify that the VM group created earlier in this exercise is selected.

19. In the unlabeled drop-down menu located between the VM Group and Host Group menus, choose the Must Run On Hosts In Group option.

20. Using the drop-down menu located under the Host Group field, verify that the Host group created earlier in this exercise is selected.

Since only a single Host Group as well as a single VM Group exist, the drop-down fields were already prepopulated as desired. If multiple groups had been created, the drop-down menus would contain them all.

EXERCISE 8.9 *(continued)*

21. Review the final configuration, which should appear similar to the following image:

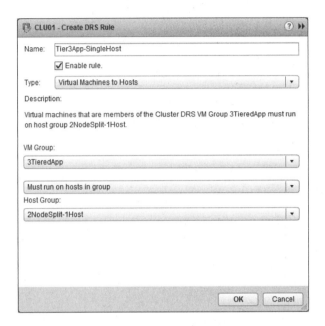

22. Click OK to add the rule. A Reconfigure Cluster task will begin, and when it completes the new rule will be listed under the DRS Rules.

23. Click the rule to view its details at the bottom of the screen.

Virtual machines that are removed from a cluster will lose their DRS group affiliations, and returning the virtual machine to the cluster will not restore them.

In step 19 of Exercise 8.9, four options are available when creating the VM-Host affinity rule. These options are as follows:

Must Run On Hosts In Group   VMs in the specified VM group are required to run on ESXi hosts in the specified host group.

Should Run On Hosts In Group   VMs in the specified VM group are preferred to run on ESXi hosts in the specified host group.

Must Not Run On Hosts In Group   VMs in the specified VM group are required to never run on ESXi hosts in the specified host group.

Should Not Run On Hosts In Group   VMs in the specified VM group are preferred to not run on ESXi hosts in the specified host group.

There are also a few caveats that need to be mentioned about VM-Host affinity rules:

- If multiple VM-Host affinity rules exist, they are applied equally.
- VM-Host affinity rules are not checked for compatibility with each other.
- DRS and HA will not violate affinity Must rules, so such rules could actually affect cluster functionality.

The best practice is to use VM-Host affinity rules sparingly and to consider using the preferential options in rules. This allows more flexibility.

Where VM-Host affinity rules are used to specify relationships between VM DRS groups and Host DRS groups, a VM-VM affinity rule applies only to individual virtual machines. Exercise 8.10 shows the steps for creating a VM-VM anti-affinity rule.

EXERCISE 8.10

Creating a VM-VM Anti-Affinity Rule

1. Connect to a vCenter Server with the vSphere Web Client.

2. Locate a cluster in the inventory. Right-click it and choose Settings from the context menu.

3. On the Manage tab, ensure that DRS Rules is selected in the left pane, and then click the Add button in the middle pane. A Create DRS Rule window will open.

4. Provide the rule with a descriptive name, and ensure that the Enable Rule check box is selected.

5. Using the drop-down menu under the Type field, choose the Separate Virtual Machines option.

6. Click the Add button to add the virtual machines to this rule. An Add Rule Member window will open.

EXERCISE 8.10 *(continued)*

7. Select two virtual machines that should not run on the same host. The final configuration should look like this:

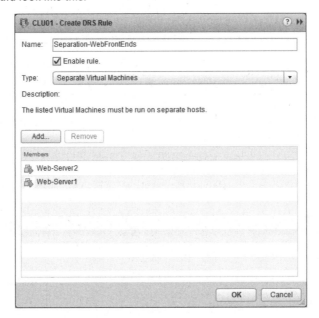

The example image assumes that two web servers are being used to provide application redundancy, and the VM-VM anti-affinity rule is used to keep them on different ESXi hosts.

8. Click OK to add the rule. A Reconfigure Cluster task will begin, and when it completes the new rule will be listed under the DRS Rules.

9. Click the rule to view its details at the bottom of the screen.

> You can disable a DRS Rule by editing the rule and deselecting the Enable Rule check box.

Just as with the VM-Host affinity rules, there is a caveat for VM-VM affinity rules. If VM-VM affinity rules conflict with each other, the newer of the conflicting rules will be disabled. For example, in Exercise 8.10, you created an anti-affinity rule. If an affinity rule were to be added with the same two virtual machines, the result would look similar to what is shown in Figure 8.6.

In Figure 8.6, a new rule was added with the name Conflicting Rule that attempted to keep the two web server virtual machines together; it conflicts with the existing

Separation–WebFrontEnds rule. That rule remains enabled, but the newer rule is not. Also note that DRS places higher priority on preventing violations of anti-affinity rules than it does on preventing violations of affinity rules. In the next section, you will see how to configure Enhanced vMotion Compatibility for a cluster.

FIGURE 8.6   Conflicting VM-VM affinity rules

Configuring Enhanced vMotion Compatibility

Enhanced vMotion Compatibility (EVC) can be used in a cluster to allow greater vMotion compatibility for the different ESXi hosts in the cluster. Configuring EVC for a cluster allows the ESXi host processors to present a baseline processor feature set known as the EVC mode. The EVC mode must be equivalent to, or a subset of, the features of the host in the cluster that contains the smallest feature set.

> Only processor features that affect vMotion will be masked by EVC. It has no effect on processor speeds or core counts.

Enabling EVC for a cluster is a simple operation, but it is important to know the following requirements for enabling EVC on a cluster:

- All hosts in the cluster must have only Intel or only AMD processors. Mixing Intel and AMD processors is not allowed.
- ESX/ESXi 3.5 update 2 or newer is required for all hosts in the cluster.
- All hosts in the cluster must be connected to the vCenter Server that is used to manage the cluster.
- vMotion networking must be configured identically for all hosts in the cluster.
- CPU features, like hardware virtualization support (AMD-V or Intel VT) and AMD No eXecute (NX) or Intel eXecute Disable (XD), should be enabled consistently across all hosts in the cluster.

Exercise 8.11 shows the steps to configure EVC on a cluster. In the interest of covering all lab environments, I will create a new cluster with no ESXi hosts for this exercise. This way, if you are using nested ESXi in your lab, you can complete the exercise. It will also allow me to show you how to enable EVC when the cluster is created.

EXERCISE 8.11

Enabling EVC for a Cluster

1. Connect to a vCenter Server with the vSphere Web Client.

2. Switch to the Hosts And Cluster view.

3. Select a datacenter object in the inventory and right-click it. Choose New Cluster from the context menu.

4. Give the cluster a descriptive and unique name. Do not enable DRS, vSphere HA, or Virtual SAN for the cluster.

5. From the EVC drop-down menu, select the Intel "Merom" Generation.

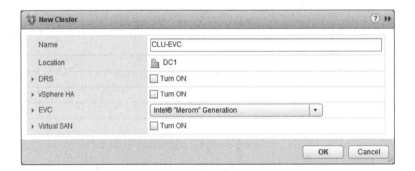

6. Click OK to create this cluster. A Create Cluster and a Configure Cluster EVC task will each begin. Wait for these tasks to complete.

   At this point, a cluster has been created with EVC enabled. The remainder of this exercise will focus on the steps required to change the EVC mode.

7. Locate the cluster you just created in the inventory. Right-click it and choose Settings from the context menu.

8. On the Manage tab, ensure that Settings is selected and that VMware EVC is selected in the left pane.

9. Review the current VMware EVC information in the middle pane.

10. Click the Edit button in the upper-right corner. A Change EVC Mode window will open.

11. From the VMware EVC mode drop-down menu, select Intel Ivy Bridge Generation. The Compatibility window should report Validation Succeeded, since there are no ESXi hosts in this cluster.

12. Click OK in the Change EVC Mode window and then verify that the Mode field reports Intel Ivy Bridge Generation in the VMware EVC section in the middle pane.

In Exercise 8.11, there were no ESXi hosts in the cluster. This allowed flexibility in creating and changing the EVC mode. In the real world, where clusters will have hosts, it is important to understand how EVC mode impacts these hosts.

Lowering the EVC mode for a cluster involves moving from a greater feature set to a lower feature set. This is often useful when introducing ESXi hosts on newer hardware into an existing cluster. It is important to remember that any virtual machines running on ESXi hosts with newer features than the EVC mode supports will need to be powered off before lowering the EVC mode.

Raising the EVC mode for a cluster involves moving from a lesser feature set to a greater feature set. This is often useful when hardware refreshes of ESXi hosts have raised the CPU baseline capability. It is important to remember that any running virtual machines may continue to run during this operation. The VMs simply will not have access to the newer CPU features of the EVC mode until they have been powered off. Also note that a reboot will not suffice, and a full power cycle of the virtual machine is required.

The following two VMware KB articles are helpful for determining both EVC compatibility and processor support:

```
http://kb.vmware.com/kb/1005764
http://kb.vmware.com/kb/1003212
```

Available EVC Modes for supported processors models are listed in VMware's Hardware Compatibility Guide:

```
http://www.vmware.com/go/hcl
```

Next we will shift our attention to monitoring our DRS/HA clusters.

Monitoring a DRS/HA Cluster

There are many options for monitoring a DRS cluster, and having the vSphere Web Client open is a great start. If there are significant problems, the cluster item in the inventory will display an alert or warning icon. An error condition is shown for a cluster in Figure 8.7.

FIGURE 8.7 Cluster with error condition

In Figure 8.7 an ESXi host in the cluster was abruptly powered off to simulate a host failure. The cluster went into an error status, and the ESXi host is listed with an alert status. This real-time information can be quite valuable.

A great deal of additional real-time information about a cluster can be obtained by simply viewing its Summary tab in the vSphere Web Client. Much more information for the error that was shown in Figure 8.7 can be obtained in the cluster's Summary tab too. This is shown in Figure 8.8.

Selecting a cluster from the inventory and viewing its Monitor tab allows you to quickly obtain a vast amount of information about the cluster. There is specific information available for Issues, Performance, Profile Compliance, Tasks, Events, Resource Allocation, vSphere DRS, vSphere HA, Utilization, and Storage Reports. Figure 8.9 shows the Utilization information for the cluster.

vSphere HA information is available on the Manage tab. It has summary information for both hosts and virtual machines, including which ESXi host is the master node and the number of hosts connected to the master node. The virtual machine information provides the number of VMs protected and unprotected by vSphere HA. There is also a Heartbeat option that can be used to view information on the datastores used for heartbeating. The final option here is Configuration Issues, where any problems with the cluster will be listed.

FIGURE 8.8   Cluster warning information

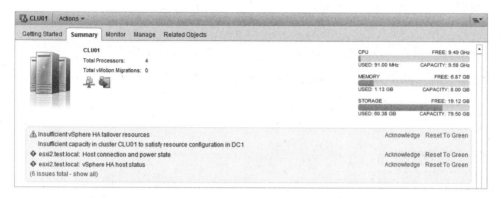

FIGURE 8.9   Cluster Utilization information

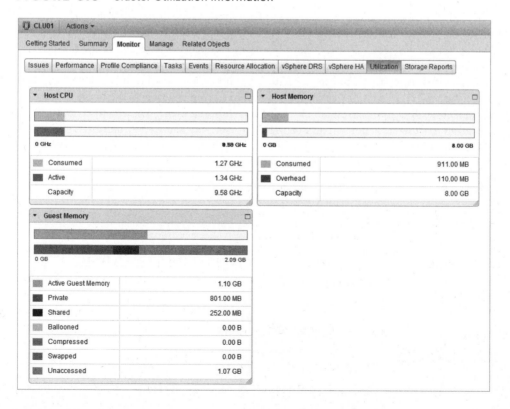

vSphere DRS information is also available on the Manage tab. It contains summary information for DRS recommendations, faults, history, CPU utilization, and memory utilization. The CPU and memory utilization tools are useful for monitoring your cluster's resource consumption. Figure 8.10 shows the CPU utilization for the cluster.

FIGURE 8.10 Cluster CPU utilization

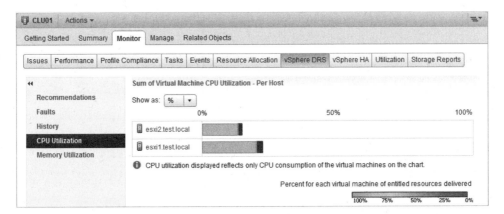

The CPU utilization will show each ESXi host in the cluster in the left column, and each of the colored boxes represents either a single virtual machine or a group of what are essentially idle virtual machines. Green boxes are good to see here! The legend at the bottom of the window shows that green means 100 percent of the entitled resources are being delivered for the VM. Any other color means the VM is not receiving all of its entitled resources. By hovering the cursor over any of these colored boxes, you can obtain the name of the virtual machine and information about its current resource usage. You can also adjust the information to show CPU percentages or MHz by using the Show As drop-down menu.

The Memory Utilization option is also useful for monitoring your cluster. Figure 8.11 shows the memory utilization.

FIGURE 8.11 Cluster memory utilization

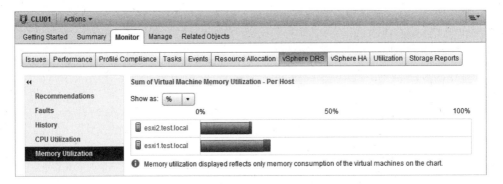

Each ESXi host in the cluster will be listed in the left column, and each of the colored boxes represents a single virtual machine. Just as with the CPU resources, hovering the cursor over any of these gray boxes will allow you to obtain the name of the virtual machine and information about its current resource usage. You can also adjust the information to show memory percentages or MB by using the Show As drop-down menu.

As you can see, the information presented in the cluster's Summary Monitor tab provides a quick and easy way to see whether your hosts are load-balanced and can often reveal which VMs are using the most resources. The information presented here also allows you to view more closely how DRS load-balances.

Alarms can also be configured in vCenter Server to help monitor your cluster. Figure 8.12 shows a filtered view of some of the vSphere HA alarm definitions.

FIGURE 8.12 vCenter alarms for vSphere HA

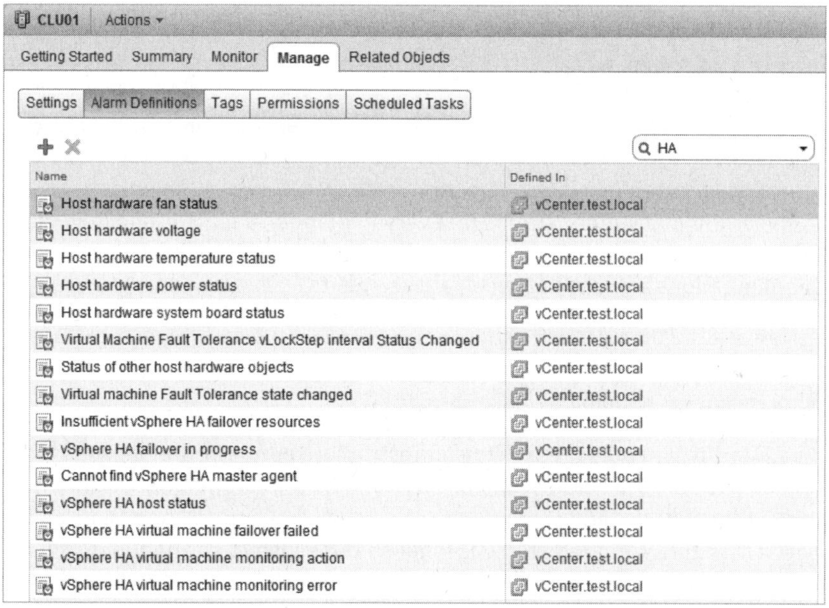

vCenter Server alarms will be covered in detail in Chapter 11, "Monitoring a vSphere Implementation and Managing vCenter Server Alarms," and many of the monitoring topics will also be revisited in Chapter 10, "Performing Basic Troubleshooting," where troubleshooting HA/DRS clusters will be covered.

In addition to the included functionality in vCenter Server, there are additional options like VMware vCenter Operations or any number of third-party solutions that can be used to monitor your clusters. These products can provide additional insight into your virtual infrastructure and are often already deployed in many environments. Operational staff members are also typically trained in using these solutions. Leveraging these existing monitoring solutions can add additional monitoring capabilities for your DRS/HA clusters.

Next, we will cover how to configure Storage DRS.

Configuring Storage DRS

Storage DRS, first introduced in vSphere 5, offers to datastores what a DRS-enabled cluster offers to ESXi hosts. When a virtual machine is deployed, it can be deployed into a cluster, and DRS will take care of the initial placement of the VM on an ESXi host. DRS can also move the virtual machine to a different host, as necessary, in order to provide the VM its entitled resources. Storage DRS provides both virtual machine placement and load balancing based on I/O and/or capacity. The goal of Storage DRS is to lessen the administrative effort involved with managing datastores by representing a pool of storage as a single resource.

 Real World Scenario

Goodbye to Spreadsheets

A virtual infrastructure administrator has multiple datastores in her infrastructure. Her environment has datastores located on a SAN, but these datastores are not consistent in their configuration. There is one disk group with fifteen SATA drives, one disk group with six 15K FC drives, and many other groups that vary in number, capacity, and drive speed. Until now, the virtual infrastructure administrator has kept spreadsheets to keep up with these disk configurations and virtual machine placements.

She also spends a lot of time dealing with complaints of slowness, identifying the latencies, and manually correcting them with Storage vMotion. Of course, after this, she has to update the spreadsheets to help her make sense of it all.

To reduce the effort this requires, the virtual infrastructure administrator decides that she will implement datastore clusters and use Storage DRS. Storage DRS will monitor her environment for capacity and I/O performance issues and correct them automatically. The virtual infrastructure administrator was relieved to be able to say goodbye to both her manual processes and the spreadsheets.

Storage DRS is made possible by the datastore cluster object, which is simply a collection of datastores with shared resources and management. There are several requirements for using datastore clusters:

- Only ESXi 5 or later hosts can be attached to any of the datastores in a datastore cluster.
- Mixing NFS and VMFS datastores in the same datastore cluster is not allowed.
- A datastore cluster cannot contain datastores shared across multiple datacenters.
- VMware recommends as a best practice that datastores with hardware acceleration enabled not be used with datastores that do not have hardware acceleration enabled.

Configuring Storage DRS starts with creating a datastore cluster. Exercise 8.12 covers the steps to create a datastore cluster and configure Storage DRS.

EXERCISE 8.12

Configuring Storage DRS

1. Connect to a vCenter Server with the vSphere Web Client.

2. Select Datastore Clusters from the left pane.

3. In the Object tab in the middle pane, click the Create A New Datastore Cluster icon. The New Datastore Cluster wizard will launch.

4. Provide a unique and descriptive name in the Datastore Cluster Name field. Ensure that the Turn On Storage DRS option is selected.

5. Select a datacenter for the placement of the Storage DRS Cluster, and then click Next to continue.

6. Choose the default Automation Level option of No Automation (Manual Mode).

   The Storage DRS automation level is similar to the automation level setting in DRS. The obvious difference is that only two settings are available with Storage DRS. Manual is used when no automation is desired, and virtual machine placement and load balancing migration recommendations will be suggested only by vCenter Server.

7. Click Next to continue.

   The following image can be used as a reference for steps 8 to 14 of this exercise.

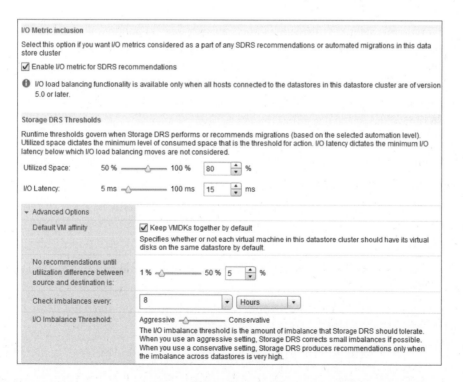

8. In Storage DRS Runtime Settings, ensure that the Enable I/O Metric For SDRS Recommendations option is selected.

   Enabling this option will allow vCenter Server to consider I/O metrics when making Storage DRS recommendations or automated migrations. In other words, this option enables I/O load balancing for the datastore cluster.

9. Review and leave the default values selected for Storage DRS Thresholds.

   The Storage DRS thresholds are similar to the migration threshold setting used in DRS. A percentage of space utilization and a millisecond value of I/O latency can each be configured to trigger Storage DRS to make a recommendation or take an automated action.

10. Expand the Advanced Options option.

11. In the Default VM Affinity section, leave the Keep VMDKs Together By Default option checked.

    This option will ensure that all virtual disks of a VM with multiple virtual disks are stored in the same datastore.

12. Leave the slider at the default value of 5% for the No Recommendations Until Utilization Difference Between Source And Destination Is option.

    This option is configured to ensure that a capacity-based recommendation is worthwhile. In other words, if the source datastore is 90 percent full and the target is 94 percent full, then don't make the move. The difference in these two percentages is the value 4. The default value of 5 percent would not allow this move to occur.

13. Use the drop-down menu to change the Check Imbalances Every value to a different value.

    This setting is used to determine the frequency that Storage DRS will check capacity and load.

14. Leave the I/O Imbalance Threshold slider at its default value.

    This setting is also similar to the migration threshold used in DRS. It is used to configure the amount of I/O imbalance that Storage DRS should tolerate.

15. Click Next to continue.

16. On the Select Hosts And Clusters screen, select a cluster to add the datastore cluster to. Click Next.

17. Select datastores to add to the datastore cluster, keeping in mind the requirements listed before the exercise.

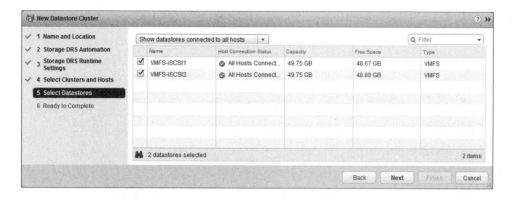

18. Click Next to continue.

19. Review the information on the Ready To Complete screen and click Finish to create the datastore cluster.

20. A Create A Datastore Cluster task will begin. Also, a Move Datastores Into A Datastore Cluster task will begin, and a Configure Storage DRS task will begin. When these tasks complete, verify that the datastore cluster is listed in the left pane.

21. Select the datastore cluster in the left pane and then select the Summary tab in the right pane.

22. The datastore cluster is now created, and existing virtual machines can be migrated to it with Storage vMotion.

You have now created a datastore cluster and enabled Storage DRS on it. In the next section, I will explain the power management features available in vSphere environments.

Enabling BIOS P/C States

You may recall from Chapter 2, where selecting a CPU power management policy for your ESXi hosts was covered, that ESXi 5.5 has four power policies available, based on the ESXi host's processor P states and C states. P states are performance states and can be utilized to save power in the ESXi host when full CPU capacity is not required. C states are power states and can be utilized to save power when the ESXi host processors have significant idle time.

You enable either the P states or C states in each ESXi host system's BIOS settings. Consult your server vendor's documentation for the specifics on configuring P states and C states. Figure 8.13 shows these settings in a Dell server's BIOS.

Configuring Host Power Management was also covered in Chapter 2, and you may remember that HPM can be leveraged to save power on a per-host basis in real time. There is another power-saving feature known as Distributed Power Management (DPM) that is also available to save even more power for hosts in DRS-enabled clusters.

FIGURE 8.13 Dell server power settings in BIOS

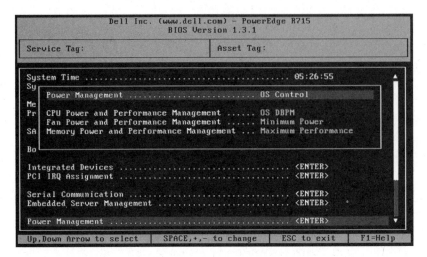

Enabling, Configuring, and Disabling Host Power Management and Distributed Power Management

Host Power Management and Distributed Power Management can be used together, to maximize the power savings in a vSphere environment. Where HPM enables real-time per-host savings, the goal of DPM is to decrease the number of powered-on ESXi hosts in the cluster. DPM works with DRS to monitor resource utilization in the cluster. If there is enough excess CPU and RAM capacity available in the cluster, DRS will vMotion virtual machines off of an ESXi host and the host will be powered off. Any ESXi host that is powered off by DPM is considered to be in Standby mode. If the resource demand later increases, then DRS will power back on the ESXi host in standby mode and virtual machines will be migrated to the host via vMotion.

DPM utilizes one of three power management protocols to communicate with the ESXi host and bring it out of standby mode:

- Intelligent Platform Management Interface (IPMI)

- Hewlett-Packard Integrated Lights-Out (iLO)

- Wake-On-LAN (WOL)

One of these protocols is required to leverage DPM, and each of these protocols requires its own hardware and configuration. Configuration is often performed in the ESXi host's system BIOS. Consult your server vendor's documentation for the specifics on configuring any of these protocols.

If an ESXi host supports multiple protocols, they will be used in the following order: IPMI, iLO, WOL.

In addition to one of these three power management protocols, the following require-ments also exist to implement DPM.

- Enterprise or Enterprise Plus licensing is required.
- A DRS-enabled cluster with at least two ESXi hosts is required.
- A vMotion interface must exist for the hosts in the DRS cluster.
- If Wake On LAN is used, the VMotion NIC must support it and Wake On LAN requires both the physical switch port and ESXi NIC to be set to autonegotiate.

 Additional consideration of how you report ESXi hosts powered down by DPM may be necessary, if you use monitoring tools in your environment.

Exercise 8.13 will cover the steps required to set up DPM in your environment. This lab will require a DRS-enabled cluster with two ESXi hosts that meet the system requirements listed above. The lab will also assume your lab has a supported power management proto-col and has been configured accordingly. If your lab does not meet these requirements, you may want to just follow along.

EXERCISE 8.13

Configuring Distributed Power Management

1. Open the vSphere Web Client and select an ESXi host from the inventory.

2. Click the Manage tab, and then select Settings from the toolbar.

3. Select Power Management from the System menu.

4. Click the Edit button.

5. Enter the IPMI or iLO username, password, IP address and MAC address. The final configuration should appear similar to the following:

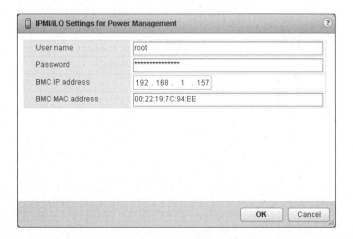

EXERCISE 8.13 *(continued)*

Note that the IP address is for the IPMI or iLO interface, and not the management address of the ESXi host. Also note that the MAC address must be entered in the following format: 01:23:45:67:89:AB.

6. Click OK to save these changes, and repeat for each ESXi host in the DRS-enabled cluster.

   Now that the ESXi hosts have been configured, the next step is to test them for their ability to enter and exit standby.

7. Right-click an ESXi host and choose All vCenter Actions ➢ Enter Standby Mode. A Confirm Standby Mode window will open. Place a check in the option to move virtual machines, if applicable, and click Yes.

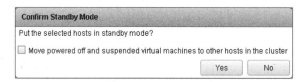

8. An Enter Standby Mode task will begin. Wait patiently for this task to complete. Once the host successfully enters standby mode its icon will update in the left pane to show a blue box with a white moon on it. The text "(standby)" will also be listed after the ESXi host name.

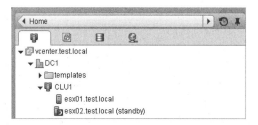

9. Right-click the ESXi host in Standby Mode and choose Power On from the context menu. An Exit Standby Mode task will begin. Wait patiently for this task to complete.

10. Repeat the Standby Mode testing for each ESXi host in the cluster.

11. Right-click the DRS-enabled cluster that contains the ESXi hosts you just tested and select Settings from the context menu.

12. Select Host Options in the left pane under Configuration and review the information in the Power Management and Last Time Exited Standby columns.

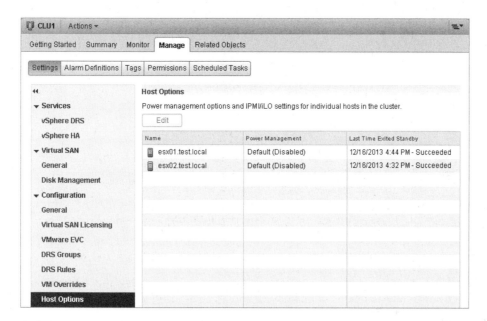

If all of the ESXi hosts in the cluster show a valid entry for the Last Time Exited Standby, then testing is complete. You are now ready to turn on DPM.

13. Right-click the DRS-enabled cluster that contains the ESXi hosts you just configured and select Settings from the context menu.

14. Select vSphere DRS in the left pane under Services, and then click the Edit button.

15. Ensure vSphere DRS is turned on and set the DRS Automation to Fully Automated.

16. Use the drop down menu to select Automatic for the Power Management option, and then expand the Power Management menu.

17. Configure the DPM Threshold to the far right, which is its most aggressive setting. Review the information below the slider to obtain more information about this setting.

EXERCISE 8.13 *(continued)*

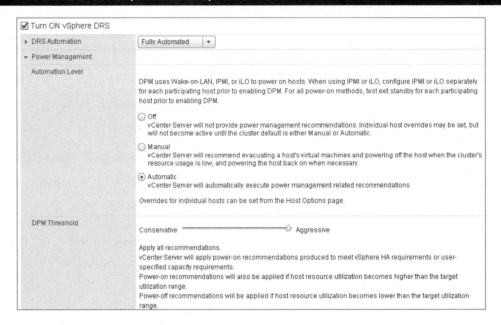

18. Click OK to implement DPM. A Reconfigure Cluster task will begin.

19. Select Host Options in the left pane under Configuration and review the information in the Power Management column now. It should have changed from Default (Disabled) to Default (Automatic).

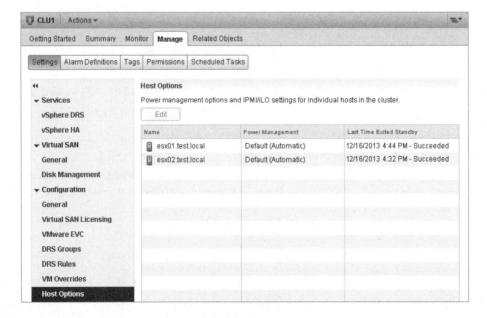

20. Select an ESXi host and click the Edit button. An Edit Host Options window will open. You can use the drop-down menu to return the Power option to Disabled. This could be a useful setting to implement for hosts that should not participate in DPM actions.

If you wait long enough and/or skew the workloads properly, you should see DPM start to work and place an ESXi host in standby mode. You can also force DPM to power back on the host by powering up new workloads or generating heavy CPU and memory requests.

In the previous lab, you set up DPM and set the DPM Threshold setting to Aggressive. While the Aggressive DPM Threshold setting is great for a lab environment, it will not always be suitable for every environment.

Determining Appropriate Power Threshold for a Given Implementation

DPM makes recommendations that range from priority-one to priority-five. These priority ratings are generated from the utilization data obtained from the DRS-enabled cluster. A priority-one recommendation is a mandatory one, where a priority-five recommendation might offer only a slight improvement. The DPM Threshold is configured by moving a slider from left to right. The far left setting of Conservative would apply only priority-one or mandatory recommendations, and each move of the slider to the right would allow additional priority ratings to be included. The far right setting of Aggressive would apply to all recommendations (priority-one through priority-five), which is why it was recommended in the previous lab.

When determining the appropriate power threshold for a given vSphere implementation, possibly the most important thing to consider is how aggressive DPM will be used. You don't want to place the environment is a constant state of power transition, and you definitely do not want to impact users. When implementing DPM in a production environment, you would likely want to start with the DPM threshold set to its most conservative setting and then monitor the cluster for a given period of time. Based on the initial results, you may then consider moving the DPM threshold slider another space to the right. This process could be repeated, until the desired or acceptable outcome is reached.

🌐 **Real World Scenario**

Going Green With DPM

A virtual infrastructure administrator has multiple ESXi hosts in his DRS-enabled cluster, and a large number of virtual machines that are used for development purposes. These virtual machines are very resource intensive and are used only during normal working hours of 8AM-6PM on weekdays. In fact, after 6PM the entire shop is typically shut down and evening work is not very common for most of the staff.

During routine troubleshooting of one of his ESXi hosts, the virtual infrastructure administrator noticed that in the daytime his ESXi hosts are consistently using 70% or more of their CPU and RAM resources. He also noticed that in the evenings the ESXi host resource utilization is consistently 10% or less. He compared this to the other ESXi hosts in the cluster and noticed the same thing. He was not surprised at these findings, but didn't think much more about them at the time.

A week later at a staff meeting, it was announced that the company was starting a green initiative. Employees were asked to come up with ways to reduce the company's energy requirements, and were told that prizes would be given for the top three initiatives. The virtual infrastructure administrator quickly thought back to the underutilized ESXi hosts.

Then he remembered reading about Distributed Power Management on `http://blogs .vmware.com`. He quickly did some additional research and discovered that his ESXi hosts met the system requirements, he had the correct licensing, and that he could implement DPM on his production cluster. He ultimately turned on DPM and helped significantly reduce the company's energy footprint, while the users were unaware of the implementation of DPM. In the end, he won a trip to VMworld for his efforts.

This concludes our discussion of creating and configuring VMware clusters.

Planning and Implementing VMware Fault Tolerance

As a VMware Certified Professional, you will be expected to know when and how to use VMware Fault Tolerance (FT). FT is used to provide higher levels of virtual machine availability than what is possible with vSphere HA. VMware FT uses VMware *vLockstep* technology to provide a replica virtual machine running on a different ESXi host. In the event of an ESXi host failure, the replica virtual machine will become active with the entire state of the virtual machine preserved. This section presents the use cases and requirements for VMware FT, and you'll learn how to configure it.

Determining Use Cases for Enabling VMware Fault Tolerance on a Virtual Machine

VMware FT can provide very high availability for virtual machines, and it is important to understand which applications are candidates for using VMware FT. There are several use cases for VMware FT:

- Applications that require high availability, particularly applications that have long-lasting client connections that would be reset by a virtual machine restart.

- Applications that have no native capability for clustering.

- Applications that could be clustered, but clustering solutions should be avoided because of their administrative and operational complexities.

- Applications that require protection for critical processes to complete. This is known as *on-demand fault tolerance*.

 Real World Scenario

On-Demand Fault Tolerance

A manufacturing company has an application that was developed in-house and is used four times a year. This application is used to provide specific quarter-end reports to the finance department. There is one report in particular that is notorious for taking many hours to complete. Recently the physical server housing this application had a motherboard failure while the report was running. As a result of this failure and the time required to repair it, the report was significantly delayed. Finance was able to complete their work on time, but many of the staff had to work through the night to make it happen.

A meeting was called between various members of IT and the business to discuss a solution for this problem. Specifically, the finance department did not want a hardware failure to delay them like this again. The virtual infrastructure administrator was present and suggested that the server be converted to a virtual machine and protected with VMware FT on an on-demand basis. This would allow the virtual machine to run as a normal virtual machine and gain the benefit of being protected with HA for normal day-to-day operations. During the four times a year that the key reports are run, the virtual infrastructure administrator enables FT for this virtual machine. The virtual machine is now protected from a physical server failure and consumes the extra resources required to provide this protection only four times a year.

It is important to remember that VMware FT will not protect virtual machines from guest OS and/or application failures. If either the guest operating system or the applications running in the guest OS fail, then the secondary VM will fail identically. It is also important to note that VMware FT has resource consumption implications. If the primary VM uses 2GB of RAM, the secondary VM will also use 2GB of RAM. There is also a significant set of requirements for using FT, which we will now discuss.

VMware Fault Tolerance Requirements

The number of requirements to use VMware FT is rather large, and for the VCP5-DCV exam it would be unreasonable to expect you to know all of them. For this section, only the requirements specifically listed in the vSphere Availability Guide have been included. There are many requirements for using VMware FT at the cluster, host, and virtual machine levels. For the cluster, these requirements include the following:

- Host certificate checking must be enabled in the vCenter Server settings.
- A minimum of two FT-certified ESXi hosts with the same FT version or host build number must be used.
- The ESXi hosts in the cluster must have access to the same datastores and networks.
- The ESXi hosts must have both Fault Tolerance logging and vMotion networking configured.
- vSphere HA must be enabled on the cluster.

In addition to the cluster requirements, the ESXi hosts have their own set of requirements:

- The ESXi hosts must have processors from an FT-compatible processor group.
- Enterprise or Enterprise Plus licensing must be in place.
- ESXi hosts must be certified for FT in the VMware HCL.
- ESXi hosts must have hardware virtualization (HV) enabled in the BIOS.

 For information on processors and guest operating systems that are supported with VMware FT, refer to the following VMware KB article: http://kb.vmware.com/kb/1008027

There are also requirements for the virtual machines that will be used with VMware FT:

- Eager zeroed thick-provisioned virtual disks and RDMs in virtual compatibility mode must be used in the virtual machine.
- Virtual machines must be on shared storage.
- The guest OS installed on the virtual machine must be on the list of supported operating systems that can be used with VMware FT.

You should also note that only virtual machines with a single vCPU are compatible with Fault Tolerance. *vSMP* is not supported. Unsupported devices, such as USB devices, parallel ports, or serial ports, cannot be attached to the virtual machine; also, incompatible features such as snapshots, Storage vMotion, and *linked clones* must not be used on virtual machines that will be protected with VMware FT.

The VMware FT requirements listed previously are not all-inclusive, and the requirements and limitations could easily consume an entire chapter. For a comprehensive and constantly updated list of the requirements and limitations of VMware FT, check my blog at http://communities.vmware.com/blogs/vmroyale/2009/05/18/vmware-fault-tolerance-requirements-and-limitations.

Now that you have seen the requirements to use VMware FT, let's move on to configuring networking for the fault tolerance logging traffic.

Configuring VMware Fault Tolerance Networking

To use VMware FT, you must meet two networking requirements. The first of these requirements is a vMotion network that will be used by ESXi hosts in the cluster. vMotion is required because the secondary VM is initially created by a vMotion of the primary VM to a different ESXi host in the cluster. Because of this design, I also recommend that you have separate 1GbE NICs for vMotion and fault tolerance logging traffic.

The fault tolerance logging traffic is the second network requirement for VMware FT. This is also a VMkernel connection type that is used to move all nondeterministic events from the primary VM to the secondary VM. Nondeterministic events include network and user input, asynchronous disk I/O, and CPU timer events. This is the connection that is used to keep the primary and secondary virtual machines in lockstep.

You created a vSwitch for vMotion use in Chapter 4 in Exercise 4.4, so you already have half of the required networking in place. In Exercise 8.14, you will create a vSwitch to be used for fault tolerance logging networking. This exercise will require one available NIC in each ESXi host in the cluster.

EXERCISE 8.14

Configuring VMware FT Logging Traffic

1. Connect to a vCenter Server with the vSphere Web Client.

2. Choose an ESXi host from the inventory.

3. Click the Manage tab and then select Networking from the toolbar on the Manage tab.

4. Click the Add Host Networking icon, which is the globe icon with the plus sign, to add ESXi host networking. The Add Networking wizard will launch.

5. Select the VMkernel Network Adapter connection type and click Next to continue.

6. Choose the New Standard Switch option and click Next.

7. On the next screen, click the plus icon to add a physical network adapter. An Add Physical Adapters To The Switch screen will appear.

EXERCISE 8.14 *(continued)*

8. In this screen, select an unused network adapter from the list in the left pane.

9. Click OK to add the physical network adapter to the vSwitch. Verify that a (New) vmnicX entry is listed in the left pane under Active Adapters.

10. Click Next to continue.

11. Provide a network label of FT. Choose a VLAN ID for this network if applicable. Choose the appropriate TCP/IP Stack for your network, and select the Fault Tolerance Logging check box.

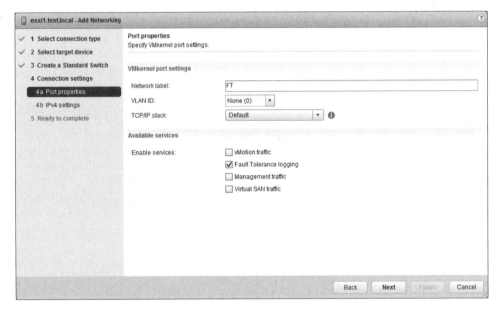

12. Click Next to continue. Provide an appropriate static IP address and subnet mask, and then click Next.

13. Review the information on the Ready To Complete screen and click the Finish button to add the new vSwitch to the ESXi host.

14. Select the vSwitch and review the information shown for accuracy.

15. Repeat steps 2–14 for each ESXi host in the cluster.

WARNING   Fault tolerance logging traffic is unencrypted and contains guest network data, guest storage I/O data, and the guest's memory contents. Because of this, fault tolerance logging traffic should always be isolated.

Now that we have the FT prerequisites covered, let's enable and disable VMware FT on a virtual machine.

Enabling and Disabling VMware Fault Tolerance on a Virtual Machine

Once all of the VMware FT prerequisites are met, the actual process of enabling FT for a virtual machine is incredibly simple. Exercise 8.15 covers the steps to enable FT for a virtual machine.

EXERCISE 8.15

Enabling FT for a Powered-Off Virtual Machine

1. Connect to a vCenter Server with the vSphere Web Client.

2. Locate a powered-off virtual machine that belongs to a cluster with ESXi hosts that have been configured for FT.

3. Right-click the virtual machine and choose the All vCenter Actions ➤ Fault Tolerance ➤ Turn On Fault Tolerance option from the context menu.

   Depending on the disk configuration of the virtual machine, you will next be presented with one of two windows. Each of these windows contains the same information about what fault tolerance does and its effect on DRS, but one of them includes additional information about the virtual machine's disks. This additional information will be displayed if the virtual disks are not in the thick-provisioned eager zeroed format. The window with the additional disk information is shown here:

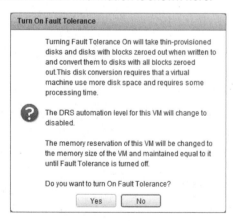

4. Review the information presented in the Turn On Fault Tolerance window and click Yes to continue.

    If the virtual disks are not in the thick-provisioned eager zeroed format, they will need to be converted to the proper format before FT can be enabled. This disk conversion operation cannot be performed if the virtual machine is powered on. If the virtual disks in the virtual machine were already in the thick-provisioned eager zeroed format, then the disk information would not have been displayed in the Turn On Fault Tolerance dialog.

5. A Turn On Fault Tolerance task will begin. When this task completes, take note of the icon for the FT-protected VM in the left pane. It has now changed to a darker shade of blue.

6. Power on the FT-protected virtual machine.

7. Select the Summary tab for the FT-protected virtual machine. Locate the Related Objects pane, and take note of the host listed here. This is the ESXi host that the FT primary VM is currently running on.

8. Locate the Fault Tolerance pane and verify the information shown there. This information should look similar to the following:

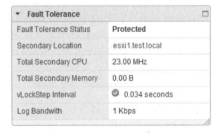

▼ Fault Tolerance	□
Fault Tolerance Status	Protected
Secondary Location	esxi1.test.local
Total Secondary CPU	23.00 MHz
Total Secondary Memory	0.00 B
vLockStep Interval	⊘ 0.034 seconds
Log Bandwith	1 Kbps

9. Review the entries in the Fault Tolerance panel, and notice that the Secondary VM location is a field in this pane.

Now that the steps to protect a VM with FT have been covered, I will cover the steps to disable FT for a VM that has been protected with it. Virtual machines protected with FT can have FT either disabled or turned off. Turning off FT for a VM will delete the secondary VM and all historical performance data. The virtual machine's DRS automation level will also be set at the cluster default settings. This option is used when FT will no longer be used for a virtual machine. Examples of this would be when a virtual machine has had its SLA modified or is due for scheduled maintenance and a snapshot is desired as part of the process.

Disabling FT for a VM will preserve the secondary VM, the configuration, and all historical performance data. You would disable FT if you might use VMware FT again in the future for this virtual machine. An example of this would be when using on-demand fault tolerance for a virtual machine. Exercise 8.16 covers the steps to disable FT for a virtual machine that is currently protected with it.

EXERCISE 8.16

Disabling FT for a Virtual Machine

1. Connect to a vCenter Server with the vSphere Web Client.

2. Locate a VM that is currently protected with FT.

3. Right-click the virtual machine and from the context menu choose All vCenter Actions ➤ Fault Tolerance ➤ Disable Fault Tolerance. A Disable Fault Tolerance dialog box will appear. Review the information presented here, and click Yes to continue.

4. A Disable Fault Tolerance task will begin. When this task completes, verify the fault tolerance status in the Fault Tolerance pane of the virtual machine's Summary tab.

6. Also notice that a Warning icon has been placed over the virtual machine in the left pane. Select the virtual machine in the left pane.

7. Select the Summary tab for the virtual machine.

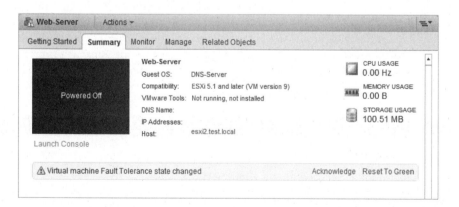

8. Use the Acknowledge Alarm and/or Reset to Green links to clear this warning.

EXERCISE 8.16 *(continued)*

9. In the left pane, note that the warning icon has now been removed from the virtual machine but that the VM icon still maintains the darker blue color.

   At this point, the VM is no longer protected by FT. If there was a time where FT protection was again required, the following steps could be used to enable FT on the virtual machine.

10. Right-click this same virtual machine and from the context menu choose All vCenter Actions ➤ Fault Tolerance ➤ Enable Fault Tolerance.

11. An Enable Fault Tolerance task will begin. When this task completes, verify the Fault Tolerance Status setting in the Fault Tolerance pane of the virtual machine's Summary tab.

Now that I have covered enabling and disabling VMware FT, let's take a moment to cover the steps required to test an FT configuration.

Testing an FT Configuration

Now that FT has been configured and a virtual machine is being protected by it, the only remaining item is verifying that FT works as expected. The only way to know whether FT will work as expected is to test failover using the built-in functions in vCenter Server or to manually fail a host.

Testing via manually failing a host is easily accomplished. If your ESXi hosts are physical servers, then you could simply pull the power cable on the host that the FT primary VM is running on. If your ESXi hosts are virtual machines, simply power off the ESXi host that the FT primary VM is running on. Either one of these approaches will guarantee an ESXi host failure. If you have many running virtual machines or simply aren't comfortable powering off your ESXi host in this way, you can also use the FT Test Failover functionality from the Fault Tolerance menu in the vSphere Client. This testing approach is preferred, since it is both fully supported and noninvasive. Exercise 8.17 shows the steps to test your FT configuration.

EXERCISE 8.17

Testing Failover of FT

1. Connect to a vCenter Server with the vSphere Web Client.

2. Locate a powered-on virtual machine that is protected by FT.

3. Select the Summary tab for the virtual machine and review the information in the Fault Tolerance pane. Take note of the fault tolerance status and the Secondary Location values.

4. Right-click the virtual machine and from the context menu choose All vCenter Actions ➤ Fault Tolerance ➤ Test Failover.

5. A Test Failover task will begin. The Fault Tolerance pane will display results like the following:

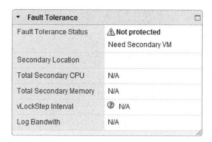

6. When the secondary VM has again been restarted, review the Fault Tolerance pane. Verify that the VM has changed ESXi hosts, and the Fault Tolerance Status is again protected.

With testing FT complete, we are ready to move on to creating and administering resource pools.

Creating and Administering Resource Pools

As a VMware Certified Professional, you should be very familiar with resource pools. Resource pools are used to partition the CPU and memory resources of ESXi hosts. They offer a convenient way to separate resources along requirements or political boundaries and also offer a way to control the resource usage of multiple virtual machines at once. This approach provides significant advantages over setting individual virtual machine limits, reservations, and shares. In this section, I will cover how resource pools work and how to configure and use them.

The Resource Pool Hierarchy

Each ESXi host or DRS-enabled cluster has a hidden root resource pool. This root resource pool is the basis for any hierarchy of shared resources that exist on standalone hosts or in DRS-enabled clusters. The root resource pool is hidden, since the resources of the ESXi host or cluster are consistent. Resource pools can contain child resource pools, vApps, virtual machines, or a combination of these objects. This allows the creation of a hierarchy of shared resources. Objects created at the same level are called *siblings*. In Figure 8.14, RP-Finance and RP-Legal are siblings. Fin-VM1 and Fin-VM2 are also siblings.

FIGURE 8.14 Resource pool hierarchy

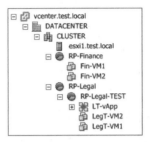

When child resource pools are created below an existing resource pool, the resource pool at the higher level is called the *parent* resource pool. In Figure 8.14, RP-Legal is a parent resource pool for the child resource pool of RP-Legal-TEST.

Each resource pool can have shares, limits, and reservations specified, in addition to specifying whether the reservation is expandable. The Expandable Reservation parameter will be defined in the next section.

You will typically not want to use resource pools to organize your virtual machines. Also use caution with resource pools, because each child resource pool you add will make the environment increasingly more difficult to understand and manage properly.

The Expandable Reservation Parameter

The Expandable Reservation parameter can be used to allow a child resource pool to request resources from its parent or ancestors if the child resource pool does not have the required resources. This provides greater flexibility when creating child resource pools. The expandable reservation is best shown in action, so Exercise 8.18 will demonstrate how it works.

EXERCISE 8.18

Configuring and Testing Expandable Reservations

1. Connect to a vCenter Server with the vSphere Web Client.

2. Select a cluster from the inventory and right-click it. Choose New Resource Pool from the context menu.

3. When the New Resource Pool window appears, enter the name **Parent Resource Pool** and use the Reservation field to set the value of 1000MHz.

4.   Deselect the Expandable Reservation setting in the CPU Resources section. The final configuration of the CPU Resources should look like this:

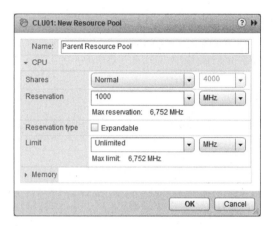

5.   Accept the defaults for all other settings and click OK to create the resource pool.

6.   A Create Resource Pool task will begin. When this task completes, verify that the new resource pool is listed under the cluster.

The parent resource pool has been created with a 1000MHz reservation, and the Expandable Reservation parameter was not selected. This setting creates a resource pool that has a static 1000MHz of CPU resources. In the following steps, a child resource pool will be created.

7.   Right-click the Parent Resource Pool resource pool created in steps 2 to 5. Choose New Resource Pool from the context menu.

8.   When the New Resource Pool window appears, enter the name **Child Resource Pool** and use the Reservation field to set the value of 500MHz.

9.   Deselect the Expandable Reservation setting in the CPU Resources section. The final configuration of the CPU Resources should look like this:

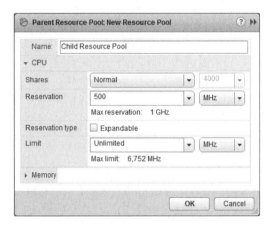

10. Accept the defaults for all other settings, and click OK to create the resource pool.

11. A Create Resource Pool task will begin. When this task completes, verify the new resource pool is listed under the first resource pool.

The child resource pool has been created with a 500MHz reservation, and the Expandable Reservation parameter was not selected. This setting creates a resource pool that has a static 500MHz of CPU resources. In the following steps, a VM will be created and powered on.

12. Right-click the Child Resource Pool resource pool and choose New Virtual Machine from the context menu.

13. Use the New Virtual Machine wizard to create any virtual machine configuration you like, but stop when you get to Step 2f - Customize Hardware.

14. Configure the VM to have a CPU Reservation setting of 750MHz, as shown in the following example:

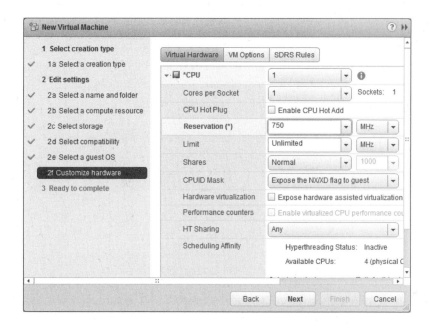

15. Finish creating the VM, and then power it on.

    You should be presented with the error messages shown here:

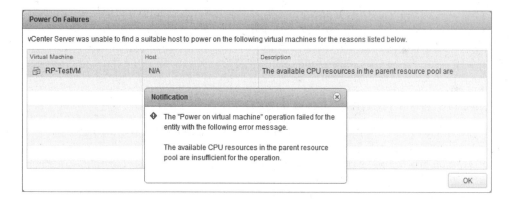

    Since this virtual machine has a reservation of 750MHz and the resource pool it belongs to has a reservation of only 500MHz, resource pool admission control prevents the virtual machine from being powered on. In the next set of steps, you will see how to configure the Child Resource Pool to use the Expandable Reservation option.

16. Right-click the Child Resource Pool object and choose Settings from the context menu.

17. On the Manage tab, click Settings on the toolbar. Ensure that CPU Resources is selected in the left pane, and then click Edit. An Edit CPU Resources window will open.

18. Select the Expandable option in the Reservation Type field.

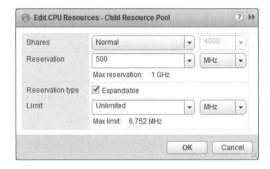

19. Click OK to save this change. An Update Resource Pool Configuration task will begin. When this task completes, power on the virtual machine that generated an error in step 15.

    You should now be presented with a running virtual machine.

The expandable reservation allowed Child Resource Pool to obtain the required resources from Parent Resource Pool to satisfy the CPU reservation of the virtual machine.

Now that I have demonstrated the Expandable Reservation parameter, I will cover the steps required to create two additional resource pools.

Creating and Removing a Resource Pool

As shown in Exercise 8.18, the actual task of creating resource pools is quite simple. Options like the expandable reservation help illustrate that the more difficult task is in understanding how resource pools work and how they will be used in your environment. In Exercise 8.19, you will create two more resource pools.

Creating a Resource Pool

1. Connect to a vCenter Server with the vSphere Web Client.

2. Select a cluster from the inventory and right-click it. Choose New Resource Pool from the context menu.

3. When the New Resource Pool window appears, enter the name **RP-Legal** and use the drop-down menu to change the Shares value to High for both the CPU and memory.

4. Ensure that the Reservation Type field's Expandable box is selected for both the CPU and memory fields. The final configuration should look like this:

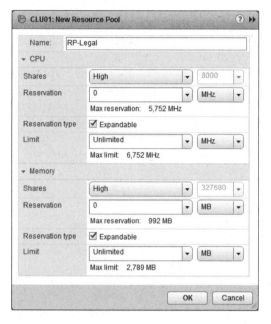

5. Click OK to create the resource pool. A Create Resource Pool task will begin. When this task completes, the resource pool is ready to be used.

6. Right-click the same cluster in the left pane and choose New Resource Pool from the context menu.

7. When the New Resource Pool window appears, enter the name **RP-Finance** and accept the defaults for all of the settings.

8. Click OK to create the resource pool. A Create Resource Pool task will begin. When this task completes, the resource pool is ready to be used. You should have a setup similar to the following:

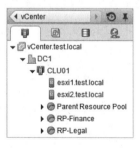

In this exercise, two resource pools were created. Assume that the cluster used in this exercise had a combined 6GHz of CPU and 30GB of RAM. In periods of resource contention, due to its high Shares value, the RP-Legal resource pool will receive 4GHz of CPU and 20GB of memory. The RP-Finance resource pool, with its lower relative Shares value, will receive 2GHz of CPU and 10GB of memory. This is because shares set to High will have twice the importance of those set to Normal. This explains the 2/3 to 1/3 ratio in this example. In periods of no resource contention, the expandable reservation allows either resource pool to have more resources as configured.

Sometimes there may be a need to delete a resource pool. The procedure to delete a resource pool is very simple. Keep in mind the implications of deleting a resource pool when working with child resource pools. Any virtual machines that are in the resource pool will be moved automatically to the parent resource pool or the root resource pool. To delete a resource pool, right-click it in the vSphere Web Client and choose All vCenter Actions ➢ Remove From Inventory from the context menu. You will be prompted to remove the resource pool, as shown in Figure 8.15.

FIGURE 8.15   Remove resource pool prompt

Click Yes to remove the resource pool. A Delete Resource Pool task will begin. When this task completes, verify that any virtual machines in the resource pool were moved as expected.

 Unless your lab has lots of resources, you may want to review the resource pools (or their reservations) created in the examples in this chapter so far.

Now that you have created a few resource pools, let's take some time to discuss how to configure resource pool attributes.

Configuring Resource Pool Attributes

Resource pools can be modified after their creation by configuring their attributes. This is useful in situations where the resource pool requirements have changed. The shares, reservation, and limit can each be modified for the resource pool. Shares, reservations, and limits were discussed in Chapter 7, but it's worth reviewing them here.

- Resource pool shares can be specified with respect to the total resources of the parent resource pool. Sibling resource pools will share the parent's resource, based on their specified share values. Virtual machines in resource pools with the highest share values will be able to consume more resources in periods of resource contention on the ESXi host.

- In addition to shares, reservations can be used to guarantee a minimum allocation of CPU and memory for the resource pool. This setting is used to claim a specific amount of the resource for the virtual machine so that these resources will always be available. Memory reservations can also be used to avoid overcommitment of physical memory resources.

- Limits are used to set an upper bound for memory and CPU resources. This prevents a virtual machine in the resource pool from using more resources than specified. This setting is by default set to Unlimited for both CPU and memory. Using this setting will ensure that the virtual machine uses close to the allocations for vCPU and memory it has been granted.

To edit a resource pool in the vSphere Web Client, right-click it and choose Settings in the context menu. You performed this in step 17 of Exercise 8.17 earlier in this chapter to view the CPU resources. The Memory Resources attributes are shown in Figure 8.16.

FIGURE 8.16   Resource pool attributes

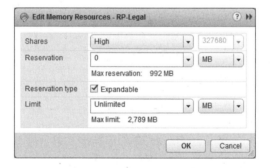

I have now shown how to configure resource pool attributes. Let's move on to adding and removing virtual machines to and from resource pools.

Adding and Removing Virtual Machines to/from a Resource Pool

Objects that can be added to a resource pool include other resource pools, vApps, and virtual machines. There are multiple options that you can use to add virtual machines to a resource pool. In Exercise 8.17, you added a virtual machine to a resource pool by right-clicking the resource pool and selecting New Virtual Machine from the context menu.

Virtual machines can also be added to resource pools, while powered on or off, by dragging and dropping them in the vSphere Web Client. Many virtual machine operations and tasks also allow you to choose the resource pool as part of the operation. They include the following:

- Creating a new virtual machine at the host, cluster, or datacenter level

- Migrating a virtual machine using vMotion or cold migration

- Deploying OVF templates

- Cloning a virtual machine

- Deploying a VM from a template

- P2V conversions with VMware Converter

Here are some caveats for adding virtual machines to a resource pool:

- If the virtual machine is powered on and the resource pool does not have adequate resources to guarantee its reservations, admission control will not allow the move to complete.

- Virtual machine–configured reservations and limits will not change.

- Virtual machine shares of high, medium, or low will be adjusted to reflect the total number of shares in the new resource pool.

- Virtual machine shares configured with a custom value will retain the custom value. A warning will appear if a significant change in total share percentage would occur.

The operations that can be used to remove a virtual machine from a resource pool are similar to the operations for adding a virtual machine to a resource pool. Virtual machines can be dragged and dropped out of resource pools, while powered on or off, using the vSphere Web Client. vMotion, cold migrations, removing a virtual machine from inventory, and deleting a virtual machine are additional ways to remove it from a resource pool.

Virtual machine operations will often provide the ability to select a resource pool, but this option will appear only if and when the resource pools are already configured.

Now let's take some time to discuss how to determine the resource pool requirements for a given vSphere implementation.

Determining Resource Pool Requirements for a Given vSphere Implementation

Determining the resource pool requirements for a given vSphere implementation involves knowing or predicting what your environment will require for resources. The requirements will depend on a variety of factors:

- The characteristics and requirements of workloads or planned workloads

- The specific terms of SLAs or other agreements that dictate performance

- Whether the resources will be divided along workload, business, or even political boundaries

- Whether the applications would benefit from expandable reservations in resource pools

- Who will own and administer the resource pools

- Whether child resource pools will be created and used

- Whether resource pools or the workloads running in them would benefit from using reservations or limits

- Whether VMware DRS will be used and the vSphere editions (Enterprise and Enterprise Plus) required

- Whether VMware HA will be used

- Whether VMware FT will be used

This is not an all-inclusive list, and each implementation will be different. The key is to know the workloads, the infrastructure layout, licensing, and how the business or organization works. Political factors or budget control may determine the design in many cases, regardless of the technical factors.

In the final section of the chapter, we will discuss evaluating appropriate shares, reservations, and limits for a resource pool based on virtual machine workloads.

Evaluating Appropriate Shares, Reservations, and Limits for a Resource Pool Based on Virtual Machine Workloads

Much like determining the resource pool requirements, evaluating the appropriate settings really means knowing your workloads. In some cases, the workloads themselves may change or have new requirements. In Exercise 8.20, you will evaluate memory reservation settings for a virtual machine that has a new requirement of being protected with VMware FT.

EXERCISE 8.20

Evaluating Memory Reservations for a VM

1. Connect to a vCenter Server with the vSphere Web Client.

2. Select a cluster from the inventory and right-click it. Choose New Resource Pool from the context menu.

3. When the New Resource Pool window appears, give it a unique name. Accept the defaults for CPU Resources.

4. Set Memory Reservation to 1024MB.

5. Deselect the Expandable Reservation setting in the Memory Resources section. The final configuration should look like this:

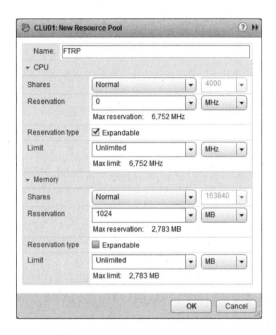

6. Click OK to create the resource pool. A Create Resource Pool task will begin.

    You have now created the new resource pool that will be used for this exercise. The next step is to add a virtual machine to it.

7. Move an existing powered-off virtual machine that is configured with a memory size of 1024MB into the resource pool or create a new virtual machine with a memory size of 1024MB. Ensure that a guest OS that is supported for use with VMware FT is used.

8. Configure the virtual machine to have a memory reservation of 1024MB. In the following example, a new VM was created.

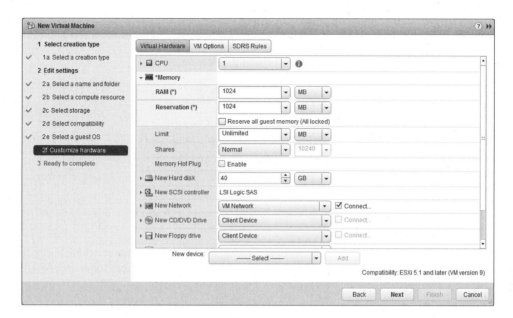

You have now added a virtual machine to the resource pool, and the virtual machine's memory reservation equals that of the resource pool.

9. Power on the virtual machine. You should receive an Insufficient Resources error message like the one shown here:

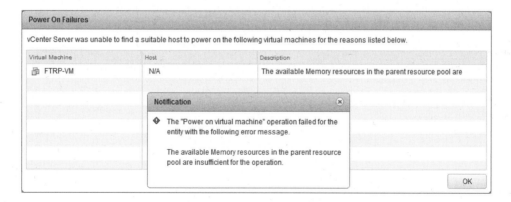

This task has failed because the virtual machine memory overhead was not taken into account. Each virtual machine has a memory overhead that is based on the number of vCPUs and memory in the VM. The error has occurred because the resource pool has a 1024MB static memory reservation and is not allowed to borrow resources from the root resource pool. In the next steps, you will configure the resource pool to have the required resources to power on the virtual machine.

EXERCISE 8.20 *(continued)*

10. Select the virtual machine in the left pane, and then select the Monitor tab. Click Resource Allocation on the toolbar, and then locate the Host Memory panel.

11. Note the value of the Overhead Reservation listed in the Host Memory panel. Round this number up to the nearest whole number.

12. Right-click the resource pool and choose the Settings option from the context menu. Edit the Memory Resources for the resource pool to add the virtual machine memory overhead value from the previous step to the current Reservation value in the Reservation field.

13. Click OK to save the changes. An Update Resource Pool Configuration task will begin. When this task completes, power on the virtual machine.

    The virtual machine should power on at this point, now that the virtual machine memory overhead has been accounted for in the resource pool reservation. In the next part of this exercise, FT will be enabled for this virtual machine.

14. Power off the virtual machine.

15. Right-click the virtual machine and choose All vCenter Actions ➢ Fault Tolerance ➢ Enable Fault Tolerance.

16. Review the information on the Turn On Fault Tolerance screen and click Yes.

17. A Turn On Fault Tolerance task will begin. When this task completes, power on the virtual machine. The same Insufficient Resources error message received in step 9 will appear for the secondary VM.

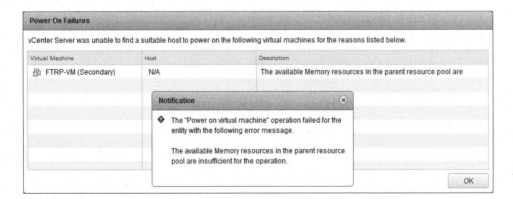

Enabling FT failed, because creating the secondary VM requires the same number of resources from the resource pool as the primary VM requires. The primary virtual machine was powered on, but the secondary could not be powered on because of the lack of available resources. In the next steps of this exercise, you will adjust the resource pool memory reservation to account for this requirement.

18. Right-click the resource pool and choose Settings from the context menu. Edit the Memory Resources for the resource pool and double the current Reservation value.

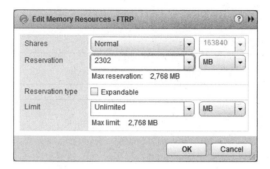

19. Click OK to save the changes. An Update Resource Pool Configuration task will begin. When this task completes, shut down the virtual machine and power it on again.

Using shares, reservations and limits can provide additional performance to your virtual machines. Another way to provide additional performance to your virtual machines is to use a new feature introduced in vSphere 5.5 called the vSphere Flash Read Cache.

Describing vSphere Flash Read Cache Architecture

vSphere Flash Read Cache allows the pooling of multiple local SSD or PCIe flash-based devices in your ESXi host to create a single consumable construct called a virtual flash resource. The virtual flash resource is also known as a flash pool or a flash volume. There are two ways the virtual flash resource can be leveraged, both of which utilize the very fast read rates of SSD and/or flash-based devices to improve host and/or virtual machine performance. ESXi host performance can be improved by using the virtual flash resource to allocate space for Virtual Flash Host Swap Cache. Virtual machine performance can be improved by configuring the Virtual Flash Read Cache for virtual disks.

vSphere Flash Read Cache is based on two major components:

- vSphere Flash Read Cache software — provides a write-through (read) cache that can increase the performance of many workloads running in virtual machines, especially for read-intensive workloads or those with high percentages of data locality requirements.

- vSphere Flash Read Cache infrastructure — resource manager and broker for Virtual Flash Resource consumption and the enforcer of admission control policies.

The architecture of vSphere Flash Read Cache is shown in Figure 8.17.

FIGURE 8.17   vSphere Flash Read Cache architecture

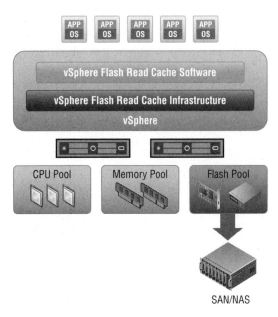

SAN/NAS

vSphere Flash Read Cache is compatible with vMotion, HA, and DRS, but there are certain system requirements that must be met.

- ESXi 5.5 and newer

- vCenter Server 5.5 and newer

- vSphere Web Client is required to manage and configure

- VM hardware version 10 (ESXi 5.5 and later compatibility)

- Each ESXi 5.5 or newer host must have a supported flash-based device listed in the HCL

- Enterprise Plus licensing

In addition to the system requirements, there are certain limitations that you should know. Table 8.3 lists these limitations:

TABLE 8.3   Virtual Flash Resource Limits

Resource	Limit
Virtual flash volumes per ESXi 5.5 host	One (local only)
SSDs or PCIe flash-based devices per virtual flash volume	8 or less

Resource	Limit
SSD or PCIe- flash-based device size	4TB or less
Virtual flash size	32TB or less

 DRS handles the initial VM placement when used with a VM configured to use vSphere Flash Read Cache, but it will not generally move these VMs as part of its load-balancing duties. Unless an ESXi host is placed into maintenance mode or there is a major imbalance in the DRS-enabled cluster, virtual machines with vSphere Flash Read Cache are considered soft affined to the host they are initially placed on.

While Enterprise Plus licensing and flash-based devices in a physical server could be obstacles for many home labs, there is a workaround for the SSD requirement that can be implemented to test vSphere Flash Read Cache. This workaround will allow you to present a VMDK to your nested ESXi host as an SSD. You will need to add the following line to your .VMX file for the nested ESXi host.

```
scsi0:1.virtualSSD = 1
```

This modification assumes that you are using SCSI controller 0 and disk ID 1. Substitute as necessary for the fake SSDs in your nested ESXi hosts. If you need assistance with editing .vmx files, refer to Exercise 7.6 in Chapter 7. The VMware Knowledge Base also has specific documents on modifying the .vmx file in the Player, Workstation, and Fusion products; see http://kb.vmware.com/kb/1714.

Take a moment to get your lab ready, because in the next section I will be covering the steps to add virtual flash resource capacity.

Adding/Removing vFlash Read Cache Resource Capacity

Whether you are initially setting up a virtual flash resource or adding capacity to an existing virtual flash resource, the procedure is very similar. when adding SSDs or PCIe flash-based devices, it is important to know that they must be used exclusively for the virtual flash resource. Exercise 8.21 covers the steps to add a virtual flash resource, or a flash pool.

EXERCISE 8.21

Adding Virtual Flash Resource Capacity

1. Connect to a vCenter Server with the vSphere Web Client.

2. Select an ESXi host with a SSD or flash-based device, and then click the Manage tab for this host.

3. Click Settings on the toolbar and select the Virtual Flash menu option.

4. Select the Virtual Flash Resource Management option, and then click the Add Capacity button.

5. Place a check in the check box beside the desired SSD or flash-based PCIe device. Note the warning at the top that states that this device will be formatted. The following image shows a fake SSD in a nested ESXi host.

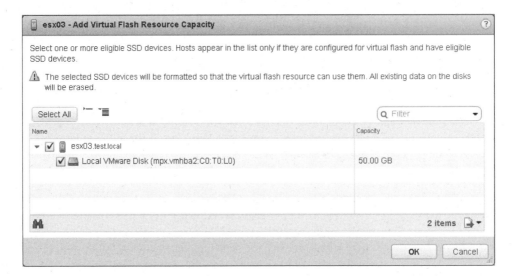

6. Click OK and a Configure Virtual Flash Resource task will begin. When this task completes, review the details of the virtual flash resource.

Virtual Flash Resource Management   [Add Capacity...] [Remove All]

Use SSD devices connected to your host to set up a virtual flash resource. After you create the resource, it can be used to allocate space for virtual flash host swap cache or to configure virtual Flash Read Cache for virtual disks.

▶ Capacity	48.80 GB free out of 49.75 GB
▶ Capacity for virtual Flash Read Cache	48.80 GB free out of 49.75 GB
File System	VFFS

Device Backing

⟳   [🔍 Filter   ▾]

Name	Capacity
Local VMware Disk (mpx.vmhba2:C0:T0:L0)	50.00 GB

🔭   1 items 📄▾

Note that when the SSD was added in the previous exercise, a VMware proprietary file system called VFFS was created on it. This is why the format warning is presented in the Add Capacity window.

To remove a virtual flash resource, or flash pool, simply click the Remove All button.

FIGURE 8.18   Remove virtual flash resource

A Remove Virtual Flash Resource task will begin, and the flash pool will now be empty.

Now that the flash pool, or virtual flash resource, has been created it can be assigned to your ESXi hosts or virtual machines. In the next section, I will cover the steps required to assign these resources to a virtual machine.

Assigning vFlash Read Cache Resources to VMDKs

Once the flash pool has been created, assigning the virtual flash read cache is a relatively simple task. The steps required to do this will be covered in Exercise 8.22.

EXERCISE 8.22

Assigning Virtual Flash Read Cache to VM

1. Connect to a vCenter Server with the vSphere Web Client.

2. Select a virtual machine that is hosted on an ESXi host with a virtual flash resource previously created.

3. Right-click the VM and choose the Edit Settings option.

4. Expand the hard disk in the virtual machine that you want to enable the virtual flash read cache resources for.

5. Click the Advanced link to the right of the Virtual Flash Read Cache option.

6. A Virtual Flash Read Cache Settings window will open. Place a check in the Enable Virtual Flash Read Cache option.

7. Enter a value for the Reservation. This is the cache size that will be used, and the recommended starting value for is 10% of the size of the VDMK.

8. Accept the default block size from the drop-down menu, or choose a size. The final configuration should look like this:

9. Click OK to accept these values, and click OK on the Edit Settings window to save the changes to the virtual machine.

10. Right-click the VM you just configured, and choose Migrate from the context menu.

11. Select the Change Host option and click Next.

12. Select a cluster and click Next.

13. Review the options on the Select Virtual Flash Read Cache Migration Settings.

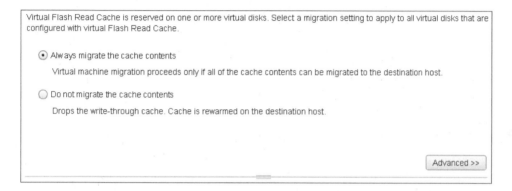

There are two available options when migrating a VM that utilizes the virtual flash read cache. The Always Migrate The Cache Contents option will result in a slower vMotion, but the cache contents will also be copied. The Do Not Migrate The Cache Contents option will result in a faster vMotion, but the VM performance could be impacted. You can also use the Advanced button to select options for individual VMDKs in the virtual machine.

14. Click Cancel.

When performing a vMotion of a virtual machine with Virtual Flash Read Cache enabled, you can only select destination ESXi hosts that have a flash pool created.

Remember that vSphere Flash Read Cache is a new feature introduced in vSphere 5.5, and be prepared to be tested on it when taking the VCP5-DCV.

Summary

This chapter focused on creating and configuring VMware clusters, with the following topics and tasks:

- Determining the appropriate failover methodology and required resources for an HA implementation
- DRS virtual machine entitlement
- Creating and deleting a cluster
- Adding and removing ESXi hosts to/from a cluster, along with adding and removing virtual machines to/from the cluster
- Enabling and disabling host monitoring and how to configure admission control
- Virtual machine and application monitoring
- Configuring automation levels for DRS and virtual machines
- Configuring migration thresholds for DRS and individual virtual machines
- Creating VM-Host and VM-VM affinity rules
- EVC and the steps to configure it
- Monitoring a DRS/HA cluster
- Configuring Storage DRS
- Enabling BIOS P/C states
- Enabling, configuring, and disabling Host Power Management and Distributed Power Management
- Determining appropriate power threshold for a given implementation

The chapter then explored planning and implementing VMware Fault Tolerance. Topics included:

- Determining the use case for enabling VMware Fault Tolerance on a virtual machine
- Identifying VMware Fault Tolerance requirements
- Configuring VMware Fault Tolerance logging networking
- Enabling and disabling VMware Fault Tolerance on a virtual machine
- Testing FT configurations

Finally, the chapter covered creating and administering resource pools:

- Describing the resource pool hierarchy
- Using the Expandable Reservation parameter
- Creating and removing resource pools
- Configuring resource pool attributes

- Adding and removing virtual machines to/from a resource pool
- Determining the resource pool requirements for a given vSphere implementation
- Evaluating appropriate shares, reservations, and limits for a resource pool based on virtual machine workloads
- Describing vSphere Flash Read Cache architecture
- Creating/Deleting vFlash Read Cache Resource Capacity
- Assigning vFlash Read Cache resources to VMDKs

Exam Essentials

Know how to create and configure VMware clusters.   Be able to determine the appropriate failover methodology and required resources for an HA implementation. Know how to describe DRS virtual machine entitlement. Understand how to create and delete a DRS/HA cluster. Be able to add and remove ESXi hosts and virtual machines from a DRS/HA cluster. Know how to enable and disable host monitoring. Be able to configure admission control for HA and virtual machines. Know how to enable, configure, and disable virtual machine and application monitoring. Understand how to configure automation levels and migration thresholds for DRS and virtual machines. Know how to create VM-Host and VM-VM affinity rules. Be able to configure EVC. Understand the different ways that a DRS/HA cluster can be monitored. Be able to configure Storage DRS.

Know how to plan and implement VMware FT.   Be able to determine the use case for enabling VMware Fault Tolerance on a virtual machine. Know the requirements and limitations of VMware FT. Be able to configure fault tolerance logging networking. Understand how to enable and disable FT for a virtual machine. Know the various ways to test an FT configuration.

Know how to create and administer resource pools.   Be able to describe the resource pool hierarchy. Understand the Expandable Reservation parameter. Be able to create and remove resource pools. Know how to configure resource pool attributes. Understand the different ways to add and remove virtual machines from a resource pool. Be able to determine resource pool requirements for a given vSphere implementation. Know how to evaluate appropriate shares, reservations, and limits for a resource pool based on virtual machine workloads. Be able to describe the vSphere Flash Read Cache architecture. Know how to create and delete vFlash Read Cache resource capacity and understand how to assign vSphere Flash Read Cache resources to virtual disks.

Review Questions

1. Which of the following are ESXi host requirements for VMware FT? (Choose all that apply.)

   A. Enterprise or Enterprise Plus licensing must be in place.

   B. ESXi hosts must be certified for FT in the VMware HCL.

   C. ESXi hosts must have hardware Virtualization (HV) enabled in the BIOS.

   D. ESXi hosts must have EVC mode enabled.

2. Which of the following are true statements about Storage DRS? (Choose two.)

   A. ESXi 4.1 and newer hosts are required.

   B. ESXi 5 and newer hosts are required.

   C. Mixing NFS and VMFS datastores is not allowed.

   D. Mixing NFS and VMFS datastores is allowed.

3. What condition must be first met to remove an ESXi host from a cluster?

   A. The host must have host monitoring disabled.

   B. The host must be in maintenance mode.

   C. The host must be disconnected from vCenter Server.

   D. None of these.

4. Which of the following are considered best practices for setting up the fault tolerance logging network? (Choose two.)

   A. Single shared 1GbE NIC for vMotion and fault tolerance logging traffic

   B. Single dedicated 1GbE NIC for fault tolerance logging traffic only

   C. Isolating the fault tolerance logging traffic

   D. Routing the fault tolerance logging traffic

5. A virtual machine has its host isolation response set to Shut Down, but this virtual machine does not have the VMware Tools installed. What will happen to this virtual machine if the ESXi host it is running on becomes isolated?

   A. It will shut down.

   B. Nothing.

   C. It will be powered off.

   D. It will be suspended.

6. You need to create an affinity rule to require a set of virtual machines to run on a specific ESXi host. Which of the following do you need to create?

   A. VM-Host affinity rule

   B. VM-Host anti-affinity rule

    C. VM-VM affinity rule

    D. VM-VM anti-affinity rule

7. When implementing VMware FT, what is the overhead percentage that is required?

    A. 5 to 10 percent

    B. 10 percent

    C. 5 to 20 percent

    D. 20 percent

8. Which of the following schedulers exist in a DRS-enabled cluster? (Choose two.)

    A. Priority scheduler

    B. Global scheduler

    C. Entitlement scheduler

    D. Local scheduler

9. Which of the following statements best describes the Expandable Reservation parameter?

    A. The Expandable Reservation parameter can be used to allow a child resource pool to request resources from its parent.

    B. The Expandable Reservation parameter can be used to allow a child resource pool to request resources from its parent or ancestors.

    C. The Expandable Reservation parameter can be used to allow a parent resource pool to request resources from its child.

    D. The Expandable Reservation parameter can be used to allow a parent resource pool to request resources from a sibling.

10. When raising the EVC mode for the cluster, which of the following statements is true? (Choose two.)

    A. Raising the EVC mode for cluster involves moving from a greater feature set to a lower feature set.

    B. Raising the EVC mode for cluster involves moving from a lower feature set to a greater feature set.

    C. Running virtual machines will need to be powered off during this operation.

    D. Running virtual machines may continue to run during this operation.

11. When using vMotion to migrate a virtual machine, the option to select a resource pool was not available for the destination. What could be a reason for this?

    A. The VM has an individual memory reservation set.

    B. vMotion does not allow this operation.

    C. Changing resource pools is not allowed.

    D. No resource pools exist in the destination.

12. In which of the following automation levels will vCenter Server inform of suggested virtual machine migrations and place the virtual machines on ESXi hosts at VM startup?

A. Manual

B. Partially automated

C. Fully automated

D. None of these

13. Which of the following admission control policies will result in an ESXi host in the cluster that is unable to run virtual machines until a failover situation occurs?

A. Host failures the cluster tolerates

B. Percentage of cluster resources reserved as failover spare capacity

C. Specify failover hosts

D. None of these

14. Which of the following are configurable resource pool attributes? (Choose all that apply.)

A. Shares

B. Reservation

C. Priority

D. Name

15. A master host has stopped receiving heartbeats from a slave host. What are the possible conditions that the slave host could be in? (Choose all that apply.)

A. Failed

B. Unprotected

C. Isolated

D. Partitioned

16. Which of the following can be used to enable and disable VMware FT for a virtual machine that contains a single eager zeroed thick-provisioned disk? (Choose all that apply.)

A. The vSphere Client for the powered-on virtual machine

B. The vSphere Client for the powered-off virtual machine

C. The vSphere Web Client for the powered-on virtual machine

D. The vSphere Web Client for the powered-off virtual machine

17. You need to test the FT configuration in your environment. Which of the following approaches is both supported and noninvasive?

A. Pull the power cables from an ESXi host that is running VMs with FT enabled.

B. Use the Web Client and right-click the secondary virtual machine. Choose the Delete From Disk option.

C. Put an ESXi host with FT VMs running on it in maintenance mode.

D. Use the Web Client and right-click a virtual machine that has FT enabled on it. Choose the Fault Tolerance Test Failover option from the context menu that appears.

18. You want DRS to use the most aggressive setting possible for the migration threshold. How do you accomplish this?

   A. Move the slider for the automation level to the far left in the DRS settings.

   B. Move the slider for the migration threshold to the far left in the DRS settings.

   C. Move the slider for the automation level to the far right in the DRS settings.

   D. Move the slider for the migration threshold to the far right in the DRS settings.

19. Which of the following is a use case for VMware FT? (Choose all that apply.)

   A. Application that requires high availability

   B. Application that has no native capability for clustering

   C. Application that requires protection for critical processes to complete

   D. Application that has persistent and long-standing connections

20. Which of the following are supported for use with vSphere Flash Read Cache? (Choose two.)

   A. SSD drive

   B. 15K SAS drive

   C. Memory

   D. Flash PCIe card

Chapter

9

Maintaining Service Levels

VCP5-DCV EXAM OBJECTIVES COVERED IN THIS CHAPTER:

✓ **1.4: Plan and Perform Upgrades of vCenter Server and VMware ESXi**

- Upgrade an ESXi Host using vCenter Update Manager

✓ **1.5: Secure vCenter Server and ESXi**

- Apply Permissions to ESXi Hosts Using Host Profiles

✓ **5.4: Migrate Virtual Machines**

- Migrate a powered-off or suspended virtual machine

- Identify ESXi host and virtual machine requirements for vMotion and Storage vMotion

- Identify Enhanced vMotion Compatibility CPU requirements

- Identify snapshot requirements for vMotion/Storage vMotion migration

- Configure virtual machine swap file location

- Migrate virtual machines using vMotion/Storage vMotion

- Utilize Storage vMotion techniques (changing virtual disk type, renaming virtual machines, etc.)

✓ **5.5: Backup and Restore Virtual Machines**

- Identify snapshot requirements

- Create/Delete/Consolidate virtual machine snapshots

- Differentiate between VDP and VDPA

- Identify VMware Data Protection requirements

- Explain VMware Data Protection sizing guidelines

- Install and Configure VMware Data Protection

- Create a backup job with VMware Date Protection

- Manage and monitor VDP capacity

- Perform a test/live full/file-level restore with VMware Data Protection

- Perform a VDR data migration

- Describe vSphere Replication architecture

- Install/Configure/Upgrade vSphere Replication

- Configure Replication for Single/Multiple VMs

- Recover a VM using vSphere Replication

- Perform a failback operation using vSphere Replication

- Determine Appropriate Backup Solution for a Given vSphere Implementation

✓ **5.6: Patch and Update ESXi and Virtual Machines**

- Identify patching requirements for ESXi hosts and virtual machine hardware/tools

- Create/Edit/Remove a Host Profile from an ESXi host

- Attach/Apply a Host Profile to an ESXi host or cluster

- Perform compliance scanning, apply Host Profiles, and remediate an ESXi host using Host Profiles

- Import/Export a Host Profile

- Install and Configure vCenter Update Manager

- Configure patch download options

- Create/Edit/Delete an Update Manager baseline

- Attach an Update Manager baseline to an ESXi host or cluster

- Scan and Remediate ESXi hosts and virtual machine hardware/tools using Update Manager

- Stage ESXi host updates

TOOLS

- vSphere Resource Management guide (Objective 5.4)

- vSphere Virtual Machine Administration guide (Objectives 5.4 and 5.6)

- VMware vSphere Examples and Scenarios guide (Objectives 5.4 and 5.6)

- Introduction to VMware vSphere Data Protection (Objective 5.5)

- vSphere Data Protection Administration Guide (Objective 5.5)

- Introduction to VMware vSphere Replication (Objective 5.5)

- VMware vSphere Replication Administration (Objective 5.5)

- VDR Data Migration Tool (Objective 5.5)

- VDP Configure Utility (Objective 5.5)

- vSphere Host Profiles guide (Objective 5.6)

- Installing and Administering VMware vSphere Update Manager guide (Objective 5.6)

- Reconfiguring VMware vSphere Update Manager (Objective 5.6)

- vSphere Update Manager Utility (Objective 5.6)

- Update Manager Web Client (Objective 5.6)

- vSphere Client/vSphere Web Client (Objectives 5.4, 5.5, and 5.6)

This chapter covers the objectives of sections 5.4 and 5.5 of the VCP5-DCV exam blueprint. Two objectives from section one of the exam blueprint have also been moved to this chapter, as they simply are in better context here. This chapter focuses on migrating virtual machines, backing up virtual machines, replicating virtual machines and patching ESXi hosts. Updating the virtual machine hardware and VMware Tools is also included.

Migrating Virtual Machines

The ability to migrate virtual machines is a feature that all virtual infrastructure administrators can appreciate. Migration is defined as the process of moving a VM from one ESXi host or datastore to another. Migration allows the virtual infrastructure to be both more dynamic and highly available. The first topic this chapter will cover is migrating powered-off or suspended virtual machines.

Migrating a Powered-Off or Suspended Virtual Machine

Before you explore the steps to migrate a powered-off virtual machine, you need to know the different types of migration. Four types of migration are possible in vCenter Server, as described in Table 9.1.

TABLE 9.1   VM migration options

Migration type	Description
Cold migration	Used to migrate a powered-off virtual machine to a new host and/or datastore. Cold migration can be used to move VMs to different datacenters.
Migrate a suspended VM	Used to migrate a suspended virtual machine to a new host and/or datastore. Suspended VMs can be migrated to different datacenters.

Migration type	Description
vMotion migration	Used to migrate a powered-on virtual machine to a new host and/or datastore with no disruption. vMotion cannot be used to move VMs to different datacenters.
Storage vMotion migration	Used to migrate the virtual disk files of a powered-on virtual machine to a new datastore with no disruption.

Migration means "move." Do not confuse migrating with copy operations such as cloning, where a new virtual machine will be created.

Exercise 9.1 covers the steps to migrate a powered-off virtual machine.

EXERCISE 9.1

Migrating a Powered-Off Virtual Machine

1. Connect to a vCenter Server with the vSphere Web Client.

2. Locate a powered-off VM in the inventory. Review the Host value in the Related Objects panel on the virtual machine's Summary tab.

3. Right-click the VM and choose Migrate from the context menu.

4. The Migrate wizard will launch. Select the Change Host option and click Next to continue.

5. Select a cluster and click the Allow Host Selection Within This Cluster check box.

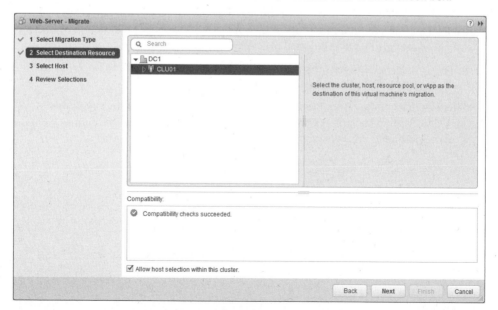

EXERCISE 9.1 *(continued)*

6. Click Next, and then select a different ESXi host than the one the VM is currently residing on. Ensure that the Compatibility checks succeed.

7. Click Next and review your selections.

8. Click Finish.

9. A Relocate Virtual Machine task will begin. When this task completes, verify that the Host value in the Related Objects panel on the virtual machine's Summary tab has been changed.

The process to migrate a suspended virtual machine is similar to that used to migrate a powered-off virtual machine. Exercise 9.2 covers the steps to migrate a suspended virtual machine.

EXERCISE 9.2

Migrating a Suspended Virtual Machine

1. Connect to a vCenter Server with the vSphere Web Client.

2. Locate a suspended VM in the inventory. Review both the Host and Storage values in the Related Objects panel on the virtual machine's Summary tab.

3. Right-click the VM and choose Migrate from the context menu.

4. The Migrate wizard will open. Select the Change Both Host And Datastore option.

5. Click Next to continue.

6. Select a cluster and note that a check appears in the Allow Host Selection Within This Cluster check box and that it is also grayed out. Click Next.

7. Select a different ESXi host than the one the VM is currently residing on. Ensure that the Compatibility checks succeed. Click Next to continue.

8. Select a different datastore than the one the VM is currently residing on. Choose the Same Format As Source option for Virtual Disk Format. Verify that Compatibility Checks Succeeded appears in the Compatibility field.

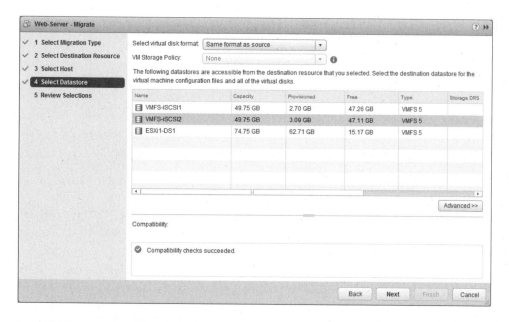

9. Click Next and review your selections.

10. Click Finish.

11. A Relocate Virtual Machine task will begin. When this task completes, verify that both the Host and Storage values in the Related Objects panel on the virtual machine's Summary tab have been changed.

12. Right-click the virtual machine in the left pane and choose Power On from the context menu.

13. Open the virtual machine console and verify that it is operating properly.

Suspended virtual machines must be able to resume execution on the target host using an equivalent instruction set. The Migrate Virtual Machine Wizard includes a compatibility check and will not allow incompatible migrations to proceed.

Now that I have covered migration and migrating powered-off and suspended virtual machines, I will move on to using vMotion. However, I will first identify the ESXi host and VM requirements for vMotion and Storage vMotion.

ESXi Host and Virtual Machine Requirements for vMotion and Storage vMotion

Before you can use vMotion or Storage vMotion, the ESXi hosts must satisfy several requirements:

- ESXi hosts must be licensed to use vMotion.
- ESXi hosts must have VMkernel networking established for the vMotion traffic.
- ESXi hosts must be licensed to use vMotion and/or Storage vMotion.

 Real World Scenario

Using Storage vMotion without a License

A virtual infrastructure administrator is building a new environment that will consist of an iSCSI SAN, three ESXi servers, vCenter Server in a virtual machine, and vSphere Essentials Plus licensing. The servers have arrived, but the SAN has been delayed. The administrator notices that the ESXi servers each contain two 300GB SAS drives.

The administrator decides to go ahead and get an early start on building out the environment. He installs ESXi on each of the three servers. He then creates a new virtual machine to install vCenter Server on and stores the virtual machine on the local storage of one of the ESXi hosts. When he installs vCenter Server, he does not enter his Essentials Plus license keys and instead elects to run the environment in evaluation mode for 60 days. He deploys another server to be used for vSphere Update Manager and also deploys the vSphere Management Appliance. All three of these virtual machines are on local storage on different ESXi hosts.

The SAN arrives a few days later, and the virtual infrastructure administrator configures the VMkernel networking for it and gets each of the three hosts connected to this shared storage. He then uses Storage vMotion to move his vCenter Server, vSphere Update Manger, and vMA virtual machines to the shared storage. Once these Storage vMotion operations are complete, he enters his vSphere Essentials Plus licensing information in vCenter Server. The 60-day evaluation mode option chosen during the vCenter Server installation allowed him to use features he was not licensed for and ultimately complete his work without waiting for the SAN to arrive.

Just as there are requirements to use vMotion and Storage vMotion on the ESXi hosts, there are virtual machine requirements for vMotion and Storage vMotion:

- Virtual machines that use raw disks for clustering cannot be migrated.
- Virtual machines that use a virtual device backed by a device that is not accessible on the destination host cannot be migrated.
- Virtual machines that use a virtual device backed by a device on the client computer cannot be migrated.

- Virtual machines that use USB pass-through devices can be migrated, but only if the devices are enabled for vMotion.

- Virtual machines that use NPIV are not supported with Storage vMotion.

- You can vMotion virtual machines that utilize NPIV, only if the RDM files are all located on the same datastore.

- Virtual machine disks must be in persistent mode or be RDMs for Storage vMotion.

- Virtual machines in the process of having a VMware Tools upgrade cannot be migrated.

Now that you understand the ESXi host and virtual machine requirements for vMotion and Storage vMotion, let's cover the Enhanced vMotion Compatibility (EVC) CPU requirements.

Enhanced vMotion Compatibility CPU Requirements

The EVC requirements were discussed in Chapter 8. As a review, the following requirements exist for EVC CPUs:

- All hosts in the cluster must have only Intel or only AMD processors. Mixing Intel and AMD processors is not allowed.

- CPU features, such as hardware virtualization support (AMD-V or Intel VT) and AMD No eXecute (NX) or Intel eXecute Disable (XD), should be enabled consistently across all hosts in the cluster.

- All of the ESXi hosts in the cluster must contain supported CPUs for the desired EVC mode.

For more information on EVC processor support, check the VMware KB article "Enhanced VMotion Compatibility (EVC) Processor Support" at

http://kb.vmware.com/kb/1003212

Supported EVC modes for different processors can be found at

www.vmware.com/go/hcl?deviceCategory=cpu

Now let's turn our attention to understanding how snapshots work with vMotion and Storage vMotion.

Snapshot Requirements for vMotion/Storage vMotion Migration

There are currently no requirements for using virtual machine snapshots with vMotion or Storage vMotion, as long as the virtual machine is located on an ESXi 5 or later host and the vSphere environment meets the vMotion or Storage vMotion requirements. Either of these two approaches can be used to migrate powered-on virtual machines with snapshots.

> If your vSphere environment has a mix of ESX or ESXi hosts running different versions, then Storage vMotion can be used only for virtual machines with snapshots if these virtual machines are running on an ESXi 5 or later host. For more information, check
>
> http://kb.vmware.com/kb/1035550.

Now let's see how to configure the virtual machine swap file location.

Configuring a Virtual Machine Swap File Location

Virtual machine swap files were discussed in detail in Chapter 7, "Managing and Administering Virtual Machines and vApps." Before we go through the steps to configure the virtual machine swap file location, here is a brief review.

The virtual machine swap (VSWP) file is created when a virtual machine is powered on. This file is used only if the ESXi host runs out of physical memory and is used to allow overcommitment of virtual memory for virtual machines running on the ESXi host. Initially the VSWP file will be equal to the amount of virtual machine–assigned memory minus the memory reservation set for the VM. These files can be large, and in some cases, such as when troubleshooting or using replication, it is better to have them in their own storage locations and not in the same working location as the virtual machine. The working location is the directory where the virtual machine's configuration files are stored.

Virtual machine swap files can be placed in the following locations:

Default   Selecting this option will store the virtual machine swap file at the default location as defined in the host or cluster where the VM currently resides.

Always Store With The Virtual Machine   Selecting this option will store the virtual machine swap file in the working location. This is the same location where the VM's configuration file is stored.

Store In The Host's Swapfile Datastore   Selecting this option will store the virtual machine swap file in the swap file datastore as defined on the host or cluster where the VM currently resides. Otherwise, the virtual swap file will be stored in the virtual machine's working location.

The virtual machine swap file location is important in migrations with vMotion, because it affects vMotion performance. For example, in migrations between ESX/ESXi 4.0 and newer hosts, if the swap file is located in a different location on the destination host, the swap file must be copied to this new location. This can slow down vMotion operations.

The virtual machine swap file location can be configured in up to three separate locations. These locations are the cluster, host, and virtual machine. Exercise 9.3 shows the steps to configure the virtual machine swap file location for each of these locations. We will begin by setting the swap file location at the cluster level and will then change the swap file location on an ESXi host that is a member of the cluster. Finally, a virtual machine will have its swap file location modified.

EXERCISE 9.3

Configuring the Virtual Machine Swap File Location

1. Connect to a vCenter Server with the vSphere Web Client.

2. Select an ESXi host that is a member of a cluster from the left pane. Select the Manage tab in the middle pane, and then select Settings from the toolbar.

3. Ensure that the Virtual Machines menu is expanded on the left, and then select the Swap File Location option.

4. Review the information for Swap File Location. Note that the Edit button is grayed out.

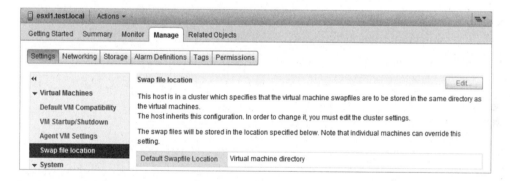

Also note that the default configuration is for the cluster to define the virtual machine swap file location.

5. Select the cluster that this ESXi host is a member of in the left pane and right-click it. Select Settings from the context menu.

6. Select the Manage tab in the middle pane, and then select Settings from the toolbar.

7. Ensure that the Configuration option is expanded on the left, and then select General. Review the information about Swap File Location.

8. Click the Edit button to the right of Swap File Location. An Edit Cluster Settings window will open.

EXERCISE 9.3 *(continued)*

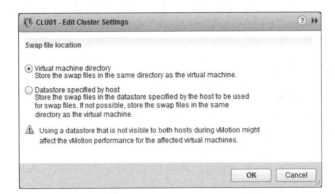

The default, and recommended, setting is to store the swap file in the same directory as the virtual machine.

9.   In the Edit Cluster Settings window, select Datastore Specified By The Host and click OK.

10. A Reconfigure Cluster task will begin.

You have changed the virtual machine swap file location for the cluster. The ESXi hosts will now need to have a datastore configured to store swap files.

11. Select the same ESXi host that was used in step 2 of this exercise and return to Virtual Machine Swapfile Location.

12. Notice that the Edit button is now active. Click it.

13. An Edit Swap File Location window will open.

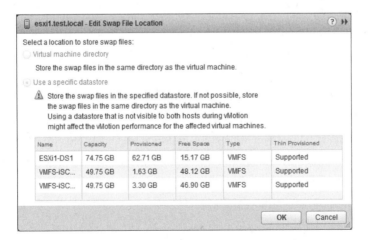

14. Select a datastore and click OK to continue. An Update Local Swap Datastore task will begin.

15. Verify that the Swap File Location setting has been updated to reflect the datastore you just selected. You might need to refresh the screen.

The virtual machine swap file location has now been configured at the ESXi host level. In the next set of steps, we will verify that this change works as expected.

16. Locate a powered-off virtual machine that is both a member of the cluster and is located on the ESXi host used in the previous steps.

17. On the virtual machine's Summary tab, locate the datastore listed in the Related Objects panel.

18. Ensure that this datastore is not the same one that you just selected in step 14 of this exercise. If it is, use another VM or migrate the currently selected VM to a different datastore before proceeding.

19. Power on the virtual machine. Note in the Related Objects panel that the datastore configured in step 14 of this exercise is now listed as an additional datastore.

20. Click this datastore in the Related Objects panel. On the Manage tab in the middle pane, ensure Files is selected on the toolbar.

21. The virtual machine's swap file will be listed in the root of the datastore, as shown here:

You will now change the virtual machine's individual swap file location setting. This setting will override the swap file location setting specified at either the ESXi host or cluster level.

22. Right-click the virtual machine and choose Edit Settings from the context menu.

23. Click VM Options in the toolbar and then expand the Advanced Settings option.

24. Change the Swap File Location setting to Virtual Machine Directory.

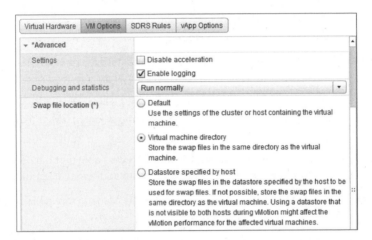

25. Click OK to save these changes. A Reconfigure Virtual Machine task will begin.

26. Power on the virtual machine again.

27. Note in the Resources pane that the datastore configured in step 14 is no longer listed.

28. Click the remaining datastore in the Related Objects panel. On the Manage tab in the middle pane, ensure that Files is selected on the toolbar.

29. The virtual machine's swap file will be listed in the root of the virtual machine's working location, as shown here:

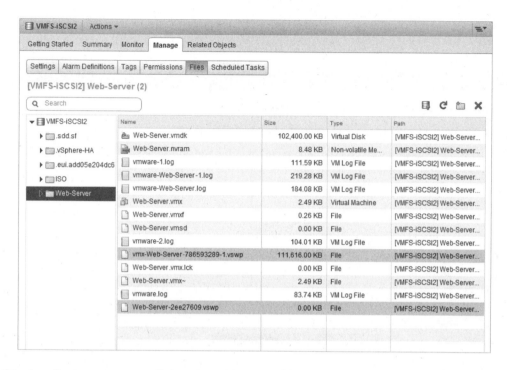

30. As a final step, restore all virtual machine swap file location settings to their defaults, which are the recommended settings from VMware.

ESXi 5 and newer hosts create a second swap file known as VMX Swap (vmx-...vswp) for VMs with virtual machine hardware version 7 or newer. The goal is to reduce the memory footprint of the VMX process and ultimately help conserve physical memory resources in the ESXi host. The VMX Swap file is by default created in the virtual machine's working directory and can only be changed by adding an advanced configuration parameter to the VM.

Now that you have seen how to configure the virtual machine swap file location, let's migrate powered-on virtual machines using vMotion and Storage vMotion.

Migrating Virtual Machines Using vMotion/ Storage vMotion

Migrating virtual machines with vMotion is a relatively simple operational task. Most virtual infrastructure administrators have surely performed a migration with vMotion, as

VMware reports that 80 percent of its customers have vMotion in use in production environments. Exercise 9.4 covers the steps to migrate a powered-on virtual machine with vMotion.

EXERCISE 9.4

Migrating a Virtual Machine with vMotion

1. Connect to a vCenter Server with the vSphere Web Client.

2. Locate a powered-on virtual machine in the left pane and select it. Make a note of which ESXi host this VM is running on.

3. Right-click the virtual machine and choose Migrate from the context menu. The Migrate window will open.

4. Select the Change Host option and click Next.

5. Select a cluster and click the Allow Host Selection Within This Cluster check box.

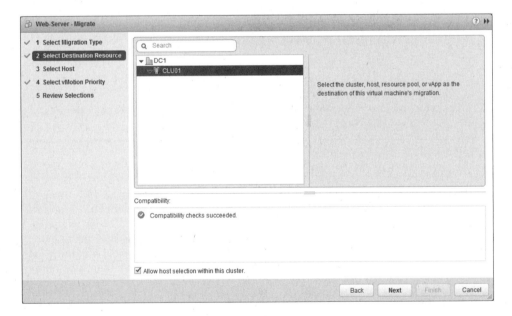

6. Click Next, and then select a different ESXi host than the one the VM is currently residing on. Ensure that the Compatibility checks succeed.

7. Accept the default and recommended vMotion priority of Reserve CPU For Optimal vMotion Performance (Recommended).

   The Perform With Available CPU Resources option can be useful if the environment is currently CPU-constrained.

8. Click Next and review your selections.

9. Click Finish.

10. A Relocate Virtual Machine task will begin. When this task completes, verify that the Host value in the Related Objects panel on the virtual machine's Summary tab has been changed.

Like using vMotion to migrate a running VM, migrating a virtual machine using Storage vMotion is also a relatively simple task. Exercise 9.5 covers the steps to migrate a virtual machine with Storage vMotion.

EXERCISE 9.5

Migrating a Virtual Machine with Storage vMotion

1. Connect to a vCenter Server with the vSphere Web Client.

2. Locate a powered-on virtual machine in the left pane and select it. Make a note of which datastore the VM currently resides on.

3. Right-click the virtual machine and choose Migrate from the context menu. The Migrate window will open.

4. Select the Change Datastore option and click Next.

5. Select a different datastore than the one the VM is currently residing on. Choose the Same Format As Source option for Virtual Disk Format. Verify that Compatibility Checks Succeeded appears in the Compatibility field.

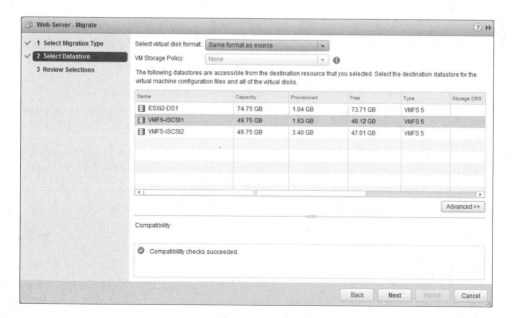

6. Click Next and review your selections.

7. Click Finish.

8. A Relocate Virtual Machine task will begin. When this task completes, verify that the Storage value in the Related Objects panel on the virtual machine's Summary tab has been changed to reflect the datastore you chose in step 5 of this exercise.

You can use additional advanced options with the Migrate wizard when you're migrating a virtual machine to a new datastore. The next section covers these advanced options.

Using Storage vMotion Techniques

The advanced options available when performing a migration using Storage vMotion can allow the virtual disk format to be changed, a storage profile to be changed, and disks and configuration files to be divided into separate datastores.

One of the more helpful options available is to rename a virtual machine in the vSphere Web Client and then cold-migrate or Storage vMotion it to another datastore. This procedure will update both the virtual machine directory and filenames to match that of the VM, once the migration is complete.

Exercise 9.6 demonstrates the advanced options that can be used to migrate a virtual machine with Storage vMotion. To simplify this exercise, use a virtual machine that has a single virtual disk assigned to it.

Performing a Storage vMotion with Advanced Techniques

1. Connect to a vCenter Server with the vSphere Web Client.

2. Locate a powered-on virtual machine in the left pane and select it. Right-click this VM and choose Edit Settings from the context menu.

3. The Edit Settings window will open. Expand Hard Disk 1, and review the Type information to determine the disk provisioning type. You will need this information later in this exercise.

   The disk type will be reported as either Thin Provision, Thick Provision Lazy Zeroed, or Thick Provision Eager Zeroed.

4. Click the Cancel button to close the Edit Settings window.

5. Right-click the virtual machine and choose Migrate from the context menu.

6. Select the Change Datastore option and click Next.

7. To access the advanced options, click the Advanced button located toward the middle-right side of the window. The view will change and look similar to this:

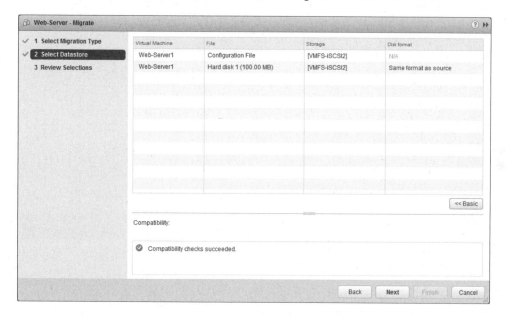

8. Select the virtual disk file by clicking it. Click in the Disk Format column in the highlighted row to access a drop-down menu.

9. Change the virtual disk format to a different type than what was shown in step 3 of this exercise.

Setting this option will change the virtual disk format as part of the migration. Note that the configuration file is listed as N/A, since it is a VMX file and not a VMDK file.

10. Click in the Storage column in the highlighted row to access a drop-down menu. Select the Browse option from the menu. The Select A Datastore Cluster Or Datastore window will open. Select a datastore that is different from the datastore location of the virtual disk file. Click OK. The final configuration should appear similar to this:

EXERCISE 9.6 *(continued)*

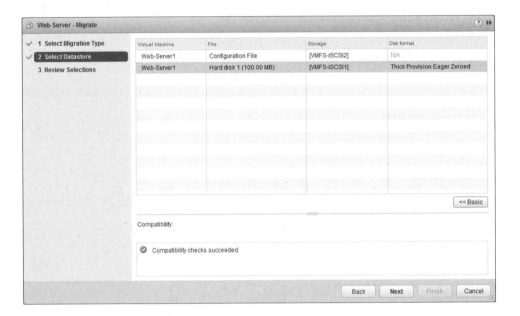

11. Click Next and review your selections.

12. Click Finish.

13. A Relocate Virtual Machine task will begin.

14. When this task completes, verify that the Storage value in the Related Objects panel on the virtual machine's Summary tab has been changed to reflect both the original datastore and the datastore you chose in step 10 of this exercise.

15. Browse each datastore and verify that the contents are as expected.

 Changing the virtual disk format with NFS servers may not always be possible. If the NFS server supports the *VAAI NAS extensions* that enable reserve space, then thick-provisioned disks on NFS are possible. If not, the option to change virtual disk formats will be grayed out.

In the next section of this chapter, we will leave migration behind and begin to look at backing up and restoring virtual machines.

Backing Up and Restoring Virtual Machines

As a VMware Certified Professional, you will be expected to know how to back up and restore virtual machines. Another common operational task that virtual infrastructure administrators must know is how and when to use VMware snapshots. In this section, I will cover snapshots, backups, replication and how to determine appropriate backup solutions.

Identifying Snapshot Requirements

Snapshots are used in vSphere to preserve state and data in a virtual machine. A virtual machine snapshot will preserve the following:

- Virtual machine settings
- Power state
- Disk state
- Memory state (optional)

Snapshots are very useful for short-term protection from changes made to a virtual machine. For example, a virtual machine can be placed in snapshot mode prior to software upgrades, operating system updates, or any virtual machine configuration changes. If the upgrade, update, or other change were to fail or otherwise be found unsuitable, then the virtual machine could be quickly and easily returned to its previous state. The key thing to remember with VMware snapshots is that they are intended for short-term use only. They are not a replacement for backups, and snapshot *delta disks* alone may not be used as backups.

To better understand why snapshots are not suitable replacements for backups, it helps to understand how snapshots work. When a snapshot is taken, a delta disk is created for the virtual disk(s) in the virtual machine. This delta disk is used for all disk writes, since the original VMDK file is placed in read-only mode to preserve its state. If the memory is also preserved in the snapshot, then the VMSN file will also contain the memory and power state. These delta disks are also referred to as *differencing* disks, and they contain only the differences between the current state and the original virtual disk or parent snapshot (if multiple snapshots are being used). This is why snapshot files cannot be used as backups. Another important thing to understand about delta disks is that they expand with each disk write and can grow to the provisioned size of the original virtual disk plus some overhead. Know that there is also a performance penalty when using snapshots. This penalty will depend on the workload, the number of snapshots used, and the duration of the snapshot(s).

Taking a snapshot will create VMDK and VMSN files. These files are detailed in Table 7.3 in Chapter 7.

When used with VMware Tools, snapshots also provide the ability to provide varying degrees of consistency for powered-on virtual machines running certain versions of the Window OS. Table 9.2 shows these abilities.

TABLE 9.2   VM snapshot consistency abilities

Guest OS	VMware Tools driver	Consistency
Windows XP 32-bit Windows 2000 32-bit	Sync Driver	File-system consistent
Windows Vista 32-bit/64-bit Windows 7 32-bit/64-bit	VMware VSS	File-system consistent
Windows 2003 32-bit/64-bit	VMware VSS	Application consistent
Windows 2008 32-bit/64-bit Windows 2008 R2	VMware VSS	Application consistent
Windows 8 32-bit/64-bit	VMware VSS	Application consistent
Windows 2012	VMware VSS	Application consistent

Windows 2008 and later snapshots will be application consistent only when the following conditions are met:

- ESX 4.1 or newer hosts are used.
- The UUID attribute is enabled.
- SCSI disks are used in the virtual machine.
- Basic disks are used. (Dynamic disks are not supported.)

VMware Tools provides drivers to allow running applications to have their I/O paused during snapshot operations. This feature, also known as *quiescing*, can be used to ensure at least some level of consistency for virtual machines that will have snapshots applied. Most backup applications leverage snapshots as part of image-level backups of virtual machines. The level of consistency achieved will vary, and it is extremely important to understand your workloads, their VSS support capability, and their specific behaviors when using them with virtual machines that will use snapshots. Just as you would with backup jobs, you will always want to test the consistency of applications when used with powered-on virtual machine snapshots. I will revisit consistency at the conclusion of this section on backups.

In addition to understanding how snapshots work, you should be aware of several restrictions when using snapshots:

- Raw disks, physical compatibility mode RDM disks, or *iSCSI initiators* being used inside a guest OS, are not supported.

- PCI vSphere Direct Path I/O devices are not supported.

 Snapshots have overheads associated with them. For more information on these overheads, see http://kb.vmware.com/kb/1012384.

Now that you are familiar with snapshots and the requirements for using them, we can move on to creating, deleting, and consolidating virtual machine snapshots.

Creating, Deleting, and Consolidating Virtual Machine Snapshots

Creating snapshots is a simple operation that can best be explained with an exercise. Exercise 9.7 covers the steps to create and revert to a snapshot.

EXERCISE 9.7

Creating a VM Snapshot and Then Reverting to It

1. Connect to a vCenter Server with the vSphere Web Client.

2. Select a powered-on virtual machine that has VMware Tools installed from the left pane and right-click it. Choose Take Snapshot from the context menu.

3. A Take VM Snapshot window will open. Provide the snapshot with a descriptive name and description.

4. Deselect the Snapshot The Virtual Machine's Memory option.

5. Ensure that the Quiesce Guest File System (Needs VMware Tools Installed) option is selected.

EXERCISE 9.7 *(continued)*

6. Click OK to create the snapshot. A Create Virtual Machine Snapshot task will begin.

7. When this task completes, right-click the VM and choose Manage Snapshots from the context menu. A Manage VM Snapshots window will open.

8. Review the information shown in the Manage VM Snapshots window, and then click the Close button in this window.

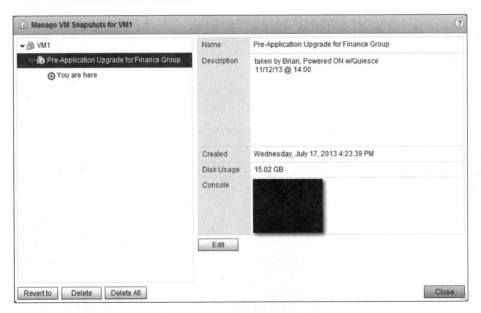

A snapshot has now been created for this virtual machine. In the next part of this exercise, you will make changes to both the virtual machine configuration and the guest OS filesystem.

9. Open the console to the virtual machine and create a directory on the root file system. Name this directory *SNAPSHOT*.

10. Edit the virtual machine's settings and click the VM Options tab.

11. Expand the Boot Options option.

12. Select the Force BIOS Setup check box.

13. Click OK and wait for the Reconfigure Virtual Machine task to complete.

In the remainder of the exercise, assume that the changes made to this VM were unsuccessful and that you would now like to return the virtual machine to its prior state.

14. Right-click the VM again and choose Revert To Latest Snapshot from the context menu.

A dialog box will appear prompting you to confirm this action.

15. Click Yes to revert to the current snapshot.

16. A Revert Snapshot task will begin. When this task completes, open the console of the virtual machine. Verify that the directory created in step 9 is not there.

17. Edit the virtual machine's settings and click the VM Options tab.

18. Expand the Boot Options option.

19. Verify that the Force BIOS Setup option is no longer selected.

20. Right-click the VM and choose the Manage Snapshots option from the context menu. Verify that the snapshot taken in step 2 of this exercise still exists.

You have now seen how to create a snapshot for a powered-on virtual machine and covered how to revert to the snapshot. Exercise 9.8 covers the steps to delete this snapshot.

EXERCISE 9.8

Deleting a Virtual Machine Snapshot

1. Connect to a vCenter Server with the vSphere Web Client.

2. Open the console of the virtual machine used in the previous exercise and create a directory on the root filesystem. Name this directory *SNAPSHOT*.

3. Edit the virtual machine's settings and click the VM Options tab.

4. Expand the Boot Options option.

5. Select the Force BIOS Setup check box.

6. Click OK and wait for the Reconfigure Virtual Machine task to complete.

   These are essentially the same steps performed in the previous exercise, but this time you should assume that the changes made to this VM were successful. The remainder of this exercise will cover the steps to commit the current state of the virtual machine by deleting the snapshot.

7. Right-click the virtual machine and choose Manage Snapshots from the context menu.

8. A Manage VM Snapshots window will open. Verify that the snapshot from the previous exercise is listed and selected.

9. Click the Delete button at the bottom of the Manage VM Snapshots window.

   A Confirm Delete window will prompt you to confirm this action.

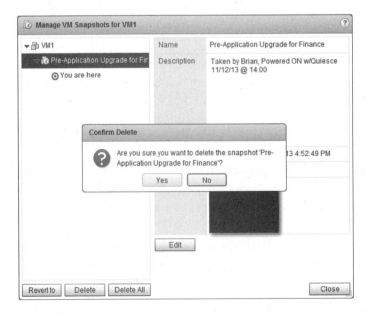

10. Click Yes to delete the snapshot.

11. A Remove Snapshot task will begin. Wait for this task to complete, and do not close the Manage VM Snapshots window.

12. When the Remove Snapshot task completes, verify that the snapshot is no longer listed in the Manage VM Snapshots window. Close the Manage VM Snapshots window.

    Deleting the snapshot will commit the current state of the virtual machine. The remainder of this exercise will verify that the changes made to the virtual machine were committed successfully.

13. Open the console of the virtual machine and verify that the SNAPSHOT directory exists on the root filesystem.

14. Edit the virtual machine's settings and click the VM Options tab.

15. Expand the Boot Options option.

16. Verify that the Force BIOS Setup option is selected.

You have now deleted a snapshot for a powered-on virtual machine. If the delete operation is successful, no further action is required. In most cases, snapshot commit operations work as expected, but there can sometimes be problems. For example, there might be inadequate datastore free space during a snapshot commit. In the past, these failed operations required either workarounds with new snapshots and the Delete All option in Snapshot Manager or placing support calls to VMware. One of the features introduced with vSphere 5 was the Consolidate option for snapshots. Consolidation essentially provides a way to notify virtual infrastructure administrators of this failed commit condition and provide a method to handle any failed snapshot commits. If a snapshot commit operation fails, a message will appear on the virtual machine's Summary tab, as shown in Figure 9.1.

FIGURE 9.1   Snapshot consolidation warning

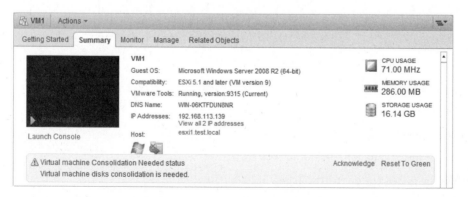

Exercise 9.9 covers the steps to consolidate virtual machine snapshots. This exercise will use Windows PowerShell and the vSphere *PowerCLI* to create the consolidate condition.

EXERCISE 9.9

Consolidating Virtual Machine Snapshots

1. Connect to a vCenter Server with the vSphere Web Client.

2. Locate a powered-on virtual machine and take a snapshot of it.

    You have now created a snapshot of the virtual machine. In the following steps, you will install the vSphere PowerCLI. The PowerCLI will be used to force a snapshot consolidate condition.

3. Ensure that you have Windows PowerShell v2 or v3 on the system that the vSphere PowerCLI will be installed on.

4. Download version 5.5 or newer of the vSphere PowerCLI from

    `https://my.vmware.com/web/vmware/details?productId=352&`
    `downloadGroup=PCLI550`

5. Once the download completes, launch the setup file.

6. A dialog box may appear stating that the VMware VIX will be installed automatically. If so, click OK to continue.

    You may also receive a message about the PowerShell execution policy, as shown here:

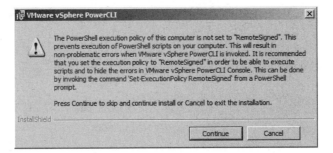

7. Review this information and then click Continue.

8. On the vSphere PowerCLI Welcome screen, click Next to begin.

9. Click Next on the Patents screen.

10. Accept the terms of the license agreement and click Next.

11. Choose the destination folder and click Next.

12. Click the Install button to install the vSphere PowerCLI.

13. When the installation completes, click Finish.

14. Using the newly created VMware vSphere PowerCLI icon on the Windows Desktop, launch the vSphere PowerCLI.

The first thing that needs to be addressed is the execution policy. This was pointed out by the installer in step 6 of this exercise. In the following steps, you will set the PowerShell execution policy to require that downloaded scripts and configuration files be signed. This is a security feature of PowerShell.

15. When the vSphere PowerCLI opens, enter the following command:

```
Set-ExecutionPolicy RemoteSigned
```

This command will change the ExecutionPolicy from its default setting of Restricted to RemoteSigned. Here's the command you'd use to find out the current setting:

```
Get-ExecutionPolicy
```

16. Review the information and then press the Y key. Press Enter to continue.

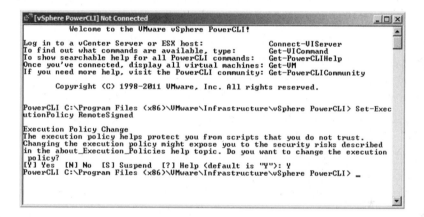

Now that the execution policy is set, you will use the vSphere PowerCLI to remove the snapshot but not commit the changes. This will result in a condition where consolidation is needed. Note that the following steps would be used only to simulate this exact condition.

17. Type the following command to connect to the vCenter Server used in step 1 of this exercise:

```
Connect-VIServer
```

18. At the Server[0] prompt, enter the FQDN of the vCenter Server and press Enter. At the Server[1] prompt, press Enter.

19. In the login dialog that opens, enter valid credentials for the vCenter Server.

20. Type the following command, replacing *<VM-Name>* with the name of the virtual machine used in step 2 of this exercise:

```
$VM = get-VM <VM_Name> | Get-View
```

21. Enter the following command to remove the snapshot but leave the delta disks:

    `$VM.RemoveAllSnapshots(0)`

22. Right-click the VM and choose Manage Snapshots from the context menu. Verify that the snapshot taken in step 2 of this exercise is no longer listed.

23. Browse the datastore that the virtual machine is located in, and confirm that there are still delta disks present for this virtual machine.

    You have now simulated a failed snapshot commit. In the remaining steps of this exercise, you will use the Consolidate function to clean up the delta disks that were left behind. This is the important part of this exercise, because all of the previous steps only created the error condition.

24. Locate the virtual machine that you have been working with in the left pane and select it. In the VM's Summary tab, review the warnings about disk consolidation.

25. Right-click the virtual machine and choose All vCenter Actions ➤ Snapshots ➤ Consolidate.

26. A Confirm Consolidate window will appear. Click the Yes button to continue.

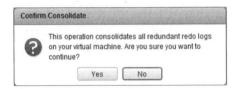

27. A Consolidate Virtual Machine Disk Files task will begin. When this task completes, verify that the message on the virtual machine's Summary tab is no longer present. You might need to refresh the screen.

28. Right-click the VM and choose Manage Snapshots from the context menu. Confirm that no snapshots are listed.

29. Open the datastore browser and navigate to the virtual machine's directory. Verify that the delta disk files have been removed.

In a real consolidation scenario, always investigate the virtual machine's datastore(s) to ensure that adequate free space is available before performing the consolidation operation.

As the discussion on snapshots ends, remember that snapshots are not intended to provide a backup solution. Fortunately, VMware provides a backup and recovery product known as VMware Data Protection.

Differentiating Between VDP and VDPA

VMware Data Protection is a disk-based backup and recovery solution that is included in all editions of vSphere except for Essentials. VMware Data Protection is based on EMC Avamar technology and automatically deduplicates backup job data to deduplication stores sized from 500GB to a maximum of 8TB.

Three components make up the VMware Data Protection solution:

- vCenter Server
- VDP Appliance
- vSphere Web Client

VMware Data Protection is available in two tiers, known as Basic and Advanced. These two tiers are more commonly referred to as VDP and VDP Advanced. While basic VDP functionality is included in all editions of vSphere, with the exception of the Essentials version, the Advanced tier requires a license key. These keys can be purchased separately or as part of certain vSphere kits, like the vSphere with Operations Management Enterprise and Enterprise Plus acceleration kits. Table 9.3 lists the feature sets available with each tier of the VMware Data Protection product.

TABLE 9.3   VDP feature set comparison

Feature	VDP	VDP Advanced
VMs supported per VDP Appliance	up to 100	up to 400
Maximum deployed size	2 TB	8 TB
Support for image-level backups	Yes	Yes
Support for individual disk backups	Yes	Yes
Support for image-level restore jobs	Yes	Yes
Support for image-level replication jobs	Yes	Yes
Support for direct to host recovery	Yes	Yes
Support for detachable data partitions	Yes	Yes
Support for file level recovery (FLR)	Yes	Yes
Support for application-level replication	No	Yes
Ability to expand current datastore	No	Yes

TABLE 9.3 VDP feature set comparison *(continued)*

Feature	VDP	VDP Advanced
Support for backup to a Data Domain system	No	Yes
Granular restore on Microsoft Servers	No	Yes
Automatic backup verification (ABV) support	No	Yes
Support for guest-level backups and restores of Microsoft SQL Servers, Exchange Servers, and SharePoint Servers	No	Yes

As you can probably gather from the table, VMware states that VDP Advanced is designed for vSphere environments of several hundred VMs. VDP Advanced is also much more likely to be able to meet all of a vSphere environment's backup needs. This could be beneficial for environments that want to use a single backup and recovery solution.

 VDP can be upgraded to VDP Advanced, but there is no backward path for VDP Advanced to be downgraded. Also be aware that with standard VDP, the deployed size cannot be changed.

Now that the differences between VDP and VDP Advanced have been covered, let's discuss sizing the VDP implementation.

Explaining VMware Data Protection Sizing Guidelines

Properly sizing the deduplication datastores is an important consideration when deploying VDP. As you will see later in this chapter in Exercise 9.10, VDP is deployed as an open virtualization application (OVA) with the destination datastores already attached. The datastore size chosen will ultimately depend on a variety of factors, including:

- The number of VMs being backed up
- The initial size of the VMs to be backed up
- The number of different OS types in the VMs
- The number of different types of workloads in the VMs
- The amount of daily I/O being generated
- The chosen retention periods for the VM data
- The anticipated growth rate for the vSphere environment

VMware states that on average 1TB of VDP datastore capacity can provide support for up to 25 virtual machines, but results will certainly vary across different vSphere environments. Because of the way unique data is added to deduplicated VDP datastores, it is also important to group similar backups together. For example, the initial backup of two

Windows Server 2012 virtual machines deployed from the same template in vCenter Server will require significantly less space on the VDP datastore than a Windows Server 2012 VM and a Linux Ubuntu 13.04 VM. Subsequent backups of any VMs will be made more efficient through the use of Changed Block Tracking (CBT) functionality and should result in less datastore consumption.

Also keep in mind some of the limitations associated with VDP, when sizing it for your vSphere environment.

- vCenter Server can support up to 10 VDP appliances.

- Only 1 VDP appliance can be deployed per ESXi host.

- Each VDP appliance supports backing up 100 VMs.

- Each VDP Advanced appliance supports backing up 400 VMs.

- Each VDP appliance can back up a maximum of 8 VMs simultaneously.

- VDP appliances operate independently of each other.

- Independent virtual disks are not supported.

- Physical compatibility mode RDMs are not supported

- Independent virtual compatibility mode RDMs are not supported

- VMs larger than 2TB that run Windows operating systems are not supported for backup with VDP.

- VMs with special characters in their names cannot be added to any VDP backup job. The following characters cannot be used: ~ ! @ $ ^ % ( ) { } [ ] | , ` # \ / : * ? < > ' "& â é ì ü ñ

VMware recommends that if you are uncertain of the VDP datastore capacity requirements, you should deploy a larger VDP appliance. The VDP datastores cannot be resized, so it is better to err on the side of excess in this case. If you run out of space on your VDP datastore, a new VDP appliance would have to be deployed to gain additional capacity.

VDP Advanced allows deduplication datastores to be expanded.

In addition to the VDP sizing, there are system requirements that need to be addressed before deploying VDP.

Identifying VMware Data Protection Requirements

As mentioned earlier in this chapter, VDP has three major components, and there are software requirements around the versions of these components. VDP has the following software requirements:

- vCenter Server: Version 5.1 or 5.5

- vSphere Web Client

- Web browser with Adobe Flash Player 11.3 or newer to access the vSphere Web Client and VDP functionality
- VMware ESX/ESXi (ESX/ESXi 4.0, 4.1, ESXi 5.0, 5.1, 5.5)

VDP 5.1 is not compatible with vCenter 5.5. Always check the VMware Product Interoperability Matrixes for VDP compatibility.

In addition to the software requirements, VDP also has system requirements for the virtual appliances. Since the VDP appliance can be deployed with three deduplication datastore sizes, the requirements vary. The VDP requirements are listed in Table 9.4.

TABLE 9.4 VDP system requirements

	500GB	**1TB**	**2TB**
Processors	Four 2GHz	Four 2GHz	Four 2GHz
Memory	4GB	4GB	4GB
Disk Space	873GB	1600GB	3100GB

The VDP Advanced appliance can be deployed with six deduplication datastore sizes, and the requirements are listed in Table 9.5.

TABLE 9.5 VDP Advanced system requirements

	500GB	**1TB**	**2TB**	**4TB**	**6TB**	**8TB**
Processors	Four 2GHz	Four 2GHz	Four 2GHz	Four 2GHz	Four 2GHz	Four 2GHz
Memory	4GB	4GB	6GB	8GB	10GB	12GB
Disk Space	873GB	1600GB	3TB	6TB	9TB	12TB

There are additional pre-installation requirements for the VDP appliances. These include the following:

- DNS A and PTR records should be created for each VDP appliance.
- Ensure that DNS A and PTR records for vCenter Server are present in the environment.
- VDP appliances obtain their time through VMware Tools, so ESXi hosts and vCenter Server should have the same time source and be configured correctly.

Beyond the system requirements, there are several other general best practices recommended by VMware when deploying VDP.

- Deploy VDP appliances on shared VMFS-5 datastores.
- Utilize virtual machine hardware version 7 or later for all VMs to ensure that Change Block Tracking is used for backups.
- Install VMware Tools in all VMs that will be protected with VDP.
- VMs being backed up must be located in the same datacenter as the VDP appliance.

Now that I have covered the sizing guidelines and system requirements for VDP, let's install and configure it.

Installing and Configuring VMware Data Protection

Installing VMware Data Protection is a very simple task, as the appliances are distributed as OVA files. We first covered deploying OVA files in Chapter 7, and Exercise 9.10 will cover the steps to deploy the VDP appliance.

EXERCISE 9.10

Installing VMware Data Protection

1. Connect to a vCenter Server with the vSphere Web Client.

2. Click the Hosts And Clusters icon.

3. Locate a datacenter object from the inventory in the left pane and right-click on it. Select the Deploy OVF Template option from the context menu.

4. A Client Integration Access Control window will open. Click Allow.

5. Click the Browse button to select the downloaded VDP .ova file and then click Next.

6. Review the OVF Template Details and click Next.

EXERCISE 9.10 *(continued)*

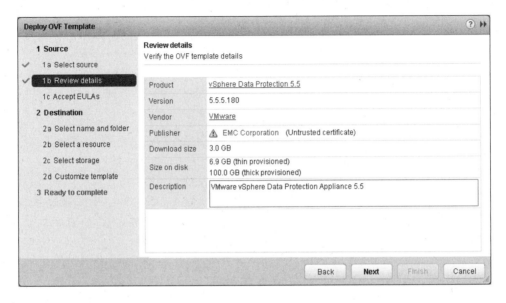

7. Accept the End User License Agreement and click Next.

8. Provide a name and select a location for the VDP Appliance. Click Next.

9. Select a cluster, host, vApp, or resource pool in which to run the deployed template and then click Next.

10. Select a virtual disk format and a datastore for the VDP appliance and click Next.

11. Select a network for the VDP appliance and then click Next.

12. The VDP Appliance does not support DHCP. Provide a gateway, DNS, IP address and Subnet Mask for the VDP appliance and then click Next.

13. Review the information presented on the Ready To Complete screen and place a check in the Power On After Deployment option. Click Finish.

14. Wait for the OVA to deploy and then open a console session and verify that the appliance boots successfully.

Now that the VDP appliance has been deployed, it will need to be configured before use. Exercise 9.11 will cover the steps to configure VDP.

EXERCISE 9.11

Configuring VMware Data Protection

1. Open a web browser and connect to the following URL:

    `https://<VDP-Appliance-IP-Address>:8543/vdp-configure/`

2. Login with username **root** and the password **changeme**. The VDP Configuration Wizard will be presented upon successful login.

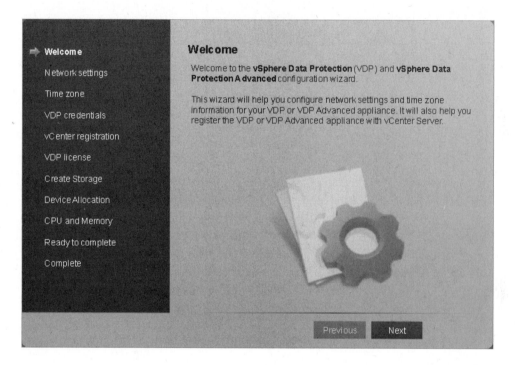

3. Click Next to begin.

4. Review the network settings and make any changes necessary. Click Next to continue. If you have not properly set up DNS A and PTR records for the VDP appliance, you will likely run into issues here.

5. Select your time zone and click Next to continue.

6. Enter a universal configuration password for the VDP appliance. Once all password requirements have been met, click Next to continue.

7. Enter the administrative credentials that will be used to register the VDP appliance with vCenter Server. If the vCenter Server username is a domain account it must be entered in the DOMAIN\USERNAME format, or you will run into issues with recent VDP tasks not displaying properly.

8. Enter the vCenter Server FQDN or IP address and modify the port number if necessary. Leave the Use vCenter For SSO Authentication option checked, if vCenter Server and vCenter SSO are installed on the same server. Remove the check from this option to specify a different vCenter SSO server. The final configuration should look similar to this:

9. You must click the Test Connection button to verify connectivity, before clicking Next to continue.

10. Click Next on the VDP Advanced license step.

11. Using the Create New Storage option, select the size of the deduplication datastore that will be created for this VDP appliance. Keep in mind the VDP system requirements discussed earlier in this chapter. Click Next.

12. In the Device Allocation step, choose where to store the VDP deduplication datastore you sized in the previous step. Also review the Provision menu options for the virtual disk format.

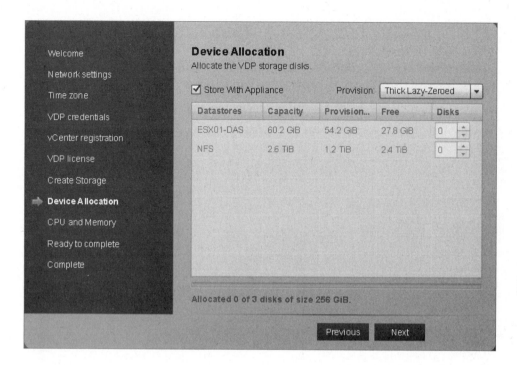

13. Click Next to continue. Review the vCPU and RAM amounts presented and click Next.

14. Review the information presented in the Ready To Complete step and decide whether or not to run the performance analysis. Note that the performance analysis could take 30 minutes to several hours to complete. Click Next. A Warning dialog will open. Review this information and click Yes.

15. Watch the VDP configuration progress as it is displayed on the Ready To Complete window.

16. When the configuration is complete, a VDP Configuration Completed window will open. Click Restart Now.

17. Open a console window for the VDP appliance and wait patiently for the Quickstart Guide to appear on the VDP appliance console. This process will take 30 minutes or more to complete.

18. Open a web browser and connect to the following URL:

    ```
    https://<VDP-Appliance-IP-Address>:8543/vdp-configure/
    ```

EXERCISE 9.11 *(continued)*

19. Login with the username **root** and the password you created in Step 6 of this exercise.

20. Review the information on the Status tab and then click the Storage tab.

21. Review the storage configuration of the VDP appliance.

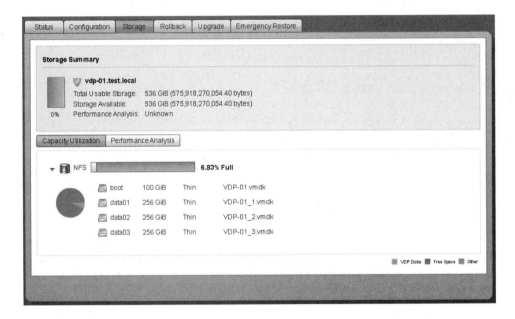

22. Review the other tabs available and then click Logout.

23. Log in to the vSphere Web Client and verify that vSphere Data Protection 5.5 is listed in the left pane.

24. Select vSphere Data Protection 5.5 in the left pane.

25. Use the VDP Appliance drop-down menu to select the VDP appliance you have been working with in this exercise and click the Connect button.

26. Verify that you can successfully connect to the VDP appliance.

Now that the VDP appliance has been installed and configured, you are ready to start backing up VMs with it.

Creating a Backup Job With VMware Data Protection

Backup jobs can be created using the VMware Data Protection user interface available in the vSphere Web Client. These backup jobs can specify the virtual machine(s), the schedule, and the retention period. Exercise 9.12 covers the steps to create a backup job with VMware Data Protection. For this exercise, choose a VM with a Windows guest OS with VMware Tools installed. This virtual machine will be used in additional exercises in this chapter.

EXERCISE 9.12

Creating a Backup Job With VDP

1. Connect to a vCenter Server with the vSphere Web Client.

2. Select vSphere Data Protection 5.5 in the left pane.

3. Use the VDP Appliance drop down menu to select the VDP appliance you have been working with in the previous exercises and click the Connect button.

4. On the Getting Started tab, under the list of Basic Tasks, click Create Backup Job. A Create A New Backup Job window will open.

5. Select the Full Image option and click Next to continue.

EXERCISE 9.12 *(continued)*

6. Expand the tree view to view most of your inventory objects. Select a data center or cluster inventory object and note that all of its contents become selected.

7. Click Clear All Selections to remove all selections.

8. Select a single virtual machine, as shown in the following image.

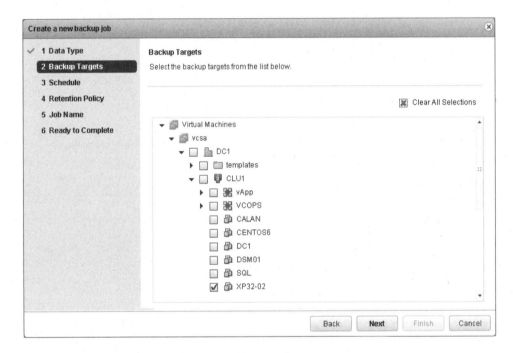

9. Click Next to continue.

10. Review the Schedule options. The following image shows the options available.

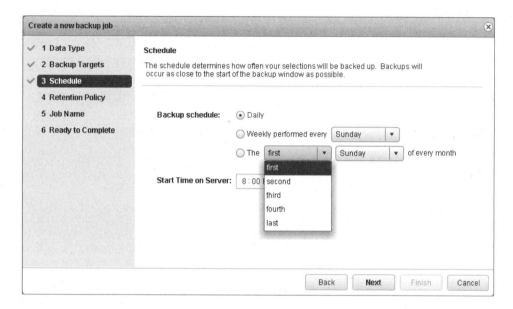

11. Select Daily for the Backup Schedule and select a Start Time. Click Next to continue.

12. Review the Retention Policy settings and then click Next to accept the default setting of 60 Days.

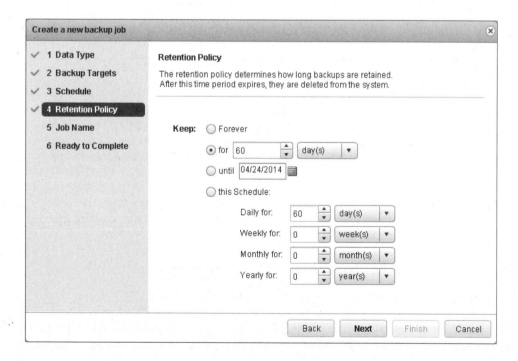

EXERCISE 9.12 *(continued)*

13. Provide a descriptive job name and click Next. The special characters blank ( ), dash (-), underscore (_) and period (.) are the only ones allowed to be used in job names.

14. Review the information on the Ready To Complete screen and click Finish to create the backup job.

15. Wait for an Info window to open that reports the backup job was created successfully. Click OK.

16. Click the Backup tab and verify that the new job is listed.

17. Click the Backup Job Actions menu to view the available options.

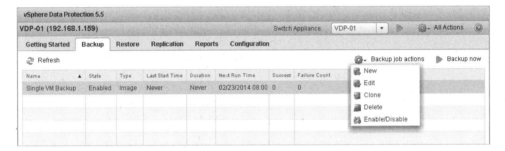

18. Click Backup Now and select Backup All Sources from the menu.

19. Review the activity in the Recent Tasks pane and click the Refresh button on the Backup tab to monitor the backup job.

 Remember that VDP deduplication stores are much more efficient when backing up similar VMs. Placing similar VMs in folders and then selecting the entire folder for backup is an effective strategy. An added bonus is that selecting a folder will also allow any new VM placed in the folder to be backed up automatically.

You have now backed up a virtual machine and sizing the VDP implementation was discussed earlier in this chapter. Next I will cover how your sizing decisions and backups meet and how this can lead to the need to monitor VDP capacity.

Managing and Monitoring VDP Capacity

VDP deduplication datastores tend to fill rapidly, as the first full download is created of each VM being backed up. This is due to the fact that each initial full backup will contain a given amount of unique data. As additional backups are performed of similar VMs the deduplication datastore usage will be less, as the amount of unique data should decrease.

Regardless of the sizing approach you use, it will always be important to monitor your VDP appliances for capacity issues. Exercise 9.13 will cover steps that can be taken to manage and monitor VDP capacity.

EXERCISE 9.13

Monitoring VDP Capacity

1.   Connect to a vCenter Server with the vSphere Web Client.

2.   Select vSphere Data Protection 5.5 in the left pane.

3.   Use the VDP Appliance drop-down menu to select the VDP appliance you have been working with in the previous exercises and click the Connect button.

4.   Select the Reports tab. Observe the value reported for Used Capacity.

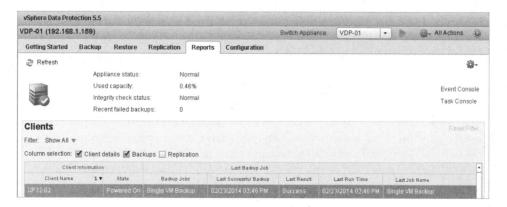

5.   Click the Configuration tab. Observe the values reported in the VDP Appliance Storage Summary panel for Capacity, Space Free, Deduplicated Size, and Non-Deduplicated Size.

6.   Once VDP has been in use for some time, you can also monitor the Alarms pane for VDP events. Check the Alarms pane in the vSphere Web Client now to ensure no VDP entries are listed.

VMware recommends that the optimal value for Used Capacity is 80% and that this value not be exceeded. Once 80% used capacity is exceeded, VDP will issue a warning event. At 95% existing backups are allowed to complete but no new backups will run. At 100% used capacity, VDP will place itself in read-only mode.

In the next section, you will see how to perform both full VM and file-level restores with VDP.

Performing a Test/Live Full/File-Level Restore with VMware Data Protection

Once vSphere Data Protection creates a backup job, restores of the entire virtual machine or individual files are possible. It is also possible to restore a backup to an entirely new virtual machine. File level restores in VDP 5.5 are performed with a web browser, and there are two modes of restore available:

Basic Login   Log in to a virtual machine that has been previously backed up by VDP. Open a web browser and connect to the Restore Client with local Administrative credentials from the guest OS. Only files from this specific virtual machine can be restored.

Advanced Login   Log in to a virtual machine that has been previously backed up by VDP. Open a web browser and connect to the Restore Client with both local Administrative credentials from the guest OS and the administrative credentials that were used to register the VDP Appliance with vCenter Server. Files from this virtual machine or any other virtual machine backed up by the VDP appliance can be browsed and restored.

Exercise 9.14 covers the steps to restore an individual file to a virtual machine. This exercise will use the virtual machine backed up in Exercise 9.12 and will cover a Windows guest OS. VMware Tools must be installed in this guest OS. VMware recommends that Internet Explorer 10 not be used to access the VDP file restore functionality.

EXERCISE 9.14

Restoring Individual Files With VDP

1. Log in to the guest OS on the virtual machine that has been previously backed up with VDP.

2. Open a web browser and connect to the following URL:

    `https://<VDP-Appliance-IP-Address>:8543/flr`

3. Enter the Username and Password of a local administrative user on this guest OS. Click Login.

    If you receive any authentication errors, either try a different web browser or verify that DNS A and PTR records exist for the guest OS.

4. Upon login, a Manage Mounted Backups window will open. Select a backup from the list of All Restore Points. Note the icon to the left of the backup name.

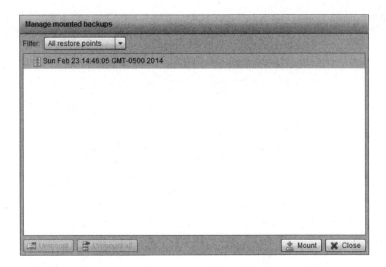

5. Click Mount to continue. The icon to the left of the backup name will now show a green status light. Click Close on the Manage Mounted Backups window.

6. Browse the directory tree in the left pane to select folders. Then select a file from the middle pane.

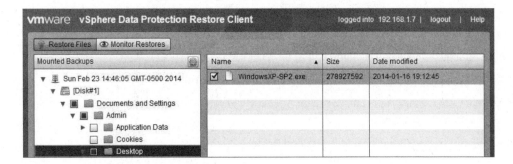

7. Once a file has been selected, click the Restore Selected Files button at the bottom of the screen. A Select Destination window will open.

8. Browse the directory tree to select a location for the file restore. In the following image, a dedicated restores directory was used.

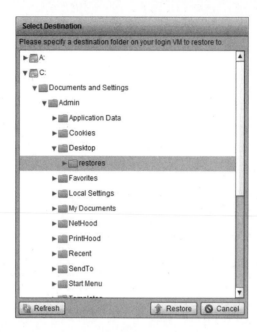

9. Click Restore. An Initiate Restore window will open. Click Yes to begin the file restore.

10. A Successfully Initiated dialog will open. Click OK.

11. Click Monitor Restores in the upper left to view the file restore status.

12. When the restore reports a Status of Success, verify the file has been restored on the guest OS file system.

13. Log out of the vSphere Data Protection Restore Client.

   You have now performed a basic login mode file level restore with VDP. In the remainder of this exercise, you will perform an advanced login mode file level restore.

14. On the vSphere Data Protection Restore Client login page, click the Advanced Login link.

15. In the Local Credentials section, enter the Username and Password of a local administrative user on this guest OS. In the vCenter Credentials section, enter the credentials of the user that registered VDP with vCenter Server.

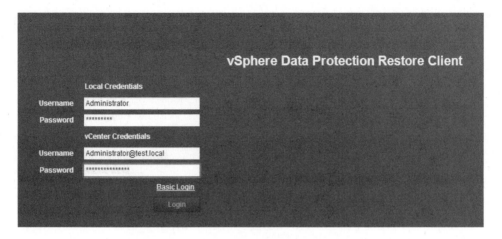

16. Click Login.

17. Upon login, a Manage Mounted Backups window will open. Select a backup from the list of All Restore Points. Note that additional VMs are available to choose from, if your VDP appliance has them available.

18. Click Mount to continue. Click Close on the Manage Mounted Backups window.

19. Click Restore Files and browse the directory tree in the left pane to select folders. Then select a file from the middle pane.

EXERCISE 9.14 *(continued)*

20. Once a file has been selected, click the Restore Selected Files button at the bottom of the screen. A Select Destination window will open.

21. Browse the directory tree to select a location for the file restore.

22. Click Restore. An Initiate Restore window will open. Click Yes to begin the file restore.

23. A Successfully Initiated dialog will open. Click OK.

24. Click Monitor Restores in the upper left to view the file restore status.

25. Wait for the restore to report a Status of Success

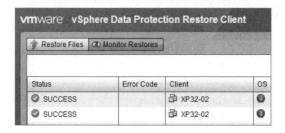

26. Verify the file has been restored on the guest OS file system.

VDP file-level restores for a Windows guest OS with VMware Tools installed have now been covered. While file-level restores may often solve a problem, sometimes an entire virtual machine may need to be restored. Exercise 9.15 covers the steps to restore a virtual machine. This exercise will restore a full virtual machine as a new virtual machine.

 With VDP 5.5 and newer, virtual machines that will be overwritten in a restore operation are not allowed to have snapshots. Failure to remove snapshots for these VMs will result in a failure of the restore.

A VM that has been previously backed up by VDP is required for this exercise.

EXERCISE 9.15

Restoring Full Virtual Machines with VDP

1. Connect to a vCenter Server with the vSphere Web Client.

2. Select vSphere Data Protection 5.5 in the left pane.

3. Use the VDP Appliance drop-down menu to select the VDP appliance you have been working with in this chapter and click the Connect button.

4. Click Restore Backup on the Getting Started tab or simply click the Restore tab.

5. Click a VM in the list to show its backups.

6.   Place a check in the checkbox beside the virtual machine backup name.

7.   Click Restore. A Restore Backup wizard will launch.

8.   Select the backup that will be restored and click Next.

9.   In the Set Restore Options, remove the check from the Restore To Original Location option and then expand the Advanced Options.

10. Provide a different name for the restored VM and verify the destination. Select an appropriate datastore for the restored VM.

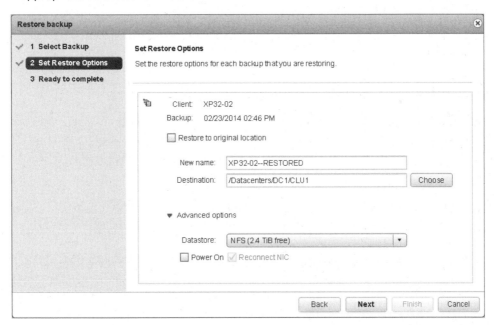

11. Click Next to continue.

12. Review the information presented on the Ready To Complete screen and click Finish.

13. Monitor the restore process from the Recent Tasks pane to verify it completes successfully.

The previous exercise allowed you to restore a backup as a new virtual machine. This functionality is also very useful for testing the restorability of your virtual machine backups, since the original does not have to be overwritten.

I have now covered the steps to restore files and full virtual machines using VMware Data Protection. Next, let's cover migrating data from the legacy VMware Data Recovery appliance into VDP.

Performing a VDR Data Migration

VMware Data Recovery (VDR) was replaced by VDP in vSphere 5.1. To ease the transition, the version of VDP that shipped in vSphere 5.1 includes a data migration tool that allows migration of the VDR restore points (backups) into VDP. Only restore points can be migrated, and jobs have to be recreated in VDP. The version of VDP that ships with vSphere 5.5 does not include this data migration tool. In order to migrate VDR data into VDP 5.5, you must first migrate your VDR data to VDP 5.1.10 and then upgrade it to VDP 5.5. For detailed information on the exact procedures required for a VDR data migration, refer to the following VMware KB article: `http://kb.vmware.com/kb/2051891`.

VMware Data Protection is a powerful feature for creating backups of your virtual machines. In the next section, I will cover another feature in vSphere that is useful for creating replicas of virtual machines.

Describing vSphere Replication Architecture

vSphere Replication was first introduced in vSphere 5.1 with the purpose of providing a native capability to continually replicate running virtual machines to another location. This location can be local, on a different datastore, or at a remote site. vSphere Replication is included in all vSphere editions except Essentials.

vSphere Replication consists of the following components:

vSphere Replication Agent This component is part of the core ESXi installation, and is responsible for sending changed data from powered-on virtual machines that are being replicated.

vSphere Replication Appliance This component contains the vSphere Replication Server and other components used to administer and manage vSphere Replication. It is paired with a single vCenter Server, and is also responsible for receiving data sent from the vSphere Replication agent.

Up to 10 vSphere Replication virtual appliances can be deployed per vCenter Server to provide load balancing and increased throughput. vSphere Replication is designed to perform an initial copy, and then use a virtual machine's changed blocks for subsequent recovery points. The next section covers the installation steps for vSphere Replication.

Installing/Configuring/Upgrading vSphere Replication

Installing the vSphere Replication appliance, which includes a vSphere Replication Server, should be a familiar process by now, as it is distributed in the OVF format. Exercise 9.16 covers the steps to deploy and configure a vSphere Replication appliance.

EXERCISE 9.16

Installing and Configuring vSphere Replication

1. Connect to a vCenter Server with the vSphere Web Client.

2. Click the Hosts And Clusters icon.

3. Locate a cluster object from the inventory in the left pane and right-click on it. Select the Deploy OVF Template option from the context menu.

4. A Client Integration Access Control window will open. Click Allow.

5. In the Deploy OVF Template window, click the Browse button to select the down-loaded vSphere Replication .ovf file. Click Next.

6. Review the OVF Template Details and click Next.

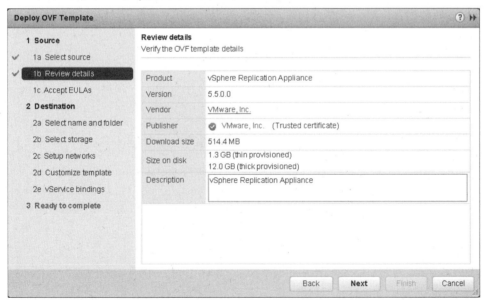

7. Accept the End User License Agreement and click Next.

8. Provide a name and select a location for the vSphere Replication Appliance. Click Next.

9. Select a virtual disk format and a datastore for the vSphere Replication appliance and click Next.

EXERCISE 9.16 *(continued)*

10. Select a Destination network, IP Protocol, and IP Allocation for the VDP appliance. If you choose the IP Allocation of Static - Manual, provide DNS, Gateway and Subnet Mask information.

11. Click Next to continue.

12. In the Customize Template screen, review any invalid values presented. You will likely need to provide an eight-character minimum administrative password and an IP address, if you chose to use a static IP address in step 10.

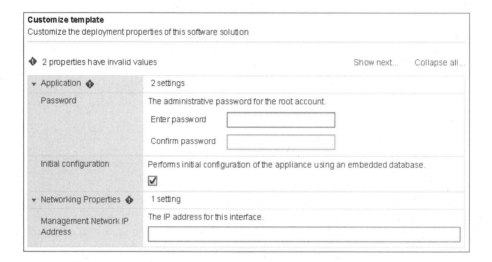

13. Correct any invalid values and click Next.

14. Review the vService Bindings information and verify that the Binding Status shows a green check. Also ensure that the vCenter Server URL listed in the Validation Message is correct. Click Next to continue.

15. Review the information presented on the Ready To Complete screen and place a check in the Power On After Deployment option.

16. Click Finish.

17. Open a console to the vSphere Replication appliance and verify that it boots properly.

18. Log out of the vSphere Client and close the web browser.

19. Open the web browser and log in to the vSphere Web Client.

20. Select the vCenter Server that the vSphere Replication appliance is registered to from the inventory in the left pane. Select the Manage tab and then click vSphere Replication on the toolbar.

21. Select About from the left menu and verify that Availability is reported as OK.

VCENTER.test.local	Actions ▾			

Getting Started   Summary   Monitor   **Manage**   Related Objects

Settings | Alarm Definitions | Tags | Permissions | Sessions | Storage Providers | Scheduled Tasks | vSphere Replication

◀◀

About

Target Sites

Replication Servers

Name:	VCENTER.test.local
Availability:	⊘ OK
Version:	5.5.0.0
Build number:	1309877
Domain name/IP:	192.168.113.179

22. Select Replication Servers from the left menu and verify that the vSphere Replication Server you just deployed reports a Status of connected.

If you are planning to replicate VMs between two sites with two vCenter Servers, you will need to repeat the steps on Exercise 9.16 to deploy another vSphere Replication appliance at the other site. For simplicity purposes, the vSphere Replication coverage in this chapter will replicate VMs between a single vCenter Server. This is possible even with a single ESXi host, as long as there are two unique datastores. The source datastore cannot be the same as the destination datastore. If you have more sites, vCenter Servers or ESXi hosts you may want to experiment with different configurations.

vSphere Replication appliances can also be upgraded. This is accomplished with an upgrade ISO image. With vSphere Replication version 5.5, neither vSphere Update Manager nor the virtual appliance management interface (VAMI) of the vSphere Replication appliance can be used to upgrade.

The upgrade process for the vSphere Replication appliance is relatively simple, but it does require that vCenter Server be version 5.5. The upgrade ISO must also be available on a datastore where it can be attached to the vSphere Replication appliance. Once the ISO is attached, log in to the vSphere Replication appliance at `https://<vSphere-Replication-Appliance>:5480` and click the Update tab.

Now that vSphere Replication is installed and configured, let's discuss configuring replication for virtual machines.

Configuring Replication for Single/Multiple VMs

Once vSphere Replication has been installed and configured, the next step is to configure replication for the virtual machines you want to protect. Part of the replication configuration for virtual machines is the defining the recovery point objective (RPO) to a certain time interval. It is also important to know that only powered-on virtual machines can be replicated. The steps to replicate virtual machines will be covered in Exercise 9.17.

EXERCISE 9.17

Configuring vSphere Replication

1. Connect to a vCenter Server with the vSphere Web Client.

2. Select the vCenter Server that the vSphere Replication appliance is registered to from the inventory in the left pane. Select the Related Objects tab and then click Virtual Machines on the toolbar.

3. Sort the virtual machines by their power state by clicking the State column.

4. Select two powered-on virtual machines by holding down either the SHIFT or CTRL key while clicking them.

5. Right-click on the highlighted VMs and select All vSphere Replication Actions ➤ Configure replication. A Configure Replication dialog will appear. Click Yes. The Configure Replication wizard will open.

6. Ensure that all VMs pass the validation check and click Next.

7. Select the vCenter Server for the Target Site. You can also use the Add Remote Site button to add a remote vCenter Server in this step. This can be the same vCenter Server that you are currently logged in to, as shown in the following image.

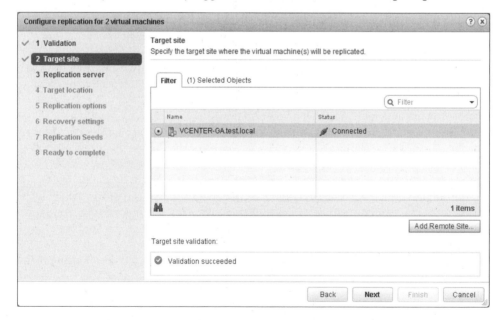

8. Ensure the Validation Succeeded message appears in Target Site Validation and click Next to continue.

9. Accept the default value of Auto-Assign vSphere Replication Server and click Next.

10. Select a Target Location. If you are using the single vCenter Server option, this must be a different datastore than the one the selected VMs are currently located on. Ensure the Validation succeeds and click Next.

11. Use the drop-down menu to select the Quiescing Method for the guest OS and/or your desired application consistency level and click Next.

12. Set the Recovery Point Objective to 15 minutes and enable the Point In Time Instances option. Configure 24 instances per day for the last 1 day, as shown here.

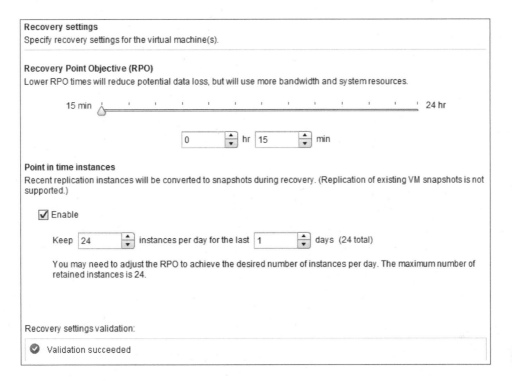

13. Ensure the Validation Succeeded message appears in Recovery Settings Validation and click Next to continue.

14. Click the How To Prepare Replication Seeds link in the upper right and review this information. Accept the default value of Do Not Use Replication Seeds and click Next to continue.

15. Review the information on the Ready To Complete Screen and click Finish.

16. Click the Monitor tab for the vCenter Server inventory object and select vSphere Replication on the toolbar.

17. Monitor the Outgoing Replications. Select individual VMs to view information specific to their replication status.

EXERCISE 9.17 *(continued)*

18. Right-click a VM and choose the Sync Now option from the context menu, if you want to create additional recovery points manually.

In the previous exercise, point-in-time instances were available as an option for replicated virtual machines. These instances allow you to recover virtual machines to specific points, and the replicated VMs will have a list of snapshots available that allow you to pick each specific point in time. A maximum of 24 point-in-time instances can be maintained for a replicated virtual machine.

> **WARNING**   In the previous exercise you configured a recovery point objective of 15 minutes, and enabled 24 point in time instances. The goal of the exercise was to create many replicas as quickly as possible, and in a production environment these same settings would likely not be recommended.

In the next section, you will recover one of the virtual machines you just enabled replication for.

Recovering a VM Using vSphere Replication

In the previous exercise, replication was configured for multiple virtual machines. These replicas will allow for the quick recovery of a recent version of the virtual machine. This feature can be useful for quickly recovering from things like viruses or human error. Exercise 9.18 will assume that something happened to one of our replicated VMs, and now it needs to be recovered.

Recovering VMs with vSphere Replication

1. Connect to a vCenter Server with the vSphere Web Client.

2. Locate one of the replicated VMs in the inventory and power it off. This is a requirement for restoring a replica, and only one VM at a time can be recovered.

3. Select the vCenter Server that the vSphere Replication appliance is registered to from the inventory in the left pane. Select the Monitor tab and then click vSphere Replication on the toolbar.

4. Select Incoming Replications in the left pane.

5. Right-click on the powered-off VM and select Recover from the context menu. A Recover Virtual Machine window will open.

6. Choose the Recover With Latest Available Data option, since this exercise assumes that the VM has been rendered unusable.

7. Ensure that the validation succeeds and click Next to continue.

8. Select a location to restore the VM. This location must be a different location than the original location of the powered-off VM. In the following image, the VM will be restored to a folder named Restored VMs.

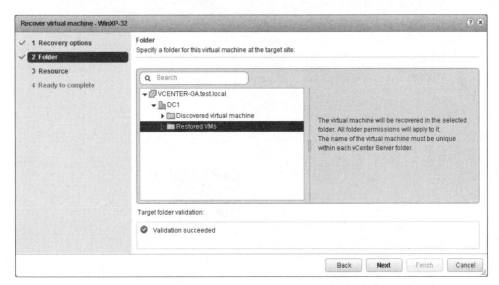

9. Ensure that the validation succeeds and click Next to continue.

10. Select a cluster or host and ensure that validation succeeds. Click Next.

11. Review the information on the Ready To Complete screen and place a check in the Power On The Virtual Machine After Recovery option.

EXERCISE 9.18 *(continued)*

12. Click Finish.

13. Monitor the Recover Virtual Machine task and when it completes verify that the VM's status reports Recovered.

14. Locate the recovered virtual machine and open a console session to it. Verify that it booted properly.

15. Edit the virtual machine's settings and reconnect the network adapter. vSphere Replication disconnects recovered VM NICs as a precaution.

16. Verify network connectivity for the recovered VM.

17. Open Snapshot Manager for the recovered VM and verify that point in time instances appear there as snapshots.

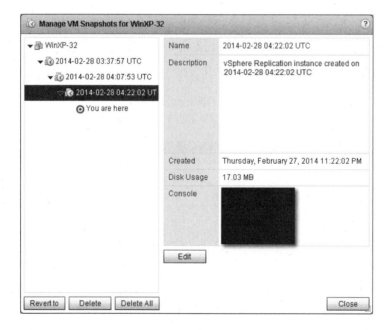

18. Delete the original VM.

19. Click the vCenter Server Monitor tab and select vSphere Replication from the toolbar. Select the Outgoing Replications menu item on the left. The original virtual machine should no longer be listed. Click Refresh if it is.

Now that the replicated virtual machine has been restored, it will need to be replicated again to provide future protection. This is known as failback, and will be the next our next topic.

Performing a Failback Operation Using vSphere Replication

As you saw in the last exercise, vSphere Replication is a powerful feature that can provide very fast recovery for virtual machines. Unfortunately, automated failback is not a feature of vSphere Replication. This means that failback is a manual process. To failback, you simply configure replication again in the reverse direction. This would be the same process you performed in Exercises 9.17 and 9.18.

So far this chapter has covered snapshots, VDP, and vSphere Replication. Each of these features provides different types of protection for your virtual machines. Knowing how these products work and when it is most appropriate to use each is important in determining an effective backup strategy for your vSphere environment.

Determining the Appropriate Backup Solution for a Given vSphere Implementation

Determining the appropriate backup solution for a given vSphere implementation will ultimately come down to understanding the workloads, the business requirements, and many more environment-specific factors. You should ask a multitude of questions:

- Will disk-based backup, tape backup, or both be used?
- If disk-based backup is used, is deduplication a requirement?
- How much data must be backed up?
- What is the estimated annual growth of backed-up data?
- With what frequency must the data be backed up?
- What are the data retention requirements?
- Is there a requirement to encrypt the backup data?
- What are the characteristics of the backup window?
- Are there SLAs in place that dictate TTR or RPO objectives?
- Is the backup solution for both VMs and physical servers?
- Are remote systems in need of backup?
- How many virtual machines must be backed up?

- How many VMs must be backed up simultaneously?
- Is vCenter Server in the environment?
- Which edition of vSphere is in use?
- What level of consistency is required for each workload?
- Are backup agents desired or required for certain workloads?
- Are the applications running in the VMs VSS-aware?
- Is VMware FT in use in the environment?
- Are file-level restores required?
- Which operating systems and versions are in the environment?
- Do any virtual machines use iSCSI initiators in the guest OS?
- Is the ability to replicate backups required?
- Are multiple definable restore points required?
- Can or should existing backup software be leveraged?
- Is the IT staff already trained in a particular backup product?
- What is the budget for the backup solution?
- Are their snapshot solutions provided by the storage vendor?
- How will the backup software be accessed and by whom?

 Real World Scenario

Choosing Backup Software

A virtual infrastructure administrator is looking for a backup solution for her new virtual infrastructure. The environment currently contains multiple virtual machines with Windows 2000, SQL Server 6.5, and a custom in-house developed application running in them. These virtual machines were *P2V* converted from older hardware that was failing, and though it's not an ideal situation, these VMs are used in production. The business requires consistent backups of these virtual machines. Currently the virtual machines are backed up with a third-party application that uses an agent to get consistent SQL Server backups.

The administrator wants to use a backup solution that can capture a complete and application-consistent image of these virtual machines. She has investigated vSphere Data Protection but discovered that application consistency was not possible for these virtual machines. She investigates the capabilities of the third-party backup application and discovers that it too will not be able to provide application-consistent image-level backups of these virtual machines.

The administrator ultimately decides to continue to use the existing third-party backup application for daily backups of the data in these virtual machines. She also decides to use the third-party software to capture an image-level backup of the virtual machine. This image-level backup will be performed monthly, during a scheduled maintenance window. This image-level backup will be taken with the application and SQL Server services stopped in order to provide an application-consistent image-level backup. This approach allows her to recover the server to within 30 days but have much more current data.

Just as with many aspects of virtualization, there is no single backup solution that will fit every environment. Finding the right solution is more about understanding the particular requirements of the environment and delivering a backup/recovery solution that can meet those exact needs.

Patching and Updating ESXi and Virtual Machines

As a VMware Certified Professional, you will be expected to know how to patch and update ESXi hosts. You will also be expected to know how to update the virtual machine hardware and VMware Tools. Both of these practices are important in ensuring a highly available and highly performing virtual infrastructure. In this section, I will cover how to keep ESXi hosts up-to-date and how to keep VMware Tools and virtual machine hardware up-to-date.

Patching Requirements for ESXi Hosts and Virtual Machine Hardware/Tools

Patching ESXi hosts can be accomplished in different ways, but the two most common methods are the following:

- Using vSphere Update Manager
- Manually with the `esxcli` command

Regardless of the method used to patch an ESXi host, the process is basically the same. The host will need to be placed in maintenance mode, and the patch or patches need to be applied and then verified. vSphere Update Manager can automate this multistep process, which can be quite helpful.

When patching ESX/ESXi hosts, vSphere Update Manager has the following requirements:

- Only ESX/ESXi 4.0 and newer hosts are supported.
- Upgrades/migrations require ESX/ESXi 4 and newer.
- vCenter Server is required.
- vSphere Update Manager requires its own database.

The esxcli command can be used from the ESXi Shell, the vMA, the vSphere PowerCLI, or the vSphere CLI. The requirements for patching ESXi hosts with the esxcli command are to ensure that you have both the access and the proper permissions to the ESXi host being patched.

Updating the VMware Tools and virtual machine hardware versions can also be accomplished in a variety of ways. These include the following:

- Using vSphere Update Manager
- Manually using the vSphere Web Client

Regardless of the method used to update the virtual machine hardware or VMware Tools, the process is the same. Windows guests will have VMware Tools uninstalled, a new version of VMware Tools will be installed, and then a reboot may or may not be required. As discussed in the upgrade sequence in Chapter 2, the VMware Tools upgrade should happen prior to the virtual machine hardware upgrade. This sequence ensures that any new virtual machine hardware will already have drivers available.

 For more information about when Windows reboots for VMware Tools installs are required, check VMware KB: http://kb.vmware.com/kb/2015163.

vSphere Update Manager has the following requirements to update virtual machine hardware versions and VMware Tools:

- ESX/ESXi 4 and newer hosts are supported.
- Virtual machine guest OS patch operations are not supported.

When manually updating the virtual machine hardware or VMware Tools with the vSphere Web Client, the requirements are to have the appropriate privileges at the virtual machine level and the guest OS level.

Although host profiles cannot be used to apply patches to ESXi hosts, they can be used to update settings on ESXi hosts. A variety of settings can be configured and checked for compliance. Using host profiles can be a powerful solution for updating configuration changes to multiple ESXi hosts. When you are patching ESX/ESXi hosts, the host profiles have the following requirements:

- Only ESX/ESXi 4 and newer hosts are supported.
- vSphere Enterprise Plus licensing is required.

Now that the requirements for patching ESX/ESXi hosts and virtual machine hardware and VMware Tools have been covered, I will show you how to create, edit, and remove a host profile from an ESXi host.

Creating, Editing, and Removing a Host Profile from an ESXi Host

Host profiles are similar to the way guest customization specifications work for templates in vCenter Server. Where the guest customization specifications are used with guest operating systems, host profiles are used to ensure consistent ESXi images. For an environment with hundreds or thousands of ESXi hosts, this could offer a significant advantage over configuring the hosts one at a time.

Host Profiles work by encapsulating the configuration of a single preconfigured ESXi host (known as the reference host) and storing it in the vCenter Server database. This configuration will include networking, security, storage, and other settings that are not host specific. For example, hostnames and IP addresses are host specific. You then attach this host profile to individual ESXi hosts or a cluster, where it can be used by vCenter Server to monitor the hosts for compliance. Noncompliant hosts can be brought into compliance by applying the host profile to them. The workflow associated with host profiles is shown in Figure 9.2.

FIGURE 9.2   The host profiles workflow

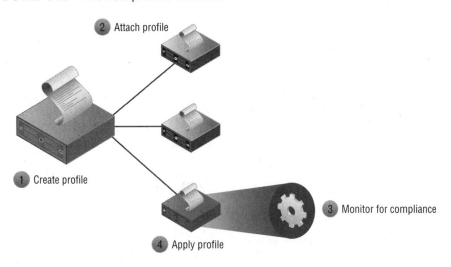

2 Attach profile

1 Create profile

3 Monitor for compliance

4 Apply profile

Host profiles are supported only for vSphere 4.0 or newer hosts and require the Enterprise Plus Edition of vSphere.

Since the first step in implementing host profiles is to create a host profile, you will do that in Exercise 9.19. This exercise will require a reference ESXi host, which is an ESXi host that is already configured and ready in your environment.

EXERCISE 9.19

Creating an ESXi Host Profile

1. Connect to a vCenter Server with the vSphere Web Client. Ensure that Enterprise Plus licensing is available or that the vCenter Server is currently running in evaluation mode.

2. Select the reference ESXi host and right-click it. Choose All vCenter Actions ➢ Host Profiles ➢ Extract Host Profile from the context menu.

3. When the Extract Host Profile wizard begins, give the host profile a descriptive name and a brief description. Click Next to continue.

4. Review the summary information on the Ready To Complete screen and click Finish. An Extract Host Profile task will start. Wait for this task to complete before continuing.

You have now created a host profile, but you will likely need to edit some of its settings. For the purpose of Exercise 9.20, assume that the NTP server in your environment has been changed. The exercise shows how to edit the NTP settings of the host profile to reflect this change.

EXERCISE 9.20

Editing an ESXi Host Profile

1. Click the Home icon at the top of the screen in the vSphere Web Client. Click the Host Profiles icon, located under the Monitoring section.

2. On the Objects tab, right-click the profile created in the previous exercise and choose Edit Settings from the context menu.

3. When the Edit Host Profile window opens, click Next on the Name And Description screen.

4. On the Edit Host Profile screen, expand the General System Settings option. Expand the Date And Time Configuration option and then select the Date And Time Configuration option. The right pane will load the settings.

If the NTP settings have been previously configured, the Time Settings drop-down menu will show Configure A Fixed NTP Configuration and show the configured NTP server below it.

5. Ensure that the drop-down menu is set to Configure A Fixed NTP Configuration and enter the new NTP server address.

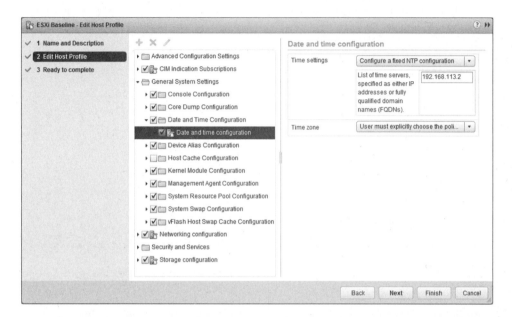

6. In the left pane, ensure the check box beside the Date And Time Configuration policy is selected.

Choosing this option ensures that a compliance check will verify this setting. In the interest of keeping this exercise simple, you should also remove the compliance check for some of the other policies. Doing this will keep the exercises that follow simple and ensure that they work. The remainder of this exercise will cover these steps.

7. Collapse the General System Settings menu. Deselect the Networking Configuration and Storage Configuration policies. The final configuration should look like this:

EXERCISE 9.20 *(continued)*

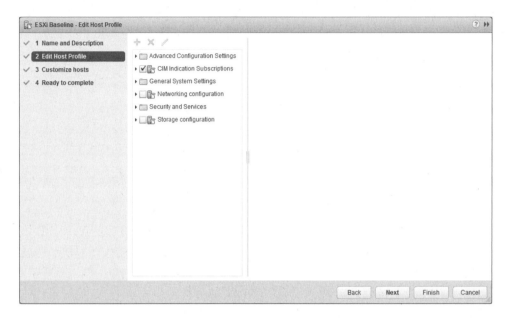

8. Click Next and wait for the changes to be validated. Click Finish on the Ready To Complete screen.

9. An Edit Host Profile task will begin. When this task completes, the host profile is ready to be used.

To remove a host profile, simply right-click it and choose All vCenter Actions ➤ Delete Profile from the context menu. You will be prompted to confirm the deletion.

You have now seen how to create, edit, and delete host profiles. The next implementation step with host profiles is to attach the host profile to an ESXi host.

Attaching and Applying a Host Profile to an ESXi Host or Cluster

Once a host profile is created, it can then be attached to another ESXi host or cluster. Exercise 9.21 shows the steps required for this.

EXERCISE 9.21

Attaching a Host Profile to Another ESXi Host

1. Connect to a vCenter Server with the vSphere Web Client. Ensure that Enterprise Plus licensing is available or that the vCenter Server is running in evaluation mode.

2. Select a different ESXi host and right-click it. Choose All vCenter Actions ➢ Host Profiles ➢ Attach Host Profile from the context menu.

3. When the Attach Host Profile window opens, select the host profile you created in Exercise 9.19. In the bottom of the window, expand both the Authentication Configuration and Network Configuration options and review the contents.

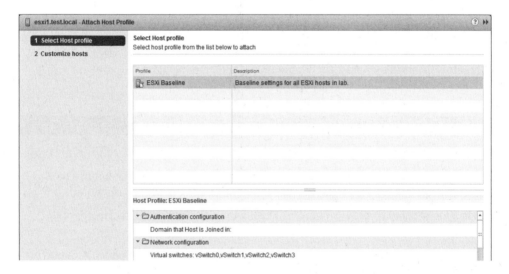

4. Click Next and then click Finish.

5. An Attach/Detach Host Profile task will start. When it completes, click the Summary tab for this ESXi host and verify that the correct host profile is listed in the Host Profile Compliance panel.

The final steps of remediating the ESXi host and applying the host profile will be covered in the next section.

Performing Compliance Scanning and Remediating an ESXi Host Using Host Profiles

If you recall, there are four steps in implementing a host profile:

1. Create

2. Attach

3. Monitor and remediate

4. Apply

In Exercise 9.19, you created a host profile by extracting it from the reference host. In Exercise 9.21, you attached the host profile to a new ESXi host, and in Exercise 9.22 you will monitor this new ESXi host for compliance and then remediate it by applying the edited host profile.

EXERCISE 9.22

Compliance Scanning and Remediating an ESXi Host

1. Connect to a vCenter Server with the vSphere Web Client. Ensure that Enterprise Plus licensing is available or that the vCenter Server is running in evaluation mode.

2. Select the secondary (or non-reference) ESXi host and then locate the Host Profile Compliance panel on its Summary tab.

3. Click the blue Check Compliance link in the Host Profile Compliance panel. A Check Compliance task will begin. When this task completes, verify that Status in the Host Profile Compliance panel reports Not Compliant. Also note that the Remediate Host option is grayed out.

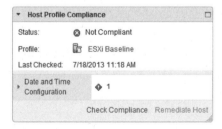

The ESXi host is not compliant in this case, because we edited the NTP server settings after we originally extracted the host profile from this ESXi host. In order for us to bring this host into compliance, it will first need to be remediated.

4. Right-click the ESXi host and choose Enter Maintenance Mode from the context menu.

5. Once the ESXi host enters maintenance mode, the blue Remediate Host link on the Host Profile Compliance panel will become active. Click that link to open the Remediate Host Based On Host Profile window.

6. Click Next and then review the Remediation Tasks listed.

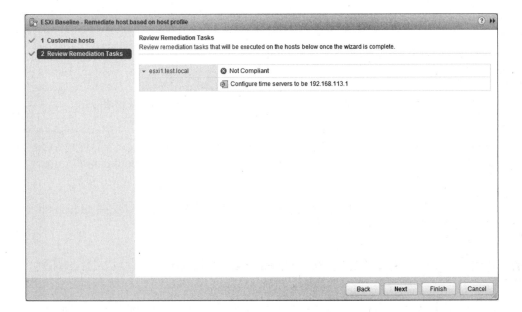

7. Click Finish to apply the host profile to the ESXi host.

8. A Remediate Hosts task will start, followed closely by a Check Compliance task. Wait for both of these tasks to complete and then verify that Host Profile Compliance is now reported as Compliant for the ESXi host.

EXERCISE 9.22 *(continued)*

9. Verify that Time Configuration for the ESXi host has been updated with the values specified in the host profile.

10. Exit maintenance mode on the ESXi host.

Now that you have applied the host profile to an additional ESXi host, you are set to leverage the power of host profiles on any additional ESXi hosts you may have in your vCenter Server inventory. Remember that the power of host profiles is in maintaining consistency across multiple ESXi hosts from a much smaller number of host profiles.

The previous lab can be tricky, depending on how similar your ESXi hosts are. You may have to edit the host profile to remove additional settings or manually correct certain issues to get the host(s) into compliance.

Now that we have worked our way through host profiles, let's examine one additional scenario in which they may be used.

Applying Permissions to ESXi Hosts Using Host Profiles

The previous exercises have demonstrated how host profiles help reduce the effort that would be required to configure your ESXi hosts manually. There are many configurable settings in host profiles, including permission changes for ESXi hosts. It is important to remember that ESXi permission changes only affect individual ESXi hosts and that ESXi hosts have no awareness of vCenter Single Sign-On (SSO). Exercise 9.23 covers the process of editing the host profile used in the previous exercises to include an ESXi host permission.

EXERCISE 9.23

Adding an ESXi Host Permission to a Host Profile

1. Connect to a vCenter Server with the vSphere Web Client. Ensure that Enterprise Plus licensing is available or that the vCenter Server is running in evaluation mode.

2. Click the Home icon at the top of the screen in the vSphere Web Client. Click the Host Profiles icon, located under the Monitoring section.

3. On the Objects tab, right-click the profile created in the previous exercise and choose Edit Settings from the context menu.

4. When the Edit Host Profile window opens, click Next on the Name And Description screen.

5. On the Edit Host Profile screen, expand the Security And Services option. Expand the Security Settings option and then expand the Authentication Configuration option. Select the Active Directory Configuration option.

6. In the right pane, from the Domain Name drop-down menu choose Configure A Fixed Domain Name.

7. Enter the name of the Active Directory domain in the domain name field.

8. From the Join Domain Method drop-down menu choose Use User Specified AD Credentials To Join The Host To Domain. The final configuration should look similar to this:

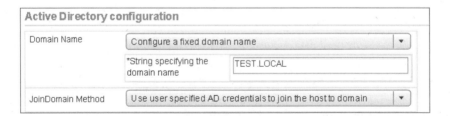

9. Click Next and wait for the changes to be validated. On the Customize Hosts screen, enter the credentials for a user with rights to join the ESXi host to the Active Directory domain.

EXERCISE 9.23 *(continued)*

ESXi Baseline - Edit Host Profile			(?) ▶▶
✓ 1 Name and Description	**Customize hosts**		
✓ 2 Edit Host Profile	The following hosts require some additional customizations:		
3 Customize hosts			
4 Ready to complete			

Host	Property Name	Path	Value
esxi2-ga.test.local	User Name	Security and Services > Security Setting...	Administrator@test.local
esxi2-ga.test.local	Password	Security and Services > Security Setting...	●●●●●●●●●●●●●●●●

Back | **Next** | Finish | Cancel

10. Wait for the changes to be validated, and then click Finish on the Ready To Complete screen.

   An Edit Host Profile task will begin. When this task completes, the host profile is ready to be used.

11. Scan an ESXi host for compliance. Verify that the host is noncompliant.

12. Remediate the host.

13. Verify the Authentication Services ➢ Domain Settings for the ESXi host.

In addition to applying permissions to ESXi hosts, another useful feature of host profiles is the ability to import and export them.

Importing/Exporting a Host Profile

Being able to import and export host profiles allows more control over ESXi host configurations. It might help to think about large distributed environments that need to have consistent ESXi host settings. The ability to import and export host profiles facilitates this capability. Exercise 9.24 shows the steps to export and import a host profile.

EXERCISE 9.24

Exporting and Importing an ESXi Host Profile

1. Click the Home icon at the top of the screen in the vSphere Web Client. Click the Host Profiles icon, located under the Monitoring section.

2. On the Objects tab, right-click the profile created in the previous exercise and choose Duplicate Host Profile from the context menu.

3. When the Duplicate Host Profile window opens, provide a Name and Description and click Next.

4. Click Finish on the Ready To Complete screen.

5. When the new host profile is listed in the Objects tab, right-click it and choose All vCenter Actions ➤ Export Host Profile.

6. Review the information on the Export Host Profile window and click Save.

7. Select a location to save the exported host profile and click Save.

8. Right-click the duplicate host profile and choose All vCenter Actions ➤ Delete.

9. Review the information on the Delete Profile window and click Yes.

10. When the host profile has been successfully deleted, click the Import Host Profile icon, which is located to the right of the Add icon. An Import Host Profile window will open.

11. Select the appropriate vCenter Server from the drop-down menu and then browse to the location of the host profile you exported earlier in this exercise.

12. Provide a name and description for the imported host profile. The final configuration should look similar to this:

13. Click OK. An Import Host Profile task will begin. Wait for this task to complete and then verify the host profile was imported successfully.

Now that we have covered host profiles in great detail, we will move on to maintaining patch levels for ESXi hosts and updates for virtual machine hardware and VMware Tools by using VMware Update Manager.

Installing and Configuring VMware vSphere Update Manager

VMware vSphere Update Manager is an automated patch management solution used to simplify the maintenance of VMware vSphere environments. Update Manager can automate patches for ESXi hosts, virtual appliances, virtual machine hardware, and VMware Tools.

Before installing Update Manager, first verify membership in the Administrators group on the system and verify that the Update Manager system requirements are met. You should have a separate drive or volume with a minimum of 120GB of disk space to store the downloaded patch files. Other prerequisites are as follows:

- vCenter Server installation media should be available.

- Microsoft.NET Framework 3.5 SP1 or newer is required.

- vCenter Server should be installed and working properly.

- A dedicated Oracle or Microsoft SQL Server database should be used. Environments smaller than 5 hosts and 50 VMs can use the bundled SQL Server 2008 R2 Express database.

- A 64-bit Windows system is required for installation.

- The Windows system cannot be an Active Directory domain controller.

- A 32-bit DSN is required for database connectivity, if you are not using the bundled SQL Express database.

- vSphere Update Manager 5.5 is compatible only with vCenter Server 5.5.

- The Update Manager server and client plug-ins must be running the same version.

- Update Manager, vCenter Server, and the vSphere Client must be running compatible versions.

- For full functionality of Update Manager, the traditional vSphere Client is required. The vSphere Web Client can be used to attach baselines and scan entities, but it cannot remediate.

 vSphere Update Manager and vCenter Server should not use the same database.

Once the prerequisites have been met for Update Manager, installation can begin. Exercise 9.25 covers the steps to install vSphere Update Manager.

EXERCISE 9.25

Installing vSphere Update Manager

1. Connect to a console session on any supported Windows server and log on with an Administrator account.

   Note that vSphere Update Manager can be installed on the vCenter Server or on its own dedicated server.

2. Launch the VMware vCenter Installer and select vSphere Update Manager from the list of vCenter Support Tools.

3. Click the Install button to begin.

4. When the installation wizard starts, select the desired language and click OK.

5. On the Welcome screen, click Next to begin.

6. Accept the terms of the license agreement and click Next.

7. Review the support information and deselect the Download Updates From Default Sources Immediately After Installation option. Click Next to continue.

8. On the vCenter Server Information screen, enter the vCenter Server name and port information. Ensure that valid credentials are entered for the connection to vCenter Server. Click Next to continue.

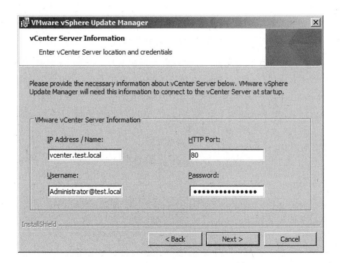

9. Choose the appropriate database/credentials; note that if you use a standalone Oracle or SQL database, a 32-bit DSN is required. Click Next to continue.

EXERCISE 9.25 *(continued)*

10. Use the drop-down menu to specify the IP address or hostname that will be used for vSphere Update Manager and select the Yes, I Have Internet Connection And I Want To Configure Proxy Settings Now option.

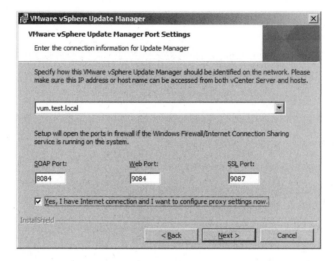

11. Click Next to continue.

12. Configure the proxy server as necessary and click Next. If you do not have a proxy server, simply deselect the Configure Proxy Settings option and click Next.

13. Select the destination folder for the Update Manager installation and the location for downloading patches.

    Note that a best practice is to change the location for patch downloads to a different volume than where the operating system is installed. This practice can help prevent OS volume disk full errors from occurring. This location can be changed after installation by manually editing the `<patchStore>` information contained in the `C:\Program Files (x86)\VMware\Infrastructure\Update Manager\vci-integrity.xml` file.

14. Click Next to continue.

15. Review the information on the Ready To Install The Program screen and click Install to install vSphere Update Manager.

16. Click Finish when the installation completes.

vSphere Update Manager has now been installed, but the vSphere Client plug-in still needs to be configured. In vSphere 5, the traditional vSphere Client is still used to configure Update Manager. The first step in configuring Update Manager is to enable the Update Manager plug-in in the vSphere Client. Exercise 9.26 covers these steps.

EXERCISE 9.26

Installing the vSphere Update Manager Client Plug-in

1. Connect to a vCenter Server with the vSphere Client.

2. Select the Plug-ins menu and then choose the Manage Plug-ins option. The Plug-in Manager window will appear.

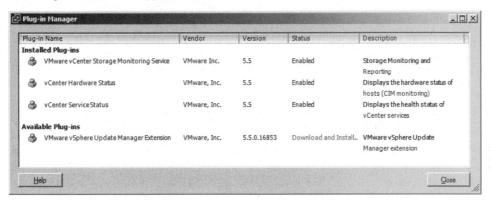

3. The VMware vSphere Update Manager Extension is listed in the Available Plug-ins section. Click the blue Download And Install link in the Status column. The Status value will change to Downloading while the file is downloaded locally.

4. When the installer launches, select the desired language and click OK to continue.

5. On the Welcome screen, click Next.

6. Accept the terms of the license agreement and click Next.

7. Click Install to begin the install.

8. Click Finish on the Installation Complete screen.

9. Verify that the VMware vSphere Update Manager Extension is now listed in the Installed Plug-ins section of the Plug-in Manager.

10. You will also be prompted with a certificate warning. Handle this as appropriate for your environment.

11. Close the Plug-in Manager.

12. Click the Home icon in the navigation bar of the vSphere Client.

13. Verify that Update Manager is now listed under Solutions And Applications.

14. Click the Update Manager icon to open Update Manager; review the interface options available.

You have now installed Update Manager and configured the plug-in in the vSphere Client. Let's next discuss how to configure its network settings in Exercise 9.27.

EXERCISE 9.27

Configuring vSphere Update Manager Network Settings

1. Connect to a vCenter Server using a vSphere Client with the vSphere Update Manager plug-in installed.

2. Click the Home icon in the navigation bar of the vSphere Client.

3. Click the Update Manager icon in the Solutions And Applications section.

4. Click the Configuration tab.

5. The Network Connectivity settings are displayed by default. Review the current settings, as shown here:

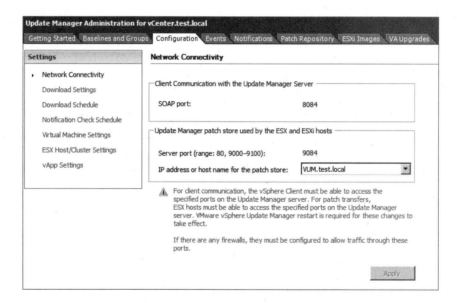

6. If the IP Address Or Host Name For The Patch Store option has a value other than an IP address, use the drop-down menu to change this value to the IP address of the system where vSphere Update Manager is installed.

   VMware recommends using an IP address here. Also note that IPv6 is not supported for scanning and/or remediation of virtual machines or virtual appliances.

7. After changing the value of the IP Address Or Host Name For The Patch Store option to the IP address of the vSphere Update Manager system, click the Apply button to save the change.

8. When the Apply button is grayed out, the change has been saved.

9. Restart the Update Manager service on the Update Manager server.

The network settings have now been configured, so let's next cover configuring the virtual machine settings. Note that the download settings will be covered in detail in the next section of this chapter.

The virtual machine settings are used to enable and disable the snapshot functionality and to define the retention period. By default, a snapshot will be taken of virtual machines before the updates are applied. This feature can be used to protect individual virtual machines in the event that an update causes a problem. By default, this snapshot will also be set to allow unlimited growth. As discussed earlier in this chapter, use caution with this default setting, because it could lead to very large snapshot files and the problems associated with them.

vSphere Update Manager can take snapshots of virtual machine hardware version 4 and newer only.

Exercise 9.28 covers the steps to configure the virtual machine settings.

EXERCISE 9.28

Configuring vSphere Update Manager Virtual Machine Settings

1. Navigate to the Update Manager Configuration tab.

2. Click the blue Virtual Machine Settings link in the Settings panel on the left.

3. Enter an acceptable value for your environment in the Keep For Hours option. This will limit the amount of time that snapshots can grow and is a good best practice to implement.

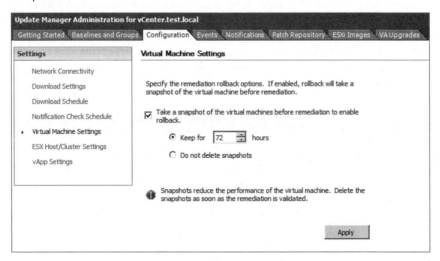

4. Click the Apply button to save these changes. When the Apply button is grayed out, the changes have been saved.

You have now configured the snapshot behavior for virtual machines used with Update Manager. I will next cover the ESXi host and cluster settings in Update Manager.

The ESXi host and cluster settings are used to control the maintenance mode behavior of ESXi hosts, cluster settings, and boot settings for ESXi hosts that use PXE boot. These settings can be configured to allow Update Manager to perform updates to ESXi hosts that are members of a cluster with DRS and/or HA enabled.

Figure 9.3 shows the default maintenance mode settings.

FIGURE 9.3 Update Manager ESXi host settings

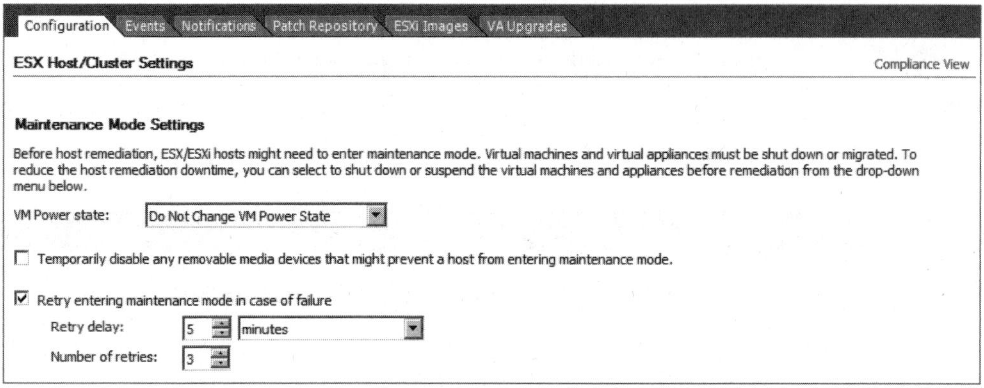

These options can be used to control how virtual machines behave when a host is placed in maintenance mode. The VM Power State drop-down menu allows the configuration to set virtual machines to power off, suspend, or be migrated. There are also retry settings in the event that the ESXi host does not successfully enter maintenance mode, as well as the ability to temporarily disable removable media devices. Each of these options can be configured to work as desired for the specific environment.

The next section of the ESXi Host/Cluster settings is the Cluster Settings. Exercise 9.29 shows how to configure these settings.

EXERCISE 9.29

Configuring vSphere Update Manager Cluster Settings

1. Navigate to the Update Manager Configuration tab.

2. Click the blue ESX Host/Cluster Settings link in the Settings panel on the left. You'll see the following settings:

Cluster Settings

Certain features might need to be temporarily disabled for cluster updates to succeed. These features will be automatically re-enabled when remediation is complete.

Update Manager does not remediate hosts on which the features are enabled.

Temporarily disable:

☑ Distributed Power Management (DPM)

☐ High Availability Admission Control

☐ Fault Tolerance (FT)

ⓘ To ensure that FT can be re-enabled, you should remediate all hosts in a cluster with the same updates at the same time. See the documentation for more details.

☐ Enable parallel remediation for hosts in cluster

☐ Migrate powered off and suspended virtual machines to other hosts in the cluster, if a host must enter maintenance mode

3. If DPM is configured on the cluster, ensure that the Distributed Power Management (DPM) option is selected. This will prevent DPM from interrupting vSphere Update Manager operations.

4. If your environment is very large, you may be able to speed the time to remediation by selecting the Enable Parallel Remediation For Hosts In Cluster option. This will allow Update Manager to update ESXi hosts simultaneously, as compared to sequentially when this option is not used.

5. Review the other settings listed here and determine whether they are suitable for your environment.

The final setting in the ESX Host/Cluster settings is PXE Booted ESXi Host Settings, which can be used to allow Update Manager to update stateless ESXi hosts. This could be useful in cases where updates do not require a host reboot. This setting is disabled by default.

The last vSphere Update Manger setting is for vApps. There is one configurable option, known as Enable Smart Reboot After Remediation. This setting is shown in Figure 9.4.

This setting is enabled by default and will attempt to fulfill the startup order listed in the vApp, if any virtual machine in the vApp is remediated and requires a reboot. This is a useful setting, since rebooting a single virtual machine in the vApp could lead to failure of a tiered application.

Now that we have configured most of the Update Manager settings, we will take some time to explore what are arguably the most important settings: the download options.

FIGURE 9.4   Update Manager vApp settings

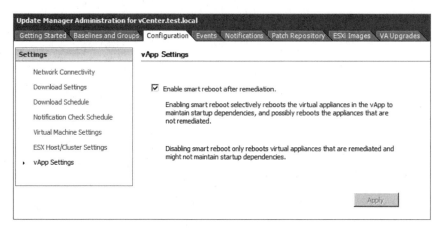

Configuring Patch Download Options

vSphere Update Manager can be configured to obtain files from three different download sources:

Direct Connection To Internet   This method can be used if Update Manager is installed on a server that has either direct or proxied Internet access.

Use A Shared Repository   This method can be used when Update Manager is installed on a server that does not have Internet access. It requires installing and configuring the Update Manager Download Service (UMDS) on an additional server that has Internet access.

Import Patches   This method can be used to import a ZIP file with the required patches.

It is important to remember that either Internet downloads or a shared repository can be used, but they cannot be used simultaneously. It is strictly an either/or option.

Exercise 9.30 covers the steps to configure the download settings for vSphere Update Manager.

EXERCISE 9.30

Configuring vSphere Update Manager Download Settings

1. Navigate to the Update Manager Configuration tab.

2. Click the blue Download Settings link in the Settings panel on the left. The default Download Settings are shown here:

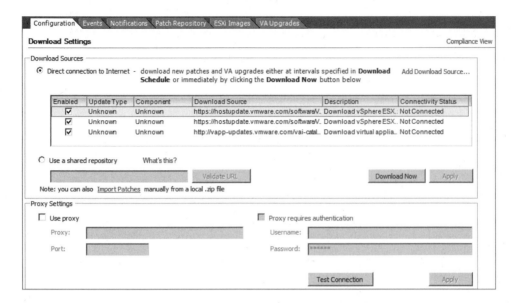

3. Skip the Download Sources settings and locate the Proxy Settings section in the lower part of the screen. These options can be configured as necessary when using the Direct Connection To Internet option in Download Settings, which we will use to download patches later in this exercise.

4. There is also a Test Connection button included to test the proxy settings. If you use a proxy server, enter its name, port number, and other values in Proxy Settings and click Test Connection to verify Internet connectivity.

5. Once you are sure that you have Internet access from the Update Manager server, turn your attention back to the top of the screen to the Download Sources settings.

6. The first option, Direct Connection To The Internet in Download Sources, is used when Update Manager is installed on a server with a connection to the Internet. Review the Enabled, Update Type, Component, Download Source, Description, and Connectivity Status columns.

7. If you recall from the Update Manager setup in Exercise 9.25, we chose not to download the files during installation. Download the files by clicking the Download Now button.

8. A dialog box will appear informing you that a download task has been started. Verify in the Recent Tasks pane that a Download Patch Definitions task has started.

9. While the patch definitions download, note the second available option in the Download Sources section, titled Use A Shared Repository. This option would be used with the UMDS mentioned earlier.

EXERCISE 9.30 *(continued)*

10. Look just below the Use A Shared Repository option, and you will see the third option, which is a blue Import Patches link.

11. When the Download Patch Definitions operation completes, browse to the directory that contains these files. If you accepted the default, the path will be C:\ProgramData\VMware\VMware Update Manager\Data\.

12. Review the directory structure and files contained here.

    Now that we have configured the proxy settings and download sources, we can set up the download schedule, which determines when Update Manager will actually download files.

13. Click the blue Download Schedule link in the Settings panel on the left.

14. Review the Download Schedule information and notice that the scheduled downloads can also be disabled using the Enable Scheduled Download check box.

15. Take note of the date and time listed for the Next Run.

16. Click the blue Edit Download Schedule link to modify the schedule.

17. The Schedule Update Download wizard will appear, as shown here:

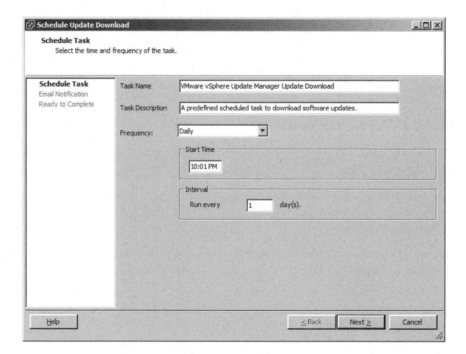

18. Change the Start Time And Interval setting to suit the needs of your environment. Click Next to continue.

19. If you want to be notified via email when new patches are downloaded, enter an email address here. Click Next.

20. Review the information on the Summary screen and click Finish to modify the schedule.

21. Verify that the new schedule appears in the Download Schedule section of the Configuration tab.

    There is one final configuration item to cover: the Notification Check Schedule option. The notification check schedule is used to check for information about patch recalls, new fixes, and alerts.

22. Click the blue Notification Check Schedule link in the Settings panel on the left.

23. Review the information and notice that the scheduled downloads can also be disabled using the Enable Scheduled Download check box.

24. You can also modify the schedule by clicking the blue Edit Notifications link to open the Schedule Update wizard.

Now that we have installed and configured Update Manager, let's discuss how to create, edit, and delete an Update Manager baseline.

Creating, Editing, and Deleting an Update Manager Baseline

vSphere Update Manager is used to scan hosts, virtual machines, and virtual appliances against a baseline or baseline group to determine their compliance level. A baseline is a collection of one or more patches, extensions, or upgrades, and a baseline group is a collection of baselines.

Baselines can be either dynamic or fixed. Dynamic baselines will update automatically as new patches are released, whereas fixed baselines are static and will not automatically include any newly released updates. Fixed baselines would typically be used when the virtual infrastructure administrator wants more control over what patches are installed.

The first type of baseline is the Host Patch baseline. Update Manager by default includes two patch baselines used for scanning hosts. These baselines can be viewed on the Update Manager Baselines And Groups tab in the Hosts view. These two host baselines are as follows:

Critical Host Patches (Predefined)   These are used to check ESX/ESXi hosts for compliance with all critical patches.

Non-Critical Host Patches (Predefined)   These are used to check ESX/ESXi hosts for compliance with all optional patches.

The second type of baseline is the Host Extension baseline, which is used to deploy VMware or third-party software. An example of this might be vendor-specific CIM providers or a multipathing plug-in.

The third type of baseline is the upgrade baseline. There's a Host Upgrade baseline, used to upgrade ESX/ESXi hosts from version 4.0 or newer to ESXi 5.5. Update Manager by default includes three upgrade baselines used for scanning virtual machines and virtual appliances. These baselines can be viewed on the Update Manager Baselines And Groups tab in the VMs/VAs view. The three upgrade baselines are as follows:

VMware Tools Upgrade To Match Host (Predefined)   Used to check virtual machines for compliance with the latest version of VMware Tools available on the ESX/ESXi 4 or newer host.

VM Hardware Upgrade To Match Host (Predefined)   Used to check the virtual hardware of a virtual machine for compliance with the most current version supported on the ESXi 5.5 host.

VA Upgrade To Latest (Predefined)   Used to check virtual appliance compliance with the latest available version of the virtual appliance.

 vSphere Update Manager cannot be used to upgrade an ESX 4 host that was upgraded from ESX 3.*x*. A fresh install will instead be required.

By the time you are reading this book, vSphere 5.5 will likely have patches available. Exercise 9.31 covers the steps to create a dynamic patch baseline for patching an ESXi 5.5 host to the latest release. This exercise will require a single ESXi 5.5 host that is not at the latest patch level.

EXERCISE 9.31

Creating a Dynamic Patch Baseline for ESXi 5.5

1. Connect to a vCenter Server using a vSphere Client with the vSphere Update Manager plug-in installed.

2. Click the Home icon in the navigation bar of the vSphere Client.

3. Click the Update Manager icon located in the Solutions And Applications section.

4. Click the Baselines And Groups tab. Note that the default view is the Hosts view.

5. On the Hosts view screen, click the blue Create link. The New Baseline Wizard will launch.

6. Give the baseline a descriptive name and provide a description for it in the Baseline Name And Description section. Ensure that the Host Patch option is selected in the Baseline Type section. The final settings should appear similar to these:

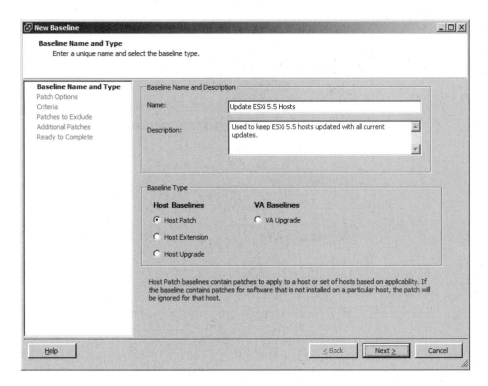

7. Click Next to continue.

8. Ensure that the Dynamic option is chosen for the baseline type and click Next to continue.

9. On the Dynamic Baseline Criteria screen, choose the Any option for the Patch Vendor. Select embeddedEsx 5.5.0 for Product. Accept the defaults for Severity and Category and do not specify any date ranges. The final settings should appear similar to these:

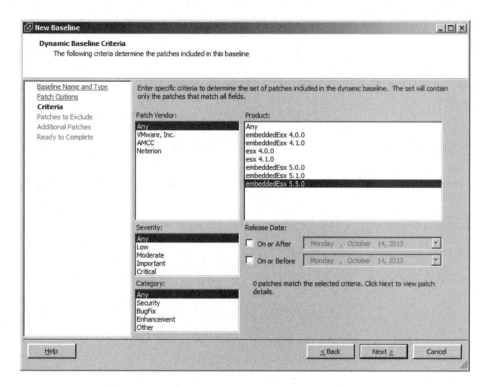

10. Note at the bottom of the screen that the number of patches that meet the selected criteria is listed. Click Next to continue.

11. On the Patches To Exclude screen, note that the available patches are listed.

    The Patch Name, Release, Type, Severity, Category, Impact, and Vendor fields provide more information about the available patches.

12. Accept the defaults and click Next.

13. On the Additional Patches screen, review the additional patches that are available in the repository. Click Next.

14. Review the information on the Ready To Complete screen. Expand Patches Matching Criteria Currently In The Repository and verify that the information listed is correct.

15. Click Finish and then verify that the new baseline is listed in the Hosts view of the baselines with the correct value in the Content column.

You have now created a dynamic baseline that can be used to update your ESXi 5.5 hosts to the latest version. I also included the Cisco Nexus 1000V in this baseline, and it's very likely that most test labs do not include this dvSwitch. If your lab does include it, then good for you! Exercise 9.32 covers how to edit the baseline just created to remove the Cisco Nexus 1000V patch.

EXERCISE 9.32

Editing a Dynamic Patch Baseline for ESXi 5.5

1. Navigate to the Update Manager Baselines And Groups tab. Note that the default view is the Hosts view.

2. On the Hosts view screen, locate the baseline created in the previous exercise. Note the value in the Content column before proceeding.

3. Right-click the baseline and choose Edit Baseline from the context menu.

4. The Edit Baseline wizard will open. Note that on the Baseline Name And Type screen, you cannot edit the baseline type. Click Next to continue.

5. Leave the baseline as Dynamic and click Next.

6. In the Dynamic Baseline Criteria settings, ensure that embeddedEsx 5.5.0 is selected for Product. Click Next.

7. On the Patches To Exclude screen, enter **Cisco** in the Patch Name, Product Or Type Contains text box to filter the results. Select the Cisco Nexus 1000V patches, and use the arrow buttons in the middle of the screen to move this patch to the Patches To Exclude section at the bottom of the screen.

    Once the patch is moved, a red X will show beside it in the leftmost column in the top portion of the screen.

EXERCISE 9.32 *(continued)*

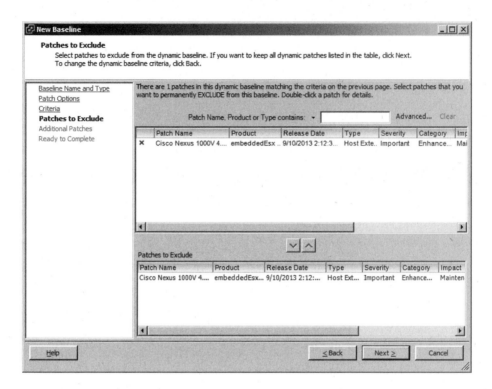

8. Click Next to continue.

9. On the Additional Patches screen, click Next.

10. Review the information on the Ready To Complete screen. Expand Patches Matching Criteria Currently In The Repository and Patches Matching Criteria To Exclude and verify that the information listed is correct.

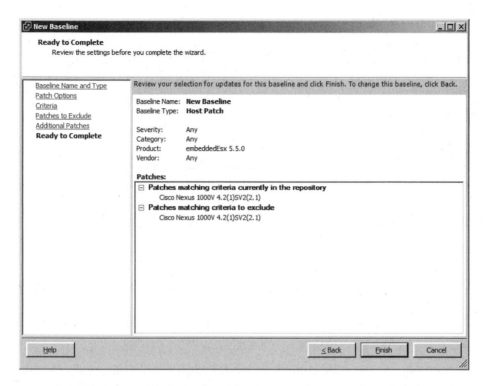

11. Click Finish and verify that the baseline is listed with the updated value in the Content column.

You have now created and edited a dynamic baseline. In the event that a baseline ever needs to be deleted, simply select the baseline to highlight it and then click the blue Delete link at the top of the screen. You will be prompted to confirm the deletion, as shown in Figure 9.5.

Now that we have created a baseline for our ESXi 5.5 hosts, the next step is to attach the baseline to an ESXi host or cluster.

Attaching an Update Manager Baseline to an ESXi Host or Cluster

Attaching a baseline to an object allows you to view compliance information and remediate the object. At this point, it is also important to know that you can also use either the vSphere Client or the vSphere Web Client for attaching baselines and scanning hosts.

FIGURE 9.5 Deleting a baseline

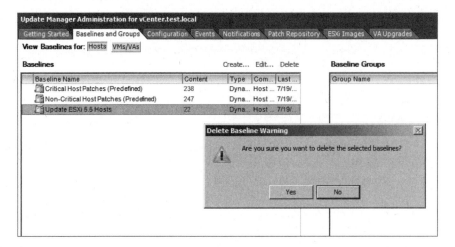

 All Update Manager configuration and remediation can only be accomplished with the traditional vSphere Client.

It is considered a best practice to attach baselines to a container object, such as a cluster, because this will help ensure consistency of all ESXi hosts in the cluster. In Exercise 9.33, this best practice will not be used. Instead, the steps to attach a baseline to a single ESXi host with the vSphere Client will be covered.

EXERCISE 9.33

Attaching a Baseline to an ESXi Host with the vSphere Client

1. Connect to a vCenter Server using a vSphere Client with the vSphere Update Manager plug-in installed.

2. Click the Home icon in the navigation bar of the vSphere Client.

3. Click the Hosts And Clusters icon.

4. Select an ESXi host in the left pane and then select the Update Manager tab in the right pane.

5. Click the blue Attach link in the upper right. The Attach Baseline Or Group window will open.

6. Select the baseline originally created in Exercise 9.32. The final configuration should appear similar to what's shown here:

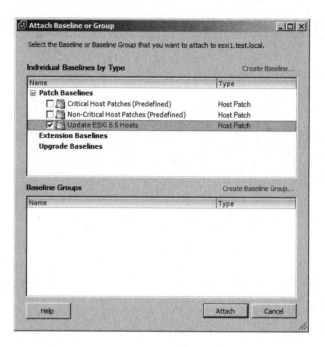

7. Click the Attach button.

8. Verify that the Update Manager tab has been updated to show the ESXi host in the lower pane.

The vSphere Web Client can also be used to attach a baseline to another ESXi host. Exercise 9.34 will cover these steps. You will need an additional ESXi host, or you will need to detach the baseline from the existing ESXi host if you want to reuse it.

EXERCISE 9.34

Attaching a Baseline to an ESXi Host with the vSphere Web Client

1. Connect to a vCenter Server with the vSphere Web Client.

2. Select an ESXi host—other than the one you selected in the previous exercise—from the inventory.

3. On the Monitor tab, click the Update Manager option on the toolbar.

4. Click the Attach button in the upper right. The Attach Baseline Or Group window will open.

5. Select the baseline originally created in Exercise 9.32. The final configuration should appear similar to what's shown here:

EXERCISE 9.34 *(continued)*

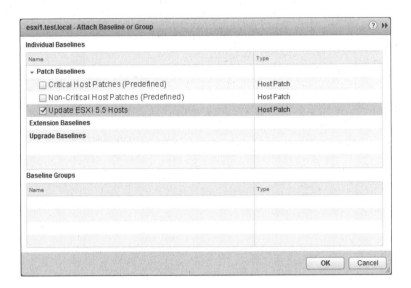

6. Click OK.

7. Verify that the Update Manager information has been updated to show the attached baseline in the lower pane.

Now that the baseline has been attached to an ESXi host, the next operation is to scan and remediate the ESXi host. The steps required to do this will be covered next.

Scanning and Remediating ESXi Hosts and Virtual Machine Hardware/Tools Using Update Manager

Scanning is how vSphere Update Manager discovers the compliance of hosts, virtual machines, or virtual appliances in the inventory. In the previous exercise, you learned how to attach a baseline to an ESXi host. The next step in patching this ESXi host is to scan it to check for compliance to the baseline you created. Scanning can be performed manually, or it can be scheduled using the Scheduled Tasks feature in vCenter Server.

ESXi host updates are all-inclusive, which means that the most recent update will contain all previous patches.

Exercise 9.35 covers the steps to perform a manual scan of an ESXi host using the vSphere Client.

EXERCISE 9.35

Manually Scanning an ESXi Host for Compliance with the vSphere Client

1. Connect to a vCenter Server using a vSphere Client with the vSphere Update Manager plug-in installed.

2. Click the Home icon in the navigation bar of the vSphere Client.

3. Click the Hosts And Clusters icon.

4. Select an ESXi host with the attached patch baseline in the left pane and choose the Scan For Updates option from the context menu that appears.

5. A Confirm Scan dialog will appear, as shown here:

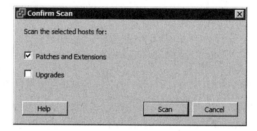

6. Ensure that the Patches And Extensions option is selected, and click the Scan button.

7. A Scan Entity task will begin. When this task completes, click the Update Manager tab in the right pane. The result should appear similar to this:

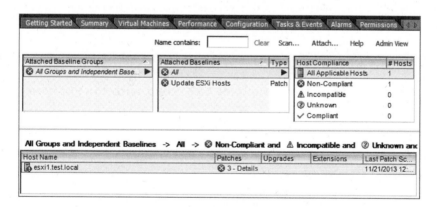

8. Verify that the ESXi host is reported as noncompliant.

The vSphere Web Client can also be used to scan an ESXi host for compliance, and Exercise 9.36 will cover these steps.

EXERCISE 9.36

Manually Scanning an ESXi Host for Compliance with the vSphere Web Client

1. Connect to a vCenter Server with the vSphere Web Client.

2. Select an ESXi host with the attached patch baseline from the inventory.

3. On the Monitor tab, click the Update Manager option on the toolbar.

4. Click the Scan button in the upper right. A Confirm Scan window will open.

5. Ensure that the Patches And Extensions option is selected, and click OK.

6. A Scan Entity task will begin. When this task completes, verify that the ESXi host is reported as noncompliant.

The next and final step in the ESXi host patching process is to remediate noncompliant hosts. Like scanning, remediating can also be performed manually or scheduled using the Scheduled Tasks feature in vCenter Server. It is also important to note that remediation is only available in the traditional vSphere Client. Exercise 9.37 covers the steps to perform a manual remediation of an ESXi host using the vSphere Client.

EXERCISE 9.37

Manually Remediating a Noncompliant ESXi Host with the vSphere Client

1. Connect to a vCenter Server using a vSphere Client with the vSphere Update Manager plug-in installed.

2. Click the Home icon in the navigation bar of the vSphere Client.

3. Click the Hosts And Clusters icon.

4. Select an ESXi host in the left pane and right-click it. Choose the Remediate option from the context menu.

5. The Remediate wizard will begin.

6. On the Remediation Selection screen, ensure that the proper baseline is selected and that the proper ESXi host is listed at the bottom of the screen.

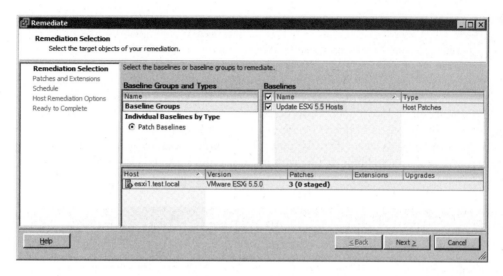

7. Click Next to continue.

8. Review the list of patches that will be applied and click Next.

9. Provide the task with a descriptive name and schedule. Ensure that the Remediate The Selected Hosts option is set to Immediately. Click Next to continue.

10. Review the Host Remediation Options settings. You may recall this same set of options from when the Update Manager configuration was originally performed.

11. Configure the Host options as appropriate for your specific test environment and click Next.

12. Review the Cluster Remediation Options settings. You may recall this same set of options from when the Update Manager configuration was originally performed.

13. Configure the Cluster options as appropriate for your specific test environment and click Next.

14. Review the information on the Ready To Complete screen and click Finish to begin the remediation of the ESXi host.

15. A Remediate Entity task will begin, and it can be followed by many others depending on how your test environment is set up.

    You should see Install, Check, Enter Maintenance Mode, Initiate Host Reboot, and Exit Maintenance Mode tasks as vSphere Update Manager remediates the host.

16. When the Remediate Entity task completes, verify that the ESXi host is reporting Compliant in the Compliance view.

As with any patching operation, always test the patches in a test environment before applying them in production.

Now that you have seen how to patch an ESXi host with Update Manager, I will show how to use Update Manager to update VMware Tools and virtual machine hardware for a VM running on this ESXi host. To accomplish the VMware Tools and virtual hardware update as a single Update Manager operation, we will first create a baseline group. Exercise 9.38 covers the steps to create the baseline group and attach it to a virtual machine. This exercise will require a virtual machine with virtual hardware version prior to 10 and an older version of VMware Tools installed.

EXERCISE 9.38

Creating a Group Baseline and Attaching It to a Virtual Machine

1. Connect to a vCenter Server using a vSphere Client with the vSphere Update Manager plug-in installed.

2. Click the Home icon in the navigation bar of the vSphere Client.

3. Click the Update Manager icon in the Solutions And Applications section.

4. Click the Baselines And Groups tab. Note that the default view is the Hosts view.

5. Switch to the VMs/VAs view by using the view toggle buttons at the top of the tab.

6. In the VMs/VAs view, locate the Baseline Groups section on the right. Click the blue Create link. The New Baseline Group Wizard will launch.

7. In the Baseline Group Type section, select Virtual Machines And Virtual Appliances Baseline Group. Give the baseline group a descriptive name and then click Next.

8. In the VA Upgrades section, ensure that the None option is selected. In the VM Hardware Upgrades section, ensure that the VM Hardware Upgrade To Match Host (Predefined) option is selected. In the VMware Tools Upgrades section, ensure that the VMware Tools Upgrade To Match Host (Predefined) option is selected. The final configuration should look like this:

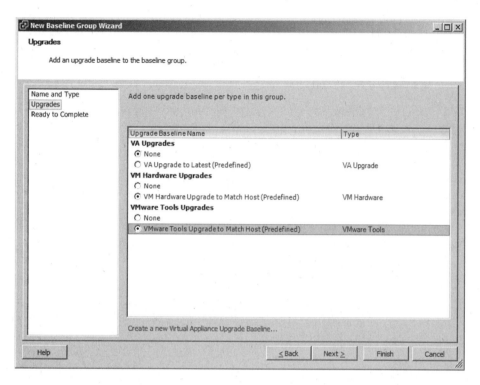

9. Click Next. Review the information on the Ready To Complete screen and then click Finish to create the baseline group.

10. Verify that the new baseline group is listed in the right pane under Baseline Groups. Expand it and ensure that both baselines are included.

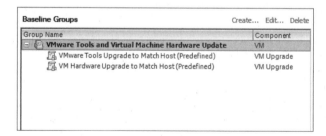

You have now created the baseline group. The next step is to attach this baseline group to a virtual machine.

EXERCISE 9.38 *(continued)*

11. Click the Home icon in the navigation bar of the vSphere Client.

12. Select the VMs And Templates icon.

13. Locate the virtual machine that will be upgraded in the left pane and select it.

14. Select the Update Manager tab from the right pane.

15. Click the blue Attach link in the upper portion of the screen.

16. An Attach Baseline Or Group window will appear. In the lower pane of this window, select the baseline group created earlier in this exercise. The final configuration will look similar to this:

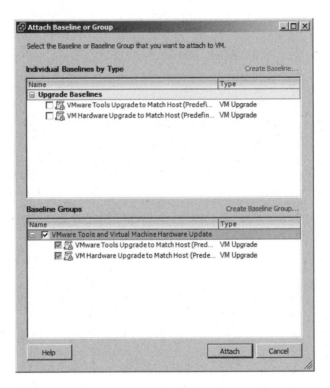

17. Click the Attach button.

18. Verify that the Update Manager tab has been updated to show the attached baseline.

The baseline group containing the predefined baselines for both VMware Tools and the virtual machine hardware has now been attached to a virtual machine. The next step is to scan the virtual machine for compliance and to remediate it. Exercise 9.39 covers these steps.

EXERCISE 9.39

Manually Scanning and Remediating a Virtual Machine

1. Connect to a vCenter Server using a vSphere Client with the vSphere Update Manager plug-in installed.

2. Click the Home icon in the navigation bar of the vSphere Client.

3. Select the VMs And Templates icon.

4. Locate the virtual machine that will be upgraded in the left pane and select it.

5. Select the Update Manager tab in the right pane.

6. Right-click the virtual machine in the left pane and choose Scan For Updates from the context menu.

7. A Confirm Scan dialog will appear. Select the VM Hardware Upgrades and VMware Tools Upgrades options.

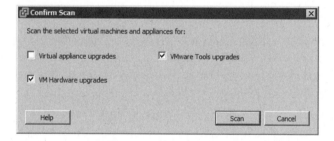

8. Click the Scan button to continue.

9. A Scan Entity task will begin. Verify that the expected results are displayed on the Update Manager tab.

10. Right-click the virtual machine and choose Remediate from the context menu.

11. The Remediate wizard will launch.

12. Ensure that the baseline group is selected and that both of the included baselines are selected. Highlight the virtual machine in the bottom pane. The final configuration should appear similar to this:

EXERCISE 9.39 *(continued)*

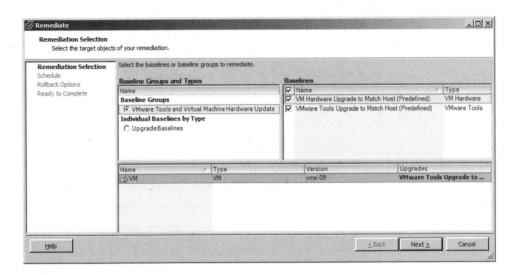

13. Click Next.

14. Provide a detailed task name and description for this operation and choose the Immediately option for the scheduling. Click Next to continue.

15. Ensure that the Take Snapshot option is enabled. You may recall these settings from when Update Manager was initially configured. Provide a detailed name and description for the snapshot and choose whether to include the virtual machine's memory as part of the snapshot. Click Next.

16. Review the information on the Ready To Complete screen and click Finish to begin the remediation.

17. A Remediate Entity task will begin, followed by a series of tasks that will be determined by which options were selected in the previous steps.

18. Watch the Recent Tasks list for entries; open the virtual machine's console, and watch the progress there as well.

19. When the Remediate Entity task completes, verify that the Compliance view reports the virtual machine as compliant.

20. Use the virtual machine's Summary tab to verify that the virtual machine hardware version and VMware Tools have both been updated.

Remediation of VMware Tools and the virtual machine hardware will initiate multiple virtual machine reboots.

In the next section of this chapter, I will cover how to stage ESXi updates.

Staging ESXi Host Updates

Earlier in this chapter, you learned how to use Update Manager to remediate an ESXi host. An additional option can be used as part of the remediation process. Staging is the process of copying the patch files to the ESXi host prior to the remediation task being run. This can save significant time in the remediation process. Exercise 9.40 covers the process to stage ESXi host updates.

EXERCISE 9.40

Staging ESXI Host Updates

1. Connect to a vCenter Server using a vSphere Client with the vSphere Update Manager plug-in installed.

2. Click the Home icon in the navigation bar of the vSphere Client.

3. Click the Hosts And Clusters icon.

4. Select an ESXi host in the left pane and right-click it. Choose the Stage Patches option from the context menu.

5. The Stage Wizard will begin.

6. On the Baseline Selection screen, ensure that the proper baseline is selected and that the proper ESXi host is listed at the bottom of the screen.

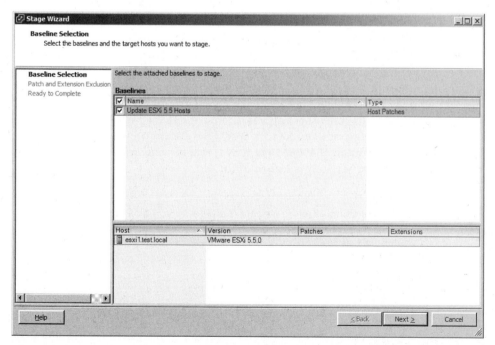

7. Click Next to continue.

8. Deselect any undesired patches and click Next.

9. Review the information on the Ready To Complete screen and click Finish to stage
    the patches to the ESXi host.

10. A Stage Patches To Entity task will begin. When the task completes, the patches have
    been successfully staged to the ESXi host.

ESX/ESXi 4 and newer hosts are supported for staging patches and extensions. PXE-booted ESXi 5 hosts are also supported, but Update Manager
will not apply an update to a PXE-booted ESXi 5 host if an update requires
a host reboot.

In addition to updating ESXi, Update Manager can be used to upgrade your ESXi hosts.

Upgrading an ESXi Host Using vSphere Update Manager

Update Manager can be used for upgrading, migrating, updating, and patching ESX/ESXi
hosts. VMware recommends that those using vCenter Server also use vSphere Update
Manager for host upgrades.

One item to be aware of, when using vSphere Update Manager, is that ESX hosts
must have more than 350MB of free space in the /boot partition to support using Update
Manager for the ESXi 5.5 upgrade. This will typically exclude ESX 4.x hosts that were
upgraded from an ESX 3.x version, and it could exclude some ESX 4.x hosts as well
depending on the partitioning scheme that was used during installation. If this free space
requirement is not met and Update Manager is not an option, you will have to use an interactive or scripted upgrade. These issues will not be present in Exercise 9.41, since we will be
using Update Manager to upgrade an ESXi 5.1 host. This exercise will require an existing
ESXi 5.1 host (with a minimum of 4096MB of RAM) that is being managed by the same
vCenter Server that Update Manager is registered to.

If you are using vSphere Update Manager to upgrade or migrate an ESX/
ESXi host to ESXi 5.5, static IP addresses are required for the hosts to
be upgraded.

EXERCISE 9.41

Upgrading an ESXi Host Using Update Manager

1. Connect to a vCenter Server using a vSphere Client with the vSphere Update Manager plug-in installed.

2. Launch Update Manager from the Home page, under the Solutions And Applications section.

3. Once Update Manager loads, click on the ESXi Images tab. In the upper-right corner locate the Import ESXi Image link and click it.

4. The Import ESXi Image wizard will launch. Click the Browse button and then locate the ESXi 5.5 image (ISO) file, as shown here:

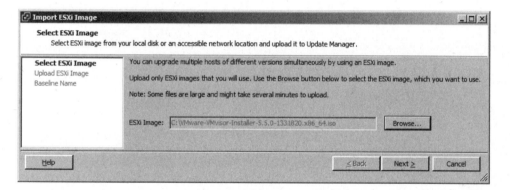

5. Click Next to continue. The image will begin to upload, and a Security Warning window will appear.

   This warning appears because a trusted certificate authority did not sign the certificate. If you trust the certificate, click the Install This Certificate check box and click the Ignore button to continue. The file upload progress will be shown in the Import ESXi Image wizard.

6. When the file upload completes, verify that the upload was successful. Review the image details, and then click Next.

7. Ensure that the Create A Baseline Using The ESXi Image check box is selected and give the baseline a name and description, as shown here:

EXERCISE 9.41 *(continued)*

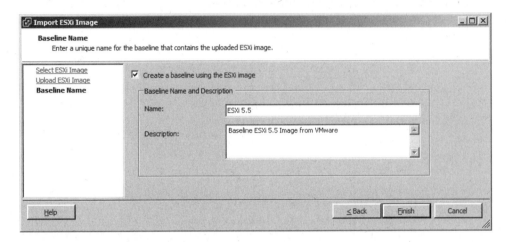

8. Click Finish to continue. Review the information in the Imported ESXi Images section of the ESXi Images tab in Update Manager and verify that everything is listed properly.

9. Select the Baselines And Groups tab and verify that the baseline we just created appears in the Baselines pane on the left.

   We are almost ready to upgrade the ESXi 5.1 host using the newly created baseline. The next step is to attach the baseline to the ESXi host.

10. Select Home from the navigation bar and then choose Hosts And Clusters in the Inventory section.

11. Select the ESXi 5.1 host and then select the Update Manager tab.

12. Click the Attach link in the upper-right corner. Select the baseline that you created in Step 7 of this exercise by clicking the check box beside it, as shown here:

Leave the Baseline Groups section blank, as this option is used to allow upgrade baselines and patch baselines to be combined. In this activity, we are only working with an upgrade baseline.

13. Click the Attach button to continue.

14. Review the information displayed in the Update Manager tab.

15. Now that the baseline has been attached, the next step is to manually initiate a scan of the ESXi 5.1 host. In the left pane, select the ESXi 5.1 host that will be upgraded to ESXi 5.5 and right-click on it. From the context menu, choose Scan For Updates.

16. A Confirm Scan window will appear. Select the Upgrades check box and then click Scan, as shown here:

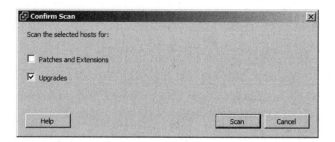

17. A Scan Entity task will appear in the Recent Tasks list. When this task completes, review the scan results and noncompliance states shown in the Update Manager tab. The results will appear similar to these:

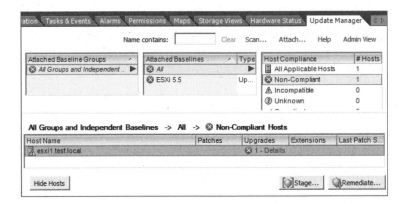

18. The final step is to remediate the noncompliant host. Right-click the ESXi 5.1 host and choose Remediate from the context menu. The Remediate wizard will begin.

19. On the Remediation Selection screen, choose the baseline created in Step 7, and then click Next.

20. Review and accept the terms of the EULA. Select the I Accept The Terms And License Agreement check box and then click Next.

21. On the next screen, if applicable check the option to remove third-party software that is incompatible with the upgrade and click Next to continue.

    Note that this option applies to only ESX/ESXi 4 hosts and can be ignored for ESXi 5 hosts.

22. Give the task a name and description and choose a time for it to run. Click Next.

    The next two screens cover *maintenance mode* and cluster remediation options. The ESXi 5.5 upgrade will obviously require the ESXi 5.1 host to be put into maintenance mode. Depending on the feature set in use in your specific VMware environment, DRS and vMotion could be used to keep VMs up and running on other hosts during this upgrade. Base your decisions on the options on these screens around the specific available features in use in your environment.

23. Review the information in the Ready To Complete screen for accuracy. If everything is correct, click Finish to begin the ESXi 5.5 upgrade.

24. A Remediate Entity task will appear in the Recent Tasks list. A series of other tasks will also appear in the Recent Tasks list while the upgrade takes place. When the Remediate Entity task completes, the upgrade is complete.

25. Review the scan results and Host Compliance states shown on the Update Manager tab. The results will appear similar to the following:

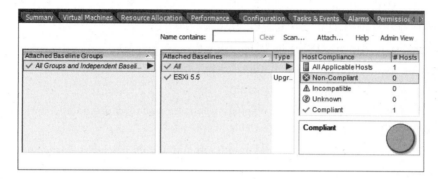

As you can see, Update Manager can simplify and automate much of the vSphere upgrade process. This capability alone makes it a very useful solution, especially when multiple ESXi hosts exist in an environment.

Summary

This chapter focused on migrating virtual machines. You learned the following:

- The procedure to migrate a powered-off or suspended virtual machine
- ESXi host and virtual machine requirements for vMotion and Storage vMotion
- Enhanced vMotion Compatibility CPU requirements
- Snapshot requirements for vMotion and Storage vMotion
- The procedure to configure the virtual machine swap file
- The procedure to migrate virtual machines using vMotion and Storage vMotion
- How to utilize Storage vMotion
- How to change virtual disk types and the virtual machine working location

Next we focused on backing up and restoring virtual machines. You learned to:

- Identify snapshot requirements.
- Create, delete, and consolidate virtual machine snapshots.
- Identify the differences between VDP and VDPA.
- Identify VMware Data Protection requirements.
- Sizing guidelines for VMware Data Protection.
- Install and configure VMware Data Protection.
- Create a backup job with VMware Date Protection.

- Manage and monitor VDP capacity.

- Perform test/live full/file-level restores with VMware Data Protection.

- Perform a VDR data migration.

- Explain the vSphere Replication architecture.

- Install/configure/upgrade vSphere Replication.

- Configure replication for single/multiple VMs.

- Recover a VM using vSphere Replication.

- Perform a failback operation using vSphere Replication. Determine an appropriate backup solution for a given vSphere implementation.

Finally, we explored patching and updating ESXi and virtual machines, focusing on these tasks:

- Identifying patching requirements for ESXi hosts, virtual machine hardware, and VMware Tools

- Creating, editing, and removing a host profile from an ESXi host

- Attaching/applying a host profile to an ESXi host

- Compliance scanning and remediation of an ESXi host using host profiles

- Applying permissions to ESXi hosts with host profiles

- Importing/Exporting host profiles

- Installing and configuring vSphere Update Manager and the patch download options

- Creating, editing, and deleting an Update Manager baseline

- Attaching an Update Manager baseline to an ESXi host

- Scanning and remediating ESXi hosts, virtual machine hardware, and VMware Tools using Update Manager

- Staging ESXi host updates and using Update Manager to perform an ESXi host upgrade

- Upgrading an ESXi host with Update Manager

Exam Essentials

Know how to migrate virtual machines.   Know how to migrate a powered-off or suspended virtual machine. Be able to identify ESXi host and virtual machine requirements for vMotion and Storage vMotion. Be able to identify Enhanced vMotion Compatibility CPU requirements and snapshot requirements for vMotion and Storage vMotion. Know how to configure the virtual machine swap file location and understand the implications of doing so. Be able to migrate virtual machines using vMotion and Storage vMotion. Know how to use Storage vMotion to change virtual disk types, rename virtual machines, and change the working directory of a virtual machine.

Know how to back up and restore virtual machines.   Be able to identify snapshot requirements and know how to create, delete, and consolidate virtual machine snapshots. Be able to differentiate between VDP and VDPA. Be able to identify VMware Data Protection requirements. Know how to explain VMware Data Protection sizing guidelines. Understand how to install and configure VMware Data Protection. Be able to create a backup job with VMware Date Protection. Know how to manage and monitor VDP capacity. Be able to perform a test/live full/file-level restore with VMware Data Protection. Know how to perform a VDR data migration. Be able to describe vSphere Replication architecture. Know how to install/configure/upgrade vSphere Replication. Understand how to configure replication for single/multiple VMs. Be able to recover a VM using vSphere Replication. Know how to perform a failback operation using vSphere Replication. Understand how to determine an appropriate backup solution for a given vSphere implementation.

Know how to patch and update ESXi and VMs.   Be able to identify patching requirements for ESXi hosts, virtual machine hardware, and VMware Tools. Know how to create, edit, and remove a host profile from an ESXi host. Know how to attach and apply a host profile to an ESXi host or cluster. Understand how to perform compliance scanning and remediation of an ESXi host using host profiles. Be able to install and configure vSphere Update Manager. Know how to configure patch download options and create, edit, and delete an Update Manager baseline. Know how to attach an Update Manager baseline to an ESXi host or cluster. Be able to scan and remediate ESXi hosts, virtual machine hardware, and VMware Tools using Update Manager. Know how to stage ESXi host updates. Be able to use Update Manager to upgrade an ESXi host.

Review Questions

1. You have a virtual machine stored on a datastore on an ESXi host's local disks. The host that this VM is running on needs maintenance, and your vCenter Server is licensed for vSphere Standard. Which of the following methods can be used to migrate this virtual machine with no downtime?

   A. Cold migration

   B. vMotion

   C. VMware Converter

   D. None of these

2. Which of the following are supported for use with snapshots?

   A. A powered-on virtual machine that is protected with VMware FT

   B. A powered-on virtual machine that has an independent disk

   C. A powered-on virtual machine with an RDM in physical compatibility mode

   D. A powered-on virtual machine with an RDM in virtual compatibility mode

3. VMware Data Protection does not support which of the following disk types? (Choose all that apply.)

   A. Independent

   B. RDM Independent - Virtual Compatibility Mode

   C. RDM Physical Compatibility Mode

   D. Eagerzeroedthick VMDK

4. A virtual infrastructure administrator plans to manually update the virtual machine hardware and VMware Tools in a maintenance window for a virtual machine with a Windows Server 2008 R2. How many times will the guest OS need to be restarted in this process?

   A. Three: one for the virtual machine hardware update and two for the VMware Tools update

   B. Three: two for the virtual machine hardware update and one for the VMware Tools

   C. Two: one for the virtual hardware and one for the VMware Tools

   D. It depends: As few as one or as many as three

5. Which of the following are available vMotion priority options? (Choose two.)

   A. Reserve CPU For Optimal vMotion Performance

   B. Limit CPU For Optimal vMotion Performance

   C. Perform With Available CPU Resources

   D. Perform With Optimal vMotion Performance

6. A cluster has the virtual machine swap file option configured to store the swap file in the datastore specified by the host. The ESXi hosts in the cluster are configured to place the swap file on a datastore named NFS-SWAP. A newly created virtual machine located in this cluster has its virtual machine swap file option configured to always store with the virtual machine. The newly created virtual machine is located on NFS-VOL1. Where will this virtual machine's swap file be located when the virtual machine is powered on?

   A. The NFS-SWAP datastore

   B. The NFS-VOL1 datastore

   C. Both NFS-SWAP and NFS-VOL1

   D. None of these

7. Which of the following are download sources that can be used with vSphere Update Manager? (Choose all that apply.)

   A. Direct Connection To Internet

   B. Use A Shared Repository

   C. Proxy Settings

   D. Import Patches

8. You want to update the VMware Tools and virtual machine hardware in one scheduled task. Which of the following will allow this?

   A. Create one scheduled task in vCenter and provide it the two update steps.

   B. Create a baseline to update the virtual machine hardware version, and VMware Tools will be automatically updated.

   C. Create a baseline group that contains both of the predefined update baselines. Schedule the remediation using the baseline group.

   D. This is not possible.

9. Which versions of vCenter Server is Update Manager 5.5 compatible with?

   A. vCenter Server 4.1 U3

   B. vCenter Server 5.0 U3

   C. vCenter Server 5.1 U2

   D. vCenter Server 5.5

10. Which versions of vCenter Server is vSphere Data Protection 5.5 compatible with?

   A. vCenter Server 4.1

   B. vCenter Server 5.0

   C. vCenter Server 5.1

   D. vCenter Server 5.5

11. You need to move a virtual machine with an active snapshot to a different datastore. You intend to use Storage vMotion to accomplish this task, and all of the hosts are ESXi 5.5. Which of the following statements is accurate for this plan?

    A. This plan will work.

    B. This plan will work, but proceed with caution.

    C. This plan will work but is unsupported.

    D. This plan will not work.

12. Which of the following are required to apply a host profile to an ESXi host? (Choose all that apply.)

    A. Enterprise Licensing

    B. Enterprise Plus Licensing

    C. ESX/ESXi host in maintenance mode

    D. vSphere Update Manager

13. A virtual infrastructure administrator has taken a single snapshot of a virtual machine. The snapshot requestor has asked that the virtual machine be reverted and he no longer needs the virtual machine to be in snapshot mode. Which set of actions should the virtual infrastructure administrator now take?

    A. Revert to the current snapshot. Delete the snapshot clicking the Delete All button in Snapshot Manager.

    B. Revert to the current snapshot.

    C. Delete the snapshot by clicking the Delete button in Snapshot Manager.

    D. None of these.

14. Which of the following are not supported for use with the VMware Data Protection File Level Restore Client? (Choose all that apply.)

    A. EXT4 file systems

    B. FAT16 and FAT32 file systems

    C. Encrypted partitions

    D. Deduplicated NTFS file systems

15. What is the proper sequence in which vSphere Update Manager processes updates?

    A. Scan object, create baseline, attach baseline, remediate object

    B. Create baseline, scan object, attach baseline, remediate object

    C. Create baseline, attach baseline, scan object, remediate object

    D. Remediate object, scan object, create baseline, attach baseline

16. You have two virtual machines that need to be moved to a new datacenter. Which of the following migrations will allow you to do this? (Choose all that apply.)

    A. Migrating a powered-off VM

    B. Migrating a suspended VM

    C. Migrating with vMotion

    D. Migrating with Storage vMotion

17. Which of the following statements are true about EVC? (Choose two.)

    A. Mixing Intel and AMD processors in the same cluster is allowed.

    B. Mixing Intel and AMD processors in the same datacenter is allowed.

    C. Mixing Intel and AMD processors in the same cluster is not allowed.

    D. Mixing Intel and AMD processors in the same datacenter is not allowed.

18. You plan to install vSphere Update Manager on a dedicated server and use a remote SQL Server database. Which of the following are required on the server that vSphere Update Manager will be installed on? (Choose two.)

    A. 32-bit operating system

    B. 64-bit operating system

    C. 32-bit DSN

    D. 64-bit DSN

19. You have a vSphere environment that uses only NFS datastores, and your storage vendor does not support the VAAI NAS extensions that enable reserve space. When you are performing a Storage vMotion, which of the following options are available? (Choose all that apply.)

    A. Change Datastore Location

    B. Change Virtual Disk Format

    C. Change Storage Profile

    D. Disable Storage DRS

20. Which of the following can be used to manage VMware Data Protection?

    A. The vSphere Web Client

    B. The vSphere Client

    C. The vSphere Client with the VMware Data Protection client plug-in

    D. vSphere Management Assistant

Chapter

10

Performing Basic Troubleshooting

VCP5-DCV EXAM OBJECTIVES COVERED IN THIS CHAPTER:

✓ **6.1: Perform Basic Troubleshooting for ESXi Hosts**

- Troubleshoot common installation issues
- Monitor ESXi system health
- Identify general ESXi host troubleshooting guidelines
- Export diagnostic information

✓ **6.2: Perform Basic vSphere Network Troubleshooting**

- Verify network configuration
- Troubleshoot physical network adapter configuration issues
- Troubleshoot virtual switch and port group configuration issues
- Verify a given virtual machine is configured with the correct network resources
- Identify the root cause of a network issue based on troubleshooting information

✓ **6.3: Perform Basic vSphere Storage Troubleshooting**

- Verify storage configuration
- Troubleshoot storage contention issues
- Troubleshoot storage over-commitment issues
- Troubleshoot iSCSI software initiator configuration issues
- Troubleshoot Storage Reports and Storage Maps
- Identify the root cause of a storage issue based on trouble-shooting information

✓ **6.4: Perform Basic Troubleshooting for HA/DRS Clusters and vMotion/Storage vMotion**

- Identify HA/DRS and vMotion requirements
- Verify vMotion/Storage vMotion configuration
- Verify HA network configuration
- Verify HA/DRS cluster configuration
- Troubleshoot HA capacity issues
- Troubleshoot HA redundancy issues
- Troubleshoot DRS load imbalance issues
- Interpret the DRS Resource Distribution Graph and Target/Current Host Load Deviation
- Troubleshoot vMotion/Storage vMotion migration issues
- Interpret vMotion Resource Maps
- Identify the root cause of a DRS/HA cluster or migration issue based on troubleshooting information

TOOLS

- vCenter Server and Host Management Guide (Objective 6.1)
- vSphere Monitoring and Performance guide (Objectives 6.1, 6.4)
- vSphere Troubleshooting guide (Objectives 6.1–6.4)
- vSphere Networking guide (Objective 6.2)
- vSphere Storage guide (Objective 6.3)
- vSphere Availability guide (Objective 6.4)
- vSphere Resource Management guide (Objective 6.4)
- vSphere Client / vSphere Web Client (Objective 6.1-6.4)

This chapter will cover the objectives of section 6 of the VCP5-DCV exam blueprint. It will focus on performing basic troubleshooting in a vSphere environment. You'll learn how to do basic troubleshooting for ESXi hosts, for vSphere networks, and for vSphere storage issues. You'll also learn how to perform basic troubleshooting for HA/DRS clusters and vMotion/Storage vMotion.

Performing Basic Troubleshooting for ESXi Hosts

The ability to troubleshoot a vSphere environment is an important skill set that any virtual infrastructure administrator should have. Knowing how to troubleshoot a vSphere environment is also important for the VCP5-DCV exam. This chapter will begin with troubleshooting common ESXi and vCenter Server installation issues.

Troubleshooting Common Installation Issues

Most of the common installation issues encountered with vCenter Server and ESXi involve not meeting the system requirements. The hardware-specific system requirements are often enforced at the software level of the installers and cannot be bypassed. Other software-specific system requirements can also prevent the installation of vCenter Server or its components. In addition, environmental factors such as networking, storage, and more can impact installation. The first step in ensuring a successful install is to meet all of the hardware, software, and environmental system requirements for both ESXi and vCenter Server.

You may also encounter installation issues related to product interoperability. You should determine prior to installation if the version of vCenter Server you plan to use is compatible with the versions of ESX/ESXi you plan to use. In addition to vCenter Server and ESXi compatibility, there are compatibility requirements for the operating system that will house the vCenter Server and requirements for specific versions of the database that will be used.

You can find the VMware product interoperability matrixes at

http://partnerweb.vmware.com/comp_guide2/sim/interop_matrix.php

ESXi hosts and all of the components they contain should be verified for compatibility using the VMware Compatbility Guide, commonly referred to as the Hardware

Compatibility List (HCL). Hardware vendors will often have their own unique set of requirements to support certain versions of ESX/ESXi, so make sure you verify your hardware (and firmware levels) with your server vendor. Also check with your vendor's documentation for any recommended BIOS settings or known issues with the version of ESXi you plan to use. Finally, ensure that any storage systems in use are listed on the HCL and are running the required firmware levels.

 You can find the VMware HCL at `www.vmware.com/go/hcl`.

Troubleshooting installation issues should begin by ensuring that system requirements are met, that product interoperability is verified, and that all components are listed on the HCL. It is also good practice to read the release notes for the version of vCenter Server and /or ESXi that is being used, since these documents often contain known issues and workarounds. Always verify downloads using the provided checksums, since corrupt media will often produce unpredictable results. Using these practices can save significant amounts of both time and effort spent troubleshooting a problem that very likely won't be solved.

Now that I have described troubleshooting common installation issues, let's discuss monitoring ESXi system health.

Monitoring ESXi System Health

The vSphere Web Client can be used to monitor system health when connected to a vCenter Server, and the vSphere Client can be used when connected directly to an ESXi host or to a vCenter Server. One of the simplest ways to monitor system health is to have the vSphere Client open and connected to an ESXi host or vCenter Server, or to have the vSphere Web Client open and connected to a vCenter Server. As health conditions occur, inventory object icons will have real-time alerts and warnings placed on them. This is often a quick and easy way for operations staff to monitor ESXi hosts. When more detail is needed, the vSphere Client or vSphere Web Client can be used to obtain this information. Remember that the approach used to discover the hardware status information is different when the vSphere Client is connected directly to an ESXi host than it is when the vSphere Client (or vSphere Web Client) is connected to a vCenter Server managing the host.

When you're connected directly to an ESXi host, select the ESXi host in the left pane and the Configuration tab in the right pane. Then select the blue Health Status link in the Hardware panel on the left. The health of the ESXi host's hardware will be shown in the right pane. Figure 10.1 shows an ESXi host in an alert state, because it has a missing power supply.

In the ESXi Health Status view, the Sensor, Status, and Reading columns are used to provide information about the sensors and their current status. The Refresh link can be used to refresh this information.

 The blue Reset Sensors link can also be used to reset sensor data. This can be useful when cumulative data needs to be cleared in order to start collecting new data.

When using the vSphere Client connected to a vCenter Server, you obtain the hardware health information in a different location. Select the ESXi host in the left pane, and select the Hardware Status tab. Figure 10.2 shows a vCenter Server–managed ESXi host in a healthy state.

FIGURE 10.1   ESXi Health Status view

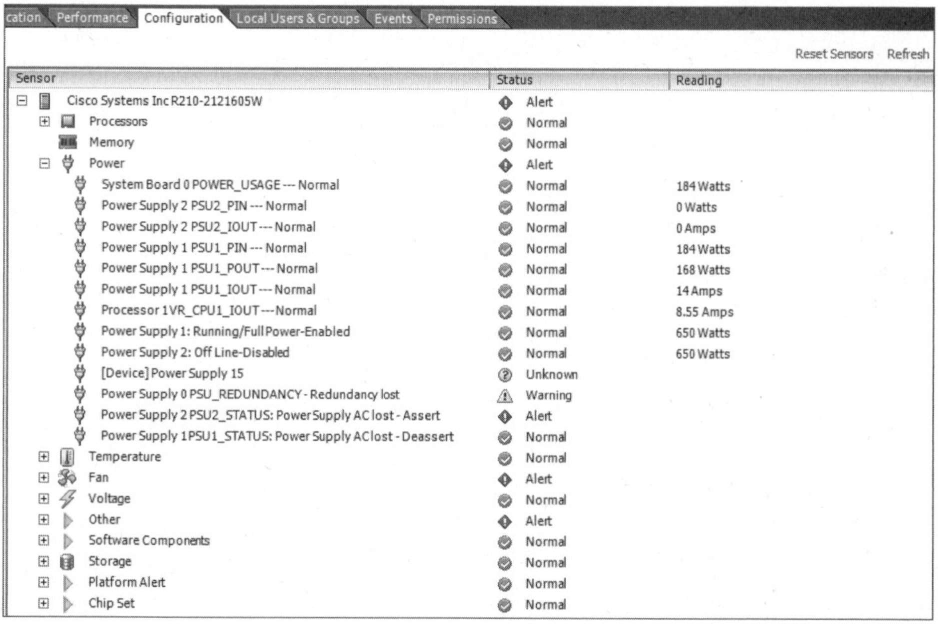

FIGURE 10.2   ESXi Hardware Status view in vCenter Server

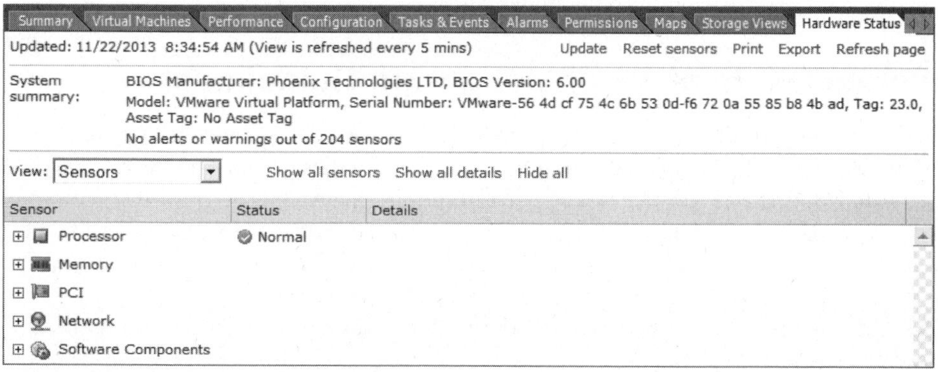

In the vCenter Server Hardware Status view, the Sensor, Status, and Details columns are used to provide information about the sensors and their current status. Notice the drop-down menu that can be used to change the View options. This allows the viewing of all sensor data, alerts, and warnings or system event logs. Also note the system summary located at the top of the tab, which includes detailed information about the host system. The blue Update link located in the upper right of the right pane can be used to refresh the information in this view, and the last update time is included at the very top left of this tab. This information can also be exported or printed using the corresponding link at the top of the tab.

When the vSphere Web Client is connected to a vCenter Server, the hardware health information appears in a slightly different location. Select the ESXi host in the left pane. Select the Monitor tab, and click Hardware Status on the toolbar. Figure 10.3 shows the ESXi host hardware information when viewed from the vSphere Web Client.

FIGURE 10.3 ESXi Hardware Status view in vCenter Server

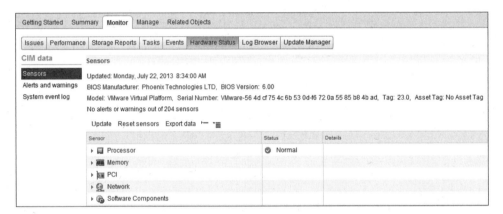

Various vendor-provided and third-party solutions are available that can be used to monitor ESXi system health. If these tools already exist in your environment, it often makes sense to leverage them when monitoring the health of your ESXi systems.

Now that you know the basics of monitoring ESXi system health, let's discuss identifying general ESXi host troubleshooting guidelines.

General ESXi Host Troubleshooting Guidelines

The health status information provided in the vSphere Client or vSphere Web Client can generally be used to start troubleshooting ESXi issues, and these clients are often where many issues will first be identified. If the issue cannot be resolved using this information, then the next location to look in is the actual ESXi log files. Some of these log files can be viewed in the vSphere Client by using the System Logs view. This view can be accessed from the Administration options on the vSphere Client home page.

The ESXi log files can also be viewed in the DCUI under the View System Logs option, as shown in Figure 10.4.

The different logs can be selected by choosing the appropriate number. All of the logs can also be accessed from /var/run/log when using the ESXi Shell.

The VirtualCenter Agent (vpxa) log option will appear in the DCUI only if the host is being managed by a vCenter Server.

FIGURE 10.4 DCUI view system logs

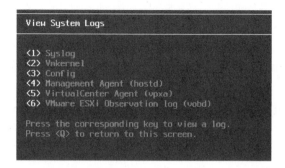

The vSphere Web Client can also be used to view ESXi host logs by accessing the Log Browser. The Log Browser is shown in Figure 10.5.

FIGURE 10.5 The vSphere Web Client Log Browser

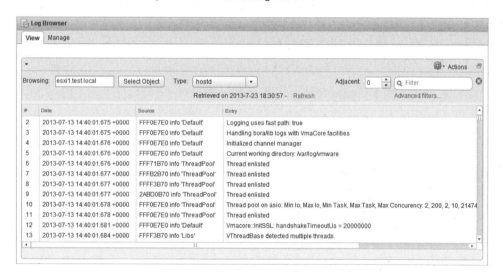

Ideally, most environments will also be configured to use a syslog server for remote logging, so this could be an additional option to use for troubleshooting ESXi hosts.

Knowing where to find the logs is great, but the order in which to troubleshoot ESXi hosts is equally important. The general troubleshooting flow for an ESXi host, as defined by VMware, is as follows:

1. Check the VMware Tools status in the virtual machine.

2. Check the ESXi host CPU usage.

3. Check the virtual machine CPU usage.

4. Check for ESXi host swapping.

5. Check storage usage.

6. Check ESXi for dropped receive packets.

7. Check ESXi for dropped transmit packets.

Now let's discuss how to export diagnostic information.

Exporting Diagnostic Information

System log files can be exported from both vCenter Server and ESXi hosts. If either the vSphere Client or vSphere Web Client is connected to a vCenter Server, the diagnostic information for all of the ESXi hosts being managed can be exported at the same time. If the vSphere Client is connected directly to an ESXi host, then only that host's diagnostic information can be exported. Exercise 10.1 covers the steps to export the diagnostic information from vCenter Server with the vSphere Web Client.

EXERCISE 10.1

Exporting System Logs from vCenter Server

1. Connect to a vCenter Server with the vSphere Web Client.

2. Select the vCenter Server root inventory object in the left pane.

3. On the Monitor tab, click the System Logs option on the toolbar.

4. Click the Export System Logs button. The Export Logs window will open.

5. Select at least one ESXi host that is in the vCenter Server inventory, and select the Include vCenter Server And vSphere Web Client Logs check box. The choices should look similar to this:

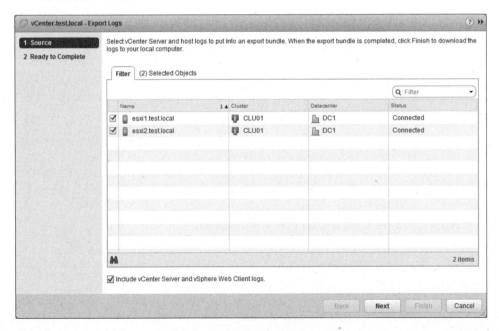

6. Click Next to continue.

7. Ensure that all of the system logs are selected by clicking the blue Select All link. Select the Gather Performance Data check box, and accept the default values for both Duration and Interval.

8. Click the Generate Log Bundle button.

9. Wait for the log bundle to be generated, and then note that the Generate Log Bundle button changes to a Download Log Bundle button.

10. Click the Download Log Bundle button.

11. Use the save procedure specific to your web browser to save the ZIP file that contains the exported logs. An animated progress bar will appear at the bottom of the Export Logs window.

12. When all files have been successfully downloaded, click the Finish button and verify that the log bundle is in the location you specified.

    Another way to generate this log bundle is to use the `vc-support.wsf` script. One advantage this method provides is the ability to collect the log bundle when VMware VirtualCenter Server service is not running. The remainder of this exercise will cover the steps to use this option.

13. Obtain local console access to the Windows system that vCenter Server is installed on.

14. Launch the `vc-support.wsf` script by choosing Start ➢ All Programs ➢ VMware ➢ Generate vCenter Server Log Bundle.

15. A Generate vCenter Server Log Bundle command window will appear, as shown here:

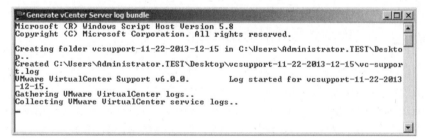

16. Take note of the lines in this command window that show the location the log bundle is being saved to. By default, this will be the current user's desktop.

17. When the command completes, verify that the log bundle has been created. Compare its contents to the bundle created in the first part of this exercise.

For vCenter Server installed on Windows, options are also available on the Windows Start menu/Start screen for exporting log bundles for the Inventory Service, Single Sign-On, and vSphere Web Client.

Diagnostic information can also be obtained for ESXi hosts from the ESXi Shell by using the following command:

```
/usr/sbin/vm-support
```

Figure 10.6 shows the output of this command.

FIGURE 10.6 vm-support command output

```
~ # /usr/sbin/vm-support
17:40:12: Creating /var/tmp/esx-esxi1.test.local-2013-11-22--17.40.tgz
17:41:35: Done.
Please attach this file when submitting an incident report.
To file a support incident, go to http://www.vmware.com/support/sr/sr_login.jsp
To see the files collected, run: tar -tzf '/var/tmp/esx-esxi1.test.local-2013-11-22--17.40.tgz'
~ # _
```

In the next section, we will cover performing basic network troubleshooting for vSphere.

Performing Basic vSphere Network Troubleshooting

Troubleshooting vSphere network connectivity is often one of the first things a virtual infrastructure administrator will do once the initial install of ESXi is complete. Networking and storage can be two of the most complex issues to troubleshoot in a virtual infrastructure, and this section will cover network troubleshooting.

Verifying Network Configuration

It is not unusual for a virtual infrastructure administrator to perform an ESXi install with one or more network cables plugged into the host. There is often consistency between similar hosts in the way the vmnics will be assigned, but sometimes this will not work as planned. One of the easiest ways to verify network connectivity is to use the Direct Console User Interface (DCUI). The DCUI's Configure Management Network feature will allow you to view which vmnic is being used by the management network connection. Figure 10.7 shows the Configure Management Network screen, which you first worked with in Chapter 2, "Planning, Installing, Configuring, and Upgrading VMware ESXi and vCenter Server."

The Configure Management Network feature shows the device name, the MAC address, and the status. Using Configure Management Network is an effective way to verify that the correct NIC is actually reported as connected.

To verify additional networking configurations, you can use the ESXi Shell. The following command can be used to list the physical network adapters' properties and status:

```
esxcli network nic list
```

FIGURE 10.7   ESXi Network Adapters for Management Network

```
Network Adapters

Select the adapters for this host's default management network
connection. Use two or more adapters for fault-tolerance and
load-balancing.


       Device Name   Hardware Label (MAC Address)   Status
  [X] vmnic0         N/A (00:0c:29:4b:8f:76)        Connected
  [ ] vmnic1         N/A (00:0c:29:4b:8f:80)        Connected (...)
  [ ] vmnic2         N/A (00:0c:29:4b:8f:8a)        Connected (...)
  [ ] vmnic3         N/A (00:0c:29:4b:8f:94)        Connected (...)





  <D> View Details  <Space> Toggle Selected      <Enter> OK  <Esc> Cancel
```

Figure 10.8 shows the output of this command from the ESXi Shell.

FIGURE 10.8   Listing NICs from the ESXi Shell

```
~ # esxcli network nic list
Name      PCI Device      Driver  Link  Speed  Duplex  MAC Address         MTU   Description
--------  --------------  ------  ----  -----  ------  -----------------   ----  -----------------
vmnic10   0000:00b:00.0   bnx2    Down      0  Half    00:10:18:a3:83:b8   1500  Broadcom Corporation
vmnic11   0000:00b:00.1   bnx2    Down      0  Half    00:10:18:a3:83:ba   1500  Broadcom Corporation
vmnic12   0000:00c:00.0   bnx2    Down      0  Half    00:10:18:a3:83:bc   1500  Broadcom Corporation
vmnic13   0000:00c:00.1   bnx2    Up     1000  Full    00:10:18:a3:83:be   1500  Broadcom Corporation
vmnic14   0000:012:00.0   igb     Up      100  Full    e8:b7:48:7b:c1:b8   1500  Intel Corporation 82
vmnic15   0000:012:00.1   igb     Up      100  Full    e8:b7:48:7b:c1:b9   1500  Intel Corporation 82
~ #
```

> If you are ever unsure which network cable is attached to a particular
> physical network adapter, you can detach the network cable and use the
> esxcli network nic list command to verify the Link status for the
> physical adapter.

In addition to listing the vmnics in the ESXi host, it is useful to view the vSwitch or
dvSwitch configuration for the ESXi host. The following commands can be used to list the
vSwitch and dvSwitch information for an ESXi host:

```
esxcli network vswitch standard list
esxcli network vswitch dvs vmware list
```

Figure 10.9 shows the output of the vSwitch command from the ESXi Shell. Note that
the format shown in this output has been modified to better fit the pages in this book.

The output of these three commands can typically be used to sort out any network configuration issues, and always remember that ping and vmkping are both available in the
ESXi Shell. While the ESXi Shell offers much functionality, in many cases it is easier to use
the vSphere Client or vSphere Web Client.

FIGURE 10.9 Listing vSwitches from the ESXi Shell

```
vSwitch0                        vSwitch1                        vSwitch2
   Name: vSwitch0                   Name: vSwitch1                  Name: vSwitch2
   Class: etherswitch               Class: etherswitch              Class: etherswitch
   Num Ports: 128                   Num Ports: 128                  Num Ports: 128
   Used Ports: 4                    Used Ports: 3                   Used Ports: 14
   Configured Ports: 128            Configured Ports: 128           Configured Ports: 128
   MTU: 1500                        MTU: 1500                       MTU: 1500
   CDP Status: listen               CDP Status: listen              CDP Status: listen
   Beacon Enabled: false            Beacon Enabled: false           Beacon Enabled: false
   Beacon Interval: 1               Beacon Interval: 1              Beacon Interval: 1
   Beacon Threshold: 3              Beacon Threshold: 3             Beacon Threshold: 3
   Beacon Required By:              Beacon Required By:             Beacon Required By:
   Uplinks: vmnic14                 Uplinks: vmnic13                Uplinks: vmnic15
   Portgroups: Management Network   Portgroups: iSCSI               Portgroups: VM Network
```

If basic management network connectivity is available, the vSphere Client or vSphere Web Client can be used to verify network configurations for the ESXi host. Network configuration was discussed in detail in Chapter 4, "Planning and Configuring vSphere Networking," but here is a brief review. Virtual machines will use virtual machine connection types, and all host-based connections will use VMkernel connection types. These host-based connections can include the management network, vMotion, FT logging, iSCSI, and NFS networking. These two connection type rules will always be the same regardless of whether a vSwitch, dvSwitch, or both are being used. Verifying these configurations can be easily performed using the information available in the vSphere Client or vSphere Web Client, and either of these clients will also report any unavailable network links.

Remember that the CDP and LLDP information provided to the vSphere Client and vSphere Web Client can be very useful in verifying network configurations.

Verifying the ESXi host network configuration is an important first step in the network troubleshooting process. The second step is to troubleshoot physical network adapter configuration issues.

Troubleshooting Physical Network Adapter Configuration Issues

Physical network adapter configuration issues can be addressed from the vSphere Client, vSphere Web Client or the ESXi Shell. As mentioned earlier, the vSphere Client or vSphere Web Client is often easier to use. The following real-world scenario can help explain why.

🌐 Real World Scenario

ESXi Shell Complications

A virtual infrastructure administrator wants to troubleshoot what she believes to be a physical network adapter configuration issue for an ESXi host that is a member of a cluster with HA and DRS enabled. This cluster is used for production systems and is monitored 24 hours a day.

The virtual infrastructure administrator uses many of the VMware best practices in her environment and leaves the ESXi Shell disabled by default for all of her ESXi hosts. Based on past experience, she knows to use the vSphere Web Client to troubleshoot this current physical network adapter issue.

Previously when troubleshooting a similar issue, she used an IP KVM to obtain console access to the ESXi host. She enabled the ESXi Shell and then logged in to the ESXi Shell. Within minutes, the operations team was calling her to report that a configuration issue was being reported on one of her ESXi hosts; they had noticed the warning for the enabled ESXi Shell access in the vSphere Client. After taking several minutes to explain to the operator that everything was okay and to ignore the error, she resumed her work. She ran the appropriate esxcli commands and identified the problem. Her phone then rang again with an emergency "production down" situation for a physical server. She quickly exited esxcli and sped off to help with the production issue. The next day, a member of the security team contacted the virtual infrastructure administrator to inquire about why the ESXi Shell had been enabled on a production system for more than 24 hours. She quickly realized that she forgot to disable the ESXi Shell before speeding off to help with the emergency situation.

When troubleshooting physical network adapter configuration issues, using the vSphere Web Client provides the same information and doesn't require as many steps or risks. The virtual infrastructure administrator learned this from her experience.

Although the esxcli command can be used to troubleshoot physical network adapter configuration issues, Exercise 10.2 demonstrates the steps required to troubleshoot physical network adapter configuration issues using the vSphere Web Client.

EXERCISE 10.2

Troubleshooting Physical Network Adapter Configuration Issues

1. Connect to a vCenter Server with the vSphere Web Client.

2. Select an ESXi host in the left pane and click the Manage tab. Then select Networking from the toolbar.

3. Select the Physical Adapters option on the left.

4. Note that the information in the right pane, as shown here, is similar to the output of the `esxcli network nic list` command in the ESXi Shell.

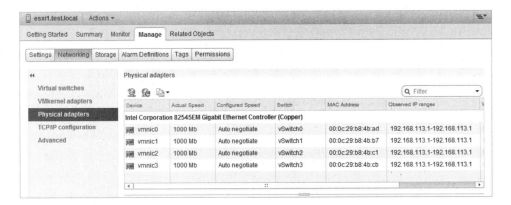

The adapters are listed by vendor, and their device names, actual speed, configured speed, switch use, MAC address, observed IP ranges, Wake On LAN support, SR-IOV status, and number of VFs are all available for troubleshooting purposes.

5. Click the Virtual Switches option on the left.

6. Choose any vSwitch or dvSwitch listed and then click the Manage Physical Network Adapter icon located above the list of virtual switches.

7. When the Manage Physical Network Adapters window opens, click one of the vmnics listed under Active Adapters.

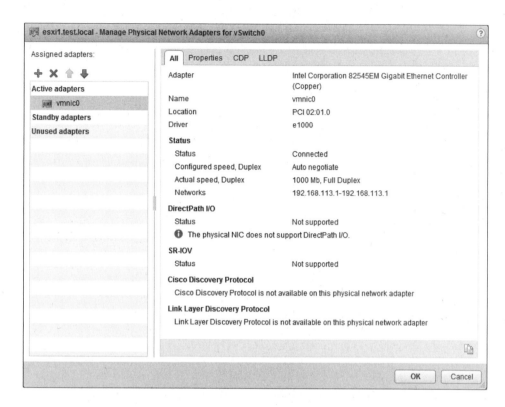

Much of the same information available in the Physical Adapters information is also available here.

8. Click Cancel to close the Manage Physical Network Adapters window.

 When certain configurations are in use, such as Route Based On IP Hash Load Balancing, it will often be necessary to involve the staff responsible for managing the upstream physical network devices. Troubleshooting the virtual switch alone might not be sufficient in these cases.

The next network troubleshooting step is to troubleshoot virtual switches.

Troubleshooting Virtual Switch and Port Group Configuration Issues

Troubleshooting virtual switch and port group configuration issues will depend on the connection type. The previous section covered troubleshooting virtual machine connections, so in this section we will troubleshoot VMkernel port group connection types. Some of these trouble-shooting steps will be the same. The steps include the following:

- Verify that the virtual switch has not lost connectivity to the physical network.

- Verify that the virtual switch has enough ports available.

- Verify that VMkernel networking is configured correctly and that the IP address and subnet mask information are both correct.

- Verify that the port group is configured to use the correct VLAN(s), if applicable.

- Verify that the correct use case is selected: vMotion, FT, management traffic, or no selection for network storage.

- If jumbo frames are used, verify that they are configured properly on the vSwitch and are enabled from end to end.

- Verify that the remote addresses can be reached with the vmkping command in the ESXi Shell.

- Verify that traffic shaping is configured properly, if applicable.

- Verify that NIC teaming is configured as required for the environment.

- Ensure that the ESXi firewall is configured correctly.

As noted, the vmkping command can be used to verify remote connections, and Exercise 10.3 demonstrates the steps for using the vmkping command from the ESXi Shell. Before beginning this exercise, locate the IP address of a storage system or another VMkernel interface on a different ESXi host. You will need this IP address for this exercise.

EXERCISE 10.3

Using the *vmkping* Command from the ESXi Shell

1. Connect to the local console of an ESXi host.

2. Press the F2 key to log in to the DCUI. Log in using the root account.

3. Scroll down to Troubleshooting Options and press the Enter key.

4. Enable ESXi Shell is selected by default. If the right pane reports ESXi Shell Is Disabled, press Enter.

5. Once the right pane reports ESXi Shell Is Enabled, press Alt+F1 to enter the ESXi Shell.

6. Log in to the ESXi Shell using the root account.

7. Type the following command and press Enter:

   vmkping

8. The output will appear similar to this:

```
~ # vmkping
vmkping [args] [host]
    args:
        -4                    use IPv4 (default)
        -6                    -use IPv6
        -c <count>            set packet count
        -d                    set DF bit on IPv4 packets
        -D                    vmkernel TCP stack debug mode
        -i <interval>         set interval (secs)
        -I <interface>        outgoing interface - for IPv6 scope or IPv4
                              (IPv4 advanced option; bypasses routing lookup)
        -N <next_hop>         set IP_NEXTHOP - requires -I option
                              (IPv4 advanced option; bypasses routing lookup)
        -s <size>             set the number of ICMP data bytes to be sent.
                              The default is 56, which translates to a 64 byte
                              ICMP frame when added to the 8 byte ICMP header.
                              (Note: these sizes does not include the IP header).
op Limit
        -v                    verbose
        -W <timeout>          set timeout to wait if no responses are
                              received (secs)

        -X                    XML output format for esxcli framework.
    NOTE: In vmkernel TCP debug mode, vmkping traverses
          VSI and pings various configured addresses.
~ #
```

9. Review the different vmkping arguments before continuing.

10. Enter the following command and press Enter, replacing *<IP Address>* with the IP address you obtained prior to the start of this exercise:

    vmkping *<IP Address>*

11. The ping should return results, indicating a success. Review these results and then type the following command and press Enter:

    exit

12. Press Alt+F2 to enter the DCUI. You may need to press the F2 key again to log in to the DCUI.

13. Disable ESXi Shell access and exit the DCUI.

Once the ESXi host has been verified to be working properly, troubleshooting virtual machines might be required.

Verifying a Given Virtual Machine Is Configured with the Correct Network Resources

When virtual machine connectivity issues arise, verifying the virtual machine network configuration might be necessary. This usually involves doing the following:

- Verify that the virtual machine has a network adapter, that it is connected, and that the virtual machine is using the correct network label in the virtual machine properties.

- Verify the virtual machine's network adapter type and check to see whether the guest OS has the required drivers installed.

- Verify that other virtual machines using the same virtual machine connection type are working properly.
- Verify the networking configuration inside the guest OS is correct, including testing the TCP/IP stack.
- Verify that the virtual switch has not lost connectivity to the physical network.
- Verify that the virtual switch has enough ports available.
- Verify that the virtual switch is configured to use the required VLAN(s).

Before we leave this section on network troubleshooting, let's take a moment to review these steps.

Identifying the Root Cause of a Network Issue Based on Troubleshooting Information

The troubleshooting techniques used to identify the root cause of a network issue are as follows:

- Verify the ESXi host network configuration.
- Verify the ESXi host physical network adapter configuration.
- Verify virtual switch and port group configuration.
- Verify VM network configuration.

Determining the root cause of an issue can sometimes be simple. It can sometimes be a long process that involves going through a number of log files, searching the VMware knowledge base, posting a discussion in the VMware Technology Network (VMTN) communities, or even opening a support request with VMware.

Now we will turn our attention to troubleshooting vSphere storage.

Performing Basic vSphere Storage Troubleshooting

Troubleshooting vSphere storage can be far more involved than troubleshooting vSphere network issues. The variety of storage options and vendors presents many unique combinations, and storage systems even have their own category in the VMware HCL. This section will cover performing basic vSphere storage troubleshooting.

Verifying Storage Configuration

Verifying the correct configuration of storage systems is an important step for the vSphere environment. Misconfigured storage can create significant problems, and it is best not to discover these problems after virtual machines are running in the environment. Storage configuration verification is a multistep process, which involves at a minimum the following:

- Verify that the host's storage adapters are listed on the HCL and used only as described in the HCL.
- Verify that the storage systems used are listed on the HCL and are at the required firmware versions.
- Verify that no configuration maximums have been exceeded.
- Verify that no ESXi patches are required for the configuration.
- Verify that SAN zoning and/or LUN masking are configured correctly.
- Verify that the storage network (Fibre Channel or Ethernet) is connected and configured properly.
- Verify that iSCSI or NFS systems are reachable via vmkping from all required ESXi hosts.
- Verify that iSCSI targets have been configured.
- Verify that iSCSI or NFS permissions are set up properly.
- Verify that authentication to iSCSI systems works properly.
- Verify that the chosen iSCSI adapter is configured properly.
- Verify that jumbo frames are set up properly.
- Verify the speed and duplex settings of network storage adapters.
- Verify that datastores are accessible and/or mounted by all required ESXi hosts.
- Verify that a supported path selection policy is being used.
- Verify VMFS versions, volume sizes, and block sizes.
- Verify that LUNs used for RDM are accessible.

Many of these verifications can take place in the vSphere Web Client, but some will have taken place in the design phase. If the storage or storage network is not under the direct responsibility of the virtual infrastructure administrator, other staff members will often need to be involved in the verification of storage configurations in vSphere. Chapter 5, "Planning and Configuring VSphere Storage," discussed how to create and verify storage configurations in detail, but the key thing to remember with verifying storage configuration is this: ensure that everything is configured in a supported configuration. For example, using a supported SAN with an unsupported path selection policy would be an undesirable storage configuration.

Always remember to read storage vendors' support statements for vSphere implementations to ensure that you use a fully supported storage configuration.

Even with the best storage configuration, you will often have to troubleshoot storage contention issues.

Troubleshooting Storage Contention Issues

With all these virtual machines accessing the same shared storage, there will inevitably be periods of contention as the virtual machines fight for resources on the storage systems. These issues can be further compounded if the SAN or NAS being used by the virtual infrastructure is also shared with other physical systems in the environment.

 Real World Scenario

Contention with Storage Not Dedicated to the vSphere Environment

A virtual infrastructure administrator wants to troubleshoot what he believes to be a storage contention issue for several of the virtual machines he is responsible for. He has collected performance data, and it appears that latency from the storage system is fairly high. Interestingly enough, he is not seeing a large number of I/O commands from the virtual machines.

The storage system is shared among other physical servers as well in this smaller environment. The virtual infrastructure administrator decides to use the tools included with the storage system to monitor it. He quickly finds that a physical file server is the culprit. He tracks it down to a backup job that was started by an operator, since this server missed its normally scheduled backup window the previous day. The backup job is canceled, and the performance of the virtual machines returns to normal.

The virtual infrastructure administrator learned that when sharing storage systems with other physical servers, or even other virtual environments, sometimes it will become necessary to troubleshoot the issue from the storage side. vSphere includes many great utilities and metrics that can be used to troubleshoot problems, but these utilities cannot be used outside of their specific realms.

As the real-world scenario showed, storage issues sometimes need to be tracked on the storage side. This can be performed with tools provided by the storage vendor or with various third-party tools. vSphere includes two ways to monitor the storage performance of the storage systems:

esxtop or resxtop   esxtop is used in the ESXi Shell to monitor storage performance, and resxtop (remote esxtop) is used in the same way from a remote environment like the vMA or vCLI. The advantage of using resxtop is that it works with the ESXi Shell and SSH both disabled.

vSphere Client / vSphere Web Client   The performance charts in the vSphere Client and the vSphere Web Client can be used to monitor storage performance.

In esxtop or resxtop, there are different screens that can be used to obtain information about the storage adapters or virtual machines. The metrics on these screens include the following:

ADAPTR	HBA name, which will be shown as vmhba#.
CMDS/s	Total number of I/O operations per second.
READS/s	Number of read I/O commands issued per second.
WRITES/s	Number of write I/O commands issued per second.
MBREAD/s	Megabytes read per second.
MBWRTN/s	Megabytes written per second.
DAVG/cmd	Average amount of time in milliseconds a device takes to service a single I/O request. The device includes the vmhba, the storage device, and any devices between.
KAVG/cmd	Average amount of time in milliseconds the VMkernel spends servicing I/O requests.
GAVG/cmd	Total latency as seen from the virtual machine. This metric is the sum of DAVG and KAVG.
LAT/rd	Average latency in milliseconds for a read I/O operation. This is a virtual machine–specific metric.
LAT/wr	Average latency in milliseconds for a write I/O operation. This is a virtual machine–specific metric.

Exercise 10.4 covers the steps to view storage contention with esxtop. Note that if you wanted to use resxtop instead, the process is identical once the remote connection has been established.

EXERCISE 10.4

Viewing Storage Contention with *esxtop*

1. Connect to the local console of an ESXi host.

2. Press the F2 key to log in to the DCUI. Log in using the root account.

3. Scroll down to Troubleshooting Options and press the Enter key.

4. Enable ESXi Shell is selected by default. If the right pane reports ESXi Shell Is Disabled, press the Enter key.

EXERCISE 10.4 *(continued)*

5. Once the right pane reports ESXi Shell Is Enabled, press Alt+F1 to enter the ESXi Shell.

6. Log in to the ESXi Shell using the root account.

7. Type the following command and press Enter on the keyboard:

   esxtop

8. When esxtop starts, press the D key. This will switch to the disk adapter screen, as shown here:

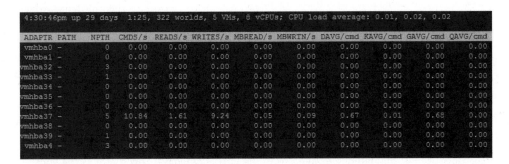

   Review the information on the disk adapter screen. Note the values listed for CMDS/s, DAVG/cmd, and KAVG/cmd. To find out which adapter is associated with the vmhba# listed, you can use the vSphere Web Client. Select an ESXi host, and then select the Storage toolbar on the Manage tab.

9. Press the V key to view the virtual machine screen.

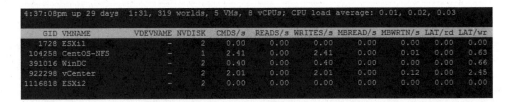

   Review the information on the virtual machine screen. Again, note the CMDS/s, but this time note the LAT/rd and LAT/wr metrics as well. The virtual machine metrics are useful when a storage adapter is reporting latency and you want to find out whether a specific virtual machine is impacted or possibly even responsible.

10. Press the Q key to exit esxtop.

11. Exit the ESXi Shell and then disable it in the DCUI.

The previous exercise focused on viewing storage contention, but in most environments storage contention will be sporadic and unpredictable. If you have a dedicated test environment, you can use tools like Iometer to create a storage contention situation. Another option would be to start multiple virtual machines that are stored on common storage simultaneously. If you have the means to re-create contention in a test environment, you can repeat the previous exercise and create the contention condition. Be sure to start monitoring with esxtop or resxtop before the contention in order to establish a proper baseline.

 You can download Iometer from www.iometer.org.

Viewing the metrics without context does not provide any value, so the following values are considered the threshold values for the metrics:

DAVG/cmd   A value greater than 20 usually indicates a problem.

KAVG/cmd   A value greater than 1 or 2 is considered high.

These are considered threshold values, but all environments and their workloads are different. What constitutes high latency in one environment or workload may not in another. It is important to establish baselines of storage latencies in order to know when something truly unusual is happening.

Whereas esxtop and resxtop provide real-time data, historical storage contention data can be viewed with the vSphere Web Client. Exercise 10.5 covers the steps to view storage contention data with the vSphere Web Client.

EXERCISE 10.5

Viewing Storage Contention Data

1. Connect to a vCenter Server with the vSphere Web Client.

2. Select an ESXi host in the left pane.

3. On the Monitor tab, select Performance on the toolbar.

4. The Overview view will load by default. In the upper portion of this view are two drop-down menus that can be used to customize the view. Make sure that the Home view is selected and that Time Range is specified as 1 Day.

5. Locate the Disk (ms) chart. It will appear similar to this:

EXERCISE 10.5 *(continued)*

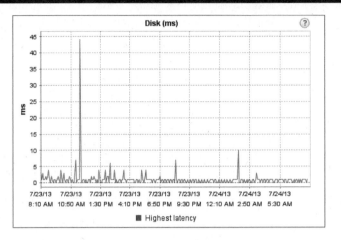

6. Note the peak value reported.

7. Repeat steps 4–6, choosing the 1 Week and 1 Month options for the Time Range. Note the peak values reported in each sampling period.

The Advanced View in performance charts can be used to obtain even more granular information about these latencies.

Besides contention on shared storage systems, another common issue is overcommitment.

Troubleshooting Storage Overcommitment Issues

With the capability of vSphere to thinly provision virtual disks, one of the very real risks is an out-of-space condition when using overcommitment with datastores. To help avoid this problem, the vCenter Server alarm Datastore Usage On Disk can be configured to alert operational staff or the virtual infrastructure administrator of this condition. Figure 10.10 shows the default settings for the Datastore Usage On Disk alarm.

Unless this preemptive action is taken, the first notice that the virtual infrastructure administrator might receive is that of crashing virtual machines on the thinly provisioned datastore(s).

If your storage system has firmware that supports *T10-based Storage APIs* – Array Integration (Thin Provisioning), you can leverage advanced warnings and errors when thresholds are realized for thinly provisioned datastores. This capability was first introduced as a hidden feature of vSphere 4. It allows virtual machines to be paused when the datastore space is exhausted, which will prevent the virtual machines from crashing or worse. When a virtual machine is paused, it can be migrated to another datastore, or space can be added or reclaimed on the current datastore. With the T10-based Storage APIs – Array Integration (Thin Provisioning) support, the first notice that the virtual infrastructure administrator will receive is likely that of warning events in vCenter Server.

FIGURE 10.10   Datastore Usage On Disk alarm

With either scenario, freeing up space is usually the solution to the out-of-space condition. Once free space is sufficient on the datastore, normal operations can resume.

Another common storage issue is troubleshooting iSCSI configuration issues.

Troubleshooting iSCSI Software Initiator Configuration Issues

Troubleshooting the iSCSI software initiator involves verifying the configuration of the iSCSI software adapter. The first step is to make sure that the iSCSI software adapter is listed in the ESXi host's storage adapters. The iSCSI initiator should also be enabled. If the iSCSI initiator is available and enabled but connectivity problems still occur, further investigation will be required.

The Network Port Binding tab can be used to verify that a VMkernel is bound to the iSCSI initiator. Figure 10.11 shows an example configuration.

If the port binding is verified, the virtual switch configuration should also be verified. These steps were discussed earlier in this chapter. Also ensure that an iSCSI target is listed on either the Dynamic Discovery or Static Discovery list available in the Targets tab of the iSCSI software adapter. Verify that these targets can be reached by using the vmkping command from the ESXi Shell. Ensure that CHAP is configured correctly, and verify that the CHAP settings are correct if they are inherited. Also ensure that any advanced settings used are well understood and used only if required.

Now that you are familiar with troubleshooting iSCSI software initiator configuration issues, let's move on to troubleshooting storage reports and storage maps.

FIGURE 10.11   VMkernel port binding details

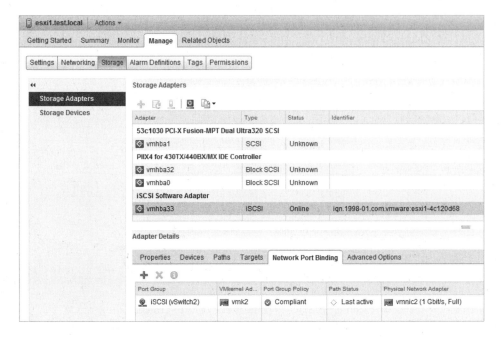

Troubleshooting Storage Reports and Storage Maps

In the traditional vSphere Client, storage reports are used to show relationships between an object and its associations with storage. Figure 10.12 shows a default Storage Report view for a virtual machine.

FIGURE 10.12   Storage report for a VM

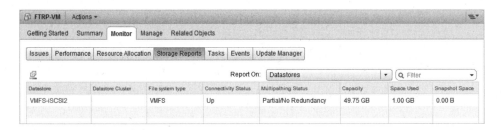

Storage maps show the relationship between a selected object and its associated virtual and physical storage entities. Figure 10.13 shows a storage map for a single virtual machine.

FIGURE 10.13   Storage map for a VM

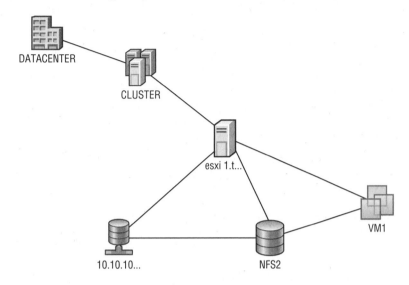

 Storage maps are available only in the vSphere Client.

Before we leave this section on storage troubleshooting, let's take a moment to identify the root cause of a storage issue based on troubleshooting information.

Identifying the Root Cause of a Storage Issue Based on Troubleshooting Information

The common storage issues are contention and overcommitment, but misconfigured storage and/or storage connections can also be problematic. As it is with network issues, determining the root cause of a storage issue can sometimes be simple. It can also be a long process that involves going through extensive log files, searching the VMware knowledge base, posting a discussion in the VMTN communities, or even opening a support request with VMware or the storage vendor.

Now that troubleshooting vSphere storage has been covered, let's turn our attention to troubleshooting clusters, vMotion, and Storage vMotion.

Performing Basic Troubleshooting for HA/DRS Clusters and vMotion/Storage vMotion

Performing basic troubleshooting for clusters with HA and DRS enabled is a key skill for any virtual infrastructure administrator. DRS and HA allow for a highly available infrastructure, along with vMotion and Storage vMotion. Keeping these functionalities working at all times is very important. The final section of this chapter will cover basic troubleshooting for clusters, vMotion, and Storage vMotion.

HA/DRS and vMotion Requirements

To ensure a properly working and supported environment, certain requirements must be met to use advanced vSphere features such as vSphere HA, DRS, and vMotion. vSphere HA has the following requirements:

- All ESX/ESXi hosts must be licensed to use vSphere HA.
- There must be at least two hosts in the cluster.
- Static IP addresses or DHCP reservations are required for all hosts in the cluster.
- A minimum of one common management network between the hosts in the cluster is required.
- All hosts must have access to the same VM networks and shared storage.
- All virtual machines in the cluster must be located on shared storage.
- VMware Tools are required in virtual machines if VM Monitoring will be used.
- Host certificate checking should be enabled.

A DRS cluster has the following requirements:

- All hosts in the DRS cluster must be licensed to use DRS.
- All hosts must have access to the same shared storage.
- All virtual machines in the cluster must be located on shared storage.
- Processor compatibilities should be maximized to most effectively use EVC.

vMotion and Storage vMotion requirements were discussed in detail in Chapter 9, "Maintaining Service Levels," so as a quick review, the vMotion requirements are as follows:

- ESXi hosts must be licensed to use vMotion.
- ESXi hosts must have VMkernel networking established for the vMotion traffic.
- Virtual machines that use raw disks for clustering cannot be migrated.

- Virtual machines that use a virtual device backed by a device that is not accessible on the destination host cannot be migrated.

- Virtual machines that use a virtual device backed by a device on the client computer cannot be migrated.

- Virtual machines that use USB pass-through devices can be migrated only if the devices are enabled for vMotion.

The Storage vMotion requirements include the following:

- ESXi hosts must be licensed to use Storage vMotion.

Virtual machine disks must be in persistent mode or be RDMs for Storage vMotion. Meeting the requirements is always important, and if all systems are compliant, it is often useful to verify the configuration of vMotion and Storage vMotion.

Verifying vMotion/Storage vMotion Configuration

Verifying the vMotion and Storage vMotion configuration involves the following:

- Verify the vSwitch/dvSwitch configuration on all ESX/ESXi source and target hosts.

- If vSwitches are used, ensure that consistent network labels are used across all hosts in the cluster.

- If dvSwitches are used, ensure that all hosts in the cluster are also members of all dvSwitches used by virtual machines.

- Verify that a Gigabit Ethernet network connection exists between all hosts that will use vMotion/Storage vMotion.

- A single Gigabit Ethernet interface should be dedicated to vMotion use.

- Verify that the vMotion traffic is on an isolated network.

- Verify that virtual machines have access to the same subnets on all ESXi hosts in the DRS cluster.

- Verify that jumbo frames are configured from end to end properly, if applicable.

The final step in verifying the vMotion and Storage vMotion configuration is to test each by performing both a vMotion and a Storage vMotion operation.

Next, let's discuss how to verify the vSphere HA network configuration.

Verifying HA Network Configuration

Ensuring that the vSphere HA networking is configured properly is essential to the proper operation of vSphere HA. The following steps can be used to verify the HA network configuration for ESXi hosts in the HA-enabled cluster:

- Verify that all hosts in the cluster have static IP addresses used for their management network(s).

- Verify that the management network redundancy is present by using NIC Teaming or creating a second management network.

- Verify that the network isolation address can be pinged from the ESXi Shell. The network isolation address is the default gateway, unless it has been manually modified.

- Verify that the upstream physical network switches support Spanning-Tree PortFast or an equivalent setting.

- Verify that consistent port group names and network labels are used on all virtual switches.

- Verify that the entire configuration is fully documented.

 For newly created HA clusters, you can power-on test virtual machines and use your configuration documentation to fail the management network connection(s). This is one of the best ways to verify the HA network configuration and to ensure that HA works as you expect it to work.

Another important aspect of verifying vSphere HA is to verify the cluster configuration.

Verifying HA/DRS Cluster Configuration

The first step in verifying a cluster configuration is to ensure that all of the system requirements have been met. This includes verifying DNS resolution and network connectivity, as discussed in the previous section. Once these prerequisites have been covered, the Summary tab for the cluster can provide a significant amount of information about both HA and DRS.

The Cluster Resources panel on the Summary tab for the cluster shows the number of hosts, total processing resources, total memory resources, total flash read cache resources, and the EVC mode. Figure 10.14 shows the Cluster Resources panel.

FIGURE 10.14   The Summary ➢ Cluster Resources panel

When the cluster has HA enabled, there will be a vSphere HA panel on the Summary tab for the cluster. This panel contains many details about the HA configuration. Figure 10.15 shows the vSphere HA panel.

In Figure 10.15, the Define Failover Capacity By Static Number Of Hosts admission control policy was used in the vSphere HA settings. Depending on the admission control policy in use, this image will differ to reflect specific information relevant to the policy.

FIGURE 10.15   The vSphere HA panel

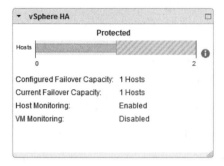

When the cluster has DRS enabled, there will also be a vSphere DRS panel on the Summary tab for the cluster. This panel contains many details about the vSphere configuration. Figure 10.16 shows the vSphere DRS panel.

FIGURE 10.16   The vSphere DRS panel

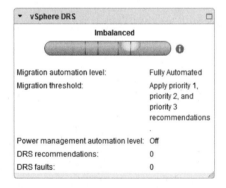

The Summary tab provides a quick overview of the cluster, but the Monitor tab can be used to obtain far more detail. This includes detail on hosts, VMs, and Advanced Runtime Info, if the Define Failover Capacity By Static Number Of Hosts admission control policy was used. Figure 10.17 shows the vSphere HA detail on the Monitor tab.

Also available on the Monitor tab, when vSphere HA is selected on the toolbar, are the Heartbeat and Configuration Issues options. Both of these settings can be used to verify HA cluster configuration.

There is also a vSphere DRS option on the toolbar in the Monitor tab. The options here include Recommendations, Faults, History, CPU Utilization and Memory Utilization.

Even after the vSphere HA configuration has been verified, it may sometimes be necessary to troubleshoot capacity issues with vSphere HA.

FIGURE 10.17 The vSphere HA Monitor tab

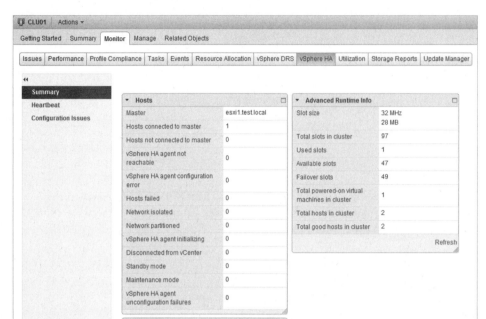

Troubleshooting HA Capacity Issues

Sometimes it will be necessary to troubleshoot capacity issues in an HA-enabled cluster. HA capacity issues will most often be related to the chosen admission control policy. An important thing to remember is that HA will consider only healthy hosts in its calculations. Hosts placed in maintenance mode or failed hosts will make a direct impact on the amount of resources available for virtual machines. These calculations need to be taken into consideration before the cluster is populated with virtual machines. The admission control policies were covered in detail in Chapter 8, "Establishing Service Levels with Clusters, Fault Tolerance, and Resource Pools," but a brief review is relevant here.

When you are using the Define Failover Capacity By Static Number Of Hosts admission control policy, a user-specified number of hosts can be defined, and vSphere HA will reserve resources to be able to fail over the virtual machines running from this number of failed hosts. The calculation used for this is based on a slot size for both CPU and memory, and the slot size is compared to the capacity of the hosts in the cluster to determine how many total slots are available. vSphere HA will then attempt to reserve enough resources to be able to satisfy the number of needed slots. If sufficient resources are no longer available, then the cluster will report that it has insufficient failover resources.

If this condition exists, further virtual machines can be prevented from powering on. To correct this condition, the unavailable ESXi hosts need to be returned to the cluster or virtual machine CPU, and memory reservations may need to be checked to ensure they are not too high.

If the CPU and/or memory reservations cannot be changed, consider using the Define Failover Capacity By Reserving A Percentage Of The Cluster Resources admission control policy.

When the Define Failover Capacity By Reserving A Percentage Of The Cluster Resources admission control policy is used, the percentages may need to be adjusted to lower values to accommodate capacity needs.

Remember that resources are finite in a vSphere environment. Setting the percentages too low in the Define Failover Capacity By Reserving A Percentage Of The Cluster Resources admission control policy can prevent HA from protecting all of your virtual machines in a failover event.

In addition to HA capacity issues, it may often be necessary to troubleshoot HA redundancy issues.

Troubleshooting HA Redundancy Issues

To troubleshoot vSphere HA redundancy issues, it is important to understand how vSphere HA works. Although vSphere HA was covered in detail in Chapter 8, here is a brief review. When host monitoring is enabled in the vSphere HA options, ESXi hosts in the cluster will exchange network heartbeats via the HA agents over their management networks. For network heartbeating, the master host monitors the status of the slave hosts. If the master host stops receiving network heartbeats from a slave host, it must determine whether the host is failed, isolated, or partitioned. To determine which type of event has occurred, the master host will try to check the slave's heartbeat region on a datastore. This is known as *datastore heartbeating* and allows the master host to better determine the true state of the slave host(s).

As discussed earlier in this chapter, redundant management network connections are preferred when using HA. As a best practice, datastore connections should always be fully redundant, regardless of whether vSphere HA is used. When only one part of a redundant connection is lost, vSphere HA should continue to work as planned. Troubleshooting vSphere HA redundancy is really more about troubleshooting network redundancy and storage connection redundancy. vSphere HA will report lost network redundancy, as shown in Figure 10.18. These warnings will stop being reported when the redundancy is restored.

FIGURE 10.18 vSphere HA configuration issues

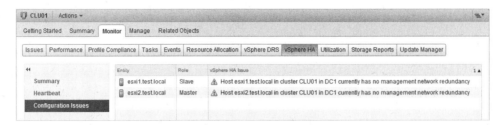

Where vSphere HA needs capacity to ensure high availability, vSphere DRS will attempt to balance workloads. It will sometimes be necessary to troubleshoot DRS load imbalance issues.

Troubleshooting DRS Load Imbalance Issues

DRS attempts to balance loads based on the resource requirements of the virtual machines running in the cluster. Imbalanced load issues can sometimes occur, usually because of certain constraints. These include the following:

- Memory contention
- CPU contention
- ESXi hosts in maintenance mode
- VM-Host affinity/anti-affinity rules
- VM-VM affinity rules

Exercise 10.6 covers the steps to manually create and correct an imbalanced load. This exercise will use a two-node DRS cluster and two virtual machines configured with identical CPU and memory settings. Each ESXi host should have one of these powered-on VMs. If your lab has more virtual machines, simply power off the additional VMs. If your lab has more than two hosts, use maintenance mode to temporarily remove the extra capacity from the cluster.

EXERCISE 10.6

Creating and Correcting a DRS Load Imbalance

1. Connect to a vCenter Server with the vSphere Web Client.

2. Select a cluster in the left pane, and use the context menu to edit the settings for this cluster.

3. On the cluster's Manage tab, click the Settings option on the toolbar.

4. Select vSphere DRS, under the Services option.

5. Review the current DRS Automation level. Click the Edit button.

6. Ensure that vSphere DRS is turned on, and then expand the DRS Automation settings.

7. Select the Fully Automated radio button in the Automation Level section.

8. Move the slider for the Migration Threshold option to the Conservative setting. The final configuration should appear exactly as shown here:

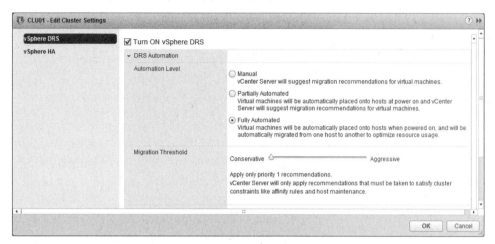

9. Click OK to save these changes. A Reconfigure Cluster task will begin. Wait for this task to complete.

    At this point, DRS has been effectively disabled, and it will not perform automated-load balancing.

10. Ensure that the cluster is selected in the left pane and click the Summary tab in the right pane.

11. Review the level that represents the Target Host Load Standard Deviation in the vSphere DRS panel. It should report a value of N/A directly above the level, and the level should imply a balanced workload. You can also hover the mouse over the Information icon to obtain the Host Load Standard Deviation values.

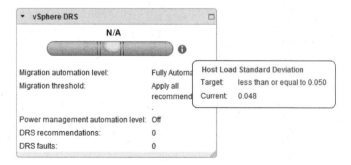

    If the Target Host Load Standard Deviation value in the vSphere DRS panel does not immediately report N/A, wait or manually refresh the screen.

12. Migrate both powered-on virtual machines to a single ESXi host in the cluster.

13. Review the Target Host Load Standard Deviation value in the vSphere DRS panel. You should now see an imbalance reported on the level.

    Now that the load is imbalanced, the remaining steps of this exercise will attempt to balance it.

14. Return to the DRS settings, and move the slider for the Migration Threshold option to the Aggressive setting.

15. Return to the cluster Summary tab.

16. Review the Target Host Load Standard Deviation level in the vSphere DRS panel. It should now report Imbalanced, where it previously stated N/A:

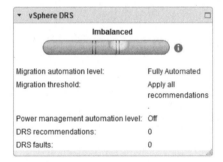

At this point, you can wait patiently for DRS to migrate one of the virtual machines. The full DRS invocation cycle of 300 seconds may have to first pass. Eventually, one of the two virtual machines should be migrated with vMotion to the other ESXi host, creating a one-to-one host-VM relationship. You can also use the Run DRS Now button by selecting a cluster in the vSphere Web Client and clicking the vSphere DRS toolbar on the Monitor tab.

17. After the vMotion completes, review the cluster Summary tab for the Current Host Load Standard Deviation value, and note that it should now report Balanced.

18. Return to the DRS settings, and move the slider for the Migration Threshold option to its default Level 3 setting.

If you are fortunate enough to have a test lab with many resources, this exercise may not work as expected beyond step 14. If the Current Host Load Standard Deviation reports Balanced at the conclusion of step 14, DRS will not migrate one of the virtual machines. If this happens, you will need to read through the exercise and understand the steps.

In the previous exercise the host standard load deviation was mentioned, and in the next section we will discuss this in more detail.

Interpreting the DRS Resource Distribution Graph and Target/Current Host Load Standard Deviation

The host load standard deviations represent the load imbalance metric of the hosts in the cluster. A Target Host Load Standard Deviation value is calculated from the configured Migration Threshold value and the available resources in the cluster. If Current Host Load Standard Deviation exceeds this value, recommendations will be generated and either applied or displayed. The automation of this action depends entirely on the automation level chosen in vSphere DRS.

The DRS host load standard deviations can also be viewed on the Cluster Summary tab in the vSphere DRS panel. To obtain this information, simply hover the mouse cursor over the information icon located to the right of the level. The host load standard deviation is shown in Figure 10.19.

FIGURE 10.19   The host load standard deviation

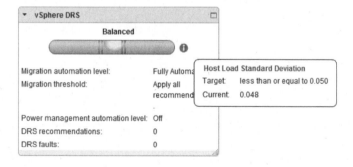

If the DRS migration threshold is set to Conservative, the Target Host Load Standard Deviation entry will report a value of N/A, since no attempt to load-balance is made when this setting is selected.

If the Current Host Load Standard Deviation value is less than or equal to the Target Host Load Standard Deviation value, DRS will report the cluster as balanced, as shown in Figure 10.19. If the Current Host Load Standard Deviation value exceeds the Target Host Load Standard Deviation value, DRS will report the cluster as imbalanced, as shown in Figure 10.20.

CPU and memory utilization for the cluster can be viewed on the cluster's Summary tab. Selecting the vSphere DRS option from the toolbar and the CPU Utilization option will allow you to view the sum of VM CPU utilization for the cluster. Figure 10.21 shows the Sum Of Virtual Machine CPU Utilization setting.

FIGURE 10.20 An imbalanced load entry

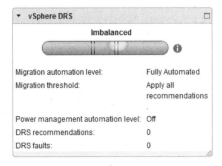

FIGURE 10.21 Cluster CPU utilization

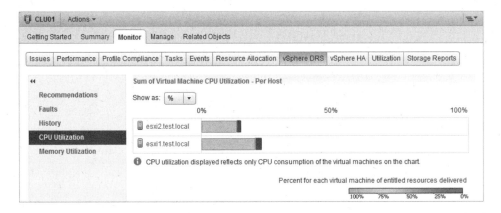

The default view used here allows you to view the CPU utilization for each ESXi host that is a member of the cluster. You can also use the % and MHz options in the drop-down menu to toggle between the different metrics. Each colored box represents either a single virtual machine or a group of what are essentially idle virtual machines. Green boxes are good to see here. The legend at the bottom of the window shows that green indicates 100 percent of the entitled resources are being delivered for the VM. Any other color means the VM is not receiving all of its entitled resources. By hovering the cursor over any of these colored boxes, you can obtain the name of the virtual machine and information about its current resource usage. This is shown in Figure 10.22.

The memory settings for the cluster are also available on the cluster's Summary tab. Selecting the vSphere DRS option from the toolbar and the Memory Utilization option will allow you to view the sum of VM Memory utilization for the cluster. Figure 10.23 shows the Sum Of Virtual Machine Memory Utilization setting.

FIGURE 10.22   Individual VM CPU Utilization

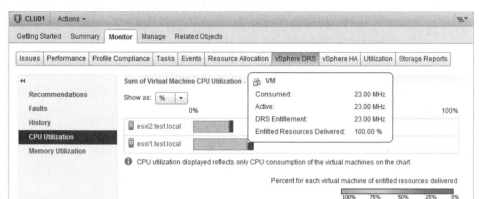

FIGURE 10.23   Cluster memory utilization

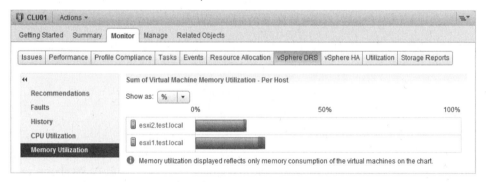

The default view used here allows you to view the memory utilization for each ESXi host that is a member of the cluster. You can also use the % and MB options in the drop-down menu to toggle between the different metrics. Just as with the CPU resources, hovering the cursor over any of these boxes will allow you to obtain the name of the virtual machine and information about its current resource usage.

In the next section we will discuss troubleshooting vMotion and Storage vMotion.

Troubleshooting vMotion/Storage vMotion Migration Issues

The first step in troubleshooting vMotion and Storage vMotion migrations is to ensure that all system requirements have been met. If vMotion and/or Storage vMotion are not working, take the following steps to troubleshoot:

- Ensure that all hosts are licensed for vMotion and/or Storage vMotion.
- Verify EVC and/or the processor compatibility of the hosts in the cluster.

- Ensure that vMotion networking exists on all hosts in the cluster.
- If vSwitches are used, ensure that consistent network labels are used across all hosts in the cluster.
- If dvSwitches are used, ensure that all hosts in the cluster are also members of all dvSwitches used by virtual machines.
- Use vmkping to verify network connectivity of the vMotion VMkernel interface for all hosts in the cluster.
- Verify that no firewalls are between hosts in the cluster.
- Verify virtual switch settings, including VLAN and MTU.
- Verify that time is synchronized across all hosts in the cluster.
- Verify that virtual machines aren't attached to devices on the local ESXi hosts.
- Ensure that the virtual machine is not in the middle of a VMware Tools installation.
- Verify required disk space is available in datastores when using Storage vMotion.
- Verify that all hosts in the cluster have access to the same shared storage.

vMotion Resource Maps are another option that can be used when you need to troubleshoot vMotion.

Interpret vMotion Resource Maps

vMotion resource maps are a quick and convenient way to visualize the relationships between a virtual machine, the ESXi hosts in the cluster, and both the datastores and networks that the virtual machine and the hosts use. It is important to remember that vMotion resource maps are available only in the traditional vSphere Client. Figure 10.24 shows the vMotion resource map for a virtual machine using datastore NFS1 and a virtual machine port group named Intranet.

vMotion resource maps are a useful tool for troubleshooting vMotion issues. In Figure 10.24, there are green circles around the ESXi hosts. These green circles represent that each host has access to the same datastores and networks. The storage and networking requirements for vMotion both pass in Figure 10.24.

As good a troubleshooting tool as the resource maps are, keep in mind that these maps can show networking and storage compatibilities only between the hosts in the cluster. In both of the previous images, the virtual machine used was connected to a host DVD-ROM that would prevent it from being migrated with vMotion. Be aware of these caveats when working with vMotion resource maps.

vMotion Resource Maps are available only in the vSphere Client.

We will conclude this chapter by summarizing how to identify the root cause of a DRS/HA cluster or migration issue based on troubleshooting information.

FIGURE 10.24   A vMotion resource map

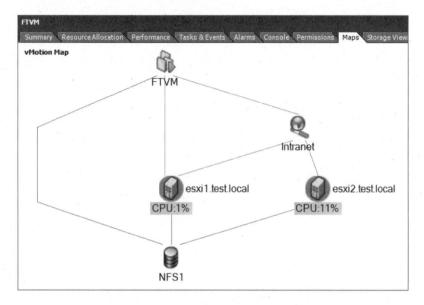

Identifying the Root Cause of a DRS/HA Cluster or Migration Issue Based on Troubleshooting Information

The troubleshooting techniques used to identify the root cause of an issue with a cluster or virtual machine migration were covered thoroughly in this chapter. Determining the root cause of these issues can sometimes be simple. It can also be a long process that involves going through a vast number of log files, searching the VMware knowledge base, posting a discussion in the VMTN communities, or even opening a support request with VMware.

Summary

This chapter focused on performing basic troubleshooting for ESXi hosts:

- Troubleshooting common ESXi installation issues
- Monitoring the ESXi system health
- General ESXi host troubleshooting guidelines
- Exporting diagnostic information

   We also discussed performing basic vSphere network troubleshooting:

- Verifying network configuration
- Verifying a given virtual machine configuration for the correct network resources

- Troubleshooting virtual switch and port group configuration issues
- Troubleshooting physical network adapter configuration issues
- Identifying the root cause of a network issue based on troubleshooting information

In addition, this chapter showed you how to perform basic vSphere storage troubleshooting:

- Verifying a storage configuration
- Troubleshooting storage contention issues
- Troubleshooting storage overcommitment issues and iSCSI software initiator configuration issues
- Troubleshooting storage reports and storage maps
- Identifying the root cause of a storage issue based on troubleshooting information

Finally, we explored performing basic troubleshooting for HA/DRS clusters and vMotion/Storage vMotion:

- HA, DRS, and vMotion requirements
- Verifying a vMotion/Storage vMotion configuration
- Verifying the HA network configuration
- HA/DRS cluster configuration verification
- Troubleshooting HA capacity and redundancy issues
- Troubleshooting DRS load imbalance issues
- Troubleshooting vMotion/Storage vMotion migration issues
- Interpreting the DRS Resource Distribution Graph and Target/Current Host Load Deviation
- Interpreting vMotion resource maps
- Identifying the root cause of a DRS/HA cluster or migration issue based on troubleshooting information

Exam Essentials

Know how to perform basic troubleshooting for ESXi.   Be able to troubleshoot common installation issues. Know how to monitor ESXi system health. Be able to identify general ESXi host troubleshooting guidelines. Understand how to export diagnostic information.

Know how to perform basic network troubleshooting.   Know how to verify a network configuration. Know how to verify whether a given virtual machine is configured with the correct network resources. Be able to troubleshoot virtual switch and port group configuration issues. Understand how to troubleshoot physical network adapter configuration issues. Be able to identify the root cause of a network issue based on troubleshooting information.

Know how to perform basic storage troubleshooting.   Know how to verify a storage configuration. Understand how to troubleshoot storage contention issues. Understand how to troubleshoot storage overcommitment issues. Be able to troubleshoot iSCSI software initiator configuration issues. Know how to troubleshoot storage reports and storage maps. Be able to identify the root cause of a storage issue based on troubleshooting information.

Know how to perform basic HA/DRS cluster, vMotion, and Storage vMotion troubleshooting.   Be able to identify HA/DRS and vMotion requirements. Know how to verify vMotion and Storage vMotion configuration. Be able to verify the HA network configuration and HA/DRS cluster configuration. Understand how to troubleshoot HA capacity issues, HA redundancy issues, and DRS load imbalance issues. Be able to troubleshoot vMotion and Storage vMotion migration issues. Understand how to interpret the DRS Resource Distribution Graph and Target/Current Host Load Deviation. Be able to interpret vMotion resource maps. Understand how to identify the root cause of a DRS/HA cluster or migration issue based on troubleshooting information.

Review Questions

1. You need to put a host in maintenance mode to replace a failed NIC card. When you attempt to put the host in maintenance mode, it gets stuck at 2 percent. Which of the following are likely reasons why the maintenance mode task will not complete?

   A. A virtual machine does not have VMware Tools installed.

   B. A virtual machine has a snapshot.

   C. A virtual machine is attached to an internal-only network.

   D. A virtual machine is attached to an ISO on a local datastore.

2. During a recent maintenance window you took a snapshot of a virtual machine. Prior to taking the snapshot you disconnected the NIC in the VM's settings. The maintenance window ended with a failure, and the VM was reverted to its previous state. Now the owner of the application on this VM reports that the application is down. What is the most likely reason?

   A. The virtual machine has the same MAC address as another virtual machine.

   B. The IP address changed for the VM.

   C. The virtual machine needs to be rebooted.

   D. The VM's NIC is disconnected.

3. Where can all of the ESXi logs be accessed from?

   A. The vSphere Client

   B. The vSphere Web Client

   C. /var/run/log from the ESXi Shell

   D. /var/vmware/log from the ESXi Shell

4. If the Define Failover Capacity By Static Number Of Hosts admission control policy is selected, which of the following panels will appear in the vSphere HA toolbar accessible from the Cluster's Monitor tab?

   A. Advanced Runtime Info

   B. Advanced Cluster Info

   C. Advanced Failure Info

   D. Advanced HA Info

5. You are troubleshooting what you believe to be a storage contention issue. Historically, the DAVG/cmd value returns an average of 7. Today that counter returns a value of 30. What statement best summarizes the situation?

   A. There is no storage contention.

   B. There is minimal storage contention but not enough to worry about.

   C. There is storage contention.

   D. None of these.

6. You have a single virtual machine that fails when using vMotion. Other virtual machines work as expected with vMotion. Which of the following troubleshooting steps should be taken? (Choose all that apply.)

   A. Verify that no firewalls are between hosts in the cluster.

   B. Verify virtual switch settings, including VLAN and MTU.

   C. Verify that the virtual machine is not attached to any devices on the local ESXi host.

   D. Verify that the virtual machine is not in the middle of a VMware Tools installation.

7. Which of the following can be used to troubleshoot vSphere HA issues? (Choose two.)

   A. The Settings toolbar on the Cluster's Manage tab

   B. The Issues toolbar on the Cluster's Manage tab

   C. The vSphere HA toolbar on the Cluster's Monitor tab

   D. The Issues toolbar on the Cluster's Monitor tab

8. Which of the following system requirements do HA, DRS, and vMotion all share? (Choose all that apply.)

   A. All hosts must be licensed to use the feature.

   B. All hosts must have access to the same shared storage.

   C. VMware Tools are required in virtual machines.

   D. VMware Tools must be the most recent version.

9. You need to export the diagnostic information for your vCenter Server and all of the ESXi hosts it manages. What is the simplest way to accomplish this task?

   A. Start ➤ Programs ➤ VMware ➤ Generate vCenter Server Log Bundle

   B. vSphere Web Client connected to vCenter Server

   C. vSphere Client connected to each ESXi host

   D. None of these

10. Which of the following is specifically used to measure virtual machine I/O latency? (Choose two.)

    A. KAVG/cmd

    B. DAVG/cmd

    C. LAT/rd

    D. LAT/wr

11. Which of the following could cause a DRS cluster to become imbalanced? (Choose all that apply.)

    A. VMs with individual memory reservations

    B. ESXi hosts in maintenance mode

    C. VM-Host affinity/anti-affinity rules

    D. VM-VM affinity rules

12. Which of the following can be viewed on a vMotion resource map? (Choose all that apply.)

   A. Virtual machine–connected devices

   B. vSwitches

   C. Datastores

   D. ESX/ESXi hosts

13. You are connected directly to an ESXi host with the vSphere Client. How do you obtain the health information for this system?

   A. Select the host and use the Hardware Status tab.

   B. Select the host and use the Configuration tab.

   C. Select the host and use the Health Status tab.

   D. Select the host and use the System Info tab.

14. Your NFS storage system firmware version does not support T10-based Storage APIs – Array Integration (Thin Provisioning). What will happen if an NFS volume fills to capacity on this storage system?

   A. Virtual machines will shut down gracefully.

   B. Virtual machines will be powered off.

   C. Virtual machines will be paused.

   D. Virtual machines will crash.

15. Which of the following is defined as the average amount of time in milliseconds a device takes to service a single I/O request?

   A. DAVG/cmd

   B. KAVG/cmd

   C. GAVG/cmd

   D. QAVG/cmd

16. You have just installed ESXi on a server and are having trouble getting management network connectivity established. When troubleshooting this issue, the network administrator has asked for the MAC address of the network adapter you are trying to use. Which of the following can be used to obtain the MAC address? (Choose all that apply.)

   A. From the ESXi Shell, run the command
   `esxcli network nic list`.

   B. The DCUI Configure Management Network feature

   C. vSphere Client

   D. vSphere Web Client

17. You are trying to install ESXi on a white-box server built from parts you bought. During the installation, the installer fails to find a hard disk. What are the most likely causes of this problem? (Choose two).

   A. The server's BIOS is not configured properly.

   B. The installation media is corrupt.

C. This server and storage controller are not on the HCL and are therefore not supported.

D. The storage controller needs a driver.

18. Which of the following are valid steps in verifying a storage configuration? (Choose all that apply.)

A. Verify the host's storage adapters are listed on the HCL and used only as described in the HCL.

B. Verify that storage systems used are listed on the HCL and are at the required firmware versions.

C. Verify that no configuration maximums have been exceeded.

D. Verify that no ESXi patches are required for the configuration.

19. Your vSphere environment uses NFS for the storage. The connectivity to the NFS server was set up with a standard vSwitch using the Route Based On IP Hash load balancing. There have recently been issues with connectivity to the NFS server. There have been no changes to the vSphere networking, and your troubleshooting has found no problems. What is the next step in troubleshooting this issue?

A. Reboot each ESXi host one at a time.

B. Restart the NFS storage system.

C. Involve the networking staff to verify that the physical switch is working properly.

D. Open a support request with VMware.

20. When viewing the VMware DRS panel on the cluster's Summary tab, the value of N/A is reported for Target Host Load Standard Deviation. Why is this?

A. Automation Level is set to Partially Automated.

B. Automation Level is set to Fully Automated.

C. Migration Threshold is set to Aggressive.

D. Migration Threshold is set to Conservative.

Chapter 11

Monitoring a vSphere Implementation and Managing vCenter Server Alarms

---

VCP5-DCV EXAM OBJECTIVES COVERED IN THIS CHAPTER:

✓ **7.1: Monitor ESXi, vCenter Server, and Virtual Machines**

- Describe how tasks and events are viewed in vCenter Server
- Create/Edit/Delete a Scheduled Task
- Configure SNMP for vCenter Server
- Configure Active Directory and SMTP settings for vCenter Server
- Configure vCenter server timeout settings
- Configure vCenter server logging options
- Create a log bundle
- Start/Stop/Verify vCenter Server service status
- Start/Stop/Verify ESXi host agent status
- Monitor/Administer vCenter Server connections
- Configure/View/Print/Export resource maps
- Explain common memory metrics
- Explain common CPU metrics
- Explain common network metrics
- Explain common storage metrics
- Identify critical performance metrics
- Compare and contrast Overview and Advanced Charts

- Create an Advanced Chart

- Determine host performance using `resxtop` and guest Performance Monitor

- Given performance data, identify the affected vSphere resource

✓ **7.2: Create and Administer vCenter Server Alarms**

- List vCenter default utilization alarms

- List vCenter default connectivity alarms

- List possible actions for utilization and connectivity alarms

- Create a vCenter utilization alarm

- Create a vCenter connectivity alarm

- Configure alarm triggers

- Configure alarm actions

- For a given alarm, identify the affected resource in a vSphere implementation

✓ **7.3: Install, Configure and Administer vCenter Operations Manager**

- Explain vCenter Operations Manager architecture

- Deploy and Configure vCenter Operations Manager appliance

- Upgrade vCenter Operations Manager

- Differentiate Major/Minor vCenter Operations Manager badges

- Understand metrics used by Major/Minor vCenter Operations Manager badges

- Monitor vSphere environment

- For a given alarm, identify the affected resource in a vSphere implementation

TOOLS

- vCenter Server and Host Management guide (Objectives 7.1, 7.2)

- vSphere Resource Management guide (Objectives 7.1, 7.2)

- vSphere Monitoring and Performance guide (Objectives 7.1, 7.2, 7.3)

- VMware vSphere Examples and Scenarios guide (Objective 7.2)

- vSphere Client / vSphere Web Client (Objectives 7.1, 7.2, 7.3)

- VMware vCenter Operations Manager Getting Started Guide – vSphere UI (Objective 7.3)

- VMware vCenter Operations Manager Getting Started Guide – Custom UI (Objective 7.3)

- VMware vCenter Operations Manager Administration Guide (Objective 7.3)

- vCenter Operations Manager Custom User Interface (Objective 7.3)

This chapter will cover the objectives of section 7 of the VCP5-DCV exam blueprint. This chapter will focus on monitoring a vSphere implementation and managing vCenter Server alarms.

Monitoring ESXi, vCenter Server, and Virtual Machines

The ongoing monitoring of virtual machines, ESXi hosts, and vCenter Server is critical to the success of any virtual infrastructure. Monitoring allows virtual infrastructure administrators to be proactive in maintaining the virtual infrastructure and to better know what is happening on a day-to-day basis. This chapter covers how to monitor virtual machines, ESXi hosts, and vCenter Server. Let's begin by describing how to view tasks and events in vCenter Server.

How Tasks and Events Are Viewed in vCenter Server

When either the vSphere Web Client or the vSphere Client is used to connect to a vCenter Server, the Recent Tasks pane is visible by default. This pane shows active tasks, in addition to tasks that were started and completed within approximately the last 10 minutes. This brief view is good for obtaining real-time task information, but it is often necessary to go back further in time.

When the vSphere Client is connected directly to an ESXi host, the Recent Tasks pane is the only task history available. You can view events in the vSphere Client connected directly to an ESXi host by selecting an object in the left pane and then using the Events tab. Figure 11.1 shows the Events tab for an ESXi host.

When the vSphere Web Client is connected to a vCenter Server, either the Tasks or Events option on the Home Page can be used to view the tasks and events. vCenter Server includes the ability to view historical task information and to create and schedule tasks. The reporting of tasks in vCenter Server can be found in the Task Console, as shown in Figure 11.2.

It is important to remember, when viewing tasks in the vSphere Web Client's Task Console, that the entries in the list will include all tasks for any inventory objects being managed by vCenter. Tasks can also be sorted by clicking the column header for the column you want to sort the data on. If you still need to be able to narrow the entries in this list, you can use the filtering options available in each view. Figure 11.3 shows a view filtered to display only the results for a virtual machine named FTRP-VM.

FIGURE 11.1 The Events tab

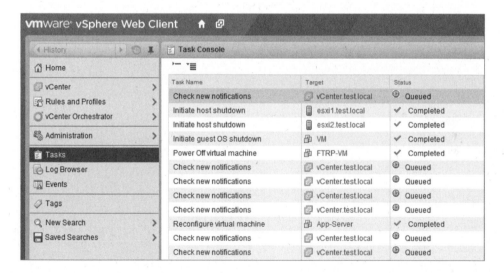

Description	Type		Date Time	User
User root@192.168.113.1 logged in as	ⓘ	info	8/1/2013 9:15:10 AM	root
User vpxuser@logged out (login time:, number of API invocations:, user agent:)	ⓘ	info	8/1/2013 8:20:57 AM	vpxuser
User vpxuser@127.0.0.1 logged in as	ⓘ	info	8/1/2013 8:20:57 AM	vpxuser
User vpxuser@logged out (login time:, number of API invocations:, user agent:)	ⓘ	info	8/1/2013 8:20:38 AM	vpxuser
User vpxuser@127.0.0.1 logged in as	ⓘ	info	8/1/2013 8:20:38 AM	vpxuser
User dcui@127.0.0.1 logged in as	ⓘ	info	8/1/2013 8:10:02 AM	dcui
The DCUI has been enabled.	ⓘ	info	8/1/2013 8:09:04 AM	
Firewall configuration has changed. Operation 'enable' for rule set ntpClient succeeded.	ⓘ	info	8/1/2013 8:09:04 AM	

FIGURE 11.2 The vCenter Server Task Console

You can obtain additional information for each task listed by clicking the entry in the list. The additional details will be displayed in the details pane below the task entries, as shown in Figure 11.4.

To view events, use exactly the same process as for tasks, but with the Event Console. Tasks and events can also be viewed for specific inventory objects. To do this, navigate to the specific inventory object in the vSphere Web Client, select the Monitor tab, and click Events on the toolbar. Figure 11.5 shows a filtered view of the events for a cluster.

FIGURE 11.3   Filtered tasks in vSphere Web Client

FIGURE 11.4   Task details

FIGURE 11.5   Cluster events

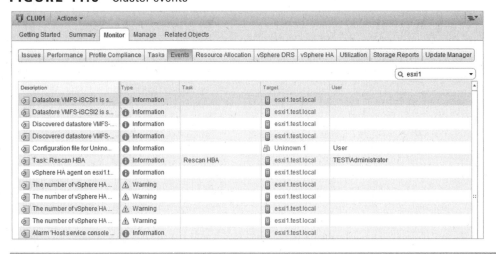

When using the traditional vSphere Client, you can adjust the number of entries displayed in the tasks and events lists. Choose Edit ➢ Client Settings and then select the Lists tab from the Client Settings window. Change the Page Size value to a number between 10 and 1000.

In addition to historical tasks and events, there is one other task view that we need to cover. Scheduled tasks in vCenter Server have their own view, which can be accessed by selecting an inventory object in the vSphere Web Client. Select the Manage tab, and then click Scheduled Tasks on the toolbar. Figure 11.6 shows the Scheduled Tasks view for the root vCenter inventory object, which includes all child objects.

FIGURE 11.6   The Scheduled Tasks view

Now that you've seen how to view events and tasks in vCenter Server and ESXi hosts, we will examine vCenter Server scheduled tasks in more detail.

Creating, Editing, and Deleting Scheduled Tasks

vCenter Server provides the ability to create scheduled tasks that can be used to perform a variety of administrative and operational tasks in the vSphere environment. The tasks available for scheduling will ultimately depend on the vSphere features and plug-ins in use, but the options include the following:

- Change the power state of a VM
- Clone a virtual machine
- Deploy a virtual machine
- Migrate a virtual machine
- Create a virtual machine
- Create a snapshot of a virtual machine
- Add a host
- Change cluster power settings
- Edit resource settings
- Check compliance of a profile
- Scan for Updates
- Remediate

Real World Scenario

Scheduling Virtual Machine Shutdowns

A virtual infrastructure administrator for a small-to-midsize business is the sole responsible person for the entire vSphere environment. He has been asked to power off a two-tiered application that runs in two virtual machines. Normally this would not be a problem, but the requested shutdown date corresponds to a time that the administrator will be on a flight. The shutdown time cannot be changed, and the application owner insists that the servers be powered off.

Rather than changing his flight plans, the administrator decides to use a scheduled task in vCenter Server to accomplish this. He creates two separate tasks to shut down the virtual machines. He schedules them according to the proper shutdown sequence for the application and configures each task to send him an email notification when it completes.

Later in the week, as the administrator is waiting for a cab at the airport, he checks his email. There are two emails, each reporting that the virtual machine was shut down successfully. The scheduled tasks in vCenter Server allowed him to accomplish his work when he couldn't physically be there to do it.

Working off the previous case study, Exercise 11.1 will cover the steps to create, edit, and delete a scheduled task in vCenter Server.

EXERCISE 11.1

Creating, Editing, and Deleting a Scheduled Task in vCenter Server

1. Connect to a vCenter Server with the vSphere Web Client.

2. Navigate to a powered-on virtual machine in the inventory.

3. Click the Manage tab, and then click Scheduled Tasks on the toolbar.

4. Click the Schedule A New Task option, and select the Shut Down Guest OS option from the context menu.

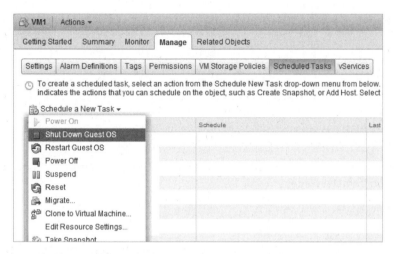

5. Click Yes in the Confirm Shut Down dialog box to continue.

   Note here that you are only confirming a shutdown task to be scheduled. The VM will not be shut down at this point.

6. Click the Scheduling Options option on the left and provide a descriptive task name and description. If your environment has SMTP configured, enter your email address in the bottom field.

   Configuring vCenter Server to use an SMTP server will be covered later in this chapter.

7. Click the Change link for the Configured Scheduler. A Configure Scheduler window will open.

8. Select the Schedule This Action To Run Later option and pick a date and time two weeks in the future. Click OK to save this schedule.

9. Review the scheduling options.

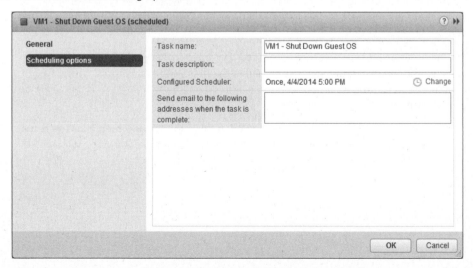

EXERCISE 11.1 *(continued)*

10. Click OK to continue. A task named Create Scheduled Task will begin. When this task completes, verify that the newly created scheduled task is listed in Scheduled Tasks.

    The scheduling of this task has now been completed. For the purposes of this exercise, assume that the task requestor has changed his mind and wants the virtual machine to be shut down at a different time. In the next part of this exercise, you will edit the scheduled task to accommodate this request.

11. Select the scheduled task created earlier in this exercise and right-click it. Choose the Edit option from the context menu.

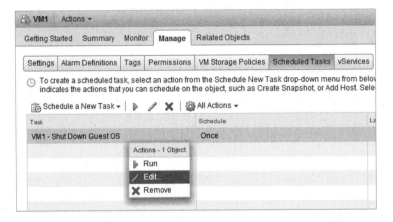

12. Click Scheduling Options and change the time of the scheduled task.

13. Click OK to save the changes made to the scheduler.

14. A task named Reconfigure Scheduled Task will begin. When this task completes, verify that the new start time is listed in Scheduled Tasks. This value will be reported in the Next Run column.

    The scheduled task has now been modified. For the purposes of this exercise, now assume that the task requestor has canceled the maintenance window entirely and no longer wants the virtual machine to be shut down. In the final part of this exercise, you will remove this scheduled task.

15. Select the scheduled task that has been used in this exercise and then click the red X icon located above the list of scheduled tasks. A confirmation dialog box will appear.

16. Click the Yes button and then verify that the scheduled task is no longer listed in Scheduled Tasks.

17. Click the Monitor tab and then click Events on the toolbar. Review the scheduled tasks from this exercise.

18. Click Tasks on the toolbar. Review the tasks from this exercise.

WARNING If the Run option is chosen from either the toolbar or the context menu of a scheduled task, the scheduled task will run immediately and you will not be prompted.

The next section covers how to configure SNMP for vCenter Server.

Configuring SNMP for vCenter Server

vCenter Server includes an SNMP agent that can be configured to send SNMP traps to up to four receivers. This agent serves as a trap emitter only. Traps will be sent when vCenter Server is started and when alarms are triggered in vCenter Server. These traps would typically be sent to other management programs, or receivers, and those applications would need to be installed and configured properly as a prerequisite to configuring SNMP in vCenter Server. If existing monitoring tools are in place that can leverage the vCenter Server SNMP data, this can be a great feature for enhancing the monitoring of vCenter Server. Configuring the SNMP settings requires the use of the vSphere Client connected to a vCenter Server. Exercise 11.2 demonstrates the steps to configure SNMP for vCenter Server.

EXERCISE 11.2

Configuring SNMP for vCenter Server

1. Connect to a vCenter Server with the vSphere Web Client.

2. Select the vCenter Server root inventory object in the left pane, and then click the Manage tab. Click Settings on the toolbar and select General in the left pane.

EXERCISE 11.2 *(continued)*

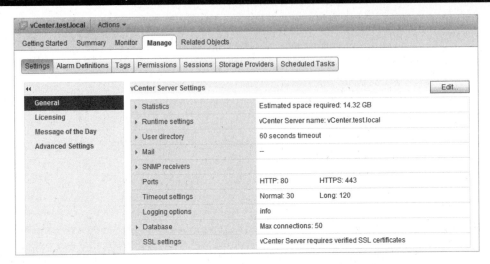

3. Click the Edit button, and an Edit vCenter Server Settings window will open.

4. Click SNMP Receivers in the left pane.

5. Enter the primary receiver URL, port information, and the community string for the primary receiver.

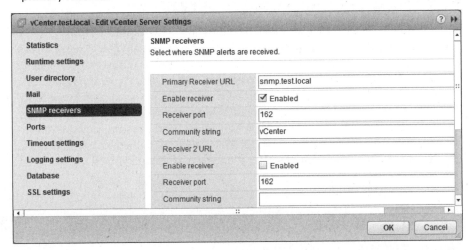

Note that to use the additional receivers, you must select the Enabled check box first.

6. Click OK to save the changes. Verify that the SNMP settings are shown in the vCenter Server Settings.

7. If your test environment has a working SNMP implementation, check to verify that vCenter Server is sending events.

Now that you have configured SNMP for vCenter Server, you will learn how to configure Active Directory and SMTP settings for vCenter Server.

Configuring User Directory and SMTP Settings for vCenter Server

vCenter Server's interactions with the user directory server that is specified as the identity source can be configured using the vCenter Server settings. The default User Directory settings are shown in Figure 11.7.

FIGURE 11.7 User directory settings

User Directory Timeout is the number of seconds specified for the connection timeout to the directory service. If you find that users and groups are not being listed, increasing the timeout interval can resolve this issue.

You can enable the Query Limit Size option to limit the number of users and groups that will be displayed in the Add Permissions dialog box when assigning permissions to inventory objects in vCenter Server. The value can be adjusted in the Query Limit Size field. Setting this value to a low number can be useful in troubleshooting situations with directory services. Note that setting the Query Limit Size value to 0 will produce the same effect as deselecting the Enabled option; with both settings there will be no limit on the maximum number of domain users and groups that will be displayed when assigning permissions in vCenter Server.

The Validation option can be enabled to periodically validate its list of known users and groups against the current list in the directory service and update its permissions accordingly. The Validation Period setting can be customized as desired, but validation will also occur at vCenter Server host startup.

vCenter Server can also be configured to use an existing SMTP server to send email in response to alarm actions. Figure 11.8 shows the vCenter Server settings for SMTP.

FIGURE 11.8   vCenter SMTP settings

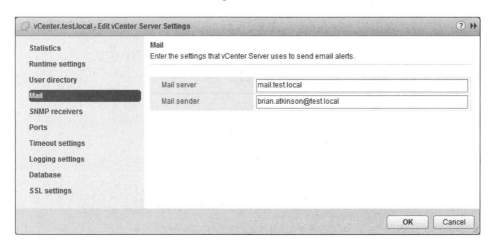

The Mail Server field can include the FQDN or IP address of the SMTP server, and the Mail Sender field must be configured with a full email address. Figure 11.8 shows a proper Mail Sender configuration.

The next section covers configuring vCenter Server timeout settings.

Configuring vCenter Server Timeout Settings

The vCenter Server timeout settings for vCenter Server operations can also be configured in the vCenter Server settings. These settings specify the interval of time after which the vSphere Web Client (or vSphere Client) will time out. The default vCenter Server timeout settings are shown in Figure 11.9.

FIGURE 11.9   vCenter timeout settings

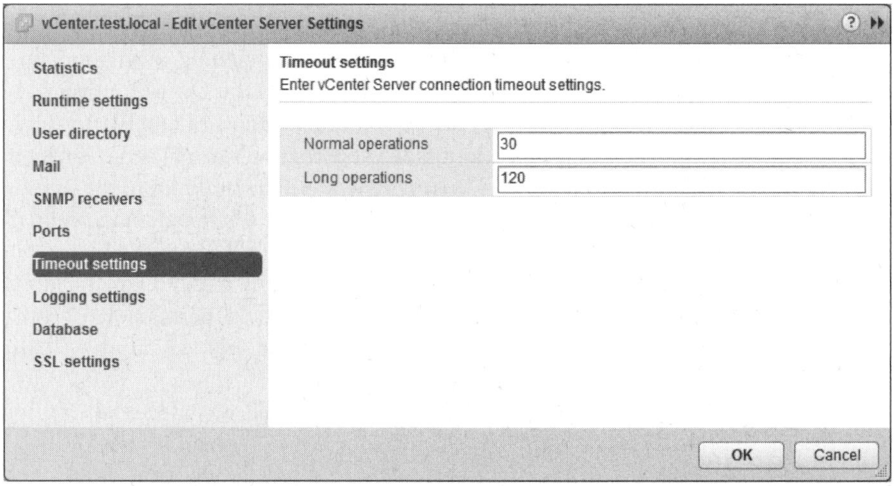

Increasing these values can sometimes be necessary for slow network links. The default value for long operations is 2 minutes, and the default value for normal operations is 30 seconds.

 WARNING   Never set the Normal Operations timeout or the Long Operations timeout to a value of 0.

The next section covers the vCenter Server logging options and their configuration.

Configuring vCenter Server Logging Options

vCenter Server logging detail can also be configured in the vCenter Server settings. There is one drop-down menu that is used to configure the logging level for vCenter Server, as shown in Figure 11.10.

FIGURE 11.10   vCenter logging options

vCenter.test.local - Edit vCenter Server Settings	② ▶▶

Statistics	**Logging settings**
Runtime settings	Select the level of detail that vCenter Server uses for log files.
User directory	
Mail	Logging options info ▼
SNMP receivers	none
Ports	error
Timeout settings	warning
Logging settings	info
Database	verbose
SSL settings	trivia

OK   Cancel

The vCenter Server logging detail is by default configured at Information (Normal Logging). The available logging levels are as follows:

None (Disable Logging)   Used to turn off logging

Error (Errors Only)   Used to display only error log entries

Warning (Errors and Warnings)   Used to display only error and warning log entries

Information (Normal Logging)   Used to display information, error, and warning log entries

Verbose (Verbose)   Used to display information, error, warning, and verbose log entries

Trivia (Trivia)   Used to display information, error, warning, verbose, and trivia log entries

Note that the exact wording of these logging levels varies slightly from the vSphere Web Client to the traditional vSphere Client. Changes made to the Logging Options section in the vCenter Server settings take effect as soon as you click OK; vCenter Server system services do not need to be restarted for this change to take effect.

The default logging level of Information would typically be used, unless there was a specific requirement to change the level of logging. Logging levels might be increased when working with VMware Support, for example.

In the next section we will review how to create a log bundle in vCenter Server.

Creating a Log Bundle

You saw how to create a log bundle for vCenter Server in Chapter 10, "Performing Basic Troubleshooting," in Exercise 10.1. As a review, Figure 11.11 shows the Export System Logs wizard that was used in Exercise 10.1 to create the vCenter Server log bundle.

FIGURE 11.11   Creating a vCenter log bundle

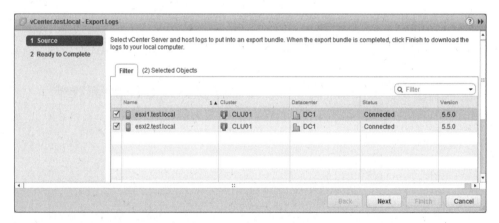

You can also create the log bundle regardless of the status of the vCenter Server services by selecting Start ➢ Programs ➢ VMware ➢ Generate vCenter Server Log Bundle from the Windows server where vCenter Server is installed. In the case of Windows 2012 you'll find the Generate vCenter Server Log Bundle tile on the start screen.

In the next section, we will discuss the vCenter Server services.

Starting, Stopping, and Verifying vCenter Server Service Status

The vCenter Server service runs as a Windows service on the server it is installed on. The service is named VMware VirtualCenter Server, and it is configured to start Automatic (Delayed Start) with the system by default. Exercise 11.3 covers the steps to verify whether the VMware VirtualCenter Server service is running and to stop and start the service.

EXERCISE 11.3

Verifying, Stopping, and Starting the VMware VirtualCenter Server Services Using the Windows Services Management Console

1. Connect to a console session on the Windows server that vCenter Server is installed on.

2. Open the vSphere Web Client and connect to vCenter Server.

3. Verify that no tasks are actively running. If there are, wait for them to complete.

4. In Windows, access the Run window or a command prompt. Type the following command in the Run window or command prompt:

    `services.msc`

5. The Services MMC snap-in will launch, as shown here:

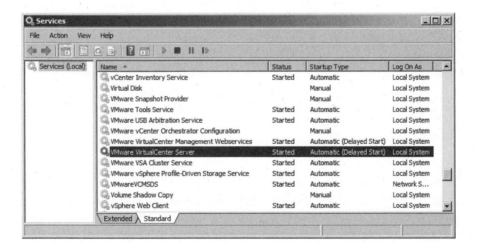

EXERCISE 11.3 *(continued)*

6. Check the Status column beside the VMware VirtualCenter Server service. If it reports Started, then vCenter Server is running.

   You have now confirmed that the VMware VirtualCenter Server service is running. In the next part of this exercise, you will manually stop the VMware VirtualCenter Server service.

7. In the Services MMC snap-in, select the VMware VirtualCenter Server service and then right-click it. Choose Stop from the context menu.

8. A Stop Other Services dialog box will appear, similar to the one shown here:

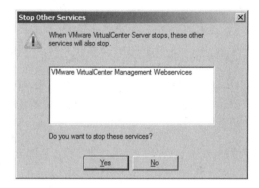

9. Note which services are going to be stopped, because they will need to be started again manually later. Click Yes to proceed.

10. Wait for the services to be stopped. Verify the Status column reports no value before continuing.

    The VMware VirtualCenter Server services have now been stopped. In the next steps, you will start the required services.

11. In the Services MMC snap-in, select the VMware VirtualCenter Server service and right-click it. Choose Start from the context menu.

12. Repeat this process for any services that were listed in the dialog box from Step 9.

    Note that your list of services can vary. Depending on the number of services and their dependencies, it can sometimes be faster and easier to simply reboot Windows.

The vCenter Service Health feature can also be used inside the vSphere Web Client connected to a vCenter Server to view vCenter Server service status information. Select the root vCenter Server object in the left pane, and then click the Monitor tab. Click Service Health on the toolbar. Figure 11.12 shows the vCenter Service Health screen.

FIGURE 11.12   The vCenter Service Health screen

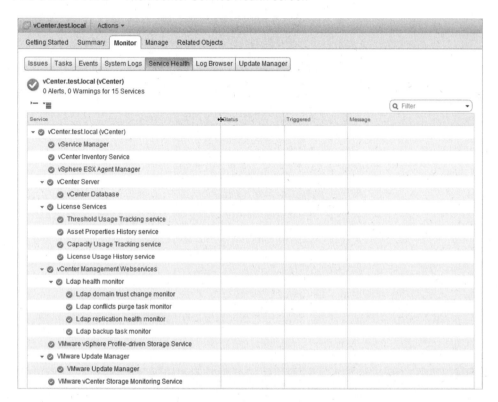

We have now covered working with the vCenter Server Service, and next you will see how to verify, stop, and start the ESXi host agent status.

Starting, Stopping, and Verifying ESXi Host Agent Status

The ESXi *host agent* communicates to the traditional vSphere Client, vCenter Server, and other vSphere interfaces through the vSphere API. The ESXi host agent runs as the hostd service in ESXi. It is installed as part of the default ESXi installation, and its architecture is shown in Figure 11.13.

FIGURE 11.13 ESXi host agent

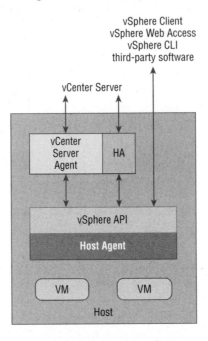

The steps to verify, stop, and start the ESXi host agent are covered in Exercise 11.4. Make sure that no active tasks are running in vCenter Server before stopping the hostd service on an ESXi host.

EXERCISE 11.4

Verifying, Stopping, and Starting the ESXi Host Agent

1. Connect to the console of an ESXi host.

2. Press the F2 key to log in to the DCUI.

3. Log in with the root account.

4. Select the View System Logs option.

5. Press the 4 key to view the Management Agent (hostd) log.

6. Press Shift+G to go to the end of the hostd log. The results should appear similar to what is shown here:

```
2011-11-29T14:33:07.165Z [33C81B90 verbose 'SoapAdapter'] Responded to service state request
2011-11-29T14:33:11.334Z [33FA5B90 verbose 'Cimsvc'] Ticket issued for CIMOM version 1.0, user root
2011-11-29T14:33:25.297Z [33C81B90 verbose 'Default'] Power policy is unset
2011-11-29T14:33:25.299Z [33A40B90 verbose 'Default'] Power policy is unset
2011-11-29T14:33:33.956Z [33D44B90 verbose 'SoapAdapter'] Responded to service state request
2011-11-29T14:33:37.167Z [33CC2B90 verbose 'SoapAdapter'] Responded to service state request
2011-11-29T14:33:55.294Z [33C81B90 verbose 'Default'] Power policy is unset
2011-11-29T14:33:55.296Z [FFBEAA90 verbose 'Default'] Power policy is unset
2011-11-29T14:34:03.958Z [3406EB90 verbose 'SoapAdapter'] Responded to service state request
2011-11-29T14:34:07.168Z [34019B90 verbose 'SoapAdapter'] Responded to service state request
2011-11-29T14:34:25.292Z [3406EB90 verbose 'Default'] Power policy is unset
2011-11-29T14:34:25.294Z [3406EB90 verbose 'Default'] Power policy is unset
<Q> Quit </> RegExp Search <H> Help
```

Pressing the G key will jump to the end of the file. Pressing it again will be similar to using the Tail command and will allow you to view the hostd log as it updates. If you are seeing current events here, then hostd is running. Remember that the time stamps will be shown in UTC, so you will need to convert them for your time zone accordingly.

7. Press the Q key to exit the hostd log viewer.

You have now verified that the hostd log has entries. In the next part of this exercise, I will cover how to use the ESXi Shell to obtain the status for the hostd service.

8. While still in the DCUI, enable the ESXi Shell in the Troubleshooting Options menu.

9. Press Alt+F1 and log in to the ESXi Shell using the root account.

10. Type the following command:

./etc/init.d/hostd status

The output should look like this:

You have now verified that the hostd service is running. The remainder of this exercise covers the steps to stop and start the hostd service.

11. To stop the hostd service, type the following command:

./etc/init.d/hostd stop

12. To start the hostd service, type the following command:

./etc/init.d/hostd start

EXERCISE 11.4 *(continued)*

13. To restart the hostd service, type the following command:

`./etc/init.d/hostd restart`

14. To restart all management services, including hostd, ntpd, sfcbd, slpd, wsman, and vobd, use the following command:

`./sbin/services.sh restart`

Note that you can restart the management agents by choosing the DCUI Troubleshooting Options option.

 For the procedure to handle hostd, if it ever becomes stuck, check the VMware KB article at `http://kb.vmware.com/kb/1005566`.

In the next section, you will see how to monitor and administer vCenter Server connections.

Monitoring and Administering vCenter Server Connections

Sessions are established in vCenter Server when users connect via the traditional vSphere Client or the vSphere Web Client. These sessions can be monitored and administered via the vSphere Web Client. Figure 11.14 shows the sessions listed in the vSphere Web Client.

FIGURE 11.14   vCenter Server sessions

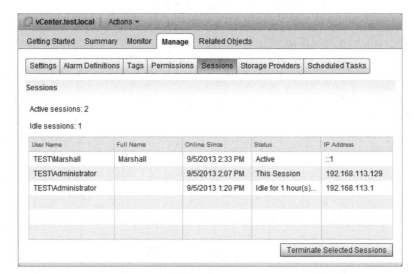

The Sessions pane shows the total count of active and idle sessions and lists the username, the user's full name, the online time, the current status, and the IP address the session connected from. Any idle or active session—except for the one currently in use—can be terminated by using the Terminate Selected Sessions button located at the bottom of the pane.

 You will not be prompted to confirm the session termination when terminating sessions from the vSphere Web Client.

A message of the day can be sent to currently active session users of vCenter Server. This message will also be sent to any newly logged-in users of the vSphere Web Client or traditional vSphere Client. This is useful when you need to notify users of events such as upcoming maintenance windows. To configure the message of the day, select vCenter Server in the left pane, and then click the Manage tab. Click Settings on the toolbar and then choose Message Of The Day in the left pane. Clicking the Edit button allows you to change the message. Figure 11.15 shows the message of the day in the vSphere Web Client.

FIGURE 11.15   Message Of The Day in vSphere Web Client

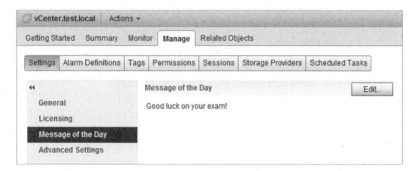

In the next section, we will cover configuring, viewing, printing, and exporting resource maps.

Configuring, Viewing, Printing, and Exporting Resource Maps

vCenter Server resource maps are used to display a visual representation of the relationships between virtual and physical resources. The following resource map views are available in vCenter Server:

- Virtual Machine Resources
- Host Resources
- Datastore Resources

- Custom

- vMotion

Chapter 10 covered vMotion resource maps. One notable difference between the vMotion resource map and the other maps is that the vMotion resource map cannot be customized. Also note that the vMotion resource map is available only in the Hosts and Clusters or VMs and Templates view when the virtual machine is selected in the left pane and the Maps tab is selected in the right pane. Resource maps are available only in the traditional vSphere Client.

Configuring resource maps begins with checking the maximum number of objects the map will display. For very large vSphere environments, this can help control the usability of the resource maps. To set the maximum number of objects, use the traditional vSphere Client menu and select the Edit ➢ Client Settings option. Select the Maps tab and change the value of Maximum Requested Topology Entities to the desired number. Figure 11.16 shows the default value of Maximum Requested Topology Entities for maps.

FIGURE 11.16 Max number of map objects

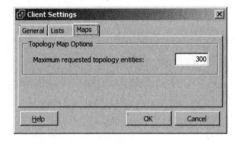

Once the maximum requested topology entities value has been configured, the resource maps are ready to be used. Exercise 11.5 covers the steps to configure, view, print, and export a resource map.

EXERCISE 11.5

Configuring, Viewing, Printing, and Exporting a Resource Map

1. Connect to a vCenter Server with the vSphere Client.

2. Click the Home icon in the navigation bar and choose Maps in the Management section. The Virtual Machine Resources view will load by default, as shown here.

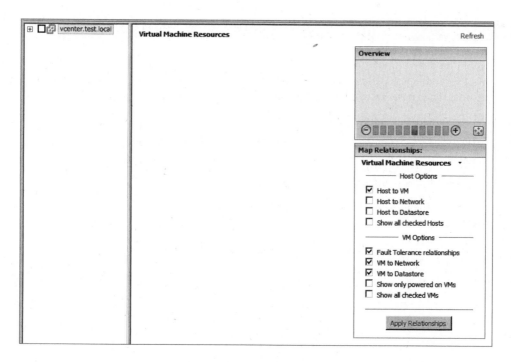

3. Using the Map Relationships panel, click the down arrow for Virtual Machine Resources to reveal the view options.

4. Select Custom Map from the menu that appears.

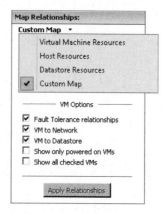

EXERCISE 11.5 *(continued)*

Note that even though there are check marks placed in several of the options in the Map Relationships panel, there are no objects placed on the map yet. This is because no object has been selected in the left pane.

5. Expand the inventory in the left pane to show all objects.

6. Select a single virtual machine in the left pane and note how the map updates immediately.

7. Click and drag any object in the map to reposition the map.

8. Right-click the virtual machine shown in the map. You should see the following context menu:

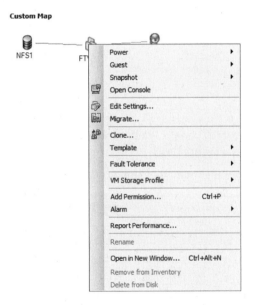

9. Press the Esc key to remove the context menu, and in the Map Relationships panel, deselect the VM To Network option.

10. Click the Apply Relationships button to apply this change.

11. Review the relationship.

12. In the Map Relationships panel, select the VM To Network option and deselect the VM To Datastore option.

13. Click the Apply Relationships button to apply this change.

14. Review the relationship.

15. Use the zoom controls in the Overview panel to zoom in and out on the map. Click the icon in the lower-right corner of the Overview panel to return to the default zoom level.

16. Deselect the virtual machine in the left pane and choose a single ESXi host instead.

17. Select the listed Host Options in the Map Relationships panel.

18. Click the Apply Relationships button and review the results. The results should look like this:

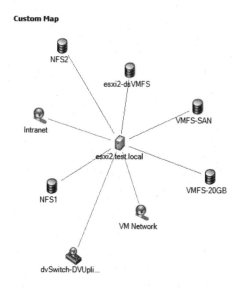

19. Print the map by choosing File ➢ Print Maps ➢ Print in the vSphere Client.

20. Export the map by choosing File ➢ Export ➢ Export Maps. You will be prompted to enter the location, name, and file type.

21. Click the Save As Type drop-down menu and review the various options available.

In the next several sections, we will discuss the common metrics used in vSphere. Let's begin with memory.

Common Memory Metrics

Memory metrics are used to track memory usage for different objects in the vSphere environment. The two most common tools used to monitor memory usage will be the vSphere

Web Client and resxtop/esxtop. Table 11.1 details the common memory metrics used for ESXi hosts as they appear in resxtop and the vSphere Web Client.

TABLE 11.1   Common memory metrics for ESXi hosts

resxtop	vSphere Web Client	Description
PMEM: total	Memory: Total Capacity	The total amount of memory installed in the ESXi host
PMEM: vmk	Memory: Used by VMkernel	The amount of memory being used by the VMkernel
PSHARE shared	Memory: Shared	The amount of physical memory that is being shared by virtual machines
SWAP curr	Memory: Swap used	The current swap file usage
ZIP zipped	Memory: Compressed	The total compressed physical memory
MEMCTL curr	Memory: Balloon	The total amount of physical memory reclaimed by ballooning

Virtual machines have their own unique set of metrics as well; Table 11.2 details these metrics.

TABLE 11.2   Common memory metrics for virtual machines

resxtop	vSphere Web Client	Description
MEMSZ	N/A	The amount of physical memory allocated to the virtual machine
%ACTV	Memory: Usage	The percentage of guest physical memory being referenced by the guest
OVHD	Memory: Overhead	The current amount of space used by the virtual machine overhead
SHRD	Memory: Shared	The amount of shared memory in physical pages
MEMCTLSZ	Memory: Balloon	The amount of physical memory reclaimed by way of ballooning
SWCUR	Memory: Swapped	The amount of memory being swapped out to disk on the ESXi host
SWR/s	Memory: Swap In Rate	The rate at which memory is being swapped in from disk on the ESXi host

resxtop	vSphere Web Client	Description
SWW/s	Memory: Swap Out Rate	The rate at which memory is being swapped out to disk on the ESXi host
CACHEUSD	Memory: Compressed	The size of the used compression memory cache
ZIP/s	Memory: Zipped Memory	The compressed memory per second
UNZIP/s	Memory: Zipped Memory	The uncompressed memory per second

Next, let's look at the common CPU metrics.

Common CPU Metrics

CPU metrics are used to track CPU usage for various objects in the vSphere environment. The two most common tools used to monitor CPU usage are the vSphere Web Client and resxtop/esxtop. Table 11.3 details the common CPU metrics used for ESXi hosts as they appear in resxtop and the vSphere Web Client.

TABLE 11.3 Common CPU metrics for ESXi Hosts

resxtop	vSphere Web Client	Description
PCPU USED (%)	CPU: Usage	The percentage of CPU usage per physical CPU (PCPU) and the percentage of CPU usage averaged over all PCPUs
PCPU UTIL (%)	CPU: Idle	The percentage of real time that the PCPU was not idle

Virtual machines have their own unique set of metrics as well; Table 11.4 details these metrics.

TABLE 11.4 Common CPU metrics for virtual machines

resxtop	vSphere Web Client	Description
%USED	CPU: Used	The percentage of physical CPU core cycles used by the virtual machine
%RDY	CPU: Ready	The percentage of time the VM was not provided CPU resources but was ready to run
%SWPWT	CPU: Swap wait	The percentage of time spent waiting for the VMkernel to swap memory

The %SWPWT metric included in the CPU metrics will often also be used when monitoring memory.

Next, let's look at the common network metrics.

Common Network Metrics

Network metrics are used to track network usage for various objects in the vSphere environment. The two most common tools used to monitor network usage are the vSphere Web Client and resxtop/esxtop. Figure 11.17 shows the common network metrics used for both ESXi hosts and virtual machines as they appear in resxtop.

FIGURE 11.17   resxtop networking metrics

```
7:55:09pm up  1:00, 302 worlds, 1 VMs, 1 vCPUs: CPU load average: 0.03, 0.04, 0.04

  PORT-ID        USED-BY    TEAM-PNIC DNAME     PKTTX/s  MbTX/s  PKTRX/s  MbRX/s  %DRPTX  %DRPRX
  16777217       Management      n/a  vSwitch0     0.00    0.00     0.00    0.00    0.00    0.00
  16777218       vmnic0            -  vSwitch0     0.79    0.00     0.98    0.00    0.00    0.00
  16777219       vmk0         vmnic0  vSwitch0     0.79    0.00     1.18    0.00    0.00    0.00
  33554433       Management      n/a  vSwitch1     0.00    0.00     0.00    0.00    0.00    0.00
  33554434       vmnic1            -  vSwitch1     0.00    0.00     1.77    0.00    0.00    0.00
  50331649       Management      n/a  vSwitch2     0.00    0.00     0.00    0.00    0.00    0.00
  50331650       vmnic5            -  vSwitch2     0.20    0.00     0.20    0.00    0.00    0.00
  50331651       vmk1         vmnic5  vSwitch2     0.20    0.00     0.39    0.00    0.00    0.00
  67108865       Management      n/a  vSwitch3     0.00    0.00     0.00    0.00    0.00    0.00
  67108866       vmnic2            -  vSwitch3     0.00    0.00     1.77    0.00    0.00    0.00
  67108867       vmk2         vmnic2  vSwitch3     0.00    0.00     0.00    0.00    0.00    0.00
  83886081       Management      n/a  vSwitch4     0.00    0.00     0.00    0.00    0.00    0.00
  83886082       vmnic3            -  vSwitch4     0.00    0.00     1.77    0.00    0.00    0.00
  83886083       4138:VM1     vmnic3  vSwitch4     0.00    0.00     0.00    0.00    0.00    0.00
```

Table 11.5 details the common network metrics used for both ESXi hosts and virtual machines.

TABLE 11.5   Common network metrics

esxtop	vSphere Web Client	Description
PKTTX/s	Network: Packets transmitted	The number of packets transmitted per second
PKTRX/s	Network: Packets received	The number of packets received per second
MbTX/s	Network: Data transmit rate	The number of megabits transmitted per second
MbRX/s	Network: Data receive rate	The number of megabits received per second

esxtop	vSphere Web Client	Description
%DRPTX	Network: Transmit packets dropped	The percentage of transmit packets that were dropped
%DRPRX	Network: Receive packets dropped	The percentage of receive packets that were dropped

Next, let's look at the common storage metrics.

Common Storage Metrics

Storage metrics are used to track storage contention, latencies, patterns, and more. The common storage metrics were discussed and used in Exercise 10.4 in Chapter 10, and they are included here as a review. Table 11.6 lists the common storage metrics used in resxtop/ esxtop and the vSphere Web Client.

TABLE 11.6 Common storage metrics

resxtop	vSphere Web Client	Description
CMDS/s	Disk: Commands issued	The total number of I/O operations per second.
READS/s	Disk: Read requests	The number of read I/O commands issued per second.
WRITES/s	Disk: Write requests	The number of write I/O commands issued per second.
MBREAD/s	Disk: Read rate	The megabytes read per second.
MBWRTN/s	Disk: Write rate	The megabytes written per second.
DAVG/cmd	Disk: Physical device command latency	The average amount of time in milliseconds a device takes to service a single I/O request. The device includes the vmhba, the storage device, and any devices between.
KAVG/cmd	Disk: Kernel command latency	The average amount of time in milliseconds the VMkernel spends servicing I/O requests.
GAVG/cmd	Disk: Command latency	The total latency as seen from the virtual machine. This metric is the sum of DAVG and KAVG.
ABRTS/s	Disk: Commands terminated	The number of commands aborted per second.
RESETS/s	Disk: Bus resets	The number of commands reset per second.

TABLE 11.6 Common storage metrics *(continued)*

resxtop	vSphere Web Client	Description
LAT/rd	Datastore: Read latency	The average latency in milliseconds for a read I/O operation; this is a VM-specific metric.
LAT/wr	Datastore: Write latency	The average latency in milliseconds for a write I/O operation; this is a VM-specific metric.

In the next section, let's look at what are considered to be critical performance metrics.

Critical Performance Metrics

Although many common metrics are used in vSphere, certain metrics are considered to be critical in monitoring the environment. These metrics also have thresholds associated with them, and several of the critical storage metrics were discussed in Chapter 10. The actual threshold values for many of these critical metrics will also be covered later in this chapter. Table 11.7 lists the critical performance metrics.

TABLE 11.7 Critical performance metrics

esxtop	vSphere Web Client	Description
SWAP curr	Memory: Swap used	The current swap file usage.
ZIP zipped	Memory: Compressed	The total compressed physical memory.
MEMCT curr	Memory: Balloon	The total amount of physical memory reclaimed by ballooning.
PCPU USED (%)	CPU: Usage	The percentage of CPU usage per PCPU and the percentage of CPU usage averaged over all PCPUs.
%RDY	CPU: Ready	The percentage of time the VM was not provided CPU resources but was ready to run.
%SWPWT	CPU: Swap wait	The percentage of time spent waiting for the VMkernel to swap memory.
%DRPTX	Network: Transmit packets dropped	The percentage of transmit packets that were dropped.
%DRPRX	Network: Receive packets dropped	The percentage of receive packets that were dropped.
CMDS/s	Disk: Commands issued	The total number of I/O operations per second.

esxtop	vSphere Web Client	Description
DAVG/cmd	Disk: Physical device command latency	The average time in milliseconds a device takes to service a single I/O request. The device includes the vmhba, the storage device, and any devices between.
KAVG/cmd	Disk: Kernel command latency	The average time in milliseconds the VMkernel spends servicing I/O requests.
GAVG/cmd	Disk: Command latency	The total latency as seen from the virtual machine. This metric is the sum of DAVG and KAVG.
ABRTS/s	Disk: Commands terminated	The number of commands aborted per second.
RESETS/s	Disk: Bus resets	The number of commands reset per second.

These metrics are deemed critical because they can be used to discover resource exhaustion, contention, or error conditions. Now that the critical performance metrics have been identified, let's discuss the overview and advanced charts that can be used to view these metrics.

Comparing and Contrasting Overview and Advanced Charts

There are two types of charts used in the vSphere Web Client, known as overview and advanced. These charts are available in two different views on the Monitor tab and Performance toolbar. Overview charts show the metrics that VMware considers the most useful for both monitoring performance and diagnosing problems. Overview charts consist of a predefined view that can be selected from a drop-down menu. The different views available depend on the object selected. Table 11.8 shows the object and associated views combinations.

TABLE 11.8 Objects and views in overview charts

Object	Views available
Datacenter	Clusters, Storage
Datastore	Storage
Cluster	Home, Resource Pools & Virtual Machines, Hosts
Host	Home, Virtual Machines
Resource Pool	Home, Resource Pools & Virtual Machines
Virtual Machine	Home, Storage, Fault Tolerance

All of these views may not always be available. For example, if no virtual machines are protected with VMware FT, the Fault Tolerance view will be unavailable in the overview charts.

A key component of the overview charts is the thumbnail charts that are presented. They are available for any child objects of the selected inventory object. Figure 11.18 shows the CPU % thumbnail chart available when an ESXi host object is selected.

FIGURE 11.18 CPU% thumbnail chart

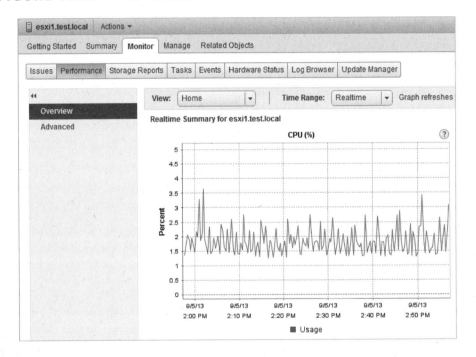

Another unique aspect of overview charts is that they are predefined, so no customization is possible, other than the time range that can be specified. Also note that the Datacenter object allows a Storage view that can show space utilization for the datastores in the datacenter. Figure 11.19 shows an overview chart with the datacenter object's Storage view.

FIGURE 11.19   Storage view in an overview chart

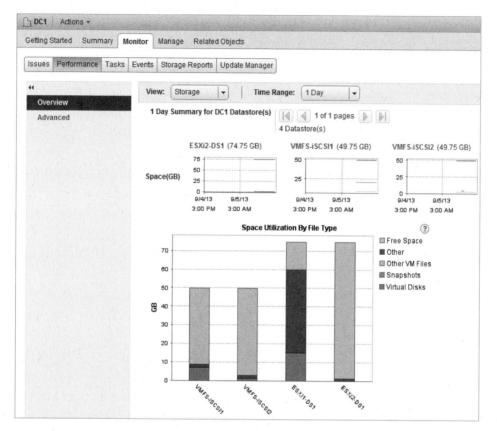

Whereas overview charts are predefined, advanced charts are extremely customizable and can allow very granular metrics to be obtained for datacenters, clusters, hosts, resource pools, and virtual machines. Advanced charts also offer the following benefits:

- Additional details can be obtained in a chart by hovering the mouse over specific data points.

- Chart data can be exported.

- Chart data can be saved as an image.

- Separate windows can be opened to view performance data.

Figure 11.20 shows the additional detail available when you hover the mouse over a specific data point. The icons used to refresh and save/export are also visible in the upper-right corner.

FIGURE 11.20   Data point detail in an advanced chart

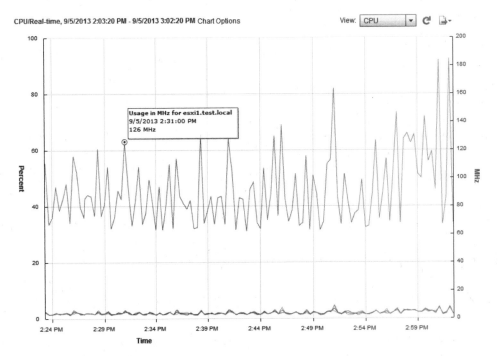

Advanced charts will be covered in more detail in the next section, including the steps to create an advanced chart.

Creating an Advanced Chart

Creating an advanced performance chart can be useful when you need to obtain more granular or specific information. The advanced charts allow you to do the following:

- Use multiple user-selected counters
- Define date/time ranges using the Custom chart option
- Select the chart type
- Select objects to use in the chart
- Save chart settings for future use

Figure 11.21 shows the Chart Options window, where an advanced chart is created.

FIGURE 11.21   Creating an advanced chart

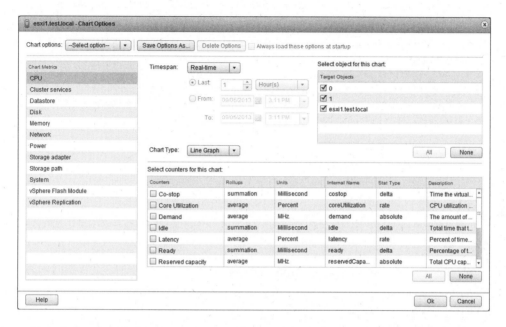

To leverage the work of creating a customized advanced chart, you'll probably want to save it to use again. Exercise 11.6 covers the steps to create and save an advanced performance chart.

EXERCISE 11.6

Creating an Advanced Performance Chart

1. Connect to a vCenter Server with the vSphere Web Client.

2. Navigate to a virtual machine in the left pane.

3. Click the Monitor tab, and then click Performance on the toolbar.

4. Click the Advanced option in the left pane to switch to the Advanced chart view.

5. Click the blue Chart Options link located in the center of the screen toward the top of the tab.

6. The Chart Options window will open. This is the window shown in Figure 11.21.

EXERCISE 11.6 *(continued)*

7. Ensure that the CPU metric is selected in the left pane and select Custom Interval from the Timespan drop-down menu.

8. Under the Timespan drop-down menu, click the Last radio button, and change the value to 3 hours.

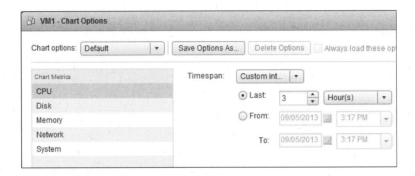

9. Accept the default Chart Type setting of Line Graph.

10. In the Target Objects panel, ensure that the virtual machine is selected by placing a check in the box beside it.

11. At the bottom of the window, select both the Usage and the Ready counters. The Counters panel should look exactly like this:

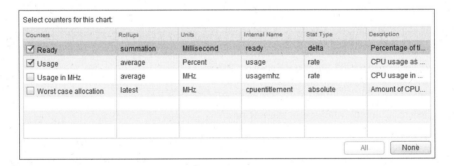

12. Click the Save Options As button located at the top of the Chart Options screen.

13. When prompted, enter a name for the chart and then click OK.

Note that the value in the Chart Options drop-down menu has now been changed to reflect the name just given to this chart.

14. Click OK and review the chart.

15. Click the Export icon. When prompted, save the chart as either an image or a CSV file.

16. Open the exported chart and review its contents.

Now that metrics and charts have been covered, we will turn our attention to using resxtop and Perfmon to determine ESXi host performance.

Determining Host Performance Using *resxtop* and Guest Perfmon

This chapter has demonstrated using esxtop, resxtop, and the vSphere Web Client performance charts to monitor ESXi hosts. One additional option for monitoring the performance of an ESXi host is to use the Windows Perfmon utility to view exported esxtop or resxtop data.

Exercise 11.7 covers the steps to use Perfmon to view exported resxtop data. This exercise will require the use of the vMA or vCLI for Linux; we will assume that the vMA is used. This exercise will also use Perfmon on Windows 2008 R2 and make use of the free WinSCP utility. WinSCP can be downloaded from http://winscp.net/.

EXERCISE 11.7

Using *resxtop* Data and Perfmon to Monitor ESXi Host Performance

1. Connect to the console or to the vMA (via SSH).

2. Log in with the vi-admin account.

3. Type the following command:

```
resxtop --server <vCENTER FQDN> --vihost <ESXi HOST FQDN> --username
<DOMAIN>\\<USERNAME> -b -d 2 -n 60 > resxtop-export.csv
```

4. Enter the user's password when prompted.

Use the FQDN of your vCenter Server and one of your ESXi hosts in the previous command. Use a domain user account that has Administrator permissions on the vCenter Server to log in.

EXERCISE 11.7 *(continued)*

Note that there are two backslashes (\\) between the domain and the username. This command will create a file containing the resxtop data in it. The -b switch is used to indicate batch mode for resxtop. The -d switch is the delay between statistics snapshots, and the -n switch is used to specify the number of iterations. Thus, in the previous example, two minutes' worth of data will be collected.

5. Wait for the previous command to complete.

6. When the command completes, enter the following command:

```
ls -l
```

7. Verify that the export file exists and appears to be a valid size (usually at least a few megabytes).

The resxtop data has now been collected. The next step is to copy the data off the vMA and onto the Windows system that Perfmon will be used on.

8. On a Windows guest, open WinSCP and connect to the vMA using the vi-admin credentials. In the right pane, locate the resxtop data file.

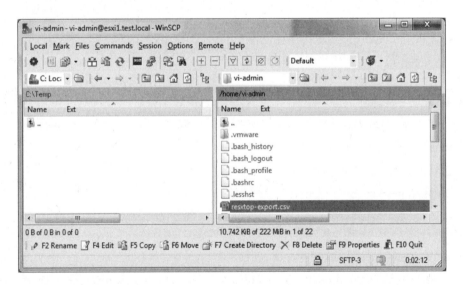

9. Select a destination directory in the left pane and copy the resxtop export file from the vMA.

The captured data file has now been copied to a Windows guest. The remainder of this exercise shows the steps to view this data with Perfmon.

10. In Windows, use the Run window or a command prompt and type the following command:

    Perfmon

11. When Performance Monitor opens, select Performance Monitor in the left pane.

12. Press Ctrl+L to open the Performance Monitor Properties window.

13. Click the Source tab and select the Log Files option for Data Source. Click the Add button and locate the resxtop data file that was copied earlier in this exercise.

    The completed configuration should look like this:

14. Click the Time Range button and verify that the time range is accurate.

15. Click the Data tab in the Performance Monitor Properties window.

16. If any Windows-specific counters are listed, remove them using the Remove button.

17. Click the Add button. The Add Counters window will appear.

EXERCISE 11.7 *(continued)*

18. Expand the Memory object in the left pane. Select the Free Mbytes counter and click the Add button at the bottom of the counter list to add this counter.

19. Expand the Physical CPU object in the left pane. Select the % Processor Time counter and click the Add button at the bottom of the counter list to add this counter.

    The final configuration should resemble the following:

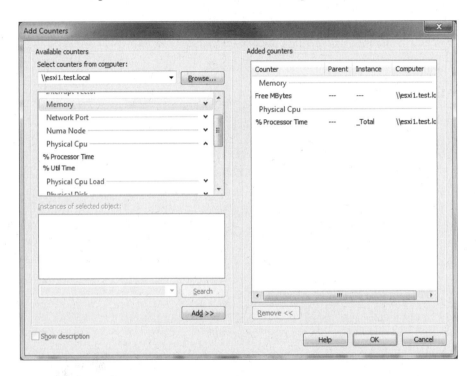

20. Click OK to close the Add Counters window.

21. Review the Counters listed in the Performance Monitor Properties window and click OK.

22. Use the Change Graph Type button in the toolbar to change to the graph type to Report.

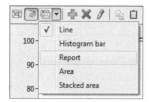

23. Review the information listed in the Report chart. It should appear similar to what is shown here:

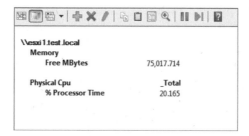

 This exercise captured an enormous amount of information from `resxtop`. When using this approach to monitor your ESXi hosts, it would likely make much more sense to configure `resxtop` to capture the data only for metrics you deem important.

Identifying the affected vSphere resource, given performance data, will be the final topic in the monitoring section of this chapter.

Given Performance Data, Identifying the Affected vSphere Resource

As seen in the previous sections, certain metrics will immediately identify affected resources in the vSphere environment. Table 11.9 shows some common metrics and their threshold values that would indicate a likely problem.

TABLE 11.9 Common metrics and affected vSphere resource

resxtop	Performance chart	Threshold
%RDY	CPU: Ready	10
%SWPWT	CPU: Swap wait	5
MEMCTLSZ	Memory: Balloon	1
SWCUR	Memory: Swapped	1
SWR/s	Memory: Swap In Rate	1
SWW/s	Memory: Swap Out Rate	1
CACHEUSD	Memory: Compressed	0
ZIP/s	Memory: Zipped Memory	0
UNZIP/s	Memory: Zipped Memory	0
%DRPTX	Network: Transmit packets dropped	1
%DRPRX	Network: Receive packets dropped	1
DAVG/cmd	Disk: Physical device command latency	25
KAVG/cmd	Disk: Kernel command latency	2
GAVG/cmd	Disk: Command latency	25
ABRTS/s	Disk: Commands terminated	1
RESETS/s	Disk: Bus resets	1

There is an excellent and constantly updated resource that details the thresholds for these and many other metrics available at www.yellow-bricks.com/esxtop/.

Now that you've seen how to identify the affected vSphere resource when given the performance data, let's discuss how to install, configure, and administer vCenter Operations Manager.

Installing, Configuring, and Administering vCenter Operations Manager

vCenter Operations Manager is VMware's integrated operations suite that brings performance monitoring, capacity monitoring, and configuration management capabilities directly into the vSphere Web Client. At its base, vCenter Operations Manager includes proactive smart alerts, intelligent operations groups, vSphere health monitoring and self-learning performance analytics. These features are all included in the Foundation edition of vCenter Operations Manager, which is a free download. There are three additional editions which can be purchased:

- Standard
- Advanced
- Enterprise

Each of these editions builds upon the capabilities of the Foundation edition of the product, similar to the way the different editions of vSphere each build upon each other. While vCenter Operations Manager contains many capabilities, for the VCP5-DCV exam you will simply be expected to know what it is, how to deploy it, how to configure it and how to use it to monitor a vSphere environment. Let's get started with an overview of the vCenter Operations Manager architecture.

Explaining vCenter Operations Manager Architecture

vCenter Operations Manager is a vApp, consisting of two virtual machines, that is deployed from an OVA file. The architecture of this vApp is shown in Figure 11.22.

FIGURE 11.22 vCenter Operations Manager vApp architecture

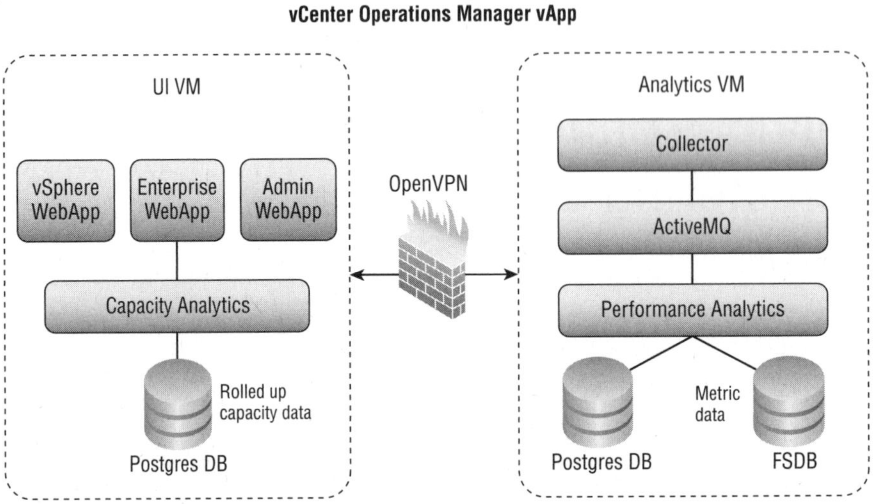

The two virtual machines in the vApp are the User Interface (UI) VM and the Analytics VM. The UI VM provides the user interface for vCenter Operations Manager and contains the following applications:

vSphere Web Application — provides summary and pre-defined views into the vSphere environment.

Enterprise Web Application (Enterprise Edition only) — provides customizable views into the vSphere environment.

Administration Web Application — provides the maintenance and management interfaces for vCenter Operations Manager.

The Analytics VM provides the data collection and processing for vCenter Operations Manager and contains the following components:

Capacity and Performance Analytics — provides real time analytics for incoming metrics, updates health scores, and generates alerts.

Capacity Collector — provides collection of all metrics and also computes derived metrics.

FileSystem Database — provides a location to store the collected metric statistics.

Postgres DB — provides a location to store all other data collected, including alerts, dynamic thresholds, events, objects, and relationships.

The same vApp is used to deploy each edition of the vCenter Operations Manager. There is also an installable version available for the Enterprise Edition that allows you to install vCenter Operations Manager on supported Windows or Linux platforms.

Now that the architecture of vCenter Operations Manager has been covered, let's deploy and configure it.

Deploying and Configuring vCenter Operations Manager Appliance

vCenter Operations Manager is deployed as a vApp, and Exercise 11.8 will cover the steps to deploy it. Note that later on in this chapter, I will cover the steps to upgrade vCenter Operations Manager. Downloading the vCenter Operations Manager vApp one version prior to the latest release will allow you to complete both the initial deployment and the upgrade exercises.

EXERCISE 11.8

Deploying vCenter Operations Manager

1. Download the vCenter Operations Manager vApp from VMware.

2. Open the vSphere Web Client and connect to a vCenter Server.

3. Verify that a Network Protocol Profile exists for the network segment where you will deploy vCenter Operations Manager. Refer to Exercise 6.19 in Chapter 6 " Creating and Deploying Virtual Machines and vApps," if you need a reference.

4. In the left pane, navigate to a DRS-enabled cluster and right-click on it. Choose the Deploy OVF Template. A Client Integration Access Control window will open. Click Allow to continue.

5. On the Select Source screen, browse to the location of the downloaded .OVA file and select it. Click Next to continue.

6. Review the details, making note of the Size On Disk field, and click Next.

7. Click the Accept button, if you agree to the terms of the end user license agreement. Click Next.

EXERCISE 11.8 *(continued)*

8. Provide a descriptive name and choose an appropriate location for the vApp to be deployed to. Click Next.

9. Select the appropriate deployment configuration size and click Next.

10. Select an appropriate virtual disk format and storage location. Click Next to continue.

11. Choose the correct network settings. Set the IP Allocation to Static - Manual, if you intend to provide static IP addresses to the VMs in the vApp or DHCP if you intend to use a DHCP server. vCenter Operations Manager does not support transient IP allocation. The configuration should look similar to this:

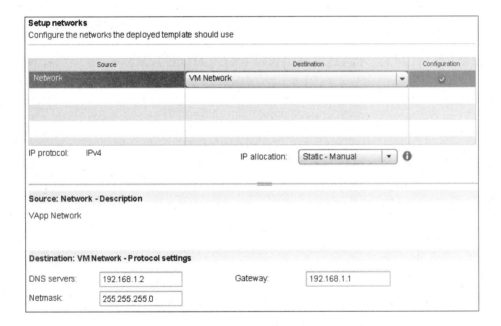

12. Click Next to continue.

13. On the Customize Template screen, review the time zone setting. If you chose the option to provide static IP addresses in the previous screen, you will need to provide those addresses now.

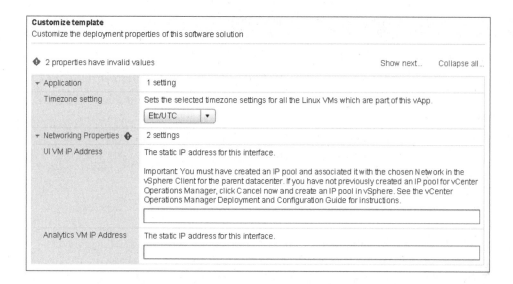

14. If applicable, enter static IP addresses for both VMs. Note that these IP addresses cannot be within the range reserved by an IP pool on this network. Click Next.

15. Review the information on the Ready To Complete screen. Place a check in the Power On After Deployment check box, and click Finish to deploy the vCenter Operations Manager vApp.

You have now deployed vCenter Operations Manager. Know that this deployment can take some time to complete, and it is not unusual for the deployment to appear to be stalled. It's best to just be patient while the deployment occurs.

 The thick provisioned eager-zeroed virtual disk format provides roughly a 10 percent performance improvement over the other two disk formats and is the VMware recommended option. VMware also recommends that snapshots not be used on the vCenter Operations Manager VMs, as their performance will typically decrease by 25-30 percent when placed in snapshot mode.

Once the vCenter Operations Manager vApp has been deployed, it will need to be configured before use. Exercise 11.9 covers the steps to configure vCenter Operations Manager.

EXERCISE 11.9

Configuring vCenter Operations Manager

1. Open a web browser and enter the IP address of the vCenter Operations Manager UI VM.

2. Log in with the default username of **admin** and the default password **admin**. The Initial Setup Wizard will open.

3. Ensure a check is in the Use Hosting vCenter Server Details option, and provide the FQDN of your vCenter Server. Provide the credentials for a user account that has administrator privileges to vCenter Server. Verify the Analytics VM IP address listed is correct, and click Next.

4. Wait for the Security Alert window to open and deal with the certificate issues accordingly.

5. Enter new passwords for both the admin and the root account and then click Next. The default administrator password is **admin**, and the default root password is **vmware**. Note that both accounts require passwords that are a minimum of eight characters and include at least one letter and one digit.

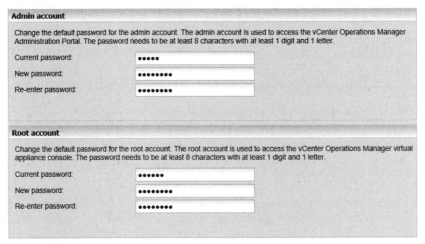

6. Click Next and then enter the requested information for the vCenter Server to monitor. This will very likely be the same vCenter Server you entered in step 3 earlier in this exercise.

Specify a vCenter Server to monitor.	
Display name:	vCenter Server (Lab)
vCenter Server address (FQDN/IP):	vcenter.test.local
Registration user:	Administrator@test.local
Registration password:	••••••••••••••••••••
Collector user (optional):	Collection@test.local
Collector password (optional):	••••••••••••••••••••

In a lab environment, using the same user account for the Registration User and Collector User is fine. In the real world, you should use separate user accounts for the Registration User and the Collector User. This can be useful in situations where you need to restrict access to what vCenter Operations Manager has access to. For example, you may want to exclude a TEST/DEV cluster in your environment. Restricting the Collector Users' access to this cluster would effectively omit these objects from being monitored in vCenter Operations Manager.

7. Click Next and review the information presented in the Import Data section. If this is the first registration of vCenter Operations Manager, then no previous registrations will be found. Click Next to continue.

8. The final screen offers the opportunity to deal with linked vCenter Servers in your environment. If you have a linked vCenter Server, select it from the drop down menu and then click Register. If you do not have vCenter Server in linked mode, simply click Finish.

9. Wait while vCenter Operations Manager is registered with vCenter Server. Once this process is complete, you will be at the vCenter Operations Manager Administration site.

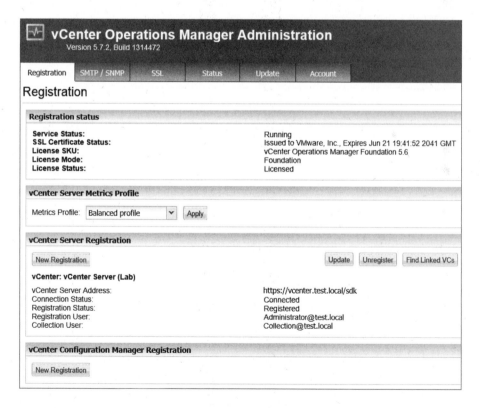

10. Take note of the License SKU, License Mode, and License Status reported under the Registration Status section. Note that vCenter Operations Manager defaults to the Foundation license mode.

EXERCISE 11.9 *(continued)*

---

11. Review the vCenter Server Registration information presented lower on the screen. Note that the both the Registration and Collector account information can be changed from here by clicking the Update button.

    This feature is useful in environments where domain user accounts used for the Register or Collector function have expiring passwords.

12. Click the SMTP/SNMP tab. Configure these options as appropriate for your environment and click the Update button to save the changes.

13. Click the Status tab and review the information presented.

14. Click the Account tab and remember that you can change the admin and/or root passwords from this location.

15. Leave vCenter Operations Manager Administration open. In the next section, you will upgrade it to the latest release.

The minimum vCenter Server privileges required for the Collector User to collect data are Global: Health and Storage Views: View.

You have configured vCenter Operations Manager and it is ready to be used in your environment. Before we start using it, let's first take a moment to upgrade it to the latest release.

Upgrading vCenter Operations Manager

Like most software, the vCenter Operations Manager vApp will periodically be updated by VMware. These updates might include things like new functionality, bug fixes and/or compatibility updates. In Exercise 11.10, I will cover the steps to upgrade your vCenter Operations Manager to the latest version. You will need to download the upgrade file (.pak) from VMware before starting this exercise. If you don't have access to the upgrade file, or if you already have the latest version of vCenter Operations Manager, you may want to just follow along on this exercise.

EXERCISE 11.10

Upgrading vCenter Operations Manager

1. Return to the vCenter Operations Manager Administration site, or open a web browser and enter the IP address of the vCenter Operations Manager UI VM.

2. Click the Update tab.

3. Browse to the download location on the local file system of the .pak file.

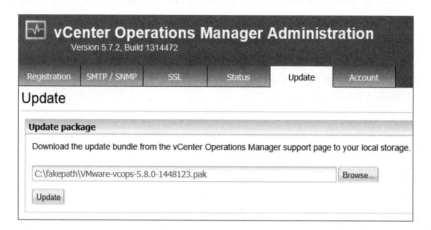

4. Click Update to begin the upgrade to the latest version. Review the information presented in the Confirm Update dialog and then click OK.

5. Wait while the .pak file is uploaded.

6. When prompted, scroll down on the vCenter Operations Manager Administration site and place a check in the I Accept The Terms Of This Agreement option. Click OK.

7. Click OK on the Confirm Update window. Note that you will be logged out of the vCenter Operations Manager Administration portal.

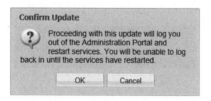

8. Wait patiently for the update to complete. When the login screen is available, log in. Click the Update tab to monitor the process of the update.

9. Note that the version number and build number listed at the top of the screen has now changed to reflect the updated version of vCenter Operations Manager.

EXERCISE 11.10 *(continued)*

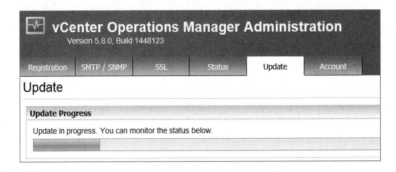

10. Wait for the update to complete and then verify the Update status message below the Update Package section.

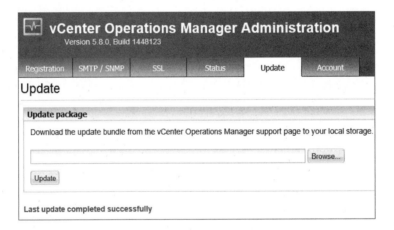

11. Open the vSphere Client. Open the Plug-In Manager and verify that the vCenter Operations Manager Plug-in is installed and enabled.

12. Open vCenter Operations Manager from the Solutions And Applications section on the vSphere Client home screen.

You have now deployed, configured and updated the vCenter Operations Manager vApp. Before we start using it, let's discuss the use of badges in vCenter Operations Manager.

Differentiating Major/Minor vCenter Operations Manager Badges

Badges are used in vCenter Operations Manager to provide an overview of the state of the virtual environment or individual objects contained within it. Badges enable you to quickly focus on specific issues in the environment. vCenter Operations Manager utilizes three major badges, and each major badge contains a subset of minor badges. There are eight minor badges. The relationship between the major and minor badges is shown in Table 11.10.

TABLE 11.10   vCenter Operations Manager major and minor badges

Major badge	Minor badges
Health	Workload, Anomalies, Faults
Risk	Time remaining, Capacity remaining, Stress
Efficiency	Reclaimable waste, Density

All of these major and minor badges will not be available in vCenter Operations Manager Foundation. Remember that each edition of vCenter Operations Manager adds additional capabilities to the Foundation version, and additional badges are only available with the licensed versions.

Scoring for the major badge health is used to show how well an inventory object is doing in real time. Health scoring ranges from 100-0, and a higher number represents a better score. The health score is derived from the three health minor badges of workload, anomalies, and faults:

- Workload — shows if an inventory object is constrained by a resource. Workload scoring ranges from 0-100 or higher. A lower score indicates a smaller workload and a score higher than 100 would indicate that an object is trying to access more resources than are currently available.

- Anomalies — shows if an inventory object is experiencing abnormal activity. Anomaly scoring ranges from 0-100, with a lower number being a better score.

- Faults — shows if an inventory object is experiencing events that may impact availability of resources. Fault scoring ranges from 0-100, with a lower number being a better score.

Scoring for the major badge risk is used to show how well an object is expected to perform in the immediate future. Risk scoring ranges from 0-100, and a lower number represents a better score. The risk score is derived from the three risk minor badges of time remaining, capacity remaining, and stress:

- Time remaining — shows the time remaining before a resource is exhausted.

- Capacity remaining — shows how many VMs can be deployed before resource exhaustion. This value is based on an average VM size. Scoring ranges from 100-0, with a higher number representing a better score.

- Stress — shows sustained resource (CPU/RAM) constraints. This value is based on if CPU and/or RAM has been over 70% for 1% of the measured time. Scoring ranges from 0-100, with a lower number representing a better score.

Scoring for the major badge efficiency is used to show virtual machine optimization opportunities or the ability to reclaim resources. The efficiency scoring ranges from 100-0, and a higher number represents a better score. The efficiency score is derived from the two efficiency minor badges of reclaimable waste and density:

- Reclaimable waste — shows resources that can be reclaimed from overprovisioned, powered-off and/or idle VMs. Scoring ranges from 0-100, and a lower number represents a better score.

- Density — shows consolidation ratios for the last seven days. A higher density score is better, generally speaking. There is no way to account for the vSphere design used, so density scores could be misleading.

Now that the major and minor badges have been discussed, let's discuss the metrics that are used to determine their values.

Understanding Metrics Used by Major/Minor vCenter Operations Manager Badges

vCenter Operations Manager collects various data points for specific resources in the vSphere environment, like CPU use. Each type of data collected is called an attribute, and a metric is an instance of an attribute. These metrics are the basis of the major and minor badges in vCenter Operations Manager, and are shown in Table 11.11.

TABLE 11.11:   vCenter Operations Manager metrics

Metric	Description
Provisioned	The specific amount of a resource. For example, host physical RAM or vCPUs in a VM.
Usable	The specific amount of a resource that can actually be used. Virtualization overhead represents the difference between the provisioned amount and the usable amount. This metric does not apply to virtual machines.
Usage	The specific amount of a resource that is consumed by an object. This value will be less than or equal to Usable.
Demand	The specific amount of a physical resource that an object could consume, assuming there is no resource contention.
Contention	This is the difference between an object's resource requirements and what it actually receives.
Limit	The maximum amount of a resource that an object can obtain.
Reservation	The guaranteed amount of a resource for an object.
Entitlement	The amount of a resource that a virtual machine can use based on a function of provisioned, limit, reservation, shares, and demand. This metric applies only to virtual machines.

Now that the badges and metrics have been covered, let's start using vCenter Operations Manager to monitor a vSphere environment.

Monitoring a vSphere Environment

Before we begin, we need to take a moment to discuss how to access the vCenter Operations Manager interface. There are two different options to choose from:

- vSphere Client
- Web browser

It is sometimes convenient to view vCenter Operations Manager from within the vSphere Client, and some of the data is even available in the vSphere Web Client, but it is often easier to use vCenter Operations Manager from a web browser. The big advantages with this approach are that you can toggle back and forth between the vSphere Client and you also get much more viewable area with the web browser.

Earlier in this chapter, I discussed the major and minor badges and the metrics these badges are based on. One additional item that needs to be covered is the color coding that is used for badges in vCenter Operations Manager. Table 11.12 shows the color coding for object health states, but the logic is the same for all other badges.

TABLE 11.12   vCenter Operations Manager color codes

Color	Description	User Action
Green	The health of the object is normal.	No attention required.
Yellow	The object is experiencing some level of problems.	Take appropriate action.
Orange	The object might have serious problems.	Take appropriate action as soon as possible.
Red	The object is either not functioning properly or will stop functioning soon.	Identify the most probable cause of the problem and act immediately.
Grey ?	No data is available.	N/A
Grey X	The object is offline.	N/A

In Exercise 11.11, I will cover the steps to monitor your environment with vCenter Operations Manager. Note that this exercise will be more of an overview of how to monitor vSphere, as the use of vCenter Operations Manager could easily span an entire book.

EXERCISE 11.11

Monitoring vSphere with vCenter Operations Manager

1. Open a web browser and enter the IP address of the vCenter Operations Manager UI VM.

2. Login as admin.

3. Note the three panes visible here. The left pane contains the vSphere environment's inventory objects. Expand World and each object contained, until you reach virtual machines. This is one way you can navigate in vCenter Operations Manager.

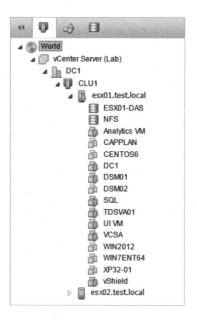

4. Also note the Groups and Datastores icons at the top of the left pane. Click the Data stores icon and expand the contents of World until you see your datastores.

5. Click the Hosts And Clusters icon at the top of the left pane to return to the default view.

6. Note that to the left of the Hosts And Clusters icon you just clicked, there is a double arrow icon that can be used to collapse this pane. Click it to collapse the object browser pane. Click the icon again to expand the object browser pane.

7. Select a cluster object in the left pane. If you have a single cluster in this environment, you will notice that the view in the middle pane refreshed but is unchanged.

8. In the middle pane, note the default view of the Environment tab. This tab provides a quick summary of the health of the vSphere environment.

EXERCISE 11.11 *(continued)*

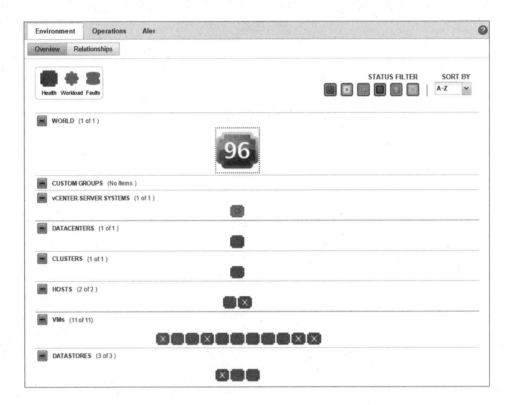

In the previous image, the vCenter Server health is shown as degraded with an orange badge. Also note that one of the ESXi hosts in this environment is shown as Powered Off, which is designated with a grey badge with an X on it.

9. Click on the Status Filter icons to show or hide objects in different states. For example, click the red bad state icon to view only those objects in a bad state.

   This default health view can allow for very efficient troubleshooting in your vSphere environment. It allows you to quickly view the scale of a problem. If the World badge is red, then you are probably not having a good day. On the other hand, if it is a single VM that is red, then you know exactly where to start troubleshooting.

10. There are also links for two of the three health minor badges at the top of the screen. Click the Workload minor badge. Note how the information changed to reflect the workload information. Also note how the badge shape changed.

11. Click the Faults badge at the top of the screen. Note how the information changes yet again to reflect the faults, and the icon also changes shape again.

12. Double-click any badge now listed on the Faults view. You will be redirected to the Operations tab which shows additional detail for the chosen object. Review any listed faults for the object. The following image shows a faulted vCenter.

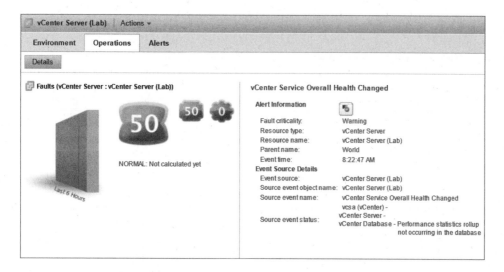

The cause of this fault was a failed database rollup job. Note how the Fault badge is the largest badge in this image.

13. Click the Health badge located to the right of the Fault badge. Notice how the Health badge now becomes larger and the health information for the object is now shown.

14. Click the Workload badge and review the information displayed. What is the most constrained resource listed in your environment?

15. Click the Alerts tab and review any alerts presented here. What alerts exist in your environment?

16. In the left pane, select a datastore. Review its health, workload and fault information.

You have seen how vCenter Operations Manager can be used to quickly identify problems in your environment. The true value of vCenter Operations Manager is that it allows the virtual infrastructure administrator to use a set of aggregated data in a visual way.

For a Given Alarm, Identify the Affected Resource In a vSphere Implementation

Identifying affected resources in a vSphere environment with vCenter Operations Manager is typically a fairly straightforward task, especially in comparison to how you might identify the same affected resources without it. Let's examine another case study to demonstrate.

Real World Scenario

Why is Virtual Machine Slow?

A virtual infrastructure administrator receives a phone call from a customer complaining of slowness in the payroll application. She happens to have the vSphere Client open and quickly looks at this VM's performance tab. She immediately notices very high CPU Ready values. She decides to open vCenter Operations Manager to get a better view of the overall environment.

On the Environment tab, she immediately notices that the cluster is in an abnormal state, and that one ESXi host is in a bad state. She also notices that many VMs are also in an abnormal state, and that one VM is in a bad state. She double-clicks the bad VM to view more information about it. The VM's health badge is red and has a value of 0. The workload badge is also red and has a value of 100, but there are 0 faults. The workload statistics show CPU at 100%. Something out of the ordinary is definitely happening with this VM.

In the left pane she sees that this VM is running on the same ESXi host as the VMs that are also in an abnormal state, including the VM that the payroll application is on. She decides to vMotion the VM with the payroll application to another host in the cluster. After confirming with the customer that the payroll application is now performing as expected, she takes the steps to eliminate the high CPU usage on the problem VM. She discovers a hung process on this server and ultimately has to perform a reset of the VM to resolve the issue.

As you can see, vCenter Operations Manager can allow affected resources in a vSphere environment to be quickly identified. This speeds resolution time, improves user experiences, and generally makes the virtual infrastructure administrator's day-to-day duties easier. vCenter Operations Manager is an excellent resource that allows virtual infrastructure administrators to proactively monitor their vSphere environments. Another effective method for staying ahead of potential problems is to utilize vCenter Server Alarms.

Creating and Administering vCenter Server Alarms

As a VMware Certified Professional, you will be expected to know how to create and administer vCenter Server alarms. vCenter Server alarms are user-configurable and allow the specification of the conditions required to trigger the alarm. vCenter Server alarms are shown in the vSphere Web Client, and they can be configured to perform a variety of actions. These alarms can be quite useful for the virtual infrastructure administrator and allow you to be more proactive in the administration of the vSphere environment. This section shows how to create and administer vCenter Server alarms.

Listing vCenter Default Utilization Alarms

Utilization alarms are used to notify the vSphere administrator of a capacity or usage issue. The default utilization alarms in vCenter Server are as follows:

- Virtual machine CPU usage
- Virtual machine memory usage
- Datastore usage on disk
- Datastore cluster is out of space
- License capacity monitoring
- License user threshold monitoring
- Thin-provisioned volume capacity threshold exceeded
- Host memory usage
- Host CPU usage
- Host service console swap rates
- Host SSD capacity exceeds the licensed limit for the VSAN
- Host virtual flash resource usage

Listing vCenter Default Connectivity Alarms

Connectivity alarms are used to notify the vSphere administrator of a connectivity issue. The default connectivity alarms in vCenter Server are as follows:

- Pre-4.1 host connected to SIOC-enabled datastore
- Cannot find vSphere HA master agent
- Network uplink redundancy degraded
- Network uplink redundancy lost
- Network connectivity lost
- Cannot connect to storage
- Host connection and power state
- Host connection failure

Listing Possible Actions for Utilization and Connectivity Alarms

vCenter Server alarms have configurable actions. Each alarm has an Actions feature that can be used to specify the action to take if the alarm is triggered. These available actions vary, depending on the alarm type monitor configured. There are nine alarm-type monitor options, which are shown in Figure 11.23.

FIGURE 11.23 Alarm-type monitor options

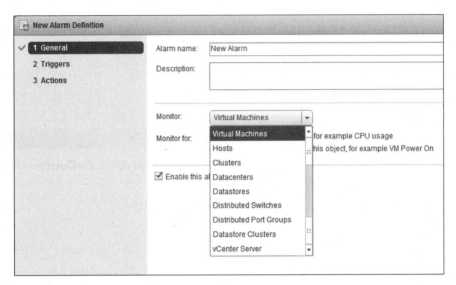

All nine of these alarm-type monitors have the following actions in common:

- Send a notification email
- Send a notification trap
- Run a command

The Host alarm-type monitor includes the following additional specific actions:

- Enter maintenance mode
- Exit maintenance mode
- Enter standby
- Exit standby
- Reboot host
- Shutdown host

The Virtual Machine alarm-type monitor includes the following additional specific actions:

- Power on VM
- Power off VM
- Suspend VM
- Reset VM
- Migrate VM

- Reboot guest on VM
- Shutdown guest on VM

Now let's examine the steps required to create a vCenter Server utilization alarm.

Creating a vCenter Utilization Alarm

Creating a vCenter Server utilization alarm is a fairly simple process that can be used to provide impressive levels of detail and automation. Exercise 11.12 covers the steps to create a vCenter Server utilization alarm for a virtual machine.

EXERCISE 11.12

Monitoring Virtual Machine CPU and Memory Usage with a vCenter Server Utilization Alarm

1. Connect to vCenter Server using the vSphere Web Client.

2. Navigate to a virtual machine in the left pane.

3. Select the Manage tab and then click Alarm Definitions on the toolbar.

4. Review the names of the listed definitions, and take note of the Defined In column. This column allows you to see which inventory object the alarm is defined on.

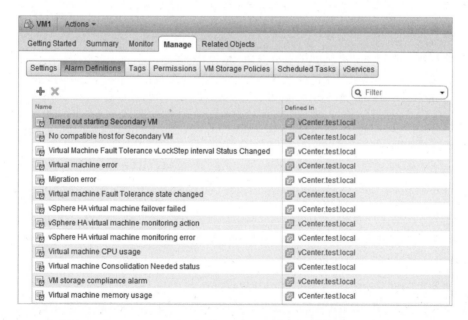

5. Click the green plus icon to add a new alarm definition. A New Alarm Definition window will open.

6. Give the alarm a unique and descriptive name and provide a description.

7. Ensure that the drop-down menu for the Monitor option is set to Virtual Machine. Ensure that Specific Conditions Or State radio button is selected in the Monitor For option.

8. Select the Enable This Alarm check box. The final configuration should look similar to this:

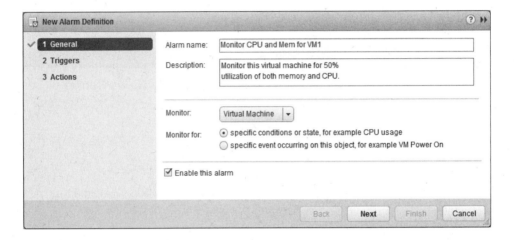

9. Click Triggers in the left pane.

10. Click the green plus icon near the top of the window.

11. An entry will appear on the list of triggers. Click this entry under the Trigger column heading to access a drop-down menu.

12. Select the VM CPU Usage option.

13. Ensure that the Operator column reports Is Above.

14. Click the Warning Condition entry and enter the values **50** and **for 1 min**.

15. Click the Critical Condition entry and enter the values **60** and **for 1 min**.

16. Click the green plus icon again.

17. Click the new entry under the Trigger column heading to access a drop-down menu.

18. Select the VM Memory Usage option.

19. Ensure that the Operator column reports Is Above.

20. Click the entry below the Warning Condition column and enter the values **50** and **for 1 min**.

21. Click the entry below the Critical Condition column and enter the values **60** and **for 1 min**.

22. Using the Trigger If drop-down menu at the top of the window, select the All option. The final configuration should look like this:

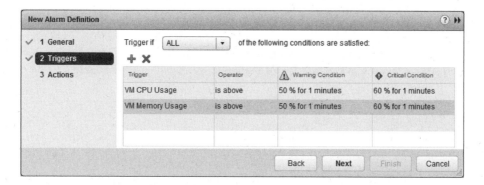

23. Click Actions in the left pane.

24. Click the green plus icon.

25. An entry will appear on the list of actions. Click this entry under the Action column heading to access a drop-down menu.

26. Select the Send A Notification Email option.

27. Click the entry below the Configuration column header and enter a valid email address to send the notification to.

28. Click the entry below each of the remaining columns and use the drop-down menu to select Once. The final configuration should look like this:

29. Click the Finish button to save this alarm. A Create Alarm Definition task will begin.

30. Review the list of alarms and verify that the new alarm is listed. Note its value in the Defined In column.

Creating the alarm at the virtual machine inventory object level makes it specific to the virtual machine. Keep in mind the most appropriate inventory object level for alarms when they are created.

The previous exercise created a utilization alarm that monitored both CPU and memory for its trigger. Either CPU or memory utilization alone would not be capable of triggering this alarm. In your test environments, you could experiment with some of the other alarm actions like Run A Command or Reboot Guest On VM on the alarm. These actions can make utilization alarms a powerful tool for managing your vSphere environment.

 Real World Scenario

Monitoring and Taking Action on Snapshots

A virtual infrastructure administrator has been asked to put a virtual machine in snapshot mode; the virtual machine is running a large database used for testing. She is reluctant to perform this task, because she knows that the snapshot will grow very large. She decides to use a vCenter Server alarm to monitor this snapshot.

She creates an alarm at the virtual machine object level so that it will apply only to this specific VM. She configures the alarm using the VM Snapshot Size (GB) trigger type. She configures the Warning value for 100 and the Alert value for 150. She adds an action of Send A Notification Email and configures it to send her an email on the normal-to-warning transition and the warning-to-alert transition.

She places the virtual machine in snapshot mode. The next day, she receives an email stating that the snapshot has reached the warning threshold. She contacts the owner of the test server and reports what she is seeing. The application owner verifies that the testing has failed and requests that the virtual machine be reverted and the snapshot deleted.

Using vCenter Server alarms allowed the virtual infrastructure administrator to keep track of the virtual machine's snapshot size without having to manually check it periodically.

Now that we have covered creating utilization alarms, we will create a vCenter Server connectivity alarm.

Creating a vCenter Connectivity Alarm

Like creating a utilization alarm, creating a vCenter Server connectivity alarm is also a fairly simple process that can be used to provide impressive levels of detail and automation. Exercise 11.13 covers the steps to create a vCenter Server connectivity alarm for a virtual machine.

EXERCISE 11.13

Monitoring Datastore Connectivity with a vCenter Server Connectivity Alarm

1. Connect to vCenter Server using the vSphere Web Client.

2. Navigate to the root vCenter Server object in the left pane.

3. Select the Manage tab and then click Alarm Definitions on the toolbar.

4. Review the names of the listed definitions, and take note of the Defined In column.

5. Click the green plus icon to add a new alarm definition. A New Alarm Definition window will open.

6. Give the alarm the name **VM Disconnected**, and provide a description for it.

7. Ensure that the drop-down menu for the Monitor option is set to Virtual Machines. Ensure that Specific Event Occurring On this Object radio button is selected in the Monitor For option.

8. Select the Enable This Alarm check box. The final configuration should look similar to this:

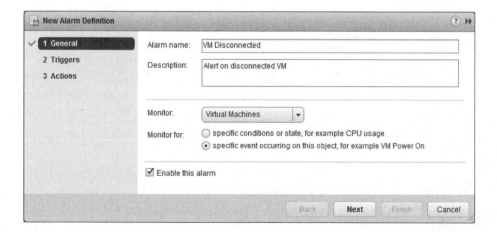

EXERCISE 11.13 *(continued)*

9. Click Triggers in the left pane.

10. Click the green plus icon near the top of the window.

11. An entry will appear on the list of triggers. Click this entry under the Trigger column heading to access a drop-down menu.

12. Select the VM Disconnected option and ensure that the Status column has a value of Alert.

13. Click the green plus icon near the bottom of the window to add a condition.

14. An entry will appear on the list of conditions. Click this entry under the Argument column heading to access a drop-down menu.

15. Select the Data Center Name option and ensure that the Operator column has a value of Equal To.

16. Click in the Value column and enter the name of your datacenter object. The final configuration should look like this:

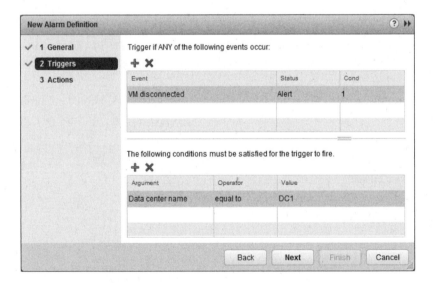

17. Click Actions in the left pane.

18. Click the green plus icon located toward the top of the window.

19. An entry will appear on the list of actions. Click this entry under the Action column heading to access a drop-down menu.

20. Select the Send A Notification Email option.

21. Click the entry below the Configuration column header and enter a valid email address to send the notification to.

22. Ensure that both the Normal To Warning and the Warning To Alert columns have the Once value selected. The final configuration should look like this:

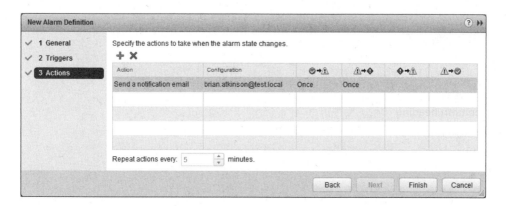

23. Click the Finish button to save this alarm. A Create Alarm Definition task will begin.

24. Review the list of alarms and verify that the new alarm is listed. Note its value in the Defined In column.

This exercise created a connectivity alarm that monitors virtual machines in a specific datacenter. In your test environments, you may want to experiment with some of the other connectivity alarms and the alarm actions to get a better understanding of the events that vCenter Server alarms can monitor and respond to.

We have now created a vCenter Server connectivity alarm. In the next section, we will explore alarm triggers in more detail.

Configuring Alarm Triggers

vCenter Server alarms consist of three parts:

- Type
- Trigger
- Action

Triggers were specifically covered in the previous two exercises, and it is important to remember that multiple trigger types can be defined in a single alarm. The trigger types can each act individually or as a group.

Keep in mind when using the Trigger If All Of The Conditions Are Satisfied option that the more trigger types that are added, the more complex the alarm becomes. Figure 11.24 shows a virtual machine–type alarm with multiple triggers defined.

FIGURE 11.24   Multiple triggers in alarm

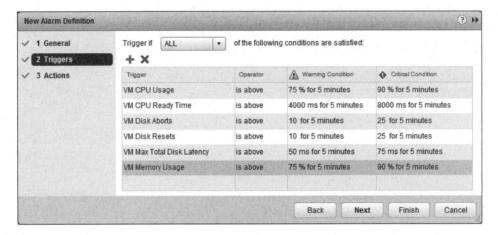

It should be fairly easy to see why this alarm would likely never be triggered!

 The VM Total Size On Disk and VM Snapshot Size triggers cannot be used in combination with any other triggers.

Next, we will discuss alarm actions in more detail.

Configuring Alarm Actions

The key thing to remember with vCenter Server alarm actions is that multiple actions can be defined on each alarm. These actions can correlate to any of the four condition changes, which are represented in the four rightmost columns as icons. The four condition changes are:

- From normal to warning (green to yellow)
- From warning to critical (yellow to red)
- From critical to warning (red to yellow)
- From warning to normal (yellow to green)

Figure 11.25 shows a virtual machine type alarm with a unique action configured for each condition change.

FIGURE 11.25   Multiple actions in alarm

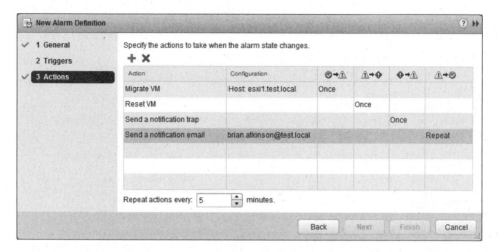

In the final section of this chapter, we will discuss identifying the affected resource in a given vSphere implementation for a given alarm.

For a Given Alarm, Identifying the Affected Resource in a vSphere Implementation

For most vCenter Server alarms, the Name column will provide sufficient detail to identify the affected resource. Figure 11.26 shows vCenter Server–triggered alarms for ESXi servers.

FIGURE 11.26   vCenter Server alarms

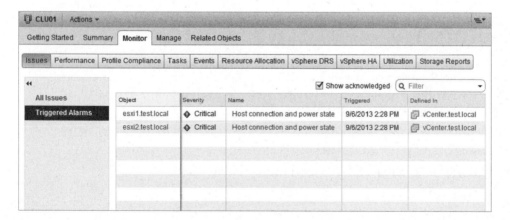

These two entries are for two ESXi hosts that had their management network connections removed. Clicking the information provided in the name column will take you to the alarm definition, where you can review the triggers to determine more information about the alarm.

Figure 11.27 shows another vCenter Server alarm scenario.

FIGURE 11.27 vCenter Server alarms for vSphere HA

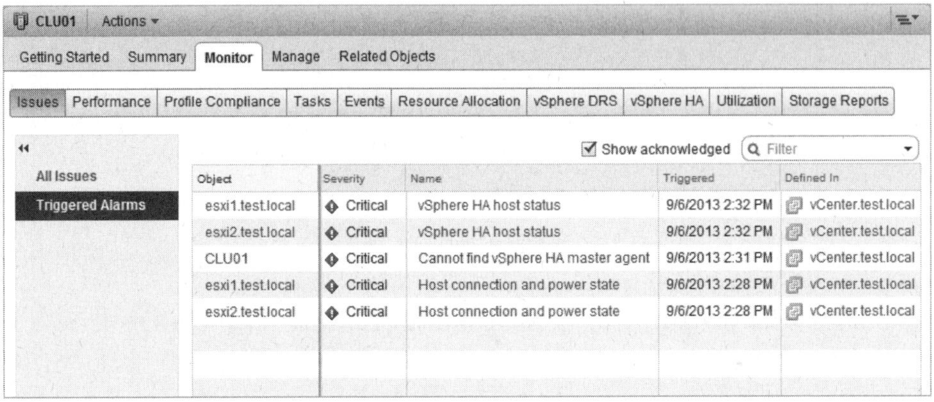

For this set of alerts, the management network was still disconnected for the ESXi host and the storage network was also disconnected. The alert about vSphere HA is not quite immediately obvious, but network connectivity should almost always be first suspected in HA alerts.

I have now covered identifying the affected resource in a vSphere implementation for a given alarm. This concludes this chapter and my coverage of the VCP5-DCV exam objectives.

Summary

This chapter focused on monitoring ESXi hosts, vCenter Server, and virtual machines; installing, configuring, and administering vCenter Server Operations Manager; and creating and administering vCenter Server alarms:

- Understanding how administrators can view tasks and events in vCenter Server

- Using critical performance metrics

- Using common memory, CPU, network, and storage metrics

- Creating overview and advanced charts

- Configuring vCenter Server settings for SNMP, User Directory Services, SMTP, logging, and timeouts

- Creating, editing, and deleting a scheduled task

- Configuring, viewing, printing, and exporting resource maps

- Understanding the vCenter Server services as well as the ESXi host agent

- Monitoring and administering vCenter Server connections

- Determining the host performance using a combination of resxtop and Windows Perfmon

- Identifying the affected vSphere resource given the performance data

The second part of this chapter focused on installing, configuring, and administering vCenter Operations Manager:

- Explaining vCenter Operations Manager Architecture

- Deploying and configuring vCenter Operations Manager vApp

- Upgrading vCenter Operations Manager

- Differentiating major/minor vCenter Operations Manager badges

- Understanding metrics used by major/minor vCenter Operations Manager badges

- Monitoring vSphere environment with vCenter Operations Manager

- Identifying the affected resource in a vSphere implementation, for a given alarm

The final part of this chapter focused on creating and administering vCenter Server alarms:

- Using the vCenter Server default utilization and connectivity alarms, along with their actions

- Creating a vCenter Server utilization and connectivity alarm and configuring alarm triggers and alarm actions

- Identifying the affected resource in a vSphere implementation for a given alarm

Exam Essentials

Know how to monitor ESXi, vCenter Server, and VMs.   Be able to describe how tasks and events are viewed in vCenter Server. Be able to identify critical performance metrics. Be able to explain common memory, CPU, network, and storage metrics. Know the difference between an overview and an advanced chart and how to create an advanced chart. Know how to configure SNMP, User Directory services, SMTP, logging, and timeout settings for vCenter Server. Be able to create, edit, and delete a scheduled task. Know how to configure, view, print, and export resource maps. Understand how to start, stop, and verify vCenter

Server services and how to start, stop, and verify the ESXi host agents. Be able to monitor and administer vCenter Server connections. Understand how to use resxtop and Windows Perfmon to determine host performance. Be able to identify the affected vSphere resource when given performance data.

Know how to install, configure and administer vCenter Operations Manager. Be able to explain the vCenter Operations Manager architecture. Know how to deploy and configure the vCenter Operations Manager appliance. Understand how to upgrade vCenter Operations Manager. Be able to differentiate between the major and minor vCenter Operations Manager badges. Understand the metrics used by the major and minor vCenter Operations Manager badges. Know how to monitor a vSphere environment with vCenter Operations Manager. Be able to identify the affected resource in a vSphere implementation, for a given alarm.

Know how to create and administer vCenter Server alarms. Be able to list vCenter Server default utilization and connectivity alarms. Be able to list the possible actions for utilization and connectivity alarms. Know how to create a vCenter utilization alarm and connectivity alarm. Understand how to configure alarm triggers and alarm actions. Be able to identify the affected resource in a vSphere implementation for a given alarm.

Review Questions

1. Which of the following can be used to restart the ESXi host agent? (Choose all that apply.)

   A. DCUI

   B. ESXi Shell

   C. vSphere Client

   D. All of these

2. You just deployed vCenter Operations Manager, and you want to change both the default admin and root passwords. Which of the following is a valid password that could be used with either of these accounts?

   A. password

   B. p@ssword

   C. passw0rd

   D. p-ssw-rd

3. When viewing the Tasks & Events tab in the vSphere Client, you notice that there are a limited number of entries, and the information available does not go back far enough. What setting could be used to adjust the number of entries?

   A. This is not possible.

   B. Edit ➤ Client Settings ➤ Lists tab.

   C. Filtering.

   D. vCenter Server Settings ➤ Administration ➤ Statistics.

4. Which of the following is defined as the percentage of time a VM was not provided CPU resources but was ready to run?

   A. %SYS

   B. %WAIT

   C. %USED

   D. %RDY

5. You need to collect resxtop data for two minutes. This data will be used in Perfmon on a Windows guest. Which of the following commands should be used?

   A.
   ```
   resxtop --server <vCENTER FQDN>
   --vihost <ESXi HOST FQDN>
   --username <DOMAIN>\\<USERNAME>
   -b -d 3 -n 120 > resxtop-export.csv
   ```

   B.
   ```
   resxtop --server <vCENTER FQDN>
   --vihost <ESXi HOST FQDN>
   ```

```
    --username <DOMAIN>\\<USERNAME>
    -b -d 120 -n 1 > resxtop-export.csv
```

  C.
```
    resxtop --server <vCENTER FQDN>
    --vihost <ESXi HOST FQDN>
    --username <DOMAIN>\\<USERNAME>
    -b -d 2 -n 60 > resxtop-export.csv
```

  D.
```
    resxtop --server <vCENTER FQDN>
    --vihost <ESXi HOST FQDN>
    --username <DOMAIN>\\<USERNAME>
    -b -d 1 -n 120 > resxtop-export.csv
```

6. You created a vCenter Server alarm at the root vCenter Server level to monitor a single virtual machine for the snapshot space used. You are now getting warnings from several VMs. What is the best way to solve this problem?

  A. Re-create the rule at the virtual machine object level.

  B. Exclude the virtual machines you don't want to see from the rule.

  C. Move the rule to the host level.

  D. None of these.

7. Which file type is used to upgrade vCenter Operations Manager?

  A. .zip

  B. .tar.gz

  C. .vib

  D. .pak

8. You collect metrics for your vSphere environment. You see %DRPRX has a value of 1. Which of the following is most likely the problem?

  A. CPU.

  B. Network.

  C. Disk.

  D. There is no problem.

9. Which of the following is defined as the average amount of time in milliseconds a device takes to service a single I/O request?

  A. DAVG/cmd

  B. GAVG/cmd

  C. KAVG/cmd

  D. None of these

10. Which of the following are major badges in vCenter Operations Manager? (Choose all that apply.)

  A. Workload

  B. Risk

C. Efficiency

D. Density

11. You notice an alarm on your vCenter Server that states vSphere HA Host Status. What is the most likely cause of this alarm?

A. Host hardware power supply failure

B. Host hardware NIC failure

C. Host hardware memory failure

D. Host hardware Fibre Channel HBA failure

12. Which of the following is an unsupported IP allocation scheme for use with the vCenter Operations Manager vApp?

A. DHCP

B. Static - Manual

C. Transient - IP Pool

D. NAT

13. Which of the following can be scheduled using the scheduled tasks feature in vCenter Server? (Choose all that apply.)

A. Cloning a VM

B. Migrating a VM

C. Adding a host

D. Deleting a VM

14. You created a vCenter Server alarm with multiple trigger types and an action to send email. One of the triggers should have fired by now, but you have not received any emails. You are receiving emails from other alarms. Which of the following is most likely the reason?

A. The Trigger If All Of The Conditions Are Satisfied option was used.

B. The Trigger If Any Of The Conditions Are Satisfied option was used.

C. SMTP is not configured in the vCenter Server settings.

D. Alarms cannot have multiple trigger types.

15. Which of the following are required to configure SMTP in the vCenter Server settings? (Choose two.)

A. IP address of SMTP server

B. Port number of SMTP server

C. SMTP server authentication information

D. Sender account

16. Which of the following make up an alarm? (Choose all that apply.)

A. Type

B. Trigger

    C. Action

    D. Condition

17. Which of the following actions do all of the alarm-type monitors have in common? (Choose all that apply.)

    A. Send a notification email

    B. Send a notification trap

    C. Run a command

    D. Enter maintenance mode

18. You need to view all events for a recent HA problem. What is the lowest-level inventory object that would be considered the best starting point?

    A. Virtual machine

    B. ESXi host

    C. Cluster

    D. vCenter Server root object

19. Which of the following metrics are used to monitor current SWAP file usage? (Choose two.)

    A. Memory: Swap Used

    B. SWAP curr

    C. SZTGT

    D. CACHEUSD

20. What are the names of the VMs contained in the vCenter Operations Manager vApp? (Choose two).

    A. UI VM

    B. WEB VM

    C. Collector VM

    D. Analytics VM

Appendix A

Answers to Review Questions

Chapter 2: Planning, Installing, Configuring, and Upgrading VMware ESXi and vCenter Server

1. C. The version of the vCenter Server Appliance shipped with vSphere 5.5 contains an embedded vPostgres database that can support up to 100 hosts and 3,000 virtual machines.

2. A. The bundled Microsoft SQL Server 2008 R2 Express edition database can be used with up to 5 VMware ESX hosts and 50 virtual machines in the inventory.

3. B. The root password is required to be at least seven characters long.

4. A. The SSO administrator in vCenter Single Sign-On shipped with vSphere 5.1 is named Admin@System-Domain.

5. A and B. vCenter Server 5.5 requires 2 vCPUs or one dual-core vCPU to be a supported configuration.

6. C. The vCenter Inventory Service, which is a part of a Simple Install of vCenter Server, is primarily used to manage the vSphere Web Client inventory objects and is not a component of vCenter Single Sign-On.

7. D. NTP is configured on ESXi hosts to ensure they each have accurate time.

8. A. vCenter Single Sign-On is always installed and/or upgraded first, when applicable.

9. B and C. ESXi 5 hosts can PXE boot and receive an IP address from a DHCP server. Then the Auto Deploy server will stream the ESXi image to the host.

10. B. ESXi 5 requires a minimum of two processor cores.

11. B and C. vCenter Server with an external SQL database requires a 64-bit DSN created for the SQL Native Client.

12. B. Mem.MemZipEnable is used to enable/disable the memory compression cache. By default the setting is 1, or enabled.

13. A, B and D. DNS and routing can be configured using the vSphere Client, the vSphere Web Client, or the DCUI.

14. C. The vSphere Web Client is a web application that can be used on Mac OS to administer vCenter Server.

15. A, B, C and D. These are the four available vCenter Server Support Tools that can be installed from the VMware vCenter Installer.

16. B and D. VMware vCenter Server Standard is used in the vSphere 5 Standard, Enterprise, and Enterprise Plus kits.

17. A. The vCenter Server Appliance requires a minimum of 7GB of disk space and a maximum of 125GB.

18. A and C. vSphere Host Power Management requires specific BIOS settings to be configured, and then the individual ESXi host can manage the power for the server.

19. D. The SSO administrator in vCenter Single Sign-On shipped with vSphere 5.5 is named Administrator@vsphere.local.

20. D. Update Manager, interactive, and scripted upgrades are the supported upgrade methods when upgrading ESX/ESXi 4.x versions to ESXi 5.

Chapter 3: Securing vCenter Server and ESXi and Identifying vSphere Architecture and Solutions

1. B. There are three default system roles: Administrator, Read-Only, and No Access.

2. C. A privilege defines individual user rights.

3. C. A role is a collection of privileges.

4. B. A permission is created by pairing a role with a user or group and associating it with an object in the vCenter Server inventory.

5. A and D. Any permission defined on a child object will override permissions propagated from parent objects, and virtual machines inherit multiple permissions.

6. B. The ESXi firewall is enabled by default and also blocks all traffic by default, except for default management services traffic.

7. A. Start And Stop With Port Usage is the setting VMware recommends.

8. C. All operations performed against an ESXi host in lockdown mode must originate from the vCenter Server that is managing the ESXi host. The exceptions are the ESXi Shell, SSH, or the Direct Console User Interface (DCUI) if these services are enabled on the ESXi host in lockdown mode.

9. B and C. Joining an ESXi host to a directory service simplifies user management and improves security by not having to share the root user account credentials.

10. B. The list of local ESXi users and groups is accessible from the vSphere Client connected directly to the ESXi host. vCenter Server has no ability to view the local ESXi accounts, and the vSphere Web Client can only connect to vCenter Server.

11. C. Active Directory security groups are the preferred method for managing permissions in vCenter Server.

12. A. The default system roles of No Access, Read-Only, and Administrator can be cloned, but they cannot be edited or removed.

13. D. There must be a group in Active Directory with the name ESX Admins, and the Active Directory user accounts that should have access to the ESXi host(s) will be placed in this group.

14. A. Horizon View is VMware's virtual desktop infrastructure solution. Site Recovery Manager is VMware's disaster recovery solution. vCenter Operations Management Suite is VMware's performance, capacity, and health monitoring solution. vCloud Director is VMware's software-defined data center provisioning solution.

15. A and C. The Virtual Machine.Snapshot Management.Create Snapshot and the Datastore. Allocate Space privileges are both required to take a snapshot of a virtual machine.

16. B and D. Storage I/O Control and Storage DRS are both included only in the Enterprise Plus Edition of vSphere 5.

17. A, B, C and D. All four of these features are available only in Enterprise or higher editions of vSphere 5.

18. A, C and D. The vSphere architecture is composed of three distinct layers: the virtualization layer, the management layer, and the interface layer.

19. A, B and D. None of these features are included with the Essentials Edition of vSphere 5.

20. A. The Enterprise Plus edition of vSphere would be required in this case, because the customer could use the Auto Deploy feature to achieve the diskless and stateless ESXi hosts.

Chapter 4: Planning and Configuring vSphere Networking

1. C. CDP information can be obtained for peer devices connected to the network adapters on vNetwork standard switches by clicking the information icon beside the vSwitch. LLDP is supported only on dvSwitches.

2. A and D. The two connection types available when creating a vSwitch are virtual machine and VMkernel. Connection types are also known as port groups.

3. A, B, C and D. All of these are common policies in both the vSwitch and the dvSwitch.

4. B and C. Virtual Switch Tagging (VST) and Virtual Guest Tagging (VGT) each require the use of trunked VLANs.

5. A, B, C and D. Any vSphere environment can make use of a vSwitch.

6. B. The Route Based On Physical NIC Load policy is available only in the dvSwitch.

7. A. Adding and removing NICs from a vSwitch with a virtual machine port group is a non-disruptive action, as long as there remains at least one active NIC.

8. D. The dvSwitch version 5.0.0 provides Network I/O Control, NetFlow, and port mirroring.

9. A and C. Add Now and Add Later are the two options presented in the wizard.

10. B. VLAN trunking allows a range of trunked VLANs to be entered, which requires only a single dvPort group in the dvSwitch.

11. A. The virtual machine will need a virtual machine port group to connect to this network, since only the ESXi host can use the VMkernel port group. The best practice would be to remove this virtual machine port group once it is no longer in use, to limit potential access to this isolated network.

12. A and D. Route Based On IP Hash requires EtherChannel, and standby adapters/uplinks must not be configured when using the Route Based On IP Hash load-balancing policy.

13. C and D. To utilize TSO in a virtual machine, either the VMXNET 2 or VMXNET 3 network adapter is required. The VMware Tools are also required to load the drivers in the guest OS, but the VMware Tools alone will not allow the VM to use TSO.

14. A, C and D. The VMkernel can be used for host-based connections such as vMotion, iSCSI, and Management traffic.

15. D. Use of the dvSwitch requires both vCenter Server and Enterprise Plus licensing.

16. B. A Distributed Virtual Uplink (dvUplink) is used to provide a level of abstraction between the physical network adapters (vmnics) on the ESXi host and the dvSwitch.

17. A. The dvSwitch provides bidirectional virtual machine traffic shaping capability.

18. A, B, C and D. Using jumbo frames in a virtual machine requires the VMXNET 2 or VMXNET 3 adapter, and the drivers provided for each by VMware Tools. Guest OS configuration changes, and ensuring that all devices on the network segment support jumbo frames is also necessary.

19. C. With static binding a dvPort is immediately assigned and reserved when the virtual machine is connected to the dvPort.

20. B, C and D. In a dvSwitch, virtual network adapters are used to provide VMkernel connections such as ESXi management traffic, vMotion, FT, iSCSI, and NFS.

Chapter 5: Planning and Configuring vSphere Storage

1. B. The software iSCSI adapter is not enabled by default.

2. A. eui.5577bd49251ddb52 is an example of a SCSI INQUIRY device identifier.

3. A, B and C. ESXi 5.5 supports booting from an iSCSI SAN LUN with a supported iSCSI HBA, a supported dependent iSCSI hardware adapter, and the ESXi software iSCSI adapter.

4. D. This question cannot be definitively answered, because the version of the ESXi host is not specified. If it was an ESXi 5 or 5.1 host, then 2TB minus 512 bytes is correct. If ESXi 5.5 were used, then 62TB is the correct answer.

5. A, C and D. The three path selection policies included by default in ESXi are Fixed, Most Recently Used, and Round Robin.

6. B. With Mutual CHAP, the target (storage system) authenticates the iSCSI adapter (initiator), and the iSCSI adapter also authenticates the target. This authentication method is also known as bidirectional.

7. C. Since the independent hardware iSCSI adapter handles the workload for both the iSCSI processing and the iSCSI traffic, it would place the least amount of additional load on the ESXi host resources.

8. B. Renaming a VMFS datastore is a non-disruptive action. Simply renaming the datastore using the vSphere Web Client would be the easiest way to rename these datastores.

9. C. LUN masking is a process performed at the SAN storage processors or ESXi host level that makes LUNs hidden from certain hosts.

10. B and C. VMFS datastores can be extended or expanded to increase their size.

11. A, B, C and D. All four are correct and represent the four vCenter Server storage filters.

12. A. VMFS-3 datastores will retain their original block size after an upgrade to VMFS-5.

13. A, B, C and D. All of these statements are prerequisites for unmounting a VMFS datastore.

14. A, B and D. The NFS server's name, the IP address or NFS UUID, the path to the NFS share, and the NFS datastore name to be used in vSphere are all required when adding an NFS datastore.

15. C and D. A Fibre Channel SAN would allow you to use both VMFS and RDM to present these large volumes to the virtual machine.

16. C. Once an NFS datastore is unmounted, the Add Storage Wizard can be used to mount it again.

17. C. The independent hardware iSCSI adapter performs the iSCSI processing and the iSCSI networking traffic on one card. These adapters are also known as iSCSI HBAs.

18. B. VMware FT requires Thick Provision Eagerly Zeroed VMDKs. This means a 50GB VMDK will consume 50GB of space both at the VMDK level and at the storage array level.

19. D. iBFT (iSCSI Boot Firmware Table) is used to communicate information about the iSCSI boot device to an ESXi host.

20. D. The Rescan Storage option from the context menu that appears when you right-click on the cluster object would scan all hosts in one operation. This would be the fastest option.

Chapter 6: Creating and Deploying Virtual Machines and vApps

1. C. The VMware Converter can be used to change the virtual hardware configuration for virtual machines, including the virtual machine hardware version.

2. B and C. New virtual machines can be configured and deployed with either the vSphere Client or the vSphere Web Client. New virtual machine hardware features, however, will be available only in the vSphere Web Client.

3. A. An RDM in Physical Compatibility Mode allows the guest OS to access the raw device directly and is used for SAN-aware applications running in a virtual machine.

4. A, B, C and D. All of these are device drivers included with the VMware Tools.

5. D. The VMware Converter is not a component of any vSphere 5.5 edition. It is a freely downloadable product available from VMWare.

6. B and C. Cloning a vApp is accomplished with either the vSphere Client or the Web Client.

7. D. The Virtual SCSI bus sharing type allows virtual disks to be shared by virtual machines located on the same ESXi host.

8. B. IP Pools are always associated with the datacenter inventory object.

9. B, C and D. The VMXNET, VMXNET 2, and VMXNET 3 NICs rely on VMware Tools to provide drivers to them.

10. A, B and C. Objects that can be added to an existing vApp include virtual machines, resource pools, and other vApps.

11. B and C. The VMware Tools are not required for any virtual machine, but they do offer advanced functionality and management for virtual machines. An automatic VMware Tools upgrade is not interactive and can reboot the guest OS without prompting.

12. B and C. Each virtual machine in the same group is started in the order specified, before the next group in the list begins. Shutdown is performed in reverse order of the start order.

13. C. All changes made to an independent nonpersistent disk are lost at VM power-off or reset.

14. A and B. Running VMware Converter with the powered on VM or importing a powered-off Hyper-V virtual machine are the two acceptable ways to accomplish this task.

15. C and D. DRS requires either the Enterprise or Enterprise Plus edition of vSphere.

16. B and D. Virtual machine hardware version 10 supports a maximum of 64 vCPUs and 1TB of RAM.

17. A, B and C. Virtual disk files can be stored with the virtual machine, or a different datastore or datastore cluster can be specified for them.

18. A, B, C and D. All of these methods can be used to convert a thin disk to a thick disk.

19. A and B. VmwareToolboxCmd.exe can be used to disable periodic time synchronization in Windows, and vmware-toolbox-cmd can be used on Linux, Solaris, and FreeBSD.

20. A and B. The vSphere Client or the vSphere Web Client can be used to obtain virtual machine console access.

Chapter 7: Managing and Administering Virtual Machines and vApps

1. A, B, C and D. All of these options are listed in the context menus when right-clicking a template using the vSphere Web Client.

2. C and D. Neither a cluster nor a resource pool is a valid content type in vCloud Connector.

3. B. Creating the VM and cloning it would be the least amount of work. Cloning can be used to avoid repetition of tasks.

4. A. Advanced parameters are added in a virtual machine's settings by clicking the VM Options toolbar item, and then navigating to Advanced ➢ Configuration Parameters ➢ Edit Configuration. These options can be configured only when the virtual machine is powered off.

5. A. The Disable Acceleration option is used to slow down a virtual machine if there is a problem running or installing software in the virtual machine.

6. B and D. The Distributed Resource Scheduler and vMotion are both supported features that can be used with USB passthrough.

7. B. vApps are built on an industry-standard format known as the Open Virtualization Format (OVF).

8. B. The option to force the virtual machine to enter the BIOS/EFI setup is one of the few options that may be configured while the virtual machine is powered on.

9. A. Templates cannot be powered on; they must first be converted to virtual machines to be powered on. After converting a template to a VM, the VM can be updated as required, powered off, and then converted to a template again.

10. A, B, C and D. Use output file, use physical serial port, use named pipe, and use network are the four available options for a new serial port configuration.

11. A, B, C and D. Virtual machine security consists of securing the virtual machine, the ESXi host(s) it runs on, the storage and Ethernet networks it uses, the vCenter Server used to manage it, the backup server used to protect it, and likely more. Each environment will be different, but securing virtual machines encompasses a lot of different parts of the infrastructure.

12. A, B and C. Shares, limits, and reservations can all be specified in the Edit Resource Settings window for a virtual machine.

13. C. When a virtual machine is converted to a template, its configuration file will have the .vmtx extension.

14. B. Windows Server 2008 R2 supports extending OS volumes, and vSphere supports hot-extending disks. Neither of these procedures requires downtime to accomplish.

15. B and C. Setting a power-on delay will provide additional time to access the BIOS setup; even better is the Force BIOS Setup option, which will ensure that the virtual machine boots into the BIOS setup.

16. A and D. Virtual machine swap files (VSWP) and virtual disk files (VMDK) can be moved to locations outside of the virtual machine working location.

17. D. The VMSD file is a database that stores information and metadata about snapshots for a virtual machine.

18. A, B and C. The vSphere Client and Web Client can both be used to create and use clones and templates while connected to vCenter Server.

19. A and C. Windows as the guest OS is always a requirement for Wake On LAN, and both the VMXNET and VMXNET 3 virtual adapters are supported.

20. A and D. Virtual appliances and vApps can both be deployed by using the Deploy OVF Template function in the Web Client.

Chapter 8: Establishing Service Levels with Clusters, Fault Tolerance, and Resource Pools

1. **A, B and C.** All of these are correct, except the EVC mode setting. EVC mode is not a requirement to use VMware FT.

2. **B and C.** Storage DRS requires ESXi 5 hosts and all NFS or all VMFS datastores.

3. **B.** ESXi hosts must be in maintenance mode before they can be removed from a cluster.

4. **B and C.** It is recommended that you have a dedicated 1GbE NIC for fault tolerance logging and that you isolate the traffic to secure it.

5. **C.** The VMware Tools are required for a proper shutdown of the guest OS, so the virtual machine without the VMware Tools would be powered off.

6. **A.** A VM-Host affinity rule can be created to require VMs in the specified VM group to run on ESXi hosts in the specified host group.

7. **C.** FT has an overhead of 5 to 20 percent that must be accounted for. This is for additional CPU, RAM, disk IO and network IO.

8. **B and D.** Enabling DRS on a cluster will create a second layer of scheduling architecture to go along with the local scheduler on each ESXi host. This second scheduler is called the global scheduler.

9. **B.** Selecting the expandable reservation allows a child resource pool to request resources from its parent or ancestors.

10. **B and D.** Raising the EVC mode for cluster involves moving from a lower feature set to a greater feature set. Virtual machines can continue to run during this operation.

11. **D.** If resource pools do not exist in the destination, the Migrate Virtual Machine Wizard will not offer you the option to select a resource pool.

12. **B.** In the partially automated automation level, vCenter Server will inform of suggested virtual machine migrations and place the virtual machines on ESXi hosts at VM startup.

13. **C.** When choosing the specify failover hosts admission control policy, no virtual machines can be powered on when they are on the specified failover hosts, unless an HA event has occurred.

14. **A, B and D.** Resource pools allow shares, reservations, and limits to be configured, and the resource pool name can be changed.

15. **A, C and D.** The slave host could be failed, isolated, or partitioned.

16. A, B, C and D. Both clients can be used to enable FT. The power state of the VM is irrelevant, since the VM's virtual disk files are already eager zeroed thick provisioned.

17. D. The Fault Tolerance Test Failover option is both noninvasive and fully supported.

18. D. The migration threshold is configured beneath the automation level settings of the DRS cluster. Moving the slider to the far right will set the migration threshold to Aggressive.

19. A, B, C and D. VMware FT can be used in all of these cases, as long as the virtual machine meets the FT requirements.

20. A and D. SSD and flash PCIe cards are supported for use with vSphere Flash Read Cache.

Chapter 9: Maintaining Service Levels

1. B. vMotion is able to change both host and datastore even with nonshared storage (using the Web Client only). Cold migration and VMware Converter would both require powering off the virtual machine.

2. D. Of the choices presented, only snapshots with RDMs in virtual compatibility mode are supported.

3. A, B and C. VMware Data Protection does not support independent disks, RDM independent disks (in virtual compatibility mode) or RDMs in physical compatibility mode.

4. D. Upgrading VMware Tools may or may not require a reboot, depending on the version of the VMware Tools and the components being upgraded in VMware Tools. A restart will be required when the virtual machine hardware is upgraded, since this requires the virtual machine to be powered off. After the VM is powered up, Windows may find new devices, again depending on which components were updated, and require another reboot. The correct answer is a minimum of one restart and a maximum of three restarts.

5. A and C. There are two options for the vMotion priority level: Reserve CPU For Optimal vMotion Performance and Perform With Available CPU Resources.

6. B. The swap file location specified on a virtual machine will override swap file settings defined at either the ESXi host or cluster level.

7. A, B and D. vSphere Update Manager can be configured with a direct connection to the Internet to use a shared repository or to import patches.

8. C. Creating a baseline group allows VMware Tools and virtual machine hardware to be updated in a single vSphere Update Manager remediation operation that can be scheduled.

9. D. Update Manager 5.5 is only compatible with vCenter Server 5.5.

10. C and D. vSphere Data Protection supports up to 10 appliances for up to 100 VMs each. vSphere Data Protection is compatible with vCenter Server versions 5.1 and 5.5.

11. A. Storage vMotion can be used to migrate a virtual machine that has snapshots, as long as the VM is located on an ESXi 5 or newer host.

12. B and C. Enterprise Plus licensing is required to use host profiles, and ESX/ESXi hosts must be placed in maintenance mode to have a host profile applied.

13. A. Reverting the virtual machine to the current snapshot will restore it to its previous state. The snapshot will still exist, so deleting it in Snapshot Manager by clicking either the Delete or Delete All button will remove the snapshot.

14. A, B, C and D. None of these are supported for use with the VMware Data Protection Recovery Restore Client.

15. C. The proper sequence is create baseline, attach baseline, scan object, and remediate object.

16. A and B. Migrating a powered-off or suspended VM to a new datacenter is supported. vMotion and Storage vMotion cannot be used to migrate VMs to different datacenters.

17. B and C. The requirement for EVC is that all hosts in the cluster must have the same brand of processors.

18. B and C. vSphere Update Manager requires a 64-bit operating system and a 32-bit DSN.

19. A, C and D. NFS servers that do not support the VAAI NAS extensions that enable reserve space will not allow the disk format to be changed, and the option to change virtual disk formats will be grayed out.

20. A. The vSphere Web Client is used to manage VMware Data Protection.

Chapter 10: Performing Basic Troubleshooting

1. D. Virtual machines attached to an ISO on local storage cannot be migrated with vMotion.

2. D. The VM's NIC was disconnected prior to the snapshot. When the VM was reverted, it had a disconnected NIC.

3. C. All of the ESXi logs are accessible from /var/run/log in the ESXi Shell.

4. A. If the Define Failover Capacity By Static Number Of Hosts admission control policy is used, there will be an Advanced Runtime Info panel available in the vSphere HA toolbar accessible from the Cluster's Monitor tab.

5. C. A DAVG/cmd value greater than 20 usually indicates a problem, and the value currently reported is nearly 4 times higher than normal. It is a safe conclusion that there is storage contention in this situation.

6. C and D. A single virtual machine is affected, so checking host-specific or network settings is simply not necessary in this case.

7. C and D. Both the Issues toolbar on the Cluster's Monitor tab and the vSphere HA tab toolbar on the Cluster's Monitor tab can be used to view all current vSphere HA issues.

8. A and B. All hosts must be licensed and have access to the same shared storage. VMware Tools are never required for these features.

9. B. If the vSphere Web Client is connected to a vCenter Server, the diagnostic information for the ESXi hosts the server manages can also be exported at the same time.

10. C and D. The LAT/rd and LAT/wr metrics are virtual machine specific and used to measure I/O latency.

11. B, C and D. Each of these can lead to a DRS cluster imbalance.

12. B, C and D. Virtual switches, datastores, hosts, and virtual machines can all be viewed in vMotion resource maps, but there is no ability to show connected devices for virtual machines.

13. B. When connected directly to an ESXi host with the vSphere Client, use the Configuration tab to view the Hardware Health Status information.

14. D. Without the T10-based Storage APIs – Array Integration (Thin Provisioning) support, virtual machines will crash if an out-of-space condition occurs.

15. A. DAVG/cmd is the average amount of time in milliseconds a device takes to service a single I/O request.

16. A and B. From the local console, the ESXi Shell or the Configure Management Network feature will show the device name, the MAC address, and the status. The vSphere Client and vSphere Web Client cannot be used if there is no management network connectivity.

17. C and D. When building a white-box server, as many parts as possible should be verified to be on the VMware HCL. When a hard disk is not seen by the ESXi installer, a missing driver is often the root cause.

18. A, B, C and D. Each of these is a valid step in verifying a storage configuration.

19. C. When certain configurations are in use, like Route Based On IP Hash Load Balancing, it will often be necessary to involve the staff responsible for managing the upstream physical network devices.

20. D. When Migration Threshold is set to Conservative, no attempt to load balance will be made by DRS. This will result in the target host load standard deviation being reported as N/A.

Chapter 11: Monitoring a vSphere Implementation and Managing vCenter Server Alarms

1. **A and B.** The ESXi Shell can be used to restart the host agent service. The DCUI Troubleshooting Options menu item can also be used to restart all management agents, including hostd.

2. **C.** The admin and root passwords must be a minimum of eight characters and include at least one letter and one digit.

3. **B.** The number of entries displayed in the tasks and events lists in the vSphere Client can be adjusted using the Edit ➢ Client Settings ➢ Lists tab.

4. **D.** %RDY or CPU Ready is used to measure the percentage of time a VM was ready to run but was not provided with CPU resources.

5. **C.** The -d switch is the delay between statistics snapshots, and the -n switch is used to specify the number of iterations. Option C will perform 60 iterations at 2-second intervals, capturing 2 minutes of data.

6. **A.** Alarms are inherited down the chain of inventory objects, so the only way to solve this problem is to re-create the alarm at the VM object level.

7. **D.** vCenter Operations Manager can be upgraded by downloading a .pak file from VMware and applying it via the vCenter Operations Manager Administration portal.

8. **B.** %DRPRX indicates that network receive packets are being dropped. This is a likely indicator of a network problem.

9. **A.** The DAVG/cmd metric is the average amount of time in milliseconds a device takes to service a single I/O request. The device includes the vmhba, the storage device, and any devices between.

10. **B and C.** Health, Risk, and Efficiency are the three major health badges in vCenter Operations Manager. Workload and Density are two of the eight minor badges.

11. **B.** vSphere HA alarms could likely be the result of a management network communication failure.

12. **C.** The transient IP allocation scheme is unsupported by vCenter Operations Manager.

13. **A, B and C.** Cloning a virtual machine, migrating a virtual machine, and adding a host are all tasks that can be scheduled in vCenter Server. There is no scheduled task to delete virtual machines.

14. A. If the Trigger If All Of The Conditions Are Satisfied option is used, then each trigger type must have the condition met before the trigger will fire. Remember that the more trigger types that are added, the more complex the alarm becomes.

15. A and D. The SMTP settings must include the FQDN or IP address of the SMTP server and the sender account.

16. A, B and C. A vCenter Server alarm consists of three parts: type, trigger, and action.

17. A, B and C. All of the alarm-type monitors have the actions of send a notification email, send a notification trap, and run a command.

18. C. All event entries for a selected object include the child objects. When troubleshooting an HA problem, the Cluster object would include events for all hosts (and virtual machines) in the cluster.

19. A and B. To monitor current swap file usage, SWAP curr is used in resxtop and esxtop, and Memory: Swap Used is used in performance charts of the vSphere Client.

20. A and D. The two VMs contained in the vCenter Operations Manager vApp are the UI VM and the Analytics VM. The name of the vApp is chosen during deployment.

Appendix B

About the Additional Study Tools

IN THIS APPENDIX:

✓ Additional study tools

✓ System requirements

✓ Using the study tools

✓ Troubleshooting

Additional Study Tools

The following sections are arranged by category and summarize the software and other goodies you'll find on the companion website. If you need help installing the items, refer to the installation instructions in the "Using the Study Tools" section of this appendix.

 You can find the additional study tools at www.sybex.com/go/vcp5dcvsg. You'll also find instructions on how to download the files to your hard drive.

Sybex Test Engine

The files contain the Sybex test engine, which includes two bonus practice exams, as well as the assessment test and the chapter review questions, which are also included in the book.

Electronic Flashcards

These handy electronic flashcards are just what they sound like. One side contains a question, and the other side shows the answer.

PDF of Glossary of Terms

We have included an electronic version of the glossary in .pdf format. You can view the electronic version of the glossary with Adobe Reader.

Adobe Reader

We've also included a copy of Adobe Reader so you can view PDF files that accompany the book's content. For more information on Adobe Reader or to check for a newer version, visit Adobe's website at www.adobe.com/products/reader/.

System Requirements

Make sure your computer meets the minimum system requirements shown in the following list. If your computer doesn't meet these requirements, you may have problems using the software and files. For the latest and greatest information, please refer to the ReadMe file located in the download.

- A PC running Microsoft Windows 98, Windows 2000, Windows NT4 (with SP4 or newer), Windows Me, Windows XP, Windows Vista, or Windows 7

- An Internet connection

Using the Study Tools

To install the items, follow these steps:

1. Download the .zip file to your hard drive, and unzip it to your desired location. You can find instructions on where to download this file at www.sybex.com/go/vcp5dcvsg.

2. Click the Start.exe file to open the study tools file.

3. Read the license agreement, and then click the Accept button if you want to use the study tools.

The main interface appears and allows you to access the content with just a few clicks.

Troubleshooting

Wiley has attempted to provide programs that work on most computers with the minimum system requirements. If a program does not work properly, the two likeliest problems are that you don't have enough memory (RAM) for the programs you want to use or you have other programs running that are affecting the installation or running of a program. If you get an error message such as "Not enough memory" or "Setup cannot continue," try one or more of the following suggestions and then try using the software again:

Turn off any antivirus software running on your computer. Installation programs sometimes mimic virus activity and may make your computer incorrectly believe that it's being infected by a virus.

Close all running programs. The more programs you have running, the less memory is available to other programs. Installation programs typically update files and programs, so if you keep other programs running, installation may not work properly.

Have your local computer store add more RAM to your computer.   This is, admittedly, a drastic and somewhat expensive step. However, adding more memory can really help the speed of your computer and allow more programs to run at the same time.

Customer Care

If you have trouble with the book's companion study tools, please call the Wiley Product Technical Support phone number at (800) 762-2974, or email them at `http://sybex.custhelp.com/`.

Index

Note to the Reader: Throughout this index **boldfaced** page numbers indicate primary discussions of a topic. *Italicized* page numbers indicate illustrations.

U

Free Online Study Tools

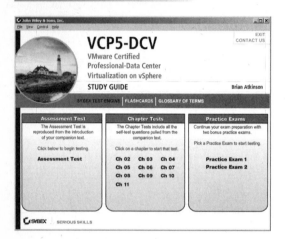

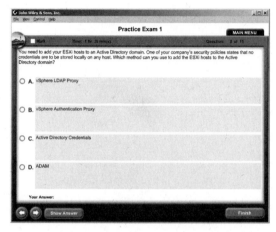

Comprehensive Study Tool Package Includes:

- **Assessment Test** to help you focus your study to specific objectives

- **Chapter Review Questions** to reinforce what you learned

- **Two VCP5-DCV Practice Exams** to test your knowledge of the material

- **Electronic Flashcards** to reinforce your learning and give you that last-minute test prep before the exam

- **Searchable Glossary** gives you instant access to the key terms you'll need to know for the exam

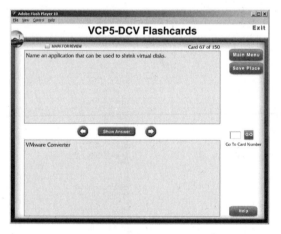

Go to www.sybex.com/go/vcp5dcvsg to register and gain access to this comprehensive study tool package.